# Reading & Writing Companion

## GRADE 10

Alaina Williams

UNITS 1–6

## studysync

studysync.com

Send all inquiries to:
BookheadEd Learning, LLC
610 Daniel Young Drive
Sonoma, CA  95476

ISBN  978-1-94-973920-6
MHID 1-94-973920-1

4 5 6 7 8 9  LWI  25 24 23 22 21

C

# Contents

Reading & Writing Companion

iii

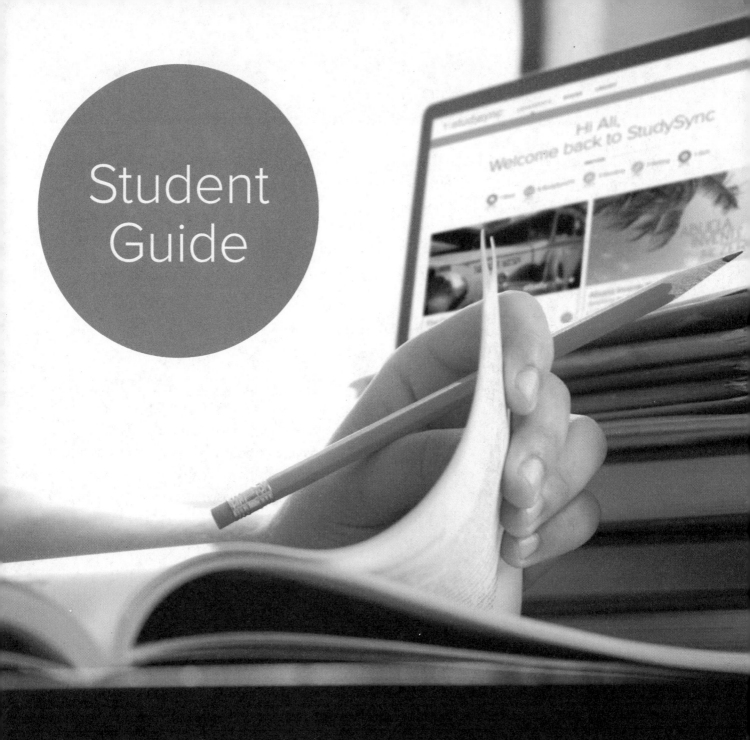

# Student Guide

## Getting Started

**W**elcome to the StudySync Reading & Writing Companion! In this book, you will find a collection of readings based on the theme of the unit you are studying. As you work through the readings, you will be asked to answer questions and perform a variety of tasks designed to help you closely analyze and understand each text selection. Read on for an explanation of each

# Close Reading and Writing Routine

In each unit, you will read texts that share a common theme, despite their different genres, time periods, and authors. Each reading encourages a closer look through questions and a short writing assignment.

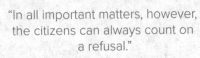

"In all important matters, however, the citizens can always count on a refusal."

Our little town does not lie on the frontier, nowhere near; it is so far from the frontier, in fact, that perhaps no one from our little town has ever been there; **desolate** highlands have to be crossed as well as wide, fertile plains. To imagine even part of the road makes one tired, and more than part one just cannot imagine. There are also big towns on the road, each far larger than ours. Ten little towns like ours laid side by side, and ten more forced down from above, still would not produce one of those enormous, overcrowded towns. If one does not get lost on the way one is bound to lose oneself in these towns, and to avoid them is impossible on account of their size.

But what is even further from our town than the frontier, if such distances can be compared at all—it's like saying that a man of three hundred years is older than one of two hundred—what is even further than the frontier is the capital. Whereas we do get news of the frontier wars now and again, of the capital we learn next to nothing—we civilians that is, for of course the government officials have very good connections with the capital; they can get news from there in as little as three months, so they claim at least.

Now it is remarkable and I am continually being surprised at the way we in our town humbly submit to all orders issued in the capital. For centuries no political change has been brought about by the citizens themselves. In the capital great rulers have superseded each other—indeed, even dynasties have been deposed or annihilated, and new ones have started; in the past century even the capital itself was destroyed, a new one was founded far away from it, later on this too was destroyed and the old one rebuilt, yet none of this had any influence on our little town. Our officials have always remained at their posts; the highest officials came from the capital, the less high from other towns, and the lowest from among ourselves—that is how it has always been and it has suited us. The highest official is the chief tax-collector, he has the rank of colonel, and is known as such. The present one is an old man; I've known him for years, because he was already a colonel when I was a child.

SKILL
Textual Evidence

*I think the narrator is talking about feeling distant from the power that rules their lives—the capital.*

*It says "we civilians" don't even get news of the capital; this is evidence of the narrator's distance from power.*

## ① Introduction

An Introduction to each text provides historical context for your reading as well as information about the author. You will also learn about the genre of the text and the year in which it was written.

## ② Notes

Many times, while working through the activities after each text, you will be asked to **annotate** or **make annotations** about what you are reading. This means that you should highlight or underline words in the text and use the "Notes" column to make comments or jot down any questions you have. You may also want to note any unfamiliar vocabulary words here.

You will also see sample student annotations to go along with the Skill lesson for that text.

## 3 First Read

During your first reading of each selection, you should just try to get a general idea of the content and message of the reading. Don't worry if there are parts you don't understand or words that are unfamiliar to you. You'll have an opportunity later to dive deeper into the text.

## 4 Think Questions

These questions will ask you to start thinking critically about the text, asking specific questions about its purpose, and making connections to your prior knowledge and reading experiences. To answer these questions, you should go back to the text and draw upon specific evidence to support your responses. You will also begin to explore some of the more challenging vocabulary words in the selection.

## 5 Skills

Each Skill includes two parts: Checklist and Your Turn. In the Checklist, you will learn the process for analyzing the text. The model student annotations in the text provide examples of how you might make your own notes following the instructions in the Checklist. In the Your Turn, you will use those same instructions to practice the skill.

### 3 THE REFUSAL — First Read

Read "The Refusal." After you read, complete the Think Questions below.

#### 4 THINK QUESTIONS

1. What can the reader infer about the tax-collector's power? Where does his power come from, and how is it expressed? Use evidence from the text to support your inferences.

2. What do you know about the relationship between the government, located in the faraway capital, and the small town? How do the villagers view the capital and the people who represent it? Cite evidence from the text to support your answer.

3. What role does the ceremony play in life in the small town? How do most townspeople feel about this custom? Support your answer with evidence from the text.

4. Use context clues to determine the meaning of **exceptional** as it is used in paragraph 5. Write your definition here and identify clues that helped you figure out its meaning.

5. Read the following dictionary entry:

   **petition**
   pe•ti•tion /pəˈtiSH(ə)n/ *noun*

   1. A formal, written request to an authority
   2. A solemn appeal to a superior
   3. An application to a court for a judicial action

   Which definition most closely matches the meaning of **petition** as it is used in paragraph 5? Write the correct definition of *petition* here and explain how you figured out the meaning.

### 5 CHARACTER — Skill: Character

Use the Checklist to analyze Character in "The Refusal." Refer to the sample student annotations about Character in the text.

#### ••• CHECKLIST FOR CHARACTER

In order to analyze how complex characters develop and interact in a text, note the following:

✓ the traits of complex characters in the text, such as a character that
  • has conflicting emotions and motivations
  • develops and changes over the course of a story or drama
  • advances the events of the plot
  • develops the central idea, or theme, through his or her actions

✓ the ways that characters respond, react, or change as the events of the plot unfold and how they interact with other characters in the story

✓ how the reactions and responses of complex characters help to advance the plot and develop the theme

To evaluate how complex characters develop and interact in a text, consider the following questions:

✓ Which characters in the text could be considered complex?

✓ Do the characters change as the plot unfolds? When do they begin to change? Which events cause them to change?

✓ How do any changes the characters undergo help to advance the plot and develop the theme?

#### ⟳ YOUR TURN

1. The narrator's description of the colonel during the reception leads the reader to conclude that—
   - ○ A. the colonel is considered to be an ordinary citizen.
   - ○ B. the colonel is openly disrespected by the townspeople.
   - ○ C. the colonel worries about losing his position as tax-collector.
   - ○ D. the colonel inspires great fear among the townspeople.

2. The crowd's reaction to the colonel's refusal reveals that in this society—
   - ○ A. the people feel dissatisfied with their government and plan to revolt.
   - ○ B. the people are glad that nothing has happened to upset their traditions.
   - ○ C. the people recognize that the colonel is a human being just as they are.
   - ○ D. the people understand that the colonel is a powerless figurehead.

3. Which detail in the passage most clearly suggests that the colonel's character may be more complex than the townspeople realize?
   - ○ A. He silently holds the two symbolic bamboo poles.
   - ○ B. He breathes deeply and conspicuously, like a frog.
   - ○ C. He drops the bamboo poles and sinks into a chair.
   - ○ D. He reveals no emotion during the reception.

## 6 Close Read & Skills Focus

After you have completed the First Read, you will be asked to go back and read the text more closely and critically. Before you begin your Close Read, you should read through the Skills Focus to get an idea of the concepts you will want to focus on during your second reading. You should work through the Skills Focus by making annotations, highlighting important concepts, and writing notes or questions in the "Notes" column. Depending on instructions from your teacher, you may need to respond online or use a separate piece of paper to start expanding on your thoughts and ideas.

## 7 Write

Your study of each selection will end with a writing assignment. For this assignment, you should use your notes, annotations, personal ideas, and answers to both the Think and Skills Focus questions. Be sure to read the prompt carefully and address each part of it in your writing.

## 8 English Language Learner

The English Language Learner texts focus on improving language proficiency. You will practice learning strategies and skills in individual and group activities to become better readers, writers, and speakers.

# Extended Writing Project and Grammar

This is your opportunity to use genre characteristics and craft to compose meaningful, longer written works exploring the theme of each unit. You will draw information from your readings, research, and own life experiences to complete the assignment.

## 1 Writing Project

After you have read all of the unit text selections, you will move on to a writing project. Each project will guide you through the process of writing your essay. Student models will provide guidance and help you organize your thoughts. One unit ends with an **Extended Oral Project** which will give you an opportunity to develop your oral language and communication skills.

## 2 Writing Process Steps

There are four steps in the writing process: Plan, Draft, Revise, and Edit and Publish. During each step, you will form and shape your writing project, and each lesson's peer review will give you the chance to receive feedback from your peers and teacher.

## 3 Writing Skills

Each Skill lesson focuses on a specific strategy or technique that you will use during your writing project. Each lesson presents a process for applying the skill to your own work and gives you the opportunity to practice it to improve your writing.

2 Literary Analysis Writing Process: Plan

3 Skill: Organizing Argumentative Writing

**••• CHECKLIST FOR ORGANIZING ARGUMENTATIVE WRITING**

As you consider how to organize your writing for your argumentative essay, use the following questions as a guide:

- Have I identified my claim or claims and the evidence that supports it?
- Have I identified reasons for my claim?
- Have I identified any counterclaims that I will need to address?
- Have I identified the textual evidence that will support my reasons?

**UNIT 1**

# The Power of Communication

Why do words matter?

Genre Focus: **FICTION**

## Texts

🔗 Paired Readings

# Extended Writing Project and Grammar

## English Language Learner Resources

# Unit 1: The Power of Communication
## Why do words matter?

**CHINUA ACHEBE**

Chinua Achebe (1930–2013) is the author of the most widely read African novel of all time, *Things Fall Apart*. The work explores the intersection of traditional Igbo culture and Western colonialism, a reflection of Achebe's upbringing in an eastern Nigerian village at the center of a substantial Christian missionary effort. Achebe chose to write in English, offering a narrative of colonization that was shown, for the first time, from the perspective of the colonized.

**HAYAN CHARARA**

The son of Lebanese immigrants, Hayan Charara (b. 1972) grew up in Detroit, Michigan. His work explores themes of Arab American identity, family, and culture. He has published poetry collections, essays, and children's books, and edited *Inclined to Speak: An Anthology of Contemporary Arab American Poetry* (2008).

**JOSEPH CONRAD**

The Polish British writer Joseph Conrad (1857–1924) drew on his real-life experience as a merchant marine to write many of his stories, including the well-known and controversial book, *Heart of Darkness*. The novel offers a brutal portrayal of colonialism as its story follows a British riverboat captain's voyage up the Congo River in pursuit of ivory. Conrad chose to write primarily in English, his third language after Polish and French. In his autobiography, Conrad called English a language "of books read, of thoughts pursued, of remembered emotions—of my very dreams!"

**PATRICK HENRY**

Patrick Henry (1736–1799) was one of the Founding Fathers of the United States, the first and sixth governor of Virginia, and a key player in the American Revolution. He is perhaps best known for his address to the Virginia Legislature in 1775, where in an effort to incite opposition to the British government, he famously declared, "give me liberty or give me death!" Henry's manner of speech mirrored rhetorical gestures of evangelical sermons, a style he'd likely been exposed to as a child during the Great Awakening.

**FRANZ KAFKA**

The writing of Czech-born, German-speaking Franz Kafka (1883–1924) is so distinctive and well-known that his name is used as an adjective. The description of a situation as *Kafkaesque* means that it resembles the bizarre and disturbing predicaments inhabited by the characters in the author's stories. Ironically, Kafka's work received little recognition or publication in his lifetime, though he would later become regarded as a major figure of 20th-century Western literature.

## MOHJA KAHF

Writer, activist, and professor Mohja Kahf (b. 1967) moved from her birthplace of Damascus, Syria, to the United States at an early age and grew up in the Midwest. Her work is shaped by both American and Arabic linguistic traditions and navigates questions of identity, diversity, and belonging. Such weight is balanced in Kahf's poems by the use of clear, accessible language paired with wit and humor.

## MARTIN LUTHER KING JR.

Dr. Martin Luther King Jr. (1929–1968) was a Baptist minister and leader of the American civil rights movement. In 1963 King and other anti-segregation demonstrators were incarcerated in Birmingham, Alabama, when their campaign of nonviolent sit-ins, marches, and boycotts was met with violence from the local police. While in jail, King began writing his now famous "Letter from Birmingham Jail" in the margins of a newspaper. For his "steadfast commitment to achieving racial justice through nonviolent action," King was awarded the Nobel Peace Prize in 1964.

## FRANCIS LA FLESCHE

Francis La Flesche (1857–1932) was a prominent Native American ethnologist who created an invaluable record of stories, songs, and rituals of the Omaha and Osage people. La Flesche was born on the Omaha Reservation and was sent by his parents to a mission school to learn English. His education and career were rooted in preserving the sophisticated and rich history of his ancestors. Much of the work was recorded on wax cylinders, the earliest commercial medium for converting and reproducing sound.

## URSULA K. LE GUIN

Ursula K. Le Guin (1929–2018) was born and raised in Berkeley, California, but lived in Portland, Oregon, from 1958 until the end of her life. She was a prolific writer known for upending the conventions of the science fiction and fantasy genres, which, at the time she started writing in the 1960s, lacked any significant racial or gender diversity. She is best known for her fantasy series, Earthsea, and her anarchist utopian allegory, *The Dispossessed*.

## JIMMY SANTIAGO BACA

Jimmy Santiago Baca (b. 1952), an American writer of Chicano and Apache descent, penned his first poems while serving a five-year prison sentence in his twenties. His poetry collection *Immigrants in Our Own Land* (1979) draws on his experience of incarceration and, like much of his work, deftly addresses themes of social justice, addiction, and community in the barrios of the American Southwest.

## PAT MORA

Pat Mora (b. 1942) is a Mexican American poet, writer, and popular national speaker. Originally from El Paso, Texas, Mora gives voice to those navigating a divided identity in the context of the border region between the United States and Mexico. Her poetry employs both English and Spanish words, addressing cultural intersection not only in theme, but through language itself.

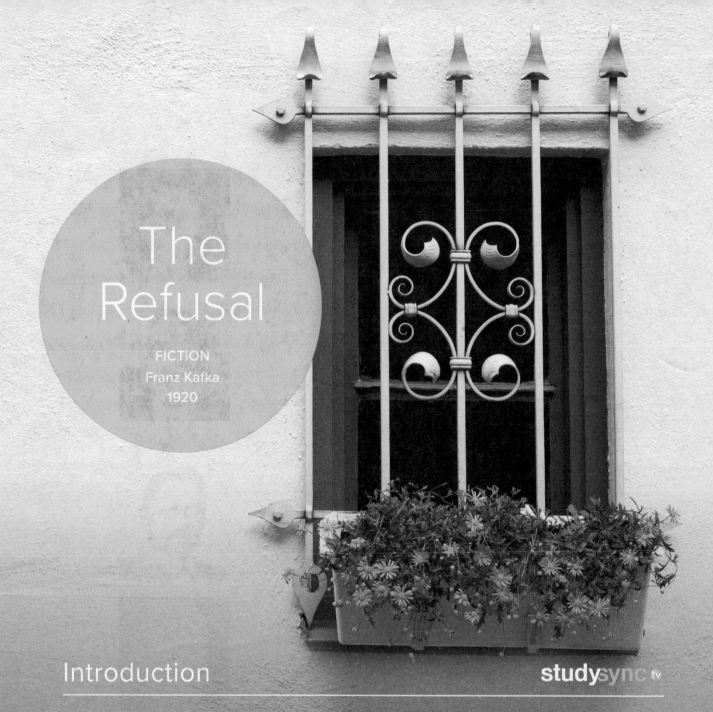

# The Refusal

FICTION
Franz Kafka
1920

## Introduction

studysync tv

B orn in a Jewish ghetto in Prague, Franz Kafka (1883–1924) allegedly burned up to 90 percent of his own work during his lifetime. Luckily, a few important pieces survived—enough to shape his legacy as one of the most influential 20th-century writers, whose depictions of bizarre and sinister events in a society under bureaucratic control coined the term 'Kafkaesque'. Written in 1920, "The Refusal" depicts a ritual ceremony in a small town controlled by a government in a faraway capital. In times of need, residents of the town appeal to the tax-collector, the town's highest ranking government official, for help. The text's themes of oppression and authoritarianism would have resonated strongly with a readership that had just endured World War I and was on the brink of another global conflict.

# "In all important matters, however, the citizens can always count on a refusal."

1    Our little town does not lie on the frontier, nowhere near; it is so far from the frontier, in fact, that perhaps no one from our little town has ever been there; **desolate** highlands have to be crossed as well as wide fertile plains. To imagine even part of the road makes one tired, and more than part one just cannot imagine. There are also big towns on the road, each far larger than ours. Ten little towns like ours laid side by side, and ten more forced down from above, still would not produce one of those enormous, overcrowded towns. If one does not get lost on the way one is bound to lose oneself in these towns, and to avoid them is impossible on account of their size.

2    But what is even further from our town than the frontier, if such distances can be compared at all—it's like saying that a man of three hundred years is older than one of two hundred—what is even further than the frontier is the capital. Whereas we do get news of the frontier wars now and again, of the capital we learn next to nothing—we civilians that is, for of course the government officials have very good connections with the capital; they can get news from there in as little as three months, so they claim at least.

3    Now it is remarkable and I am continually being surprised at the way we in our town humbly submit to all orders issued in the capital. For centuries no political change has been brought about by the citizens themselves. In the capital great rulers have superseded each other—indeed, even dynasties have been deposed or annihilated, and new ones have started; in the past century even the capital itself was destroyed, a new one was founded far away from it, later on this too was destroyed and the old one rebuilt, yet none of this had any influence on our little town. Our officials have always remained at their posts; the highest officials came from the capital, the less high from other towns, and the lowest from among ourselves—that is how it has always been and it has suited us. The highest official is the chief tax-collector, he has the rank of colonel, and is known as such. The present one is an old man; I've known him for years, because he was already a colonel when I was a child. At first he rose very fast in his career, but then he seems to have advanced no further; actually, for our little town his rank is good enough, a higher rank would be out of place. When I try to recall him I see him sitting on the veranda of his house in the Market Square, leaning back, pipe in mouth. Above him

Franz Kafka is German

[Surreal]

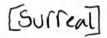

Skill:
Textual Evidence

*I think the narrator is talking about feeling distant from the power that rules their lives—the capital.*

*It says "we civilians" don't even get news of the capital; this is evidence of the narrator's distance from power.*

Copyright © BookheadEd Learning, LLC

*On one hand the colonel is the most powerful man in town, but on the other hand it seems like he didn't try to be so powerful; he just went along with becoming the top official just like the rest of the town did. What motivates him?*

from the roof flutters the imperial flag; on the sides of the veranda, which is so big that minor military maneuvers are sometimes held there, washing hangs out to dry. His grandchildren, in beautiful silk clothes, play around him; they are not allowed down in the Market Square, the children there are considered unworthy of them, but the grandchildren are attracted by the square, so they thrust their heads between the posts of the banister and when the children below begin to quarrel they join the quarrel from above.

4    This colonel, then, commands the town. I don't think he has ever produced a document entitling him to this position; very likely he does not possess such a thing. Maybe he really is chief tax-collector. But is that all? Does that entitle him to rule over all the other departments in the administration as well? True, his office is very important for the government, but for the citizens it is hardly the most important. One is almost under the impression that the people here say: "Now that you've taken all we possess, please take us as well." In reality, of course, it was not he who seized the power, nor is he a tyrant. It has just come about over the years that the chief tax-collector is automatically the top official, and the colonel accepts the tradition just as we do.

5    Yet while he lives among us without laying too much stress on his official position, he is something quite different from the ordinary citizen. When a delegation comes to him with a request, he stands there like the wall of the world. Behind him is nothingness, one imagines hearing voices whispering in the background, but this is probably a delusion; after all, he represents the end of all things, at least for us. At these receptions he really was worth seeing. Once as a child I was present when a delegation of citizens arrived to ask him for a government subsidy because the poorest quarter of the town had been burned to the ground. My father the blacksmith, a man well respected in the community, was a member of the delegation and had taken me along. There's nothing exceptional about this, everyone rushes to spectacles of this kind, one can hardly distinguish the actual delegation from the crowd. Since these receptions usually take place on the veranda, there are even people who climb up by ladder from the Market Square and take part in the goings-on from over the bannister. On this occasion about a quarter of the veranda had been reserved for the colonel, the crowd kept filling the rest of it. A few soldiers kept watch, some of them standing round him in a semicircle. Actually a single soldier would have been quite enough, such is our fear of them. I don't know exactly where these soldiers come from, in any case from a long way off, they all look very much alike, they wouldn't even need a uniform. They are small, not strong but agile people, the most striking thing about them is the prominence of their teeth which almost overcrowd their mouths, and a certain restless twitching of their small narrow eyes. This makes them the terror of the children, but also their delight, for again and again the children long to be frightened by these teeth, these eyes, so as to be able to run away in horror. Even grownups probably never quite lose this

childish terror, at least it continues to have an effect. There are, of course, other factors contributing to it. The soldiers speak a dialect utterly incomprehensible to us, and they can hardly get used to ours—all of which produces a certain shut-off, unapproachable quality corresponding, as it happens, to their character, for they are silent, serious, and **rigid.** They don't actually do anything evil, and yet they are almost unbearable in an evil sense. A soldier, for example, enters a shop, buys some trifling object, and stays there leaning against the counter; he listens to the conversations, probably does not understand them, and yet gives the impression of understanding; he himself does not say a word, just stares blankly at the speaker, then back at the listeners, all the while keeping his hand on the hilt of the long knife in his belt. This is revolting, one loses the desire to talk, the customers start leaving the shop, and only when it is quite empty does the soldier also leave. Thus wherever the soldiers appear, our lively people grow silent. That's what happened this time, too. As on all solemn occasions the colonel stood upright, holding in front of him two poles of bamboo in his outstretched hands. This is an ancient custom implying more or less that he supports the law, and the law supports him. Now everyone knows, of course, what to expect up on the veranda, and yet each time people take fright all over again. On this occasion, too, the man chosen to speak could not begin, he was already standing opposite the colonel when his courage failed him and, muttering a few excuses, he pushed his way back into the crowd. No other suitable person willing to speak could be found, albeit several unsuitable ones offered themselves; a great commotion ensued and messengers went in search of various citizens who were well-known speakers. During all this time the colonel stood there motionless, only his chest moving visibly up and down to his breathing. Not that he breathed with difficulty, it was just that he breathed so conspicuously, much as frogs breathe—except that with them it is normal, while here it was **exceptional.** I squeezed myself through the grownups and watched him through a gap between two soldiers, until one of them kicked me away with his knee. Meanwhile the man originally chosen to speak had regained his composure and, firmly held up by two fellow citizens, was delivering his address. It was touching to see him smile throughout this solemn speech describing a grievous misfortune—a most humble smile which strove in vain to elicit some slight reaction on the colonel's face. Finally he formulated the request—I think he was only asking for a year's tax exemption, but possibly also for timber from the imperial forests at a reduced price. Then he bowed low, as did everyone else except the colonel, the soldiers, and a number of officials in the background. To the child it seemed ridiculous that the people on the ladders should climb down a few rungs so as not to be seen during the significant pause and now and again peer inquisitively over the floor of the veranda. After this had lasted quite a while an official, a little man, stepped up to the colonel and tried to reach the latter's height by standing on his toes. The colonel, still motionless save for his deep breathing, whispered something in his ear, whereupon the little man clapped

Skill:
Text-Dependent
Responses

*The townspeople are
terrified of the soldiers,
who come from far
away and speak an
unfamiliar language.*

NOTES

his hands and everyone rose. "The **petition** has been refused," he announced. "You may go." An undeniable sense of relief passed through the crowd, everyone surged out, hardly a soul paying any special attention to the colonel, who, as it were, had turned once more into a human being like the rest of us. I still caught one last glimpse of him as he wearily let go of the poles, which fell to the ground, then sank into an armchair produced by some officials, and promptly put his pipe in his mouth.

6   This whole occurrence is not isolated, it's in the general run of things. Indeed, it does happen now and again that minor petitions are granted, but then it invariably looks as though the colonel had done it as a powerful private person on his own responsibility, and it had to be kept all but a secret from the government—not **explicitly** of course, but that is what it feels like. No doubt in our little town the colonel's eyes, so far as we know, are also the eyes of the government, and yet there is a difference which it is impossible to comprehend completely.

7   In all important matters, however, the citizens can always count on a refusal. And now the strange fact is that without this refusal one simply cannot get along, yet at the same time these official occasions designed to receive the refusal are by no means a formality. Time after time one goes there full of expectation and in all seriousness and then one returns, if not exactly strengthened or happy, nevertheless not disappointed or tired. About these things I do not have to ask the opinion of anyone else, I feel them in myself, as everyone does; nor do I have any great desire to find out how these things are connected.

8   As a matter of fact, there is, so far as my observations go, a certain age group that is not content—these are the young people roughly between seventeen and twenty. Quite young fellows, in fact, who are utterly incapable of foreseeing the consequences of even the least significant, far less a revolutionary, idea. And it is among just them that discontent creeps in.

"The Refusal" by Franz Kafka, translated by Tania and James Stern; from THE COMPLETE STORIES by Franz Kafka, edited by Nahum N. Glatzer, copyright © 1946, 1947, 1948, 1949, 1954, 1958, 1971 by Penguin Random House LLC. Used by permission of Schocken Books, an imprint of the Knopf Doubleday Publishing Group, a division of Penguin Random House LLC. All rights reserved.

# Skill:
# Text-Dependent Responses

Use the Checklist to analyze Text-Dependent Responses in "The Refusal." Refer to the sample student annotations about Text-Dependent Responses in the text.

## ••• CHECKLIST FOR TEXT-DEPENDENT RESPONSES

In order to cite strong and thorough textual evidence that supports an analysis, consider the following:

✓ Inferences are sound and logical assumptions about information in a text that is not explicitly or directly stated by the author.

- Read closely and critically and consider why an author gives or excludes particular details and information.

- Apply your own knowledge, experiences, and observations along with textual evidence to help you figure out what the author does not state directly.

- Cite several pieces of textual evidence that offer the strongest, most thorough and comprehensive support for your analysis.

✓ To make a point, authors often provide explicit evidence of a character's feelings or motivations, or the reasons behind an historical event in a nonfiction text.

- Explicit evidence is stated directly in the text and must be cited accurately to support a text-dependent response or analysis.

To cite strong and thorough textual evidence that supports an analysis, consider the following questions:

✓ Can the question be answered by citing explicit evidence in the text, such as a direct cause-and-effect relationship?

✓ If I infer things in the text that the author does not state directly, what evidence from the text, along with my own experiences and knowledge, can I use to support my analysis?

✓ Have I used textual evidence that offers the strongest support for my analysis? How do I know?

Please note that excerpts and passages in the StudySync® library and this workbook are intended as touchstones to generate interest in an author's work. The excerpts and passages do not substitute for the reading of entire texts, and StudySync® strongly recommends that students seek out and purchase the whole literary or informational work in order to experience it as the author intended. Links to online resellers are available in our digital library. In addition, complete works may be ordered through an authorized reseller by filling out and returning to StudySync® the order form enclosed in this workbook.

Reading & Writing Companion    5

# Skill:
# Text-Dependent Responses

Reread paragraph 3 of "The Refusal." Then, using the Checklist on the previous page, answer the multiple-choice questions below.

## ⟳ YOUR TURN

1. In paragraph 3, the narrator reveals that the tax-collector's grandchildren "are not allowed down in the Market Square." Which commentary best responds to this textual evidence?

   ○ A  The tax-collector's grandchildren are special and considered far above the status of the townspeople's children.

   ○ B  The tax-collector's grandchildren think they are better than the townspeople's children and refuse to play with them.

   ○ C  The tax-collector's grandchildren adore their grandfather but look down on the townspeople's children.

   ○ D  The tax-collector's grandchildren are spoiled by the time and attention lavished on them and do not like to play with other children.

2. Which quotation from the text best supports a reader's response that claims "although the villagers have no power of their own, events in the faraway capital have little effect on them"?

   ○ A  "Now it is remarkable and I am continually being surprised at the way we in our town humbly submit to all orders issued in the capital."

   ○ B  "For centuries no political change has been brought about by the citizens themselves."

   ○ C  "In the capital great rulers have superseded each other—indeed, even dynasties have been deposed or annihilated, and new ones have started . . ."

   ○ D  ". . . in the past century even the capital itself was destroyed, a new one was founded far away from it, later on this too was destroyed and the old one rebuilt, yet none of this had any influence on our little town."

# First Read

Read "The Refusal." After you read, complete the Think Questions below.

---

## ☁ THINK QUESTIONS

1. What can the reader infer about the tax-collector's power? Where does his power come from, and how is it expressed? Use evidence from the text to support your inferences.

2. What do you know about the relationship between the government, located in the faraway capital, and the small town? How do the villagers view the capital and the people who represent it? Cite evidence from the text to support your answer.

3. What role does the ceremony play in life in the small town? How do most townspeople feel about this custom? Support your answer with evidence from the text.

4. Use context clues to determine the meaning of **exceptional** as it is used in paragraph 5. Write your definition here and identify clues that helped you figure out its meaning.

5. Read the following dictionary entry:

   **petition**
   pe•ti•tion /pə'tiSH(ə)n/ *noun*

   1. A formal, written request to an authority
   2. A solemn appeal to a superior
   3. An application to a court for a judicial action

   Which definition most closely matches the meaning of **petition** as it is used in paragraph 5? Write the correct definition of *petition* here and explain how you figured out the meaning.

Please note that excerpts and passages in the StudySync® library and this workbook are intended as touchstones to generate interest in an author's work. The excerpts and passages do not substitute for the reading of entire texts, and StudySync® strongly recommends that students seek out and purchase the whole literary or informational work in order to experience it as the author intended. Links to online resellers are available in our digital library. In addition, complete works may be ordered through an authorized reseller by filling out and returning to StudySync® the order form enclosed in this workbook.

Reading & Writing Companion    **7**

# Skill:
# Textual Evidence

Use the Checklist to analyze Textual Evidence in "The Refusal." Refer to the sample student annotations about Textual Evidence in the text.

## ••• CHECKLIST FOR TEXTUAL EVIDENCE

In order to support an analysis by citing evidence that is explicitly stated in the text, do the following:

✓ Read the text closely and critically.

✓ Identify what the text says explicitly.

✓ Find the most relevant textual evidence that supports your analysis.

✓ Consider why an author explicitly states specific details and information.

✓ Cite the specific words, phrases, sentences, or paragraphs from the text that support your analysis.

In order to interpret implicit meanings in a text by making inferences, do the following:

✓ Combine information directly stated in the text with your own knowledge, experiences, and observations.

✓ Cite the specific words, phrases, sentences, or paragraphs from the text that lead to and support this inference.

In order to cite textual evidence to support an analysis of what the text says explicitly as well as inferences drawn from the text, consider the following questions:

✓ Have I read the text closely and critically?

✓ What inferences am I making about the text?

✓ What textual evidence am I using to support these inferences?

✓ Am I quoting the evidence from the text correctly?

✓ Does my textual evidence logically relate to my analysis or the inference I am making?

Copyright © BookheadEd Learning, LLC

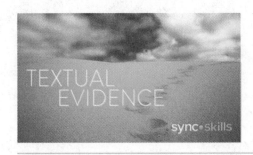

# Skill:
# Textual Evidence

Reread paragraph 5 of "The Refusal." Then, using the Checklist on the previous page, answer the multiple-choice questions below.

## ⟳ YOUR TURN

1. Which of the following statements from the text provides the best evidence for the inference that the soldiers are seen as beastlike and inhuman?

   ○ A. "Thus wherever the soldiers appear, our lively people grow silent."

   ○ B. "This is revolting, one loses the desire to talk, the customers start leaving the shop, and only when it is quite empty does the soldier also leave."

   ○ C. "A soldier, for example, . . . listens to the conversations, probably does not understand them, and yet gives the impression of understanding. . . ."

   ○ D. "They are small, not strong but agile people, the most striking thing about them is the prominence of their teeth which almost overcrowd their mouths, and a certain restless twitching of their small narrow eyes."

2. Which of the following facts provides the best textual evidence for the inference that the people of the village do not hope for change?

   ○ A. They find it very difficult to request things from the colonel.

   ○ B. Even the colonel sinks into his chair after the ceremony.

   ○ C. They are comforted by a predictable refusal.

   ○ D. Even very reasonable requests are always refused.

Please note that excerpts and passages in the StudySync® library and this workbook are intended as touchstones to generate interest in an author's work. The excerpts and passages do not substitute for the reading of entire texts, and StudySync® strongly recommends that students seek out and purchase the whole literary or informational work in order to experience it as the author intended. Links to online resellers are available in our digital library. In addition, complete works may be ordered through an authorized reseller by filling out and returning to StudySync® the order form enclosed in this workbook.

Reading & Writing
Companion

9

# Skill:
# Character

Use the Checklist to analyze Character in "The Refusal." Refer to the sample student annotations about Character in the text.

## ••• CHECKLIST FOR CHARACTER

In order to analyze how complex characters develop and interact in a text, note the following:

- ✓ the traits of complex characters in the text, such as a character that

  - has conflicting emotions and motivations
  - develops and changes over the course of a story or drama
  - advances the events of the plot
  - develops the central idea, or theme, through his or her actions

- ✓ the ways that characters respond, react, or change as the events of the plot unfold and how they interact with other characters in the story

- ✓ how the reactions and responses of complex characters help to advance the plot and develop the theme

To evaluate how complex characters develop and interact in a text, consider the following questions:

- ✓ Which characters in the text could be considered complex?

- ✓ Do the characters change as the plot unfolds? When do they begin to change? Which events cause them to change?

- ✓ How do any changes the characters undergo help to advance the plot and develop the theme?

# Skill:
# Character

Reread paragraph 5 of "The Refusal." Then, using the Checklist on the previous page, answer the multiple-choice questions below.

## ↻ YOUR TURN

1. The narrator's description of the colonel during the reception leads the reader to conclude that—

   ○ A. the colonel is considered to be an ordinary citizen.
   ○ B. the colonel is openly disrespected by the townspeople.
   ○ C. the colonel worries about losing his position as tax-collector.
   ○ D. the colonel inspires great fear among the townspeople.

2. The crowd's reaction to the colonel's refusal reveals that in this society—

   ○ A. the people feel dissatisfied with their government and plan to revolt.
   ○ B. the people are glad that nothing has happened to upset their traditions.
   ○ C. the people recognize that the colonel is a human being just as they are.
   ○ D. the people understand that the colonel is a powerless figurehead.

3. Which detail in the passage most clearly suggests that the colonel's character may be more complex than the townspeople realize?

   ○ A. He silently holds the two symbolic bamboo poles.
   ○ B. He breathes deeply and conspicuously, like a frog.
   ○ C. He drops the bamboo poles and sinks into a chair.
   ○ D. He reveals no emotion during the reception.

Please note that excerpts and passages in the StudySync® library and this workbook are intended as touchstones to generate interest in an author's work. The excerpts and passages do not substitute for the reading of entire texts, and StudySync® strongly recommends that students seek out and purchase the whole literary or informational work in order to experience it as the author intended. Links to online resellers are available in our digital library. In addition, complete works may be ordered through an authorized reseller by filling out and returning to StudySync® the order form enclosed in this workbook.

Reading & Writing
Companion

11

# Close Read

Reread "The Refusal." As you reread, complete the Skills Focus questions below. Then use your answers and annotations from the questions to help you complete the Write activity.

## ◎ SKILLS FOCUS

1. Paragraph 3 of "The Refusal" contains descriptions of the capital and the small town in which the story is set. Explain what you can infer about how the setting might affect the characters.

2. Analyze the townspeople's attitudes toward the soldiers and the colonel. Use textual evidence to explain what the different attitudes suggest about the characters' roles and interactions in the story.

3. In paragraph 7, the narrator reveals his feelings about the events in the town. Explain what you can infer about his character from this revelation and discuss how the details the narrator supplies help to advance the plot.

4. The young people in the final paragraph of the story are described as "discontent." Explain the likely source of their unhappiness and why this fact helps make them complex.

5. Discuss how the characters in "The Refusal" use language, or avoid using language, and how communication affects the events in the story.

## ✏ WRITE

LITERARY ANALYSIS: How does the author use the historical setting to create complex yet believable characters? Choose one or two characters to focus on and use evidence from the text to support your response.

Copyright © BookheadEd Learning, LLC

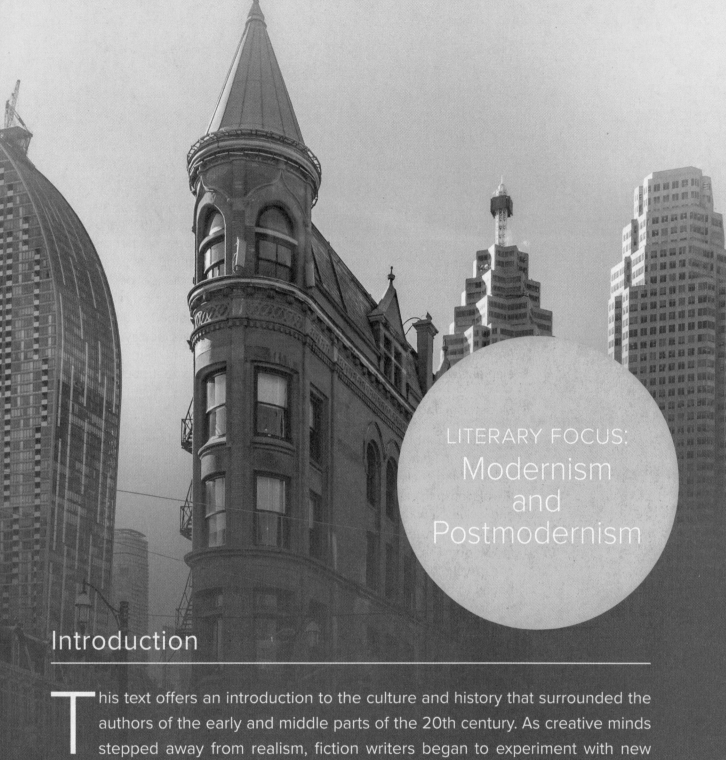

# Modernism and Postmodernism

## Introduction

This text offers an introduction to the culture and history that surrounded the authors of the early and middle parts of the 20th century. As creative minds stepped away from realism, fiction writers began to experiment with new approaches to narrative, plot, character, and theme. This informational text helps audiences understand how art and works of literature written in different periods of the 20th century compare. What makes *Things Fall Apart* so different from *Heart of Darkness*? This overview gives insight into the new ideas and modern interests that informed the writers who lived through World War I and World War II to see a new world before their eyes and across the page.

# "Just how real is it?"

1    Think about your favorite reality show. Just how real is it? The stakes seem high, but will the winner actually be America's top model or chef or fashion designer or survivor? What's really going on when participants express their feelings directly into a camera? Surely they know that millions of people will be watching them. Even though the word *reality* is in the title, most reality shows are in fact carefully constructed narratives pieced together by directors and producers. The dramatic confrontations, the way viewers identify with or vilify the participants, the self-aware finales, and the fragmented storylines are all elements with roots in literary periods known as modernism and postmodernism.

## Modernism and the Modern World

2    The literature of the nineteenth century was characterized by realism. Novelists, in particular, created stories with characters and plots that faithfully reflected the challenges and issues of their time. With the Second Industrial Revolution in the late 1800s, daily life became more fast-paced, mechanized, and urban. New research and analysis by scientists such as Charles Darwin and Albert Einstein and the psychoanalyst Sigmund Freud helped usher in the Modern Era. This era was a time of science and progress, rational thought and psychology. After World War I (1914–1918), traditional class structures began to break down in Europe and the United States. Modern writers felt alienated from the stable, pre-war world they had previously known.

3    As a result, many rejected realism, the practice of representing or depicting people, places, and situations as close to how they look in real life as possible. Instead, their works explored the subjective **interiority** of a narrator's inner life and the **fragmentation** of time. Virginia Woolf's *Mrs. Dalloway* and James Joyce's *Ulysses* are classic examples of modernism. The novels lack linear plot, chronology, and a reliable narrator. Instead, writers used **stream of consciousness** to move the narrative forward. With stream of consciousness, writers endeavor to mimic natural human patterns of thought which can shift quickly from one thought or observation to the next in a seemingly random or chaotic manner. This technique makes modernist novels highly stylized, reflecting the author's unique voice. Much like the literature, modernist art also rejected realism and hinted at characters' inner worlds, as in Picasso's painting *Girl Before A Mirror*, whose colorful distortions depict a girl looking inward as she stands in front of a mirror, perhaps self-consciously.

*Girl Before A Mirror* by Pablo Picasso (1932)

## Postmodernism and the Post-War World

4   With the end of World War II in 1945 came the collapse of European colonialism, the emergence of new nations, and the rise of multicultural voices by authors with new stories to tell and new ways to tell them. Postmodern literature regularly features everyday language, narrative fragmentation, and **experimentalism**.

5   Postmodern texts often have unexpected and challenging structures. Other times, authors use conventional structures, but subvert an existing story by modifying its genre or form, or updating it in some other way. In some examples of postmodernist literature, each chapter in a novel might tell the story from a different character's experience, or the story might start in the middle of the narrative and never reach a satisfying conclusion, as in Julio Cortazar's story "House Taken Over." Like the participants in a reality show, postmodern authors and their narrators are ironic; they understand that they—and the readers—are "in on" the act of storytelling. They reveal their self-awareness through quoting, referring to, or **parodying** other texts. For example, Seth Grahame-Smith updated Jane Austen's *Pride and Prejudice* by adding zombies, mixing two genres and putting his own spin on the classic and well-known novel. Unlike modernist writers, postmodernist writers focus on **exteriority**. They are frequently more interested in the external world and its social and cultural constructs than in a character's inner thoughts and feelings. They often convey the complexity of the postmodern world by using **multiplication** or several narrators. Each narrator has his or her own unique and often conflicting perspectives. Sometimes a postmodern author inserts himself or herself—or a character that is very close to him or her—into the narrative. In postmodern art such as Escher's *Convex and Concave*, the artist

plays with perspective much like postmodern writers, but in this case by carefully constructing vanishing points so that one could see a different exterior world with each turn of the piece.

*Convex and Concave* by M.C. Escher, 1955

## Major Concepts

|  | Modernist Literature | Postmodernist Literature |
|---|---|---|
| **Point of View** | The focus is on the author's subjective style and point of view. | The focus is on the reader's experience of reading the text and the author's awareness of that experience. |
| **Character** | The author uses interiority, stream of consciousness, and inner monologue to explore the narrator's or character's psychology. | The author may concentrate on exteriority, often through a third-person omniscient narrator who focuses on the social or physical world. |
| **Narrative Coherence** | The author may employ unreliable narrators, nonlinear time sequences, and complicated language. | The author creates multiplication of meaning through multiple narrators with multiple perspectives on the same issue. |
| **Themes** | Themes often include alienation, escapism, and unstable or fragmented identity. Franz Kafka's story "The Refusal" is a classic example of the modernist themes of alienation and uncertain identity. | Themes often reflect collective voices and multicultural experiences. |

6

## Style and Form

7

| | Modernist Literature | Postmodernist Literature |
|---|---|---|
| **Language** | The author often uses uncommon, sophisticated, or made-up language to express a subjective experience or point of view. | The author uses clear, everyday language to engage the audience and offset the often complicated narrative structure. |
| **Narration** | Stories are often presented in a subjective, often fragmented or nonlinear way. As an example, consider the complicated logic of Marlow, the narrator of Joseph Conrad's *Heart of Darkness*. | Stories are often presented in a fragmented or nonlinear way by an ironic narrator or multiple narrators. Chinua Achebe explores the opposing but equally sympathetic perspectives of Okonkwo and his father in *Things Fall Apart*. |
| **Genre** | Modernist writers experiment with storytelling elements, such as linear plot structures and character, but generally do not break from established genres. In modernism, literature is still considered an art form. | Postmodernist writers show self-awareness of genre forms by quoting or parodying other texts. Postmodern texts mix and give equal weight to "high culture" and popular culture. |

8   Though different in style and form, modernist and postmodernist literature reflect a complicated and ever-changing reality. Modernists examined the world through a deeply subjective lens, while postmodernists tend to be more interested in a multiplicity of voices and experiences. Postmodernist texts continue to challenge readers and evolve into new forms today. Where do you notice the influence of modernism and postmodernism in popular culture?

# Literary Focus

Read "Literary Focus: Modernism and Postmodernism." After you read, complete the Think Questions below.

## ☁ THINK QUESTIONS

1. What are the major differences between modernist and postmodernist works in terms of how authors craft their characters? Cite evidence from the text that backs up your explanations.

2. What effect did both world wars have on the literature that followed? Explain, using evidence from the text to support your inferences.

3. Think of two or three texts you have read in school that were written in the 20th century. Write down their titles and explain, based on the information here, whether you think they are modernist or postmodernist works. Use evidence from this text to support your assertions.

4. The word **fragmentation** stems from the Latin *frangere*, meaning "to break or shatter." With this information in mind, determine the meaning of *fragmentation* as it is used within the context of an informational text about literature. Cite any words or phrases from the text that were helpful in coming to your conclusion.

5. Use context clues to determine the meaning of the word **exteriority**. Write your definition here, along with the words or phrases that were most helpful in determining the word's meaning. Finally, check a dictionary to confirm your understanding.

# I Am Offering This Poem

POETRY
Jimmy Santiago Baca
1979

## Introduction

The tender words of this poem give little hint of the poet's rough life, but Jimmy Santiago Baca (b. 1952) says he doesn't know if he'd be alive today if he hadn't found poetry. Born in New Mexico of Apache and Chicano descent, Baca was abandoned by his parents as a toddler and later sent to an orphanage, which he fled at the age of 13 to live on the streets. By the time he was 21, Baca was in jail for drugs. It was there he began to turn his life around, learning to read and write poetry while serving a six-and-a-half-year prison sentence. Since his release, he has dedicated his life to teaching others the saving grace of writing.

*His gift to others is his words*

# "I am offering this poem to you . . ."

1  I am offering this poem to you,
2  since I have nothing else to give.
3  Keep it like a warm coat
4  when winter comes to cover you,
5  or like a pair of thick socks
6  the cold cannot bite through,

7  I love you,

8  I have nothing else to give you,
9  so it is a pot full of yellow corn
10 to warm your belly in winter,
11 it is a scarf for your head, to wear
12 over your hair, to tie up around your face,

13 I love you,

14 Keep it, treasure this as you would
15 if you were lost, needing **direction**,
16 in the wilderness life becomes when **mature**;
17 and in the corner of your drawer,
18 tucked away like a cabin or **hogan**
19 in **dense** trees, come knocking,
20 and I will answer, give you directions,
21 and let you warm yourself by this fire,
22 rest by this fire, and make you feel safe

23 I love you,

24 It's all I have to give,
25 and all anyone needs to live,
26 and to go on living inside,
27 when the world outside

28   no longer cares if you live or die;
29   remember,
30   I love you

By Jimmy Santiago Baca, from IMMIGRANTS IN OUR OWN LAND, copyright ©1979 by Jimmy Santiago Baca. Reprinted by permission of New Directions Publishing Corp.

---

## ✏ WRITE

PERSONAL RESPONSE:  Often, people give gifts that are tangible or material. However, in this poem, the gift is one of words. How does what you read influence your opinion on what makes a good gift? Cite evidence from the poem as well as from your personal experience to support your opinion.

Please note that excerpts and passages in the StudySync® library and this workbook are intended as touchstones to generate interest in an author's work. The excerpts and passages do not substitute for the reading of entire texts, and StudySync® strongly recommends that students seek out and purchase the whole literary or informational work in order to experience it as the author intended. Links to online resellers are available in our digital library. In addition, complete works may be ordered through an authorized reseller by filling out and returning to StudySync® the order form enclosed in this workbook.

Reading & Writing Companion   21

# She Unnames Them

FICTION
Ursula K. Le Guin
1985

## Introduction

Ursula K. Le Guin (1929–2018) was a beloved and influential science-fiction author. Deeply engaged with issues of feminism and the environment, she won the Hugo and Nebula awards for her novel *The Left Hand of Darkness*. Le Guin's short story "She Unnames Them" reimagines a foundational passage from the Book of Genesis in which Adam names the different animals he encounters. Le Guin's story, however, has a modern twist—it is narrated from the perspective of Eve, the first woman. In this brief tale, Le Guin's use of descriptive language enhances her perspectives on gender barriers, inequality, and identity.

# "Most of them accepted namelessness . . ."

1   Most of them accepted namelessness with the perfect indifference with which they had so long accepted and ignored their names. Whales and dolphins, seals and sea otters consented with particular grace and **alacrity**, sliding into anonymity as into their element. A faction of yaks, however, protested. They said that "yak" sounded right, and that almost everyone who knew they existed called them that. Unlike the ubiquitous creatures such as rats and fleas, who had been called by hundreds or thousands of different names since Babel, the yaks could truly say, they said, that they had a *name*. They discussed the matter all summer. The councils of the elderly females finally agreed that though the name might be useful to others it was so redundant from the yak point of view that they never spoke it themselves and hence might as well dispense with it. After they presented the argument in this light to their bulls, a full consensus was delayed only by the onset of severe early blizzards. Soon after the beginning of the thaw, their agreement was reached and the designation "yak" was returned to the donor.

2   Among the domestic animals, few horses had cared what anybody called them since the failure of Dean Swift's[1] attempt to name them from their own vocabulary. Cattle, sheep, swine, asses, mules, and goats, along with chickens, geese, and turkeys, all agreed enthusiastically to give their names back to the people to whom—as they put it—they belonged.

3   A couple of problems did come up with pets. The cats, of course, **steadfastly** denied ever having had any name other than those self-given, unspoken, ineffably personal names which, as the poet Eliot[2] said, they spend long hours daily contemplating—though none of the contemplators has ever admitted that what they contemplate is their names and some onlookers have wondered if the object of that meditative gaze might not in fact be the Perfect, or Platonic, Mouse. In any case, it is a moot point now. It was with the dogs, and with some parrots, lovebirds, ravens, and mynahs, that the trouble arose. These verbally talented individuals insisted that their names were

NOTES

Skill:
Allusion

*I know that Babel is a story in the Bible. I also know Adam gives all the animals their names in the Bible. I wonder if the animals losing their names has something to do with the story of Adam.*

---

1. **Dean Swift** Anglo-Irish author Jonathan Swift, whose satirical novel *Gulliver's Travels* imagines a race of talking horses
2. **Eliot** American/British poet T.S. Eliot, who wrote the poem "The Naming of Cats"

NOTES

important to them, and flatly refused to part with them. But as soon as they understood that the issue was precisely one of individual choice, and that anybody who wanted to be called Rover, or Froufrou, or Polly, or even Birdie in the personal sense, was perfectly free to do so, not one of them had the least objection to parting with the lowercase (or, as regards German creatures, uppercase) generic appellations "poodle," "parrot," "dog," or "bird," and all the Linnaean qualifiers that had trailed along behind them for two hundred years like tin cans tied to a tail.

4  The insects parted with their names in **vast** clouds and swarms of ephemeral syllables buzzing and stinging and humming and flitting and crawling and tunneling away.

5  As for the fish of the sea, their names dispersed from them in silence throughout the oceans like faint, dark blurs of cuttlefish ink, and drifted off on the currents without a trace.

Skill:
Theme

*In this section I notice that by unnaming all the animals, Eve has changed her relationship with them. She thinks about how she feels closer to them because she has removed all of their labels. These thoughts show a theme that labels can be a barrier to equality.*

6  NONE were left now to unname, and yet how close I felt to them when I saw one of them swim or fly or trot or crawl across my way or over my skin, or stalk me in the night, or go along beside me for a while in the day. They seemed far closer than when their names had stood between myself and them like a clear barrier: so close that my fear of them and their fear of me became one same fear. And the attraction that many of us felt, the desire to smell one another's smells, feel or rub or caress one another's scales or skin or feathers or fur, taste one another's blood or flesh, keep one another warm—that attraction was now all one with the fear, and the hunter could not be told from the hunted, nor the eater from the food.

7  This was more or less the effect I had been after. It was somewhat more powerful than I had anticipated, but I could not now, in all conscience, make an exception for myself. I **resolutely** put anxiety away, went to Adam, and said, "You and your father lent me this—gave it to me, actually. It's been really useful, but it doesn't exactly seem to fit very well lately. But thanks very much! It's really been very useful."

8  It is hard to give back a gift without sounding **peevish** or ungrateful, and I did not want to leave him with that impression of me. He was not paying much attention, as it happened, and said only, "Put it down over there, O.K.?" and went on with what he was doing.

9  One of my reasons for doing what I did was that talk was getting us nowhere, but all the same I felt a little let down. I had been prepared to defend my decision. And I thought that perhaps when he did notice he might be upset and want to talk. I put some things away and fiddled around a little, but he

continued to do what he was doing and to take no notice of anything else. At last I said, "Well, goodbye, dear. I hope the garden key turns up."

10  He was fitting parts together, and said, without looking around, "O.K., fine, dear. When's dinner?"

11  "I'm not sure," I said. "I'm going now. With the—" I hesitated, and finally said, "With them, you know," and went on out. In fact, I had only just then realized how hard it would have been to explain myself. I could not chatter away as I used to do, taking it all for granted. My words now must be as slow, as new, as single, as tentative as the steps I took going down the path away from the house, between the dark-branched, tall dancers motionless against the winter shining.

Copyright © 1985 by Ursula K. Le Guin. First appeared in "The New Yorker" in 1985, reprinted in author's own collection BUFFALO GALS AND OTHER ANIMAL PRESENCES. Reprinted by permission of Curtis Brown, Ltd.

Please note that excerpts and passages in the StudySync® library and this workbook are intended as touchstones to generate interest in an author's work. The excerpts and passages do not substitute for the reading of entire texts, and StudySync® strongly recommends that students seek out and purchase the whole literary or informational work in order to experience it as the author intended. Links to online resellers are available in our digital library. In addition, complete works may be ordered through an authorized reseller by filling out and returning to StudySync® the order form enclosed in this workbook.

Reading & Writing Companion  25

SHE UNNAMES THEM

# First Read

Read "She Unnames Them." After you read, complete the Think Questions below.

 ## THINK QUESTIONS

1. What was the narrator's intention for "unnaming" the animals? Refer to paragraphs 6 and 7 and use evidence from the text to support your answer.

2. What can you infer about Adam and Eve's relationship? Use evidence from the last three paragraphs of the story to defend your answer.

3. Why did the narrator decide to leave Adam at the end of the story? Cite specific evidence from the text in your answer.

4. What is the meaning of the word **peevish** as it is used in the text? Write your best definition here, along with a brief explanation of how you arrived at its meaning.

5. Read the following dictionary entry:

**vast**

vast /vast/

*adjective*

1. of very great extent or quantity; immense

*noun*

2. an immense space

Use context to determine which of these definitions most closely matches the use of **vast** in "She Unnames Them." Write the definition here and explain how you figured it out.

# Skill:
# Allusion

Use the Checklist to analyze Allusion in "She Unnames Them." Refer to the sample student annotations about Allusion in the text.

## ••• CHECKLIST FOR ALLUSION

In order to identify an allusion, note the following:

- ✓ clues in a specific work that suggest a reference to previous source material

- ✓ when the author references previous source material

- ✓ the theme, event, character, or situation in a text to which the allusion adds information

To better understand the source material an author used to create a new work, do the following:

- ✓ use a print or digital resource to look up the work and any other allusions

- ✓ list details about the work or allusion that are related to the new work

To analyze how an author draws on and transforms source material in a specific work of fiction, consider the following questions:

- ✓ What theme/event/character from another work is referenced in the fiction I am reading? How do I know?

- ✓ How does that theme/event/character change or transform in this new text?

- ✓ What does the modern version of the story add to the earlier story?

Please note that excerpts and passages in the StudySync® library and this workbook are intended as touchstones to generate interest in an author's work. The excerpts and passages do not substitute for the reading of entire texts, and StudySync® strongly recommends that students seek out and purchase the whole literary or informational work in order to experience it as the author intended. Links to online resellers are available in our digital library. In addition, complete works may be ordered through an authorized reseller by filling out and returning to StudySync® the order form enclosed in this workbook.

Reading & Writing Companion

27

# Skill:
# Allusion

Reread paragraphs 7–9 of "She Unnames Them" and the excerpts from the text below. Then, write the letter for each Biblical allusion that best relates to the excerpt provided.

## ⟳ YOUR TURN

| | Excerpt Options |
|---|---|
| **A** | There is no clear allusion. |
| **B** | And Adam said, This is now bone of my bones, and flesh of my flesh: she shall be called Woman, because she was taken out of Man. |
| **C** | Therefore the Lord God sent him forth from the garden of Eden, to till the ground from whence he was taken. |

| Excerpt from "She Unnames Them" | Excerpt from the Bible |
|---|---|
| "You and your father lent me this – gave it to me, actually. It's been really useful, but it doesn't exactly seem to fit very well lately. But thanks very much! It's really been very useful." | |
| One of my reasons for doing what I did was that talk was getting us nowhere, but all the same I felt a little let down. | |
| At last I said, "Well, goodbye, dear. I hope the garden key turns up." | |

# Skill:
# Theme

Use the Checklist to analyze Theme in "She Unnames Them." Refer to the sample student annotations about Theme in the text.

## ••• CHECKLIST FOR THEME

In order to identify a theme or central idea of a text, note the following:

✓ the subject of the text and a theme that might be stated directly in the text

✓ details in the text that help to reveal theme

- the title and chapter headings

- details about the setting

- the narrator's or speaker's tone

- characters' thoughts, actions, and dialogue

- the central conflict in a story's plot

- the climax, or turning point in the story

- the resolution of the conflict

- changes in characters, setting, or plot events

✓ specific details that shape and refine the theme

To determine a theme or central idea of a text and analyze in detail its development over the course of the text, including how it emerges and is shaped and refined by specific details, consider the following questions:

✓ How do details of setting, characters, and plot events lead to a message about life?

✓ What is a theme of the text? How and when does it emerge?

✓ Is there more than one theme? How do I know?

✓ What specific details shape and refine the theme?

✓ How does each theme develop over the course of the text?

Skill:
Theme

Reread paragraphs 8–11 of "She Unnames Them." Then, using the Checklist on the previous page, answer the multiple-choice questions below.

## ⟳ YOUR TURN

1. This question has two parts. First, answer Part A. Then, answer Part B.

   **Part A:** Identify the theme that most clearly emerges from the details in the passage.

   ○ A.  Achieving freedom sometimes requires us to enter into the unknown.

   ○ B.  The transition from childhood to adulthood is often a sad one.

   ○ C.  Leaving an important relationship behind can create a sense of grief and loss.

   ○ D.  Language is a powerful force because it can unite us with others.

   **Part B:** Which of Eve's actions helps BEST to develop the theme identified in Part A?

   ○ A.  She doubts her choice to leave her name and Adam behind.

   ○ B.  She stops worrying about explaining her choices to others.

   ○ C.  For the first time, Eve's fear overcomes her.

   ○ D.  She feels more certain of how to express herself than ever.

# Skill:
# Compare and Contrast

Use the Checklist to analyze Compare and Contrast in "She Unnames Them."

## ••• CHECKLIST FOR COMPARE AND CONTRAST

In order to determine how to compare and contrast a text to its source material, use the following steps:

✓ First, choose works of literature in which the author draws on and transforms elements from another source, such as theme in John Green's *The Fault in Our Stars* and Shakespeare's *Romeo and Juliet*, or Ovid's poems on Greek and Roman mythology and their influence on Shakespeare.

✓ Next, identify literary elements that are comparable in the text and its source:

- the series of events that make up each plot
- connections between the characters and what motivates them
- the theme in each work
- the message or ideas the authors want to communicate to readers

✓ Finally, explain ways the author transforms the source material, perhaps by updating certain aspects of the plot or changing a character's traits.

To analyze how an author draws on and transforms source material in order to compare and contrast, consider the following questions:

✓ How does the author draw from the source material?

✓ How does the author transform the source material?

✓ How do the literary elements in the text compare to its source?

# Skill:
# Compare and Contrast

Reread paragraphs 9–11 from "She Unnames Them" and lines 14–23 from "I Am Offering This Poem." Then, using the Checklist on the previous page, complete the chart on the next page to compare and contrast the passages. Write the letter for each sentence in the correct column.

## ⟳ YOUR TURN

| | Observation Options |
|---|---|
| A | Words matter to the narrator and speaker. |
| B | Words seem hard to say. |
| C | The words from the speaker to the recipient are warm and caring. |
| D | For the narrator and speaker, words are meaningful and powerful. |
| E | Both show a relationship between two people. |
| F | The relationship is a strong one. |
| G | Words flow easily. |
| H | The words between the narrator and her partner are distant and cold. |
| I | The relationship is ending. |

Reading & Writing Companion

| "She Unnames Them" | Both | "I Am Offering This Poem" |
|---|---|---|
|  |  |  |
|  |  |  |
|  |  |  |

# SHE UNNAMES THEM

# Close Read

Reread "She Unnames Them." As you reread, complete the Skills Focus questions below. Then use your answers and annotations from the questions to help you complete the Write activity.

## ◎ SKILLS FOCUS

1. Discuss the ways in which Le Guin alludes to the Book of Genesis in the Bible and how she makes it new through her story.

2. Explain the main theme of "She Unnames Them" and describe how the specific details shape and refine the theme over the course of the story.

3. The narrator of "I Am Offering This Poem" says, in the final stanza,

   It's all I have to give,
   and all anyone needs to live,

and to go on living inside,
when the world outside
no longer cares if you live or die;

Explain what the narrator of "She Unnames Them" believes she is giving to the natural world, and why.

4. In Genesis in the Bible, Adam is tasked with naming all the animals. Explain why, based on Le Guin's story, Eve may want to use the power of words in a negative sense, by "unnaming."

## ✏ WRITE

COMPARE AND CONTRAST: Philosopher Suzanne K. Langer said, "The very notion of giving something a name was the vastest generative idea that was ever conceived." The plot of "She Unnames Them," which centers on the voluntary unnaming of Eve and the animals, plays an important role in communicating a theme concerning hierarchy. Using "She Unnames Them" and "I Am Offering This Poem" as sources, discuss how writers use language to develop themes and ideas and how those words give the themes and ideas power.

# The Story of a Vision

FICTION
Francis La Flesche
1901

## Introduction

Francis La Flesche (1857–1932) was the first Native American to work for the Smithsonian Institution as a professional anthropologist. His fiction and his ethnography offer invaluable documents of Omaha and Osage tribal cultures. Most of La Flesche's short stories, including "The Story of a Vision," are based on the rich folktales of the Omaha tribe that defined the author's childhood. La Flesche integrates the tribe's belief system into much of his writing—especially that of spirit, retribution, community, and omens—which makes "A Story of a Vision" that much more enchanting.

# "In the old days, many strange things came to pass in the life of our people . . ."

NOTES

1 Each of us, as we gathered at the lodge of our storyteller at dusk, picked up an armful of wood and entered. The old man who was sitting alone, his wife having gone on a visit, welcomed us with a pleasant word as we threw the wood down by the fire-place and busied ourselves rekindling the fire.

Omaha Dance

2 Ja-bae-ka and Ne-ne-ba, having nothing to do at this moment, fell to scuffling. "You will be fighting if you keep on," warned the old man.

3 "Stop your fooling and come and sit down," scolded Wa-du-pa. "You're not in your own house."

4 The flames livened up cheerily and cast a **ruddy** glow about us when Wa-du-pa said,

5 "Grandfather, the last time we were here, you told us the myth of the eagle and the wren; we liked it, but now we want a true story, something that really happened, something you saw yourself."

6 "How thirsty I am!" said the old man irrelevantly. "I wonder what makes me so dry."

7 "Quick!" said Wa-du-pa, motioning to Ja-bae-ka, "Get some water!"

8 The lad peered into one kettle, squinted into another, and then said, "There isn't any."

9 "Then go, get some!" arose a number of voices.

10 "Why don't some of you go?" Ja-bae-ka **retorted,** picking up one of the kettles.

11 "Take both!" someone shouted.

12 Ja-bae-ka approached the door grumbling. As he grasped the heavy skin portier to make his way out, he turned and said, "Don't begin until I come back."

13  We soon heard his heavy breathing in the long entrance way. "It's moonlight, just like day!" he exclaimed, as he set the kettles down and thrust his cold hands into the flames with a twisting motion. "The boys and girls are having lots of fun sliding on the ice."

14  "Let them slide, we don't care!" ejaculated Wa-du-pa as he dipped a cup into the water and handed it to the old man, who put it to his lips and made a gulping sound as he drank, the lump in his throat leaping up and down at each swallow. At the last draught, he expelled his pent-up breath with something like a groan, set the cup down, wiped his lips with the back of his hand, and asked, "A real true story—something that I saw myself; that's what you want, is it?"

15  "Yes, grandfather," we sang out in chorus. "A story that has you in it!"

16  His face brightened with a smile and he broke into a gentle laugh, nodding his head to its rhythm.

17  After a few moments' **musing,** and when we boys had settled down, the old man began: "Many, many winters ago, long before any of you were born, our people went on a winter hunt, away out among the sand hills where even now we sometimes go. There was a misunderstanding between the leaders, so that just as we reached the hunting grounds the tribe separated into two parties, each going in a different direction.

18  "The weather was pleasant enough while on the journey, but a few days after the departure of our friends, a heavy storm came upon us. For days and nights the wind howled and roared, threatening to carry away our tents, and the snow fell thick and fast, so that we could not see an arm's length; it was waist deep and yet it kept falling. No hunting could be done; food grew scarcer and scarcer, and the older people became alarmed.

19  "One afternoon as my father, mother and I were sitting in our tent eating from our last kettle of corn, there came a lull and we heard with startling distinctness a man singing a song of augury. We paused to listen, but the wind swept down again and drowned the voice.

20  "'A holy man seeking for a sign,' said my father. 'Son, go and hear if he will give us words of courage.'

21  "My father was lame and could not go himself, so I waded through the heavy drifts and with much difficulty reached the man's tent, where many were already gathered to hear the predictions. I held my breath in awe as I heard the holy man say:

22 "'For a moment the wind ceased to blow, the clouds parted, and in the rift I saw standing, in mid air against the blue sky, the spirit of the man who was murdered last summer. His head was bowed in grief and although he spoke not, I know from the vision that the anger of the storm gods was moved against us for not punishing the murderer. Silently the spirit lifted an arm and pointed beyond the hills. Then I found that I too was in midair. I looked over the hilltops and beheld a forest, where shadowy forms like those of large animals moved among the trees. I turned once more to the spirit, but the clouds had come together again.

23 "'Before dawn to-morrow the storm will pass away, then let the runners go to the forest that I saw and tell us whether or not there is truth in the words that I have spoken.'

24 "As predicted, the wind ceased to blow and the snow to fall. Runners were hastily sent to the forest, and the sun was hardly risen when one of them returned with the good news that the shadowy forms the holy man had seen were truly those of buffalo.

25 "The effect of the news upon the camp was like magic, faces brightened, the gloomy **forebodings** that clouded the minds of the older people fled as did the storm, and laughter and pleasantries enlivened the place. The hunters and boys were soon plodding through the snow toward the forest, and before dark every one returned heavily laden, tired and hungry, but nonetheless happy. The fires burned brightly that night, and men told stories until it was nearly morning.

26 "The forest of the vision was a bag of game; every few days the hunters went there and returned with buffalo, elk, or deer, so that even the poorest man had plenty for his wife and children to eat.

27 "All this time nothing had been heard from the party that separated from us before the storm. One night when I came home from a rabbit hunt, I found my mother and father packing up pemican and jerked meat as though for a journey. I looked inquiringly at the pack as I ate my supper; bye and bye my mother told me that a man had just come from the other camp with the news that the people had exhausted their supplies and, as they could find no game, they were suffering for want of food. My sister and her husband were in that camp, and I was told to carry the pack to them.

28 "My father had arranged with a young man bound on a similar errand to call for me early in the morning, so I went to bed as soon as I had finished eating to get as much sleep and rest as possible. It was well that I did, for long before dawn creaking footsteps approached our tent and the man called out, 'Are you ready?' I quickly slipped on my leggings and moccasins, put on my robe, slung the pack over my shoulders, and we started.

NOTES

29 "To avoid the drifts, we followed the ridges, but even there the snow lay deep, and we were continually breaking through the hard crust. My friend turned every mishap into a joke and broke the **monotony** of our travel with humorous tales and incidents. Late at night we camped in the bend of a small, wooded stream. We gathered a big pile of dry branches, kindled a roaring fire, and roasted some of the jerked meat. When supper was over, we dried our moccasins, then piling more wood on the fire, we wrapped ourselves up in our robes and went to sleep.

30 "I do not know how long we might have slept had we not been wakened by the howling of hundreds of wolves not far away from us. 'They're singing to the morning star!' said my friend. 'It is near day, so we must be up and going.'

31 "We ate a little of the pemican, helped each other to load, and again we started. Before night we were overtaken by other men and boys who were also going to the relief of their friends in the other camp, where we arrived just in time to save many of the people from starving.

32 "How curious it was that the predictions of the holy man should come true— the stopping of the storm before morning, the forest, and the shadowy forms of animals. Stranger still was the death of the murderer. This took place, we were told by the people we had rescued, on the very night of the augury in our camp. They said, as the man was sitting in his tent that night, the wind suddenly blew the door flap violently aside, an expression of terror came over his face, he fell backward, and he was dead.

33 "In the old days, many strange things came to pass in the life of our people, but now we are getting to be different."

34 Wa-du-pa thanked the storyteller, and we were about to go when Ne-ne-ba, pointing to Ja-bae-ka, whispered, "He's gone to sleep! Let's scare him."

35 The old man fell into the spirit of the fun, so we all tip-toed to the back part of the lodge where it was dark and watched, as the flames died down to a blue flickering. We could see the boy's head drop lower and lower until his nose nearly touched his knee. Just then a log on the fire suddenly tumbled from its place, broke in two, sent up a shower of crackling sparks, and Ja-bae-ka awoke with a start. He threw up his head, looked all around, and thinking he was left alone in the darkened lodge, took fright and rushed to the door with a cry of terror. We ran out of our hiding places with shouts of laughter and overtook Ja-bae-ka outside the door, where we teased him about going to sleep and being afraid in the dark.

36 Suddenly he turned upon Ne-ne-ba and said, "You did that, you rascal! I'll pay you back sometime."

WRITE

LITERARY ANALYSIS:  In this short story, the Grandfather relates a story in order to convey an important life lesson to the youth of his tribe. Determine and analyze the theme of this story, including how the theme emerges and is shaped by details of character and setting.

# Heart of Darkness

FICTION
Joseph Conrad
1899

## Introduction

Prior to his career as an author, Joseph Conrad (1857–1924) was a member of both the French and British naval forces. His experiences as a sailor and seaman included journeys to India, Australia, and Africa—and it was during these travels that Conrad became inspired to write about the horrors of colonialism. One of his most controversial and memorable works, *Heart of Darkness* is derived from his time in the Congo Free State, ruled at the time by King Leopold II of Belgium, where Conrad purportedly came face-to-face with the depths of madness found in colonialism, the African jungle, and the human psyche. The story follows river-boat captain Charles Marlow along the Congo River in his pursuit of ivory, a journey that brings him into contact with cannibals, crazed traders, and the enigmatic, rogue

# "We penetrated deeper and deeper into the heart of darkness."

## from Chapter II

1   "It's a wonder to me yet. Imagine a blindfolded man set to drive a van over a bad road. I sweated and shivered over that business considerably, I can tell you. After all, for a seaman, to scrape the bottom of the thing that's supposed to float all the time under his care is the unpardonable sin. No one may know of it, but you never forget the thump—eh? A blow on the very heart. You remember it, you dream of it, you wake up at night and think of it—years after—and go hot and cold all over. I don't pretend to say that steamboat floated all the time. More than once she had to wade for a bit, with twenty cannibals splashing around and pushing. We had enlisted some of these chaps on the way for a crew. Fine fellows—cannibals—in their place. They were men one could work with, and I am grateful to them. And, after all, they did not eat each other before my face: they had brought along a **provision** of hippo-meat which went rotten, and made the mystery of the wilderness stink in my nostrils. Phoo! I can sniff it now. I had the manager on board and three or four pilgrims with their staves—all complete. Sometimes we came upon a station close by the bank, clinging to the skirts of the unknown, and the white men rushing out of a tumble-down hovel, with great gestures of joy and surprise and welcome, seemed very strange,—had the appearance of being held there captive by a spell. The word ivory would ring in the air for a while—and on we went again into the silence, along empty reaches, round the still bends, between the high walls of our winding way, reverberating in hollow claps the ponderous beat of the stern-wheel. Trees, trees, millions of trees, massive, immense, running up high; and at their foot, hugging the bank against the stream, crept the little begrimed steamboat, like a sluggish beetle crawling on the floor of a lofty portico. It made you feel very small, very lost, and yet it was not altogether depressing, that feeling. After all, if you were small, the grimy beetle crawled on—which was just what you wanted it to do. Where the pilgrims imagined it crawled to I don't know. To some place where they expected to get something, I bet! For me it crawled toward Kurtz—exclusively; but when the steam-pipes started leaking we crawled very slow. The reaches opened before us and closed behind, as if the forest had stepped leisurely across the water to bar the way for our return. We penetrated deeper and deeper into the heart of darkness. It was very quiet there. At

night sometimes the roll of drums behind the curtain of trees would run up the river and remain sustained faintly, as if hovering in the air high over our heads, till the first break of day. Whether it meant war, peace, or prayer we could not tell. The dawns were heralded by the descent of a chill stillness; the woodcutters slept, their fires burned low; the snapping of a twig would make you start. We were wanderers on a prehistoric earth, on an earth that wore the aspect of an unknown planet. We could have fancied ourselves the first of men taking possession of an accursed inheritance, to be subdued at the cost of **profound** anguish and of excessive toil. But suddenly, as we struggled round a bend, there would be a glimpse of rush walls, of peaked grass-roofs, a burst of yells, a whirl of black limbs, a mass of hands clapping, of feet stamping, of bodies swaying, of eyes rolling, under the droop of heavy and motionless foliage. The steamer toiled along slowly on the edge of a black and incomprehensible frenzy. The prehistoric man was cursing us, praying to us, welcoming us—who could tell? We were cut off from the comprehension of our surroundings; we glided past like phantoms, wondering and secretly appalled, as sane men would be before an enthusiastic outbreak in a madhouse. We could not understand, because we were too far and could not remember, because we were traveling in the night of first ages, of those ages that are gone, leaving hardly a sign—and no memories.

2   "The earth seemed unearthly. We are accustomed to look upon the shackled form of a conquered monster, but there—there you could look at a thing monstrous and free. It was unearthly, and the men were—No, they were not inhuman. Well, you know, that was the worst of it—this suspicion of their not being inhuman. It would come slowly to one. They howled, and leaped, and spun, and made horrid faces; but what thrilled you was just the thought of their humanity—like yours—the thought of your remote kinship with this wild and passionate uproar. Ugly. Yes, it was ugly enough; but if you were man enough you would admit to yourself that there was in you just the faintest trace of a response to the terrible frankness of that noise, a dim suspicion of there being a meaning in it which you—you so remote from the night of first ages—could comprehend. And why not? The mind of man is capable of anything—because everything is in it, all the past as well as all the future. What was there after all? Joy, fear, sorrow, devotion, valor, rage—who can tell?—but truth—truth stripped of its cloak of time. Let the fool gape and shudder—the man knows, and can look on without a wink. But he must at least be as much of a man as these on the shore. He must meet that truth with his own true stuff—with his own inborn strength. Principles? Principles won't do. **Acquisitions**, clothes, pretty rags— rags that would fly off at the first good shake. No; you want a deliberate belief. An appeal to me in this fiendish row—is there? Very well; I hear; I admit, but I have a voice too, and for good or evil mine is the speech that cannot be silenced. Of course, a fool, what with sheer fright and fine sentiments, is always safe. Who's that grunting? You wonder I didn't go ashore for a howl and a dance? Well, no—I didn't. Fine sentiments, you say? Fine sentiments, be

hanged! I had no time. I had to mess about with white-lead and strips of woolen blanket helping to put bandages on those leaky steam-pipes—I tell you. I had to watch the steering, and **circumvent** those snags, and get the tin-pot along by hook or by crook. There was surface-truth enough in these things to save a wiser man. And between whiles I had to look after the savage who was fireman. He was an improved specimen; he could fire up a vertical boiler. He was there below me, and, upon my word, to look at him was as edifying as seeing a dog in a parody of breeches and a feather hat, walking on his hind-legs. A few months of training had done for that really fine chap. He squinted at the steam-gauge and at the water-gauge with an evident effort of intrepidity—and he had filed teeth too, the poor devil, and the wool of his pate shaved into queer patterns, and three ornamental scars on each of his cheeks. He ought to have been clapping his hands and stamping his feet on the bank, instead of which he was hard at work, a thrall to strange witchcraft, full of improving knowledge. He was useful because he had been instructed; and what he knew was this—that should the water in that transparent thing disappear, the evil spirit inside the boiler would get angry through the greatness of his thirst, and take a terrible vengeance. So he sweated and fired up and watched the glass fearfully (with an **impromptu** charm, made of rags, tied to his arm, and a piece of polished bone, as big as a watch, stuck flatways through his lower lip), while the wooded banks slipped past us slowly, the short noise was left behind, the interminable miles of silence—and we crept on, towards Kurtz. But the snags were thick, the water was **treacherous** and shallow, the boiler seemed indeed to have a sulky devil in it, and thus neither that fireman nor I had any time to peer into our creepy thoughts.

---

✏ WRITE

---

LITERARY ANALYSIS: *Heart of Darkness* is narrated from the perspective of a European exploring Africa. The passage conveys his perspective on his journey into the unknown as he experiences new regions of the globe. How does the author characterize the narrator through the historical setting? In your response, cite textual evidence to support your analysis.

# Things Fall Apart

FICTION
Chinua Achebe
1958

## Introduction

———————————————————————————————

Nigerian writer and Igbo chieftain Chinua Achebe (1930–2013) was a towering figure in African literature. Achebe's writing captures the traditional rhythms of his West African ancestors through language and dialogue; his works focus mainly on African identity, the effects of colonialism, and the preservation of culture. *Things Fall Apart*, his 1958 masterwork, tells the story of Okonkwo, the well-respected leader of a Nigerian village until—as the title would suggest—things take a turn for the worse. In this excerpt from the first chapter, readers are introduced to a father and son who are very different from one another.

# "... Okonkwo's fame had grown like a bush-fire ..."

NOTES

## Chapter One

1   Okonkwo was well known throughout the nine villages and even beyond. His fame rested on solid personal achievements. As a young man of eighteen he had brought honor to his village by throwing Amalinze the Cat. Amalinze was the great wrestler who for seven years was unbeaten, from Umuofia to Mbaino. He was called the Cat because his back would never touch the earth. It was this man that Okonkwo threw in a fight which the old men agreed was one of the fiercest since the founder of their town engaged a spirit of the wild for seven days and seven nights.

2   The drums beat and the flutes sang and the **spectators** held their breath. Amalinze was a wily craftsman, but Okonkwo was as slippery as a fish in water. Every nerve and every muscle stood out on their arms, on their backs and their thighs, and one almost heard them stretching to breaking point. In the end, Okonkwo threw the Cat.

3   That was many years ago, twenty years or more, and during this time Okonkwo's fame had grown like a bush-fire in the harmattan. He was tall and huge, and his bushy eyebrows and wide nose gave him a very **severe** look. He breathed heavily, and it was said that, when he slept, his wives and children in their houses could hear him breathe. When he walked, his heels hardly touched the ground and he seemed to walk on springs, as if he was going to pounce on somebody. And he did pounce on people quite often. He had a slight stammer and whenever he was angry and could not get his words out quickly enough, he would use his fists. He had no patience with unsuccessful men. He had had no patience with his father.

4   Unoka, for that was his father's name, had died ten years ago. In his day he was lazy and **improvident** and was quite incapable of thinking about tomorrow. If any money came his way, and it seldom did, he immediately bought gourds of palm-wine, called round his neighbors and made merry. He always said that whenever he saw a dead man's mouth he saw the folly of not eating what one had in one's lifetime. Unoka was, of course, a debtor,

Skill:
Theme

*Okonkwo's father was irresponsible. However, I infer that Unoka had worth: he liked joy. I see a theme about the difficulty of reconciling a parent's good and bad traits.*

and he owed every neighbor some money, from a few cowries to quite substantial amounts.

5    He was tall but very thin and had a slight stoop. He wore a **haggard** and mournful look except when he was drinking or playing on his flute. He was very good on his flute, and his happiest moments were the two or three moons after the harvest when the village musicians brought down their instruments, hung above the fireplace. Unoka would play with them, his face beaming with blessedness and peace. Sometimes another village would ask Unoka's band and their dancing egwugwu[1] to come and stay with them and teach them their tunes. They would go to such hosts for as long as three or four markets, making music and feasting. Unoka loved the good fare and the good fellowship, and he loved this season of the year, when the rains had stopped and the sun rose every morning with dazzling beauty. And it was not too hot either, because the cold and dry harmattan wind was blowing down from the north. Some years the harmattan was very severe and a **dense** haze hung on the atmosphere. Old men and children would then sit round log fires, warming their bodies. Unoka loved it all, and he loved the first kites that returned with the dry season, and the children who sang songs of welcome to them. He would remember his own childhood, how he had often wandered around looking for a kite sailing leisurely against the blue sky. As soon as he found one he would sing with his whole being, welcoming it back from its long, long journey, and asking it if it had brought home any lengths of cloth.

6    That was years ago, when he was young. Unoka, the grown-up, was a failure. He was poor and his wife and children had barely enough to eat. People laughed at him because he was a loafer, and they swore never to lend him any more money because he never paid back. But Unoka was such a man that he always succeeded in borrowing more, and piling up his debts.

Excerpted from *Things Fall Apart* by Chinua Achebe, published by Anchor Books.

NOTES

 Skill:
Point of View

*Although Okonkwo's father Unoka is a debtor, he is accepted and welcomed into surrounding villages for his talent with music during plentiful times of the year. He finds great joy in playing his flute, and his life is tied to the natural cycles of the land and harvest in a way that isn't common in the U.S. anymore. The story continues to be told from an outsider's perspective.*

1.  **egwugwu** masked elders of the community who represent ancestral gods

# First Read

Read *Things Fall Apart*. After you read, complete the Think Questions below.

 **THINK QUESTIONS**

1. According to the narrator, Okonkwo "had no patience with unsuccessful men." What do you think is Okonkwo's definition of success? Support your answer with evidence from the text.

2. Explain what the following sentence reveals about Unoka's priorities: "He always said that whenever he saw a dead man's mouth he saw the folly of not eating what one had in one's lifetime." Refer to details from the text to support your answer.

3. What can you infer about the relationship between father and son when Unoka was alive? Support your answer with evidence that is directly stated as well as with ideas you have gathered from clues in the text.

4. Use context clues to determine the meaning of the word **haggard** as it is used in *Things Fall Apart*. Write your definition of *haggard* here and explain how you figured it out.

5. Read the following dictionary entry:

**dense**
dense / dens/

*adjective*

1. unintelligent; slow to learn or comprehend
2. difficult to understand due to complexity of ideas, especially in a text
3. being closely packed together so that it is difficult to move or see through

Decide which definition best matches **dense** as it is used in *Things Fall Apart*. Write that definition of *dense* here and indicate which clues from the text helped you determine the meaning.

# Skill:
# Theme

Use the Checklist to analyze Theme in *Things Fall Apart*. Refer to the sample student annotations about Theme in the text.

## ••• CHECKLIST FOR THEME

In order to identify a theme or central idea of a text, note the following:

✓ the subject of the text and a theme that might be stated directly in the text

✓ details in the text that help to reveal theme

- the title and chapter headings
- details about the setting
- the narrator's or speaker's tone
- characters' thoughts, actions, and dialogue
- the central conflict in a story's plot
- the climax, or turning point in the story
- the resolution of the conflict
- shifts in characters, setting, or plot events

✓ specific details that shape and refine the theme

To determine a theme or central idea of a text and analyze in detail its development over the course of the text, including how it emerges and is shaped and refined by specific details, consider the following questions:

✓ What is a theme of the text? How and when does it emerge?

✓ What specific details shape and refine the theme?

✓ How does the theme develop over the course of the text?

# Skill:
# Theme

Reread paragraph 6 of *Things Fall Apart*. Then, using the Checklist on the previous page, answer the multiple-choice questions below.

## ↻ YOUR TURN

1. What does paragraph 6 suggest most clearly about Unoka's personality?

   ○ A. He grew more amusing as he got older.
   ○ B. He was finally forced to work for his livelihood.
   ○ C. He was seen as more of a burden to those around him.
   ○ D. He lost the ability to talk people into lending him money.

2. From the evidence in paragraph 6, what inference can you make most clearly about Okonkwo's childhood?

   ○ A. Okonkwo grew up eager to follow in his father's footsteps.
   ○ B. Okonkwo felt ashamed of his father's lifestyle.
   ○ C. Okonkwo vowed to repay his father's many debts.
   ○ D. Okonkwo was thin and weak from lack of food.

3. The contrast between father and son supports the theme that—

   ○ A. children tend to be stronger and more successful than their parents.
   ○ B. we are often labeled with the reputation that our parents had.
   ○ C. family relationships have a strong effect on our worldview.
   ○ D. children of failures are less likely to work hard or save money.

# Skill:
# Point of View

Use the Checklist to analyze Point of View in *Things Fall Apart*. Refer to the sample student annotations about Point of View in the text.

## ••• CHECKLIST FOR POINT OF VIEW

In order to identify the point of view or cultural experience reflected in a work of literature from outside the United States, note the following:

- ✓ the pronouns the narrator or speaker uses

- ✓ what the narrator or speaker knows and reveals

- ✓ the country of origin of the characters and author

- ✓ moments in the work that reflect a cultural experience not common in the United States by drawing on reading from world literature, such as

  - a drama written by Ibsen or Chekov or other international authors
  - a story that reflects an indigenous person's experience in another country

To analyze the point of view or a cultural experience reflected in a work of literature from outside the United States, drawing on a wide reading of world literature, consider the following questions:

- ✓ What is the country of origin of the author of the text? Of the characters in the text?

- ✓ What texts have you read previously from these nations or cultures? How does this help you analyze the point of view of this text?

- ✓ How does this text use point of view to present a different cultural experience than that of the United States?

Please note that excerpts and passages in the StudySync® library and this workbook are intended as touchstones to generate interest in an author's work. The excerpts and passages do not substitute for the reading of entire texts, and StudySync® strongly recommends that students seek out and purchase the whole literary or informational work in order to experience it as the author intended. Links to online resellers are available in our digital library. In addition, complete works may be ordered through an authorized reseller by filling out and returning to StudySync® the order form enclosed in this workbook.

Reading & Writing Companion    51

# Skill:
# Point of View

Reread paragraphs 2 and 3 of *Things Fall Apart*. Then, using the Checklist on the previous page, answer the multiple-choice questions below.

## ⟳ YOUR TURN

1. What does this excerpt suggest about the importance of wrestling and strength in the setting of *Things Fall Apart*?

   ○ A. Wrestling is considered an inferior sport that is looked down upon greatly.

   ○ B. Wrestling used to be very important, but in the decades since Okonkwo defeated Amalinze people have stopped caring as much.

   ○ C. Being a strong wrestling champion is a widely respected feat.

   ○ D. Okonkwo is famed for his patience and strength.

2. Who is the narrator, and are there any clues as to his or her perspective on the story?

   ○ A. Unoka, Okonkwo's father, is the narrator, and he is disappointed that his son never had any patience for him.

   ○ B. The narrator is anonymous. The knowledge of Okonkwo's emotions and rumors about his family suggest an omniscient narrator.

   ○ C. Okonkwo is narrating, and he felt ashamed of his father's lifestyle.

   ○ D. The narrator is European and exploring villages in Africa for the first time.

# Close Read

Reread *Things Fall Apart*. As you reread, complete the Skills Focus questions below. Then use your answers and annotations from the questions to help you complete the Write activity.

## ◎ SKILLS FOCUS

1. Discuss details from the opening of this novel that suggest experiences specific to a particular culture outside the United States.

2. Identify clues that suggest that Unoka was "an unsuccessful man." Using these details, explain what it means to be successful in the Igbo culture and how this develops a theme.

3. The title of Achebe's novel comes from a poem called "The Second Coming" written by Irish poet William Butler Yeats. In the poem the speaker says,

   *Things fall apart; the centre cannot hold;*
   *Mere anarchy is loosed upon the world,. . .*

   Based on this excerpt, discuss why Achebe may have alluded to Yeats's poem in his title.

4. Consider what it means to be a man in *Things Fall Apart* and in *Heart of Darkness*. Then explain how Okonkwo, Marlow, and the other male characters are similar in their show of masculinity—and how Unoka is different.

5. In the Native American story "The Story of a Vision," the storyteller says, "In the old days, many strange things came to pass in the life of our people, but now we are getting to be different." Explain how the narrators of *Heart of Darkness* and *Things Fall Apart* use language to develop themes around what is strange, different, or incomprehensible.

## ✎ WRITE

LITERARY ANALYSIS: Compare related themes in *Heart of Darkness* and *Things Fall Apart* about masculinity. Respond by analyzing how the authors represent different cultural perspectives and what the details reveal about the worlds the characters live in.

Please note that excerpts and passages in the StudySync® library and this workbook are intended as touchstones to generate interest in an author's work. The excerpts and passages do not substitute for the reading of entire texts, and StudySync® strongly recommends that students seek out and purchase the whole literary or informational work in order to experience it as the author intended. Links to online resellers are available in our digital library. In addition, complete works may be ordered through an authorized reseller by filling out and returning to StudySync® the order form enclosed in this workbook.

Reading & Writing Companion 53

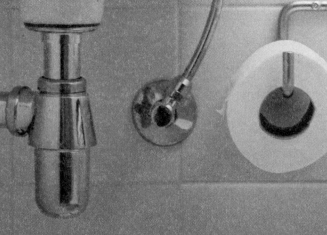

My Grandmother Washes Her Feet in the Sink of the Bathroom at Sears

POETRY
Mohja Kahf
2003

# Introduction

Five times a day, it is the duty of a practicing Muslim to answer the ritual call to prayer. But in the big box stores of the American Midwest, this can get a little complicated. In this poem by Syrian American writer Mohja Kahf (b. 1967), the speaker explores, from a distinctly Arab American perspective, what happens when a clash of civilizations occurs in the bathroom of a department store.

# "I can see a clash of civilizations brewing in the Sears bathroom"

NOTES

1  My grandmother puts her feet in the sink
2  of the bathroom at Sears
3  to wash them in the **ritual** washing for prayer,
4  *wudu,*
5  because she has to pray in the store or miss
6  the **mandatory** prayer time for Muslims
7  She does it with great poise, balancing
8  herself with one plump matronly arm
9  against the automated hot-air hand dryer,
10 after having removed her support knee-highs
11 and laid them aside, folded in thirds,
12 and given me her purse and her packages to hold
13 so she can accomplish this august ritual
14 and get back to the ritual of shopping for housewares

15 Respectable Sears **matrons** shake their heads and frown
16 as they notice what my grandmother is doing,
17 an affront to American porcelain,
18 a contamination of American Standards[1]
19 by something foreign and unhygienic
20 requiring civic action and possible use of disinfectant spray
21 They fluster about and flutter their hands and I can see
22 a clash of **civilizations** brewing in the Sears bathroom

23 My grandmother, though she speaks no English,
24 catches their meaning and her look in the mirror says,
25 *I have washed my feet over Iznik tile in Istanbul*
26 *with water from the world's ancient irrigation systems*
27 *I have washed my feet in the bathhouses of Damascus[2]*
28 *over painted bowls imported from China*
29 *among the best families of Aleppo[3]*

---

1. **American Standard**  a brand that manufactures kitchen and bathroom plumbing fixtures
2. **Damascus**  the capital of Syria
3. **Aleppo**  the most populous city in Syria

30 *And if you Americans knew anything*

31 *about civilization and cleanliness,*

32 *you'd make wider washbasins, anyway*

33 My grandmother knows one **culture**—the right one,

34 as do these matrons of the Middle West. For them,

35 my grandmother might as well have been squatting

36 in the mud over a rusty tin in vaguely tropical squalor,

37 Mexican or Middle Eastern, it doesn't matter which,

38 when she lifts her well-groomed foot and puts it over the edge.

39 "You can't do that," one of the women protests,

40 turning to me, "Tell her she can't do that."

41 "We wash our feet five times a day,"

42 my grandmother declares hotly in Arabic.

43 "My feet are cleaner than their sink.

44 Worried about their sink, are they? I

45 should worry about my feet!"

46 My grandmother nudges me, "Go on, tell them."

47 Standing between the door and the mirror, I can see

48 at multiple angles, my grandmother and the other shoppers,

49 all of them decent and goodhearted women, diligent

50 in cleanliness, grooming, and **decorum**

51 Even now my grandmother, not to be rushed,

52 is delicately drying her pumps with tissues from her purse

53 For my grandmother always wears well-turned pumps

54 that match her purse, I think in case someone

55 from one of the best families of Aleppo

56 should run into her—here, in front of the Kenmore display

57 I smile at the midwestern women

58 as if my grandmother has just said something lovely about them

59 and shrug at my grandmother as if they

60 had just apologized through me

61 No one is fooled, but I

62 hold the door open for everyone

63 and we all emerge on the sales floor

64 and lose ourselves in the great common ground

65 of housewares on markdown.

"My Grandmother Washes Her Feet in the Sink of the Bathroom at Sears," in *E-mails from Scheherazad*, by Mohja Kahf. Gainesville: University Press of Florida, 2003, pp. 26–28. Reprinted with permission of the University Press of Florida.

**WRITE**

PERSONAL RESPONSE: In "My Grandmother Washes Her Feet in the Sink of the Bathroom at Sears," the speaker feels conflicted about two sets of cultural expectations. Write a personal narrative about a time you felt stuck between two sets of expectations. In your personal narrative, describe the conflict, what you felt about the dynamic, and how you responded.

Please note that excerpts and passages in the StudySync® library and this workbook are intended as touchstones to generate interest in an author's work. The excerpts and passages do not substitute for the reading of entire texts, and StudySync® strongly recommends that students seek out and purchase the whole literary or informational work in order to experience it as the author intended. Links to online resellers are available in our digital library. In addition, complete works may be ordered through an authorized reseller by filling out and returning to StudySync® the order form enclosed in this workbook.

Reading & Writing Companion     57

# In Between Cultures: A Granddaughter's Advantage

ARGUMENTATIVE TEXT
Hayan Charara
2018

## Introduction

Hayan Charara (b. 1972) is a Lebanese American poet, essayist, children's book author and editor whose work explores themes of Arab American identity, family, and culture. In this essay, Charara takes a close look at "My Grandmother Washes Her Feet in the Sink of the Bathroom at Sears" by Syrian American author Mohja Kahf. In Kahf's poem, the speaker explores, from a distinctly Arab American perspective, what happens when a clash of civilizations occurs in the bathroom of a department store. Charara explores Kahf's representation of the speaker's "in-between" identity and supports the poet's position that a life lived in-between yields great insight and understanding.

# "Mirrors reflect ourselves back to us, helping to reveal what we might otherwise overlook."

1    For over a century Americans have been making choices at Sears. GE or Frigidaire? White or stainless steel? Extended warranty or take your chances? Likewise, the speaker in Mohja Kahf's "My Grandmother Washes Her Feet in the Sink of the Bathroom at Sears" must choose from a host of available **options**, not the least of which is "a clash of civilizations" or "the great common ground." Through her portrayal of the granddaughter, Kahf challenges the commonly held belief that hyphenated Americans are torn between two cultures.

2    Confronted by customers who "shake their heads and frown" at her grandmother, who washes her feet in preparation for prayer, the speaker becomes an intermediary between two sides, East and West, each of which "knows one culture—the right one." The speaker must reconcile seemingly irreconcilable **perspectives**: on the one hand, that of the customers, who view the grandmother's act as "an affront to American porcelain, / a contamination of American Standards," and on the other hand, that of the grandmother herself, who, "though she speaks no English, / catches their meaning," takes offense, and, in Arabic, asks her granddaughter to hurl a "hotly" declared retort:

3    "My feet are cleaner than their sink.
Worried about their sink, are they? I
should worry about my feet!"

4    The granddaughter keeps this indignant response to herself. Her goal is to de-escalate the conflict, if not altogether resolve it, a task complicated by her identity. She belongs not to one or the other side, but to a bit of both. She is Arab and American, "foreign" and domestic. She literally stands in the middle, "between the door and the mirror," a difficult position to be in, for sure, one in which a person may feel torn. But doors not only close off spaces; they open into them. Mirrors reflect ourselves back to us, helping to reveal what we might otherwise overlook. In this way, the granddaughter's in-between identity provides her with a unique perspective—she sees both sides—and this proves to be advantageous.

Please note that excerpts and passages in the StudySync® library and this workbook are intended as touchstones to generate interest in an author's work. The excerpts and passages do not substitute for the reading of entire texts, and StudySync® strongly recommends that students seek out and purchase the whole literary or informational work in order to experience it as the author intended. Links to online resellers are available in our digital library. In addition, complete works may be ordered through an authorized reseller by filling out and returning to StudySync® the order form enclosed in this workbook.

Reading & Writing
Companion

59

5     Though tense, the drama between the grandmother and customers hardly rises to the level of epic conflict between cultures, and while a divide does exist between the two sides, it is not a chasm—the disagreement is grounded in lack of understanding, lack of knowledge, and lack of familiarity, which are not insurmountable obstacles. The women, in fact, have much in common. The speaker recognizes this, even if the women do not. For instance, both the grandmother and the women present themselves (and are represented by the speaker) as dignified women, "all of them decent and goodhearted." Despite their differences, cultural or otherwise, both sides also value "cleanliness, grooming, and decorum." And last but not least, both the grandmother and the "matrons" practice the same distinctive American act of consumerism—not Islam or Christianity, but a secular faith, one that welcomes adherents of all stripes, regardless of race, class, ethnicity, or even religious persuasion. As for consumerism, Sears is one of its oldest sects, replete with houses of worship (department stores), observances (blowout sales and holiday events), rules and obligations (see return policy on the back of your receipt), and even a "sacred" text (the Sears catalog). Whatever the grandmother and "matrons" do not know about each other's cultures, customs, or rituals, they know how to be good consumers. This unites them. It will be "housewares on markdown" that they lose themselves in, and they will come together "on the sales floor."

6     If anyone deserves credit for this coming together, however, it is not Sears, Roebuck, and Company, it is the granddaughter. Her in-between identity plays a central role in the bridge-building taking place. The granddaughter is a hyphenated American, perhaps American-born, certainly reared long enough in the United States as to be recognized by the matrons as American, or American enough. Not so with the grandmother, whose look (is she wearing a hijab?) and/or behavior (the sink incident) mark her as not American and definitely not American enough. For this reason, when one of the matrons protests the grandmother's **perceived** breach of bathroom etiquette, the woman turns immediately to the granddaughter to translate the demand, "Tell her she can't do that." The matron presumes that the grandmother "speaks no English" (she is right) but, more significantly, she assumes that the granddaughter does. The poet gives no explanation for why, so we can only guess. Perhaps the granddaughter is not visibly Muslim (no hijab?) or she simply acts more "American" (she doesn't wash her feet in a sink?). Whatever the reason, the matrons judge the granddaughter to be approachable, to be more like them than not. They regard her as a go-between.

7     So, too, does the grandmother. The grandmother also uses the granddaughter as a mediator, nudging her to "Go on, tell them." The back-and-forth between grandmother and matrons transforms the Sears bathroom into a mini-United

Nations. At the center of the debate between East and West is the granddaughter, a member of two cultures: one supposedly foreign, the other domestic. Historically, the granddaughter's predicament has been viewed as disadvantageous: she is stuck between a rock and a hard place, caught or trapped between cultures. Like generations of immigrants before her, she may feel pressure to overcome the difference, to choose sides—to assimilate.

8  That being so, the impulse may be to view the granddaughter's in-betweenness as unenviable. But this would be a mistake. In *Reflections On Exile*, Edward W. Said points out:

9  "Most people are principally aware of one culture, one setting, one home; exiles are aware of at least two, and this plurality of vision gives rise to an awareness of simultaneous dimensions, an awareness that is—to borrow a phrase from music—contrapuntal[1]."

10  Viewed from this perspective, the granddaughter holds an advantage over her grandmother and the matrons. In embracing her in-between **status**, her vision of the world shifts from being singular to plural. She can articulate and inhabit more than one culture, and she moves freely between them, between the "foreign" and domestic, planting her feet firmly on either side of the border. She speaks Arabic and English simultaneously, she negotiates linguistic and cultural differences effortlessly, and she code-switches freely ("sink" to "washbasin," "the ritual washing for prayer" to "*wudu,*" "bathhouses" to "bathrooms"). At the poem's end, it is difficult to imagine a reader feeling uneasy with how the grandmother uses the bathroom sink. At the very least, the act can no longer be seen as unhygienic or warranting cultural warfare. This is because of the granddaughter, who acts as an intermediary for the matrons, the grandmother, and the reader.

11  Ultimately, the granddaughter is neither foreign nor domestic. She is somewhere between. We use a variety of terms to describe people in this position, including *foreigner, exile, refugee, immigrant,* and *descendant of immigrants*. Uncomfortable though the role may be at times—especially during a confrontation in a public bathroom—the granddaughter takes it up without hesitation. In fact, she appears to relish her in-betweenness. Such positioning (as in-between cultures) allows the speaker insight that is lost on her grandmother and the matrons. *They* are so sure of their one right culture, that they appear to be stuck and at a disadvantage. In her role as intermediary, the granddaughter uses a simple gesture and a smile to resolve the conflict. She "hold[s] the door open for everyone" and creates a common ground without having to utter a single word. The women are finally able to "lose" their preconceived notions about one another and **emerge** together onto

---

1.  **contrapuntal**  in music, referring to two independent melodic lines played simultaneously

Copyright © BookheadEd Learning, LLC

"common ground." The granddaughter has opened the door "for everyone" by using her unique ability to communicate across language and culture.

Hayan Charara is the author of three poetry collections and a children's book, and editor of *Inclined to Speak,* an anthology of contemporary Arab American poetry. He teaches literature and creative writing at the University of Houston.

## ✏ WRITE

DISCUSSION: Reading a piece of literary criticism can help a reader develop or sharpen his or her own interpretation of a piece of literature. What insights about the poem did this essay provide? How did reading this essay change or deepen your interpretation of the poem? What strategies for close reading can you learn from this essay? How will you apply these strategies in the future? Prepare for your discussion by selecting several pieces of textual evidence from the essay or the poem and by preparing original analysis to reference while sharing your ideas with your peers.

# Letter from Birmingham Jail

ARGUMENTATIVE TEXT
Martin Luther King Jr.
1963

## Introduction

r. Martin Luther King Jr. (1929–1968) was one of the leaders of the civil rights movement in America in the 1950s and '60s. "Letter from Birmingham Jail" lays out his eloquent argument for change, written in the midst of the efforts to protest Jim Crow laws and racial violence in Birmingham, Alabama. Knowing that they would be arrested, King and other members of the Alabama Christian Movement for Human Rights and the Southern Christian Leadership Conference used picketing, sit-ins, and marches to demand change. Nine days into this campaign, King was arrested alongside other prominent protesters. King's letter, written four days later in his jail cell on the margins of newspapers and on smuggled paper, responded to a newspaper article titled "A Call to Unity" in which eight white clergymen suggested that civil rights should be gained through the court system and not via protest. The

# "Oppressed people cannot remain oppressed forever."

NOTES

> *Note: The text you are about to read contains offensive language. Remember to be mindful of the thoughts and feelings of your peers as you read and discuss this text. Please consult your teacher for additional guidance and support.*

16 April 1963
My Dear Fellow Clergymen:

1    While confined here in the Birmingham city jail, I came across your recent statement calling my present activities "unwise and untimely." Seldom do I pause to answer criticism of my work and ideas. If I sought to answer all the criticisms that cross my desk, my secretaries would have little time for anything other than such correspondence in the course of the day, and I would have no time for constructive work. But since I feel that you are men of genuine good will and that your criticisms are sincerely set forth, I want to try to answer your statement in what I hope will be patient and reasonable terms.

2    I think I should indicate why I am here in Birmingham, since you have been influenced by the view which argues against "outsiders coming in." I have the honor of serving as president of the Southern Christian Leadership Conference, an organization operating in every southern state, with headquarters in Atlanta, Georgia. We have some eighty five affiliated organizations across the South, and one of them is the Alabama Christian Movement for Human Rights. Frequently we share staff, educational and financial resources with our affiliates. Several months ago the affiliate here in Birmingham asked us to be on call to engage in a nonviolent direct action program if such were deemed necessary. We readily **consented**, and when the hour came we lived up to our promise. So I, along with several members of my staff, am here because I was invited here. I am here because I have organizational ties here.

3    But more basically, I am in Birmingham because injustice is here. Just as the prophets of the eighth century B.C. left their villages and carried their "thus saith the Lord" far beyond the boundaries of their home towns, and just as the Apostle Paul left his village of Tarsus and carried the gospel of Jesus Christ to the far corners of the Greco Roman world, so am I compelled to carry the

**Skill:**
**Primary and Secondary Sources**

*Here I see King referring to stories from the Bible. I know the Bible is a primary source because it is considered an original firsthand account. King's use of it makes it a secondary source for me because he is interpreting a primary source. He uses the Bible to liken the freedom movement to the spreading of the gospel in early Christianity.*

gospel of freedom beyond my own home town. Like Paul, I must constantly respond to the Macedonian call for aid.

4 Moreover, I am **cognizant** of the interrelatedness of all communities and states. I cannot sit idly by in Atlanta and not be concerned about what happens in Birmingham. Injustice anywhere is a threat to justice everywhere. We are caught in an inescapable network of mutuality, tied in a single garment of destiny. Whatever affects one directly, affects all indirectly. Never again can we afford to live with the narrow, provincial "outside agitator" idea. Anyone who lives inside the United States can never be considered an outsider anywhere within its bounds.

5 You deplore the demonstrations taking place in Birmingham. But your statement, I am sorry to say, fails to express a similar concern for the conditions that brought about the demonstrations. I am sure that none of you would want to rest content with the superficial kind of social analysis that deals merely with effects and does not grapple with underlying causes. It is unfortunate that demonstrations are taking place in Birmingham, but it is even more unfortunate that the city's white power structure left the Negro community with no alternative.

6 In any nonviolent campaign there are four basic steps: collection of the facts to determine whether injustices exist; negotiation; self purification; and direct action. We have gone through all these steps in Birmingham. There can be no gainsaying the fact that racial injustice engulfs this community. Birmingham is probably the most thoroughly segregated city in the United States. Its ugly record of brutality is widely known. Negroes have experienced grossly unjust treatment in the courts. There have been more unsolved bombings of Negro homes and churches in Birmingham than in any other city in the nation. These are the hard, brutal facts of the case. On the basis of these conditions, Negro leaders sought to negotiate with the city fathers. But the latter consistently refused to engage in good faith negotiation.

7 Then, last September, came the opportunity to talk with leaders of Birmingham's economic community. In the course of the negotiations, certain promises were made by the merchants—for example, to remove the stores' humiliating racial signs. On the basis of these promises, the Reverend Fred Shuttlesworth and the leaders of the Alabama Christian Movement for Human Rights agreed to a **moratorium** on all demonstrations. As the weeks and months went by, we realized that we were the victims of a broken promise. A few signs, briefly removed, returned; the others remained.

8 As in so many past experiences, our hopes had been blasted, and the shadow of deep disappointment settled upon us. We had no alternative except to prepare for direct action, whereby we would present our very bodies as a

Skill: Arguments and Claims

*King makes the claim that injustice matters wherever it happens. He uses reasoning to support his claim, arguing that all communities are interrelated. He concludes that everyone should protest any acts of injustice in the country.*

Skill: Primary and Secondary Sources

*King speaks in biblical terms to develop his concept of justice, comparing the freedom movement to the struggle of early Christians. The people in the movement lay their bodies down for their beliefs in the same way as early Christians.*

NOTES

means of laying our case before the conscience of the local and the national community. Mindful of the difficulties involved, we decided to undertake a process of self purification. We began a series of workshops on nonviolence, and we repeatedly asked ourselves: "Are you able to accept blows without retaliating?" "Are you able to endure the ordeal of jail?" We decided to schedule our direct action program for the Easter season, realizing that except for Christmas, this is the main shopping period of the year. Knowing that a strong economic-withdrawal program would be the by product of direct action, we felt that this would be the best time to bring pressure to bear on the merchants for the needed change.

**Skill:**
**Rhetoric**

*King offers logical reasoning, showing evidence of all the times they changed the timing of protests to be thoughtful to the community. With this rhetorical device he strengthens his claim that the movement could not wait any longer.*

9    Then it occurred to us that Birmingham's mayoral election was coming up in March, and we speedily decided to postpone action until after election day. When we discovered that the Commissioner of Public Safety, Eugene "Bull" Connor, had piled up enough votes to be in the run off, we decided again to postpone action until the day after the run off so that the demonstrations could not be used to cloud the issues. Like many others, we waited to see Mr. Connor[1] defeated, and to this end we endured postponement after postponement. Having aided in this community need, we felt that our direct action program could be delayed no longer.

10   You may well ask: "Why direct action? Why sit ins, marches and so forth? Isn't negotiation a better path?" You are quite right in calling for negotiation. Indeed, this is the very purpose of direct action. Nonviolent direct action seeks to create such a crisis and foster such a tension that a community which has constantly refused to negotiate is forced to confront the issue. It seeks so to dramatize the issue that it can no longer be ignored. My citing the creation of tension as part of the work of the nonviolent resister may sound rather shocking. But I must confess that I am not afraid of the word "tension." I have earnestly opposed violent tension, but there is a type of constructive, nonviolent tension which is necessary for growth. Just as Socrates felt that it was necessary to create a tension in the mind so that individuals could rise from the bondage of myths and half truths to the unfettered realm of creative analysis and objective appraisal, so must we see the need for nonviolent gadflies to create the kind of tension in society that will help men rise from the dark depths of prejudice and racism to the majestic heights of understanding and brotherhood.

11   The purpose of our direct action program is to create a situation so crisis packed that it will inevitably open the door to negotiation. I therefore concur with you in your call for negotiation. Too long has our beloved Southland been bogged down in a tragic effort to live in monologue rather than dialogue.

---

1.  **Mr. Connor** Eugene "Bull" Connor, the segregationist mayoral candidate and Commissioner of Public Safety that used dogs and water hoses on black civil rights activists

12    One of the basic points in your statement is that the action that I and my associates have taken in Birmingham is untimely. Some have asked: "Why didn't you give the new city administration time to act?" The only answer that I can give to this query is that the new Birmingham administration must be prodded about as much as the outgoing one, before it will act. We are sadly mistaken if we feel that the election of Albert Boutwell as mayor will bring the millennium to Birmingham. While Mr. Boutwell is a much more gentle person than Mr. Connor, they are both segregationists, dedicated to maintenance of the **status quo**. I have hope that Mr. Boutwell will be reasonable enough to see the futility of massive resistance to desegregation. But he will not see this without pressure from devotees of civil rights. My friends, I must say to you that we have not made a single gain in civil rights without determined legal and nonviolent pressure. Lamentably, it is an historical fact that privileged groups seldom give up their privileges voluntarily. Individuals may see the moral light and voluntarily give up their unjust posture; but, as Reinhold Niebuhr has reminded us, groups tend to be more immoral than individuals.

13    We know through painful experience that freedom is never voluntarily given by the oppressor; it must be demanded by the oppressed. Frankly, I have yet to engage in a direct action campaign that was "well timed" in the view of those who have not suffered unduly from the disease of segregation. For years now I have heard the word "Wait!" It rings in the ear of every Negro with piercing familiarity. This "Wait" has almost always meant "Never." We must come to see, with one of our distinguished jurists, that "justice too long delayed is justice denied."

14    We have waited for more than 340 years for our constitutional and God given rights. The nations of Asia and Africa are moving with jetlike speed toward gaining political independence, but we still creep at horse and buggy pace toward gaining a cup of coffee at a lunch counter. Perhaps it is easy for those who have never felt the stinging darts of segregation to say, "Wait." But when you have seen vicious mobs lynch your mothers and fathers at will and drown your sisters and brothers at whim; when you have seen hate filled policemen curse, kick and even kill your black brothers and sisters; when you see the vast majority of your twenty million Negro brothers smothering in an airtight cage of poverty in the midst of an affluent society; when you suddenly find your tongue twisted and your speech stammering as you seek to explain to your six-year-old daughter why she can't go to the public amusement park that has just been advertised on television, and see tears welling up in her eyes when she is told that Funtown is closed to colored children, and see ominous clouds of inferiority beginning to form in her little mental sky, and see her beginning to distort her personality by developing an unconscious bitterness toward white people; when you have to concoct an answer for a five-year-old son who is asking: "Daddy, why do white people treat colored people so mean?"; when you take a cross-country drive and find it necessary

Skill:
Rhetoric

*This passage grabbed me because it is so upsetting! The injustices that King describes here cause a strong emotional reaction. I think it would be hard for someone to not be moved by what King describes here.*

Reading & Writing
Companion

to sleep night after night in the uncomfortable corners of your automobile because no motel will accept you; when you are humiliated day in and day out by nagging signs reading "white" and "colored"; when your first name becomes "n-----," your middle name becomes "boy" (however old you are) and your last name becomes "John," and your wife and mother are never given the respected title "Mrs."; when you are harried by day and haunted by night by the fact that you are a Negro, living constantly at tiptoe stance, never quite knowing what to expect next, and are plagued with inner fears and outer resentments; when you are forever fighting a degenerating sense of "nobodiness"—then you will understand why we find it difficult to wait. There comes a time when the cup of endurance runs over, and men are no longer willing to be plunged into the abyss of despair. I hope, sirs, you can understand our legitimate and unavoidable impatience.

**Skill:**
**Arguments and**
**Claims**

*King uses reasoning to defend his argument that "one has a moral responsibility to disobey unjust laws." He cites the opinion of St. Augustine in his reasoning, quoting the expert opinion of someone who will appeal to his audience.*

15 You express a great deal of anxiety over our willingness to break laws. This is certainly a legitimate concern. Since we so diligently urge people to obey the Supreme Court's decision of 1954[2] outlawing segregation in the public schools, at first glance it may seem rather paradoxical for us consciously to break laws. One may well ask: "How can you advocate breaking some laws and obeying others?" The answer lies in the fact that there are two types of laws: just and unjust. I would be the first to advocate obeying just laws. One has not only a legal but a moral responsibility to obey just laws. Conversely, one has a moral responsibility to disobey unjust laws. I would agree with St. Augustine that "an unjust law is no law at all."

16 Now, what is the difference between the two? How does one determine whether a law is just or unjust? A just law is a man-made code that squares with the moral law or the law of God. An unjust law is a code that is out of harmony with the moral law. To put it in the terms of St. Thomas Aquinas: An unjust law is a human law that is not rooted in eternal law and natural law. Any law that uplifts human personality is just. Any law that degrades human personality is unjust. All segregation statutes are unjust because segregation distorts the soul and damages the personality. It gives the segregator a false sense of superiority and the segregated a false sense of inferiority. Segregation, to use the terminology of the Jewish philosopher Martin Buber, substitutes an "I it" relationship for an "I thou" relationship and ends up relegating persons to the status of things. Hence segregation is not only politically, economically and sociologically unsound, it is morally wrong and sinful. Paul Tillich has said that sin is separation. Is not segregation an existential expression of man's tragic separation, his awful estrangement, his terrible sinfulness? Thus it is that I can urge men to obey the 1954 decision of the Supreme Court, for it is morally

2. **Supreme Court's decision of 1954** the landmark Supreme Court case *Brown v. Board of Education* which declared state laws that segregated schools by race to be unconstitutional

NOTES

right; and I can urge them to disobey segregation ordinances, for they are morally wrong.

17    Let us consider a more concrete example of just and unjust laws. An unjust law is a code that a numerical or power majority group compels a minority group to obey but does not make binding on itself. This is difference made legal. By the same token, a just law is a code that a majority compels a minority to follow and that it is willing to follow itself. This is sameness made legal.

18    Let me give another explanation. A law is unjust if it is inflicted on a minority that, as a result of being denied the right to vote, had no part in enacting or devising the law. Who can say that the legislature of Alabama which set up that state's segregation laws was democratically elected? Throughout Alabama all sorts of devious methods are used to prevent Negroes from becoming registered voters, and there are some counties in which, even though Negroes constitute a majority of the population, not a single Negro is registered. Can any law enacted under such circumstances be considered democratically structured?

19    Sometimes a law is just on its face and unjust in its application. For instance, I have been arrested on a charge of parading without a permit. Now, there is nothing wrong in having an ordinance which requires a permit for a parade. But such an ordinance becomes unjust when it is used to maintain segregation and to deny citizens the First-Amendment privilege of peaceful assembly and protest.

20    I hope you are able to see the distinction I am trying to point out. In no sense do I advocate evading or defying the law, as would the rabid segregationist. That would lead to anarchy. One who breaks an unjust law must do so openly, lovingly, and with a willingness to accept the penalty. I submit that an individual who breaks a law that conscience tells him is unjust, and who willingly accepts the penalty of imprisonment in order to arouse the conscience of the community over its injustice, is in reality expressing the highest respect for law.

21    Of course, there is nothing new about this kind of civil disobedience. It was evidenced sublimely in the refusal of Shadrach, Meshach and Abednego to obey the laws of Nebuchadnezzar, on the ground that a higher moral law was at stake. It was practiced superbly by the early Christians, who were willing to face hungry lions and the excruciating pain of chopping blocks rather than submit to certain unjust laws of the Roman Empire. To a degree, academic freedom is a reality today because Socrates practiced civil disobedience. In our own nation, the Boston Tea Party represented a massive act of civil disobedience.

NOTES

22    We should never forget that everything Adolf Hitler did in Germany was "legal" and everything the Hungarian freedom fighters did in Hungary was "illegal." It was "illegal" to aid and comfort a Jew in Hitler's Germany. Even so, I am sure that, had I lived in Germany at the time, I would have aided and comforted my Jewish brothers. If today I lived in a Communist country where certain principles dear to the Christian faith are suppressed, I would openly advocate disobeying that country's antireligious laws.

23    I must make two honest confessions to you, my Christian and Jewish brothers. First, I must confess that over the past few years I have been gravely disappointed with the white moderate. I have almost reached the regrettable conclusion that the Negro's great stumbling block in his stride toward freedom is not the White Citizen's Counciler[3] or the Ku Klux Klanner, but the white moderate, who is more devoted to "order" than to justice; who prefers a negative peace which is the absence of tension to a positive peace which is the presence of justice; who constantly says: "I agree with you in the goal you seek, but I cannot agree with your methods of direct action"; who paternalistically believes he can set the timetable for another man's freedom; who lives by a mythical concept of time and who constantly advises the Negro to wait for a "more convenient season." Shallow understanding from people of good will is more frustrating than absolute misunderstanding from people of ill will. Lukewarm acceptance is much more bewildering than outright rejection.

24    I had hoped that the white moderate would understand that law and order exist for the purpose of establishing justice and that when they fail in this purpose they become the dangerously structured dams that block the flow of social progress. I had hoped that the white moderate would understand that the present tension in the South is a necessary phase of the transition from an obnoxious negative peace, in which the Negro passively accepted his unjust plight, to a substantive and positive peace, in which all men will respect the dignity and worth of human personality. Actually, we who engage in nonviolent direct action are not the creators of tension. We merely bring to the surface the hidden tension that is already alive. We bring it out in the open, where it can be seen and dealt with. Like a boil that can never be cured so long as it is covered up but must be opened with all its ugliness to the natural medicines of air and light, injustice must be exposed, with all the tension its exposure creates, to the light of human conscience and the air of national opinion before it can be cured.

25    In your statement you assert that our actions, even though peaceful, must be condemned because they **precipitate** violence. But is this a logical assertion? Isn't this like condemning a robbed man because his possession of money

3. **White Citizen's Counciler** a member of a White Citizens Council, groups that were formed after, and in continued opposition to, the Supreme Court's desegregation of schools

precipitated the evil act of robbery? Isn't this like condemning Socrates because his unswerving commitment to truth and his philosophical inquiries precipitated the act by the misguided populace in which they made him drink hemlock[4]? Isn't this like condemning Jesus because his unique God consciousness and never ceasing devotion to God's will precipitated the evil act of crucifixion? We must come to see that, as the federal courts have consistently affirmed, it is wrong to urge an individual to cease his efforts to gain his basic constitutional rights because the quest may precipitate violence. Society must protect the robbed and punish the robber.

26  I had also hoped that the white moderate would reject the myth concerning time in relation to the struggle for freedom. I have just received a letter from a white brother in Texas. He writes: "All Christians know that the colored people will receive equal rights eventually, but it is possible that you are in too great a religious hurry. It has taken Christianity almost two thousand years to accomplish what it has. The teachings of Christ take time to come to earth." Such an attitude stems from a tragic misconception of time, from the strangely irrational notion that there is something in the very flow of time that will inevitably cure all ills. Actually, time itself is neutral; it can be used either destructively or constructively. More and more I feel that the people of ill will have used time much more effectively than have the people of good will. We will have to repent in this generation not merely for the hateful words and actions of the bad people but for the appalling silence of the good people. Human progress never rolls in on wheels of inevitability; it comes through the tireless efforts of men willing to be co workers with God, and without this hard work, time itself becomes an ally of the forces of social stagnation. We must use time creatively, in the knowledge that the time is always ripe to do right. Now is the time to make real the promise of democracy and transform our pending national elegy into a creative psalm of brotherhood. Now is the time to lift our national policy from the quicksand of racial injustice to the solid rock of human dignity.

27  You speak of our activity in Birmingham as extreme. At first I was rather disappointed that fellow clergymen would see my nonviolent efforts as those of an extremist. I began thinking about the fact that I stand in the middle of two opposing forces in the Negro community. One is a force of complacency, made up in part of Negroes who, as a result of long years of oppression, are so drained of self respect and a sense of "somebodiness" that they have adjusted to segregation; and in part of a few middle-class Negroes who, because of a degree of academic and economic security and because in some ways they profit by segregation, have become insensitive to the problems of the masses. The other force is one of bitterness and hatred, and it comes perilously close to advocating violence. It is expressed in the various

4. **hemlock** a lethal drink made from a poisonous plant of the same name

NOTES

black nationalist groups that are springing up across the nation, the largest and best known being Elijah Muhammad's Muslim movement. Nourished by the Negro's frustration over the continued existence of racial discrimination, this movement is made up of people who have lost faith in America, who have absolutely repudiated Christianity, and who have concluded that the white man is an incorrigible "devil."

28    I have tried to stand between these two forces, saying that we need emulate neither the "do nothingism" of the complacent nor the hatred and despair of the black nationalist. For there is the more excellent way of love and nonviolent protest. I am grateful to God that, through the influence of the Negro church, the way of nonviolence became an integral part of our struggle.

29    If this philosophy had not emerged, by now many streets of the South would, I am convinced, be flowing with blood. And I am further convinced that if our white brothers dismiss as "rabble rousers" and "outside agitators" those of us who employ nonviolent direct action, and if they refuse to support our nonviolent efforts, millions of Negroes will, out of frustration and despair, seek solace and security in black nationalist ideologies—a development that would inevitably lead to a frightening racial nightmare.

30    Oppressed people cannot remain oppressed forever. The yearning for freedom eventually manifests itself, and that is what has happened to the American Negro. Something within has reminded him of his birthright of freedom, and something without has reminded him that it can be gained. Consciously or unconsciously, he has been caught up by the Zeitgeist[5], and with his black brothers of Africa and his brown and yellow brothers of Asia, South America and the Caribbean, the United States Negro is moving with a sense of great urgency toward the promised land of racial justice. If one recognizes this vital urge that has engulfed the Negro community, one should readily understand why public demonstrations are taking place. The Negro has many pent up resentments and latent frustrations, and he must release them. So let him march; let him make prayer pilgrimages to the city hall; let him go on freedom rides—and try to understand why he must do so. If his repressed emotions are not released in nonviolent ways, they will seek expression through violence; this is not a threat but a fact of history. So I have not said to my people: "Get rid of your discontent." Rather, I have tried to say that this normal and healthy discontent can be channeled into the creative outlet of nonviolent direct action. And now this approach is being termed extremist.

31    But though I was initially disappointed at being categorized as an extremist, as I continued to think about the matter I gradually gained a measure of satisfaction from the label. Was not Jesus an extremist for love: "Love your enemies, bless

5. **Zeitgeist** the spirit or climate of a specific age or culture (Origin: German)

them that curse you, do good to them that hate you, and pray for them which despitefully use you, and persecute you." Was not Amos an extremist for justice: "Let justice roll down like waters and righteousness like an ever flowing stream." Was not Paul an extremist for the Christian gospel: "I bear in my body the marks of the Lord Jesus." Was not Martin Luther an extremist: "Here I stand; I cannot do otherwise, so help me God." And John Bunyan: "I will stay in jail to the end of my days before I make a butchery of my conscience." And Abraham Lincoln: "This nation cannot survive half slave and half free." And Thomas Jefferson: "We hold these truths to be self evident, that all men are created equal . . ." So the question is not whether we will be extremists, but what kind of extremists we will be. Will we be extremists for hate or for love? Will we be extremists for the preservation of injustice or for the extension of justice? In that dramatic scene on Calvary's hill three men were crucified. We must never forget that all three were crucified for the same crime—the crime of extremism. Two were extremists for immorality, and thus fell below their environment. The other, Jesus Christ, was an extremist for love, truth and goodness, and thereby rose above his environment. Perhaps the South, the nation and the world are in dire need of creative extremists.

32   I had hoped that the white moderate would see this need. Perhaps I was too optimistic; perhaps I expected too much. I suppose I should have realized that few members of the oppressor race can understand the deep groans and passionate yearnings of the oppressed race, and still fewer have the vision to see that injustice must be rooted out by strong, persistent and determined action. I am thankful, however, that some of our white brothers in the South have grasped the meaning of this social revolution and committed themselves to it. They are still all too few in quantity, but they are big in quality. Some—such as Ralph McGill, Lillian Smith, Harry Golden, James McBride Dabbs, Ann Braden and Sarah Patton Boyle—have written about our struggle in eloquent and prophetic terms. Others have marched with us down nameless streets of the South. They have languished in filthy, roach infested jails, suffering the abuse and brutality of policemen who view them as "dirty n------lovers." Unlike so many of their moderate brothers and sisters, they have recognized the urgency of the moment and sensed the need for powerful "action" antidotes to combat the disease of segregation.

33   Let me take note of my other major disappointment. I have been so greatly disappointed with the white church and its leadership. Of course, there are some notable exceptions. I am not unmindful of the fact that each of you has taken some significant stands on this issue. I commend you, Reverend Stallings, for your Christian stand on this past Sunday, in welcoming Negroes to your worship service on a nonsegregated basis. I commend the Catholic leaders of this state for integrating Spring Hill College several years ago.

34 But despite these notable exceptions, I must honestly reiterate that I have been disappointed with the church. I do not say this as one of those negative critics who can always find something wrong with the church. I say this as a minister of the gospel, who loves the church; who was nurtured in its bosom; who has been sustained by its spiritual blessings and who will remain true to it as long as the cord of life shall lengthen.

35 When I was suddenly catapulted into the leadership of the bus protest in Montgomery, Alabama, a few years ago, I felt we would be supported by the white church. I felt that the white ministers, priests and rabbis of the South would be among our strongest allies. Instead, some have been outright opponents, refusing to understand the freedom movement and misrepresenting its leaders; all too many others have been more cautious than courageous and have remained silent behind the anesthetizing security of stained glass windows.

36 In spite of my shattered dreams, I came to Birmingham with the hope that the white religious leadership of this community would see the justice of our cause and, with deep moral concern, would serve as the channel through which our just grievances could reach the power structure. I had hoped that each of you would understand. But again I have been disappointed.

37 I have heard numerous southern religious leaders admonish their worshipers to comply with a desegregation decision because it is the law, but I have longed to hear white ministers declare: "Follow this decree because integration is morally right and because the Negro is your brother." In the midst of blatant injustices inflicted upon the Negro, I have watched white churchmen stand on the sideline and mouth pious irrelevancies and sanctimonious trivialities. In the midst of a mighty struggle to rid our nation of racial and economic injustice, I have heard many ministers say: "Those are social issues, with which the gospel has no real concern." And I have watched many churches commit themselves to a completely other worldly religion which makes a strange, un-Biblical distinction between body and soul, between the sacred and the secular.

38 I have traveled the length and breadth of Alabama, Mississippi and all the other southern states. On sweltering summer days and crisp autumn mornings I have looked at the South's beautiful churches with their lofty spires pointing heavenward. I have beheld the impressive outlines of her massive religious education buildings. Over and over I have found myself asking: "What kind of people worship here? Who is their God? Where were their voices when the lips of Governor Barnett dripped with words of interposition and nullification? Where were they when Governor Wallace gave a clarion call for defiance and hatred? Where were their voices of support when bruised and weary Negro men and women decided to rise from the dark dungeons of complacency to the bright hills of creative protest?"

Copyright © BookheadEd Learning, LLC

39   Yes, these questions are still in my mind. In deep disappointment I have wept over the laxity of the church. But be assured that my tears have been tears of love. There can be no deep disappointment where there is not deep love. Yes, I love the church. How could I do otherwise? I am in the rather unique position of being the son, the grandson and the great grandson of preachers. Yes, I see the church as the body of Christ. But, oh! How we have blemished and scarred that body through social neglect and through fear of being nonconformists.

40   There was a time when the church was very powerful—in the time when the early Christians rejoiced at being deemed worthy to suffer for what they believed. In those days the church was not merely a thermometer that recorded the ideas and principles of popular opinion; it was a thermostat that transformed the mores of society. Whenever the early Christians entered a town, the people in power became disturbed and immediately sought to convict the Christians for being "disturbers of the peace" and "outside agitators."' But the Christians pressed on, in the conviction that they were "a colony of heaven," called to obey God rather than man. Small in number, they were big in commitment. They were too God-intoxicated to be "astronomically intimidated." By their effort and example they brought an end to such ancient evils as infanticide and gladiatorial contests. Things are different now. So often the contemporary church is a weak, ineffectual voice with an uncertain sound. So often it is an archdefender of the status quo. Far from being disturbed by the presence of the church, the power structure of the average community is consoled by the church's silent—and often even vocal—**sanction** of things as they are.

41   But the judgment of God is upon the church as never before. If today's church does not recapture the sacrificial spirit of the early church, it will lose its authenticity, forfeit the loyalty of millions, and be dismissed as an irrelevant social club with no meaning for the twentieth century. Every day I meet young people whose disappointment with the church has turned into outright disgust.

42   Perhaps I have once again been too optimistic. Is organized religion too inextricably bound to the status quo to save our nation and the world? Perhaps I must turn my faith to the inner spiritual church, the church within the church, as the true *ecclesia* and the hope of the world. But again I am thankful to God that some noble souls from the ranks of organized religion have broken loose from the paralyzing chains of conformity and joined us as active partners in the struggle for freedom. They have left their secure congregations and walked the streets of Albany, Georgia, with us. They have gone down the highways of the South on tortuous rides for freedom. Yes, they have gone to jail with us. Some have been dismissed from their churches, have lost the support of their bishops and fellow ministers. But they have acted in the faith that right defeated is stronger than evil triumphant. Their witness has been the spiritual salt that has preserved the true meaning of the gospel in these troubled times. They have carved a tunnel of hope through the dark mountain of disappointment.

NOTES

43  I hope the church as a whole will meet the challenge of this decisive hour. But even if the church does not come to the aid of justice, I have no despair about the future. I have no fear about the outcome of our struggle in Birmingham, even if our motives are at present misunderstood. We will reach the goal of freedom in Birmingham and all over the nation, because the goal of America is freedom. Abused and scorned though we may be, our destiny is tied up with America's destiny. Before the pilgrims landed at Plymouth, we were here. Before the pen of Jefferson etched the majestic words of the Declaration of Independence across the pages of history, we were here. For more than two centuries our forebears labored in this country without wages; they made cotton king; they built the homes of their masters while suffering gross injustice and shameful humiliation—and yet out of a bottomless vitality they continued to thrive and develop. If the inexpressible cruelties of slavery could not stop us, the opposition we now face will surely fail. We will win our freedom because the sacred heritage of our nation and the eternal will of God are embodied in our echoing demands.

44  Before closing I feel impelled to mention one other point in your statement that has troubled me profoundly. You warmly commended the Birmingham police force for keeping "order" and "preventing violence." I doubt that you would have so warmly commended the police force if you had seen its dogs sinking their teeth into unarmed, nonviolent Negroes. I doubt that you would so quickly commend the policemen if you were to observe their ugly and inhumane treatment of Negroes here in the city jail; if you were to watch them push and curse old Negro women and young Negro girls; if you were to see them slap and kick old Negro men and young boys; if you were to observe them, as they did on two occasions, refuse to give us food because we wanted to sing our grace together. I cannot join you in your praise of the Birmingham police department.

45  It is true that the police have exercised a degree of **discipline** in handling the demonstrators. In this sense they have conducted themselves rather "nonviolently" in public. But for what purpose? To preserve the evil system of segregation. Over the past few years I have consistently preached that nonviolence demands that the means we use must be as pure as the ends we seek. I have tried to make clear that it is wrong to use immoral means to attain moral ends. But now I must affirm that it is just as wrong, or perhaps even more so, to use moral means to preserve immoral ends. Perhaps Mr. Connor and his policemen have been rather nonviolent in public, as was Chief Pritchett in Albany, Georgia, but they have used the moral means of nonviolence to maintain the immoral end of racial injustice. As T. S. Eliot has said: "The last temptation is the greatest treason: To do the right deed for the wrong reason."

46  I wish you had commended the Negro sit inners and demonstrators of Birmingham for their sublime courage, their willingness to suffer and their

NOTES

amazing discipline in the midst of great provocation. One day the South will recognize its real heroes. They will be the James Merediths, with the noble sense of purpose that enables them to face jeering and hostile mobs, and with the agonizing loneliness that characterizes the life of the pioneer. They will be old, oppressed, battered Negro women, symbolized in a seventy-two-year-old woman in Montgomery, Alabama, who rose up with a sense of dignity and with her people decided not to ride segregated buses, and who responded with ungrammatical profundity to one who inquired about her weariness: "My feets is tired, but my soul is at rest." They will be the young high school and college students, the young ministers of the gospel and a host of their elders, courageously and nonviolently sitting in at lunch counters and willingly going to jail for conscience' sake. One day the South will know that when these disinherited children of God sat down at lunch counters, they were in reality standing up for what is best in the American dream and for the most sacred values in our Judeo-Christian heritage, thereby bringing our nation back to those great wells of democracy which were dug deep by the founding fathers in their formulation of the Constitution and the Declaration of Independence.

47 Never before have I written so long a letter. I'm afraid it is much too long to take your precious time. I can assure you that it would have been much shorter if I had been writing from a comfortable desk, but what else can one do when he is alone in a narrow jail cell, other than write long letters, think long thoughts and pray long prayers?

48 If I have said anything in this letter that overstates the truth and indicates an unreasonable impatience, I beg you to forgive me. If I have said anything that understates the truth and indicates my having a patience that allows me to settle for anything less than brotherhood, I beg God to forgive me.

49 I hope this letter finds you strong in the faith. I also hope that circumstances will soon make it possible for me to meet each of you, not as an integrationist or a civil-rights leader but as a fellow clergyman and a Christian brother. Let us all hope that the dark clouds of racial prejudice will soon pass away and the deep fog of misunderstanding will be lifted from our fear drenched communities, and in some not too distant tomorrow the radiant stars of love and brotherhood will shine over our great nation with all their scintillating beauty.

Yours for the cause of Peace and Brotherhood,

Martin Luther King, Jr.

Please note that excerpts and passages in the StudySync® library and this workbook are intended as touchstones to generate interest in an author's work. The excerpts and passages do not substitute for the reading of entire texts, and StudySync® strongly recommends that students seek out and purchase the whole literary or informational work in order to experience it as the author intended. Links to online resellers are available in our digital library. In addition, complete works may be ordered through an authorized reseller by filling out and returning to StudySync® the order form enclosed in this workbook.

Reading & Writing
Companion          77

LETTER FROM
BIRMINGHAM JAIL

# First Read

Read "Letter from Birmingham Jail." After you read, complete the Think Questions below.

## ☁ THINK QUESTIONS

1. According to Dr. King, why is he in Birmingham? List at least three reasons, using evidence from the text to support your response.

2. What does Dr. King mean when he says, "Injustice anywhere is a threat to justice everywhere?" What examples does he give of this concept? Include evidence from paragraphs 5–7 in your response.

3. According to Dr. King, what is the goal of direct nonviolent action?

4. Keeping in mind that the Latin root *cog* means "to learn," use context to determine the definition of the adjective **cognizant**. Once you are finished, use a print or an online dictionary to confirm the definition.

5. Use context to determine the meaning of the Latin phrase **status quo**. Then write your definition here, explaining how you determined its meaning.

# Skill:
# Primary and Secondary Sources

Use the Checklist to analyze Primary and Secondary Sources in "Letter from Birmingham Jail." Refer to the sample student annotations about Primary and Secondary Sources in the text.

## ••• CHECKLIST FOR PRIMARY AND SECONDARY SOURCES

In order to analyze and differentiate between primary and secondary sources, do the following:

✓ examine the source, noting the title, author, and date of publication, if applicable

✓ identify the genre of the source

- examples of primary sources include letters, diaries, journals, speeches, eyewitness interviews, oral histories, memoirs, and autobiographies
- examples of secondary sources include encyclopedia articles, newspaper and magazine articles, biographies, documentary films, history books, and textbooks

If the source meets one or more of the following criteria, it is considered a primary source:

✓ original, firsthand account of an event or time period

✓ writing that takes place during the event or time period

If the source meets one or more of the following criteria, it is considered a secondary source:

✓ a book or an article that analyzes and interprets primary sources

✓ a secondhand account of an historical event

✓ a book or an article that interprets or analyzes creative work

To analyze a primary or secondary source, including how it addresses themes and concepts in a text, ask the following questions:

✓ Is the source reliable and credible in its presentation of information? How do I know?

✓ How does the source address themes and concepts, such as patriotism?

✓ What gives this source historical or literary significance?

# Skill:
# Primary and Secondary Sources

Reread paragraph 10 of "Letter from Birmingham Jail." Then, using the Checklist on the previous page, answer the multiple-choice questions below.

## ⟳ YOUR TURN

1. What primary source does King use to support his argument?

   ○ A. The questions that the readers might ask
   ○ B. Socrates' views on tension
   ○ C. King's views on tension
   ○ D. The fact that the community has refused to negotiate

2. For readers of King's letter, is the above reference a primary or secondary source?

   ○ A. It's a secondary source because King is referencing a primary source.
   ○ B. It's a primary source because King is referencing a historical figure.
   ○ C. It's a secondary source because King is referencing a secondary source.
   ○ D. It's a primary source because King, the author, is a historical figure.

3. How does King's reference to a primary source contribute to making his letter a document of literary and historical significance?

   ○ A. By referencing a primary source, King is stating a new and unique idea.
   ○ B. By referencing Socrates, King is debating one of the greatest minds in history.
   ○ C. King builds on a powerful theme originally stated by Socrates, an important thinker.
   ○ D. King is helping to convince people of Socrates' argument.

# Skill:
# Arguments and Claims

Use the Checklist to analyze Arguments and Claims in "Letter from Birmingham Jail." Refer to the sample student annotations about Arguments and Claims in the text.

## ••• CHECKLIST FOR ARGUMENTS AND CLAIMS

In order to identify a speaker's or author's argument and claims, note the following:

- ✓ clues that reveal the author's opinion in the title, opening remarks or introductory paragraph, or concluding statement or paragraph

- ✓ the specific situation or circumstances about which the author is writing

- ✓ declarative statements that come before or follow a speaker's anecdote, story, or example

To delineate an author's argument and specific claims, do the following:

- ✓ note the information that the author introduces in sequential order

- ✓ note how the author structures his or her writing (claim, evidence, and conclusion)

- ✓ describe the author's argument in your own words

To analyze and evaluate the argument and specific claims, consider the following questions:

- ✓ Does the author support each claim with reasoning and evidence?

- ✓ Is the reasoning sound and the evidence sufficient?

- ✓ Do the author's claims work together to support the his or her overall argument?

- ✓ Which claims are not supported, if any?

Please note that excerpts and passages in the StudySync® library and this workbook are intended as touchstones to generate interest in an author's work. The excerpts and passages do not substitute for the reading of entire texts, and StudySync® strongly recommends that students seek out and purchase the whole literary or informational work in order to experience it as the author intended. Links to online resellers are available in our digital library. In addition, complete works may be ordered through an authorized reseller by filling out and returning to StudySync® the order form enclosed in this workbook.

Reading & Writing
Companion

81

# Skill:
# Arguments and Claims

Reread paragraphs 30 and 31 of "Letter from Birmingham Jail." Then, using the Checklist on the previous page, answer the multiple-choice questions below.

## ↻ YOUR TURN

1. This question has two parts. First, answer Part A. Then, answer Part B.

   **Part A:** Which claim does King make most clearly in paragraph 30?

   - ○ A. When people are oppressed there will always come a time when they inevitably fight for their freedom.
   - ○ B. Germans began the freedom movement.
   - ○ C. People of Africa, Asia, South America, and the Caribbean are all fighting together for freedom.
   - ○ D. Violence is inevitable and only a matter of time.

   **Part B:** Which of the following details BEST provides reason to support the claim in Part A?

   - ○ A. "one should readily understand why public demonstrations are taking place"
   - ○ B. "let him make prayer pilgrimages to the city hall"
   - ○ C. "The Negro has many pent up resentments and latent frustrations, and he must release them."
   - ○ D. "he has been caught up by the Zeitgeist"

2. This question has two parts. First, answer Part A. Then, answer Part B.

   **Part A:** Which claim does King make most clearly in paragraph 31?

   - ○ A. Jesus would have also been condemned by the church.
   - ○ B. Extremism is always right.
   - ○ C. King is refuting the idea that he is an extremist.
   - ○ D. Extremism is a good thing for virtuous causes.

   **Part B:** Based on your answer in Part A, how does King defend his claim?

   - ○ A. King defends his claim with facts about the Civil War.
   - ○ B. King defends his claim with expert opinions about historical figures.
   - ○ C. King defends his claim by reasoning that everyone should be like historical figures.
   - ○ D. King defends his claim by reasoning that many revered historical figures were extremists.

# Skill:
# Rhetoric

Use the Checklist to analyze Rhetoric in "Letter from Birmingham Jail." Refer to the sample student annotations about Rhetoric in the text.

## ••• CHECKLIST FOR RHETORIC

In order to determine an author's point of view or purpose in a text and analyze how an author uses rhetoric, note the following:

✓ Rhetoric refers to the persuasive use of language in a text or speech, and authors or speakers may use different rhetorical devices to advance a purpose or a specific point of view:

- logical reasoning, supported by evidence, facts, or statistics
- an emotional plea by personalizing a situation or occurrence
- reminding readers or listeners of their shared values and beliefs

✓ An author or speaker may be objective or biased, and the use of rhetoric may communicate his or her point of view, or attitude toward a topic, to readers.

To analyze how an author or speaker uses rhetoric, consider the following questions:

✓ Does the author or speaker employ rhetoric in the text? If so, what kind?

✓ How does the author or speaker try to persuade readers? Are there any emotional pleas meant to evoke sympathy, or does the author only present facts and statistics?

✓ How does the author's or speaker's use of rhetoric reveal his or her purpose for writing?

✓ What does the use of rhetoric disclose about the author's or speaker's point of view toward the subject?

Please note that excerpts and passages in the StudySync® library and this workbook are intended as touchstones to generate interest in an author's work. The excerpts and passages do not substitute for the reading of entire texts, and StudySync® strongly recommends that students seek out and purchase the whole literary or informational work in order to experience it as the author intended. Links to online resellers are available in our digital library. In addition, complete works may be ordered through an authorized reseller by filling out and returning to StudySync® the order form enclosed in this workbook.

Reading & Writing
Companion
83

# Skill:
# Rhetoric

Reread paragraphs 44–46 of "Letter from Birmingham Jail." Then, using the Checklist on the previous page, answer the multiple-choice questions below.

## ↻ YOUR TURN

1. Identify the effect of the logical reasoning that King employs in paragraph 44.

   ○ A. It refutes the idea that the Birmingham police have been keeping "order" and "preventing violence."
   ○ B. It shows King's disappointment in the clergymen who think that the Birmingham police have been peaceful.
   ○ C. It explains why the actions of the Birmingham police are inherently wrong.
   ○ D. It is used to explain why the actions of the protestors are just.

2. What does King's emotional appeal in paragraph 46 accomplish?

   ○ A. It contrasts the protesters in Birmingham with protesters in other Southern cities.
   ○ B. It highlights the positive traits of the people who are protesting for greater freedoms.
   ○ C. It clarifies the idea that there are various ways to protest injustice.
   ○ D. It emphasizes the moral evil of the people who oppose extending civil rights to all.

3. Why does King refer to the American dream and sacred Judeo-Christian values at the end of paragraph 46?

   ○ A. It explains how the protestors are seen in the South.
   ○ B. It describes why the clergymen are wrong.
   ○ C. It highlights the shared values between the protestors and the clergymen.
   ○ D. It highlights the courage and resolve of those participating in the protest movement.

# Close Read

Reread "Letter from Birmingham Jail." As you reread, complete the Skills Focus questions below. Then use your answers and annotations from the questions to help you complete the Write activity.

## ◎ SKILLS FOCUS

1. In paragraph 15, identify two examples of primary sources cited by Dr. King. Explain how each source helps him reinforce his argument.

2. Identify the claim that Dr. Martin Luther King Jr. makes in paragraph 21. Explain how his use of an appeal supports that claim.

3. Identify the rhetorical device and the type of appeal that King uses in paragraph 26. Explain how they are intended to affect the reader.

4. Explain the rhetorical shift in paragraphs 38–39. Explain the purpose of this device in King's argument.

5. Identify the conclusion of King's letter. Describe the appeal King uses to help create a convincing conclusion to his argument and make his words matter.

## ✎ WRITE

RHETORICAL ANALYSIS: One reason that "Letter from Birmingham Jail" remains one of the best-known texts of the civil rights era is because of the powerful rhetoric that Dr. Martin Luther King Jr. uses to advocate for nonviolent resistance to racism. Write a response in which you delineate and evaluate King's argument, his specific claims, his rhetorical appeals, his use of sources, and his argument's conclusion. Support your analysis with evidence from the text.

Please note that excerpts and passages in the StudySync® library and this workbook are intended as touchstones to generate interest in an author's work. The excerpts and passages do not substitute for the reading of entire texts, and StudySync® strongly recommends that students seek out and purchase the whole literary or informational work in order to experience it as the author intended. Links to online resellers are available in our digital library. In addition, complete works may be ordered through an authorized reseller by filling out and returning to StudySync® the order form enclosed in this workbook.

Reading & Writing Companion  85

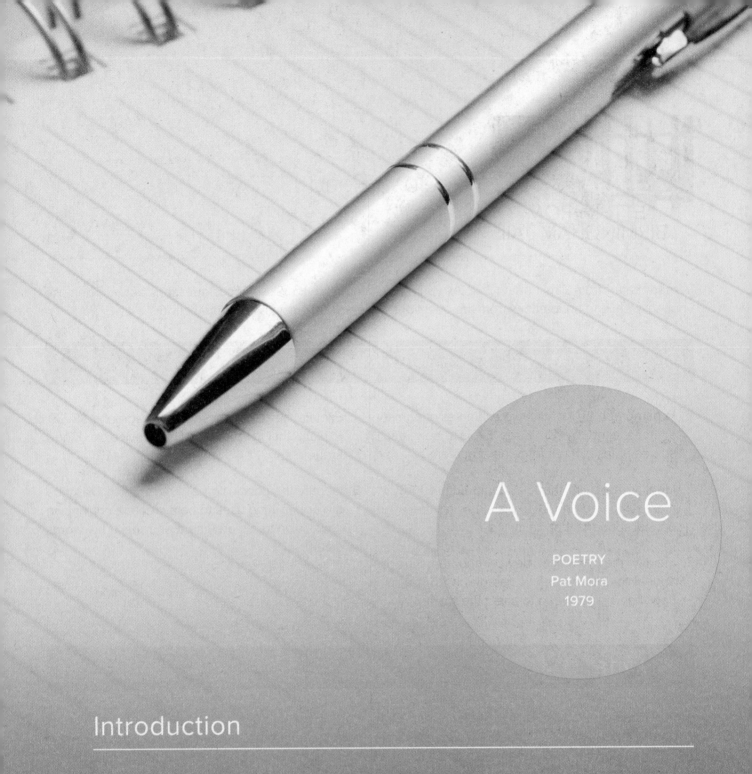

# A Voice

POETRY
Pat Mora
1979

## Introduction

Author Pat Mora (b. 1942) grew up along the border between the United States and Mexico, and her writing contains great insight into the diverse perspectives of the region. In ten moving stanzas, the speaker of "A Voice" tells the story of how her mother learned a new language and assimilated into American culture—and the impact her mother's experiences have had on her own life. On the border between two markedly different countries, her mother's displacement is felt both culturally and physically, among her family and loved ones, as well as in her own heart.

# "'How did I do it?' you ask me now."

NOTES

1    Even the lights on the stage **unrelenting**
2    as the desert sun couldn't hide the other
3    students, their eyes also unrelenting,
4    students who spoke English every night

5    as they ate their meat, potatoes, gravy.
6    Not you. In your house that smelled like
7    rose powder, you spoke Spanish formal
8    as your father, the **judge** without a courtroom

9    in the country he floated to in the dark
10    on a flatbed truck. He walked slow
11    as a hot river down the narrow hall
12    of your house. You never dared to race past him,

13    to say, "Please move," in the language
14    you learned effortlessly, as you learned to run,
15    the language forbidden at home, though your mother
16    said you learned it to fight with the neighbors.

17    You liked winning with words. You liked
18    writing speeches about **patriotism** and **democracy**.
19    You liked all the faces looking at you, all those eyes.
20    "How did I do it?" you ask me now. "How did I do it

21    when my parents didn't understand?"
22    The family story says your voice is the voice
23    of an aunt in Mexico, spunky as a peacock.
24    Family stories sing of what lives in the blood.

25    You told me only once about the time you went
26    to the state capitol, your family proud as if
27    you'd been named governor. But when you looked
28    around, the only Mexican in the auditorium,

NOTES

29   you wanted to hide from those strange faces.
30   Their eyes were pinpricks, and you faked
31   hoarseness. You, who are never at a loss
32   for words, felt your breath stick in your throat

33   like an ice-cube. "I can't," you whispered.
34   "I can't." Yet you did. Not that day but years later.
35   You taught the four of us to speak up.
36   This is America, Mom. The undo-able is done

37   in the next **generation**. Your breath moves
38   through the family like the wind
39   moves through the trees.

"A Voice" is reprinted with permission from the publisher of "My Own True Name" by Pat Mora (© 2000 Arte Público Press - University of Houston)

## ✏ WRITE

LITERARY ANALYSIS: In "A Voice," the speaker shares her fear of how others might perceive her at a speech contest due to her background. How does the speaker's characterization of her mother convey her attitude toward her background?

# Speech to the Second Virginia Convention

ARGUMENTATIVE TEXT
Patrick Henry
1775

studysync TV

# Introduction

Patrick Henry (1736–1799) was an orator, attorney, twice governor of Virginia and one of the Founding Fathers of the United States. Given on the eve of America's Revolutionary War, Patrick Henry's "Speech to the Second Virginia Convention" articulated his radical views with carefully constructed language and emotional appeals. Hoping to convince Virginia's House of Burgesses to pass a resolution of independence against Britain and to provide military support for the cause, Henry appealed to the patriotism of those in attendance—including George Washington, Thomas Jefferson, and many more. Today, Henry is best remembered

# "I know not what course others may take; but as for me, give me liberty or give me death!"

 Skill:
Author's Purpose
and Point of View

*Henry makes a point of being respectful, even though it's clear he's going to say things that others don't agree with. To show how serious this is, Henry makes the point that this a question of freedom vs. slavery.*

1   Mr. President, no man thinks more highly than I do of the patriotism, as well as abilities, of the very worthy gentlemen who have just **addressed** the House. But different men often see the same subject in different lights; and, therefore, I hope it will not be thought disrespectful to those gentlemen if, entertaining as I do, opinions of a character very opposite to theirs, I shall speak forth my sentiments freely, and without reserve. This is no time for ceremony. The question before the House is one of awful moment to this country. For my own part, I consider it as nothing less than a question of freedom or slavery; and in **proportion** to the magnitude of the subject ought to be the freedom of the debate. It is only in this way that we can hope to arrive at truth, and fulfill the great responsibility which we hold to God and our country. Should I keep back my opinions at such a time, through fear of giving offence, I should consider myself as guilty of treason towards my country, and of an act of disloyalty toward the majesty of heaven, which I revere above all earthly kings.

2   Mr. President, it is natural to man to indulge in the illusions of hope. We are apt to shut our eyes against a painful truth, and listen to the song of that siren[1] till she transforms us into beasts. Is this the part of wise men, engaged in a great and arduous struggle for liberty? Are we **disposed** to be of the number of those who, having eyes, see not, and, having ears, hear not, the things which so nearly concern their temporal salvation? For my part, whatever anguish of spirit it may cost, I am willing to know the whole truth; to know the worst, and to provide for it.

Give me liberty, or give me death!, lithograph (1876) from the Library of Congress

---

1. **the song of that siren** a reference to the Sirens of Greek Mythology, who sang so beautifully that men were mesmerized and led to their ends

3   I have but one lamp by which my feet are guided; and that is the lamp of experience. I know of no way of judging of the future but by the past. And judging by the past, I wish to know what there has been in the conduct of the British ministry for the last ten years, to justify those hopes with which gentlemen have been pleased to solace themselves, and the House? Is it that insidious smile with which our petition has been lately received[2]? Trust it not, sir; it will prove a snare to your feet. Suffer not yourselves to be betrayed with a kiss. Ask yourselves how this gracious reception of our petition comports with these war-like preparations which cover our waters and darken our land. Are fleets and armies necessary to a work of love and reconciliation? Have we shown ourselves so unwilling to be reconciled, that force must be called in to win back our love? Let us not deceive ourselves, sir. These are the implements of war and **subjugation**; the last arguments to which kings resort. I ask, gentlemen, sir, what means this martial array, if its purpose be not to force us to submission? Can gentlemen assign any other possible motive for it?

4   Has Great Britain any enemy, in this quarter of the world, to call for all this accumulation of navies and armies? No, sir, she has none. They are meant for us; they can be meant for no other. They are sent over to bind and rivet upon us those chains which the British ministry have been so long forging. And what have we to oppose to them? Shall we try argument? Sir, we have been trying that for the last ten years. Have we anything new to offer upon the subject? Nothing. We have held the subject up in every light of which it is capable; but it has been all in vain. Shall we resort to entreaty and humble supplication? What terms shall we find which have not been already exhausted? Let us not, I beseech you, sir, deceive ourselves. Sir, we have done everything that could be done, to avert the storm which is now coming on. We have petitioned; we have remonstrated; we have supplicated; we have prostrated ourselves before the throne, and have implored its interposition to arrest the tyrannical hands of the ministry and Parliament. Our petitions have been slighted; our remonstrances have produced additional violence and insult; our supplications have been disregarded; and we have been spurned, with contempt, from the foot of the throne. In vain, after these things, may we indulge the fond hope of peace and reconciliation. There is no longer any room for hope. If we wish to be free, if we mean to preserve inviolate those inestimable privileges for which we have been so long contending, if we mean not basely to abandon the noble struggle in which we have been so long engaged, and which we have pledged ourselves never to abandon until the glorious object of our contest shall be obtained, we must fight! I repeat it, sir, we must fight! An appeal to arms and to the God of Hosts is all that is left us!

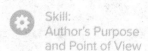

Skill:
Author's Purpose
and Point of View

Henry tries to persuade the House that the only option is for the colonists to fight if they truly want freedom from British rule. He uses powerful rhetoric and repeated phrases to lead up to his forceful three-word message at the end.

---

2. **Is it that insidious smile with which our petition has lately been received** the "petition" here being a protest by the First Continental Congress against new tax laws

Copyright © BookheadEd Learning, LLC

Skill:
Language, Style,
and Audience

Patrick Henry's continued questions emphasize his message that the time for action has come. He carefully chooses phrases such as "holy cause of liberty" and "invincible" to persuade his audience that the colonists' cause is just.

5     They tell us, sir, that we are weak; unable to cope with so **formidable** an adversary. But when shall we be stronger? Will it be the next week, or the next year? Will it be when we are totally disarmed, and when a British guard shall be stationed in every house? Shall we gather strength by irresolution and inaction? Shall we acquire the means of effectual resistance, by lying supinely on our backs, and hugging the delusive phantom of hope, until our enemies shall have bound us hand and foot? Sir, we are not weak if we make a proper use of those means which the God of nature hath placed in our power. Three millions of people, armed in the holy cause of liberty, and in such a country as that which we possess, are invincible by any force which our enemy can send against us. Besides, sir, we shall not fight our battles alone. There is a just God who presides over the destinies of nations; and who will raise up friends to fight our battles for us. The battle, sir, is not to the strong alone; it is to the vigilant, the active, the brave. Besides, sir, we have no election. If we were base enough to desire it, it is now too late to retire from the contest. There is no retreat but in submission and slavery! Our chains are forged! Their clanking may be heard on the plains of Boston! The war is inevitable and let it come! I repeat it, sir, let it come. It is in vain, sir, to extenuate the matter. Gentlemen may cry, Peace, Peace but there is no peace. The war is actually begun! The next gale that sweeps from the north will bring to our ears the clash of resounding arms! Our brethren are already in the field! Why stand we here idle? What is it that gentlemen wish? What would they have? Is life so dear, or peace so sweet, as to be purchased at the price of chains and slavery? Forbid it, Almighty God! I know not what course others may take; but as for me, give me liberty or give me death!

# First Read

Read "Speech to the Second Virginia Convention." After you read, complete the Think Questions below.

 **THINK QUESTIONS**

1. Who is Patrick Henry's audience for this speech, and what is the occasion or historical situation in which he is giving the speech? Support your answer with evidence from the text.

2. According to paragraph 4, what efforts have the American colonists already made to negotiate with Britain? Were those efforts successful? Support your answer with evidence from the text.

3. Henry claims that the British view the Americans as "weak." How does he respond to this criticism? Use evidence from paragraph 5 to support your response.

4. The Latin prefix *sub-* means "under," and the Latin word *jugus* means "yoke." With this information in mind and using context clues from the text, write your best definition of the word **subjugation** here.

5. Use context clues to determine the meaning of the word **formidable** as it is used in the speech. Write your definition of *formidable* here and explain how you figured it out.

Please note that excerpts and passages in the StudySync® library and this workbook are intended as touchstones to generate interest in an author's work. The excerpts and passages do not substitute for the reading of entire texts, and StudySync® strongly recommends that students seek out and purchase the whole literary or informational work in order to experience it as the author intended. Links to online resellers are available in our digital library. In addition, complete works may be ordered through an authorized reseller by filling out and returning to StudySync® the order form enclosed in this workbook.

Reading & Writing
Companion

93

# Skill: Author's Purpose and Point of View

Use the Checklist to analyze Author's Purpose and Point of View in "Speech to the Second Virginia Convention." Refer to the sample student annotations about Author's Purpose and Point of View in the text.

## ••• CHECKLIST FOR AUTHOR'S PURPOSE AND POINT OF VIEW

In order to identify the author's or speaker's purpose and point of view, do the following:

- ✓ Note the evidence that the author or speaker offers to support his or her point of view.

- ✓ Clarify if the author or speaker includes any fallacious reasoning or errors in logic that invalidate or overturn an argument, such as drawing a conclusion based on information that is inconclusive or questionable.

- ✓ Determine whether the author or speaker offers distorted or exaggerated evidence to support a point of view.

- ✓ Examine whether the author or speaker uses figurative language or other descriptive words in order to intensify an emotion.

- ✓ Identify the author's use of rhetoric, or the art of speaking and writing persuasively, such as using repetition to drive home a point.

To evaluate the author's or speaker's purpose and point of view, consider the following questions:

- ✓ How does the author or speaker convey, or communicate, information in the text?

- ✓ Does the author or speaker use figurative or emotional language? What effect does it have on the author's point of view?

- ✓ Are charts, graphs, maps, and other graphic aids referred to or included in the text?

- ✓ How does the author use rhetoric to try and persuade readers or the audience to accept a specific point of view or opinion? Is the use of rhetoric successful? Why or why not?

AUTHOR'S PURPOSE AND POINT OF VIEW

sync•skills

# Skill: Author's Purpose and Point of View

Reread paragraph 2 of "Speech to the Second Virginia Convention." Then, using the Checklist on the previous page, answer the multiple-choice questions below.

## ⟳ YOUR TURN

1. What is Henry's purpose of starting this paragraph with "Mr. President"?

   ○ A. Henry knows the president is the only one in the audience he needs to convince.

   ○ B. Henry shows he has has given up on his attempt to persuade his audience.

   ○ C. Henry separates himself and the president from the rest of the audience he is addressing.

   ○ D. Henry shows respect for the audience and its leader in order to gain their respect and attention.

2. Which of the following quotes in this paragraph best achieves Henry's purpose to persuade the audience to join him in his fight for American independence?

   ○ A. "Mr. President, it is natural to man to indulge in the illusions of hope."

   ○ B. "Is this the part of wise men, engaged in a great and arduous struggle for liberty?"

   ○ C. "For my part, whatever anguish of spirit it may cost, I am willing to know the whole truth; to know the worst, and to provide for it."

   ○ D. "We are apt to shut our eyes against a painful truth, and listen to the song of that siren till she transforms us into beasts."

3. Which of the following best states Henry's point of view in this paragraph?

   ○ A. Give the British a second chance in the hope that their behavior will improve.

   ○ B. Do whatever can possibly be done to avoid the outbreak of war.

   ○ C. Face the painful truth of the current situation and prepare to respond to it.

   ○ D. Accept the current situation but plan to revisit the issue in the future.

Please note that excerpts and passages in the StudySync® library and this workbook are intended as touchstones to generate interest in an author's work. The excerpts and passages do not substitute for the reading of entire texts, and StudySync® strongly recommends that students seek out and purchase the whole literary or informational work in order to experience it as the author intended. Links to online resellers are available in our digital library. In addition, complete works may be ordered through an authorized reseller by filling out and returning to StudySync® the order form enclosed in this workbook.

Reading & Writing Companion    95

# Skill:
# Language, Style, and Audience

Use the Checklist to analyze Language, Style, and Audience in "Speech to the Second Virginia Convention." Refer to the sample student annotations about Language, Style, and Audience in the text.

## ••• CHECKLIST FOR LANGUAGE, STYLE, AND AUDIENCE

In order to determine an author's style, do the following:

✓ Identify and define any unfamiliar words or phrases.

✓ Analyze the surrounding words and phrases as well as the context in which the specific words are being used.

✓ Note the audience—both intended and unintended—and possible reactions to the author's word choice and style.

✓ Examine your reaction to the author's word choice and how the author's choice affected your reaction.

In order to analyze the cumulative impact of word choice on meaning and tone, ask the following questions:

✓ How did your understanding of the writer's language change during your analysis?

✓ How does the writer's cumulative word choice impact or create meaning in the text?

✓ How does the writer's cumulative word choice impact or create a specific tone in the text?

✓ What images, feelings, or ideas do the writer's cumulative word choices evoke?

✓ How could various audiences interpret this language? What different possible emotional responses can you list?

# Skill:
# Language, Style, and Audience

Reread paragraph 5 of "Speech to the Second Virginia Convention." Then, using the Checklist on the previous page, answer the multiple-choice questions below.

## YOUR TURN

1. Think about the metaphor of chains ("Our chains are forged!"). What is the most likely purpose of that metaphor?

   ○ A.  The metaphor is intended to frighten the colonists into submission to Britain.

   ○ B.  The metaphor reminds colonists of the harsh way in which the British punish criminals.

   ○ C.  The metaphor is intended to warn colonists about the danger of going to war with Britain.

   ○ D.  The metaphor reinforces the idea that the British will not grant freedom to the colonists.

2. Near the end of the paragraph, Patrick Henry phrases his thoughts in the form of questions and exclamations. What purpose does that language serve?

   ○ A.  The language expresses Henry's anger over the past actions of the British.

   ○ B.  The language captures Henry's passion and his belief that now is the time for action.

   ○ C.  The language encourages Henry's audience to seek God's help in the coming war.

   ○ D.  The language begs Henry's audience to prepare to protect themselves and their families.

Please note that excerpts and passages in the StudySync® library and this workbook are intended as touchstones to generate interest in an author's work. The excerpts and passages do not substitute for the reading of entire texts, and StudySync® strongly recommends that students seek out and purchase the whole literary or informational work in order to experience it as the author intended. Links to online resellers are available in our digital library. In addition, complete works may be ordered through an authorized reseller by filling out and returning to StudySync® the order form enclosed in this workbook.

Reading & Writing
Companion

97

# COMPARE AND CONTRAST
sync•skills

# Skill:
# Compare and Contrast

Use the Checklist to analyze Compare and Contrast in "Speech to the Second Virginia Convention."

## ••• CHECKLIST FOR COMPARE AND CONTRAST

In order to compare and contrast informational texts, including seminal U.S. documents of historical and literary significance, do the following:

✓ Choose two or more seminal, groundbreaking, or influential documents of literary and historical significance, such as Franklin Roosevelt's Four Freedoms Speech or Martin Luther King, Jr.'s "Letter from Birmingham Jail."

✓ Identify the main idea in each document and the themes and concepts outlined in each text.

✓ Compare and contrast two or more of these documents and note the similarities and differences between them, including how they address related themes and concepts.

To analyze seminal U.S. documents, including how they address related themes and concepts, consider the following questions:

✓ Are the texts I have chosen considered to be seminal U.S. documents of both historical and literary significance?

✓ What themes or concepts are apparent in each of these documents?

✓ Have I determined the main idea in each document? What details support it?

✓ How are the ideas, themes, and concepts in these documents similar and different?

# Skill:
# Compare and Contrast

Reread paragraph 24 of King's "Letter from Birmingham Jail" and paragraph 5 of Henry's "Speech to the Second Virginia Convention." Then, using the Checklist on the previous page, answer the multiple-choice questions below.

## ⟳ YOUR TURN

1. Which of the following best summarizes the central ideas of King's letter and Henry's speech and how they are related?

   ○ A. King and Henry both are calling to fight for the freedom of oppression in the U.S. using whatever means necessary.

   ○ B. King is advocating for the acceptance of the status quo in the U.S. while Henry is is not, although both of them are addressing themes of oppression in seminal fictional texts.

   ○ C. In seminal U.S. historical documents, King and Henry are both speaking directly to their opponents to advocate further action to end oppression.

   ○ D. Henry thinks the only way to make change in America is with violence while King hopes to make change using words, so the documents are not related.

2. Which of the following statements regarding literary devices in each historical document is true?

   ○ A. King uses metaphors and similes to strengthen his argument, while Henry speaks in plain language.

   ○ B. King uses metaphors and similes to strengthen his argument, while Henry uses questioning and hyperbole to strengthen his speech.

   ○ C. Neither Henry nor King use literary devices but instead use factual statements only.

   ○ D. Henry's speech is a metaphor for slavery, whereas King uses similes to describe the civil rights era.

Please note that excerpts and passages in the StudySync® library and this workbook are intended as touchstones to generate interest in an author's work. The excerpts and passages do not substitute for the reading of entire texts, and StudySync® strongly recommends that students seek out and purchase the whole literary or informational work in order to experience it as the author intended. Links to online resellers are available in our digital library. In addition, complete works may be ordered through an authorized reseller by filling out and returning to StudySync® the order form enclosed in this workbook.

Reading & Writing
Companion

99

# Close Read

Reread "Speech to the Second Virginia Convention." As you reread, complete the Skills Focus questions below. Then use your answers and annotations from the questions to help you complete the Write activity.

## ◎ SKILLS FOCUS

1. In paragraph 1, identify words and phrases Patrick Henry uses to justify his speaking "freely, and without reserve." Explain how you would characterize the language and what it suggests about both Henry's audience and the situation facing the colonists.

2. In paragraph 3, Henry mentions the "war-like preparations" the British appear to be making. Describe Henry's ultimate purpose in discussing these preparations and how it helps advance his argument.

3. In paragraph 4, discuss how Henry's use of repetition, or repeated words or phrases, in his rhetoric helps advance his purpose and point of view.

4. At the close of his "Letter from Birmingham Jail," Martin Luther King, Jr. says, "Let us all hope that the dark clouds of racial prejudice will soon pass away and the deep fog of misunderstanding will be lifted from our fear drenched communities, and in some not too distant tomorrow the radiant stars of love and brotherhood will shine over our great nation with all their scintillating beauty." Compare and contrast the closing from this significant U.S. historic letter with Henry's message and rhetoric in paragraph 5 of his speech.

5. This speech by Patrick Henry is one of the most famous in U.S. history. Describe how Henry's language and style, as well as his awareness of his time and his audience, help to reinforce and enhance his message.

**WRITE**

RHETORICAL ANALYSIS: In the fifth stanza of Pat Mora's poem "A Voice," the speaker says,

> *You liked winning with words. You liked*
> *writing speeches about patriotism and democracy.*
> *You liked all the faces looking at you, all those eyes.*
> *"How did I do it?" you ask me now. . . .*

"Winning with words" is a goal in persuasive writing and speaking, and both Patrick Henry and Martin Luther King, Jr. use language to advocate for their ideas. Reflecting on Mora's poem and the shared concepts and themes in King's "Letter from Birmingham Jail" and Henry's "Speech to the Second Virginia Convention," discuss how a person's choice of words may be a matter of "life" and "death."

Please note that excerpts and passages in the StudySync® library and this workbook are intended as touchstones to generate interest in an author's work. The excerpts and passages do not substitute for the reading of entire texts, and StudySync® strongly recommends that students seek out and purchase the whole literary or informational work in order to experience it as the author intended. Links to online resellers are available in our digital library. In addition, complete works may be ordered through an authorized reseller by filling out and returning to StudySync® the order form enclosed in this workbook.

Reading & Writing Companion **101**

Extended
Writing
Project and
Grammar

EXTENDED
WRITING
PROJECT
LITERARY ANALYSIS
WRITING

# Literary Analysis Writing Process: Plan

| PLAN | DRAFT | REVISE | EDIT AND PUBLISH |
|---|---|---|---|

The texts you have read in this unit grapple with the power of words. Language emerges in these texts as a powerful force, serving as a tool to unite past and future generations or operating as a means of achieving justice.

## WRITING PROMPT

### What is the power of language?

Select two or three works from this unit in which individuals' language has a powerful impact on themselves, another individual, or their community. In a literary analysis essay, make a claim about what exactly is the power of language and explain how that power is demonstrated in each of the selections. Cite evidence from the texts you have selected to support your position.

### Writing to Sources

As you gather ideas and information from the texts in the unit, be sure to:

- include a claim;
- address counterclaims;
- use evidence from multiple sources; and
- avoid overly relying on one source.

### Introduction to Literary Analysis Writing

A literary analysis consists of certain elements, including the following:

- a claim, or thesis
- valid reasons or points that support the claim
- textual evidence to support the reasons and the claim
- original commentary to explain the significance of the textual evidence

In a literary analysis, a writer analyzes how literary elements and devices work together to create meaning in one or more works of literature. Literary analysis is considered a form of argumentative writing in that the writer expresses a claim that states his or her position, or interpretation of the literary work, and then provides textual evidence and original commentary as justification for the claim.

Before you get started on your own literary analysis, read this essay that one student, Caroline, wrote in response to the writing prompt. As you read the Model, highlight and annotate the features of literary analysis writing that Caroline included in her essay.

NOTES

## ☰ STUDENT MODEL

### The Power of Language

1   There is an old saying that "sticks and stones may break my bones, but words will never hurt me," but it isn't true. Words can be much more dangerous than sticks or stones. Words may not kill a person instantly, like a weapon—but, like a tool, they can shape the world. Words are powerful. They can change history by calling people to action. They can also change people's minds. The authors of "She Unnames Them," "Letter from Birmingham Jail," and "Speech to the Second Virginia Convention" all want to change the world, and they use words to bring about that change.

2   In "She Unnames Them" by Ursula K. Le Guin, Eve shows how powerful a name is even when it does not fit its owner. She explains that most of the animals never cared about the names Adam had given them. Yet some of the animals, especially pets and yaks, debate whether or not to keep their names. By unnaming the animals, Eve feels an unexpected "powerful" effect. She feels closer to but also more afraid of the animals. Then she realizes that she "could not now, in all conscience, make an exception for [herself]." She must give up her own name. Not wanting to seem ungrateful, she gives her name back to Adam. She tells him that it's "been really useful, but it doesn't exactly seem to fit very well lately." Adam does not seem to be listening. It is possible that Adam does not understand the power of words, probably because he is the one who gave Eve and the animals their names. Eve, however, now understands the power of language. As she leaves the garden, she realizes that her words must "be as slow, as new, as single, as tentative as the steps I took." Language is powerful, and the author confirms this idea by implying that Eve plans to use it carefully from now on.

3   While Le Guin seems to suggest using words with caution, revolutionary patriot Patrick Henry uses logical appeals and vivid language to persuade his audience in "Speech to the Second

Virginia Convention." When Henry delivered the speech in 1775, he was taking a big risk. The purpose of Henry's speech was to persuade his audience to declare independence from Britain. What Henry is suggesting is treasonous, but he feels so strongly about the "question of freedom or slavery" that he considers it treason to hold back his opinions. Henry shows respect for his audience by referring to them as "sir" and "gentlemen," but he argues that they are not seeing the world clearly. They are like people "who, having eyes, see not, and, having ears, hear not." He guides his listeners to see his point of view through logic. He asks rhetorical questions and then answers them. Yet it is his emotional language that is more persuasive. Throughout his speech, Henry uses the image of heavy chains to argue that the Americans are enslaved to Britain. He asks, "Is life so dear, or peace so sweet, as to be purchased at the price of chains and slavery?" He declares that "if we wish to be free," then "we must fight!" He ends his speech by speaking for himself: "I know not what course others may take; but as for me, give me liberty or give me death!" It is as if he does not care whether the others follow him; he knows that he will take courageous action.

4    Like Patrick Henry, Martin Luther King Jr. uses powerful language to address an injustice. King wrote "Letter from Birmingham Jail" after being arrested during a peaceful protest against racial segregation. King's letter is a response to white people who think that African Americans should not protest against inequality but should wait for it to be handled in the courts. Like Henry, King addresses his audience directly. For example, he asks questions: "You may well ask: 'Why direct action? Why sit ins, marches and so forth? Isn't negotiation a better path?'" He uses logic to explain how he ended up in jail. However, the most persuasive part of his argument comes from his use of powerful language to explain what injustice feels like to African Americans who experience "the stinging darts of segregation." He describes the pain of being told to be patient when "you have seen hate filled policemen curse, kick and even kill your black brothers and sisters." He expresses the pain of having to tell his daughter that she can't go to an amusement park because she is black and of having to live a life "plagued with inner fears and outer resentments." Yet he ends his letter by imagining a day in which "the South will recognize its real heroes"—those people who peacefully and courageously fought for their civil rights. He describes them as

Please note that excerpts and passages in the StudySync® library and this workbook are intended as touchstones to generate interest in an author's work. The excerpts and passages do not substitute for the reading of entire texts, and StudySync® strongly recommends that students seek out and purchase the whole literary or informational work in order to experience it as the author intended. Links to online resellers are available in our digital library. In addition, complete works may be ordered through an authorized reseller by filling out and returning to StudySync® the order form enclosed in this workbook.

Reading & Writing Companion    105

"bringing our nation back to those great wells of democracy which were dug deep by the founding fathers." As a result of King's powerful language, others could share his vision of the world as it is and as it might be.

5    Words are everywhere. It's easy to tune them out or think that they don't mean much. But when life turns serious, and there are injustices and wrongs to fix, people rely on the power of words. In "Speech to the Second Virginia Convention" and "Letter from Birmingham Jail," Patrick Henry and Martin Luther King Jr. describe terrible injustices and challenge their audiences to think about the world in a new way and to take action. In "She Unnames Them," Eve recognizes the power of naming and finds freedom by giving up a name she didn't choose. She decides that she's up to the challenge of using language thoughtfully and carefully instead of chattering. All have learned, as have we in reading these three selections, that language can be an important and powerful tool for changing the world in serious ways.

# ✏ WRITE

Writers often take notes about their ideas before they sit down to write an essay. Think about what you've learned so far about literary analysis to help you begin prewriting.

- **Purpose:** Think about the texts you have read in this unit. What two or three works would you like to explore further in a literary analysis?

- **Audience:** Who will read your literary analysis? What type of language and style should you use for this audience?

- **Textual Evidence:** Is there any particular passage that immediately comes to mind that exemplifies the power of language?

- **Analysis:** What do you think that passage suggests about the power of language?

- **Claim:** How can you use the passage you have identified and your commentary on it to begin to formulate the claim of your literary analysis?

## Response Instructions

Use the questions in the bulleted list to write a one-paragraph summary. Your summary should help guide you in the planning and writing of your literary analysis essay.

Don't worry about including all of the details now; focus only on the most essential and important elements. You will refer to this short summary as you continue through the steps of the writing process.

Please note that excerpts and passages in the StudySync® library and this workbook are intended as touchstones to generate interest in an author's work. The excerpts and passages do not substitute for the reading of entire texts, and StudySync® strongly recommends that students seek out and purchase the whole literary or informational work in order to experience it as the author intended. Links to online resellers are available in our digital library. In addition, complete works may be ordered through an authorized reseller by filling out and returning to StudySync® the order form enclosed in this workbook.

Reading & Writing Companion  **107**

# Skill: Organizing Argumentative Writing

## ••• CHECKLIST FOR ORGANIZING ARGUMENTATIVE WRITING

As you consider how to organize your writing for your argumentative essay, use the following questions as a guide:

- Have I identified my claim or claims and the evidence that supports it?

- Have I identified reasons for my claim?

- Have I identified any counterclaims that I will need to address?

- Have I identified the textual evidence that will support my reasons?

Follow these steps to organize your argumentative essay in a way that establishes clear relationships among claim(s), counterclaims, reasons, and evidence:

- Identify your precise, or specific, claim or claims and the reasons to support each one.

- Identify textual evidence that will support each reason.

- Identify any counterclaims, as needed.

- Choose an organizational structure that establishes clear relationships among claims, reasons, and the evidence presented to support your claim.

## ♻ YOUR TURN

Read the quotations from a student's literary analysis essay on "In Between Cultures: A Granddaughter's Advantage" below. Then, complete the chart by matching each quotation with its correct place in the outline.

| Quotation Options | |
|---|---|
| A | Likewise, the speaker in Mohja Kahf's "My Grandmother Washes Her Feet in the Sink of the Bathroom at Sears" must choose from a host of available **options**, not the least of which is "a clash of civilizations" or "the great common ground." |
| B | Through her portrayal of the granddaughter, Kahf challenges the commonly held belief that hyphenated Americans are torn between two cultures. |
| C | The speaker must reconcile seemingly irreconcilable perspectives: on the one hand, that of the customers. . . . |
| D | In this way, the granddaughter's in-between identity provides her with a unique perspective—she sees both sides—and this proves to be advantageous. |
| E | If anyone deserves credit for this coming together, however, it is not Sears, Roebuck, and Company, it is the granddaughter. |
| F | The granddaughter has opened the door "for everyone" by using her unique ability to communicate across language and culture. |

| Outline | Quotation |
|---|---|
| Introductory Statement: | |
| Thesis: | |
| Main Idea/Reason 1: | |
| Main Idea/Reason 2: | |
| Main Idea/Reason 3: | |
| Conclusion: | |

Please note that excerpts and passages in the StudySync® library and this workbook are intended as touchstones to generate interest in an author's work. The excerpts and passages do not substitute for the reading of entire texts, and StudySync® strongly recommends that students seek out and purchase the whole literary or informational work in order to experience it as the author intended. Links to online resellers are available in our digital library. In addition, complete works may be ordered through an authorized reseller by filling out and returning to StudySync® the order form enclosed in this workbook.

Reading & Writing Companion 109

## ↻ YOUR TURN

Complete the chart below by writing a short summary of what will happen in each section of your literary analysis.

| My Literary Analysis | |
|---|---|
| Purpose, Audience, Topic, Context: | |
| Introductory Statement: | |
| Thesis: | |
| Main Idea/Reason 1: | |
| Main Idea/Reason 2: | |
| Main Idea/Reason 3: | |

# Skill:
# Thesis Statement

Copyright © BookheadEd Learning, LLC

## ••• CHECKLIST FOR THESIS STATEMENT

Before you begin writing your thesis statement for your argumentative essay, ask yourself the following questions:

- What is the prompt asking me to write about?
- What claim do I want to make about the topic of this essay?
- Is my claim precise? How is it specific to my topic?
- Does my thesis statement introduce the body of my essay?
- Where should I place my thesis statement?

Here are some methods to introduce and develop a topic as well as a precise claim:

- think about your central claim of your essay

  > identify a clear claim you want to introduce, thinking about:

     o how closely your claim is related to your topic and specific to your supporting details

     o any alternate or opposing claims (counterclaims)

  > identify as many claims and counterclaims as you intend to prove

- your thesis statement should:

  > let the reader anticipate the content of your essay

  > begin your essay in an organized manner

  > present your opinion clearly

  > respond completely to the writing prompt

- consider the best placement for your thesis statement

  > if your response is short, you may want to get right to the point and present your thesis statement in the first sentence of the essay

  > if your response is longer (as in a formal essay), you can build up your thesis statement and place it at the end of your introductory paragraph

YOUR TURN

Read the sentences below. Then, complete the chart by sorting them into those that are thesis statements and those that are supporting details.

| | Sentence Options |
|---|---|
| A | When making an argument, an author's rhetoric can have as much of an impact on the audience as the content of the ideas. |
| B | Names demonstrate the power of language. |
| C | Dr. Martin Luther King Jr.'s "Letter from Birmingham Jail" is effective because it uses powerful imagery such as "the stinging darts of segregation." |
| D | Language is always a powerful tool, but it is most powerful when effective imagery is used to paint a picture in readers' or listeners' minds. |
| E | In "She Unnames Them," Eve realizes she must give up her own name because it no longer fits her. |
| F | Patrick Henry asks and answers rhetorical questions in order to persuade people that independence from Britain is a good idea. |

| Thesis Statements | Supporting Details |
|---|---|
| | |
| | |
| | |
| | |

✏ WRITE

Use the steps in the checklist to draft a thesis statement for your literary analysis.

# Skill: Reasons and Relevant Evidence

## ••• CHECKLIST FOR REASONS AND RELEVANT EVIDENCE

As you begin to determine what reasons and relevant evidence will support your claim(s), use the following questions as a guide:

- Is my claim precise, specific, and clearly stated?

- How is my claim different from any alternate or opposing claims? How can I make my claim more specific to my topic and ideas?

- What are the relationships between the claims, counterclaims, reasons, and evidence I have presented? What kinds of transitional devices or organizational patterns might improve these relationships?

- What is my counterclaim? How can I use it to strengthen my claim?

Use the following steps as a guide to help you introduce a precise claim(s), distinguish the claim(s) from alternate or opposing claims, and create an organization that establishes clear relationships among argument elements:

- identify the precise claim or claims you will make in your argument, refine it by:

  > eliminating any gaps of information or vague ideas

  > using vocabulary that clarifies your ideas

  > evaluating how it is distinguished, or different, from other claims and counterclaims on your topic

- assess any connections between your claim and the counterclaim, which is another claim made to refute or disprove a previous claim

- choose or create an organizational pattern, such as compare and contrast, that will establish clear relationships among claim(s), counterclaims, reasons, and evidence

## ⟳ YOUR TURN

Read each piece of textual evidence from "She Unnames Them" below. Then, complete the chart by sorting them into those that are relevant and those that are not relevant to the writing topic of "the power of language."

| | Textual Evidence |
|---|---|
| A | They seemed far closer than when their names had stood between myself and them like a clear barrier: so close that my fear of them and their fear of me became one same fear. |
| B | I put some things away and fiddled around a little, but he continued to do what he was doing and to take no notice of anything else. |
| C | But as soon as they understood that the issue was precisely one of individual choice, and that anybody who wanted to be called Rover, or Froufrou, or Polly, or even Birdie in the personal sense, was perfectly free to do so . . . |
| D | He was fitting parts together, and said, without looking around, "O.K., fine dear. When's dinner?" |

| Relevant Evidence | Not Relevant Evidence |
|---|---|
| | |
| | |

## ⟳ YOUR TURN

Complete the chart below by identifying 1) three texts you may want to write about; 2) reasons for choosing each text; and 3) relevant evidence from each text to help develop your own writing ideas.

| Text | Reasons | Relevant Evidence |
|---|---|---|
| | | |
| | | |
| | | |
| | | |
| | | |

# Literary Analysis Writing Process: Draft

| PLAN | DRAFT | REVISE | EDIT AND PUBLISH |
|------|-------|--------|------------------|

You have already made progress toward writing your literary analysis. Now it is time to draft your literary analysis.

## ✏ WRITE

Use your plan and other responses in your Binder to draft your literary analysis. After rereading the prompt, you may also think of new ideas as you begin drafting. Feel free to explore those new ideas as you have them. You can also ask yourself these questions to ensure that your writing is focused, organized, and developed:

**Draft Checklist:**

☐ **Focused**: Have I introduced my claim clearly in a thesis statement? Have I included only relevant evidence to support my claim, and nothing extraneous that might confuse my readers?

☐ **Organized**: Have I organized my analysis in a way that makes sense with the texts I have chosen? Have I established clear relationships among claims, counterclaims, reasons, and evidence?

☐ **Developed**: Have I clearly stated reasons that support my claim? Have I identified counterclaims and alternate claims in a way my audience can follow? Is my evidence sufficient?

Before you submit your draft, read it over carefully. You want to be sure that you've responded to all aspects of the prompt.

Here is Caroline's draft of her literary analysis. As you read, notice how Caroline develops her draft to be focused, organized, and developed. As Caroline continues to revise and edit her literary analysis, she will introduce counterclaims, find and improve weak spots in her writing, as well as correct any language or punctuation mistakes.

NOTES

### ☰ STUDENT MODEL: FIRST DRAFT

**The Power of Language**

~~Words are powerful things. They can change the world. They can change people's minds. Words can hurt just as much as stick or stones, as the old saying goes. The authors of "She Unnames Them," "Letter from Birmingham Jail," and "Speech to the Second Virginia Convention" all want to change the world, so they use their words.~~

There is an old saying that "sticks and stones may break my bones, but words will never hurt me," but it isn't true. Words can be much more dangerous than sticks or stones. Words may not kill a person instantly, like a weapon—but, like a tool, they can shape the world. Words are powerful. They can change history by calling people to action. They can also change people's minds. The authors of "She Unnames Them," "Letter from Birmingham Jail," and "Speech to the Second Virginia Convention" all want to change the world, and they use words to bring about that change.

In "She Unnames Them" by Ursula K. Le Guin, Eve learns that most of the animals never cared about the names Adam had given them. By unaming the animals, Eve feels an unexpected "powerful" effect. She feels closer to but also more afraid of the animals. She realizes that she must renounce her own name. She tries to give her name back to Adam. He doesn't seem to be listening; because he pays no attention to her words. As she leaves the garden, she realizes that her words must "be as slow, as new, as single, as tentative as the steps I took."

Patrick Henry uses strong language to get his listeners to change their minds in "Speech to the Second Virginia Convention." When he delivered the speech in 1775, he was taking a big risk. The purpose of his speech was to persuade his audience to declare independence from Britain. What Henry is suggesting is treasonous, but he feels so

### Skill:
### Introductions

*Caroline understands that she needs to add a more interesting "hook." She decides to start with an old saying, rather than placing this saying several sentences into the paragraph. Next, she decides to add sentences to help explain how and why words are powerful and even dangerous. Last, she crafts a stronger, clearer claim and a more complete introductory paragraph.*

strongly about "the question of freedom or slavery" that he considers it is treason to hold back his opinions. Henry shows respect for his audience, but he argues that they are not seeing the world clearly. He guides his listeners to see his point of view through logic. He asks rhetorical questions and then answers them. Yet it is his emotional language that is more persuasive. Throughout his speech, he uses the image of heavy chains to argue that the Americans are enslaved to Britian. He asks, "is life so dear, or peace so sweet, as to be purchased at the price of chains and slavery?" He declares that "if we wish to be free" then "we must fight!" he ends his speech by speaking for himself: "I know not what course others may take; but as for me, give me liberty or give me death! It was like he didn't care whether the others folow him, he knows what he will do. He has convinced himself to take couragous action.

~~King wrote "Letter from Birmingham Jail" after being arrested during a peacefull protest against racial segregation. His letter is a response to white people. They think that African Americans should not protest against inequality. Instead they should wait for it to be handled in the courts. King addresses his audience directly and asks questions. He uses logic to explain how he ended up in jail. The most persuasive part of his argument comes from his use of powerful language to explain what injustice feels like to African Americans. He expresses the pain of having to tell his daughter that she can't go to an amusement park because she is black. he paints a picture of a world that is unjust and dangerous for people of color. He ends his letter by imagining a day in which "the South will recognize its real heroes." He is talking about those people who peacefully—And courageously— fought for their civil Rights.~~

Like Patrick Henry, Martin Luther King Jr. uses powerful language to address an injustice. King wrote "Letter from Birmingham Jail" after being arrested during a peaceful protest against racial segregation. King's letter is a response to white people who think that African Americans should not protest against inequality but should wait for it to be handled in the courts. Like Henry, King addresses his audience directly. For example, he asks questions: "You may well ask, 'Why direct action? Why sit ins, marches and so forth? Isn't negotiation a better path?'" He uses logic to explain how he ended up in jail. However, the most persuasive part of his argument comes

 Skill: Transitions

*Caroline's new topic sentence—"Like Patrick Henry, Martin Luther King Jr. uses powerful language to address an injustice"—introduces the main idea developed in this paragraph. The transition "Like Patrick Henry" makes a connection to another author whose text Caroline discusses in an earlier paragraph.*

NOTES

from his use of powerful language to explain what injustice feels like to African Americans who experience "the stinging darts of segregation." He describes the pain of being told to be patient when "you have seen hate filled policemen curse, kick and even kill your black brothers and sisters." He expresses the pain of having to tell his daughter that she can't go to an amusement park because she is black and of having to live a life "plagued with inner fears and outer resentments." Yet he ends his letter by imagining a day in which "the South will recognize its real heroes"—those people who peacefully and courageously fought for their civil rights. He describes them as "bringing our nation back to those great wells of democracy which were dug deep by the founding fathers." As a result of King's powerful language, others could share his vision of the world as it is and as it might be.

All three authors want to change the world, so they use their words. The selections "She Unnames Them," "Speech to the Second Virginia Convention," and "Letter from Birmingham Jail," all use powerful words to say important stuff about the world. Patrick Henry and Martin Luther King Jr. talk about injustices and challenge their audiences to think about the world in a new way. The character of Eve recognizes the power of naming and finds freedom by giving up her name.

Words are everywhere. It's easy to tune them out or think that they don't mean much. But when life turns serious, and there are injustices and wrongs to fix, people rely on the power of words. In "Speech to the Second Virginia Convention" and "Letter from Birmingham Jail," Patrick Henry and Martin Luther King Jr. describe terrible injustices and challenge their audiences to think about the world in a new way and to take action. In "She Unnames Them," Eve recognizes the power of naming and finds freedom by giving up a name she didn't choose. She decides that she's up to the challenge of using language thoughtfully and carefully instead of chattering. All have learned, as have we in reading these three selections, that language can be an important and powerful tool for changing the world in serious ways.

Skill:
Conclusions

Caroline notices that her conclusion simply restates her original claim almost exactly as it appears in the introduction. She rephrases the claim in the conclusion to show the depth of her knowledge about the topic. She adds some of her own thoughts in order to make an impression on the audience at the end.

# Skill:
# Introductions

## ••• CHECKLIST FOR INTRODUCTIONS

Before you write your introduction, ask yourself the following questions:

- What is my claim? Have I recognized opposing claims that disagree with mine or have a different perspective? How can I use them to make my own claim more precise?

- How can I introduce my topic? How have I organized complex ideas, concepts, and information to make important connections and distinctions?

- How will I "hook" my reader's interest? I might:

  > start with an attention-grabbing statement

  > begin with an intriguing question

Below are two strategies to help you introduce your precise claim and topic clearly in an introduction:

- Peer Discussion

  > Talk about your topic with a partner, explaining what you already know and your ideas about your topic.

  > Write down notes and talk about how to state your claim or thesis.

  > Briefly state your precise claim or thesis, establishing how it is different from alternative claims and counterclaims about your topic.

  > Ask about ideas to "hook" a reader.

- Freewriting

  > Freewrite for 10 minutes about your topic. Don't worry about grammar, punctuation, or having fully formed ideas. The point of freewriting is to discover ideas.

  > Review your notes and draft your claim or thesis.

  > Establish how your thesis is different from alternate claims about your topic.

  > Brainstorm ways to "hook" your reader.

## ↻ YOUR TURN

Choose the best answer to each question.

1. Which of the following belongs in an introductory paragraph?

   ○ A. a concluding statement to sum up the argument
   ○ B. a list of reasons to support a claim
   ○ C. relevant supporting evidence to justify a claim
   ○ D. a thesis statement containing a claim

2. Below is Caroline's introduction from a previous draft. The meaning of the underlined sentence is unclear. How can she rewrite the underlined sentence to make her idea clearer?

   > <u>Words are only made of air and sound but are so important.</u> They can change the world and people's minds. Words can hurt just as much as stick or stones, like that old saying goes. The authors of "She Unnames Them," "Letter from Birmingham Jail," and "Speech to the Second Virginia Convention" all try to change the world by using their words.

   ○ A. Words are powerful tools.
   ○ B. Words are made of nothing, but they have a big impact.
   ○ C. Words can be whispered or shouted.
   ○ D. Words are things that most people can't live without.

## ✎ WRITE

Use the questions in the checklist to revise the introduction of your literary analysis to meet the needs of the purpose, audience, topic, and context.

# Skill:
# Transitions

## ••• CHECKLIST FOR TRANSITIONS

Before you revise your current draft to include transitions, think about:

- the key ideas you discuss in your body paragraphs
- the relationships among your claim(s), reasons, and evidence
- the relationship between your claim(s) and counterclaims
- the logical progression of your argument

Next, reread your current draft and note areas in your essay where:

- the relationships between your claim(s), counterclaims, and the reasons and evidence are unclear, identifying places where you could add linking words or other transitional devices to make your argument more cohesive. Look for:

  > sudden jumps in your ideas

  > breaks between paragraphs where the ideas in the next paragraph are not logically following from the previous

Revise your draft to use words, phrases, and clauses to link the major sections of the text, create cohesion, and clarify the relationships between claim(s) and reasons, between reasons and evidence, and between claim(s) and counterclaims, using the following the questions as a guide:

- Are there unifying relationships between the claims, reasons, and the evidence I present in my argument?
- How do my claim(s) and counterclaims relate?
- Have I clarified, or made clear, these relationships?
- What linking words (such as conjunctions), phrases, or clauses could I add to my argument to clarify the relationships between the claims, reasons, and evidence I present?

**YOUR TURN**

Choose the best answer to each question.

1. Below is a body paragraph from a previous draft of Caroline's literary analysis. Caroline has not included an effective topic sentence. Which of the following could replace the underlined sentence in this body paragraph and provide the most effective transition to the ideas that follow?

> <u>In "She Unnames Them," the main character is the first woman Eve.</u> Eve understands that the names that Adam has given her and all of the world's creatures don't fit them. Without telling Adam, she unnames all the animals and herself. She is surprised by the powerful feeling she gets when names are removed. She tries to give back her name, but Adam doesn't listen. Eve wishes she could explain her decision to him. In the end, Eve realizes that her own words do matter. They are too precious to waste on someone who doesn't listen.

- ○ A. In "She Unnames Them," the main character is the first woman Eve, who frees the animals from their names and gives up her own name as an act of rebellion.
- ○ B. Authors tend to think that words are important because words are the way they communicate their ideas to others.
- ○ C. In "She Unnames Them," the characters are unable to use words to communicate well with each other, and as a result, the story is difficult to read.
- ○ D. In "She Unnames Them," the author uses the character of Eve to demonstrate how words can have great power and should be used sparingly.

2. Below is a body paragraph from a previous draft of Caroline's literary analysis. Caroline would like to add a transition word or phrase to help readers move from sentence 4 to sentence 5. Which of these is the most effective transition to add to the beginning of sentence 5?

> (1) Like Martin Luther King Jr., Patrick Henry uses powerful language to address injustice in "Speech to the Second Virginia Convention." (2) Henry's purpose was to persuade members of the convention to rebel against the king of England. (3) He feels so strongly about "the question of freedom or slavery" that he considers it treason to hold back his opinions. (4) He uses both logical and emotional appeals. (5) His emotional appeal is more effective. (6) When Henry declares "give me liberty or give me death," he shows his true, heartfelt feelings. (7) Even readers today feel moved by the passion behind his words.

○ A.  Finally,

○ B.  However,

○ C.  Therefore,

○ D.  As a result,

 **WRITE**

Use the questions in the checklist to revise one of your body paragraphs in order to clarify its claim or counterclaim and add cohesion and establish relationships between ideas through the use of transitions.

Please note that excerpts and passages in the StudySync® library and this workbook are intended as touchstones to generate interest in an author's work. The excerpts and passages do not substitute for the reading of entire texts, and StudySync® strongly recommends that students seek out and purchase the whole literary or informational work in order to experience it as the author intended. Links to online resellers are available in our digital library. In addition, complete works may be ordered through an authorized reseller by filling out and returning to StudySync® the order form enclosed in this workbook.

Reading & Writing
Companion

**123**

# Skill:
# Conclusions

## ••• CHECKLIST FOR CONCLUSIONS

Before you write your conclusion, ask yourself the following questions:

- How can I restate the thesis or main idea?
- How can I write my conclusion so that it supports and follows from the information I presented?
- How can I communicate the importance of my topic? What information do I need?

Below are two strategies to help you provide a concluding statement or section that follows from and supports the information or explanation presented:

- Peer Discussion

  > After you have written your introduction and body paragraphs, talk with a partner about what you want readers to remember; take notes.

  > Think about how you can articulate, or express, the significance of your topic in the conclusion.

    o Restate any ideas from people who are experts on your topic.

    o Note possible implications if something is done or is not accomplished.

  > Rephrase your claim to show the depth of your knowledge and support for the information you presented.

  > Write your conclusion.

- Freewriting

  > Freewrite for 10 minutes to discover ideas about what to include in your conclusion. Don't worry about grammar, punctuation, or having fully formed ideas.

  > Follow the last three steps as you would for Peer Discussion, above.

YOUR TURN

Choose the best answer to each question.

1. Which of the following belongs in a concluding paragraph?

   ○ A. a statement to sum up the argument and demonstrate that a claim is valid, or true
   ○ B. reasons and relevant evidence to support a claim
   ○ C. transitions to link major sections of text
   ○ D. a "hook" and the first appearance of the thesis statement containing a claim

2. Below is Caroline's conclusion from a previous draft. Her closing sentence is weak. Which of these sentences could replace her final sentence, which is underlined, to provide a more effective closing to her literary analysis?

   All three authors show the power of language. The authors of "She Unnames Them," "Speech to the Second Virginia Convention," and "Letter from Birmingham Jail" use words to say something important about the world. Patrick Henry and Martin Luther King Jr. talk about injustices and challenge their audiences to think. Eve understands that because language is powerful, she will use it carefully from now on. <u>Because our words are important and precious, we should think carefully before speaking.</u>

   ○ A. Don't you think it's important to use powerful words when it's time to change the world?
   ○ B. These three selections help show that words can be powerful tools for changing the world.
   ○ C. Let's watch how we use our words at all times because they are so important.
   ○ D. Like Eve, maybe we should all choose our words more carefully in the future.

✎ WRITE

Use the questions in the checklist to revise the conclusion of your literary analysis to meet the needs of the purpose, audience, topic, and context.

Please note that excerpts and passages in the StudySync® library and this workbook are intended as touchstones to generate interest in an author's work. The excerpts and passages do not substitute for the reading of entire texts, and StudySync® strongly recommends that students seek out and purchase the whole literary or informational work in order to experience it as the author intended. Links to online resellers are available in our digital library. In addition, complete works may be ordered through an authorized reseller by filling out and returning to StudySync® the order form enclosed in this workbook.

Reading & Writing Companion    125

# Literary Analysis Writing Process: Revise

| PLAN | DRAFT | REVISE | EDIT AND PUBLISH |
|------|-------|--------|------------------|

You have written a draft of your literary analysis. You have also received input from your peers about how to improve it. Now you are going to revise your draft.

## ← REVISION GUIDE

Examine your draft to find areas for revision. Keep in mind your purpose and audience as you revise for clarity, development, organization, and style. Use the guide below to help you review:

| Review | Revise | Example |
|--------|--------|---------|
| **Clarity** | | |
| Label each pronoun to make it clear to whom you are referring. | Use the authors' or characters' names to identify who you are talking about. | When ~~he~~ Henry delivered the speech in 1775, he was taking a big risk. The purpose of ~~his~~ Henry's speech was to persuade his audience to declare independence from Britain. |
| **Development** | | |
| Identify the textual evidence that supports your claims and include commentary. Annotate places where you feel that there is not enough textual evidence to support your ideas or where you have failed to provide commentary. | Focus on a single idea or claim and add your personal reflections in the form of commentary or support in the form of textual evidence. | Henry shows respect for his audience by referring to them as "sir" and "gentlemen," but he argues that they are not seeing the world clearly. They are like people "who, having eyes, see not, and, having ears, hear not." |

| Review | Revise | Example |
|---|---|---|
| **Organization** | | |
| Review your body paragraphs. Identify and annotate any sentences that don't flow in a clear or logical way. | Reorganize or rewrite sentences so that each paragraph progresses in a logical sequence, starting with a clear topic sentence and including transitions as needed. Delete details that are repetitive or not essential to the claim. | By unnaming the animals, Eve feels an unexpected "powerful" effect. She feels closer to but also more afraid of the animals. ~~She~~ Then she realizes that she must renounce her own name. When she ~~She~~ tries to give her name back to Adam, ~~.~~ ~~He~~ he does not seem to be listening~~;~~ ~~because he pays no attention to her words~~. |
| **Style: Word Choice** | | |
| Look for everyday words and phrases that could be replaced with academic language, such as literary terms, or more precise language. | Replace everyday language with academic terms, such as *logical appeal*, *persuade*, and *audience*. | Patrick Henry uses ~~strong~~ logical appeals and vivid language to ~~get his listeners to change their minds~~ persuade his audience in "Speech to the Second Virginia Convention." |
| **Style: Sentence Effectiveness** | | |
| Read your literary analysis aloud. Annotate places where you have too many long or short sentences in a row. | Shorten longer sentences for clarity or emphasis. Revise short sentences by linking them together. | His letter is a response to white people. ~~They~~ who think that African Americans should not protest against inequality~~.~~ ~~Instead they~~ but should wait for it to be handled in the courts. |

## ✏️ WRITE

Use the guide above, as well as your peer reviews, to help you evaluate your literary analysis to determine areas that should be revised.

# STYLE

## Skill:
## Style

## ••• CHECKLIST FOR STYLE

First, reread the draft of your literary analysis essay and identify the following:

- slang, colloquialisms, contractions, abbreviations, or a conversational tone

- areas where you could use domain-specific or academic language in order to help persuade or inform your readers

- the use of first person (*I*) or second person (*you*)

- areas where you could vary sentence structure and length, emphasizing compound, complex, and compound-complex sentences

- statements that express judgment or emotion, rather than an objective tone that relies on facts and evidence

- incorrect uses of the conventions of standard English for grammar, spelling, capitalization, and punctuation

Establish and maintain a formal style in your essay, using the following questions as a guide:

> Have I avoided slang in favor of academic language?

> Did I consistently used a third-person perspective, using third-person pronouns (*he*, *she*, *they*)?

> Have I maintained an objective tone without expressing my own judgments and emotions?

> Have I used varied sentence lengths and different sentence structures?

   o Where should I make some sentences longer by using conjunctions to connect independent clauses, dependent clauses, and phrases?

   o Where should I make some sentences shorter by separating independent clauses?

> Did I follow the conventions of standard English?

**YOUR TURN**

Choose the best answer to each question.

1. Below is a section from a previous draft of Caroline's literary analysis. She wants to add some style to the paragraph. Which sentence could she add after sentence 4 to achieve that goal?

> (1) Patrick Henry's "Speech to the Second Virginia Convention" is a stirring call to war. (2) He begins by addressing his audience directly and politely. (3) He asks and answers rhetorical questions to help his listeners see the logic of his thinking. (4) However, he also uses emotional appeals effectively. (5) He declares that "there is no retreat but submission and slavery!" (6) He exclaims that no matter what the others at the convention will do, his choice is "give me liberty or give me death!"

- ○ A. I think Henry's speech is basically a call for his colleagues at the convention to commit treason.
- ○ B. Henry's mixture of logical and emotional appeals makes his argument interesting to read.
- ○ C. Henry's use of the metaphor of the chains effectively illustrates his passionate stance.
- ○ D. Henry allows his own personal feelings to erupt throughout the speech.

2. Caroline wants to improve the topic sentence of a paragraph from a previous draft of her literary analysis. She wants the topic sentence to use formal style to more clearly express her analysis. Which sentence is a better replacement for the underlined sentence?

> I get the feeling that Eve's relationship with language is the focus of the story "She Unnames Them." Eve discovers that most of the animals do not care about their names. The names are unnecessary. She feels an unexpected "powerful" effect from taking away their names. Then she realizes that she must give up her own name. She is not sure how she feels about it. It doesn't "fit," but she doesn't want to seem "ungrateful."

- ○ A. Eve's decision to unname the animals and leave the garden is a rewriting of an ancient biblical tale.
- ○ B. I think Eve's determination to unname the animals and herself falters when she must speak to Adam in person.
- ○ C. Eve's main discovery in the story is that language, especially names, can be powerful, and she is right.
- ○ D. Eve's uncertainty about her relationship to language indicates an inner conflict that is key to understanding the story.

Please note that excerpts and passages in the StudySync® library and this workbook are intended as touchstones to generate interest in an author's work. The excerpts and passages do not substitute for the reading of entire texts, and StudySync® strongly recommends that students seek out and purchase the whole literary or informational work in order to experience it as the author intended. Links to online resellers are available in our digital library. In addition, complete works may be ordered through an authorized reseller by filling out and returning to StudySync® the order form enclosed in this workbook.

Reading & Writing Companion

**129**

WRITE

Use the steps in the checklist to add to or revise the language of your thesis, use of textual evidence, and a paragraph or section of your analysis to demonstrate a formal style and objective tone.

# Grammar: Basic Spelling Rules I

## Examples

| Rule | Text | Explanation |
| --- | --- | --- |
| When adding a suffix that begins with a vowel to a word that ends with a silent **e**, usually drop the **e**.<br><br>When adding a suffix that begins with a consonant to a word that ends with a silent **e**, keep the **e**. | Therefore **begrudging** neither augury<br>Nor other **divination** that is thine,<br>O save thyself, thy country, and thy king,<br>Save all from this **defilement** of blood shed.<br><br>*Oedipus Rex* | *Begrudging* drops the final silent *e* of *begrudge*, because the suffix starts with a vowel.<br><br>*Divination* drops the final silent *e* of *divine*, because the suffix starts with a vowel.<br><br>*Defilement* keeps the silent *e*, because the suffix starts with a consonant. |
| Always keep the original spelling of the word when you add a prefix. | It is the Nation's resilience, not its rigidity, that Texas sees reflected in the flag—and it is that resilience that we **reassert** today.<br><br>Texas v. Johnson | The prefix *re-* does not change the spelling of the base word *assert*. |
| When **i** and **e** appear after a **c**, the **e** usually comes before the **i**.<br><br>However, there are exceptions to this rule. | Let us not, I beseech you, sir, **deceive** ourselves.<br><br>Speech to the Second Virginia Convention | When following a c, e comes before i. |
| When a word ends in a consonant + **y**, change the **y** to **i** before adding a suffix. | America is rapidly losing its position as leader of the world simply because the Democratic Administration has **pitifully** failed to provide effective leadership.<br><br>Remarks to the Senate in Support of a Declaration of Conscience | The y at the end of *pity* is changed to an i before adding the suffix -*fully*. |

## ↻ YOUR TURN

1. How should the spelling error in this sentence be corrected?

> The democratic rules of debate and voting are violated when Napoleon has the conciet to use his trained dogs to viciously attack Snowball, seize control, and monopolize power.

○ A. Change **conciet** to **conceit**.
○ B. Change **violated** to **violateed**.
○ C. Change **monopolize** to **monopalize**.
○ D. No change needs to be made to this sentence.

2. How should the spelling error in this sentence be corrected?

> The bedraggled chihuahua in the torrential rain was the most pityable creature imaginable.

○ A. Change **torrential** to **torrencial**.
○ B. Change **pityable** to **pitiable**.
○ C. Change **imaginable** to **imagineable**.
○ D. No change needs to be made to this sentence.

3. How should the spelling error in this sentence be corrected?

> By constantly discusing their shared dream, Ryne and Lennie inspire themselves to work toward an incredibly difficult goal.

○ A. Change **constantly** to **constanly**.
○ B. Change **discusing** to **discussing**.
○ C. Change **incredibly** to **incredibally**.
○ D. No change needs to be made to this sentence.

4. How should the spelling error in this sentence be corrected?

> Technological advances have brought miraculous solutions to problems as well as consequences that could not be forseen.

○ A. Change **Technological** to **Technologycal**.
○ B. Change **solutions** to **soluteions**.
○ C. Change **forseen** to **foreseen**.
○ D. No change needs to be made to this sentence.

# Grammar: Independent and Dependent Clauses

A clause is a group of words that has both a subject (noun) and a predicate (verb). A clause can function as a sentence by itself or as part of a sentence.

**Independent or Main Clause**

An independent clause is also called a main clause. An independent or main clause has a subject and a predicate and expresses a complete thought. It can stand alone as a sentence.

| Incorrect | Correct |
|---|---|
| visited the beach | The family visited the beach. |
| the sleepy teen | The sleepy teen turned off his alarm clock. |

**Dependent or Subordinate Clause**

A dependent clause is also called a subordinate clause. A dependent or subordinate clause has a subject and a predicate, but it does not express a complete thought. It cannot stand alone as a sentence.

Dependent, or subordinate, clauses usually begin with a subordinating conjunction, such as *when*, *since*, *because*, *after*, or *while*. They may also begin with a relative pronoun, such as *who*, *whose*, *whom*, *which*, *that*, or *what*, or with a relative adverb, such as *when*, *where*, or *why*. In some subordinate clauses, the connecting word also serves as the subject of the clause.

| Text | Explanation |
|---|---|
| Never shall I forget that night, the first night in camp, **that turned my life into one long night seven times sealed.**<br><br>*Night* | **That** is a relative pronoun. It stands in for the noun *night*. It begins the subordinate clause. **Turned** is the verb in the subordinate clause. It tells what the night did. |
| Do I have the right to represent the multitudes **who have perished**?<br><br>Nobel Prize Acceptance Speech | **Who** is a relative pronoun. It stands in for the noun *multitudes*. It begins the subordinate clause. **Perished** is the verb in the subordinate clause. Along with the auxiliary verb **have**, it tells what happened to the multitudes. |

## ⟳ YOUR TURN

1. How should this sentence be changed?

> Because Jim and Clare went to a Chicago Cubs' game that was played in Wrigley Field.

- ○ A. Insert a period after **game**.
- ○ B. Delete the word **because**.
- ○ C. Replace **that** with **which**.
- ○ D. No change needs to be made to this sentence.

2. How should this sentence be changed?

> The movie that Sue rented was very creepy.

- ○ A. Delete **was very creepy**.
- ○ B. Insert **since** before **the**.
- ○ C. Delete **that Sue rented**.
- ○ D. No change needs to be made to this sentence.

3. How should this sentence be changed?

> Chili is Lila's favorite food it's cold outside.

- ○ A. Insert **whenever** before **chili**.
- ○ B. Insert **when** after **food**.
- ○ C. Insert **that** after **chili**.
- ○ D. No change needs to be made to this sentence.

4. How should this sentence be changed?

> Becka's orange shirt, which Tom had given her for her birthday.

- ○ A. Delete **Becka's orange shirt**.
- ○ B. Insert a **comma** and **ripped** after **birthday**.
- ○ C. Replace **which** with **because**.
- ○ D. No change needs to be made to this sentence.

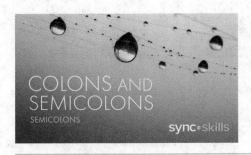

COLONS AND
SEMICOLONS
SEMICOLONS
sync•skills

# Grammar: Semicolons

A semicolon [;] connects groups of words in a sentence. Most often, a semicolon is used to join independent clauses that are not already connected with a comma and a coordinating conjunction, such as *and*, *but*, *so*, or *or*. When a semicolon is used in this way, do not use a coordinating conjunction as well. Also, keep in mind that both sentence parts need to be independent clauses.

| Correct | Incorrect |
|---|---|
| Sonia was deeply committed to doing her work well; she consistently applied all her abilities to the task at hand. | Sonia was deeply committed to doing her work well; and she consistently applied all her abilities to the task at hand. |
| Tom Hanks is a talented and appealing actor, especially in the movie *Forrest Gump*. | Tom Hanks is a talented and appealing actor; especially in the movie *Forrest Gump*. |

Follow these additional rules when using semicolons:

| Rule | Text |
|---|---|
| When a semicolon is used between independent clauses, the clauses must be closely related in thought. | The few birds seen anywhere were moribund; they trembled violently and could not fly. *Silent Spring* |
| Use a semicolon to join two independent clauses with a conjunctive adverb (such as *however*) or another transition word or phrase (such as *for example*). A comma may follow the transition word or phrase. | The animals listened first to Napoleon, then to Snowball, and could not make up their minds which was right; indeed, they always found themselves in agreement with the one who was speaking at the moment. *Animal Farm* |
| Use a semicolon to separate items in a series when one or more of the items already contains commas. | She survives him, as do his brothers Malachy and Alphie, both of Manhattan, and his brother Mike, of San Francisco; his daughter, Maggie McCourt of Burlington, Vt.; and three grandchildren. "Frank McCourt, Whose Irish Childhood Illuminated His Prose, Is Dead at 78" |

## ⟳ YOUR TURN

1. What change would correct the error in this sentence?

> The old car needed new tires, furthermore, the paint was scratched, and the fender was bent.

- ○ A. Change the comma after *tires* to a semicolon.
- ○ B. Change the comma after *furthermore* to a semicolon.
- ○ C. Change the comma after *scratched* to a semicolon.
- ○ D. No change needs to be made to this sentence.

2. What change would correct the error in this sentence?

> Jack has never been deliberately unkind; he is pleasant to everyone; friend or foe.

- ○ A. Change the semicolon after *unkind* to a comma.
- ○ B. Change both semicolons to commas.
- ○ C. Change the semicolon after *everyone* to a comma.
- ○ D. No change needs to be made to this sentence.

3. What change would correct the error in this sentence?

> Janey's family moved into their new house along with Princess, their dog, Ginger, their cat; and Mason, their hamster.

- ○ A. Change the comma after *dog* to a semicolon.
- ○ B. Change the semicolon after *cat* to a comma.
- ○ C. Insert a semicolon after *house*.
- ○ D. No change needs to be made to this sentence.

4. What change would correct the error in this sentence?

> Miguel's pirate costume was wonderful; he had even trained his pet parrot, Petey, to ride on his shoulder.

- ○ A. Change the semicolon after *wonderful* to a comma.
- ○ B. Change the commas around *Petey* to semicolons.
- ○ C. Insert a semicolon after *ride*.
- ○ D. No change needs to be made to this sentence.

# Literary Analysis Writing Process: Edit and Publish

| PLAN | DRAFT | REVISE | EDIT AND PUBLISH |
|------|-------|--------|------------------|

You have revised your literary analysis essay based on your peer feedback and your own examination.

Now, it is time to edit your literary analysis essay. When you revised, you focused on the content of your literary analysis. You probably looked at your essay's claim, your organization, your supporting details and textual evidence, and your word choice. When you edit, you focus on the mechanics of your literary analysis essay, paying close attention to things like spelling, grammar, and punctuation. You can also edit to be sure your writing maintains a formal style and objective tone.

**Use the checklist below to guide you as you edit:**

☐ Have I spelled everything correctly?

☐ Have I correctly used capitalization throughout my essay?

☐ Have I used semicolons correctly to link closely related independent clauses and to create sentence variety?

☐ Have I used a consistent verb tense throughout the essay?

☐ Do I have any sentence fragments or run-on sentences?

☐ Have I maintained a formal style and objective tone?

**Notice some edits Caroline has made:**

- Replaced a pronoun to clarify a reference.

- Corrected her spelling after her spellchecker flagged some misspelled words.

- Checked and corrected her capitalization of words at the beginnings of sentences, following dashes, and in direct quotations.

- Correctly used a semicolon to correct a comma splice and show a connection between two complete thoughts.

- Changed a verb from past to present tense for consistency.

- Eliminated a contraction to maintain a formal style.

Throughout his speech, ~~he~~ Henry uses the image of heavy chains to argue that the Americans are enslaved to ~~Britian~~ Britain. He asks, "~~is~~ Is life so dear, or peace so sweet, as to be purchased at the price of chains and slavery?" He declares that "if we wish to be free" then "we must fight!" ~~hH~~He ends his speech by speaking for himself: "I know not what course others may take; but as for me, give me liberty or give me death!" It is ~~like~~ as if he ~~didn't~~ does not care whether the others ~~folow~~ follow him~~;~~; he knows ~~what he will do. He has convinced himself to~~ that he will take ~~couragous~~ courageous action.

---

## ✏ WRITE

Use the questions on the previous page, as well as your peer reviews, to help you evaluate your literary analysis essay to determine areas that need editing. Then edit your literary analysis text to correct those errors.

Once you have made all your corrections, you are ready to publish your work. You can distribute your writing to family and friends, hang it on a bulletin board, or post it on your blog. If you publish online, share the link with your family, friends, and classmates.

# Roosevelts on the Radio

## Introduction

A week after his inauguration, President Franklin Delano Roosevelt gave his first "fireside chat" to the nation over the radio. He, along with First Lady Eleanor, began an unprecedented series of radio addresses delivered directly to the American people. Their influence changed how Americans expect their politicians to communicate.

# V VOCABULARY

### broadcasting
communicating to the public through radio or television

### proficiency
expertise or skill

### constituents
people who live and vote in an area

### infamy
the state of being well-known for disgraceful character or actions

### goodwill
a kind or helpful feeling

NOTES

# ≡ READ

1. Every Saturday morning from 2009 to 2016, Americans could turn on their radios and hear a weekly address from President Barack Obama. The practice of using the radio to reach Americans started in the 20th century. Franklin Delano Roosevelt was president from 1933 to 1945. He, along with his wife Eleanor, pioneered and perfected **broadcasting** from the Oval Office.

2. President Roosevelt and his wife Eleanor Roosevelt each made about 300 radio appearances during his 12 years in office. By 1940, most American homes had a radio. The radio was a great way for the president to reach people. It was inexpensive and efficient. He could speak directly to **constituents** without going through journalists.

3. Of all his radio appearances, President Roosevelt is most famous for his "fireside chats." These were a series of informal speeches to the nation. (The president did not sit next to a roaring fire during these chats. He sat at his desk behind microphones.) President Roosevelt needed to reassure a country reeling from the Great Depression. As a result, the tone of his chats was different than most

NOTES

presidential speeches. He opened with the welcoming greeting "my friends." He did not use forceful language. Instead, he spoke calmly.

4   The chats were very successful. President Roosevelt was asked to speak every month or every week. He refused. He gave only a few chats a year. He wanted to make them special events. It worked. By some estimates, his most popular broadcasts reached 70 percent of radio listeners. He was a natural, confident speaker. The chats helped to increase public opinion of him.

5   Mrs. Roosevelt, on the other hand, was not a natural public speaker. Yet she became a popular radio personality too. Mrs. Roosevelt did 13 radio shows for women in 1932. After the success of those shows, she was regularly asked to do more. Mrs. Roosevelt talked about topics ranging from the challenges working women face to world peace. She rarely spoke directly about her husband's policies. Her popularity built **goodwill** for him.

6   Some people thought that Mrs. Roosevelt's radio shows were inappropriate for a First Lady. They were sponsored. She was paid for them. But not all of her radio appearances were for money. Both Roosevelts regularly appeared on air to host events and support charities.

7   The Roosevelts were very connected to the American people thanks to their radio **proficiency**. They got a lot of mail. President Roosevelt could receive 8,000 letters a day. Some previous administrations only received 200 letters in a week. Mrs. Roosevelt received 300,000 letters and postcards in 1933 alone. Many of the letters were negative. The Roosevelts were both hated and loved, like any politicians. But many letters were heartbreaking requests for help during hard times.

8   On December 7, 1941, the Japanese bombed the American naval base Pearl Harbor. Many Americans know the speech that President Roosevelt gave the next day. He called December 7 "a date which will live in **infamy**." The night of the attack, Mrs. Roosevelt addressed the nation. She had a regular Sunday night program. She spoke frankly to worried mothers and nervous young adults. She encouraged them to keep their spirits high. She said she was confident in the country.

9   President Roosevelt continued his "fireside chats" and radio broadcasts throughout World War II. When he died in 1945, most Americans grieved. They felt he had personally guided them through the challenges of the past decade.

10  Mrs. Roosevelt returned to the radio with a daily show in 1948. When television became more popular than radio, she appeared on television often. Polls ranked Mrs. Roosevelt as the most admired woman in the United States after her death in 1962. Thanks to radio, the Roosevelts had been welcomed into American homes. They left their mark.

# First Read

Read the text. After you read, complete the Think Questions below.

## ☁ THINK QUESTIONS

1. Which two presidents are compared in the text?

   The text compares _____

   _____.

2. Write two or three sentences to describe the "fireside chats."

   The fireside chats were _____

   _____.

3. Why did Americans grieve when Roosevelt died in 1945? Support your answer with evidence from the text.

   Americans grieved because _____

   _____.

4. Use context to confirm the meaning of the word *proficiency* as it is used in "Roosevelts on the Radio." Write your definition of *proficiency* here.

   *Proficiency* means _____

   _____.

   A context clue is _____

   _____.

5. What is another way to say that fireside chats created *goodwill* toward the Roosevelts?

   Fireside chats _____

   _____.

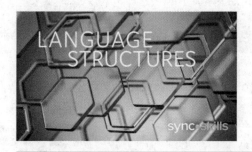

# Skill:
# Language Structures

## ★ DEFINE

In every language, there are rules that tell how to **structure** sentences. These rules define the correct order of words. In the English language, for example, a **basic** structure for sentences is subject, verb, and object. Some sentences have more **complicated** structures.

You will encounter both basic and complicated **language structures** in the classroom materials you read. Being familiar with language structures will help you better understand the text.

## ••• CHECKLIST FOR LANGUAGE STRUCTURES

To improve your comprehension of language structures, do the following:

✓ Monitor your understanding.

- Ask yourself: Why do I not understand this sentence? Is it because I do not understand some of the words? Or is it because I do not understand the way the words are ordered in the sentence?

✓ Break down the sentence into its parts.

- In English, many sentences share this basic pattern: subject + verb + object.

  > The **subject** names who or what is doing the action.

  > The **verb** names the action or state of being.

  > The **object** answers questions such as Who?, What?, Where?, and When?

- Ask yourself: What is the action? Who or what is doing the action? What details do the other words provide?

✓ Confirm your understanding with a peer or teacher.

Please note that excerpts and passages in the StudySync® library and this workbook are intended as touchstones to generate interest in an author's work. The excerpts and passages do not substitute for the reading of entire texts, and StudySync® strongly recommends that students seek out and purchase the whole literary or informational work in order to experience it as the author intended. Links to online resellers are available in our digital library. In addition, complete works may be ordered through an authorized reseller by filling out and returning to StudySync® the order form enclosed in this workbook.

Reading & Writing Companion    143

**YOUR TURN**

Read paragraph 8 from "Roosevelts on the Radio." Then, complete the chart by sorting the words and phrases into the "Subject," "Verb," and "Object" columns. The first row has been done as an example.

---

**from "Roosevelts on the Radio"**

On December 7, 1941, the Japanese bombed the American naval base Pearl Harbor. Many Americans know the speech that President Roosevelt gave the next day. He called December 7 "a date which will live in infamy." The night of the attack, Mrs. Roosevelt addressed the nation. She had a regular Sunday night program.

---

| Options | | | |
|---|---|---|---|
| know | December 7 "a date which will live in infamy" | Many Americans | He |
| a regular Sunday night program | She | the speech | Mrs. Roosevelt |
| the nation | had | called | addressed |

---

| Sentence | Subject | Verb | Object |
|---|---|---|---|
| On December 7, 1941, the Japanese bombed the American naval base Pearl Harbor. | the Japanese | bombed | the American naval base Pearl Harbor |
| Many Americans know the speech that President Roosevelt gave the next day. | | | |
| He called December 7 "a date which will live in infamy." | | | |
| The night of the attack, Mrs. Roosevelt addressed the nation. | | | |
| She had a regular Sunday night program. | | | |

# Skill:
# Conveying Ideas

## ★ DEFINE

**Conveying** ideas means communicating a **message** to another person. When speaking, you might not know what word to use to convey your ideas. When you do not know the exact English word, you can try different strategies. For example, you can ask for help from classmates or your teacher. You may use gestures and physical movements to act out the word. You can also try using **synonyms** or **defining** and describing the meaning you are trying to express.

## ••• CHECKLIST FOR CONVEYING IDEAS

To convey ideas for words you do not know when speaking, use the following learning strategies:

- ✓ Request help.
- ✓ Use gestures or physical movements.
- ✓ Use a synonym for the word.
- ✓ Describe what the word means using other words.
- ✓ Give an example of the word you want to use.

## ⟳ YOUR TURN

Match each example with the correct strategy for conveying the meaning of the word *confident*.

| A | The person uses the similar word *self-assured*. |
|---|---|
| B | The person mimes standing up straight and looking fearless. |
| C | The person explains that the word means "feeling sure of oneself." |
| D | The person says it is like when you have studied thoroughly and know you will do well on a test. |

| Strategies | Examples |
|---|---|
| Use gestures or physical movements. | |
| Use a synonym for the word. | |
| Describe what the word means using other words. | |
| Give an example of the word you want to use. | |

# Close Read

## ✏ WRITE

INFORMATIONAL: President Franklin Delano Roosevelt and his wife, Eleanor, used radio to communicate with the American people. In a short essay, explain why the "fireside chats" were successful. Use evidence from the text to convey your ideas. Pay attention to and edit for spelling patterns as you write.

**Use the checklist below to guide you as you write:**

☐ How did the Roosevelts use the radio?

☐ Who listened to the "fireside chats"?

☐ What made the chats popular?

**Use the sentence frames to organize and write your informational text.**

Many Americans had _____.

President Roosevelt's fireside chats were _____

_____.

President Roosevelt was a _____ speaker.

The tone of the broadcasts was _____.

The fireside chats improved _____ of him.

Please note that excerpts and passages in the StudySync® library and this workbook are intended as touchstones to generate interest in an author's work. The excerpts and passages do not substitute for the reading of entire texts, and StudySync® strongly recommends that students seek out and purchase the whole literary or informational work in order to experience it as the author intended. Links to online resellers are available in our digital library. In addition, complete works may be ordered through an authorized reseller by filling out and returning to StudySync® the order form enclosed in this workbook.

Reading & Writing Companion    147

# The Dinner of the Lion

FICTION

## Introduction

lion demands honor and respect from animals who are destined to be his dinner. Will they bow before him and be eaten? Or will one of them come

## V VOCABULARY

**dread**

a strong feeling of fear or worry

**logic**

a reasonable way of thinking

**diminish**

to decrease or reduce

**measure**

action taken as a way to achieve a goal

**flattery**

praise that is insincere

## ☰ READ

NOTES

1   The water was pure, and the grass was green. Life was marvelous for the animals in the Seven Hills, until the lion moved in. He believed he was the strongest and the most beautiful of all animals. His long, yellow mane rippled in the breeze like a flag announcing his greatness.

2   Lion believed he could do whatever he liked. He liked making others afraid. He insisted on being called "His Lordship." Even worse, he devoured two or three animals every day, creating great **dread** among them all. They became so frightened that they could hardly eat. The quality of the lion's meals **diminished**. His Lordship roared in fury, and the sound echoed in the hills like nearby thunder.

3   The fearful animals held a meeting. It would be easier to please the lion if only one animal were eaten a day. Then more might survive to see their children grow up. Weasel was sent to negotiate with His Lordship.

4 "Your honor," he began, "we fear for your health. The quality of your meals is poor. We suggest that, instead of you hunting down two or three of us, we will bring you one plump and extremely tender animal every day. You won't have to waste your time hunting. You are too great for such nonsense."

5 His Lordship, soaking up **flattery** like a sponge, agreed, adding a threat: "My meal must arrive on time. Bring it with the honor that is due me. I am great and deserve respect! If you disappoint me, I will eat all of you in a single day." Weasel retired from His Lordship's presence, bowing in obedience.

6 When Weasel reported back to the animals, they were torn between two feelings. It was better that only one of them got eaten every day. However, if His Lordship was not happy, they would all die. Only Hare saw the faulty **logic**.

7 "If he ate all of us," Hare explained, "there would be no more food. He would die too. He enjoys threatening others with extreme, but unlikely **measures**."

8 The animals still lived in fear of angering His Lordship. Each day they picked a name from a bowl to see who would be on the day's menu. Each one worried, thinking, "Tomorrow it may be my turn. I will never see my children again."

9 Everyone worried except Hare. When it was his turn, he seemed as tranquil as a summer breeze. He said, "I have a plan."

10 Hare dashed to the river and jumped in. Then he rolled around on the riverbank until his whole body except for his head was covered with smelly mud. Satisfied, Hare strolled toward His Lordship's den. He began to run when he got close. Appearing out of breath, he threw himself at His Lordship's feet.

11 "How dare you present me with a dirty meal!" His Lordship bellowed.

12 "Forgive me, oh great His Lordship who is the Greatest," Hare panted. "I am not the dinner. Another lion stole the delicious hare I was bringing you! He was bigger and stronger than you. His yellow mane blew so beautifully in the breeze."

13 His Lordship screamed in fury. "I am the GREATEST! No other lion is allowed in these hills! Show me that evil lion, and I will destroy him!"

14 Hare led the way to the old well. "He took your dinner and jumped in," Hare said, pretending to be frightened.

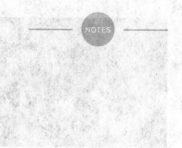

15 His Lordship looked into the well, and Hare peered over the edge at the same time. They saw the reflections of a lion and a neat, clean hare's head. "I will smash you because I am the Great Lion who owns these hills!" shrieked His Lordship. With that he hurled himself into the well and was never seen again.

16 The animals had a pleasant party that evening, and Hare lived to see his children, his grandchildren, and even his great grandchildren grow up.

# First Read

Read the story. After you read, complete the Think Questions below.

## ☁ THINK QUESTIONS

1. What was life like for the animals before Lion moved in?

   Life for the animals was _____

   _____.

2. Why are the animals scared of the lion?

   All the animals are afraid because _____

   _____.

3. How does Hare trick His Lordship?

   Hare tricks His Lordship by _____

   _____.

4. Use context to confirm the meaning of the word *logic* as it is used in "The Dinner of the Lion." Write your definition of *logic* here.

   *Logic* means _____

   _____.

   A context clue is _____

   _____.

5. What is another way to say that the rain *diminished*?

   The rain _____

   _____.

# Skill:
# Analyzing Expressions

## ★ DEFINE

When you read, you may find English expressions that you do not know. An **expression** is a group of words that communicates an idea. Three types of expressions are idioms, sayings, and figurative language. They can be difficult to understand because the meanings of the words are different from their **literal**, or usual, meanings.

An **idiom** is an expression that is commonly known among a group of people. For example, "It's raining cats and dogs" means it is raining heavily. **Sayings** are short expressions that contain advice or wisdom. For instance, "Don't count your chickens before they hatch" means do not plan on something good happening before it happens. **Figurative** language is when you describe something by comparing it with something else, either directly (using the words *like* or *as*) or indirectly. For example, "I'm as hungry as a horse" means I'm very hungry. None of the expressions are about actual animals.

## ••• CHECKLIST FOR ANALYZING EXPRESSIONS

To determine the meaning of an expression, remember the following:

✓ If you find a confusing group of words, it may be an expression. The meaning of words in expressions may not be their literal meaning.

  • Ask yourself: Is this confusing because the words are new? Or because the words do not make sense together?

✓ Determining the overall meaning may require that you use one or more of the following:

  • context clues

  • a dictionary or other resource

  • teacher or peer support

✓ Highlight important information before and after the expression to look for clues.

## ⟳ YOUR TURN

Read paragraphs 5–9 from the story. Then, complete the multiple-choice questions below.

---

from **"The Dinner of the Lion"**

His Lordship, soaking up flattery like a sponge, agreed, adding a threat: "My meal must arrive on time. Bring it with the honor that is due me. I am great and deserve respect! If you disappoint me, I will eat all of you in a single day." Weasel retired from His Lordship's presence, bowing in obedience.

When Weasel reported back to the animals, they were torn between two feelings. It was better that only one of them got eaten every day. However, if His Lordship was not happy, they would all die. Only Hare saw the faulty logic.

"If he ate all of us," Hare explained, "there would be no more food. He would die too. He enjoys threatening others with extreme, but unlikely measures."

The animals still lived in fear of angering His Lordship. Each day they picked a name from a bowl to see who would be on the day's menu. Each one worried, thinking, "Tomorrow it may be my turn. I will never see my children again."

Everyone worried except Hare. When it was his turn, he seemed as tranquil as a summer breeze. He said, "I have a plan."

---

1. In paragraph 5, which sentence contains figurative language?

   ○ A. His Lordship, soaking up flattery like a sponge, agreed, adding a threat: "My meal must arrive on time."

   ○ B. "I am great and deserve respect!"

   ○ C. "If you disappoint me, I will eat all of you in a single day."

   ○ D. Weasel retired from His Lordship's presence, bowing in obedience.

2. Which word in paragraph 5 is a clue that one thing is being compared to another?

   ○ A. like

   ○ B. adding

   ○ C. due

   ○ D. single

3.  If Hare seems "as tranquil as a summer breeze," how does he act?

    ○ A.  cleverly
    ○ B.  hotly
    ○ C.  freely
    ○ D.  calmly

4.  Which figurative language best describes Lion?

    ○ A.  as happy as a clam
    ○ B.  as dry as a bone
    ○ C.  as greedy as a pig
    ○ D.  as busy as a bee

# Skill:
# Retelling and Summarizing

## ★ DEFINE

You can retell and summarize a text after reading to show your understanding. **Retelling** is telling a story again in your own words. **Summarizing** is giving a short explanation of the most important ideas in a text.

Keep your retelling or summary **concise**. Only include important information and key words from the text. By summarizing and retelling a text, you can improve your comprehension of the text's ideas.

## ••• CHECKLIST FOR RETELLING AND SUMMARIZING

In order to retell or summarize a text, note the following:

✓ Identify the main events of the text.

- Ask yourself: What happens in this text? What are the main events that happen at the beginning, the middle, and the end of the text?

✓ Identify the main ideas in a text.

- Ask yourself: What are the most important ideas in the text?

✓ Determine the answers to the six WH questions.

- Ask yourself: After reading this text, can I answer Who?, What?, Where?, When?, Why?, and How? questions.

## ↻ YOUR TURN

Read paragraphs 12–15 from the story. Then, complete the multiple-choice questions below.

from **"The Dinner of the Lion"**

"Forgive me, oh great His Lordship who is the Greatest," Hare panted. "I am not the dinner. Another lion stole the delicious hare I was bringing you! He was bigger and stronger than you. His yellow mane blew so beautifully in the breeze."

His Lordship screamed in fury. "I am the GREATEST! No other lion is allowed in these hills! Show me that evil lion, and I will destroy him!"

Hare led the way to the old well. "He took your dinner and jumped in," Hare said, pretending to be frightened.

His Lordship looked into the well, and Hare peered over the edge at the same time. They saw the reflections of a lion and a neat, clean hare's head. "I will smash you because I am the Great Lion who owns these hills!" shrieked His Lordship. With that he hurled himself into the well and was never seen again.

1. Who must be included in a summary of these paragraphs?

   ○ A. the two lions
   ○ B. Weasel and Hare
   ○ C. Hare and His Lordship
   ○ D. His Lordship and the imaginary lion

2. Which sentence best summarizes why His Lordship is angry?

   ○ A. He thinks that Hare has tricked him again.
   ○ B. He believes that another lion stole his dinner.
   ○ C. He knows that Hare is just pretending to be afraid.
   ○ D. He wants to eat Hare, but Hare is too small.

Please note that excerpts and passages in the StudySync® library and this workbook are intended as touchstones to generate interest in an author's work. The excerpts and passages do not substitute for the reading of entire texts, and StudySync® strongly recommends that students seek out and purchase the whole literary or informational work in order to experience it as the author intended. Links to online resellers are available in our digital library. In addition, complete works may be ordered through an authorized reseller by filling out and returning to StudySync® the order form enclosed in this workbook.

Reading & Writing
Companion

157

3. Which statement is the main idea in these paragraphs?

○ A. Hare manages to trick His Lordship and save himself.

○ B. His Lordship is so greedy that he tries to eat another lion.

○ C. Hare uses His Lordship to get rid of the evil lion.

○ D. His Lordship proves that he is the greatest.

4. What is the best summary of these paragraphs?

○ A. When His Lordship wants food, he calls for Hare to bring it. Hare lies about the disappearance of the food, and instead of feeding him, he pushes the lion into a well.

○ B. His Lordship is about to eat Hare when the clever rabbit tells him about a fatter, juicier rabbit down in a well. The lion peers into the well and jumps in, never to be seen again.

○ C. Hare convinces His Lordship that he was not the meal the lion was supposed to eat. The lion becomes enraged and leaps into a well, never to be seen again.

○ D. To save himself from being eaten, Hare pretends that another lion stole His Lordship's meal. He leads the lion to a well. His Lordship sees his reflection and jumps in, never to be seen again.

# Close Read

---

### ✏ WRITE

NARRATIVE: Retell the fable from the point of view of the Lion. How does he perceive the problem and the solutions? Use the characters, settings, and sequence of events from the original text. Pay attention to verb tenses as you write.

**Use the checklist below to guide you as you write.**

☐ Imagine that you are the lion. What problems do you face in Seven Hills?

☐ From Lion's point of view, what do you think about Weasel's solution?

☐ How do your feelings change as new events happen?

**Use the sentence frames to organize and write your narrative.**

When I first came to Seven Hills, I believed that I_____

_____.

When the animals got scared and stopped eating, I felt very _____

_____.

I was glad when Weasel _____. But when Hare arrived all muddy,

I felt _____. His story about the other lion made me feel

_____, because _____.

# :: studysync®

ASSIGNMENTS    BINDER    LIBRARY

## Moving Forward

# UNIT 2

# Moving Forward

## How does culture influence your goals?

Genre Focus: **ARGUMENTATIVE**

## Texts

 Paired Readings

# Extended Writing Project and Grammar

## English Language Learner Resources

# Unit 2: Moving Forward
## How does culture influence your goals?

**CHINUA ACHEBE**

Novelist, professor, and activist Chinua Achebe (1930–2013) was raised in the Igbo town of Ogidi in Nigeria. During the Biafran War, a civil war in which the region of Biafra broke away from Nigeria in 1967, Achebe acted as an ambassador for the people of the new nation. Many of the writer's stories draw from the history of Igbo people, and Achebe believes the storyteller's role is to preserve memories and give voice to the oppressed.

**AMANDA GORMAN**

In addition to being a published poet, the first-ever United States Youth Poet Laureate Amanda Gorman (b. 1998) is also an activist, a *New York Times* columnist, and a student at Harvard University. She grew up in Los Angeles, at an "odd intersection" where "the black 'hood met black elegance met white gentrification met Latin culture met wetlands." She plans to run for president of the United States in 2036.

**RASHEMA MELSON**

For most of high school, Rashema Melson (b. 1996) lived with her mother and siblings in a Washington, DC, homeless shelter. Her hard work as a student earned her the title of valedictorian of the graduating class of 2014 at Anacostia High School, and a scholarship to Georgetown University. When she enrolled in a summer academic program, she was removed from the list of residents at her shelter and moved into the dorms a week earlier than her peers. Her story made national news in 2015.

**LOUISE MUNSON**

Playwright Louise Munson credits her mother, a classics professor, for an early education in storytelling. Munson grew up hearing Greek myths as her bedtime stories in her home of Princeton, New Jersey. She seeks inspiration in her writing by reading all genres—poetry, fiction, non-fiction, and plays. She currently lives in Los Angeles, where she writes for theater and television.

## PLATO

Ancient Greek philosopher and writer Plato (ca. 427–ca. 347 BCE) was born of noble Athenian lineage and grew up during the Peloponnesian War. He founded the Academy in Athens, an open-air space for lectures that became the model for institutions of higher learning in the Western world. Plato's written work takes the form of dialogue or discussion, and often features his teacher Socrates as a speaker.

## ELLEN JOHNSON SIRLEAF

The first elected female head of state in Africa, Ellen Johnson Sirleaf (b. 1938), served as president of Liberia from 2006–2018. She attended grade school in Liberia and earned degrees in accounting, economics, and public policy from institutions in the United States. Throughout her career, she has been recognized by *Forbes, Newsweek, Time* and the *Economist* as one of the most powerful women in the world, and was awarded the Nobel Peace Prize in 2011.

## RIGOBERTA MENCHÚ TUM

Rigoberta Menchú Tum (b. 1959) is an indigenous human rights activist from the ki'che' community of Chimel in the Guatemalan highlands. As a young girl, she traveled with her father throughout the rural communities of Guatemala to educate residents about their rights and encourage them to organize. After much of Tum's family was killed during the Guatemalan Civil War, Tum sought exile in Mexico, where she continued to organize resistance against oppression.

## ELIE WIESEL

At the age of fifteen, Elie Wiesel (1928–2016) was deported from Romania to the German concentration camp at Auschwitz, where his youngest sister and parents were killed. After World War II, Wiesel moved to Paris to work as a journalist and began to write about his experiences in the Holocaust about ten years later, publishing nearly thirty books in his lifetime. When Wiesel was awarded the Nobel Peace Prize in 1986, the committee called him a "messenger to mankind."

## VÁLMÍKI

The ancient epic poem the *Rámáyana* is attributed to the Sanskrit poet Válmíki, who names himself in the text as the author. Válmíki, a Hindu sage, created the verse form sloka in which most great Indian epics have since been written. Válmíki was born along the banks of the Ganges in India and is said to have lived as a hunter before becoming a religious scholar and writer. Artistic depictions of the poet typically portray him in the act of writing, usually with a peacock feather as a pen.

## Introduction

This informational text provides readers with specific cultural and historical information about the worlds of ancient and classical literature. Dominant societies of this time typically held reason, critical thinking, and philosophy in the highest esteem. Many of the earliest written works were epic poems like the *Odyssey* and the *Rámáyana*. In societies that were bolstered by oral traditions, increasingly global, and determined to pursue perfection in both art and literature, epics provided a rich foundation of knowledge and wisdom from which we still draw inspiration to this day.

# "They were concerned with making moral choices and using reason to make sense of a chaotic world."

1   The global nature of our lives today is not terribly different from life in the ancient and classical worlds. We certainly can travel and communicate faster than people did 2,500 years ago, but even back then people were telling similar kinds of stories, striving for similar ideals, and asking themselves similar questions about the nature of being human. Just as the classical world of Ancient Greece had epics like the *Odyssey*, we have stories of modern day heroes and heroines who embark on journeys or battles of their own in order to pursue an ideal. We witness these pursuits in films like *Star Wars* and *Spider-Man*, as well as in texts like *Divergent* and *Wild: From Lost to Found on the Pacific Crest Trail*, the story of Cheryl Strayed's journey hiking the Pacific Crest Trail

## Ancient World

2   Ancient civilizations around the world contributed to the development of the modern cultures we see today. Of these cultures, ancient Greece is considered the foundation of the Western world. Ideas about democracy, **philosophy**, science, medicine, literature, and the other arts all spring from the Greek islands in the Mediterranean. Modern Western literature and storytelling have their roots in the oral tradition of the ancient Greeks, dating from around 800–500 BCE. During this period, before writing was widespread, stories were shared orally as entertainment and instruction. The most important works of Ancient Greece are the **epic poems** *Iliad* and *Odyssey*, both ascribed to the Greek poet Homer. These long narrative poems tell the stories of early military battles and overseas journeys. Peopled with human heroes and divine figures, they were and continue to be considered part history, part mythology, part moral instruction, and full-on entertainment.

## Classical World

3   The classical period began around 500 By this time, Greek culture had grown increasingly sophisticated and influential in the Mediterranean region. A democratic system of rule had been established in Athens, the Greek capital city. Drama became a recognized art form in which small groups of actors and singers stood before audiences to act out exciting and thought-provoking

tales of noble life. The sub-genres of tragedy and comedy emerged, including the masterpiece of Greek tragedies, *Oedipus Rex* by Sophocles. This play tells the story of a king who tries to change his fate, only to accidentally fulfill it. Also during this period, the Greek thinkers Socrates, Plato, and Aristotle made an impact on the study of knowledge and existence, or philosophy. Through dialogues and discussions, they explored new ways of thinking critically about the world and humanity's place in it.

4   Eventually the Greek empire waned, and the Roman empire rose in the Mediterranean and beyond. Roman writers and artists adapted Greek forms, modifying them to their own tastes. For example, Roman sculptures of the human form became less idealized and more realistic. As during the Greek golden age, the high point of Rome's own golden age of literature was an epic poem. Virgil's *Aeneid*, like Homer's *Odyssey*, describes a hero's memorable journey and encounters with the gods.

5   The ancient and classical worlds were global places. In the mid 300s BCE, Alexander the Great expanded Greek influence as far east as India and Persia. At its height, the Roman empire included Britain, most of Europe, North Africa, and the Middle East. Each empire included people who spoke different languages and practiced different customs and religions. As a result, many texts from different regions of the world during this period have surprisingly similar themes and structures. The parables of Jesus, like the fables of the Greek writer Aesop, were simple tales with clear morals or lessons for listeners. The epics of Greece, Rome, and India all featured gods and goddesses intermingling with the human heroes, important battles, and a focus on the pursuit of ideals. Even though Greco-Roman and Indian epics like the *Odyssey* and the *Rámáyana* were written in completely different places, they both take place in a mythological past and involve gods populating the human earth. They describe the journeys of heroes who face battle, turmoil, and the prospect of victory. These themes can be seen in *Battle at Lanka*, which portrays an important battle featured in the Rámáyana.

*Battle at Lanka, Ramayana* by Sahib Din, 17th century.

Copyright © Bookheaded Learning, LLC

Winged Victory of Somothrace, ca. 220–185 BCE

6  **Major Concepts**

- **Focus on Classical Values —** The artists, poets, and philosophers of the ancient and classical periods valued reason or rational thinking over emotion or passion. They sought to achieve the **ideal** or most perfect form in their works, whether it be a sculpture of the idealized human form or an epic poem about an ideal hero. The pursuit of the ideal can be seen through the famous sculpture, the *Winged Victory of Samothrace*, which shows the goddess of Victory braced against a strong wind as she stands on a ship. Poets and artists communicated these values in both form and content. For example, epic poems and tragedies may have episodes of passion and action, but these dramatic moments are always balanced out by a clear theme about the importance of rational behavior and moral actions. In their lectures, philosophers argued about how to attain these ideals in an imperfect world. Architects built structures that were perfectly balanced and symmetrical.

Please note that excerpts and passages in the StudySync® library and this workbook are intended as touchstones to generate interest in an author's work. The excerpts and passages do not substitute for the reading of entire texts, and StudySync® strongly recommends that students seek out and purchase the whole literary or informational work in order to experience it as the author intended. Links to online resellers are available in our digital library. In addition, complete works may be ordered through an authorized reseller by filling out and returning to StudySync® the order form enclosed in this workbook.

Reading & Writing
Companion

169

- **Purpose** — Epic poems, plays, and philosophical texts all were meant to serve the purpose of teaching a lesson or inspiring audiences to think. Even an exciting epic poem, such as the *Rámáyana* from India, invited listeners to contemplate the influences of fate, the gods, and history on their world. Despite the inclusion of mythological figures in the literature and artwork of the period, the works themselves are not fantasy or myths; they were deeply informed by and reflective of the philosophy of the day. They were concerned with making moral choices and using reason to make sense of a chaotic world.

- **Emerging Genres** — The literature of the ancient and classical periods was wide ranging in its genres. Poetic forms included lyric poetry, odes, and epic narrative poems, such as the *Odyssey* and the *Rámáyana*. Dramas included tragedies like Sophocles' political play *Antigone* and comedies like Aristophanes' *The Birds*. Plato's *Dialogues* are recreated conversations between Plato and his teacher Socrates in which they explore, through the exchange of questions and answers, how to live an ethical life. Aesop's fables were short humorous stories about non-human characters that ended with an explicit moral or lesson.

### Style and Form

7 ### Allegory

- **Allegory** is a form of storytelling with hidden levels of meanings that the author wants readers or listeners to discern. Unlike Aesop's fables, which end with an explicitly stated lesson or moral, part of Plato's *Republic* is an allegory. "The Allegory of the Cave" employs symbolism and analogies that readers must recognize and decode in order to understand the meaning. In the text, Socrates presents his ideas on education by using the analogy of prisoners literally being led from a dark, shadowy cave to the sunlight outside. As a result, the *Republic* is both a straightforward story about prisoners in a cave and an examination of how we humans perceive reality.

8 ### Epic Poem

- An epic is a long narrative poem about one particular hero's deeds. Epic poetry of the ancient and classical periods was primarily created to transmit the values and traditions of the poet's culture. While not considered historical documents today, ancient epic poems were once the most effective method for recording and passing down details about historical events from long ago.

- The epic was a common genre in regions all around the globe during the classical period. Many epic poems from the period that survive were written thousands of miles apart in different languages and reflect different cultural traditions. Yet, these epics have many surprising similarities. For example, here are several ways in which the *Rámáyana*, an Indian epic poem written in Sanskrit around 300 BCE by the poet Valmiki, and Homer's *Iliad* are similar:

> They both focus on a hero from a noble family.

> The action in each poem is inspired by jealousy.

> The heroes are helped—and hindered—by gods and goddesses.

> Both epics highlight the values of the culture.

## Formal and Restrained

- The literature and other art of the ancient and classical periods is characterized by a **formal** and **restrained** style. A glance at any piece of classical Greek or Roman art or architecture makes that style clear. It is perfectly balanced and symmetrical and hardly adorned, which can be seen in the Parthenon, a famous Greek temple built in 480 BCE. Classical artists strove to achieve an ideal, and therefore did not include excess features that could throw the piece off balance or reveal any awkward human flaw. Likewise, classical authors employed a restrained style in their poetry and prose. True to the philosophy of the time, they prized balance and order in their language and in the structure of their poems and plots. Dramas follow Aristotle's unities, strict rules that dictated that a play must focus on one action over the course of one day in a single location. All the messy action happens offstage and then is described in formal language for the audience by a member of the chorus. In epic poems, passionate actions are often counseled against or result in terrible consequences.

The Parthenon, built in 480 BCE

10 Ancient and classical artists, poets, and philosophers responded to the chaos of their world by using reason in pursuit of the ideal. Epic poems bridged mythology and history and transmitted a culture's values across generations. Philosophers developed many of the ideas that are the foundation of Western culture today. Where do you notice the influence of ancient and classical literature in today's world?

# Literary Focus

Read "Literary Focus: The Classics." After you read, complete the Think Questions below.

## ☁ THINK QUESTIONS

1. How does the purpose of most ancient and classical literature connect to or reflect the ideals of those time periods? Explain, citing evidence from the text to support your response.

2. Explain the characteristics of an epic poem. How were these poems different from popular forms of poetry that we see today? Can you think of any epic poems from other periods of literature that are not mentioned in this text? Be sure to cite evidence from the text in your explanations.

3. Why might it be important that an increasingly global world emphasize reason and morality over emotions and passion? Explain, citing evidence from the text that supports your assertions.

4. The word **formal** comes from the Latin *forma*, meaning "shape." With this information in mind, determine the definition of *formal* as it is used in this context, along with an explanation of how you arrived at its meaning. Finally, consult a dictionary to confirm your understanding.

5. Use context clues to determine the meaning of the word **restrained**. Write your definition here, along with the words or phrases that were most helpful in arriving at your conclusion. Then consult a dictionary to confirm your understanding.

Please note that excerpts and passages in the StudySync® library and this workbook are intended as touchstones to generate interest in an author's work. The excerpts and passages do not substitute for the reading of entire texts, and StudySync® strongly recommends that students seek out and purchase the whole literary or informational work in order to experience it as the author intended. Links to online resellers are available in our digital library. In addition, complete works may be ordered through an authorized reseller by filling out and returning to StudySync® the order form enclosed in this workbook.

Reading & Writing Companion    **173**

# The Power of the Hero's Journey

INFORMATIONAL TEXT
Louise Munson
2018

## Introduction

The scholar Joseph Campbell (1904–1987) is best remembered for *The Hero with a Thousand Faces*, his magnum opus in which he explains how mythical protagonists both ancient and modern follow uncannily similar paths from beginning to end. Campbell's monomyth theory is a 17-point chronological structure that includes landmarks labeled "The Belly of the Whale" and "The Magic Flight," tracing the shared arcs of character and plot that form the blueprints of our most

# "While happy enough, deep down he or she feels there's *something* missing."

1  To begin a hero's journey, "we must be willing to let go of the life we planned so as to have the life that is waiting for us." At least, that's what comparative mythologist Joseph Campbell said—and he should know. While not an actual sailor, like Ulysses, nor an armored King Arthur, Campbell took his own hero's journey through chronicles of mythology. Writing in *The Hero With A Thousand Faces*, published in 1949, Campbell stated that all stories from all cultures are essentially the same. To exemplify this idea, he came up with the Monomyth, which uses 17 steps to outline a hero's journey.

Joseph Campbell

2  Since it was published, Campbell's book has come to be revered by academics, authors, and filmmakers because it is a blueprint that helps unlock the structure and meaning of almost every story ever told. Knowing the plot points also helps us write new ones. Just think about the popular stories of our lifetime: *Star Wars, The Matrix,* and *Lord of the Rings*—they all utilize the steps Campbell outlined in *The Hero With A Thousand Faces*. The **archetype** of the hero's journey is important because it helps us understand the common building blocks human beings have used to tell stories across time and cultures.

Skill: Informational Text Structure

*The second paragraph seems to contain the essay's thesis: The hero's journey is important because it helps us understand the essential components of human stories. I wonder how the writer will present or explain those components.*

THE HERO'S JOURNEY

STAGE ONE: DEPARTURE

1 THE CALL TO ADVENTURE · 2 REFUSAL OF THE CALL · 3 SUPERNATURAL AID · 4 CROSSING THE FIRST THRESHOLD

STAGE TWO: INITIATION

5 THE BELLY OF THE WHALE · 6 THE ROAD OF TRIALS · 7 THE MEETING WITH THE GODDESS · 8 WOMAN AS THE TEMPTRESS · 9 ATONEMENT WITH THE FATHER · 10 APOTHEOSIS

STAGE THREE: RETURN

11 THE ULTIMATE BOON · 12 REFUSAL OF THE RETURN · 13 THE MAGIC FLIGHT · 14 RESCUE FROM WITHOUT · 15 THE CROSSING OF THE RETURN THRESHOLD · 16 MASTER OF THE TWO WORLDS · 17 FREEDOM TO LIVE

NOTES

**The Hero's Journey:**

**Stage One: Departure**

**1.** The Call to Adventure

3  Many stories open with our would-be hero living an ordinary life. While happy enough, deep down he or she feels there's something missing. Then, suddenly, there's a call to crisis! This call interrupts the ordinary world, and requires our hero to leave his or her ordinary life and jump into action. Remember how, in order to protect her sister Prim, Katniss volunteered to be a Tribute for the Hunger Games? After Katniss answers this call, we know her world will never be the same.

**2.** Refusal of the Call

4  Although Katniss skipped this step, most of the time the hero initially refuses the call. While ordinary life is boring, the hero prefers boredom and routine because change is scary. However, refusing the call doesn't make it go away. Instead, the knock just gets louder, and if the hero continues to refuse, he or she suffers the consequences. Frodo is a good example of this because he loves his comfortable life in the Shire and doesn't want to leave. It is only after he is almost killed by the Ringwraiths that he realizes he will never be safe as long as the One Ring exists. Refusing the call means staying stuck and not growing. That wouldn't make for a very good story, would it?

**3.** Supernatural Aid

5  Once the hero answers the call, the universe sends help in the form of a mentor—often an old man, a wizard, or Robin Williams—who provides divine power or protection against, as Campbell puts it, "the dragon forces he [or she] is about to pass." Sometimes the mentor is the same figure that started the whole thing in the first place with the call to adventure. Luke Skywalker is given Yoda, Will Hunting is given an insightful therapist, and Harry Potter actually gets two supernatural aids: Hagrid and Albus Dumbledore. All of these mentors help our heroes understand themselves and harness their powers for the journey to come.

**4.** The Crossing of the First **Threshold**

6  Now prepared for the journey ahead, the hero still has to face the "threshold guardian" before he can pass into the dangerous unknown. Usually deceitful, the guardian is not who he or she appears to be, but he or she often possesses wisdom our hero needs. In *The Matrix,* Morpheus is the threshold guardian, and he presents Neo with a tough choice: the blue pill or the red pill. If the hero decides to cross the threshold, he enters into a new world, where the rules are different and the stakes are life and death.

---

**Skill:
Summarizing**

*I highlight the key details: The hero may at first refuse an adventure because changing his or her life is scary, but refusing the call would mean the hero would be stuck in the old life and would lose a chance for a good story.*

**Skill:
Context Clues**

*What does deceitful mean? In this sentence it's being used to describe the "threshold guardian." The suffix -ful shows the word is an adjective, describing the guardian.*

---

## Stage Two: Initiation

**5.** The Belly of the Whale

7    By passing the first threshold, the hero is transformed into another state of being. As Campbell puts it, "The hero . . . is swallowed into the unknown and would appear to have died." Sometimes, he or she is literally swallowed by a monster or creature. Other times, it's more metaphorical. Think of *Star Wars,* when the Millennium Falcon is sucked into the Death Star by a tractor beam. This part of the journey is the hero's rebirth, where he or she must spend time going inward.

**6.** The Road of Trials

8    After being spit out of the belly of the whale, the hero must continue his or her transformation by facing a series of tests sent by symbolic figures. The hero or heroine usually fails one or more of these tests. Remember how even though it was fun to watch him try, Luke failed at first in his Jedi training? This is the exciting part where the hero hones his or her skills. There are preliminary victories, but most importantly, we learn about the shortcomings within the hero that he or she must eventually overcome.

**7.** The Meeting with the Goddess

9    Next, the hero encounters the Queen Goddess of the World, who represents the feminine and the entire universe, good and bad alike. This encounter serves to make the hero whole. In mythology, this test is represented by someone of the opposite sex (a goddess, or god). As Campbell puts it, "The meeting with the goddess (who is **incarnate** in every woman) is the final test of the talent of the hero to win the **boon** of love." Remember when Jake meets the goddess Neytiri in *Avatar?* She protects him from harm, teaches him about the Na'vis, and they fall in love.

**8.** Woman as the Temptress

10    Here is where the hero faces material or physical temptations that could lure him or her to abandon his or her quest. The hero must make a choice: give in to worldly temptations, or stay the course. The temptations faced by the hero do not always come in the form of a female character. Sometimes, temptation can come in the form of an object. For Harry Potter in *Harry Potter and the Sorcerer's Stone*, the temptation manifests as the Sorting Hat lures him to join Slytherin House. In *Star Wars,* Luke is similarly tempted by the dark side of the Force. A hero must "surpass the temptations of [their] call, and soar to the immaculate ether beyond."

**9.** Atonement with the Father

11    This is the center point of our journey, when the hero must finally confront the person or thing that holds power over his or her life (remember the inner shortcomings that were left unchecked in Step 6?). In many myths, this

"self-generated double monster" is symbolized by the father or father figure. Every step before this one has led to this encounter, where the hero must accept all the terrible things in the universe, and in return is shown the bliss of the world. In *Star Wars*, this is when Luke confronts Darth Vader.

### 10. Apotheosis

12 In return for pushing past fear, the hero is elevated and enlightened. He or she keeps the best of both the mother and father, rejecting their flaws. In *Harry Potter and the Sorcerer's Stone,* this happens when Harry realizes the wizard within him and becomes immune to Voldemort's aggression. By achieving the seemingly impossible (in Step 9), the hero discovers newfound power.

### Stage Three: Return

### 11. The Ultimate Boon

13 Having advanced past the previous steps, the hero finally achieves the main purpose of his or her journey—the ultimate boon. At times it means avenging someone or destroying something (the One Ring, the Death Star). Other times the ultimate boon comes in the form of a holy grail or the elixir of life itself. For Harry Potter, his ultimate boon is defeating Voldemort and discovering the Sorcerer's Stone.

### 12. Refusal of the Return

14 Now that the hero has been enlightened, he or she might not feel like returning to his or her old life, but the adventurer "still must return with [a] life-transmuting trophy." In the 2011 film version of *Little Red Riding Hood,* Valerie refuses to return to live with her family after slaying the Big Bad Wolf. Still, most heroes *do* eventually return home, feeling a responsibility to share their new wisdom so others may benefit.

### 13. The Magic Flight

15 If the hero decides to go home, this is when he or she must figure out *how*. Dorothy is faced with this dilemma throughout her heroine's journey in *The Wizard of Oz*. Sometimes the return is dangerous, especially if the hero must escape with the boon and face further obstacles. This last stage can also be a comical pursuit, like in *Toy Story* when Buzz flies into Andy's car after defeating Sid.

### 14. Rescue from Without

16 If the hero can't get home without help, or refuses to return, he or she might need some help from friends and allies. The ally who steps in to save the hero at this stage often comes as a surprise. A good example of this can be found in Marvel's *The Avengers*, when Iron Man, after making a heroic

sacrifice and taking out the enemy, nearly falls to his death before Hulk swoops in and saves him at the last minute.

**15.** The Crossing of the Return Threshold

17  To complete the adventure, the hero "must survive the impact of the world." In other words, this is where the adventurer figures out how to keep the wisdom gained on the quest while integrating back into ordinary life. Not so easy! Remember how, in *The Incredibles*, they return home after defeating Omnidroid only to discover that Syndrome has abducted Jack-Jack? Just when you think the journey's over . . .

**16.** Master of the Two Worlds

18  The hero's ultimate goal is to represent both the human and divine in a single being. Heroes become masters when they conquer all fear by defeating external foes and internal doubt. Mastering two worlds can also involve a hero achieving balance within or reconciling opposing internal forces. In *Aliens*, Ripley unites her maternal instincts to protect an orphan girl with her warrior drive.

**17.** Freedom to Live

19  The hero can now live in harmony with the universe. Freed from the constraints of fear, he or she can finally live in the moment. In *Star Wars,* Luke earns his Freedom to Live when he becomes one with the Force and is able to impart his wisdom to others.

**Conclusion**

20  Recognizing Campbell's Hero's Journey in stories across time and cultures can help us better understand the archetypal structure of books and movies. The hero monomyth serves a more personal purpose as we reflect on our own journeys through life. Using this lens allows us to view the trials we face with a fresh perspective while also giving us more compassion for our fellow travelers.

Please note that excerpts and passages in the StudySync® library and this workbook are intended as touchstones to generate interest in an author's work. The excerpts and passages do not substitute for the reading of entire texts, and StudySync® strongly recommends that students seek out and purchase the whole literary or informational work in order to experience it as the author intended. Links to online resellers are available in our digital library. In addition, complete works may be ordered through an authorized reseller by filling out and returning to StudySync® the order form enclosed in this workbook.

Reading & Writing Companion

**179**

THE POWER OF THE
HERO'S JOURNEY

# First Read

Read "The Power of the Hero's Journey." After you read, complete the Think Questions below.

 **THINK QUESTIONS**

1. What is the conflict at the heart of the hero's life as they know it and their eventual destiny? How do Frodo Baggins and Katniss Everdeen exemplify this stage of the hero's journey?

2. According to the text, what is "Atonement with the Father"?

3. Explain the significance of the theme of home within Campbell's theory of the Hero's Journey.

4. What do you think the word **threshold** means as it is used in the text? Write your best definition here, along with a brief explanation of the context clues that helped you arrive at the definition.

5. The Latin root *in-* means "into" and the Latin root *caro* means "flesh." Keeping this in mind, what do you think the word **incarnate** means? What are some other words with the same roots, and what do they mean? Write your best answer here.

# Skill:
# Context Clues

Use the Checklist to analyze Context Clues in "The Power of the Hero's Journey." Refer to the sample student annotations about Context Clues in the text.

## ••• CHECKLIST FOR CONTEXT CLUES

In order to use context as a clue to the meaning of a word or phrase, note the following:

- ✓ clues about the word's part of speech

- ✓ clues in the surrounding text about the word's meaning

- ✓ words with similar denotations that seem to differ slightly in meaning

- ✓ signal words that cue a type of context clue, such as:

  - *comparably, related to,* or *similarly* to signal a comparison context clue

  - *on the other hand, however,* or *in contrast* to signal a contrast context clue

  - *by reason of, because,* or *as a result* to signal a cause-and-effect context clue

To determine the meaning of words or phrases as they are used in a text, consider the following questions:

- ✓ What is the meaning of the overall sentence, paragraph, or text?

- ✓ How does the position of the word in the sentence help me define it?

- ✓ How does the word function in the sentence? What clues help identify the word's part of speech?

- ✓ What clues in the text suggest the word's definition?

- ✓ What do I think the word means?

To verify the preliminary determination of the meaning of the word or phrase based on context, consider the following questions:

- ✓ Does the definition I inferred make sense within the context of the sentence?

- ✓ Which of the dictionary's definitions makes sense within the context of the sentence?

Please note that excerpts and passages in the StudySync® library and this workbook are intended as touchstones to generate interest in an author's work. The excerpts and passages do not substitute for the reading of entire texts, and StudySync® strongly recommends that students seek out and purchase the whole literary or informational work in order to experience it as the author intended. Links to online resellers are available in our digital library. In addition, complete works may be ordered through an authorized reseller by filling out and returning to StudySync® the order form enclosed in this workbook.

Reading & Writing
Companion

181

# Skill:
# Context Clues

Reread section 5 of "The Power of the Hero's Journey." Then, using the Checklist on the previous page, answer the multiple-choice questions below.

## ⟳ YOUR TURN

1. This question has two parts. First, answer Part A. Then, answer Part B.

   **Part A:** Based on context clues in the passage, what is most likely the meaning of the word *transformed*?

   ○ A.  made powerful

   ○ B.  created by gods

   ○ C.  changed in form

   ○ D.  defeated by outside forces

   **Part B:** Which of these context clues from the text BEST support the meaning identified in Part A?

   ○ A.  ". . . passing the first threshold."

   ○ B.  ". . . into another state of being."

   ○ C.  "The hero . . . is swallowed into the unknown and would appear to have died."

   ○ D.  "This part of the journey is the hero's rebirth, where he or she must spend time going inward."

2. Which definition of *transform* from a dictionary would support the answer to Question 1?

   ○ A.  *adjective* Powerful; having great power over others.

   ○ B.  *verb* To change the form or appearance of something.

   ○ C.  *noun* A significant change or shift.

   ○ D.  *verb* To conquer or subdue.

INFORMATIONAL
TEXT STRUCTURE

sync·skills

# Skill:
# Informational Text Structure

Use the Checklist to analyze Informational Text Structure in "The Power of the Hero's Journey." Refer to the sample student annotations about Informational Text Structure in the text.

## ••• CHECKLIST FOR INFORMATIONAL TEXT STRUCTURE

In order to identify an author's ideas or claims in the text, note the following:

- ✓ the writer's claim or thesis, usually in an introductory paragraph

- ✓ the evidence the writer uses to support his or her claim or thesis

- ✓ specific statements that contain the main ideas or claims of the argument

- ✓ individual paragraphs and sentences that

  - develop an author's ideas or claims

  - clarify and refine an author's ideas or claims

- ✓ how an idea or claim is made clearer, or refined, in larger portions of text

To analyze in detail how an author's ideas or claims are developed and refined by particular sentences, paragraphs, or larger portions of a text, consider the following questions:

- ✓ What is the overall structure of the text?

- ✓ What are the author's main ideas or claims? Where do I see them?

- ✓ How are the author's ideas and claims developed in larger portions of the texts?

- ✓ How are these claims or ideas developed and refined by particular sentences in the text?

- ✓ What specific sentences and paragraphs refine or develop the author's overall claim or ideas?

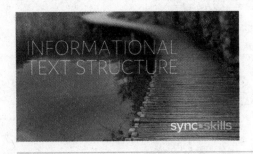

# Skill:
# Informational Text Structure

Reread paragraphs 16–20 of "The Power of the Hero's Journey." Then, using the Checklist on the previous page, answer the multiple-choice questions below.

## 🔄 YOUR TURN

1. Identify the type of structure example the author uses in the excerpt in addition to the overall sequential text structure.

   ○ A. In step 14, the author uses a compare-and-contrast example to discuss Iron Man and Hulk in *The Avengers*.

   ○ B. In step 15, the author uses compare-and-contrast to detail plot points in *The Incredibles*.

   ○ C. In step 16, the author uses a problem-solution example to explain how Ripley conquers her fears and defeats the Alien Queen in *Aliens*.

   ○ D. In step 17, the author uses a problem-solution example to discuss how Luke becomes one with the Force.

2. The essay's conclusion develops and supports the author's claim or thesis by —

   ○ A. introducing the final step in the hero's journey.

   ○ B. summarizing the major steps in the hero's journey.

   ○ C. restating the universal relevance of the hero's journey.

   ○ D. explaining the value of understanding the hero's journey.

# Skill:
# Summarizing

Use the Checklist to analyze Summarizing in "The Power of the Hero's Journey." Refer to the sample student annotations about Summarizing in the text.

## ••• CHECKLIST FOR SUMMARIZING

In order to determine what to include in an objective summary of a text, note the following:

✓ for nonfiction, note the central idea and how it is developed over the course of the text

✓ include only those relevant, specific details connected to the central idea or necessary for understanding the text

✓ answer the basic questions *who, what, where, when, why,* and *how*

✓ stay objective and do not add your own personal thoughts, judgments, or opinions to the summary, avoiding

  • phrases such as "I think" or "I feel"
  • value words such as *good, bad, best, worst, interesting, beautiful, stupid, awesome,* or *terrible*

✓ write as concisely, or briefly, as possible

To provide an objective summary of a text, consider the following questions:

✓ Does my summary include how the theme or central idea is developed over the course of the text?

✓ Did I include only those details that help develop the central idea or are key to understanding the text?

✓ What are the answers to basic *who, what, where, when, why,* and *how* questions in this text?

✓ Is my summary objective, or do I need to remove words and phrases that show my own thoughts, judgments, and personal opinions?

✓ Is my summary concise?

# Skill:
# Summarizing

Reread steps 11–12 of "The Power of the Hero's Journey." Then, using the Checklist on the previous page, answer the multiple-choice questions below.

## ↻ YOUR TURN

1. Which detail from step 12 is the most important to include in a summary?

   ○ A. The hero is now enlightened.

   ○ B. In *Little Red Riding Hood*, Valerie refuses to return home.

   ○ C. Initially the hero may refuse to return home.

   ○ D. The hero has wisdom that may benefit others.

2. What is the best summary of the information in step 11?

   ○ A. Harry Potter's ultimate boon was defeating Voldemort and discovering the Sorcerer's Stone.

   ○ B. Once completing the previous steps, the hero gets the "ultimate boon." This boon can take many forms, either getting something, destroying something, or avenging someone.

   ○ C. Once completing the previous steps, the hero gets the "ultimate boon," which is really cool, though some boons are better than others.

   ○ D. Once completing the previous steps, the hero gets the "ultimate boon."

THE POWER OF THE
HERO'S JOURNEY

# Close Read

Reread "The Power of the Hero's Journey." As you reread, complete the Skills Focus questions below. Then use your answers and annotations from the questions to help you complete the Write activity.

## ◎ SKILLS FOCUS

1. Explain how the headings of the various sections of the article help to structure the information presented by the author.

2. Explain how the graphics contribute to the information in the text.

3. Use context to determine the meaning of *manifests* as it is used in section number 8 of the article. Cite evidence to support your inference.

4. Write a brief, objective summary of the key ideas surrounding the hero's journey as discussed in the article.

5. Think about how the idea of a hero's journey is tied to culture. Use your summary and examples from the article to discuss how cultural ideas influence the journeys of various heroes.

## ✎ WRITE

EXPLANATORY ESSAY: Apply the archetype of the hero's journey to a text or movie you have encountered. Using a specific text structure, explain how this text or movie communicates a few key aspects of the hero's journey. Use textual evidence from the article to support your explanation.

# The Gathering Place

POETRY
Amanda Gorman
2017

## Introduction

Amanda Gorman (b. 1999) describes herself as a poet, activist, and change-maker. At 19, she was the first-ever Youth Poet Laureate of the United States. She published her first poetry book, *The One for Whom Food Is Not Enough*, in 2015. She is a student at Harvard, has worked with the U.N., and started a community platform focused on literacy and youth activism. "The Gathering Place" was written by Gorman for the Social Good Summit in 2017.

# "we be united, we be good, / we do good, we are good / as we should"

1 On the corner of East 92nd and Lexington
2 Under congested **incandescence** of pulsing city
3 the world bends itself into a village.
4 Here: our great gathering place.

5 A space on hot, laughing earth
6 Where we stretch room for others beside us
7 where closed doors are far too tight for
8 the giant that is hope to grow.
9 Every idea an open sea
10 Every voice a boat voyaging the bank of blue.

11 We, a village, a dancing city,
12 meet among the music of concrete and steel
13 where subway cars, ride the beat of hustle and heel.

14 In this village we string together the continents
15 in the palm of one building
16 With one microphone, we streak
17 across the globe like an eclipse
18 We strike our plans into stone
19 and from this we build a summit worth climbing,
20 a goal worth reaching,
21 a world worth building.

22 Like this place,
23 Our village is one of striking shapes and deeds
24 where cultures and languages **jive** like seeds

25 Village to Cynthia Erivo[1], London miracle, whose voice rips
26 open the sky from the mountaintop of the stage
27 Village to Pete Cashmore[2], who at my age built

---

1. **Cynthia Erivo** a well known Broadway actress from England
2. **Pete Cashmore** the founder of the blog site *Mashable*, which he started at age 19

28 a gathering site for the courageously curious and **obstinately** obsessive
29 Village to ElsaMarie D'Silva[3], who took her own pain to carve
30 out a thick roof of voices for assaulted women.

31 These are the types of villagers we are—
32 We eat away our hunger
33 With our appetite for goodness
34 we breathe rivers into throats
35 with our voices for change.

36 Today
37 in the spine of this meeting ground,
38 new city, new village, we've reached a summit,
39 and are ready to loudly name another.
40 This be hope, this be home,
41 we are hope, we are home,
42 we be **vigilant**,
43 we be united, we be good,
44 we do good, we are good,
45 as we should
46 in the place where a millennium stood
47 for what we understood
48 was
49 right.

50 On the corner of hope and drive,
51 Under the question of open sky
52 sprawls our great gathering site.

53 In this village
54 We make the globe a little smaller
55 So we can dream bigger,
56 so the dream need not wait.

57 Here in this gathering,
58 we do good so that the world
59 might be great.

By Amanda Gorman, 2017. Used by permission of Amanda Gorman.

3. **ElsaMarie D'Silva** a former aviation professional who went on to found Safecity.in and the Red Dot Foundation, both of which work toward gender equality and ending violence against women

**WRITE**

NARRATIVE: U.S. Youth Poet Laureate Amanda Gorman performed this poem at the Social Good Summit to convey her perspective on how to create meaningful change so that the world can become a better place. Write a narrative involving a setting, real or imagined, that conveys your ideal world.

# Rámáyana

POETRY
Válmíki
(translated by Ralph T. H. Griffith)
Circa 400 BCE

## Introduction

One of the great epics of India, the *Rámáyana* existed for years in oral tradition before the Hindu sage and poet Válmíki recorded the story in verse sometime around the 5th century BCE. A vast tale of intrigue, ferocious battles, and the triumph of good over evil, the *Rámáyana* serves as an integral part of the Hindu canon, and its many versions continue to shape cultures and societies worldwide. In the following excerpt, the poet Válmíki summarizes the general arc of the epic: from Ráma's banishment at the hands of his father's wife, Kaikeyi, to his battle with the demon Rávana and his ascension to the throne.

# "The life of Ráma, great and good, Roaming with Sítá in the wood."

NOTES

Rama and Lakshmana Search in Vain for Sita

Canto[1] III. The Argument.

1  The hermit thus with watchful heed
2  Received the poem's pregnant seed,
3  And looked with eager thought around
4  If fuller knowledge might be found.
5  His lips with water first bedewed,
6  He sate, in **reverent** attitude
7  On holy grass, the points all bent
8  Together toward the orient;
9  And thus in meditation he
10 Entered the path of poesy[2].
11 Then clearly, through his virtue's might,
12 All lay discovered to his sight,
13 Whate'er befell, through all their life,
14 Ráma, his brother, and his wife:
15 And Das'aratha and each queen
16 At every time, in every scene:
17 His people too, of every sort;

Skill:
Media

*The poem is a summary of the major events of the story, and the tapestry shows sections of the story.*

1. **Canto** in medieval or epic poetry, one division or section of a longer poem
2. **poesy** poetry and its inspiration

NOTES

18 The nobles of his princely court:
19 Whate'er was said, whate'er decreed,
20 Each time they sate each plan and deed:
21 For holy thought and fervent rite
22 Had so refined his keener sight
23 That by his **sanctity** his view
24 The present, past, and future knew,
25 And he with mental eye could grasp,
26 Like fruit within his fingers clasp,
27 The life of Ráma, great and good,
28 Roaming with Sítá in the wood.
29 He told, with secret-piercing eyes,
30 The tale of Ráma's high **emprise**,
31 Each listening ear that shall entice,
32 A sea of pearls of highest price.
33 Thus good Válmíki, sage divine,
34 Rehearsed the tale of Raghu's line,
35 As Nárad, heavenly saint, before
36 Had traced the story's outline o'er.
37 He sang of Ráma's princely birth,
38 His kindness and heroic worth;
39 His love for all, his patient youth,
40 His gentleness and constant truth,
41 And many a tale and legend old
42 By holy Vis'vámitra told.
43 How Janak's child he wooed and won,
44 And broke the bow that bent to none.
45 How he with every virtue fraught
46 His namesake Ráma met and fought.
47 The choice of Ráma for the throne;
48 The malice by Kaikeyí shown,
49 Whose evil counsel marred the plan
50 And drove him forth a banished man.
51 How the king grieved and groaned, and cried,
52 And swooned away and pining died.
53 The subjects' woe when thus bereft;
54 And how the following crowds he left:
55 With Guha talked, and firmly stern
56 Ordered his driver to return.
57 How Gangá's farther shore he gained;
58 By Bharadvája entertained,
59 By whose advice he journeyed still
60 And came to Chitrakúta's hill.
61 How there he dwelt and built a cot;
62 How Bharat journeyed to the spot;
63 His earnest supplication made;
64 Drink-offerings to their father paid;

Skill:
Media

*While the tapestry shows events mentioned in the poem, the character names are missing.*

Skill: Poetic
Elements and
Structure

*The first two lines end in a rhyme. The next two lines have a different rhyme. So, the rhyme scheme is aa, bb, cc, dd, ee, and so on. The effect is to make the poem sound almost like a song when read aloud.*

  Reading & Writing
Companion

NOTES

65    The sandals given by Ráma's hand,

66    As emblems of his right, to stand:

67    How from his presence Bharat went

68    And years in Nandigráma spent.

69    How Ráma entered Dandak wood

70    And in Sutíkhna's presence stood.

71    The favour Anasúyá showed,

72    The wondrous balsam she bestowed.

73    How Sárabhangá's dwelling-place

74    They sought; saw Indra face to face;

75    The meeting with Agastya gained;

76    The heavenly bow from him obtained.

77    How Ráma with Virádha met;

78    Their home in Panchavata set.

79    How S'úrpanakhá underwent

80    The mockery and disfigurement.

81    Of Trígirá's and Khara's fall,

82    Of Rávana roused at vengeance call,

83    Márícha doomed, without escape;

84    The fair Videhan lady's rape.

85    How Ráma wept and raved in vain,

86    And how the Vulture-king was slain.

87    How Ráma fierce Kabandha slew;

88    Then to the side of Pampá drew,

89    Met Hanumán, and her whose vows

90    Were kept beneath the greenwood boughs.

91    How Raghu's son, the lofty-souled,

92    On Pampá's bank wept uncontrolled,

93    Then journeyed, Rishyamúk to reach,

94    And of Sugríva then had speech.

95    The friendship made, which both had sought:

96    How Báli and Sugríva fought.

97    How Báli in the **strife** was slain,

98    And how Sugríva came to reign.

99    The treaty, Tára's wild lament;

100    The rainy nights in watching spent.

101    The wrath of Raghu's lion son;

102    The gathering of the hosts in one.

103    The sending of the spies about,

104    And all the regions pointed out.

105    The ring by Ráma's hand bestowed;

106    The cave wherein the bear abode.

107    The fast proposed, their lives to end;

108    Sampati gained to be their friend.

109    The scaling of the hill, the leap

110    Of Hanumán across the deep.

111    Ocean's command that bade them seek

Nineteenth century art based on the *Rámáyana*

112   Maináka of the lofty peak.
113   The death of Sinhiká, the sight
114   Of Lanká with her palace bright
115   How Hanumán stole in at eve;
116   His plan the giants to deceive.
117   How through the square he made his way
118   To chambers where the women lay,
119   Within the Aśoka garden came
120   And there found Ráma's captive dame.
121   His colloquy with her he sought,
122   And giving of the ring he brought.
123   How Sítá gave a gem o'erjoyed;
124   How Hanumán the grove destroyed.
125   How giantesses trembling fled,
126   And servant fiends were smitten dead.
127   How Hanumán was seized; their **ire**
128   When Lanká blazed with hostile fire.
129   His leap across the sea once more;
130   The eating of the honey store.
131   How Ráma he consoled, and how
132   He showed the gem from Sítá's brow.
133   With Ocean, Ráma's interview;
134   The bridge that Nala o'er it threw.
135   The crossing, and the sitting down
136   At night round Lanká's royal town.
137   The treaty with Vibhíshan made:
138   The plan for Rávana's slaughter laid.
139   How Kumbhakarna in his pride
140   And Meghanáda fought and died.
141   How Rávana in the fight was slain,
142   And captive Sítá brought again.
143   Vibhíshan set upon the throne;
144   The flying chariot Pushpak shown.
145   How Brahmá and the Gods appeared,
146   And Sítá's doubted honour cleared.
147   How in the flying car they rode
148   To Bharadvája's cabin abode.
149   The Wind-God's son sent on afar;
150   How Bharat met the flying car.
151   How Ráma then was king ordained;
152   The legions their discharge obtained.
153   How Ráma cast his queen away;
154   How grew the people's love each day.
155   Thus did the saint Válmíki tell
156   Whate'er in Ráma's life befell,
157   And in the closing verses all
158   That yet to come will once befall.

# First Read

Read the *Rámáyana*. After you read, complete the Think Questions below.

**THINK QUESTIONS**

1. Why does the king grieve? Explain, citing evidence.

2. Who is the speaker? Describe what you know about the speaker from the beginning of the poem.

3. Identify two or three main characters and describe their significance to the narrative.

4. Use context clues to determine the meaning of **strife**. Write your best definition here, explaining what clues helped you to figure out its meaning.

5. Use context clues to determine the meaning of **ire**. Write your best definition in your own words, explaining how you figured out its meaning.

Please note that excerpts and passages in the StudySync® library and this workbook are intended as touchstones to generate interest in an author's work. The excerpts and passages do not substitute for the reading of entire texts, and StudySync® strongly recommends that students seek out and purchase the whole literary or informational work in order to experience it as the author intended. Links to online resellers are available in our digital library. In addition, complete works may be ordered through an authorized reseller by filling out and returning to StudySync® the order form enclosed in this workbook.

Reading & Writing Companion  197

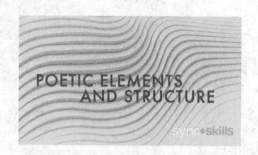

# Skill: Poetic Elements and Structure

Use the Checklist to analyze Poetic Elements and Structure in the *Rámáyana*. Refer to the sample student annotations about Poetic Elements and Structure in the text.

## ••• CHECKLIST FOR POETIC ELEMENTS AND STRUCTURE

In order to identify a poet's choices concerning how to structure a poem, order events within it, and manipulate time, note the following:

- ✓ the forms and overall structures of the poem

- ✓ the rhyme, rhythm and meter, if present

- ✓ lines and stanzas in the poem that suggest its meaning

- ✓ ways that the poem's structures connects to its meaning

- ✓ lines and stanzas where the poet manipulated time to create an effect such as mystery, tension, or surprise

- ✓ how the poet ordered events to create an effect such as mystery, tension, or surprise

To analyze how a poet's choices concerning how to structure a poem, order events within it, and manipulate time create such effects as mystery, tension, or surprise, consider the following questions:

- ✓ How does the poet structure his or her poem? How does he or she order events within the poem? How does he or she manipulate time?

- ✓ What effects, such as mystery, tension, or surprise, does the poet create through his or her choices?

- ✓ How does the poet's choice of form or structure affect the overall meaning of the poem?

# Skill: Poetic Elements and Structure

Reread lines 133–146 of the *Rámáyana*. Then, using the Checklist on the previous page, answer the multiple-choice questions below.

## ↻ YOUR TURN

1. Based on this selection, which of the following statements best describes an aspect of the poem's structure?

   ○ A. The poem is divided into stanzas with equal numbers of lines.
   ○ B. The poem has an irregular meter and an irregular rhyme scheme.
   ○ C. The poem punctuates the end of most lines to suggest different types of pauses.
   ○ D. The poem uses periods and capitalization within the lines to indicate scene shifts.

2. A slant rhyme is formed when words do not exactly rhyme, but they come close to rhyming. An example of a slant rhyme is the words *life* and *lies*. Which of the following pairs of lines show a slant rhyme?

   ○ A. lines 133–134
   ○ B. lines 137–138
   ○ C. lines 141–142
   ○ D. lines 145–146

3. Which of the following most accurately describes the effect of the break in meter in line 138?

   ○ A. The shift in meter creates a sense of excitement about the plan to slaughter Rávana.
   ○ B. The shift in meter lends the poem forward momentum.
   ○ C. The shift in meter emphasizes a neutral tone.
   ○ D. The shift in meter creates a sense of tension and sadness about the plan to slaughter Rávana.

# Skill: Media

Use the Checklist to analyze Media in the *Rámáyana*. Refer to the sample student annotations about Media in the text.

In order to determine the representation of a subject or a key scene in two different artistic mediums, do the following:

✓ note the artistic medium and its features

✓ identify what is emphasized or absent in each treatment of a subject or a key scene

✓ examine why the same subject receives completely different treatments in different media

✓ consider sources, as a story about a historical event might refer, directly or indirectly, to letters, paintings, plays, or photographs from the same place and time as the events that took place

To analyze the representation of a subject or a key scene in two different artistic mediums, including what is emphasized or absent in each treatment, consider the following questions:

✓ Is the content informational or fictional? How does this affect the treatment of the key scene or subject?

✓ What are the strengths and weaknesses of each artistic medium? How does this affect the treatment of the key scene or subject?

✓ What is emphasized and what is absent, or left out of each medium's version of events?

# Skill:
# Media

Reread lines 85–104 of the *Rámáyana* and review the photograph of the tapestry in the digital lesson. Then, using the Checklist on the previous page, answer the multiple-choice questions below.

## ↻ YOUR TURN

1. Which line could we see depicted in the bottom left quadrant of the tapestry?

   ○ A. "And of Sugríva then had speech. / The friendship made, which both had sought: . . ."

   ○ B. "The sending of the spies about, / And all the regions pointed out."

   ○ C. "How Ráma wept and raved in vain, / . . ."

   ○ D. "The treaty, Tára's wild lament; / The rainy nights in watching spent."

2. What information is missing in the poem about Sugriva and Báli that is included in the tapestry?

   ○ A. Báli and Sugríva fight to the death.

   ○ B. Báli and Sugriva are monkeys.

   ○ C. After fighting, Báli and Sugríva form a protective alliance.

   ○ D. Báli and Sugriva are brothers.

3. Which lines of the poem are depicted in the center left panel of the tapestry?

   ○ A. "Then to the side of Pampá drew, / . . ."

   ○ B. "The wrath of Raghu's lion son; / . . ."

   ○ C. "And how the Vulture-king was slain."

   ○ D. "How Báli and Sugríva fought. / How Báli in the strife was slain, . . ."

Please note that excerpts and passages in the StudySync® library and this workbook are intended as touchstones to generate interest in an author's work. The excerpts and passages do not substitute for the reading of entire texts, and StudySync® strongly recommends that students seek out and purchase the whole literary or informational work in order to experience it as the author intended. Links to online resellers are available in our digital library. In addition, complete works may be ordered through an authorized reseller by filling out and returning to StudySync® the order form enclosed in this workbook.

Reading & Writing
Companion

201

# Close Read

Reread the *Rámáyana*. As you reread, complete the Skills Focus questions below. Then use your answers and annotations from the questions to help you complete the Write activity.

## ◎ SKILLS FOCUS

1. Explain how the poet's choices of rhyming couplets and eight beats per line affect the message and reading of the poem. Use textual evidence to support your ideas.

2. Identify and explain the theme or message of this canto from Válmíki's *Rámáyana*. Use textual evidence to support your response.

3. Having read this summary section in the *Rámáyana* and examined the tapestry of events noted in the poem, explain what is emphasized in each medium. Then explain what each medium accomplishes that the other cannot. Cite textual evidence and descriptions of the tapestry to explain your ideas.

4. Near the end of "The Gathering Place," the speaker says,

   *In this village*
   *We make the globe a little smaller*
   *So we can dream bigger,*
   *so the dream need not wait.*

   Reread lines 142–154 of the *Rámáyana*, which tells what happens after Sítá is brought home. Compare and contrast how both "The Gathering Place" and the *Rámáyana* deal with ways that a cultural community affects our goals. Use textual evidence to support your response.

## ✎ WRITE

LITERARY ANALYSIS: Both the poet Válmíki in the *Rámáyana* and poet Amanda Gorman in "The Gathering Place" present a view about what it means to create positive change in a community. However, they do so through different poetic forms—Válmíki through the form of an ancient epic narrative poem and Amanda Gorman through the form of a contemporary free verse poem. Compare and contrast the ways that each poet conveys a message about community, and also analyze each poet's use of metrics and rhyme schemes to communicate this message. Use textual evidence to support your response.

# Republic

ARGUMENTATIVE TEXT

Plato
(translated by Benjamin Jowett)
Circa 380 BCE

## Introduction

Comprising ten books, the *Republic* is one of Plato's longest works, setting forth his ideas on government and justice in both political and personal terms. Using his late mentor, Socrates, as his voice, in characteristic "Socratic" dialogues, Plato explores relationships between concepts such as rationality and desire, leaving behind an enduring philosophy of human thought and action. In this excerpt, Socrates presents his ideas on education through the analogy of being led from the shadows

# "To them, I said, the truth would be literally nothing but the shadows of the images."

BOOK VII

1 AND now, I said, let me show in a figure how far our nature is enlightened or unenlightened: Behold! human beings living in an underground den, which has a mouth open toward the light and reaching all along the den; here they have been from their childhood, and have their legs and necks chained so that they cannot move, and can only see before them, being prevented by the chains from turning round their heads. Above and behind them a fire is blazing at a distance, and between the fire and the prisoners there is a raised way; and you will see, if you look, a low wall built along the way, like the screen which **marionette** players have in front of them, over which they show the puppets.

2 I see.

3 And do you see, I said, men passing along the wall carrying all sorts of vessels, and statues and figures of animals made of wood and stone and various materials, which appear over the wall? Some of them are talking, others silent.

4 You have shown me a strange image, and they are strange prisoners.

5 Like ourselves, I replied; and they see only their own shadows, or the shadows of one another, which the fire throws on the opposite wall of the cave?

6 True, he said; how could they see anything but the shadows if they were never allowed to move their heads?

7 And of the objects which are being carried in like manner they would only see the shadows?

8 Yes, he said.

9 And if they were able to converse with one another, would they not suppose that they were naming what was actually before them?

10  Very true.

11  And suppose further that the prison had an echo which came from the other side, would they not be sure to fancy when one of the passers-by spoke that the voice which they heard came from the passing shadow?

12  No question, he replied.

13  To them, I said, the truth would be literally nothing but the shadows of the images.

14  That is certain.

15  And now look again, and see what will naturally follow if the prisoners are released and **disabused** of their error. At first, when any of them is liberated and compelled suddenly to stand up and turn his neck round and walk and look toward the light, he will suffer sharp pains; the glare will distress him, and he will be unable to see the realities of which in his former state he had seen the shadows; and then conceive someone saying to him, that what he saw before was an illusion, but that now, when he is approaching nearer to being and his eye is turned toward more real existence, he has a clearer vision— what will be his reply? And you may further imagine that his instructor is pointing to the objects as they pass and requiring him to name them—will he not be perplexed? Will he not fancy that the shadows which he formerly saw are truer than the objects which are now shown to him?

16  Far truer.

17  And if he is compelled to look straight at the light, will he not have a pain in his eyes which will make him turn away to take refuge in the objects of vision which he can see, and which he will conceive to be in reality clearer than the things which are now being shown to him?

18  True, he said.

19  And suppose once more, that he is reluctantly dragged up a steep and rugged ascent, and held fast until he is forced into the presence of the sun himself, is he not likely to be pained and irritated? When he approaches the light his eyes will be **dazzled**, and he will not be able to see anything at all of what are now called realities.

20  Not all in a moment, he said.

21  He will require to grow accustomed to the sight of the upper world. And first he will see the shadows best, next the reflections of men and other objects

Skill: Central or Main Idea

*Plato spends up until paragraph 13 describing the situation of the people in the cave; here he seems to state his central idea that what they perceive is the truth, in reality, is just shadows of the truth.*

Skill: Context Clues

*I usually think of rugged as meaning "strong and determined." But the context clues here are not positive. Being dragged, held, and forced connotes something difficult and challenging.*

in the water, and then the objects themselves; then he will gaze upon the light of the moon and the stars and the spangled heaven; and he will see the sky and the stars by night better than the sun or the light of the sun by day?

22 Certainly.

23 Last of all he will be able to see the sun, and not mere reflections of him in the water, but he will see him in his own proper place, and not in another; and he will contemplate him as he is.

24 Certainly.

25 He will then proceed to argue that this is he who gives the season and the years, and is the guardian of all that is in the visible world, and in a certain way the cause of all things which he and his fellows have been accustomed to behold?

26 Clearly, he said, he would first see the sun and then reason about him.

27 And when he remembered his old habitation, and the wisdom of the den and his fellow-prisoners, do you not suppose that he would felicitate himself on the change, and pity him?

28 Certainly, he would.

• • •

29 Imagine once more, I said, such an one coming suddenly out of the sun to be replaced in his old situation; would he not be certain to have his eyes full of darkness?

30 To be sure, he said.

31 And if there were a contest, and he had to compete in measuring the shadows with the prisoners who had never moved out of the den, while his sight was still weak, and before his eyes had become steady (and the time which would be needed to acquire this new habit of sight might be very considerable), would he not be ridiculous? Men would say of him that up he went and down he came without his eyes; and that it was better not even to think of ascending; and if any one tried to loose another and lead him up to the light, let them only catch the offender, and they would put him to death.

32 No question, he said.

Skill: Central or Main Idea

Plato is building on his central idea here. Now a man that has seen the truth returns to the cave, but the people ridicule him. This seems to say that once enlightened, those still unenlightened would be hostile to the truth.

33    This entire allegory, I said, you may now append, dear Glaucon[1], to the previous argument; the prison-house is the world of sight, the light of the fire is the sun, and you will not misapprehend me if you interpret the journey upwards to be the ascent of the soul into the intellectual world according to my poor belief, which, at your desire, I have expressed—whether rightly or wrongly God knows. But, whether true or false, my opinion is that in the world of knowledge the idea of good appears last of all, and is seen only with an effort; and, when seen, is also inferred to be the universal author of all things beautiful and right, parent of light and of the lord of light in this visible world, and the immediate source of reason and truth in the intellectual; and that this is the power upon which he who would act rationally either in public or private life must have his eye fixed.

34    I agree, he said, as far as I am able to understand you.

35    Moreover, I said, you must not wonder that those who attain to this beatific vision are unwilling to descend to human affairs; for their souls are ever hastening into the upper world where they desire to dwell; which desire of theirs is very natural, if our allegory may be trusted.

36    Yes, very natural.

. . .

37    But then, if I am right, certain professors of education must be wrong when they say that they can put a knowledge into the soul which was not there before, like sight into blind eyes.

38    They undoubtedly say this, he replied.

39    Whereas, our argument shows that the power and capacity of learning exists in the soul already; and that just as the eye was unable to turn from darkness to light without the whole body, so too the instrument of knowledge can only by the movement of the whole soul be turned from the world of becoming into that of being, and learn by degrees to endure the sight of being, and of the brightest and best of being, or in other words, of the good.

. . .

40    You remember, I said, how the rulers were chosen before?

41    Certainly, he said.

---

1. **Glaucon** Plato's older brother, also a philosopher

42   The same natures must still be chosen, and the preference again given to the surest and the bravest, and, if possible, to the fairest; and, having noble and generous tempers, they should also have the natural gifts which will facilitate their education.

43   And what are these?

44   Such gifts as **keenness** and ready powers of acquisition; for the mind more often faints from the severity of study than from the severity of gymnastics: the toil is more entirely the mind's own, and is not shared with the body.

. . .

45   Suppose, I said, the study of philosophy to take the place of gymnastics and to be continued diligently and earnestly and exclusively for twice the number of years which were passed in bodily exercise—will that be enough?

46   Would you say six or four years? he asked.

47   Say five years, I replied; at the end of the time they must be sent down again into the den and compelled to hold any military or other office which young men are qualified to hold: in this way they will get their experience of life, and there will be an opportunity of trying whether, when they are drawn all manner of ways by temptation, they will stand firm or flinch.

48   And how long is this stage of their lives to last?

49   Fifteen years, I answered; and when they have reached fifty years of age, then let those who still survive and have distinguished themselves in every action of their lives and in every branch of knowledge come at last to their **consummation**: the time has now arrived at which they must raise the eye of the soul to the universal light which lightens all things, and behold the absolute good; for that is the pattern according to which they are to order the State and the lives of individuals, and the remainder of their own lives also; making philosophy their chief pursuit, but, when their turn comes, toiling also at politics and ruling for the public good, not as though they were performing some heroic action, but simply as a matter of duty;

Marble statuette of Socrates

and when they have brought up in each generation others like themselves and left them in their place to be governors of the State, then they will depart to the Islands of the Blest and dwell there; and the city will give them public

memorials and sacrifices and honour them, if the Pythian oracle[2] consent, as demigods[3], but if not, as in any case blessed and divine.

50   You are a sculptor, Socrates, and have made statues of our governors faultless in beauty.

51   Yes, I said, Glaucon, and of our governesses too; for you must not suppose that what I have been saying applies to men only and not to women as far as their natures can go.

52   There you are right, he said, since we have made them to share in all things like the men.

53   Well, I said, and you would agree (would you not?) that what has been said about the State and the government is not a mere dream, and although difficult not impossible, but only possible in the way which has been supposed; that is to say, when the true philosopher kings are born in a State, one or more of them, despising the honours of this present world which they deem mean and worthless, esteeming above all things right and the honour that springs from right, and regarding justice as the greatest and most necessary of all things, whose ministers they are, and whose principles will be exalted by them when they set in order their own city?

---

2. **Pythian oracle**  prophet of the greek god Apollo
3. **demigods**  those more perfect and powerful than humans, but less so than the gods

# First Read

Read the *Republic*. After you read, complete the Think Questions below.

1. Why are the shadows "truer" than the objects outside of the cave? Cite evidence from the text to support your answer.

2. Think about the physical sensation of blinking into bright light after being in the dark. Is it pleasant or painful? How does this thematically connect to Plato's allegory? Cite evidence from the text to support your answer.

3. Who is speaking? Who are the people engaged in dialogue in this text?

4. Use context clues to determine the meaning of **disabused** in the text. Write your best definition of *disabused* here, and explain how you came to it.

5. Use context clues to determine the meaning of **keenness**. If it helps, verify your answer in a dictionary. Then, write a sentence about Plato's philosophy on learning using the word *keenness* here.

# Skill:
# Context Clues

Use the Checklist to analyze Context Clues in the *Republic*. Refer to the sample student annotations about Context Clues in the text.

## ••• CHECKLIST FOR CONTEXT CLUES

In order to use context as a clue to the meaning of a word or phrase, note the following:

✓ clues about the word's part of speech

✓ clues in the surrounding text about the word's meaning

✓ words with similar denotations that seem to differ slightly in meaning

✓ signal words that cue a type of context clue, such as:

- *comparably, related to*, or *similarly* to signal a comparison context clue
- *on the other hand, however,* or *in contrast* to signal a contrast context clue
- *by reason of, because*, or *as a result* to signal a cause-and-effect context clue

To determine the meaning of a word or phrase as they are used in a text, consider the following questions:

✓ What is the meaning of the overall sentence, paragraph, or text?

✓ How does the position of the word in the sentence help me define it?

✓ How does the word function in the sentence? What clues help identify the word's part of speech?

✓ What clues in the text suggest the word's definition?

✓ What do I think the word means?

To verify the preliminary determination of the meaning of the word or phrase based on context, consider the following questions:

✓ Does the definition I inferred make sense within the context of the sentence?

✓ Which of the dictionary's definitions makes sense within the context of the sentence?

# Skill:
# Context Clues

Reread paragraph 33 of the *Republic*. Then, using the Checklist on the previous page, answer the multiple-choice questions below.

## ↻ YOUR TURN

1. The dictionary definition of *light* is "what makes vision possible." Which of the following most closely addresses its meaning as used in the text?

   ○ A. The meaning is negative because it is associated with "fire." As it is used, *light* means "danger."

   ○ B. The meaning is negative because it is associated with "prison-house." As it is used, *light* means "a feeling of being stuck."

   ○ C. The meaning is positive because it is associated with "misapprehend." As it is used, *light* means "a feeling of being misunderstood."

   ○ D. The meaning is positive because it is associated with "sun." As it is used, *light* means "enlightenment."

2. What do context clues around the word *universal* indicate about its meaning in this sentence?

   ○ A. "Author of all things beautiful and right" indicates that *universal* means "all the planets near us."

   ○ B. "Author of all things beautiful and right" indicates that *universal* means "covering all" or "all encompassing."

   ○ C. "And, when seen" indicates that *universal* denotatively means "something you come to see."

   ○ D. "Truth in the intellectual" indicates that *universal* means "intellectual."

# Skill:
# Textual Evidence

Use the Checklist to analyze Textual Evidence in the *Republic*. Refer to the sample student annotations about Textual Evidence in the text.

Copyright © BookheadEd Learning, LLC

## ••• CHECKLIST FOR TEXTUAL EVIDENCE

In order to support an analysis by citing evidence that is explicitly stated in the text, do the following:

- ✓ Read the text closely and critically.

- ✓ Identify what the text says explicitly.

- ✓ Find the most relevant textual evidence that supports your analysis.

- ✓ Consider why an author explicitly states specific details and information.

- ✓ Cite the specific words, phrases, sentences, or paragraphs from the text that support your analysis.

In order to interpret implicit meanings in a text by making inferences, do the following:

- ✓ Combine information directly stated in the text with your own knowledge, experiences, and observations.

- ✓ Cite the specific words, phrases, sentences, or paragraphs from the text that led to and support this inference.

In order to cite textual evidence to support an analysis of what the text says explicitly as well as inferences drawn from the text, consider the following questions:

- ✓ Have I read the text closely and critically?

- ✓ What inferences am I making about the text?

- ✓ What textual evidence am I using to support these inferences?

- ✓ Am I quoting the evidence from the text correctly?

- ✓ Does my textual evidence logically relate to my analysis or the inference I am making?

# Skill:
# Textual Evidence

Reread paragraphs 15–24 of the *Republic*. Then, using the Checklist on the previous page, answer the multiple-choice questions below.

## ⟳ YOUR TURN

1. Which of the following excerpts is the strongest piece of evidence to support the claim that the enlightenment process is painful and stressful?

   ○ A. "He will be unable to see the realities of which in his former state he had seen the shadows,"

   ○ B. "At first, when any of them is liberated and compelled suddenly to stand up and turn his neck round and walk and look toward the light, he will suffer sharp pains; the glare will distress him,"

   ○ C. "But that now, when he is approaching nearer to being and his eye is turned toward more real existence,"

   ○ D. "Will he not fancy that the shadows which he formerly saw are truer than the objects which are now shown to him?"

2. In paragraphs 17–19, which statement best supports the idea that someone would have a hard time accepting new truths and would want to revert back to their old beliefs?

   ○ A. "Which will make him turn away to take refuge in the objects of vision which he can see, and which he will conceive to be in reality clearer than the things which are now being shown to him?"

   ○ B. "When he approaches the light his eyes will be **dazzled**, and he will not be able to see anything at all of what are now called realities."

   ○ C. "And suppose once more, that he is reluctantly dragged up a steep and rugged ascent, and held fast until he is forced into the presence of the sun himself,"

   ○ D. "is he not likely to be pained and irritated?"

3. Which of the following excerpts is the best textual evidence for the argument that enlightenment must be a gradual process?

   ○ A. "He will require to grow accustomed to the sight of the upper world."

   ○ B. "Certainly."

   ○ C. "Last of all he will be able to see the sun, and not mere reflections of him in the water,"

   ○ D. "And first he will see the shadows best, next the reflections of men and other objects in the water, and then the objects themselves,"

# Skill:
# Central or Main Idea

Use the Checklist to analyze Central or Main Idea in the *Republic*. Refer to the sample student annotations about Central or Main Idea in the text.

## ••• CHECKLIST FOR CENTRAL OR MAIN IDEA

In order to determine a central idea of a text, note the following:

- ✓ the central or main idea, if it is explicitly stated

- ✓ key details and supporting ideas that connect to the author's point or message

- ✓ ways that details develop and refine the central idea

- ✓ ways that the author builds on ideas to communicate a message

To determine a central idea of a text and analyze its development over the course of the text, including how it emerges and is shaped and refined by specific details, consider the following questions:

- ✓ What main idea(s) do the details in each paragraph explain or describe?

- ✓ What bigger idea do all the paragraphs support?

- ✓ What is the best way to state the central idea?

- ✓ How do the supporting ideas and details help develop and refine the central idea over the course of the text?

- ✓ How might you summarize the text and message? What details would you include?

Please note that excerpts and passages in the StudySync® library and this workbook are intended as touchstones to generate interest in an author's work. The excerpts and passages do not substitute for the reading of entire texts, and StudySync® strongly recommends that students seek out and purchase the whole literary or informational work in order to experience it as the author intended. Links to online resellers are available in our digital library. In addition, complete works may be ordered through an authorized reseller by filling out and returning to StudySync® the order form enclosed in this workbook.

Reading & Writing Companion   **215**

# Skill:
# Central or Main Idea

Reread paragraphs 37–44 of the *Republic*. Then, using the Checklist on the previous page, answer the multiple-choice questions below.

## ⟳ YOUR TURN

1. This question has two parts. First, answer Part A. Then, answer Part B.

   **Part A:** What is the central idea of this excerpt?

   ○ A. Teachers must put knowledge into their students.

   ○ B. People inherently have the capacity to learn.

   ○ C. The process of learning is a difficult one.

   ○ D. People are inherently unenlightened.

   **Part B:** Which supporting detail BEST helps to shape this central idea?

   ○ A. "They undoubtedly say this, he replied."

   ○ B. "Learn by degrees to endure the sight of being, and of the brightest and best of being, or in other words, of the good."

   ○ C. "Professors of education must be wrong when they say that they can put a knowledge into the soul which was not there before."

   ○ D. "The eye was unable to turn from darkness to light without the whole body."

2. Which statement about paragraphs 40–44 shows how the central idea is further developed?

   ○ A. Intellectuals should also practice gymnastics.

   ○ B. There should be no standards for the people who are chosen for intellectual study.

   ○ C. There should be high standards for the people who are chosen for intellectual study.

   ○ D. Intellectual study is a toil on the mind and the body.

# Close Read

Reread the *Republic*. As you reread, complete the Skills Focus questions below. Then use your answers and annotations from the questions to help you complete the Write activity.

## ◎ SKILLS FOCUS

1. Identify what Plato says he intends to show in the first paragraph. Cite evidence to explain how that purpose relates to the figure Plato describes.

2. State the meaning of the multiple-meaning word *converse* in paragraph 9 and identify context clues that helped you figure out the meaning.

3. In paragraph 33, Socrates explains his allegory. In your own words, restate what Socrates says. Then explain the central or main idea of the allegory, citing evidence and details to show how it emerges over the course of the text.

4. Explain what this section of Plato's *Republic* reveals about the culture of ancient Greece that is relevant for our culture today. Cite textual evidence to support your ideas.

## ✎ WRITE

RHETORICAL ANALYSIS: Analyze how Plato develops his central idea concerning the necessity of education. How does Plato's use of dialogue and specific details help to achieve his purpose?

Please note that excerpts and passages in the StudySync® library and this workbook are intended as touchstones to generate interest in an author's work. The excerpts and passages do not substitute for the reading of entire texts, and StudySync® strongly recommends that students seek out and purchase the whole literary or informational work in order to experience it as the author intended. Links to online resellers are available in our digital library. In addition, complete works may be ordered through an authorized reseller by filling out and returning to StudySync® the order form enclosed in this workbook.

Reading & Writing Companion    217

# Valedictorian Address at Anacostia High School

INFORMATIONAL TEXT
Rashema Melson
2014

## Introduction

Graduating first in her class from Anacostia High School in Washington, D.C.—while living at a homeless shelter—Rashema Melson defied the odds and became an inspiration for many. Despite her difficult living situation, Melson was determined to prioritize her education; she would work long days attending classes, studying, and even participating in sports after school, spending more than 12 hours at school each day before returning to the shelter to be with her mother and siblings. In her 2014 valedictory speech, Melson reveals the life lessons she learned throughout her journey as well as the people who have played a significant

# "I say life is endless; turn up, earn it up, but don't burn it up."

1   Welcome to Anacostia's Class of 2014 **commencement** exercises. The two years I have spent at Anacostia have been wonderful, and I could not have asked for a better experience.

2   I have been taken care of by the best principal, teachers, and coaches in the city. These educators actually care about our wellbeing: it is not just a paycheck to them. I feel as if I have walked into the arms of a second family. They are a security blanket that covers us wherever we are.

3   During my journey, I have made wonderful friends, sweated, cried, succeeded on the court and track and in the classroom. I have to shout out my family for always supporting me and being by my side. I have to shout out my school for always being available and helping me when I was in a jam. Also, for pushing me when I felt as if I was about to give up. My amazing track coach, Ms. Perry, was like a mother, sister, and best friend to me at the same time. She has always been someone who I could come to for whatever and whenever—no matter the time of day—and when I needed an ear for my problems and advice, as well. I love her so much. She is definitely a life-changer. Mrs. Sugarman, my wonderful counselor who not only told me to follow my heart but helped me to as well. I adore her. Mr. Smith, Anacostia's excellent D.C. CAP[1] advisor, who helped me get through the tough, frustrating college process without a problem. Without him, I probably would not have even applied and made it through, especially the financial aid portions. I would also like to thank Mr. Debon, Coach June, Coach Crows, Ms. Freeman, Coach Shackleford, Coach Thomas, Mr. Mooner, and Ms. Witherspoon, who have supported me every step of the way. And I would be **remiss** if I didn't thank all of the community partners and [inaudible] supporters I have gained over the past month.

4   Throughout my journey here, I have learned that time doesn't wait, pity, or judge for or to anyone, and life is not fair. Life is not fair. But despite that harsh reality, you must keep striving for success through the pain, tears, and feeling of lost hope.

---

1.  **CAP** College Access Program

5   People say life is short; live it up. I say life is endless; turn up, earn it up, but don't burn it up. Your life decisions lead you to where you end up.

6   For the longest, I was in the struggle, trying my best, but started to think that it would never be over. I started to give up. But then, God gave me a sign that He wasn't putting me through this to punish me, but to show others how to be **resilient** and persistent in the goals of life.

7   I see a promising future ahead, and I didn't do it all alone. I had gracious help for which I will be forever grateful.

8   Before I receive my diploma and head on to Georgetown, I just wanted to leave you all with a piece of advice. Class of 2014, always be who you truly are inside. Never be afraid to go after your dreams. And regardless of the negative forecast that has been predicted upon us, beat the odds, and let the sun shine.

9   The future lies within reach of our hands, and if we keep striving and don't let anyone knock us off our path, or **deter** us from our goals, we can do anything we put our mind to. No matter what. Resilience, **perseverance**, discipline, determination, and dedication is the key to your success. Each step we take is paved with possibilities. Now, go unlock the doors to your future.

By Rashema Melson, 2014. Used by permission of Rashema Melson.

---

## ✏ WRITE

CORRESPONDENCE: In this high school valedictorian speech, Rashema Melson reflects on adults who have made a positive impact on her life, such as her track coach, who she says "has always been someone who I could come to for whatever and whenever—no matter the time of day—and when I needed an ear for my problems and advice as well." Think of someone who has provided guidance and support in your life. Next, write a letter to that person explaining the impact he or she has had on your life. Be sure to provide specific examples of this person's support, just as Rashema Melson does when referencing her track coach.

# Methods of Motivation

ARGUMENTATIVE TEXT
2018

## Introduction

Can you imagine living a life without any rewards? All of us crave them—whether it's a parent's approval, a high-five from our coach, or a promotion at work. But what do we lose when our yearning for rewards and recognition becomes our dominant source of motivation? In the two essays presented here, the authors examine the benefits of internal versus external sources of motivation. Their essays pose questions about what drives people to perform, achieve, and improve. As you read their arguments, ask yourself, what motivates *you*?

# "Stimulation-based motivation often appeals to our most basic needs."

NOTES

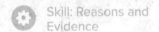
**Skill:** Reasons and Evidence

*I see the author directly state her claim that intrinsic motivation is better than extrinsic motivation. She then goes on to provide evidence to support this claim by listing the three kinds of intrinsic motivation.*

**Methods of Motivation: What's more effective—intrinsic or extrinsic motivation?**

**Point: A Job Well Done Is Its Own Reward**

1   If you are energized and actively working toward a goal, you are *motivated* to reach that goal. Lately, employers and educators have recognized the vital importance of **intrinsic** motivation—working toward a goal because it is inspiring, exciting, fascinating, and satisfying. Intrinsic motivation is the best way to ensure creative problem solving and steady, continuous achievement.

**Examples of Intrinsic Motivation**

2   It is possible to break down intrinsic motivation into three basic types:

- Knowledge-based. If you perform a task purely for the joy of learning or the satisfaction of understanding something, your motivation is knowledge-based.

- Accomplishment-based. If you perform a task for the pleasure of completing, creating, or achieving a goal, your motivation is accomplishment-based.

- Stimulation-based. If you perform a task because of the excitement or gratification it gives you, your motivation is stimulation-based.

3   Imagine that you are planning a trip and hope to learn some key phrases in Italian so that you can explore Rome with some degree of understanding. Your motivation is knowledge-based; just the satisfaction of learning those phrases is enough to motivate you to complete your task.

4   Anyone who enjoys completing crossword puzzles understands motivation that is accomplishment-based. Filling in that last square gives you a feeling of success; you need no other reward.

5  Stimulation-based motivation often appeals to our most basic needs. If you cook a delicious meal for yourself, your key motivation is the stimulus to eat something delectable.

6  It is certainly true that a certain element of extrinsic reward can add to the enjoyment of these various tasks. You can show off your finished crossword puzzle and receive praise, or you can reward yourself with an Italian ice for having learned twenty new Italian phrases. The most effective source of your motivation is internal, however; you are interested in the task and do it just for the sake of doing it.

**Intrinsic Motivation in the Workplace**

7  Shrewd employers refuse to tie every workplace achievement to an extrinsic reward. It would be expensive, and it might result in employees' ceasing to work hard unless they **anticipate** some kind of remuneration. Instead, employers should emphasize the kinds of intrinsic motivation that make workers want to be productive.

8  Some businesses offer flexibility of scheduling and more autonomy, so that workers feel empowered to make choices and decisions. Some workplaces offer professional development that gives workers a feeling of accomplishment and appeals to their joy in learning. Others ensure that all staff are cognizant of the business's goals and how each worker fits into the realization of those goals. Allowing opportunities for collaboration and interaction with others can appeal to workers' stimulation-based motivation. Using intrinsic motivation to engage employees is an effective way for companies to get their employees to do great work. Providing workers a sense of choice and a feeling of progress are two ways to ensure they are intrinsically motivated. Every employee is motivated by a sense of control and progress. If employees feel successful and empowered to make an impact on the organization, they will feel excited to come to work and try their best.

9  Of course, there are still extrinsic rewards involved in work of any kind because they remind employees of their value. No professional works for free, and everyone expects to be compensated, praised, and thanked for a job well done. However, extrinsic rewards are not sufficient. Employers must supplement them with intrinsic motivators to ensure that employees feel engaged and trusted. According to a Gallup report, employees who are asked by their managers to share in the company's process of setting goals are almost four times more likely to feel engaged at work than other employees. This statistic demonstrates intrinsic motivation is the primary tool for creating motivation and a strong work environment for employees. Not only does this type of intrinsic motivator empower employees to feel trusted by their superiors, but it also costs a company nothing.

NOTES

 Skill: Reasons and Evidence

*I see the author support her claim here by reasoning that employers must supplement extrinsic motivation with intrinsic motivators. She cites evidence from a Gallup report that backs up this reasoning.*

**Intrinsic Motivation in the Classroom**

10    The philosophy of Lehman Alternative Community School in Ithaca, New York, is to encourage "students to use freedom responsibly, and to make educational choices appropriate to their individual levels of development." LACS long ago got rid of gold stars, stickers, and even most grades in favor of intrinsic motivation. At an All School Meeting every week, students make decisions on issues facing the school. They make choices about their courses of study and reflect on their learning and achievement. They complete community projects and take trips outside the classroom.

11    Experimental and field research shows that students are more likely to complete a task and more likely to take on a challenge if they are intrinsically motivated. They are also more likely to retain the concepts learned. Students need to feel competent, and they need to feel connected to a task. The more they can make decisions and choices around their learning, the greater their intrinsic motivation becomes. A 2015 study that looked at low-income high school students from low-income high schools (64.7 percent from immigrant families) found that intrinsic motivation consistently predicted their intention to pursue health-related careers. It seems likely that intrinsic motivation is a key predictor of everyone's employment paths, no matter what his or her background might be.

12    Not every school can be as enlightened as LACS, but every school should try. Teachers must either **incorporate** intrinsic motivation into their classrooms or be left with a system of rewards and punishments that stifles creativity and students' desire to learn. Teachers' behaviors may even affect student achievement. A 2014 study that clustered intermediate-level students into three groups—high intrinsic and high extrinsic motivation, high intrinsic and low extrinsic motivation, and low intrinsic and high extrinsic motivation—found that the students who were primarily intrinsically motivated outperformed their fellow students and showed the greatest increase in achievement over the course of a school year.

13    Some people argue that extrinsic rewards can help a child build intrinsic motivation by associating a positive feeling with a task the child finds unappealing. For example, if a parent takes his or her child out to ice cream after every swim lesson, that parent might assume that the child will eventually learn to love swimming. However, research has disproven this argument in favor of extrinsic motivation. In fact, incentivizing a child's behavior with rewards actually lessens their intrinsic motivation and makes the child less likely to pursue the activity on his or her own in the future.

### Fun and the Brain

14   Scientists have performed some interesting recent experiments in the area of neuroscience to study how the brain reacts to "boring" and "fun" tasks and to try to determine the neural mechanisms of intrinsic motivation. In a 2015 study of 16 Chinese graduate and undergraduate students, who were hooked up to electrodes and faced with two separate tasks, researchers found a significant difference in electrophysiological response depending on the task being offered. So clearly the brain is most motivated by fun—a biological reason to rely on intrinsic motivation to achieve and succeed as we work and learn.

Skill: Logical
Fallacies

*I think this is misleading. It's a generalization not to describe the tasks and the actual results. The author claims this is a reason for intrinsic motivation. How credible is the author's argument without sufficient evidence?*

# "If you want someone to perform a task, you have to give them a reward . . ."

**Skill: Logical Fallacies**

*The author uses exaggeration in assuming "everyone" feels this way and then concludes they "have to" be rewarded. It's an either/or fallacy. The author assumes that someone won't complete a task without a reward, when it's also possible someone might.*

### Counterpoint: Positive Reinforcement Is Powerful

### Rewards: Simple, but Effective

15    Everyone loves recognition. For that reason, the best way to get your children, your students, or your workers to do what you want them to do is to reward them for doing it. Without it, however, the people in your life simply have no reason to perform up to their potential or to your expectations. If you want someone to perform a task, you have to give them a reward or else they won't have a reason to feel invested in the task. A common concern with offering extrinsic rewards is that they are expensive and time-consuming to purchase and assemble. It's not reasonable to expect teachers to spend their own money on candy or prizes to give their students just to get them to do their homework. Similarly, parents should not have to bribe their children with expensive toys or an allowance just to get them to clean their rooms. What people need to understand is that rewards need not be monetary, edible, or even **tangible**; it could be as simple as a word of praise or a round of applause. Research has proven that praise from a teacher has the power to improve student behavior and enhance academic achievement. Praise is an example of an extrinsic motivator that costs nothing to a teacher, but has a significant impact on a student.

### Operant Conditioning

16    The American psychologist and behaviorist B.F. Skinner is widely associated with the theory of operant conditioning, which connects learning to behavioral changes in response to environmental stimuli. According to Skinner, when a certain response pattern is rewarded, the individual learns to respond similarly in the future. One classic experiment had

*Pigeons in a box developed by Skinner used to research operant conditioning.*

pigeons conditioned to hop as food was presented at 15-second intervals. Skinner defined motivation in terms of such reinforcement, explaining that behavior that receives reinforcement will recur, and behavior that receives punishment will cease to occur. Reinforcement may be positive, as in the addition of something pleasant such as praise or treats. It may be negative, as in the removal of something pleasant when a certain behavior occurs. Punishment, too, may involve application of something unfavorable or removal of something favorable.

|  | PUNISHMENT (REDUCING BEHAVIOR) | REINFORCEMENT (INCREASING BEHAVIOR) |
|---|---|---|
| POSITIVE (ADDING) | ADDING SOMETHING TO REDUCE BEHAVIOR | ADDING SOMETHING TO INCREASE BEHAVIOR |
| NEGATIVE (TAKING AWAY) | TAKING SOMETHING AWAY TO REDUCE BEHAVIOR | TAKING SOMETHING AWAY TO INCREASE BEHAVIOR |

17　Extrinsic motivation, then, is a form of operant conditioning, because it relies on a reward system to stimulate a preferred response. For example, a well-known grocery store chain that regularly ranks high on Fortune's list of 100 top places to work offers scholarship programs for loyal employees and special awards that employees can give to co-workers who are living up to the store's values. Such motivators are examples of positive reinforcement. The store offers a certain form of negative reinforcement as well—most employees participate in community service programs because to avoid doing so might lead to certain unpleasant judgments by fellow employees.

**The Perks of Perks**

18　We have all seen the awe-inducing photographs of some of Silicon Valley's most famous businesses—the day care centers, the state-of-the-art gyms, the meditation rooms and arcades, the free food and recording studios. Those businesses do not spend their money foolishly. They want to **incentivize** their workers to feel comfortable working long hours, and they know they are competing with other businesses that can offer good workers solid benefits, so they do their best to create an environment that is fun and playful and offers extrinsic motivation to stay and work. The usual benefits of dental insurance and two-week vacations seem old-fashioned as businesses strive to engage employees and ensure their loyalty.

### Rewards vs. Intrinsic Motivation

19 Psychologists have posited for decades that rewards can, over time, decrease a person's internal desire to do a task. They based this notion on a couple of studies that showed children becoming less interested in a "fun" task after they were rewarded for doing it. However, a 1994 review of the research determined that any negative effects of rewards took place only under very restricted and easily avoided conditions. Intrinsic motivation is excellent if it exists, but it appears quite likely from this review that verbal rewards may enhance intrinsic motivation and that physical rewards do not affect it. After all, if you enjoy a job that you are doing as a volunteer, would you be likely to despise it suddenly if you were offered a paycheck for the same work?

### Effective Use of Rewards

20 You may be thinking about students you know whose parents paid them for each A they received on a report card and wondering whether that sort of reward is ever appropriate. After all, the grade itself is a form of extrinsic motivation, or at least it should be. It is certainly possible for rewards to go too far and for students or workers to become addicted to them and to function primarily in hopes of an expected reward. But it is also possible to use rewards more effectively to attain the behavior you are striving for. Some psychologists suggest using surprise rewards as a very successful means of bumping up motivation. For instance, Mark Lepper and David Greene's 1973 psychological study on preschoolers found that children who received a surprise reward for drawing were more likely to draw on their own than those who received no reward and those who received an expected reward. **Judicious** use of extrinsic motivation can lead to happier, more productive children, students, and workers, and it doesn't even need to cost a lot.

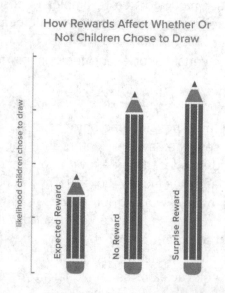

How Rewards Affect Whether Or Not Children Chose to Draw

POINT/COUNTERPOINT:
**METHODS OF
MOTIVATION**

# First Read

Read "Methods of Motivation." After you read, complete the Think Questions below.

## ☁ THINK QUESTIONS

1. What does the Point essay author think about classroom environments that focus primarily on extrinsic motivation? Refer to specific evidence to support your answer.

2. What is the Counterpoint essay author's opinion about extrinsic motivation in classroom environments? Give evidence.

3. Using information from both essays, explain one reason why rewards can be effective and one reason why rewards might fail.

4. Use context clues to determine the meaning of **anticipate** as it is used in paragraph 7 of the Point essay. Write your own definition of *anticipate* and explain how you figured it out.

5. The Latin word *judicium* means "judgment." With this information in mind, what do you think the word **judicious** means? Use context clues and your knowledge of word patterns and relationships to support your thinking and write your best definition here.

Please note that excerpts and passages in the StudySync® library and this workbook are intended as touchstones to generate interest in an author's work. The excerpts and passages do not substitute for the reading of entire texts, and StudySync® strongly recommends that students seek out and purchase the whole literary or informational work in order to experience it as the author intended. Links to online resellers are available in our digital library. In addition, complete works may be ordered through an authorized reseller by filling out and returning to StudySync® the order form enclosed in this workbook.

Reading & Writing
Companion     **229**

# Skill:
# Reasons and Evidence

Use the Checklist to analyze Reasons and Evidence in "Methods of Motivation." Refer to the sample student annotations about Reasons and Evidence in the text.

## ••• CHECKLIST FOR REASONS AND EVIDENCE

In order to identify the reasons and evidence that support an author's claim(s) in an argument, note the following:

✓ the argument the author presents in the text and identify the claim

✓ the reasons and evidence the author includes that support the claim

✓ if the evidence supports the claim and is complete and comprehensive

✓ if the author introduces irrelevant evidence, not related to the claim, and that does not support it

✓ reasons and evidence that have been distorted or exaggerated, as well as examples of fallacious reasoning, or errors in logic such as personal attacks

To assess whether the reasoning is sound and the evidence is relevant and sufficient, consider the following questions:

✓ What kind of argument is the author making?

✓ Is the reasoning, or the thinking behind the claims, sound and valid?

✓ Are the reasons and evidence the author presents to support the claim sufficient, or is more evidence needed? Why or why not?

✓ Does the author introduce irrelevant evidence, not related to the claim? How do you know?

✓ How can you tell if there is any fallacious reasoning, or evidence that is distorted or exaggerated?

REASONS
AND
EVIDENCE

sync•skills

# Skill:
# Reasons and Evidence

Reread paragraphs 18–20 of "Methods of Motivation." Then, using the Checklist on the previous page, answer the multiple-choice questions below.

## ↻ YOUR TURN

1. This question has two parts. First, answer Part A. Then, answer Part B.

   **Part A:** What reason does the author give to support his claim in paragraph 18?

   ○ A. Businesses in Silicon Valley waste money on extrinsic motivators.

   ○ B. The businesses in Silicon Valley use extrinsic motivators to incentivize their employees to stay and work.

   ○ C. Employees in Silicon Valley are more productive.

   ○ D. All employers should provide daycare to their employees.

   **Part B:** Which evidence from the text BEST supports your response from Part A?

   ○ A. "they do their best to create an environment that is fun and playful and offers extrinsic motivation to stay and work"

   ○ B. "Those businesses do not spend their money foolishly."

   ○ C. "The usual benefits of dental insurance and two-week vacations seem old-fashioned"

   ○ D. "they know they are competing with other businesses that can offer good workers solid benefits"

2. In paragraph 19, what evidence does the author use to rebut the counter argument that studies showed extrinsic rewards decrease a person's desire to do a task?

   ○ A. studies showing children lost interest after being rewarded

   ○ B. studies that utilized a "fun" task

   ○ C. evidence from a follow-up review

   ○ D. psychologist reports

3. The author rebuts the idea that extrinsic motivation can go too far by reasoning that _____.

    ○ A.  money is an appropriate reward for good grades

    ○ B.  addicted workers only work for greater and greater rewards

    ○ C.  gold stars go a long way in motivating students and workers to achieve

    ○ D.  thoughtful extrinsic motivation can lead to both happiness and productivity

# Skill:
# Logical Fallacies

Use the Checklist to analyze Logical Fallacies in "Methods of Motivation." Refer to the sample student annotations about Logical Fallacies in the text.

## ••• CHECKLIST FOR LOGICAL FALLACIES

In order to identify a speaker's reasoning, point of view, and use of evidence and rhetoric, note the following:

✓ the evidence that the speaker offers to support his or her point of view

✓ any fallacious reasoning, or errors in logic and reasoning, as well as distorted, or misleading, information

✓ whether the speaker employs the use of exaggeration, especially when citing facts or statistics

✓ the author setting up a false premise, such as either/or, making a situation absolute when that does not have to be the case

✓ the author's use of rhetoric and what it contributes to the speaker's point of view

To evaluate a speaker's point of view, reasoning, and use of evidence and rhetoric, consider the following questions:

✓ Where does the speaker state a clear point of view?

✓ What reasons does the speaker offer to support his or her point of view?

✓ Does the speaker offer any examples of fallacious reasoning or distorted evidence? What were they, and how do they affect the speaker's point of view?

✓ Are there any instances of distorted or exaggerated evidence? In what ways is the evidence exaggerated or distorted, and how does it affect the claim?

✓ Does the author set up a false premise, assuming that only one view is possible?

✓ Are there rhetorical devices? What do they contribute to the speaker's point of view?

# Skill:
# Logical Fallacies

Reread paragraph 12 of "Methods of Motivation." Then, using the Checklist on the previous page, answer the multiple-choice questions below.

## ⟳ YOUR TURN

1. The argument that teachers must incorporate intrinsic motivation or be left with a rewards and punishment system that stifles students' desire to learn is a logical fallacy because _____.

   - ○ A. it is a piece of evidence
   - ○ B. it accounts for multiple possibilities
   - ○ C. it is a faulty piece of evidence
   - ○ D. it does not account for any other possibilities

2. Analyzing the effect of the author's use of the logical fallacy in this paragraph allows the reader to _____.

   - ○ A. correct the author's errors
   - ○ B. research evidence about the topic
   - ○ C. evaluate the effectiveness of the author's argument
   - ○ D. become an expert on the issue being discussed

3. What effect does the use of the logical fallacy in this paragraph have on the credibility of the author's argument?

   - ○ A. It strengthens the argument because it shows that the author carefully researched the results.
   - ○ B. It strengthens the argument because it shows that the author has narrowed the potential conclusions.
   - ○ C. It weakens the argument because it shows that the author may have failed to consider all outcomes.
   - ○ D. It weakens the argument because it shows that the author has based the argument on an incorrect idea.

POINT/COUNTERPOINT:
## METHODS OF MOTIVATION

# Close Read

Reread "Methods of Motivation." As you reread, complete the Skills Focus questions below. Then use your answers and annotations from the questions to help you complete the Write activity.

## ◎ SKILLS FOCUS

1. State the central claim of each argument and cite two examples of evidence in support of each claim.

2. Identify an example of a logical fallacy in each argument and explain why it is an example of fallacious reasoning.

3. In "Valedictorian Address at Anacostia High School" the speaker states, "The future lies within reach of our hands, and if we keep striving and not let anyone knock us off our path, or deter us from our goals, we can do anything we put our mind to." Compare this statement to the two central ideas from "Methods of Motivation" and analyze which central idea it most closely supports. Make sure to use textual evidence to support your answer.

4. Analyze the different points of view in the point/counterpoint essays from "Methods of Motivation" and explain what each author's view has to say about culture and goals.

## ✏ WRITE

DISCUSSION: This text presents differing perspectives on how to best motivate individuals to achieve their goals. In your opinion, what is the most effective way your family, school, or community can help students build and maintain motivation to achieve their goals? As you formulate your own position, defend or challenge a perspective you read about in the text. Prepare to discuss this question with your peers by writing down your thoughts about this question, as well as your reasoning and any relevant examples or textual evidence that informs your opinion. As you listen to others, evaluate each speaker's point of view and use of evidence, and identify any fallacious reasoning.

Please note that excerpts and passages in the StudySync® library and this workbook are intended as touchstones to generate interest in an author's work. The excerpts and passages do not substitute for the reading of entire texts, and StudySync® strongly recommends that students seek out and purchase the whole literary or informational work in order to experience it as the author intended. Links to online resellers are available in our digital library. In addition, complete works may be ordered through an authorized reseller by filling out and returning to StudySync® the order form enclosed in this workbook.

Reading & Writing
Companion
**235**

# Remarks at the UN General Assembly

ARGUMENTATIVE TEXT
Ellen Johnson Sirleaf
2015

## Introduction

Ellen Johnson Sirleaf (b. 1938) is a Nobel Peace Prize winner and the first woman elected to lead an African nation. Born in Liberia's capital, she received an education in the United States at Madison Business College and Harvard University before returning to serve in the Liberian president's cabinet. After the government was taken over in a coup, she fled to the United States, but returned to Liberia in 1985 to run for a senate seat. In 1997, she ran for the presidency and finished in second place; finally, in 2005, she won the election and became the President of Liberia, serving until 2018. The following text is an address she delivered to the United Nations General Assembly, discussing gender equality and empowerment for women in the Post-2015 Development Agenda.

# "There is no doubt that progress has been made."

NOTES

1    Mr. President of the General Assembly and Madame Executive Director, I thank you for the invitation. I could do no less than respond favorably to join you and the women of the world in this truly monumental year.

2    In 1995, we came together in Beijing, 17,000 governments from all over the world and 26,000 activists to envision a world where women and girls have equal rights, freedom and opportunity in all **spheres** of life. This year marks the 20th anniversary of that historic event, when we adopted the Beijing Declaration and Platform for Action.

3    At a summit in January in Addis Ababa, members of the African Union promoted a stakeholders consultation on the progress and challenges relating to women advancement in the year 2015, designated by them as the year of Women Empowerment and Development in promotion of Agenda 2063.

4    In February 2015, San Diego, women leaders of the global community declared 2015 a year for Gender Equality and Women Empowerment.

5    In Rio, world leaders reaffirmed their commitment to ensure women's equal rights, access to opportunity and participation in leadership in the economy, security and political decision making.

6    In a few months, members of the United Nations will adopt a post-2015 development agenda which will call once again for more concrete action in advocating Gender Equality & Empowerment of Women & Girls for a transformative world.

7    There is no doubt that progress has been made. In the 20 years since Beijing, more girls are educated, rural women have found their voices, more women hold professional positions, more women are chief executives in the private sector, more women are in parliament, and in **exceptionally** high percentage such as in Rwanda, more women are vying for high political office and some of us have finally broken the glass ceiling.

8    Yet, as the San Diego Conference points out, the current pace of change has been much too slow, much too slow, so that at the current pace it will take 81 years to achieve gender equity in the workplace where the highest echelon remains largely male, and it will take 75 years to reach remuneration between men and women for work of equal value and more than 30 to reach gender balance in decision making.

9    This simply is a clear **manifestation** of an unjust world that seeks to leave women behind. It is not enough to make nice speeches, hold international meetings, issue communiqués and declarations. Women leaders have said unequivocally, it is time for equality and have issued a call for action, to achieve Planet 5050 by 2030. This call seeks a commitment to address 12 **critical** areas of concern—essentially calls for the protection, education and training for women and girls, ensuring access to information and the factors for production; especially for rural women; removing the constraints that lead to participation, in decision making at all levels in the society.

10   As we continue negotiation for a post-2015 development agenda, our call for women empowerment and equality must go beyond rhetoric, must set the goals that are realistic and achievable and design the monitoring and evaluation systems that motivate countries to action. This was the success of the MDGs (Millennium Development Goals)[1], the spirit of progress and competition in the achievement of goals. Let us do the same in the next global goal for women.

11   Liberia has a history of **turbulent** times but in 2013 for the first time in two decades we celebrated ten consecutive years of peace and two successful general elections. Then came 2014 and we were hit by Ebola, an enemy that threatened all the gains of the past 10 years. Once again the Liberian people rose to the task. Today we can report that there are no new cases anywhere in the country for over 13 days.

12   When the next five years celebration of Beijing takes place in 2020, I would have served and left a better country than I found. I want to thank all of you who provided the motivation and support that enabled me to break the glass ceiling. I hope that we will all work toward ensuring that the African Union does not return to male domination. Thank you.

---

1. **MDGs (Millennium Development Goals)** the UN's 15-year goals outlined at the Millennium Summit in 2000

WRITE

PERSONAL RESPONSE: In "Remarks at the UN General Assembly," the speaker, Ellen Johnson Sirleaf, argues for the need for widespread change she hopes to see continue in her society. Taking a cue from Sirleaf's rhetoric, write a speech you would like to deliver to advocate for change. In your speech, allude to or directly refer to examples from this and other speeches, letters, and texts you have read to help support your claims.

Please note that excerpts and passages in the StudySync® library and this workbook are intended as touchstones to generate interest in an author's work. The excerpts and passages do not substitute for the reading of entire texts, and StudySync® strongly recommends that students seek out and purchase the whole literary or informational work in order to experience it as the author intended. Links to online resellers are available in our digital library. In addition, complete works may be ordered through an authorized reseller by filling out and returning to StudySync® the order form enclosed in this workbook.

Reading & Writing
Companion

239

# A Plea for Global Education

ARGUMENTATIVE TEXT
Rigoberta Menchú Tum
and Global Vision
1993

## Introduction

Rigoberta Menchú Tum (b. 1959) is an activist, writer, and politician, and the winner of the 1992 Nobel Peace Prize. Born in war-torn Guatemala to a poor indigenous family, Menchú graduated from middle school and became an activist campaigning against human rights violations by the Guatemalan army. She had grown up witnessing widespread genocide of the Mayan people by the Guatemalan government, and her family were all brutally murdered in conflicts stemming from the civil war. In 1981, Menchú was exiled and escaped to Mexico, where she organized against indigenous oppression and war in Guatemala. When the war ended in 1996, Menchú continued to work toward bringing war criminals to justice. In this interview from 1993, shortly after being awarded the Nobel Peace Prize, Menchú advocates for international cooperation, respect for indigenous peoples, and for the power and necessity of global education.

# "No people can flourish who do not know their own past."

## WHAT IS YOUR MESSAGE TO HUMANKIND?

1   We are living in a troubled world, in a time of great uncertainty. It's a time to reflect about many things, especially about humankind as a whole, and the balance between collective values and individual values.

2   The world right now is preoccupied with business, buying and selling and making money. But solutions can be found in our community, among the indigenous peoples[1] who are the victims of terrible repression and violations of the law in many parts of the world. You can find experience, people who have educated themselves, and a whole side of science which is not well known.

3   There is a big change going on in the way people see the world: change in the concept of development, in the way people live together. But for this change to bear fruit, we need education on a global scale. Humankind will not recover from its mistakes without global education. The United Nations, human rights organisations, indigenous peoples, and all the countries of the world should **concentrate** their efforts on education. Solutions will come when the world becomes educated about global values, the common values of its inhabitants and communities.

4   We have to focus on solutions in this time of great challenges. If we just wait around, the problems will overwhelm us. We need to take the initiative, to launch local, regional and global projects, to unite our efforts, and really listen to indigenous peoples. We have to listen to people to find out what they want, to discover the solutions they have to offer for the future.

## WHAT SHOULD BE DONE TO PROTECT INDIGENOUS PEOPLES?

5   It is very important to understand that we indigenous peoples don't need "protection." What we do need is simply to be allowed to exist, to live, to let our own culture develop, and to recover the meaning of our own history. Indigenous peoples have always depended on their traditional wisdom and culture. Our

---

1.  **indigenous peoples**  communities of people who are native to the area in which they live

NOTES

cosmological vision, our way of thinking, our lifestyle have empowered us to survive through many difficult times in the past. Now that we stand at the close of the twentieth century, this fact should send a very clear message to the conscience of the world. We indigenous people reaffirm our struggle to survive!

6    To me, the most important thing is that indigenous people still possess a balance, an equilibrium with Mother Nature, a balance between human life and the earth itself. For us, the Earth is the source of knowledge, of historical memory, of life! But the rest of the world does not share this vision, and so they keep on destroying Mother Earth. Indigenous people aren't strange. We may be special, but we are also part of the modern world in which we all live. We are part of the diversity of cultures, the plurality of races, the mixture of societies on all the continents where we live today. Indigenous people are not some myth from the past, a myth that survives only in legends and in ruins!

7    You should find out what indigenous people can contribute toward a global vision, a vision of nature, of development, of community based on the oral **transmission** of our ancestors' knowledge from generation to generation. You should also look at the way we think about nature. Around the world, there have been many struggles in which indigenous peoples have played an important role. But their names are never mentioned, their contributions have been ignored. Others have given new names to these concerns which indigenous peoples have always cared about.

8    The fact that indigenous people are among the most marginalised of the marginalised people on Earth, among those whose rights have been violated for so long, is a call to conscience. I hope this call will be answered in the new millennium which now awaits us.

9    The time has come now to stop feeling sorry for all the wrongs that have been done to indigenous people. The time has come to go beyond blame, beyond sympathy with our cause, beyond identifying with our world-view. It's time to implement programmes—alternative projects and technologies that combine the benefits of science and the benefits of nature, that respect the traditional ethno-botanical knowledge of peasants and the age-old experience through which they have survived—and to combine these with the advances of technology and science. We indigenous peoples have nothing against the innovations of technology and science when they are shown to be appropriate. But we are against such innovations if they are applied in opposition to the values which indigenous people protect, which are those of life, nature, and historical memory.

10 No people can flourish who do not know their own past. The past is a good foundation for the present, and an inspiration for the future. People owe it to history and to the present to prepare for the future. Finally, I sincerely hope that now, at the end of the twentieth century, indigenous people will never again be forced into extinction on the face of this Earth. We need international law, national legislation, the legal protection of our human rights, as well as the respect and acceptance of society in general, in order to face the future.

11 To listen to indigenous peoples is to listen to the women and to those who know how to love this earth. We may be only a small grain of sand, but it is one which will prove important for the challenges humankind must face in the next millennium.

**WHAT DO YOU FEEL ABOUT HUMAN RIGHTS?**

12 Among the nations which have suffered the most widespread human rights abuses, unpunished **atrocities**, murders, terror and fear, is Guatemala. The recent historical events in Guatemala have fragmented the culture of the Mayas in many places. Displacement, refuge, exile are daily facts of life in my country. However, these things have also allowed us to learn something more in our experience of the world. In Guatemala today, there are some very courageous women who are making a stand, indigenous women, who are leading the struggle! We believe the war in Guatemala is no disgrace for the Mayas. It's a disgrace for the people of Guatemala . . .

13 Unfortunately, the rest of the world has turned a blind eye on the situation. Atrocities still go unpunished, and many governments have helped to cover up the problem. I think it's important to say this, because the Guatemalan people know it, and we feel offended again and again when we realise that our country has been silenced. This has also made us aware of the plight of other people. Solidarity between nations must be militant, constant, and continuous. There is a need for international organisations to which the victims can turn for help, to which people can go to defend their lives and to protect their human rights.

14 Finally, I believe that peace in Guatemala is not a myth. Peace in Guatemala is not a myth, neither is it a myth for Central America, or for the people of this continent or other continents. Rather, it is a process which requires effort and consciousness-raising around the world, especially among those in governments and in large organisations who have the power to make important decisions.

15 Peace requires work in the heart of the small society that is Guatemala. But Guatemala is also part of humankind, and what has been going on in Guatemala is a very bad example for the world and for future generations. I

hope that the world will one day acknowledge its responsibility and will not be indifferent to any war, no matter where it happens, or to any violation of human rights, no matter where it may occur, because the massacre in the Quiché[2] is a wound in the heart of humankind.

**WHAT IS GOING ON IN GUATEMALA NOW?** (i.e. March 1993)

16    It's a very complex situation. The war is officially over, yet there are continuous assassinations, enormous suffering and grinding poverty. But the greatest problem in Guatemala is that most people cannot participate in the political negotiations, because they don't speak Spanish! An emergency parliament needs to be formed immediately to address the problem. **Blatant** disregard for the law is rampant. We must put an end not only to these violations of law, but also to the suppression of truth, to the repression and persecution of over a million civilians who take part in our self-defence patrols.

17    About a million people have been displaced within the country. Some have sought refuge in the mountains, where they suffer a great deal of bombing. Over two hundred thousand Guatemalans are refugees. Many people have been forced to permanently abandon their farms or leave their towns. In other words, the war is not just the armed conflict which occurs every day, but it's also the general persecution which afflicts the whole economy and society, and which also—as a routine matter—limits our freedom of speech. In the end, the people of Guatemala are paying a very high price for all of this. If we don't recognise the **magnitude** of the problem in Guatemala, we will never come to grips with the whole issue of development both in Central America and throughout the continent. Guatemala has suffered a lot of repression, and especially, many unpunished crimes. I would say that ninety percent of the people who suffer from the war, the widows and the orphaned children in the streets, are indigenous people. This is a fact. It's not only a racial issue; it is just a reality which happens to fall on the heads of the indigenous people.

Global Vision Foundation interview translated by Michael O'Callaghan. Used by permission of the Global Vision Foundation.

2. **the massacre in the Quiché** an organized slaughter of native Guatemalans in the jungle by the Guatemalan military

WRITE

PERSONAL RESPONSE: This text opens with the question, "What is your message to humankind?" What is Rigoberta Menchú's response to this question? What would your message to humankind be? How did reading this text shape your perspective on your own message to humankind?

# The Perils of Indifference

INFORMATIONAL TEXT
Elie Wiesel
1999

## Introduction

Elie Wiesel (1928–2016) was born in the Carpathian Mountains in Romania. At the age of 15, Wiesel—along with his mother, father, and three sisters—was relocated to a confinement ghetto. Two months later, they were all shipped to a concentration camp, Auschwitz, where his mother and younger sister were murdered upon arrival. Wiesel and his two older sisters were the only members of his family that survived the Holocaust; he went on to lead a life dedicated to writing, activism and Judaism. His most famous book, *Night*, was published in 1960 and narrates his experiences in the concentration camps in vivid detail. Wiesel was the recipient of dozens of awards, including the Nobel Peace Prize, for his efforts on behalf of victims of ethnic and religious persecution worldwide. In this speech, delivered at the White House before President Bill Clinton, his staff, and members of Congress, Wiesel implores listeners to follow the kinder nature of their hearts.

# "Indifference is not a beginning; it is an end."

1   Mr. President, Mrs. Clinton, members of Congress, Ambassador Holbrooke, Excellencies, friends:

2   Fifty-four years ago to the day, a young Jewish boy from a small town in the Carpathian Mountains woke up, not far from Goethe's beloved Weimar[1], in a place of eternal infamy called Buchenwald. He was finally free, but there was no joy in his heart. He thought there never would be again. Liberated a day earlier by American soldiers, he remembers their rage at what they saw. And even if he lives to be a very old man, he will always be grateful to them for that rage, and also for their compassion. Though he did not understand their language, their eyes told him what he needed to know—that they, too, would remember, and bear witness.

 Skill:
Word Meaning

*What is* infamy? *The* fam *might be related to* famous. *Since there was no joy in the boy's heart, this is a clue that* infamy *has a negative meaning. It is also the object of the preposition* of, *so it's a noun.*

3   And now, I stand before you, Mr. President—Commander-in-Chief of the army that freed me, and tens of thousands of others—and I am filled with a profound and **abiding** gratitude to the American people. "Gratitude" is a word that I cherish. Gratitude is what defines the humanity of the human being. And I am grateful to you, Hillary, or Mrs. Clinton, for what you said, and for what you are doing for children in the world, for the homeless, for the victims of injustice, the victims of destiny and society. And I thank all of you for being here.

4   We are on the threshold of a new century, a new millennium. What will the legacy of this vanishing century be? How will it be remembered in the new millennium? Surely it will be judged, and judged severely, in both moral and metaphysical terms. These failures have cast a dark shadow over humanity: two World Wars, countless civil wars, the senseless chain of assassinations (Gandhi, the Kennedys, Martin Luther King, Sadat, Rabin), bloodbaths in Cambodia and Algeria, India and Pakistan, Ireland and Rwanda, Eritrea and Ethiopia, Sarajevo and Kosovo; the inhumanity in the gulag and the tragedy of Hiroshima. And, on a different level, of course, Auschwitz and Treblinka. So much violence; so much **indifference**.

5   What is indifference? Etymologically, the word means "no difference." A strange and unnatural state in which the lines blur between light and darkness,

1.   **Goethe's beloved Weimar**   a German city which was at the heart of a literary and cultural movement called Weimar Classicism

dusk and dawn, crime and punishment, cruelty and compassion, good and evil. What are its courses and inescapable consequences? Is it a philosophy? Is there a philosophy of indifference conceivable? Can one possibly view indifference as a virtue? Is it necessary at times to practice it simply to keep one's sanity, live normally, enjoy a fine meal and a glass of wine, as the world around us experiences **harrowing** upheavals?

6    Of course, indifference can be tempting—more than that, seductive. It is so much easier to look away from victims. It is so much easier to avoid such rude interruptions to our work, our dreams, our hopes. It is, after all, awkward, troublesome, to be involved in another person's pain and despair. Yet, for the person who is indifferent, his or her neighbor are of no consequence. And, therefore, their lives are meaningless. Their hidden or even visible anguish is of no interest. Indifference reduces the Other to an abstraction.

7    Over there, behind the black gates of Auschwitz, the most tragic of all prisoners were the "Muselmanner[2]," as they were called. Wrapped in their torn blankets, they would sit or lie on the ground, staring vacantly into space, unaware of who or where they were—strangers to their surroundings. They no longer felt pain, hunger, thirst. They feared nothing. They felt nothing. They were dead and did not know it.

8    Rooted in our tradition, some of us felt that to be abandoned by humanity then was not the ultimate. We felt that to be abandoned by God was worse than to be punished by Him. Better an unjust God than an indifferent one. For us to be ignored by God was a harsher punishment than to be a victim of His anger. Man can live far from God—not outside God. God is wherever we are. Even in suffering? Even in suffering.

9    In a way, to be indifferent to that suffering is what makes the human being inhuman. Indifference, after all, is more dangerous than anger and hatred. Anger can at times be creative. One writes a great poem, a great symphony. One does something special for the sake of humanity because one is angry at the injustice that one witnesses. But indifference is never creative. Even hatred at times may elicit a response. You fight it. You denounce it. You disarm it.

10   Indifference elicits no response. Indifference is not a response. Indifference is not a beginning; it is an end. And, therefore, indifference is always the friend of the enemy, for it benefits the aggressor—never his victim, whose pain is magnified when he or she feels forgotten. The political prisoner in his cell, the hungry children, the homeless refugees—not to respond to their plight, not to relieve their solitude by offering them a spark of hope is to exile them from human memory. And in denying their humanity, we betray our own.

---

2. **Muselmanner** a slang term referring to those who have been starved and exhausted to the point of accepting their own impending death

Skill:
Informational
Text Structure

*Wiesel claims that indifference to another human's suffering takes away one's own humanity. He continues using a cause and effect structure, adding details to refine his claim.*

11   Indifference, then, is not only a sin, it is a punishment.

12   And this is one of the most important lessons of this outgoing century's wide-ranging experiments in good and evil.

13   In the place that I come from, society was composed of three simple categories: the killers, the victims, and the bystanders. During the darkest of times, inside the ghettoes and death camps—and I'm glad that Mrs. Clinton mentioned that we are now commemorating that event, that period, that we are now in the Days of Remembrance—but then, we felt abandoned, forgotten. All of us did.

14   And our only miserable consolation was that we believed that Auschwitz and Treblinka were closely guarded secrets; that the leaders of the free world did not know what was going on behind those black gates and barbed wire; that they had no knowledge of the war against the Jews that Hitler's armies and their accomplices waged as part of the war against the Allies. If they knew, we thought, surely those leaders would have moved heaven and earth to **intervene**. They would have spoken out with great outrage and conviction. They would have bombed the railways leading to Birkenau, just the railways, just once.

15   And now we knew, we learned, we discovered that the Pentagon knew, the State Department knew. And the illustrious occupant of the White House then, who was a great leader—and I say it with some anguish and pain, because, today is exactly 54 years marking his death—Franklin Delano Roosevelt died on April the 12th, 1945. So he is very much present to me and to us. No doubt, he was a great leader. He mobilized the American people and the world, going into battle, bringing hundreds and thousands of valiant and brave soldiers in America to fight fascism, to fight dictatorship, to fight Hitler. And so many of the young people fell in battle. And, nevertheless, his image in Jewish history—I must say it—his image in Jewish history is flawed.

16   The depressing tale of the St. Louis is a case in point. Sixty years ago, its human cargo—nearly 1,000 Jews—was turned back to Nazi Germany. And that happened after the Kristallnacht[3], after the first state sponsored pogrom[4], with hundreds of Jewish shops destroyed, synagogues burned, thousands of people put in concentration camps. And that ship, which was already in the shores of the United States, was sent back. I don't understand. Roosevelt was a good man, with a heart. He understood those who needed help. Why didn't he allow these refugees to disembark? A thousand people—in America, the great country, the greatest democracy, the most generous of all new nations in modern history. What happened? I don't understand. Why the indifference, on the highest level, to the suffering of the victims?

---

3. **Kristallnacht**  a night riot and massacre against Jewish citizens that occured on the 9th and 10th of November, 1938
4. **pogrom**  Russian for "devastation"; violent, destructive, racially-motivated attack on a community

17   But then, there were human beings who were sensitive to our tragedy. Those non-Jews, those Christians, that we call the "Righteous Gentiles," whose selfless acts of heroism saved the honor of their faith. Why were they so few? Why was there a greater effort to save SS murderers after the war than to save their victims during the war? Why did some of America's largest corporations continue to do business with Hitler's Germany until 1942? It has been suggested, and it was documented, that the Wehrmacht could not have conducted its invasion of France without oil obtained from American sources. How is one to explain their indifference?

18   And yet, my friends, good things have also happened in this traumatic century: the defeat of Nazism, the collapse of communism, the rebirth of Israel on its ancestral soil, the demise of apartheid, Israel's peace treaty with Egypt, the peace accord in Ireland. And let us remember the meeting, filled with drama and emotion, between Rabin and Arafat that you, Mr. President, **convened** in this very place. I was here and I will never forget it.

19   And then, of course, the joint decision of the United States and NATO to intervene in Kosovo and save those victims, those refugees, those who were uprooted by a man, whom I believe that because of his crimes, should be charged with crimes against humanity.

20   But this time, the world was not silent. This time, we do respond. This time, we intervene.

21   Does it mean that we have learned from the past? Does it mean that society has changed? Has the human being become less indifferent and more human? Have we really learned from our experiences? Are we less insensitive to the plight of victims of ethnic cleansing and other forms of injustices in places near and far? Is today's justified intervention in Kosovo, led by you, Mr. President, a lasting warning that never again will the deportation, the terrorization of children and their parents, be allowed anywhere in the world? Will it discourage other dictators in other lands to do the same?

22   What about the children? Oh, we see them on television, we read about them in the papers, and we do so with a broken heart. Their fate is always the most tragic, inevitably. When adults wage war, children perish. We see their faces, their eyes. Do we hear their pleas? Do we feel their pain, their agony? Every minute one of them dies of disease, violence, famine.

23   Some of them—so many of them—could be saved.

24   And so, once again, I think of the young Jewish boy from the Carpathian Mountains. He has accompanied the old man I have become throughout these years of quest and struggle. And together we walk towards the new millennium, carried by profound fear and extraordinary hope.

# First Read

Read "The Perils of Indifference." After you read, complete the Think Questions below.

 **THINK QUESTIONS**

1. Why does Elie Wiesel say he was grateful that the American soldiers who liberated him from the concentration camp felt rage at what they saw? Explain.

2. In paragraph 6, Elie Wiesel states, "Indifference reduces the Other to an abstraction." What do you think he means by this? Explain.

3. In his closing statements, Wiesel refers to his life as a quest, which implies that he has been in search of something. What do you think this is? Give evidence from the speech.

4. Using context clues, write your own definition for the word **harrowing** as it appears in the fifth paragraph of the speech. Explain how you arrived at your definition.

5. The word **intervene** is derived from the Latin word *intervenire*. The first part of the word *inter* means "between." Using this knowledge, along with context clues and your knowledge of word patterns and relationships, write your best definition for the word *intervene* here. Then verify your meaning using a print or digital dictionary.

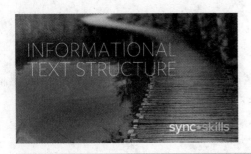

# Skill:
# Informational Text Structure

Use the Checklist to analyze Informational Text Structure in "The Perils of Indifference." Refer to the sample student annotations about Informational Text Structure in the text.

## ••• CHECKLIST FOR INFORMATIONAL TEXT STRUCTURE

In order to identify an author's ideas or claims in the text, note the following:

- ✓ the writer's claim or thesis

- ✓ the evidence the writer uses to support his or her claim or thesis

- ✓ specific statements that contain the main ideas or claims of the argument

- ✓ individual paragraphs and sentences that

  - develop an author's ideas or claims

  - clarify and refine an author's ideas or claims

- ✓ how an idea or claim is made clearer, or refined, in larger portions of text

To analyze in detail how an author's ideas or claims are developed and refined by particular sentences, paragraphs, or larger portions of a text, consider the following questions:

- ✓ What are the author's main ideas or claims?

- ✓ How are the author's ideas and claims developed in larger portions of the texts?

- ✓ How are these claims or ideas developed and refined by particular sentences in the text?

- ✓ What specific sentences and paragraphs refine or develop the author's overall claim or ideas?

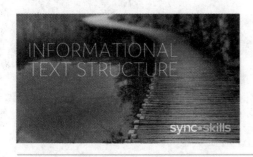

# Skill:
# Informational Text Structure

Reread paragraphs 20–24 of "The Perils of Indifference." Then, using the Checklist on the previous page, answer the multiple-choice questions below.

## 🔁 YOUR TURN

1. Which sentence(s) from the speech show how Wiesel uses cause and effect to make the conclusion of his argument effective?

   ○ A. "But this time, the world was not silent. This time, we do respond. This time, we intervene."
   ○ B. "Does it mean that we have learned from the past? Does it mean that society has changed?"
   ○ C. "When adults wage war, children perish. We see their faces, their eyes. Do we hear their pleas?"
   ○ D. "He has accompanied the old man I have become throughout these years of quest and struggle."

2. Which quote from this excerpt **best** supports Wiesel's clear claim that we must intervene when someone elsewhere is suffering from violence?

   ○ A. "Has the human being become less indifferent and more human?"
   ○ B. "Oh, we see them on television, we read about them in the papers, and we do so with a broken heart."
   ○ C. "Some of them—so many of them—could be saved."
   ○ D. "And so, once again, I think of the young Jewish boy from the Carpathian Mountains. He has accompanied the old man I have become throughout these years of quest and struggle."

# Skill:
# Word Meaning

Use the Checklist to analyze Word Meaning in "The Perils of Indifference." Refer to the sample student annotations about Word Meaning in the text.

••• CHECKLIST FOR WORD MEANING

In order to find the pronunciation of a word or determine or clarify its precise meaning or its part of speech, do the following:

- ✓ determine the word's part of speech in context

- ✓ use context clues to make a preliminary determination of the meaning of the word

- ✓ consult general and specialized reference materials, both print and digital

  - • locate the word through parts of speech to understand usage

  - • use the pronunciation guide and say the word aloud

- ✓ verify the preliminary determination of the meaning of a word or phrase by reading all of the definitions, and then decide which definition makes sense within the context of the text

In order to determine the etymology of different words, and the way in which their meanings have changed throughout history, do the following:

- ✓ use reference materials, such as a dictionary, to determine the word origin and history

- ✓ consider how the historical context of the word clarifies its usage

To determine a word's part of speech, pronunciation, precise meaning, or etymology, consider the following questions:

- ✓ What is the word describing? What inferred meanings can I make?

- ✓ How is the word being used in the phrase or sentence?

- ✓ Which definition makes sense in the sentence?

- ✓ How can the word's origin and history help me clarify its precise meaning or usage?

## Skill:
## Word Meaning

Reread paragraph 13 of "The Perils of Indifference." Then, using the Checklist on the previous page, answer the multiple-choice questions below.

## ⟳ YOUR TURN

1. *Composed* is what part of speech?

   ○ A. noun
   ○ B. verb
   ○ C. adjective
   ○ D. adverb

2. What is the precise meaning of the word *composed* as used in the sentence in paragraph 13?

   ○ A. write or create, as a work of art, as with music
   ○ B. calm or settle oneself or one's features or thoughts
   ○ C. to make up or form parts of a whole
   ○ D. prepare, as a text, for printing by setting up the letters and other characters in the order to be printed

3. How can the etymology of *composed* help in learning the word's meaning?

   ○ A. To pose is to stand.
   ○ B. *Composed* sounds like *decompose*.
   ○ C. A composer puts together pieces of music into a whole.
   ○ D. *Comp* is the start of the word *computer*.

THE PERILS
OF INDIFFERENCE

# Close Read

Reread "The Perils of Indifference." As you reread, complete the Skills Focus questions below. Then use your answers and annotations from the questions to help you complete the Write activity.

## ◎ SKILLS FOCUS

1. Choose two or three paragraphs of the speech and analyze in detail how Elie Wiesel's claims about indifference are refined and shaped. Cite evidence from the text as you explain the structure of the speech.

2. In paragraph 13, Elie Wiesel speaks of "ghettoes." Use a print and digital reference to determine the pronunciation, part of speech, etymology, and precise meaning of the word *ghetto*. Then discuss how this word relates to Wiesel's argument.

3. In her "Remarks at the UN General Assembly," Ellen Johnson Sirleaf states of troubles in her country, "It is not enough to make nice speeches, hold international meetings, issue communiqués and declarations." In "A Plea for Global Education," Rigoberta Menchú Tum says, "We have to focus on solutions in this time of great challenges. If we just wait around, the problems will overwhelm us." Explain how these speakers' comments connect to the ideas that Wiesel discusses in his address.

4. Explain how Wiesel's cultural experience has influenced his central idea or goal in delivering this speech. Cite evidence from the text to support your understanding.

## ✏ WRITE

RHETORICAL ANALYSIS: Elie Wiesel asks his audience to consider an important concept: the "inescapable consequences of indifference." What is his claim about the consequences of indifference? How does he use structural elements of his argument, such as appeals and a conclusion, to develop his argument? Quote and paraphrase evidence from the speech to support your response.

# Night

INFORMATIONAL TEXT
Elie Wiesel
1955

## Introduction

In his autobiographical account of a Jewish teenager and his father struggling to stay alive in a World War II concentration camp, Nobel Prize-winner Elie Wiesel (1928–2016) delivers an impact that few readers can ever forget. In this excerpt, the narrator describes his first night at Birkenau and its indelible physical and mental effects on him, then and since.

# "We were incapable of thinking. Our senses were numbed, everything was fading into a fog."

**From Section 3**

1   Never shall I forget that night, the first night in camp, that turned my life into one long night seven times sealed.

2   Never shall I forget that smoke.

3   Never shall I forget the small faces of the children whose bodies I saw transformed into smoke under a silent sky.

4   Never shall I forget those flames that consumed my faith forever.

5   Never shall I forget the **nocturnal** silence that deprived me for all eternity of the desire to live.

6   Never shall I forget those moments that murdered my God and my soul and turned my dreams to ashes.

7   Never shall I forget those things, even were I condemned to live as long as God Himself.

8   Never.

9   The barrack we had been assigned to was very long. On the roof, a few bluish skylights. I thought: This is what the **antechamber** of hell must look like. So many crazed men, so much shouting, so much brutality.

10  Dozens of inmates were there to receive us, sticks in hand, striking anywhere, anyone, without reason. The orders came:

11  "Strip! Hurry up! *Raus!* Hold on only to your belt and your shoes . . ."

12  Our clothes were to be thrown on the floor at the back of the barrack. There was a pile there already. New suits, old ones, torn overcoats, rags. For us it meant true equality: nakedness. We trembled in the cold.

Copyright © BookheadEd Learning, LLC

13    A few SS officers[1] wandered through the room, looking for strong men. If vigor was that appreciated, perhaps one should try to appear sturdy? My father thought the opposite. Better not to draw attention. (We later found out that he had been right. Those who were selected that day were incorporated into the Sonder-Kommando, the Kommando working in the crematoria. Béla Katz, the son of an important merchant of my town, had arrived in Birkenau with the first transport, one week ahead of us. When he found out that we were there, he succeeded in slipping us a note. He told us that having been chosen because of his strength, he had been forced to place his own father's body into the furnace.)

14    The blows continued to rain on us:

15    "To the barber!"

16    Belt and shoes in hand, I let myself be dragged along to the barbers. Their clippers tore out our hair, shaved every hair on our bodies. My head was buzzing; the same thought surfacing over and over: not to be separated from my father.

17    Freed from the barbers' clutches, we began to wander about the crowd, finding friends, acquaintances. Every encounter filled us with joy—yes, joy: Thank God! You are still alive!

18    Some were crying. They used whatever strength they had left to cry. Why had they let themselves be brought here? Why didn't they die in their beds? Their words were **interspersed** with sobs.

19    Suddenly someone threw his arms around me in a hug: Yehiel, the Sigheter rebbe's brother. He was weeping bitterly. I thought he was crying with joy at still being alive.

20    "Don't cry, Yehiel," I said. "Don't waste your tears . . ."

21    "Not cry? We're on the threshold of death. Soon, we shall be inside . . . Do you understand? Inside. How could I not cry?"

22    I watched darkness fade through the bluish skylights in the roof. I no longer was afraid. I was overcome by fatigue.

23    The absent no longer entered our thoughts. One spoke of them—who knows what happened to them?—but their fate was not on our minds. We were incapable of thinking. Our senses were numbed, everything was fading into

1. **SS officers** officers in the *Schutzstaffel*, a division of the Nazi military under Adolf Hitler

a fog. We no longer clung to anything. The instincts of self-preservation, of self-defense, of pride, had all deserted us. In one terrifying moment of **lucidity**, I thought of us as damned souls wandering through the void, souls condemned to wander through space until the end of time, seeking **redemption**, seeking oblivion, without any hope of finding either.

24  Around five o'clock in the morning, we were expelled from the barrack. The Kapos were beating us again, but I no longer felt the pain. A glacial wind was **enveloping** us. We were naked, holding our shoes and belts. An order:

25  "Run!" And we ran. After a few minutes of running, a new barrack.

26  A barrel of foul-smelling liquid stood by the door. Disinfection. Everybody soaked in it. Then came a hot shower. All very fast. As we left the showers, we were chased outside. And ordered to run some more. Another barrack: the storeroom. Very long tables. Mountains of prison garb. As we ran, they threw the clothes at us: pants, jackets, shirts . . .

27  In a few seconds, we had ceased to be men. Had the situation not been so tragic, we might have laughed. We looked pretty strange! Meir Katz, a colossus, wore a child's pants, and Stern, a skinny little fellow, was floundering in a huge jacket. We immediately started to switch.

28  I glanced over at my father. How changed he looked! His eyes were veiled. I wanted to tell him something, but I didn't know what.

29  The night had passed completely. The morning star shone in the sky. I too had become a different person. The student of Talmud, the child I was, had been consumed by the flames. All that was left was a shape that resembled me. My soul had been invaded—and devoured—by a black flame.

30  So many events had taken place in just a few hours that I had completely lost all notion of time. When had we left our homes? And the ghetto? And the train? Only a week ago? One night? *One single night?*

31  How long had we been standing in the freezing wind? One hour? A single hour? Sixty minutes? Surely it was a dream.

Excerpted from *Night* by Elie Wiesel, published by Hill and Wang.

WRITE

NARRATIVE: In this excerpt from *Night*, Elie Wiesel vows never to forget his painful memories. Write a narrative about a character, real or imagined, who commits to remembering something painful. In your narrative, provide insight as to the effect of these memories on the character.

Please note that excerpts and passages in the StudySync® library and this workbook are intended as touchstones to generate interest in an author's work. The excerpts and passages do not substitute for the reading of entire texts, and StudySync® strongly recommends that students seek out and purchase the whole literary or informational work in order to experience it as the author intended. Links to online resellers are available in our digital library. In addition, complete works may be ordered through an authorized reseller by filling out and returning to StudySync® the order form enclosed in this workbook.

Reading & Writing Companion   **261**

# Civil
# Peace

FICTION
Chinua Achebe
1972

## Introduction

C hinua Achebe (1930–2013) was a Nigerian novelist, poet, essayist and lecturer. Amid some controversy, Achebe chose to write in English, "the language of colonizers," in order to reach the broadest possible audience. He is best known for his 1958 novel *Things Fall Apart,* which remains to this day the most widely read work of African literature. In the short story presented here, "Civil Peace," Achebe provides a true-to-life description of Nigeria in the early 1970s,

# "Jonathan and his family were now completely paralysed by terror."

1    Jonathan Iwegbu counted himself extraordinarily lucky. "Happy survival!" meant so much more to him than just a current fashion of greeting old friends in the first hazy days of peace. It went deep to his heart. He had come out of the war with five inestimable blessings—his head, his wife Maria's head and the heads of three out of their four children. As a bonus he also had his old bicycle—a miracle too but naturally not to be compared to the safety of five human heads.

2    The bicycle had a little history of its own. One day at the height of the war it was commandeered "for urgent military action." Hard as its loss would have been to him he would still have let it go without a thought had he not had some doubts about the genuineness of the officer. It wasn't his disreputable rags, nor the toes peeping out of one blue and one brown canvas shoes, nor yet the two stars of his rank done obviously in a hurry in biro, that troubled Jonathan; many good and heroic soldiers looked the same or worse. It was rather a certain lack of grip and firmness in his manner. So Jonathan, suspecting he might be **amenable** to influence, rummaged in his raffia bag and produced the two pounds with which he had been going to buy firewood which his wife, Maria, retailed to camp officials for extra stock-fish and corn meal, and got his bicycle back. That night he buried it in the little clearing in the bush where the dead of the camp, including his own youngest son, were buried. When he dug it up again a year later after the surrender all it needed was a little palm-oil greasing. "Nothing puzzles God," he said in wonder.

3    He put it to immediate use as a taxi and accumulated a small pile of Biafran[1] money ferrying camp officials and their families across the four-mile stretch to the nearest tarred road. His standard charge per trip was six pounds and those who had the money were only glad to be rid of some of it in this way. At the end of a fortnight he had made a small fortune of one hundred and fifteen pounds.

4    Then he made the journey to Enugu and found another miracle waiting for him. It was unbelievable. He rubbed his eyes and looked again and it was still

---

1. **Biafran** from Biafra, a secessionist African state

NOTES

standing there before him. But, needless to say, even that monumental blessing must be accounted also totally inferior to the five heads in the family. This newest miracle was his little house in Ogui Overside. Indeed nothing puzzles God! Only two houses away a huge concrete edifice some wealthy contractor had put up just before the war was a mountain of rubble. And here was Jonathan's little zinc house of no regrets built with mud blocks quite intact! Of course the doors and windows were missing and five sheets off the roof. But what was that? And anyhow he had returned to Enugu early enough to pick up bits of old zinc and wood and soggy sheets of cardboard lying around the neighbourhood before thousands more came out of their forest holes looking for the same things. He got a **destitute** carpenter with one old hammer, a blunt plane and a few bent and rusty nails in his tool bag to turn this assortment of wood, paper and metal into door and window shutters for five Nigerian shillings or fifty Biafran pounds. He paid the pounds, and moved in with his overjoyed family carrying five heads on their shoulders.

5  His children picked mangoes near the military cemetery and sold them to soldiers' wives for a few pennies—real pennies this time—and his wife started making breakfast akara balls for neighbours in a hurry to start life again. With his family earnings he took his bicycle to the villages around and bought fresh palm-wine which he mixed generously in his rooms with the water which had recently started running again in the public tap down the road, and opened up a bar for soldiers and other lucky people with good money.

6  At first he went daily, then every other day and finally once a week, to the offices of the Coal Corporation where he used to be a miner, to find out what was what. The only thing he did find out in the end was that the little house of his was even a greater blessing than he had thought. Some of his fellow ex-miners who had nowhere to return at the end of the day's waiting just slept outside the doors of the offices and cooked what meal they could **scrounge** together in Bournvita tins. As the weeks lengthened and still nobody could say what was what Jonathan discontinued his weekly visits altogether and faced his palm-wine bar.

7  But nothing puzzles God. Came the day of the windfall when after five days of endless scuffles in queues and counter-queues in the sun outside the Treasury he had twenty pounds counted into his palms as ex-gratia award for the rebel money he had turned in. It was like Christmas for him and for many others like him when the payments began. They called it (since few could manage its proper official name) *egg-rasher*[2].

8  As soon as the pound notes were placed in his palm Jonathan simply closed it tight over them and buried fist and money inside his trouser pocket. He had

_____

2. **egg-rasher**  a colloquial pronunciation of the Latin "ex gratia," which means "as a favor"

to be extra careful because he had seen a man a couple of days earlier collapse into near-madness in an instant before that oceanic crowd because no sooner had he got his twenty pounds than some heartless **ruffian** picked it off him. Though it was not right that a man in such an extremity of agony should be blamed yet many in the queues that day were able to remark quietly on the victim's carelessness, especially he pulled out the innards of his pocket and revealed a hole in it big enough to pass a thief's head. But of course he had insisted that the money had been in the other pocket, pulling it out too to show its comparative wholeness. So one had to be careful.

9  Jonathan soon transferred the money to his left hand and pocket so as to leave his right free for shaking hands should the need arise, though by fixing his gaze at such an elevation as to miss all approaching human faces he made sure that the need did not arise, until he got home.

10  He was normally a heavy sleeper but that night he heard all the neighbourhood noises die down one after another. Even the night watchman who knocked the hour on some metal somewhere in the distance had fallen silent after knocking one o'clock. That must have been the last thought in Jonathan's mind before he was finally carried away himself. He couldn't have been gone for long, though, when he was violently awakened again.

11  'Who is knocking?' whispered his wife lying beside him on the floor.

12  "I don't know," he whispered back breathlessly.

13  The second time the knocking came it was so loud and imperious that the rickety old door could have fallen down.

14  "Who is knocking?" he asked then, his voice parched and trembling.

15  "Na tief-man and him people," came the cool reply. "Make you hopen de door." This was followed by the heaviest knocking of all.

16  Maria was the first to raise the alarm, then he followed and all their children.

17  *"Police-o! Thieves-o! Neighbours-o! Police-o! We are lost! We are dead! Neighbours, are you asleep? Wake up! Police-o!"*

18  This went on for a long time and then stopped suddenly. Perhaps they had scared the thief away. There was total silence. But only for a short while.

19  "You done finish?" asked the voice outside. "Make we help you small. Oya, everybody!"

20  *"Police-o! Tief-man-o! Neighbours-o! we done loss-o! Police-o! . . ."*

21    There were at least five other voices besides the leader's.

22    Jonathan and his family were now completely paralysed by terror. Maria and the children sobbed inaudibly like lost souls. Jonathan groaned continuously.

23    The silence that followed the thieves' alarm vibrated horribly. Jonathan all but begged their leader to speak again and be done with it.

24    "My frien," said he at long last, "we don try our best for call dem but I tink say dem all done sleep-o . . . So wetin we go do now? Sometaim you wan call soja? Or you wan make we call dem for you? Soja better pass police. No be so?"

25    "Na so!" replied his men. Jonathan thought he heard even more voices now than before and groaned heavily. His legs were sagging under him and his throat felt like sand-paper.

26    "My frien, why you no de talk again. I de ask you say you wan make we call soja?"

27    "No."

28    "Awrighto. Now make we talk business. We no be bad tief. We no like for make trouble. Trouble done finish. War done finish and all the katakata wey de for inside. No Civil War again. This time na Civil Peace. No be so?"

29    "Na so!" answered the horrible chorus.

30    'What do you want from me? I am a poor man. Everything I had went with this war. Why do you come to me? You know people who have money. We . . .'

31    "Awright! We know say you no get plenty money. But we sef no get even anini. So derefore make you open dis window and give us one hundred pound and we go commot. Orderwise we de come for inside now to show you guitar-boy like dis . . ."

32    A volley of automatic fire rang through the sky. Maria and the children began to weep aloud again.

33    "Ah, missisi de cry again. No need for dat. We done talk say we na good tief. We just take our small money and go nwayorly. No molest. Abi we de molest?"

34    "At all!" sang the chorus.

35    "My friends," began Jonathan hoarsely. "I hear what you say and I thank you. If I had one hundred pounds . . ."

36    "Lookia my frien, no be play we come play for your house. If we make mistake and step for inside you no go like am-o. So derefore . . ."

37 "To God who made me; if you come inside and find one hundred pounds, take it and shoot me and shoot my wife and children. I swear to God. The only money I have in this life is this twenty-pounds *egg-rasher* they gave me today . . ."

38 "OK. Time de go. Make you open dis window and bring the twenty pound. We go manage am like dat."

39 There were now loud murmurs of dissent among the chorus: 'Na lie de man de lie; e get plenty money . . . Make we go inside and search properly well . . . Wetin be twenty pound? . . .

40 ''Shurrup!" rang the leader's voice like a lone shot in the sky and silenced the murmuring at once. "Are you dere? Bring the money quick!"

41 "I am coming," said Jonathan fumbling in the darkness with the key of the small wooden box he kept by his side on the mat.

42 At the first sign of light as neighbours and others assembled to **commiserate** with him he was already strapping his five-gallon demijohn to his bicycle carrier and his wife, sweating in the open fire, was turning over akara balls in a wide clay bowl of boiling oil. In the corner his eldest son was rinsing out dregs of yesterday's palm wine from old beer bottles.

43 "I count it as nothing," he told his sympathizers, his eyes on the rope he was tying. "What is *egg-rasher*? Did I depend on it last week? Or is it greater than other things that went with the war? I say, let *egg-rasher* perish in the flames! Let it go where everything else has gone. Nothing puzzles God."

"Civil Peace" from GIRLS AT WAR by Chinua Achebe, copyright © 1972, 1973 by Chinua Achebe. Used by permission of Doubleday, an imprint of the Knopf Doubleday Publishing Group, a division of Random House LLC. All rights reserved.

### ✏ WRITE

RESEARCH: This story is set shortly after the Biafran War in Nigeria. Conduct brief research on the impact of the Biafran War on the Nigerian people. Then, write a short report in which you summarize important information you learned in your research, and explain how what you learned shapes your understanding of the story you read, "Civil Peace."

Please note that excerpts and passages in the StudySync® library and this workbook are intended as touchstones to generate interest in an author's work. The excerpts and passages do not substitute for the reading of entire texts, and StudySync® strongly recommends that students seek out and purchase the whole literary or informational work in order to experience it as the author intended. Links to online resellers are available in our digital library. In addition, complete works may be ordered through an authorized reseller by filling out and returning to StudySync® the order form enclosed in this workbook.

Reading & Writing Companion    267

Extended
Writing
Project and
Grammar

EXTENDED
WRITING
PROJECT
INFORMATIVE
WRITING

# Informative Writing Process: Plan

| PLAN | DRAFT | REVISE | EDIT AND PUBLISH |
|------|-------|--------|------------------|

Conflict often arises when the wants of one individual clash with those of another. These individual wants may also represent the desires of a larger community. When we examine an individual's goals, we often gain a way to understand the community and culture from which he or she comes.

## WRITING PROMPT

**How does community influence our goals?**

From this unit or the previous unit, select three texts in which communities face a challenge. In an informative essay, describe the challenge and how specific individuals aim to help their communities overcome that challenge. Analyze how the goals of the individual are connected to the goals of their community.

**Writing to Sources**

As you gather ideas and information from the texts in the unit, be sure to:

- use evidence from multiple sources; and

- avoid overly relying on one source.

Please note that excerpts and passages in the StudySync® library and this workbook are intended as touchstones to generate interest in an author's work. The excerpts and passages do not substitute for the reading of entire texts, and StudySync® strongly recommends that students seek out and purchase the whole literary or informational work in order to experience it as the author intended. Links to online resellers are available in our digital library. In addition, complete works may be ordered through an authorized reseller by filling out and returning to StudySync® the order form enclosed in this workbook.

Reading & Writing Companion

**269**

## Introduction to Informative Writing

Informative writing examines a topic and conveys ideas and information through comparisons, descriptions, and explanations. Good informative writing includes a clear thesis statement with supporting details—such as definitions, quotations, examples, and facts—that clarify and support the thesis statement. The characteristics of informative writing include:

- an introduction with a topic, main idea, and thesis statement

- appropriate formatting to organize complex ideas, concepts, or information

- body paragraphs with supporting details

- transitions between and within paragraphs

- a formal style and objective tone

- a conclusion that follows from the information presented

As you continue with this Extended Writing Project, you will receive more instruction and practice at crafting each of the characteristics of informative writing to create your own informative essay.

Before you get started on your own informative essay, read this informative essay that one student, Theo, wrote in response to the writing prompt. As you read the Model, highlight and annotate the features of informative writing that Theo included in his essay.

## ≡ STUDENT MODEL

### A Community's Survival Depends on Individuals' Goals

1   Imagine that the worst has happened to a community—a war, a hurricane, or a devastating fire. People flee or are taken away. What happens to the community? By definition, a community is a place where individuals live together and share common characteristics or goals. When a community faces challenges, the individuals can try to keep it going. If enough individuals make it their goal to work together, they can keep the community alive. This important idea is a subject of many kinds of writing, from news reports to memoirs, as well as fiction and poetry, and the knowledge the authors share can be helpful in a variety of ways. In the selections *Night*, "Civil Peace," and "The Gathering Place," each community has a few individuals who are doing the best they can for the greater good, but if they do not work together, the community might not survive.

2   In the memoir *Night*, Elie Wiesel describes how his community and his family were destroyed by hate and hopelessness during World War II. He, his family, and his community were arrested and sent to concentration camps because they were Jewish. In these camps, the prisoners form a new community, and the goal of each person is no doubt to survive. When a weeping friend appears, Wiesel thinks the man is crying with joy to be alive. Instead, the friend explains that he is crying because "we're on the threshold of death." The man's hopelessness causes Wiesel to stop thinking as an individual. He describes the community's shock and pain: "We were incapable of thinking. . . . We no longer clung to anything." The hope of survival is fading. Yet the next morning, Wiesel and his father are still alive. Stunned, they realize that only one night has passed. Wiesel speaks of himself as "I" again. He wants to tell his father "something, but I didn't know what." It's possible that at this moment, Wiesel realizes that he must survive, and as a result he becomes "I" again. In the end, Wiesel lived through the war to tell this story. In *Night*, he speaks

as an individual for his lost communities, and this information is something he wants future generations to understand and remember.

3    As in *Night*, the community in Chinua Achebe's story "Civil Peace" has been through a terrible war, but now people must figure out how to live in peacetime. While Wiesel shows the need for community through a real-life war experience, Achebe's fictional situation still feels very real. The main character, Jonathan Iwegbu, considers himself "extraordinarily lucky" for the following reason: he has survived with "his head, his wife Maria's head and the heads of three out of their four children." With these "blessings" and the "miracle" of his bicycle, Jonathan is eager to start life over. Still, there are problems in the community. When robbers threaten to kill Jonathan and his family, the police don't help and neither do Jonathan's neighbors. The neighbors only "assembled to commiserate" in the morning, when it was safe. Despite this, Jonathan maintains a positive attitude. Jonathan knows that possessions and money do not last, saying the money counted "as nothing." Yet he might also suspect that the community cannot survive if people do not help out one another in times of danger. He will get by because of God's "blessings" and because he is willing to work hard, but not because his community is willing to help one another.

4    Like the setting in "Civil Peace," the urban community in "The Gathering Place" by poet Amanda Gorman faces many challenges, but it is strong thanks to the common goals and good work of its members. The poem's speaker refers to her community on "the corner of East 92nd and Lexington" as "our great gathering place" (lines 1, 4). The speaker never refers to herself using the pronoun *I*; she speaks of "we." She writes that her community meets "among the music of concrete and steel" (12) and "build[s] a summit worth climbing, / a goal worth reaching" (19–20). Then she names real-life individuals whose efforts have helped the community, including Cynthia Erivo, Pete Cashmore, and ElsaMarie D'Silva. Each person has contributed to making the community safe and strong by speaking out or building something. As a result, the speaker declares that "we are hope, we are home . . . we be united, we be good." (41–43). Through poetry, Gorman explores what is possible when the individuals' goals make a community—and the whole world—a better place to live.

5    As the authors of *Night*, "Civil Peace," and "The Gathering Place" show, a community can be a concentration camp, a former war zone, or a city neighborhood, but the people living there cannot thrive if they do not have one another's backs. The people in these communities have things in common, but they are not always united in a key goal: their collective survival. In *Night*, the men in the concentration camp all want to survive, but they are too hopeless and afraid to help one another. In "Civil Peace," the community is still at war in peacetime as robbers roam the streets and neighbors and police will not help. However, the community in "The Gathering Place" is successful because people do work together to fight for justice. When individuals share a common goal and are able to work together, they keep the community alive even under the worst circumstances.

# ✏ WRITE

Writers often take notes about story ideas before they sit down to write. Think about what you've learned so far about informative writing to help you begin prewriting.

- **Purpose**: What texts do you want to write about, and what challenges do the communities in them face?
- **Audience**: Who is your audience, and what is their connection to the topic of your essay? How will you engage them in your point of view?
- **Introduction**: How will you clearly introduce the topic and the main idea of your essay? What language can you use that is both precise and intriguing? What is your unique controlling idea about the three texts? How can you word this controlling idea clearly and concisely as a thesis statement?
- **Supporting Evidence and Details**: What textual evidence might you use to add substance to your essay? Where did you find this information? Which details are essential to support your thesis and which details can you leave out?
- **Text Structure**: What strategies will you use to organize your response to the prompt? How can you ensure that the progression of ideas is logical and well developed?
- **Formal Style**: What type of language and sentence constructions will you use to create a formal style for your academic audience?
- **Conclusion**: How does the information in the body of your essay relate to your thesis? How can you connect the ideas presented in your essay to a greater concept or to society in a thoughtful way?

## Response Instructions

Use the questions in the bulleted list to write a one-paragraph summary. Your summary should describe what you will write about in your essay like the one above.

Don't worry about including all of the details now; focus only on the most essential and important elements. You will refer back to this short summary as you continue through the steps of the writing process.

# Skill:
# Organizing Informative Writing

## ••• CHECKLIST FOR ORGANIZING INFORMATIVE WRITING

As you begin to organize your writing for your informative essay, use the following questions as a guide:

- What is my topic? How can I summarize the main idea?

- What is the logical order of my ideas, concepts, and information? Do I see a pattern that is similar to a specific text structure?

- Do I make important connections and distinctions within the material I want to present?

- Which organizational structure should I use to present my information?

- How might using graphics, headings, or some form of multimedia help to present my information?

Here are some important connections and distinctions that you can make through organizing complex ideas, concepts, and information and aid comprehension:

- definitions, such as the connections and distinctions between qualities of a subject or examples

- classifications, such as the distinctions between subcategories of a topic

- comparisons, such as the connections and distinctions between two texts, ideas, or concepts

- cause-and-effect relationships, such as understanding the connection between what happened and why

- sequences, such as the connections between events and processes

**YOUR TURN**

Read the informational text titles below. Then, complete the chart by writing the organizational structure that would best convey the ideas of each text.

| Organizational Structure Options | | | | |
|---|---|---|---|---|
| steps in a process in sequential order | chronological | cause-and-effect | categories and subcategories | problem-and-solution |

| Informational Text Title | Organizational Structure |
|---|---|
| "The Life and Legacy of Marie Curie" | |
| "How Crayons are Made" | |
| "How V-Chips Made It Possible for Parents to Control Their Kids' TV Viewing" | |
| "A Guide to Thailand's Wildlife" | |
| "The Effects of Sports on Students' Lives" | |

## ↻ YOUR TURN

Complete the chart below by writing a short summary of what you will focus on in each paragraph of your essay.

| Paragraph | Summary |
| --- | --- |
| Introduction | |
| Body Paragraph 1 | |
| Body Paragraph 2 | |
| Body Paragraph 3 | |
| Conclusion | |

Please note that excerpts and passages in the StudySync® library and this workbook are intended as touchstones to generate interest in an author's work. The excerpts and passages do not substitute for the reading of entire texts, and StudySync® strongly recommends that students seek out and purchase the whole literary or informational work in order to experience it as the author intended. Links to online resellers are available in our digital library. In addition, complete works may be ordered through an authorized reseller by filling out and returning to StudySync® the order form enclosed in this workbook.

Reading & Writing Companion    277

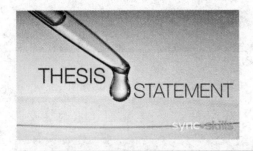

# Skill:
# Thesis Statement

## ••• CHECKLIST FOR THESIS STATEMENT

Before you begin writing your thesis statement, ask yourself the following questions:

- What is the prompt asking me to write about?

- What claim do I want to make about the topic of this essay?

- Is my claim precise? How is it specific to my topic? Does my thesis statement introduce the body of my essay?

- Where should I place my thesis statement?

Here are some methods to introduce and develop a topic as well as a precise claim:

- think about your central claim of your essay

  > identify a clear claim you want to introduce, thinking about:

   o the sources you will use to support it

   o how closely your claim is related to your topic and specific to your supporting details

  > identify claims and counterclaims you intend to prove, as needed

- your thesis statement should:

  > let the reader anticipate the content of your essay

  > begin your essay in an organized manner

  > present your opinion clearly

  > respond completely to the writing prompt

- consider the best placement for your thesis statement.

  > if your response is short, you may want to get right to the point and present your thesis statement in the first sentence of the essay

  > if your response is longer (as in a formal essay), you can build up to your thesis statement and place it at the end of your introductory paragraph

## ↻ YOUR TURN

Read the sentences below. Then, complete the chart by sorting them into those that are thesis statements and those that are statements of facts.

| | Options |
|---|---|
| A | The community members in "Civil Peace," such as the protagonist's neighbors and the police, do not work together in order to survive. |
| B | The short story "Civil Peace" shows that even if a community survives a disaster, individuals must protect each other if the community is to remain successful. |
| C | Although they are different genres, Amanda Gorman's "A Gathering Place" and Elie Wiesel's "The Perils of Indifference" both center on the topic of communities. |
| D | *Night* by Elie Wiesel is the memoir of a Holocaust survivor who was imprisoned in the Nazi Germany concentration camps at Auschwitz and Buchenwald. |
| E | The narrator's shifts in point of view in *Night* show how his attitude toward himself and his community change throughout his experience, ultimately proving that challenges facing a community force its members to think of their shared experience. |
| F | Communities thrive when individuals share a common goal, which both Elie Wiesel and Amanda Gorman demonstrate in their reflections. |

| Thesis Statement | Statement of Fact |
|---|---|
| | |
| | |
| | |

## ✏ WRITE

Use the questions in the checklist to draft a thesis statement for your informative essay.

# Skill:
# Supporting Details

As you look for supporting details to develop your topic, claim, or thesis statement, ask yourself the following questions:

- What is my main idea about this topic?

- What does a reader need to know about the topic in order to understand the main idea?

- What details will support my thesis?

- Is this information necessary to the reader's understanding of the topic? What other kinds of information could I provide?

- Does this information relate to my thesis and help to develop and refine my key concept or idea?

- Are the supporting details I have included sufficient to support my thesis or claim?

- Where can I find better evidence that will provide stronger support for my point?

Here are some suggestions for how you can develop your topic:

- review your thesis or claim

- consider your main idea

- consider what your audience may already know about the topic

- note what the audience will need to know to understand the topic

- be sure to consult credible sources

- use different types of supporting details, such as:

  > well-chosen and sufficient facts that are specific to your topic, enhance your discussion, and fully support your thesis or claim

  > extended definitions to explain difficult concepts, terms, or ideas

  > concrete details and examples that will add descriptive and detailed material to your topic

  > quotations to directly connect your thesis statement or claim to the text

## ⟳ YOUR TURN

Choose the best answer to each question.

1. Theo wants to improve the supporting details in a paragraph about *Night*, from a previous draft of his informative essay. How can he rewrite the underlined sentence to provide more specific support?

> Like the speaker in "A Gathering Place," Elie Wiesel stops being an individual and speaks for the community. He knows what all the prisoners are thinking and feeling. <u>They are hopeless and can't function</u>. His insight reveals that the prisoners share not only a common goal but also a common fear.

- ○ A. Wiesel evokes the prison camp as a hellish place that is full of fog and fear.
- ○ B. Wiesel describes them as "incapable of thinking," "numbed," and "deserted" by their instincts for "self-preservation."
- ○ C. Wiesel says, "I thought of us as damned souls wandering through the void, souls condemned to wander . . ."
- ○ D. Wiesel has a "terrifying moment of lucidity" in which he realizes that he and all the other prisoners will die.

2. Theo would like to add a supporting detail to a previous draft of his paragraph about "Civil Peace." Which quotation could best follow and provide support for the last sentence?

> Jonathan's attitude is an example for the whole community as it recovers after the war. Even after he has been robbed, he counts his blessings. He holds no grudges against his neighbors who did not come to his aid. As he prepares for another day's work, he reminds the community of what's important.

- ○ A. "I hear what you say and I thank you."
- ○ B. "Nothing puzzles God."
- ○ C. Money is "nothing. . . . Let it go where everything else has gone."
- ○ D. "I say, let the *egg-rasher* perish in the flames!"

## ✎ WRITE

Use the questions in the checklist to revise the supporting details in your informative essay.

# Informative Writing Process: Draft

| PLAN | DRAFT | REVISE | EDIT AND PUBLISH |
|------|-------|--------|------------------|

You have already made progress toward writing your informative essay. Now it is time to draft your informative essay.

## ✏ WRITE

Use your plan and other responses in your Binder to draft your informative essay. You may also have new ideas as you begin drafting. Feel free to explore those new ideas as you have them. You can also ask yourself these questions to ensure that your writing is focused, organized, and developed:

**Draft Checklist:**

☐ **Focused**: Have I stated my thesis clearly? Have I included only relevant information and details that support my thesis, and nothing extraneous that might confuse my readers?

☐ **Organized**: Does my choice of organizational structure make sense? Does my writing show cohesion so that my ideas within and across paragraphs are clearly connected?

☐ **Developed**: Are all of my ideas clearly developed? Will readers be able to follow my train of thought with ease and understanding?

Before you submit your draft, read it over carefully. You want to be sure that you've responded to all aspects of the prompt.

Here is Theo's draft of his informative essay. As you read, notice how Theo develops his draft to be focused, organized, and developed. As he continues to revise and edit his essay, Theo will find and improve weak spots in his writing, as well as correct any language or punctuation mistakes.

## ≡ STUDENT MODEL: FIRST DRAFT

### A Community's Survival Depends on Individuals' Goals

~~When a community faces challenges, people try to keep going. If enough people work together, they can keep the community alive. There is a kind of community in each of the selections: "The Gathering Place," *Night*, and "Civil Peace." In each comunity a few people do the best they can. Their goal is to survive. They want their community to survive too. But that won't happen if they don't work together. The authors all show that individuals working together is the key to a community's survival.~~

Imagine that the worst has happened to a community—a war, a hurricane, or a devastating fire. People flee or are taken away. What happens to the community? By definition, a community is a place where individuals live together and share common characteristics or goals. When a community faces challenges, the individuals can try to keep it going. If enough individuals make it their goal to work together, they can keep the community alive. This important idea is a subject of many kinds of writing, from news reports to memoirs, as well as fiction and poetry, and the knowledge the authors share can be helpful in a variety of ways. In the selections *Night*, "Civil Peace," and "The Gathering Place," each community has a few individuals who are doing the best they can for the greater good, but if they do not work together, the community might not survive.

In *Night* Elie Wiesel describes how his community was destroyed by hate during World War II he, his family, and his comunity were arrested because they were Jews and sent to concentration camps. The prisoners form a new community. The goal: survival. After all survival is the what every living creature wants. Weisel thinks his friend is crying with joy. He is crying because "we're on the threshold of death." He is hopeless. Wiesel stops thinking as an individual. He describes the community's shock and pain. Hope is fading. When Wiesel and his father are still alive the next day they are stunned to

Skill:
Introductions

*Theo adds a hook by using descriptive details to set the scene for his audience and engage his audience in his topic. He follows the hook with an engaging question designed to imply that his purpose for writing is to provide an answer to this question.*

realize that one night has passed. Wiesel speaks of himself as "I" again. He wants to tell his father "something" It's possible that Wiesel realizes that he must survive. He becomes "I" again. Wiesel lived through the really terrible and frightening experience of war to tell this story and to speak as an individual for his lost communities.

The community in Chinua Achebe's story ("A Civil Peace") has been through a terrible war now peple must figure out how to live in piece time. The main character, Jonathan Iwegbu. He considers himself "extraordinarily lucky": because he has survived with "his head, his wife Maria's head and the heads of three out of their four children." Jonathan has "blessings" and the "miracle" of his bicycle. Jonathan is eager to start life over. There are problems in the community. Money is scarce. People get robbed. Robbers threaten to kill Jonathan and his family. The police don't help and neither do Jonathan's neighbors. Jonathan is on his own. He negotiated with the robbers and gives them all his money. The neighbors only "assembled to commiserate" in the morning, when it was safe. Jonathan maintains a positive attitude. Yet he might also suspect that the community can't survive if people don't help out one another in times of danger. He will get by because of God's "blessings" and because he is willing to work hard, not because his community is willing to help one another.

The urban comunity in "The Gathering Place" by Amanda Gorman, faces a lot of challenges. But it is strong because it's members have common goals and do good work. The poem's speaker calls it a gathering place. The speaker uses the pronoun *we* instead of *I*. The speaker talks about what "we do." They have meeting and set goals. ~~Then the speaker names people who helped the community. Each person has given back to help make the community safe and strong by speaking out or building something. The person speaking in the poem says: "we are hope, we are home . . . we be united, we be good." In this community everbody's goals make the community— and the whole world—a better place to live.~~

Then she names real-life individuals whose efforts have helped the community, including Cynthia Erivo, Pete Cashmore, and ElsaMarie D'Silva. Each person has contributed to making the community safe and strong by speaking out or building something. As a result, the

**Skill: Precise Language**

*Theo added specific names to identify "real-life individuals" and add an authentic element.*

speaker declares that "we are hope, we are home . . . we be united, we be good." (41–43). Through poetry, Gorman explores what is possible when the individuals' goals make a community—and the whole world—a better place to live.

~~The people in the selections *Night*, "Civil Peace," and "The Gathering Place" show a community can be a city neighborhood, a concentration camp, or a former war zone. They want their community to survive but that can't happen if they don't work together and they mostly don't share the same goals. The peple in the camp are helpless. The community in "Civil Peace" is still at war with robbers roaming the streets and people won't help. Only the community in the poem survives because people work together.~~

As the authors of *Night*, "Civil Peace," and "The Gathering Place" show, a community can be a concentration camp, a former war zone, or a city neighborhood, but the people living there cannot thrive if they do not have one another's backs. The people in these communities have things in common, but they are not always united in a key goal: their collective survival. In *Night*, the men in the concentration camp all want to survive, but they are too hopeless and afraid to help one another. In "Civil Peace," the community is still at war in peacetime as robbers roam the streets and neighbors and police will not help. However, the community in "The Gathering Place" is successful because people do work together to fight for justice. When individuals share a common goal and are able to work together, they keep the community alive even under the worst circumstances.

**Skill: Transitions**

Theo's concluding paragraph is missing a transition that might better link it to the body paragraph that precedes it. The transition he adds—"As the authors of *Night*, 'Civil Peace,' and 'The Gathering Place' show"—smooths out a logical progression of his argument and helps to clarify the relationships among texts and ideas.

**Skill: Conclusions**

Theo revises his conclusion by adding an observation about what a community is, and this observation connects to his original thesis as well as the texts he used as sources. He supports his observation by summing up the key points from his essay. He moves the restatement of his thesis to the last sentence in the paragraph, reinforcing his main message.

# Skill:
# Introductions

## ••• CHECKLIST FOR INTRODUCTIONS

Before you write your introduction, ask yourself the following questions:

• What is my claim? Have I recognized opposing claims that disagree with mine or use a different perspective? How can I use them to make my own claim more precise?

• How can I introduce my topic? How have I organized complex ideas, concepts, and information to make important connections and distinctions?

• How will I "hook" my reader's interest? I might:

  > start with an attention-grabbing statement

  > begin with an intriguing question

  > use descriptive words to set a scene

Below are two strategies to help you introduce your precise claim and topic clearly in an introduction:

• Peer Discussion

  > Talk about your topic with a partner, explaining what you already know and your ideas about your topic.

  > Write notes about the ideas you have discussed and any new questions you may have.

  > Review your notes and think about what will be your claim or controlling idea.

  > Briefly state your precise claim or thesis, establishing how it is different from other claims about your topic.

  > Write a possible "hook."

• Freewriting

  > Freewrite for 10 minutes about your topic. Don't worry about grammar, punctuation, or having fully formed ideas. The point of freewriting is to discover ideas.

  > Review your notes and think about what will be your claim or thesis.

  > Briefly state your precise claim or thesis, establishing how it is different from other claims about your topic.

  > Write a possible "hook."

**YOUR TURN**

Choose the best answer to each question.

1. Below is Theo's introduction from a previous draft. The meaning of the underlined sentence is unclear. How can he rewrite the underlined sentence to make his idea clearer?

> When a community faces challenges, people try to keep going. If enough people work together on a common goal, they can keep the community alive. The people in the communities in *Night*, "Civil Peace" and "The Gathering Place" are doing their best to stay alive during and after war and to fight injustices. <u>Survival won't happen if they don't work together</u>.

○ A. A community is a real place but also a concept that depends on its people.

○ B. Each community is like a drowning person, and it is saved only when people throw it a line.

○ C. The survival of each community happens only when they rally around a common cause.

○ D. Each community's survival depends on its members' shared common goals.,

2. The following introduction is from a previous draft of Theo's essay. Theo would like to add a hook to catch his audience's attention. Which sentence could he add before the first sentence to help achieve this goal?

> When a community faces challenges, people try to keep going. If enough people work together, they can keep the community alive. There is a kind of community in each of the selections: "The Gathering Place," *Night*, and "Civil Peace." In each comunity a few people do the best they can. Their goal is to survive. They want their community to survive too. But that won't happen if they don't work together.

○ A. The soul of a community is the struggle of its people to survive.

○ B. A community can take many forms depending on its organization.

○ C. A hurricane can challenge any community, no matter how well organized.

○ D. Which communities do you belong to? Can they survive?

 **WRITE**

Use the questions in the checklist to revise the introduction of your informative essay to meet the needs of the purpose, audience, topic, and context.

# Skill:
# Transitions

Copyright © Bookheaded Learning, LLC

## ••• CHECKLIST FOR TRANSITIONS

Before you revise your current draft to include transitions, think about:

- the key ideas you discuss
- the major sections of your essay
- the organizational structure of your essay
- the relationships among complex ideas and concepts

Next, reread your current draft and note areas in your essay where:

- the organizational structure is not yet apparent

  > For example, if you are comparing and contrasting two texts, your explanations about how two texts are similar and different should be clearly stated

- the relationship between ideas from one paragraph to the next is unclear

  > For example, describing a process in sequential order should clarify the order of steps using transitional words like *first, then, next,* and *finally*

- your ideas are not creating cohesion, or uniting together as a whole
- your transition is inappropriate or too similar to other transitions

Revise your draft to use appropriate and varied transitions to link the major sections of your essay, create cohesion, and clarify the relationships among complex ideas and concepts, using the following questions as a guide:

- What kind of transitions should I use to make the organizational structure clear to readers?
- Are my transitions linking the major sections of my essay?
- What transitions create cohesion, or a united whole, among complex ideas and concepts?
- Are my transitions varied and appropriate?

## ♻ YOUR TURN

Choose the best answer to each question.

1. Below is a body paragraph from a previous draft of Theo's informative essay. Theo has not included an effective topic sentence. Which of the following could replace the underlined sentence in this body paragraph and provide the most effective transition to the ideas that follow?

> As in *Night*, the community in Chinua Achebe's story "Civil Peace" has been through a terrible war, but now people must figure out how to live in peacetime. <u>Wiesel and Achebe both write about surviving a war and then worry how they will survive the peace that follows</u>. The main character, Jonathan Iwegbu, considers himself "extraordinarily lucky" for the following reason: he has survived with "his head, his wife Maria's head and the heads of three out of their four children." With these "blessings" and the "miracle" of his bicycle, Jonathan is eager to start life over. Still, there are problems in the community. When robbers threaten to kill Jonathan and his family, the police don't help and neither do Jonathan's neighbors. The neighbors only "assembled to commiserate" in the morning, when it was safe. Despite this, Jonathan maintains a positive attitude. Jonathan knows that possessions and money do not last, saying the money counted "as nothing." Yet he might also suspect that the community cannot survive if people do not help out one another in times of danger. He will get by because of God's "blessings" and because he is willing to work hard, but not because his community is willing to help one another.

- ○ A. While Wiesel went through a real war, Achebe is only writing about a fictional war.
- ○ B. While Wiesel discusses how prisoners stuck together in bad times, Achebe believes that he doesn't need his neighbors to survive.
- ○ C. While Wiesel shows how prisoners fail to survive a death camp, Achebe emphasizes how the war makes people survive.
- ○ D. While Wiesel shows the need for community through a real-life war experience, Achebe's fictional situation still feels very real.

Please note that excerpts and passages in the StudySync® library and this workbook are intended as touchstones to generate interest in an author's work. The excerpts and passages do not substitute for the reading of entire texts, and StudySync® strongly recommends that students seek out and purchase the whole literary or informational work in order to experience it as the author intended. Links to online resellers are available in our digital library. In addition, complete works may be ordered through an authorized reseller by filling out and returning to StudySync® the order form enclosed in this workbook.

Reading & Writing
Companion

**289**

2. Below is a body paragraph from a previous draft of Theo's informative essay. Theo would like to add a transition word or phrase to help readers move from sentence 4 to sentence 5. Which of these is the most effective transition to add to the beginning of sentence 5?

> (1) In the memoir *Night*, Elie Wiesel describes how his community and his family were destroyed by hate and hopelessness during World War II. (2) He, his family, and his community were arrested and sent to concentration camps because they were Jewish. (3) In these camps, the prisoners form a new community, and the goal of each person is no doubt to survive. (4) When a weeping friend appears, Weisel thinks the man is crying with joy to be alive. (5) The friend explains that he is crying because "we're on the threshold of death." (6) The man's hopelessness causes Wiesel to stop thinking as an individual. (7) He describes the community's shock and pain: "We were incapable of thinking. . . . We no longer clung to anything." (8) The hope of survival is fading. . . .

- ○ A. Nevertheless,
- ○ B. Instead,
- ○ C. In addition,
- ○ D. At first

## ✏ WRITE

Use the questions in the checklist to revise one paragraph of your informative essay draft to include stronger transitions between ideas and sentences. Underline each of the transitions you add.

# Skill:
# Precise Language

## ••• CHECKLIST FOR PRECISE LANGUAGE

As you consider precise language and domain-specific vocabulary related to a complicated subject or topic, use the following questions as a guide:

- What information am I trying to convey or explain to my audience?

- What key concepts need to be explained or understood?

- Have I determined the complexity of the subject matter and whether any ideas, words, or domain-specific vocabulary need additional explanation?

- How can I use more specific, precise vocabulary in my explanation for greater accuracy?

- What can I refine or revise in my word choice to enhance meaning and clarify understanding of my topic's complex ideas, concepts, and information?

Here are some suggestions that will help guide you in using precise language and domain-specific vocabulary to manage the complexity of the topic:

- determine the topic or area of study you will be writing about

- determine the complexity of the subject matter and whether any words or domain-specific vocabulary need additional explanation in order to manage the difficulty of the topic

- substitute vague, general, or overused words and phrases with more precise, descriptive, and domain-specific language

**YOUR TURN**

Read the precise words, from Elie Wiesel's *Night*, below. Then, complete the chart by matching each precise word with its vague and imprecise word to demonstrate your understanding of how to use precise language, instead of vague terms.

| Precise Word Options | | | | |
|---|---|---|---|---|
| **A** | disinfection | **F** | SS officers | |
| **B** | Talmud | **G** | colossus | |
| **C** | clutches | **H** | threshold | |
| **D** | Kapos | **I** | glacial | |
| **E** | barrack | **J** | oblivion | |

| Vague or Imprecise Word | Precise Word |
|---|---|
| icy | |
| hands | |
| giant | |
| cleaning | |
| edge | |
| ending | |
| guards | |
| building | |
| holy books | |
| secret police | |

YOUR TURN

Complete the chart below by writing your own precise words to replace the vague or imprecise language.

| Vague or Imprecise Language | Precise Language |
| --- | --- |
| interesting buildings | |
| movement from an earthquake | |
| a big group of people | |
| a loud noise | |
| sad faces | |

# Skill:
# Conclusions

## ••• CHECKLIST FOR CONCLUSIONS

Before you write your conclusion, ask yourself the following questions:

- How can I restate the thesis or main idea?
- How will my conclusion support and follow from the information I presented?
- How can I communicate the importance of my topic? What information do I need?

Below are two strategies to help you provide a concluding statement or section that follows from and supports the information or explanation presented:

- Peer Discussion
  - > after you have written the introduction and body paragraphs, talk with a partner about what you want readers to remember; take notes
  - > think about how you can articulate, or express, the significance of your topic in the conclusion
    - o restate any ideas from people who are experts on your topic
    - o note possible implications if something is done or is not accomplished
  - > rephrase your main idea to show the depth of your knowledge and support for the information you presented
  - > write your conclusion

- Freewriting
  - > freewrite for 10 minutes about what you might include in your conclusion, without worrying about grammar or mechanics
  - > think about how you can articulate, or express, the significance of your topic in the conclusion
    - o restate any ideas from experts on your topic
    - o note possible implications if something is done or is not accomplished
  - > rephrase your main idea to show depth of knowledge and support for information you presented
  - > write your conclusion

## ⟳ YOUR TURN

Choose the best answer to each question.

1. Below is Theo's conclusion from an early draft. What is one obvious omission that Theo needs to include as he continues to revise?

> The people in the selections *Night*, "Civil Peace," and "The Gathering Place" want their community to survive but that can't happen if they don't work together and they mostly don't share the same goals. The community in "Civil Peace" is still at war with robbers roaming the streets and people won't help. Only the community in the poem survives because people work together.

   ○ A. Theo neglects to discuss community, which is part of his thesis.
   ○ B. Theo discusses only one of the texts, "Civil Peace," rather than all three.
   ○ C. Theo needs to discuss other texts outside of the three mentioned in his topic sentence.
   ○ D. Theo neglects to mention the community in *Night*.

2. The following conclusion is from a previous draft of Theo's essay. Theo would like to add a thought-provoking quote to leave his audience with a lasting impression. Which sentence could he add after the last sentence to help achieve this goal?

> The texts show that a community's success depends on its members working toward a common goal. The communities in *Night*, "Civil Peace," and "A Gathering Place" have mixed success. The prisoners are too helpless to work toward a common goal. The community in "Civil Peace" is basically still at war. Only the community in "A Gathering Place" thrives because its members work together to fight for common goals.

   ○ A. The texts truly show that when individuals in a community work together, they can "build a summit worth climbing."
   ○ B. The texts truly show that "nothing puzzles God."
   ○ C. The texts truly show what happens when "the instincts of self-preservation, of self-defense, of pride" desert us.
   ○ D. The texts truly show that there is no excuse for not cooperating.

## ✎ WRITE

Use the questions in the checklist to revise the conclusion of your informative essay to meet the needs of the purpose, audience, topic, and context.

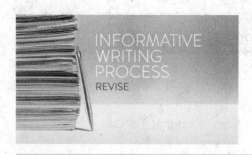

# Informative Writing Process: Revise

| PLAN | DRAFT | REVISE | EDIT AND PUBLISH |
|---|---|---|---|

You have written a draft of your informative essay. You have also received input from your peers about how to improve it. Now you are going to revise your draft.

## ◀◀ REVISION GUIDE

Examine your draft to find areas for revision. Keep in mind your purpose and audience as you revise for clarity, development, organization, and style. Use the guide below to help you review:

| Review | Revise | Example |
|---|---|---|
| **Clarity** | | |
| Highlight any place in your essay where irrelevant information or sentence structure hinders clarity. | Remove irrelevant information from sentences. | Wiesel lived through the ~~really terrible and frightening experience of~~ war to tell this story ~~and to speak as an individual for his lost communities.~~ |
| **Development** | | |
| Identify places where you need details in support of your thesis. Think of details, examples, and quotations from the text you could incorporate to add support, along with your own commentary. | Focus on a single idea and add details, examples, or quotations from the text, as well as original commentary, to better develop your idea. | Despite this, Jonathan maintains a positive attitude. Jonathan knows that possessions and money do not last, saying the money counted "as nothing." Yet he might also suspect that the community can't survive if people don't help out one another in times of danger. |

| Review | Revise | Example |
|---|---|---|
| **Organization** | | |
| Review whether your text structure supports your purpose. Annotate places where the organization can be improved. | Rewrite by adding a transition between paragraphs to make the text structure clearer to readers. | Like the setting in "Civil Peace," the ~~The~~ urban comunity in "The Gathering Place" by Amanda Gorman faces a lot of challenges. |
| **Style: Word Choice** | | |
| Look for opportunities to replace casual or everyday language with academic vocabulary. | Select sentences to rewrite using academic vocabulary. | Each person has ~~given back to help make~~ contributed to making the community safe and strong by speaking out or building something. As a result, the ~~The person speaking in the poem says~~ speaker declares that "we are hope, we are home . . . we be united, we be good." |
| **Style: Sentence Effectiveness** | | |
| Review your essay for choppy sentences. Create compound sentences by joining main clauses with a comma and a coordinating conjunction. Create complex sentences by combining subordinating clauses and main clauses. | Rewrite choppy sentences to form compound or complex sentences by moving a phrase or clause and using coordinating and subordinating conjunctions. | With these ~~Jonathan has~~ "blessings" and the "miracle" of his bicycle~~.~~, Jonathan is eager to start life over. Still, there ~~There~~ are problems in the community. Money is scarce~~.~~, and people ~~People~~ get robbed. When robbers ~~Robbers~~ threaten to kill Jonathan and his family~~.~~, the ~~The~~ police don't help, and neither do Jonathan's neighbors. |

## ✏ WRITE

Use the guide above, as well as your peer reviews, to help you evaluate your informative essay to determine areas that should be revised.

# Skill:
# Style

## ••• CHECKLIST FOR STYLE

First, reread the draft of your informative essay and identify the following:

- slang, colloquialisms, contractions, abbreviations, or a conversational tone
- areas where you could use subject-specific or academic language in order to help persuade or inform your readers
- the use of first person (*I*) or second person (*you*)
- areas where you could vary sentence structure and length, emphasizing compound, complex, and compound-complex sentences
- statements that express judgment or emotion, rather than an objective tone that relies on facts and evidence
- incorrect uses of the conventions of standard English for grammar, spelling, capitalization, and punctuation

Establish and maintain a formal style in your essay, using the following questions as a guide:

- Have I avoided slang in favor of academic language?
- Did I consistently used a third-person perspective, using third-person pronouns (*he, she, they*)?
- Have I maintained an objective tone without expressing my own judgments and emotions?
- Have I used varied sentence lengths and different sentence structures?
  - > Where should I make some sentences longer by using conjunctions to connect independent clauses, dependent clauses, and phrases?
  - > Where should I make some sentences shorter by separating independent clauses?
- Did I follow the conventions of standard English?

## YOUR TURN

Choose the best answer to each question.

1. Below is a section from a previous draft of Theo's essay. The underlined sentence lacks a formal style. What changes should Theo make to improve the formal style of the sentence?

> The neighbors only "assembled to commiserate" in the morning, when it was safe. Jonathan maintains a positive attitude. <u>Yet he might also suspect that the community can't survive if people don't help out one another in times of danger.</u> He will get by because of God's "blessings" and because he is willing to work hard, not because his community is willing to help one another.

- ○ A. Change *might* to *will*
- ○ B. Change *can't* and *don't* to *cannot* and *do not*
- ○ C. Change *people* to *community*
- ○ D. Change *help out* to *help*

2. Theo wants to make sure his essay has an objective tone. How can he best revise the underlined sentence to make it more objective?

> Like the setting in "Civil Peace," the urban community in "The Gathering Place" by poet Amanda Gorman faces many challenges, but it is strong thanks to the common goals and good work of its members. I can relate to the poem's powerful speaker refers to her community on "the corner of East 92nd and Lexington" as "our great gathering place" (lines 1, 4). <u>The awesome speaker never refers to herself using the pronoun I; she speaks of "we."</u>

- ○ A. The awesome speaker never refers to herself in the first person.
- ○ B. The awesome speaker refers to herself using the pronoun "we."
- ○ C. The awesome speaker never refers to herself.
- ○ D. The speaker never refers to herself using the pronoun *I*; she speaks of "we."

## ↻ YOUR TURN

Complete the chart by revising the sentences below to achieve a more formal style and objective tone.

| Sentence | Revision |
|---|---|
| Although I really liked the story, the characters made decisions that hurt others. | |
| The coolest lesson from the article was that money alone can't make a difference without leaders who know what to do with it and where it can go. | |
| Nobody's perfect, sure, but this story shows that if you don't at least try to learn from your mistakes, what's the point? | |

# Grammar: Parallel Structure

Lists usually have a parallel structure to make them easy to remember and to show that all the listed items have equal weight. Parallel structures in sentences are like lists. They create a pattern among ideas of equal weight. Sentences that could have parallel structures but don't may sound awkward or confusing.

| Not Parallel | Parallel |
|---|---|
| Marjorie is intelligent, capable, and **she has good sense**. | Marjorie is intelligent, capable, and **sensible**. |
| Gorillas have a mostly vegetarian diet, **so they eat fruit**, **the leaves**, **seeds**, and **also the** stems of a variety of plants, also consuming some termites and caterpillars. | Gorillas have a mostly vegetarian diet, **eating** the **fruit**, **leaves**, **seeds**, and **stems** of a variety of plants **and consuming** some **insects**, **such as** termites and caterpillars. |

Some sentences can have more than one parallel structure, such as parallel verbs and parallel direct objects. Parallelism can be employed as a rhetorical device to emphasize ideas, establish rhythm, and make a text or speech more memorable.

| Text | Explanation |
|---|---|
| There will be **more shuttle flights** and **more shuttle crews** and, yes, **more volunteers**, **more civilians**, **more teachers** in space.<br><br>Address to the Nation on the Explosion of the Space Shuttle Challenger by Ronald Reagan | The predicate nominatives all begin with the word *more*, which gives them parallel structure. Repetition of this word emphasizes its positive connotations. |
| As part of an exchange program, we now have an exhibition touring your country that shows how information technology is **transforming** our lives — **replacing** manual labor with robots, **forecasting** weather for farmers, or **mapping** the genetic code of DNA for medical researchers.<br><br>Address to Students at Moscow State University by Ronald Reagan | The series of present participles, *transforming*, *replacing*, *forecasting*, and *mapping*, establishes parallel structure in this sentence. |

Please note that excerpts and passages in the StudySync® library and this workbook are intended as touchstones to generate interest in an author's work. The excerpts and passages do not substitute for the reading of entire texts, and StudySync® strongly recommends that students seek out and purchase the whole literary or informational work in order to experience it as the author intended. Links to online resellers are available in our digital library. In addition, complete works may be ordered through an authorized reseller by filling out and returning to StudySync® the order form enclosed in this workbook.

Reading & Writing Companion    301

## ↻ YOUR TURN

1. How should this sentence be changed?

> Carla spent the whole morning in her grandparents' attic looking through trunks of old clothes, cartons of fading photographs, and boxes of cassette tapes.

- ○ A. Insert **old** before cassette tapes.
- ○ B. Add **through** before boxes.
- ○ C. Delete **in her grandparents' attic**.
- ○ D. No change needs to be made to this sentence.

2. How should this sentence be changed?

> Students in the after-school program can play sports, homework, or do arts and crafts.

- ○ A. Delete **do**.
- ○ B. Replace **play** with **do**.
- ○ C. Insert **finish** before **homework**.
- ○ D. No change needs to be made to this sentence.

3. How should this sentence be changed?

> To be considered exemplary, students need to arrive on time, hand in their assignments when they are due, and reporting bullying and other inappropriate behavior among their peers.

- ○ A. Insert **and** after **time**.
- ○ B. Change **hand** to **handing**.
- ○ C. Change **reporting** to **report**.
- ○ D. No change needs to be made to this sentence.

4. How should this sentence be changed?

> On his first day of school, Lester wore a flannel shirt, black jeans, sneakers, and his new binder.

- ○ A. Insert **carried** after **and**.
- ○ B. Delete **On his first day of school**.
- ○ C. Change **and** to **with**.
- ○ D. No change needs to be made to this sentence.

# Grammar: Prepositions and Prepositional Phrases

## Preposition

A preposition is a word that connects a noun or a pronoun to another word in a sentence. A compound preposition consists of more than one word.

| Common Prepositions | | | | | |
|---|---|---|---|---|---|
| above | at | by | in | outside | toward |
| across | before | down | inside | over | under |
| after | below | during | like | since | until |
| against | beside | except | of | through | up |
| along | between | excepting | on | throughout | with |
| around | but (except) | from | out | to | within |

| Compound Prepositions | | | | | |
|---|---|---|---|---|---|
| according to | apart from | because of | in addition | in front of | on account |
| ahead of | as to | by means of | to | instead of | of |

Prepositions often act like adjectives or adverbs, showing *which, when, where,* or *how* something is.

| Text | Explanation |
|---|---|
| Henry Avenue curved **around** the perimeter **of** a low bluff overlooking the Aberjona marsh.<br><br>A Civil Action | The preposition **around** tells *where* Henry Avenue curved. It connects *perimeter* and *curved*. The preposition **of** tells *which* perimeter. It connects *low bluff* and *perimeter*. |

## Prepositional Phrase

A prepositional phrase is a group of words that begins with a preposition and ends with a noun or pronoun, which is called the object of the preposition. The phrases *to the game, for my aunt and uncle,* and *according to scientists* are examples of prepositional phrases. Sentences can have more than one prepositional phrase.

## ↻ YOUR TURN

1. Which word should fill the blank in this sentence?

> Although he was also an actor, Shakespeare rose _____ fame as a playwright.

○ A.  in

○ B.  to

○ C.  after

○ D.  None of the above.

2. Which word should fill the blank in this sentence?

> Shakespeare's theater, the Globe Theater, was a multileveled space, and many audience members stood _____ the stage to watch the plays.

○ A.  in front of

○ B.  afterward

○ C.  on account of

○ D.  None of the above.

3. How should this sentence be changed?

> Shakespeare's audience did not sit quietly to watch plays and would even throw food toward the stage since the actors if they did not like the play.

○ A.  Insert the pronoun **they** after the preposition **toward**.

○ B.  Replace the preposition **since** with the preposition **at**.

○ C.  Insert the noun **people** after the preposition **to**.

○ D.  No change needs to be made to this sentence.

4. How should this sentence be changed?

> Unlike contemporary theaters, where the same show can run for many years, productions in Shakespeare's day lasted a short time before they were replaced.

○ A.  Replace the preposition **for** with the preposition **across**.

○ B.  Insert the noun **plays** after the preposition **before**.

○ C.  Insert the pronoun **it** after the preposition **in**.

○ D.  No change needs to be made to this sentence.

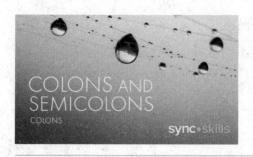

# Grammar: Colons

Colons [:] have several uses. Follow these rules when using a colon:

| Rule | Text |
|---|---|
| Use a colon to introduce a list, especially after a statement that uses words such as *these*, *the following*, or *as follows*. | We mourn seven heroes: Michael Smith, Dick Scobee, Judith Resnik, Ronald McNair, Ellison Onizuka, Gregory Jarvis, and Christa McAuliffe.<br><br>Address to the Nation on the Explosion of the Space Shuttle *Challenger* |
| Use a colon to introduce material that illustrates, explains, or restates the preceding material. The complete sentence after the colon is generally lowercase. | "And that's why people jump higher when they have a drop step or a few steps: they use the velocity of the descent toward the ground to compress the tendon, just like a spring."<br><br>The Sports Gene |
| Use a colon between the hour and minute of the precise time. | A Back Alley - 11:00 p.m.<br>(Maria appears at the window above him which opens onto the escape.)<br><br>*West Side Story* |

Do **not** use a colon to introduce a list if the list immediately follows a verb or a preposition.

| Text | Incorrect |
|---|---|
| The meal includes salad, soup, a main course, and dessert. | The meal includes: salad, soup, a main course, and dessert. |
| I went to the movie with Carmen, Celeste, and Carol. | I went to the movie with: Carmen, Celeste, and Carol. |

## ↻ YOUR TURN

1.  Where should a colon be added to correct the sentence?

    > William found this quotation to write as the conclusion to his essay on bravery "Behold the Turtle. He makes progress only when he sticks his neck out."

    - ○ A. after the word *quotation*
    - ○ B. after the word *essay*
    - ○ C. after the word *bravery*
    - ○ D. No change needs to be made to this sentence.

2.  Where should a colon be added to correct the sentence?

    > The weight of our problems lay before us we couldn't go backward and the unknown was ahead.

    - ○ A. after the word *us*
    - ○ B. after the word *couldn't*
    - ○ C. after the word *backward*
    - ○ D. No change needs to be made to this sentence.

3.  Where should a colon be added to correct the sentence?

    > "Don't forget to stop by the store and buy a jar of pickles, some ketchup, and mayonnaise for the picnic," said Mother.

    - ○ A. after the word *forget*
    - ○ B. after the word *buy*
    - ○ C. after the word *picnic*
    - ○ D. No change needs to be made to this sentence.

4.  Where should a colon be added to correct the sentence?

    > Ann added the following items to her notepad a toothbrush, toothpaste, shampoo, soap, deodorant, a comb, and a brush.

    - ○ A. after the word *following*
    - ○ B. after the word *items*
    - ○ C. after the word *notepad*
    - ○ D. No change needs to be made to this sentence.

# Informative Writing Process: Edit and Publish

| PLAN | DRAFT | REVISE | EDIT AND PUBLISH |
|------|-------|--------|------------------|

You have revised your informative essay based on your peer feedback and your own examination.

Now, it is time to edit your informative essay. When you revised, you focused on the content of your informative essay. You probably looked at your essay's supporting details, its introduction and conclusion, and your use of precise language. When you edit, you focus on the mechanics of your informative essay, paying close attention to elements such as grammar, punctuation, and style.

## Use the checklist below to guide you as you edit:

☐ Have I checked for errors in parallel structure in my essay?

☐ Have I used colons correctly in my essay?

☐ Have I used prepositional phrases correctly to create transitions and add variety?

☐ Have I used formal style throughout the essay?

☐ Do I have any sentence fragments or run-on sentences?

☐ Have I spelled everything correctly?

## Notice some edits Theo has made:

- Created parallel structure by placing the settings in the same order as the selections.

- Eliminated contractions to maintain a formal style.

- Changed a sentence to include a colon that emphasizes a main idea.

- Moved a prepositional phrase to create a stronger transition.

- Corrected his spelling after his spellchecker flagged some misspelled words.

As the authors of *Night*, "Civil Peace," and "The Gathering Place" show, a community can be ~~a city neighborhood, a concentration camp, or a former war zone~~ **a concentration camp, a former war zone, or a city neighborhood**, but the ~~peple~~ **people** living there ~~can't~~ **cannot** thrive if they ~~don't~~ **do not** have one another's backs. The people in these communities have things in common, but they are not always united in ~~their goals~~ **a key goal: their collective survival**. In *Night*, the men in the ~~concentration~~ **concentration** camp all want to survive, but they are too hopeless and afraid to help one another. **In "Civil Peace,"** the community ~~in "Civil Peace"~~ is still at war in peacetime as robbers roam the streets and neighbors and police ~~won't~~ **will not** help.

---

# ✏ WRITE

Use the questions above, as well as your peer reviews, to help you evaluate your informative essay to determine areas that need editing. Then edit your informative essay to correct those errors.

Once you have made all your corrections, you are ready to publish your work. You can distribute your writing to family and friends, hang it on a bulletin board, or post it on your blog. If you publish online, share the link with your family, friends, and classmates.

# The Peasant Revolt

INFORMATIONAL TEXT

## Introduction

Many hardships and burdens had been placed on the French peasants in the late 1700s. How did they respond? What did they do to show their discontent?

##  VOCABULARY

**extravagant**

extremely high in cost, very lavish

**stormed**

attacked and captured suddenly and without warning

**endure**

suffer pain or difficulty over a period of time

**deeds**

signed, legal documents

**suppressed**

put down or ended something, often by force

NOTES

## ≡ READ

1 The population of France at the beginning of the eighteenth century was more than twenty million people. The majority, about eighty percent, was concentrated in rural areas, villages, and very small cities.

2 People who owned bits of land and people who worked in the countryside were known as peasants. There were many levels of peasants, which differed dramatically in status and wealth. Peasants who were in the best position rented land to others and lived off the profits. On the opposite end were desperate day workers looking only for enough food and a place to rest. In the middle were independent farmers, renters, and sharecroppers. In years with poor harvests, ninety percent of the peasants barely had enough to feed their families.

3 Another group living in the countryside was the nobles and non-nobles who owned **extravagant** manor houses. They lived off the work of the peasants. The stark contrast between the peasant group and the nobles and non-nobles group was one of the factors leading to the French Revolution.

4   Year after year the peasants had grown poorer. Droughts caused catastrophe and famine. Peasants had no voice in government. They **endured** great hardships and endless inequalities like paying heavy taxes. They were required to pay a land tax and a poll tax to the State. The lord of the manor demanded rents and contributions. The clergy collected tithes, or a percentage of income and harvest. The government, deeply in debt, also taxed essential items like salt. Furthermore, peasants were the only class that could be forced into military service. Understandably, the peasants felt intense anger. They resented those who **suppressed** them and endangered their families.

5   Then the riots began. On July 14, 1789, the citizens of Paris, terrified that troops of King Louis XVI might attack them, **stormed** the Bastille, a fortress in the city. More than 100 people died. People in the countryside heard the news. Rumors spread like wildfire. The peasants, hearing of the capture of the Bastille, decided that social change just might be possible. A small flame of hope was ignited.

6   Peasants also heard stories of troops gathering with the blessings of King Louis XVI. The troops would be sent to the countryside to kill peasants and stop rebellions. Something called the "Great Fear" mobilized the countryside and destroyed many lives.

7   Mass hysteria, fed by wild rumors, spread across rural France. Peasants believed in an "aristocratic conspiracy." That is, frightened nobles would hire armed men, or "brigands," to burn crops, steal food, and attack the villages. Peasants feared that their homes would be burned. They would lose what little they had. Misinformation flowed across the countryside like water after a heavy storm. No one bothered to verify the rumors. They all seemed possible and probably true.

8   Peasants formed armed groups to defend their fields and their homes. They were driven by fear. Terrified peasants began attacking manors. They burned grain, looted manors, and leveled walls that separated them from the lord. Most importantly, they found and destroyed **deeds** that dictated the dues peasants had to pay the lord. Peasants loathed paying the dues demanded by the lord. They no longer wanted to live on the edge of potential starvation. They despised the class system that made them the lowest of the low. They wanted the manor system destroyed.

9   George Lefebvre, noted French historian, commented that the uprising in Paris and the threat of brigands was magnified because it was harvest time. No one had any doubt that the aristocrats were paying the brigands. Was that a fact? Probably not, but the rebellion continued and eventually ended the reign of the monarchy in France.

# First Read

Read the text. After you read, complete the Think Questions below.

## ☁ THINK QUESTIONS

1. What was life like for most peasants in France during the 1700s?

   Most peasants were _____

   _____.

2. When did the citizens of Paris storm the Bastille?

   They stormed the Bastille on _____.

3. What was the "Great Fear"? Include a line from the text to support your response.

   The "Great Fear" was _____

   _____.

4. Use context to confirm the meaning of the word *deeds* as it is used in "The Peasant Revolt." Write your definition of *deeds* here.

   *Deeds* means _____.

   A context clue is _____.

5. If soldiers *stormed* a city, what did they do?

   The soldiers _____.

# Skill: Analyzing Expressions

## ★ DEFINE

When you read, you may find English expressions that you do not know. An **expression** is a group of words that communicates an idea. Three types of expressions are idioms, sayings, and figurative language. They can be difficult to understand because the meanings of the words are different from their **literal**, or usual, meanings.

An **idiom** is an expression that is commonly known among a group of people. For example, "It's raining cats and dogs" means it is raining heavily. **Sayings** are short expressions that contain advice or wisdom. For instance, "Don't count your chickens before they hatch" means do not plan on something good happening before it happens. **Figurative** language is when you describe something by comparing it with something else, either directly (using the words *like* or *as*) or indirectly. For example, "I'm as hungry as a horse" means I'm very hungry. None of the expressions are about actual animals.

## ••• CHECKLIST FOR ANALYZING EXPRESSIONS

To determine the meaning of an expression, remember the following:

✓ If you find a confusing group of words, it may be an expression. The meaning of words in expressions may not be their literal meaning.

- Ask yourself: Is this confusing because the words are new? Or because the words do not make sense together?

✓ Determining the overall meaning may require that you use one or more of the following:

- context clues
- a dictionary or other resource
- teacher or peer support

✓ Highlight important information before and after the expression to look for clues.

**YOUR TURN**

Read the following excerpt from "The Peasant Revolt." Then complete the multiple-choice questions below.

---

from **"The Peasant Revolt"**

Mass hysteria, fed by wild rumors, spread across rural France. Peasants believed in an "aristocratic conspiracy." That is, frightened nobles would hire armed men, or "brigands," to burn crops, steal food, and attack the villages. Peasants feared that their homes would be burned. They would lose what little they had. Misinformation flowed across the countryside like water after a heavy storm. No one bothered to verify the rumors. They all seemed possible and probably true.

---

1. Which sentence contains figurative language?
   - ○ A. "Mass hysteria, fed by wild rumors, spread across rural France."
   - ○ B. "Peasants believed in an 'aristocratic conspiracy.'"
   - ○ C. "Peasants feared that their homes would be burned."
   - ○ D. "They would lose what little they had."

2. Which sentence contains figurative language?
   - ○ A. "Misinformation flowed across the countryside like water after a heavy storm."
   - ○ B. "No one bothered to verify the rumors."
   - ○ C. "They all seemed possible and probably true."
   - ○ D. All of these sentences contain figurative language.

3. What two things does the author compare in this sentence? *Misinformation flowed across the countryside like water after a heavy storm.*
   - ○ A. The author compares misinformation to a storm.
   - ○ B. The author compares misinformation to water.
   - ○ C. The author compares the countryside to a storm.
   - ○ D. The author compares the countryside to water.

4. In what way are the two things alike in this sentence? *Misinformation flowed across the countryside like water after a heavy storm.*

   ○ A. Both are moving quickly.

   ○ B. Both can get very deep.

   ○ C. Both dampen the earth.

   ○ D. Both allow things to grow.

5. How could you restate the literal language as figurative language in the following sentence? *No one bothered to verify the rumors.*

   ○ A. No one bothered to check the rumors.

   ○ B. No one bothered to verify the rumors. Like many rumors, they may or may not have been true.

   ○ C. No one bothered to verify the rumors, but they believed the rumors as if they were true.

   ○ D. Like a game of telephone, rumors may have changed as they passed from person to person.

# Skill: Sharing Information

## ★ DEFINE

**Sharing** information involves asking for and giving information. The process of sharing information with other students can help all students learn more and better understand a text or a topic. You can share information when you participate in **brief** discussions or **extended** speaking assignments.

## ••• CHECKLIST FOR SHARING INFORMATION

When you have to speak for an extended period of time, as in a discussion, you ask for and share information. To ask for and share information, you may use the following sentence frames:

✓ To ask for information:

- What do you think about _____?

- Do you agree that _____?

- What is your understanding of _____?

✓ To give information:

- I think _____.

- I agree because _____.

- My understanding is _____.

## ⟳ YOUR TURN

Watch the "Civil Peace" StudySyncTV episode. After watching, sort the following statements from the episode into the chart below.

| | Statements |
|---|---|
| A | Jonathan tells the thieves that the only money he has is a twenty-pound egg-rasher. |
| B | Jonathan knows that he can control only his own attitude and actions. |
| C | Even if Jonathan is terrified, by the next day, he's made sense of it. |
| D | When Jonathan dug up his bicycle after the surrender, all it needed was a little palm-oil greasing. |
| E | Jonathan probably worried about whether the bicycle would still work. |
| F | Jonathan repeats the phrase, "Nothing puzzles God." |

| Information from "Civil Peace" | Shared Information |
|---|---|
| | |
| | |
| | |

Please note that excerpts and passages in the StudySync® library and this workbook are intended as touchstones to generate interest in an author's work. The excerpts and passages do not substitute for the reading of entire texts, and StudySync® strongly recommends that students seek out and purchase the whole literary or informational work in order to experience it as the author intended. Links to online resellers are available in our digital library. In addition, complete works may be ordered through an authorized reseller by filling out and returning to StudySync® the order form enclosed in this workbook.

Reading & Writing
Companion

317

# Close Read

---

## ✏ WRITE

INFORMATIONAL: In a paragraph, share the information you learned in "The Peasant Revolt" to explain the factors that contributed to the French Revolution. Why were the peasants resentful of their situation? What did they do about it? What was the result? Pay attention to and edit for subject-verb agreement.

**Use the checklist below to guide you as you write.**

☐ How did the peasants live?

☐ What did the nobles do?

☐ How did fear and rumors cause trouble?

**Use the sentence frames to organize and write your informational text.**

Before the Revolution began, the peasants felt _____.

They felt this way because _____.

In Paris, citizens _____. The peasants in the countryside _____.

They reacted by _____. They wanted to _____.

# Learning a Second Language: Is It Worth It?

ARGUMENTATIVE TEXT

## Introduction

Many students in America are getting the opportunity to learn a second language. Some might be learning Spanish, French, or even Chinese. Knowing a second language has its advantages, but there are some factors to consider before dedicating your time to becoming bilingual. This debate focuses on both the positives and negatives of learning a second language so you can decide what's the best option for you.

## V VOCABULARY

**opportunity**

a chance that makes
something possible

**bilingual**

being able to speak two
languages

**expand**

to become larger (physically) or
more developed (an idea)

**fluent**

being able to speak or write a
language well

**value**

the importance or worth of
something

NOTES

## ☰ READ

**Point: Learning a second language is valuable.**

1   When I was younger, I thought the moon was made out of cheese. In third grade, I learned the truth. Although I was disappointed at first, this information opened up many **opportunities** for me to learn. It **expanded** my mind and my world (actually, my universe).

2   When people are willing to open their minds to something new, there's no limit on its **value**. Learning a second language is the perfect example of this. Like learning about the moon, I think that learning a second language expands not only one's mind, but his or her world as well.

3   Learning a second language makes you smarter. Language learning exercises the muscles on the left side of your brain that are also used to solve math and other logical problems. Therefore, knowing more than one language helps your brain work better. Studies have shown that **bilingual** students score higher on state exams, too.

4   Knowing a language can take you somewhere new. You can meet new friends on the other side of the world. You might be able to watch movies and TV shows in a different language. Charlemagne said, "To know two languages is to possess a second soul." This means that knowing more than one language makes it easier to make connections to people from different cultures.

5   Lastly, learning a second language opens up doors for your future. This is especially true when it's time to find a job. Employers are more likely to hire bilingual people. People who know more than one language can communicate well, solve problems, and get along with many different people.

6   Learning a second language is very valuable. It's the best way to open up your universe. Once you learn a new language, it can take you beyond your greatest goals. Maybe it can even take you to the moon.

**Counterpoint: Learning a second language is not worth the time and money.**

7   There's a saying, "Time is money." There's nothing more valuable than time. You better make sure you're doing something worthwhile with your time. Learning a second language is not the best way to spend your time. Language learning isn't for everybody. Knowing more than one language can be valuable, but learning a new language is not worth the time and money.

8   Unless someone learns a second language as a child, it's a lot harder to actually become bilingual. Studies have shown that it's much more difficult for anyone over the age of five to learn a second language. It takes years of practice to be **fluent**, even if you study the language for many hours each day.

9   The time spent learning a second language might be better spent learning a different hobby or talent. These talents or hobbies can be useful when you get a job. For example, taking a debate class can help me become a lawyer. Taking choir lessons can help me become a singer. Someone might have a talent that is never used because of the time spent learning a language.

10  Lastly, taking language classes can cost a lot of money. Schools have budgets, or certain amounts of money, that they need to spend on courses. Instead of giving language classes a big portion of the money, schools should spend their money on other courses. Spending money on science, math, and reading would be money well-spent. If you wanted to learn a second language outside of school, you would have to pay for a tutor, books, and other materials. Some people choose to travel to another country to learn a second language. These trips can be very costly as well.

11  Learning a second language can be a great experience, but not if it takes time and money away from exploring other opportunities.

# First Read

Read "Learning a Second Language: Is It Worth It?" After you read, complete the Think Questions below.

## ☁ THINK QUESTIONS

1. What does the Point writer think about learning a second language?

   The Point writer thinks that _____

   _____ .

2. According to the Point writer, how does learning a second language take you somewhere new?

   You can meet _____

   You can watch _____

3. According to the Counterpoint writer, what do studies show about learning a second language? Include a line from the text to support your response.

   Studies show that learning a second language _____

   _____ .

4. Use context to confirm the meaning of the word *fluent* as it is used in "Learning a Second Language: Is It Worth It?" Write your definition of *fluent* here.

   *Fluent* means _____ .

   A context clue is _____

5. What is another way to say that an object has *value*?

   An object has value if it _____ .

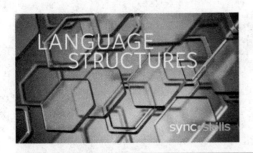

# Skill:
# Language Structures

## ★ DEFINE

In every language, there are rules that tell how to **structure** sentences. These rules define the correct order of words. In the English language, for example, a basic structure for sentences is subject, verb, and object. Some sentences have more complicated structures.

You will encounter both basic and complicated **language structures** in the classroom materials you read. Being familiar with language structures will help you better understand the text.

## ••• CHECKLIST FOR LANGUAGE STRUCTURES

To improve your comprehension of language structures, do the following:

✓ Monitor your understanding.

- Ask yourself: Why do I not understand this sentence? Is it because I do not understand some of the words? Or is it because I do not understand the way the words are ordered in the sentence?

✓ Break down the sentence into its parts.

- Pay attention to comparatives and superlatives. The **comparative** form compares two things. The **superlative** form compares more than two things.

- Ask yourself: Are there comparatives or superlatives in this sentence? What are they comparing?

✓ Confirm your understanding with a peer or teacher.

**YOUR TURN**

Complete the chart by writing the correct words into the "Comparative" and "Superlative" columns.

| Word Options | | | | |
|---|---|---|---|---|
| higher | worst | highest | kindest | more valuable |
| kinder | most valuable | most interesting | worse | more interesting |

| Adjective | Comparative | Superlative |
|---|---|---|
| kind | | |
| high | | |
| interesting | | |
| bad | | |
| valuable | | |

# Skill:
# Supporting Evidence

---

## ★ DEFINE

In some informational or argumentative texts, the author may share an opinion. This **opinion** may be the author's **claim** or **thesis**. The author must then provide readers with **evidence** that supports his or her opinion. Supporting evidence can be details, examples, or facts that agree with the author's claim or thesis.

Looking for supporting evidence can help you confirm your understanding of what you read. Finding and analyzing supporting evidence can also help you form your own opinions about the subject.

---

## ••• CHECKLIST FOR SUPPORTING EVIDENCE

In order to find and analyze supporting evidence, do the following:

✓ Identify the topic and the author's claim or thesis.

- Ask yourself: What is this mostly about? What is the author's opinion?

✓ Find details, facts, and examples that support the author's claim or thesis.

- Ask yourself: Is this detail important? How does this detail relate to the thesis or claim?

✓ Analyze the supporting evidence.

- Ask yourself: Is this evidence strong? Do I agree with the evidence?

Please note that excerpts and passages in the StudySync® library and this workbook are intended as touchstones to generate interest in an author's work. The excerpts and passages do not substitute for the reading of entire texts, and StudySync® strongly recommends that students seek out and purchase the whole literary or informational work in order to experience it as the author intended. Links to online resellers are available in our digital library. In addition, complete works may be ordered through an authorized reseller by filling out and returning to StudySync® the order form enclosed in this workbook.

Reading & Writing
Companion

325

**YOUR TURN**

Read paragraphs 7–9 from "Learning a Second Language;" Is It Worth It? Then complete the multiple-choice questions below.

---

from **"Learning a Second Language: Is It Worth It?"**

There's a saying, "Time is money." There's nothing more valuable than time. You better make sure you're doing something worthwhile with your time. Learning a second language is not the best way to spend your time. Language learning isn't for everybody. Knowing more than one language can be valuable, but learning a new language is not worth the time and money.

Unless someone learns a second language as a child, it's a lot harder to actually become bilingual. Studies have shown that it's much more difficult for anyone over the age of five to learn a second language. It takes years of practice to be **fluent,** even if you study the language for many hours each day.

The time spent learning a second language might be better spent learning a different hobby or talent. These talents or hobbies can be useful when you get a job. For example, taking a debate class can help me become a lawyer. Taking choir lessons can help me become a singer. Someone might have a talent that is never used because of the time spent learning a language.

---

1. What is the main claim of this section?

   ○ A. "There's a saying, 'Time is money.'"
   ○ B. "Learning a new language is not worth the time and money."
   ○ C. "Unless someone learns a second language as a child, it's a lot harder to actually become bilingual."
   ○ D. "It takes years of practice to be fluent."

2. Paragraphs 8 and 9 provide supporting evidence about—

   ○ A. talents or hobbies that can be useful when you get a job.
   ○ B. the financial cost of learning a language.
   ○ C. how language skills cannot help you get a job.
   ○ D. the time it takes to learn a new language.

3. The author could best support his or her claim in paragraph 8 by adding—

    ○ A.  an image of a child reading.

    ○ B.  a story about young children learning a second language from grandparents.

    ○ C.  a graph showing that it takes longer to learn new languages as we get older.

    ○ D.  a study indicating that bilingual people take less time to complete tasks.

4. The author supports the claim that there may be better ways to spend time than studying a new language by—

    ○ A.  quoting an expert.

    ○ B.  providing statistics.

    ○ C.  giving a personal story.

    ○ D.  giving examples.

Please note that excerpts and passages in the StudySync® library and this workbook are intended as touchstones to generate interest in an author's work. The excerpts and passages do not substitute for the reading of entire texts, and StudySync® strongly recommends that students seek out and purchase the whole literary or informational work in order to experience it as the author intended. Links to online resellers are available in our digital library. In addition, complete works may be ordered through an authorized reseller by filling out and returning to StudySync® the order form enclosed in this workbook.

Reading & Writing Companion   327

# Close Read

## ✏ WRITE

ARGUMENTATIVE: This text presents arguments for and against learning new languages. Which side do you agree with the most? Write a paragraph that clearly states your position and supports it with evidence. Pay attention to and edit for spelling rules.

**Use the checklist below to guide you as you write.**

☐ What is each author's argument?

☐ What do you think about each argument?

☐ In your opinion, which reasons and evidence are the strongest?

**Use the sentence frames to organize and write your argument.**

I agree with the (Point/Counterpoint) author who argues that _____.

This author's strongest reason is that _____.

The author supports this opinion with _____.

This is convincing because I believe that _____.

Reading this text helped me decide what I think because _____.

# studysync®

ASSIGNMENTS    BINDER    LIBRARY

# The Persistence of Memories

**UNIT 3**

# The Persistence of Memories

How does the past impact the future?

Genre Focus: INFORMATIONAL

## Texts

Paired Readings

# Extended Writing Project and Grammar

## English Language Learner Resources

# Unit 3: The Persistence of Memory
## How does the past impact the future?

**KIMBERLY BLAESER**

Born on the White Earth Reservation in Minnesota to parents of Anishinaabe and German descent, Kimberly Blaeser (b. 1955) now lives in rural Wisconsin. A member of the Minnesota Chippewa tribe, Blaeser's poems, essays, and works of fiction offer glimpses into Native American life and culture. A reviewer in the *Notre Dame Review* notes that Blaeser's writing "remains cognizant of the continued colonization of the continent by other means."

**ALLISON ADELLE HEDGE COKE**

Poet and educator Allison Adelle Hedge Coke (b. 1958) grew up in various locations around North America. Being of Huron, Cherokee, French Canadian, and Portuguese descent, her heritage features prominently in her work. Best known for her memoir, *Rock, Ghost, Willow, Deer* (2004), Hedge Coke's writing articulates the ways in which land, history, and identity are entwined, and sheds light on the stories that have been left out of dominant historical narratives.

**SALVADOR DALÍ**

Spanish visual artist Salvador Dalí (1904–1989) would self-induce a hallucinatory state to dream up the Surrealist imagery for which he is best known. He developed his signature style in the late 1920s after joining the Paris Surrealists and discovering Sigmund Freud's writings on sexuality and the subconscious. In his biography on Dalí, Ian Gibson conducts a psychoanalytic reading of the artist's life and work based on the anxiety he experienced as a youth.

**SIGMUND FREUD**

Sigmund Freud (1865–1939) was an Austrian neurologist who founded psychoanalysis, a set of theories and techniques around human behavior and personality that gained widespread popularity around the turn of the twentieth century. In 1900, Freud published *The Interpretation of Dreams*, in which he analyzed dreams according to his theory of the unconscious. Initially met with skepticism, Freud's ideas have proven to be highly influential in academia and popular culture alike.

**RACHEL KOLB**

Rachel Kolb is a writer, scholar, and disability advocate who was born with profound bilateral hearing loss. Her essays and nonfiction works address themes of language, communication, and social attitudes toward disability. Kolb's obsession as a writer is thinking about how language shapes our understanding of the world and how it might be possible to represent deafness and disability on the page.

**NGO TU LAP**

Ngo Tu Lap (b. 1962) and his family were forced to evacuate Hanoi, Vietnam, soon after his birth due to the impending threat of the Vietnam War. In his numerous collections of poems, works of fiction, and essay collections, Lap delves into his own personal experiences of the war and the feelings of grief and estrangement that it induced. Now a professor of film theory and criticism, Lap continues to emphasize imagery and figurative language in his writing.

## EDNA ST. VINCENT MILLAY

After graduating from Vassar College in 1917, Edna St. Vincent Millay (1892–1950), lived a quintessentially bohemian lifestyle in Greenwich Village in New York City, epitomizing the modern, liberated woman of the 1920s. Millay, who called herself Vincent from a young age, came to be known for her progressive political stances, her frank commentary on taboo topics like feminism, and her distinct writing style, which combined modernist attitudes with traditional poetic forms.

## MICHAEL PRICE

Michael Price is a science journalist based in San Diego, California, who has written articles on a wide range of topics for popular science publications. His article "Facial expressions—including fear—may not be as universal as we thought" (2016) refutes the so-called "universality thesis" of human emotion and expression that went virtually unchallenged since psychologists in the 1960s affirmed Charles Darwin's findings on the subject from the 1870s.

## SANTHA RAMA RAU

Santha Rama Rau (1923–2009) was an Indian-born, Western-educated author and journalist, whose work gained popularity in the United States in the decades following World War II and India's independence. Her extensive travels throughout Africa, Asia, and Russia informed much of her writing, which included travelogues, novels, a memoir, and a *Time-Life* cookbook. One way her work functions now is as a document of the residual effects of British colonialism in the American public sphere.

## MARJANE SATRAPI

Although she was raised by Westernized parents and has lived abroad since she was fifteen, Marjane Satrapi (b. 1969) firmly identifies as Iranian. In an interview, she compares her relationship with her native country to her relationship with her mother, saying, "She is me and I am her." *Persepolis* (2000, 2001), Satrapi's graphic memoir in two parts, tells the story of her childhood growing up in Tehran, focusing on the gaps and junctures between East and West before, during, and after the 1979 Iranian Revolution.

## REBECCA SKLOOT

Science writer Rebecca Skloot is best known for her book, *The Immortal Life of Henrietta Lacks* (2010) about a woman whose cells, taken without her knowledge in 1951 while she was suffering from cervical cancer, wound up playing a key role in the development of important medical technologies including the polio vaccine and in vitro fertilization. Skloot's book, while it recognizes the importance of Lacks's unwitting contribution, raises questions about medical ethics and the racial politics of medicine.

## ARUNDHATI ROY

Author, actress, and political activist Arundhati Roy (b. 1961) is best known for her semi-autobiographical novel *The God of Small Things* (1997) about the caste, class, and religious systems that shape interpersonal relationships in her native India. Heavily involved in environmental and human rights causes, Roy has also written politically oriented nonfiction that addresses some of the problems India faces in the age of global capitalism.

## Introduction

This informational text provides readers with background information about the historical and cultural context that gave rise to surrealism. As war dominated the beginning of the 20th century, artists responded to this bleak and violent landscape by turning inward, to a world of infinite possibility and creativity, of dreams and the unconscious mind. Inspired by the theories of Sigmund Freud, surrealist artists and writers like André Breton, Frida Kahlo, Salvador Dalí, and Guillaume Apollinaire experimented with strange new forms and styles. This period of surrealism in literature and the arts sought to transcend the limits of the conscious mind and provoke emotions in audiences around the world.

# "It is dream-like, fantastical, and without a clear meaning. But it evokes an emotional response."

1    Have you ever been in a situation where you experienced something that was unexpected or strange—not frightening or dangerous—but just kind of weird or nonsensical? For example, you see a woman dressed in a Statue of Liberty costume buying oranges at the grocery store and it's not Halloween. Or maybe you see a man wearing a top hat and walking a rooster on a leash in your neighborhood park. Afterward, as you think about what you saw or talk with friends, you say, "That was surreal." What does it mean when something is surreal? A surreal experience doesn't make sense. It's not rational or logical. It is dream-like, fantastical, and without a clear meaning. But it evokes an emotional response. Today, we can apply the label *surreal* to incomprehensible experiences and artworks because of the artistic period known as surrealism.

## Surrealism: New Art for a Broken World

2    At the end of the nineteenth century, western European nations were at the height of their powers. It was a time of prosperity—the cities of London, Paris, and Berlin were capitals of commerce and art. It was an age that prized rational thinking and realism above all else. However, the outbreak of World War I in 1914 shattered that world. Four years later, millions of people were dead, and land was scarred by trenches and battles. The artists and writers who emerged in the postwar period wanted a new way of thinking about the world and representing it in their art. They found their inspiration in the works of the German psychoanalyst Sigmund Freud. By studying his patients' dreams, Freud concluded that a person's unconscious mind was as important as his or her conscious mind. According to Freud, the unconscious mind, with its **bizarre** dreams, hazy memories, and impolite impulses, deeply influences the way people behave in the world. In 1924, French poet and critic André Breton took Freud's idea of the **unconscious** versus **conscious** and applied it to art and literature. Breton believed that rational thought and realism kept artists and writers from accessing their creativity. As he explained in *The Surrealist Manifesto*, **surreality** was the joining of outward reality with the dreams and fantasy from one's unconscious mind. Thus, surrealism became a movement of artists and writers who tapped into their unconscious minds to make art that was strange and fantastical.

Please note that excerpts and passages in the StudySync® library and this workbook are intended as touchstones to generate interest in an author's work. The excerpts and passages do not substitute for the reading of entire texts, and StudySync® strongly recommends that students seek out and purchase the whole literary or informational work in order to experience it as the author intended. Links to online resellers are available in our digital library. In addition, complete works may be ordered through an authorized reseller by filling out and returning to StudySync® the order form enclosed in this workbook.

Reading & Writing Companion    335

3   Surrealism lent itself well to the visual arts. Some artists, such as Salvador Dalí, René Magritte, Joan Miró, Paul Nash, and Max Ernst focused on painting, while others, like American photographer Man Ray and sculptor Jean Arp focused on other media. The work of these artists was often difficult to interpret and considered **avant garde**, or ahead of its time. Despite this difficulty, surrealism spread from its emergence in Europe in the 1920s around the world. The personal works of renowned Mexican artist Frida Kahlo and the elaborate collages and films of American artist Joseph Cornell were heavily shaped by the surrealists.

### Surrealists' Style

4   Each of the surrealists had a distinct style of exploring and expressing the unconscious, but ultimately they fell into two groups. Some, like Dalí and Magritte, created works that incorporated identifiable objects from the real world but arranged them in strange, often nightmarish scenes. A classic example is Dalí's *The Persistence of Memory*, which features several clocks that appear to be melting in a desert setting. Viewers recognize the clocks, but the fact that they are melting and in a desert is irrational and unsettling. Magritte's paintings are characterized by faceless men and women standing against a blue sky filled with white, fluffy clouds. Their faces are often obscured by a cloth or replaced by an object, such as an apple. First-time viewers usually experience confusion as they gaze at the images, and they struggle to make an interpretation. Other surrealists, like Miró and Arp preferred to create surreal art that they considered "organic" or "absolute." Their works mixed abstract shapes, colorful blobs, and chaotic lines that evoke a strong response in viewers and can not be easily described or interpreted. Max Ernst's *Ubu Imperator* reflects these features. Comprised of a red, tower-like structure with arms that seems to be spinning on a top, this painting defies easy interpretation.

*Ubu Imperator* by Max Ernst, 1923

5   The great Spanish artist Pablo Picasso's style was partly borrowed from and reinforced by the surrealists. Picasso did not need to tap into his unconscious

to unleash his creative genius, yet one of his most memorable works, *Guernica*, which he painted in 1937, is considered a surrealist masterpiece. Painted in black and white like a photograph, it combines disturbing symbols, such as a bull's head and a wounded horse, and contorted human-like figures to convey the pain and betrayal of the bombardment of a Spanish town by Nazi and Italian forces. Like *Guernica*, Paul Nash represents the chaos of war in his painting *Totes Meer* (German for "Dead Sea"). He depicts an aircraft graveyard from World War II as a sea of metal plane parts, with wings replacing waves breaking against the shore.

*Totes Meer (Dead Sea)* by Paul Nash, 1942

6   Many surrealist artists were also writers. Like surrealist art, surrealist poetry was deeply influenced by the unconscious: The poetry was characterized by the **juxtaposition** or unexpected placement of contrasting words, ideas, and symbols. The effect of the juxtaposition was surprising. For example, Breton's poem "Freedom of Love" describes his wife by juxtaposing unusual and unsettling imagery: "My wife with the hair of a wood fire . . . With the waist of an otter in the teeth of a tiger." Breton and Dalí used automatic writing or **automatism** to tap into their unconscious minds. Automatic writing might be compared to freewriting. The result is often chaotic and full of bizarre descriptions and incomplete or meandering sentences, as in Dali's partly fictional autobiography.

7   French poet and writer Guillaume Apollinaire actually coined the term 'surrealism' and his book of poetry, *Calligrammes,* is considered one of the most important of the twentieth century. Apollinaire's surrealist poems are known for their unusual shapes, as the construction of the lines often mirrors the content of the poem. For instance, in the calligramme "La Colombe Poignardée et le Jet D'Eau," which translates to 'The Stabbed Dove and the Fountain of Water,' the lines form the shape of a dove and a fountain of water. In Apollinaire's poem "Visée," or 'Aim,' about warfare, the lines spread across the page like bullets emanating from a fortress.

Calligrammes by Guillaume Apollinaire.

8 **Major Concepts**

- **The Conscious and The Unconscious**—By emphasizing dream and fantasy elements in their work, surrealist artists attempted to bridge the real world and the unconscious. Surrealists drew on Sigmund Freud's theories about the unconscious mind that were based on his work with dreams.

- **Representing the Unconscious**—Surrealist painters, sculptors, and photographers created visual works using imagery that defied interpretation and even description. Surrealist writers invented bizarre or illogical plot events and dreamlike descriptions that defied readers' expectations.

9 **Style and Form**

- **Real Versus Surreal**—Some surrealist artwork featured clear and obvious representations of objects and people from the real world. For example, Dalí's work often includes landscapes and natural objects. Magritte's work incorporated recognizable human forms. Surrealist artists and writers incorporated imagery and metaphors that were outlandish, complicated, strange, and shocking.

- **Breaking from Tradition**—Surrealist writers focused not on plot and other traditional genre characteristics; instead they focused on abstract, dreamlike, or fantasy language, imagery, and structures that defied logic and interpretation. Surrealist writing used bizarre juxtapositions of words and images to express contrasting and often inexplicable ideas.

10 Surrealism emerged in a world destroyed by war. Its followers rejected the philosophy, politics, and the artistic and literary principles of previous generations. They wanted to create art and literature that was absolute, pure, and a reflection of their unconscious minds. Surrealism thrived for two decades, but after a second world war, people craved stability, and the art

world moved in a different direction. Some artists today, like the Japanese novelist Haruki Murakami and the American filmmaker David Lynch, continue to borrow dreamlike plots and fantastical characters and events from the surrealists. Many recent movies and shows incorporate these surrealistic elements to engage viewers and to reveal a character's unconscious. As a consumer of popular culture, where do you notice the influence of surrealism?

# Literary Focus

Read "Literary Focus: Surrealism." After you read, complete the Think Questions below.

 **THINK QUESTIONS**

1. What is the definition of *surrealism*? Explain why the paintings by Max Ernst and Paul Nash are examples of surrealism.

2. Why did surrealists take up Freud's ideas about the unconscious mind? Explain, citing evidence from the text and the images to support your response.

3. What did Salvador Dalí contribute to surrealism? Explain, citing specific examples.

4. Use context clues to determine the meaning of the word **juxtaposition**. Write your best definition, along with the words and phrases that were most helpful in determining the word's meaning. Then, check a dictionary to confirm your understanding.

5. The word ***avant-garde*** is a French word that literally means "advance guard." The word was used in English in a military context for centuries before it became associated with the art world. With this information in mind, write your best definition of the word **avant garde** as it is used in this text. Cite any words or phrases that were particularly helpful in coming to your conclusion.

# By Any Other Name

INFORMATIONAL TEXT
Santha Rama Rau
1951

## Introduction

Novelist and memoirist Santha Rama Rau (1923–2009) was born in India to a distinguished family of doctors and civil servants. She grew up at a time when India was being ruled by the British, and in her autobiography, Rau explores the power dynamic that existed between the British Empire and Indians. In the excerpt, Rau details the treatment Indian children received at an Anglo Indian school.

# "It was an entirely usual, wonderful evening."

1   At the Anglo-Indian day school in Zorinabad to which my sister and I were sent when she was eight and I was five and a half, they changed our names. On the first day of school, a hot, windless morning of a north Indian September, we stood in the headmistress's study and she said, "Now you're the new girls. What are your names?"

2   My sister answered for us. "I am Premila, and she"—nodding in my direction— "is Santha."

3   The headmistress had been in India, I suppose, fifteen years or so, but she still smiled her helpless inability to cope with Indian names. Her rimless half-glasses glittered, and the precarious bun on the top of her head trembled as she shook her head. "Oh, my dears, those are much too hard for me. Suppose we give you pretty English names. Wouldn't that be jolly? Let's see, now— Pamela for you, I think." She shrugged in a baffled way at my sister. "That's as close as I can get. And for you" she said to me, "how about Cynthia? Isn't that nice?"

4   My sister was always less easily **intimidated** than I was, and while she kept a stubborn silence, I said, "Thank you," in a very tiny voice.

5   We had been sent to that school because my father, among his responsibilities as an officer of the civil service, had a tour of duty to perform in the villages around that steamy little provincial town, where he had his headquarters at that time. He used to make his shorter inspection tours on horseback, and a week before, in the stale heat of a typically post monsoon day, we had waved goodbye to him and a little procession—an assistant, a secretary, two bearers, and the man to look after the bedding rolls and luggage. They rode away through our large garden, still bright green from the rains, and we turned back into the twilight of the house and the sound of fans whispering in every room.

6   Up to then, my mother had refused to send Premila to school in the British-run establishments of that time, because, she used to say, "you can bury a dog's tail for seven years and it still comes out curly, and you can take a Britisher

away from his home for a lifetime and he still remains insular." The examinations and degrees from entirely Indian schools were not, in those days, considered valid. In my case, the question had never come up, and probably never would have come up if Mother's extraordinary good health had not broken down. For the first time in my life, she was not able to continue the lessons she had been giving us every morning. So our Hindi books were put away, the stories of the Lord Krishna as a little boy were left in midair, and we were sent to the Anglo-Indian school.

7   That first day at school is still, when I think of it, a remarkable one. At that age, if one's name is changed, one develops a curious form of dual personality. I remember having a certain **detached** and disbelieving concern in the actions of "Cynthia," but certainly no responsibility. Accordingly, I followed the thin, erect back of the headmistress down the veranda to my classroom feeling, at most, a passing interest in what was going to happen to me in this strange, new atmosphere of School.

8   The building was Indian in design, with wide verandas opening onto a central courtyard, but Indian verandas are usually white-washed, with stone floors. These, in the tradition of British schools, were painted dark brown and had matting on the floors. It gave a feeling of extra intensity to the heat.

9   I suppose there were about a dozen Indian children in the school—which contained perhaps forty children in all—and four of them were in my class. They were all sitting at the back of the room, and I went to join them.

10  I sat next to a small, solemn girl who didn't smile at me. She had long, glossy black braids and wore a cotton dress, but she still kept on her Indian jewelry—a gold chain around her neck, thin gold bracelets, and tiny ruby studs in her ears. Like most Indian children, she had a rim of black kohl around her eyes. The cotton dress should have looked strange, but all I could think of was that I should ask my mother if I couldn't wear a dress to school, too, instead of my Indian clothes. I can't remember too much about the proceedings in class that day, except for the beginning. The teacher pointed to me and asked me to stand up. "Now, dear, tell the class your name." I said nothing.

11  "Come along," she said, frowning slightly. "What's your name, dear?"

12  "I don't know," I said, finally.

13  The English children in front of the class—there were about eight or ten of them—giggled and twisted around in their chairs to look at me. I sat down quickly and opened my eyes very wide, hoping in that way to dry them off. The little girl with the braids put out her hand and very lightly touched my arm. She still didn't smile.

14   Most of that morning I was rather bored. I looked briefly at the children's drawings pinned to the wall, and then concentrated on a lizard clinging to the ledge of the high, barred window behind the teacher's head. Occasionally it would shoot out its long yellow tongue for a fly, and then it would rest, with its eyes closed and its belly palpitating, as though it were swallowing several times quickly. The lessons were mostly concerned with reading and writing and simple numbers—things that my mother had already taught me—and I paid very little attention. The teacher wrote on the easel blackboard words like "bat" and "cat," which seemed babyish to me: only "apple" was new and incomprehensible.

15   When it was time for the lunch recess, I followed the girl with braids out onto the veranda. There the children from the other classes were assembled. I saw Premila at once and ran over to her, as she had charge of our lunchbox. The children were all opening packages and sitting down to eat sandwiches. Premila and I were the only ones who had Indian food—thin wheat chapatties, some vegetable curry, and a bottle of buttermilk. Premila thrust half of it into my hand and whispered fiercely that I should go and sit with my class, because that was what the others seemed to be doing.

16   The enormous black eyes of the little Indian girl from my class looked at my food longingly, so I offered her some. But she only shook her head and plowed her way solemnly through her sandwiches.

17   I was very sleepy after lunch, because at home we always took a siesta. It was usually a pleasant time of day, with the bedroom darkened against the harsh afternoon sun, the drifting off into sleep with the sound of Mother's voice reading a story in one's mind, and, finally, the shrill, fussy voice of the ayah waking one for tea.

18   At school, we rested for a short time on low, folding cots on the veranda, and then we were expected to play games. During the hot part of the afternoon we played indoors, and after the shadows had begun to lengthen and the slight breeze of the evening had come up we moved outside to the wide courtyard.

19   I had never really grasped the system of competitive games. At home, whenever we played tag or guessing games, I was always allowed to "win"— "because," Mother used to tell Premila, "she is the youngest, and we have to allow for that." I had often heard her say it, and it seemed quite reasonable to me, but the result was that I had no clear idea of what "winning" meant.

20   When we played twos-and-threes that afternoon at school, in accordance with my training, I let one of the small English boys catch me, but was naturally rather puzzled when the other children did not return the courtesy. I ran about

for what seemed like hours without ever catching anyone, until it was time for school to close. Much later I learned that my attitude was called "not being a good sport," and I stopped allowing myself to be caught, but it was not for years that I really learned the spirit of the thing.

21 When I saw our car come up to the school gate, I broke away from my classmates and rushed toward it yelling, "Ayah! Ayah!" It seemed like an eternity since I had seen her that morning—a wizened, affectionate figure in her white cotton sari, giving me dozens of urgent and useless instructions on how to be a good girl at school. Premila followed more **sedately**, and she told me on the way home never to do that again in front of the other children.

22 When we got home we went straight to Mother's high, white room to have tea with her, and I immediately climbed onto the bed and bounced gently up and down on the springs. Mother asked how we had liked our first day of school. I was so pleased to be home and to have left that peculiar Cynthia behind that I had nothing whatever to say about school, except to ask what "apple" meant. But Premila told Mother about the classes, and added that in her class they had weekly tests to see if they had learned their lessons well.

23 I asked, "What's a test?"

24 Premila said, "You're too small to have them. You won't have them in your class for donkey's years." She had learned the expression that day and was using it for the first time. We all laughed enormously at her wit. She also told Mother, in an aside, that we should take sandwiches to school the next day. Not, she said, that she minded. But they would be simpler for me to handle.

25 That whole lovely evening I didn't think about school at all. I sprinted barefoot across the lawns with my favorite playmate, the cook's son, to the stream at the end of the garden. We quarreled in our usual way, waded in the tepid water under the lime trees, and waited for the night to bring out the smell of the jasmine. I listened with fascination to his stories of ghosts and demons, until I was too frightened to cross the garden alone in the semidarkness. The ayah found me, shouted at the cook's son, scolded me, hurried me in to supper—it was an entirely usual, wonderful evening.

26 It was a week later, the day of Premila's first test, that our lives changed rather abruptly. I was sitting at the back of my class, in my usual inattentive way, only half listening to the teacher. I had started a rather guarded friendship with the girl with the braids, whose name turned out to be Nalini (Nancy in school).

27 The three other Indian children were already fast friends. Even at that age it was apparent to all of us that friendship with the English or Anglo-Indian children was out of the question. Occasionally, during the class, my new friend

and I would draw pictures and show them to each other secretly. The door opened sharply and Premila marched in. At first, the teacher smiled at her in a kindly and encouraging way and said, "Now, you're little Cynthia's sister?"

28 Premila didn't even look at her. She stood with her feet planted firmly apart and her shoulders rigid, and addressed herself directly to me. "Get up," she said. "We're going home."

29 I didn't know what had happened, but I was aware that it was a crisis of some sort. I rose obediently and started to walk toward my sister.

30 "Bring your pencils and your notebook," she said.

31 I went back to them, and together we left the room. The teacher started to say something just as Premila closed the door, but we didn't wait to hear what it was.

32 In complete silence we left the school grounds and started to walk home. Then I asked Premila what the matter was. All she would say was "We're going home for good."

33 It was a very tiring walk for a child of five and a half, and I dragged along behind Premila with my pencils growing sticky in my hand.

34 I can still remember looking at the dusty hedges, and the tangles of thorns in the ditches by the side of the road, smelling the faint fragrance from the eucalyptus trees and wondering whether we would ever reach home. Occasionally a horse-drawn tonga passed us, and the women, in their pink or green silks, stared at Premila and me trudging along on the side of the road. A few coolies and a line of women carrying baskets of vegetables on their heads smiled at us. But it was nearing the hottest time of day, and the road was almost deserted. I walked more and more slowly, and shouted to Premila, from time to time, "Wait for me!" with increasing **peevishness**. She spoke to me only once and that was to tell me to carry my notebook on my head, because of the sun.

35 When we got to our house the ayah was just taking a tray of lunch into Mother's room. She immediately started a long, worried questioning about what are your children doing back here at this hour of the day.

36 Mother looked very startled and very concerned, and asked Premila what had happened.

37 Premila said, "We had our test today, and she made me and the other Indians sit at the back of the room, with a desk between each one."

38    Mother said, "Why was that, darling?"

39    "She said it was because Indians cheat." Premila added. "So I don't think we should go back to that school."

40    Mother looked very distant, and was silent a long time. At last she said, "Of course not, darling." She sounded displeased.

41    We all shared the curry she was having for lunch, and afterward I was sent off to the beautifully familiar bedroom for my siesta. I could hear Mother and Premila talking through the open door.

42    Mother said, "Do you suppose she understood all that?"

43    Premila said, "I shouldn't think so. She's a baby."

44    Mother said, "Well, I hope it won't bother her."

45    Of course, they were both wrong. I understood it perfectly, and I remember it all very clearly. But I put it happily away, because it had all happened to a girl called Cynthia, and I never was really particularly interested in her.

By Santha Rama Rau, 1951. Used by permission of Jai Bowers, sole proprietor of the Estate of Santha Rama Rau.

---

### ✎ WRITE

PERSONAL RESPONSE:  In this short memoir, the narrator's personal growth relates to her name. To what extent do you believe our names affect our experience of life? Quote evidence from the text and use personal anecdotes to support your opinion.

Please note that excerpts and passages in the StudySync® library and this workbook are intended as touchstones to generate interest in an author's work. The excerpts and passages do not substitute for the reading of entire texts, and StudySync® strongly recommends that students seek out and purchase the whole literary or informational work in order to experience it as the author intended. Links to online resellers are available in our digital library. In addition, complete works may be ordered through an authorized reseller by filling out and returning to StudySync® the order form enclosed in this workbook.

Reading & Writing
Companion                    347

# Rituals of Memory

INFORMATIONAL TEXT
Kimberly Blaeser
1985

## Introduction

Kimberly Blaeser (b. 1955) is an essayist and poet who worked as a journalist prior to receiving her PhD at University of Notre Dame. Blaeser, whose parents are of German and Anishinaabe descent, was raised on the White Earth Reservation and is a member of the Minnesota Chippewa Tribe. In 2017, she became poet laureate of Wisconsin due to her contributions and achievements in literature. Much of Blaeser's work explores Native American identity and culture. In this essay, she examines the way her mixed heritage and cultural influences came together to impact her as a child.

# "No matter how far our experience takes us from our origins, our lives remain connected."

1   Memory begins with various wonders. For my friend Mary, it began with hair. Her hair grew tightly curled, so strong the spirals defied taming. Brushing and combing brought tears. When Mary tried to run her fingers through her hair as she saw others do, her fingers became hopelessly captured by the curls: Hair, she **deduced**, must grow in loops, out of our head at one point, back into it at another. Because her locks had never been cut, the loops never broken, her fingers became entangled in the loops. Perhaps that story delights me because it stands as a wonderful example of our always innocent attempts to explain the world. Or perhaps because it seems a fine metaphor for the looped relationships of family, place, and community, the innate patterns of ourselves that always keep us returning. No matter how long our lives, no matter how far our experience takes us from our origins, our lives remain connected, always loop back to that center of our identity, our spirit.

2   I believe we belong to the circle and, for our survival, we will return in one way or another to renew those rhythms of life out of which our sense of self has **emerged**. Some of us have a physical place and a people we return to. We also have what Gerald Vizenor calls the "interior landscapes" of our imaginative and spiritual lives. Perhaps our strongest link to the sacred center, the pulsing core of being, is memory and the storytelling and ceremonies that feed it—our own rituals of memory. My memories entangle themselves oddly among the roots of several cultures: Native American, perhaps foremost in my mind, but also a German Catholic background, the culture of rural America, the close looping of small towns in the Midwest, and what I guess could be called Minnesota wilderness culture. But these several cultures did not always exist in opposition or in isolation from one another. I remember Memorial Day celebrations when my father joined the Legionnaires[1] in their visits to all the graveyards in Mahnomen and Nay-Tah-Waush. Uniformed, sometimes sweating in the early summer heat, they marched to the sites, stood at attention as taps was played, and then, as a gesture of salute to the fallen veterans, they shot over the graves. Each year, through late morning and early afternoon, we followed the men on these tours. We stood, moved to

NOTES

Skill: Informational Text Structure

*The author begins the first paragraph with a broad statement about memory and an extended metaphor. The last sentence expresses a main idea that ties all the previous details together. It must be the main idea.*

---

1. **Legionnaires** refers in this context to members of the American Legion, a war veterans' organization with roughly two million members around the world

**Skill: Language, Style, and Audience**

*Here I see the author use the phrase "out of ordinary time" and then repeat the word* oblivious. *The words accumulate to generate a feeling of awe and spiritual connection. This is an important concept in the essay.*

**Skill: Figurative Language**

*The figurative meaning of* loop *extends here to mean "humanity" and pride in shared ancestry. I also see a euphemism in the phrase "darker place of memory" to refer to the deaths recalled on Memorial Day.*

goose bumps by the lonely trumpet tune, scrambling with all the other children for spent casings when each ceremony was concluded. The last site on their schedule was the Indian burial grounds close to the BAB landing. As a child I saw nothing unusual about a dozen American Legionnaires marching back on the little wooded path and paying solemn respect to those Indian warriors who I would later realize were really of another nation. On this march through the tall grasses and hazelnut bushes that crowded the path, my older brother and I often fell in step. Several times I marched beside Sig Tveit and his trumpet, his arm linked through mine.

3   We stood, all of us—those descended from settlers of Norwegian, German, or other European origins, and those descended from Anishinaabe or other Indian people. Together in a moment out of ordinary time, we paused in the little opening at the wooden grave houses, **oblivious** to the wood ticks, which must later be picked carefully from our clothes and our flesh, oblivious to the buzzing of mosquitoes or sand flies, oblivious as well to the more trivial tensions of contemporary politics. We stood together in a great ceremonial loop of our humanity, in our need to remember our ancestors and the lives they lived, together in our desire to immerse ourselves in their honor, to always carry those memories forward with us, to be ourselves somehow made holy by the ritual of those memories. We emerged quiet from those little woods, from that darker place of memory, into the too bright sunshine of a late May day in the twentieth century.

4   And then we arrived back at the sandy beach. The men brought out drinks from the trunks of their cars, laughter and talk sprang up, picnic foods came out, and people would disperse again—to their own families.

5   I don't know if the Legionnaires still march back into the woods each year. I like to believe they do. For that kind of experience has helped me keep balance when the strands of my mixed heritage seem to pull one against another. However unconscious, it was a moment of crossover, a moment when the borders of culture were nullified by the greater instincts of humanity to remember and to give honor. Perhaps the Memorial Days of those early years have become one of the watermarks of my life because they brought to ceremonial focus the many tellings of the past that filled up the hours and days of my childhood. As children, we were never so much taught as storied. All work and play had memories attached.

6   "Indians," Ed Castillo says, "can hold more than one thing sacred." With school being my double life. I went to Catholic grade school, where I earned a reputation for being quiet, obedient, pious, and bright. I learned my Baltimore Catechism[2]—"Who made you?"

2. **Catechism** a summary of Christian principles and doctrines written in the form of questions and answers

7   *"God made me." "Why did God make you?" "God made me because he loves me."*—learned my singsong phonics——*ba be bi bu, ca ci ca cu, da de di da du*——studied my spelling—*i before e, except after c, or when it sounds like a as in neighbor and weigh.* In between school days, we gathered hazelnuts, went partridge hunting, fished, had long deer-hunting weekends, went to powwows, went spearing and ice fishing, played canasta and whist, learned the daisy chain, beaded on looms, made fish house candles, sausage, and quilts. No one then questioned the necessity or value of our school education, but somehow I grew up knowing it wasn't the only—maybe not even the most important—education I would need, and sometimes we stole time from that education for the other one. My parents might keep us home from school or come and get us midday for some more lovely adventure on a lake or in the woods. I'm still thankful for those stolen moments, because now I know by heart not only the Hail Mary, the Our Father, and the National Anthem, but the misty prayers water gives off at dawn and the ancient song of the loon: I recognize not only the alphabet and the parts of the English sentence, but the silhouetted form of the shipoke[3] and the **intricate** language of a beaver's teeth and tail.

8   My life at school and in the Catholic Church is officially recorded and documented—dates of baptism, First Communion and confirmation, quarterly grade reports, attendance records—just as my academic life is later documented at universities in Minnesota, Indiana, and Wisconsin. But for my other education, practical and spiritual, I have no grades or degrees, no certificates to commemorate the annual rituals. I have some **tangibles** of those processes—a jingle dress, fans of feathers, sometimes photos—but mostly I have stories, dreams, and memories.

*The Persistence of Memory* by surrealist painter Salvador Dalí

By Kimberly Blaeser, 2000. From *Here First: Autobiographical Essays by Native American Writers* (Random House). Used by permission of Kimberly Blaeser.

---

3. **shipoke**  a dark-colored bird belonging to the heron family

Skill:
Informational
Text Structure

*The signal word but suggests a compare-and-contrast structure—school versus practical and spiritual education. The last sentence makes a good conclusion because it's poetic and reinforces the underlying main idea about memories and identity.*

# First Read

Read "Rituals of Memory." After you read, complete the Think Questions below.

## ☁ THINK QUESTIONS

1. The author frequently revisits her memories of certain people and places. Describe the people and places, supporting your description with evidence from the text.

2. During the author's youth, how did the American Legionnaires pay tribute to fallen Indian warriors? Explain, citing evidence from the text.

3. The author values her academic experiences but describes other experiences that were equally important for her learning. What were those experiences? Cite evidence from the text in your answer.

4. The Latin root *oblivisci* means "to forget." With this information in mind, what do you think **oblivious** means? Write your best definition of the word *oblivious*.

5. What is the meaning of the word **tangibles** as it is used in the text? Write your best definition, along with a brief explanation of how you arrived at its meaning.

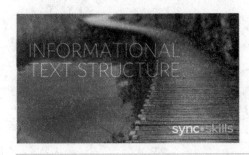

# Skill:
# Informational Text Structure

Use the Checklist to analyze Informational Text Structure in "Rituals of Memory." Refer to the sample student annotations about Informational Text Structure in the text.

## ••• CHECKLIST FOR INFORMATIONAL TEXT STRUCTURE

In order to identify an author's ideas or claims in the text, note the following:

✓ specific statements that contain the main ideas or claims of the argument

✓ individual paragraphs and sentences that

• develop an author's ideas or claims

• clarify and refine an author's ideas or claims

✓ how an idea or claim is made clearer, or refined, in larger portions of text

To analyze in detail how an author's ideas or claims are developed and refined by particular sentences, paragraphs, or larger portions of a text, consider the following questions:

✓ What are the author's main ideas or claims?

✓ How are the author's ideas and claims developed in larger portions of the texts?

✓ How are these claims or ideas developed and refined by particular sentences in the text?

✓ What specific sentences and paragraphs refine or develop the author's overall claim or ideas?

# Skill:
# Informational Text Structure

Reread paragraph 2 of "Rituals of Memory." Then, using the Checklist on the previous page, answer the multiple-choice questions below.

## ⟳ YOUR TURN

1. Which characteristics of the text best suggest the structure the author uses to describe her Memorial Day experiences?

   ○ A. The author's use of the past tense indicates a sequential text structure.

   ○ B. The author's use of signal words and phrases, such as "then" and "the last site," indicates a sequential text structure.

   ○ C. The author's explanation about the purpose of Memorial Day and how it made the spectators feel indicates a cause and effect text structure.

   ○ D. The author's statement introducing the meaning of Memorial Day, followed by details about the day itself, indicates a main idea and details text structure.

2. Which of the following sentences further refines the author's main idea and purpose for writing?

   ○ A. "I believe we belong to the circle and, for our survival, we will return in one way or another to renew those rhythms of life out of which our sense of self has emerged."

   ○ B. "But these several cultures did not always exist in opposition or in isolation from one another."

   ○ C. "We stood, moved to goose bumps by the lonely trumpet tune, scrambling with all the other children for spent casings when each ceremony was concluded."

   ○ D. "Several times I marched beside Sig Tveit and his trumpet, his arm linked through mine."

# Skill:
# Figurative Language

Use the Checklist to analyze Figurative Language in "Rituals of Memory." Refer to the sample student annotation about Figurative Language in the text.

## ••• CHECKLIST FOR FIGURATIVE LANGUAGE

In order to determine the meaning of a figure of speech in context, note the following:

- ✓ words that mean one thing literally and suggest something else
- ✓ similes, metaphors, or personification
  - • extended metaphors extend a metaphor or similar comparison throughout a text
- ✓ figures of speech, including
  - • oxymorons, or a figure of speech in which apparently contradictory terms appear in conjunction, such as
    - > a description such as "deafening silence"
    - > sayings such as "seriously funny"
  - • euphemisms, or a mild or indirect word or expression substituted for one considered to be too harsh when referring to something unpleasant or embarrassing, such as
    - > saying someone has "passed away" instead of "died"
    - > using the term "correctional facility" instead of "prison"

In order to interpret a figure of speech in context and analyze its role in the text, consider the following questions:

- ✓ Where is there figurative language language in the text and what seems to be the purpose of the author's use of it?
- ✓ Why does the author use a figure of speech rather than literal language?
- ✓ How do euphemisms or oxymorons affect the meaning of the text?
- ✓ How does the figurative language develop the message or theme of the literary work?

Please note that excerpts and passages in the StudySync® library and this workbook are intended as touchstones to generate interest in an author's work. The excerpts and passages do not substitute for the reading of entire texts, and StudySync® strongly recommends that students seek out and purchase the whole literary or informational work in order to experience it as the author intended. Links to online resellers are available in our digital library. In addition, complete works may be ordered through an authorized reseller by filling out and returning to StudySync® the order form enclosed in this workbook.

Reading & Writing Companion    355

# Skill:
# Figurative Language

Reread paragraph 5 of "Rituals of Memory." Then, using the Checklist on the previous page, answer the multiple-choice questions below.

## ⟳ YOUR TURN

1. This question has two parts. First, answer Part A. Then, answer Part B.

   **Part A:** Based on the context clues in this passage, what is the best meaning of the figure of speech "the strands of my mixed heritage"?

   ○ A.  an extended metaphor, related to hair, for the idea that the parts of her racial and ethnic backgrounds are not completely blended

   ○ B.  a simile to show that parts of her are in constant struggle with one another

   ○ C.  a euphemism for "mixed race" to demonstrate a feeling of struggle within herself

   ○ D.  another way of saying that her identity is smooth and untangled, like straight hair

   **Part B:** Which quote BEST supports the meaning of the figure of speech from Part A?

   ○ A.  "seem to pull one against another"

   ○ B.  "that kind of experience has helped me keep balance"

   ○ C.  "it was a moment of crossover"

   ○ D.  "the borders of culture were nullified by the greater instincts of humanity to remember and to give honor"

2. The word *watermarks* literally refers to a mark that shows the level to which water has risen in a container, or to a barely visible design on paper to identify a paper's maker. The best figurative meaning for the word *watermarks* as it is used in the context of paragraph 5 is—

   ○ A.  designs on paper

   ○ B.  stains on the body

   ○ C.  imprints on identity

   ○ D.  loops of community

3. The author uses the word *storied* literally to refer to the way in which the children were told stories of their family history. Which of the following is the most accurate analysis of the significance of the word *storied* as it is used by the author?

○ A. *Storied* evokes a feeling of intelligence, which is supported by context clues such as "work and play" and "those early years."

○ B. *Storied* is contrasted with *taught* to evoke a feeling of celebration and the idea of legends, which is supported by context clues such as "ceremonial" and "tellings of the past."

○ C. *Storied* figuratively means "taught" because it evokes an image of conflict, which is supported by context clues such as "pull" and "crossover."

○ D. *Storied* figuratively refers to powerlessness and an image of not having control, which is supported by context clues such as "early years" and "play."

Please note that excerpts and passages in the StudySync® library and this workbook are intended as touchstones to generate interest in an author's work. The excerpts and passages do not substitute for the reading of entire texts, and StudySync® strongly recommends that students seek out and purchase the whole literary or informational work in order to experience it as the author intended. Links to online resellers are available in our digital library. In addition, complete works may be ordered through an authorized reseller by filling out and returning to StudySync® the order form enclosed in this workbook.

Reading & Writing Companion

357

# Skill:
# Language, Style, and Audience

Use the Checklist to analyze Language, Style, and Audience in "Rituals of Memory." Refer to the sample student annotation about Language, Style, and Audience in the text.

## ••• CHECKLIST FOR LANGUAGE, STYLE, AND AUDIENCE

In order to determine an author's style, do the following:

✓ Identify and define any unfamiliar words or phrases as well as unusual phrasing.

✓ Analyze the surrounding words and phrases as well as the context in which the specific words are being used.

✓ Examine word choices to determine the author's attitude toward his or her subject.

✓ Note the audience—both intended and unintended—and possible reactions to the author's word choice and style.

✓ Examine your reaction to the author's word choice and how the author's choice affected your reaction.

✓ Determine how the language affects the meaning, or the author's message or purpose.

To analyze the cumulative impact of word choice on meaning and tone, ask the following questions:

✓ How did my understanding of the writer's language change as a result of analysis?

✓ How do the writer's cumulative word choices impact or create meaning in the text?

✓ How do the writer's cumulative word choices impact or create a specific tone in the text?

✓ What images, feelings, or ideas do the writer's cumulative word choices evoke?

✓ How could various audiences interpret this language? What different possible emotional responses can you list?

✓ How do the author's word choices help to support his or her message or purpose?

# Skill:
# Language, Style, and Audience

Reread paragraphs 6 and 7 of "Rituals of Memory." Then, using the Checklist on the previous page, answer the multiple-choice questions below.

## YOUR TURN

1. What is cumulative effect of the imagery and descriptions in paragraphs 6 and 7 on the meaning of the text?

   ○ A. The author shows that Native Americans were Christians and believed in God.
   ○ B. The author reveals the complex education she experienced as a Native American.
   ○ C. The author shows that formal schooling was vital to her success.
   ○ D. The author shows how fun her upbringing was.

2. In paragraph 7, the author lists activities she did, and later lists the kinds of things she learned "by heart." What is the cumulative effect of the lists on the tone of the text?

   ○ A. The lists give a light-hearted tone to the text.
   ○ B. The lists offer a tone of anger to the text.
   ○ C. The lists describe her learning in an appreciative tone.
   ○ D. The lists describe her learning in a mocking tone.

Please note that excerpts and passages in the StudySync® library and this workbook are intended as touchstones to generate interest in an author's work. The excerpts and passages do not substitute for the reading of entire texts, and StudySync® strongly recommends that students seek out and purchase the whole literary or informational work in order to experience it as the author intended. Links to online resellers are available in our digital library. In addition, complete works may be ordered through an authorized reseller by filling out and returning to StudySync® the order form enclosed in this workbook.

Reading & Writing Companion    359

# RITUALS OF MEMORY

# Close Read

Reread "Rituals of Memory." As you reread, complete the Skills Focus questions below. Then use your answers and annotations from the questions to help you complete the Write activity.

## ◎ SKILLS FOCUS

1. Choose one of the longer paragraphs from "Rituals of Memory." Explain how the author's ideas about memory are shaped and refined by particular sentences in the paragraph.

2. Choose two examples of words the author uses in a figurative way. Explain the effect of this language on your understanding of her key ideas about memory.

3. Select a repeated word or phrase the author uses in "Rituals of Memory." Analyze the cumulative effect of the author's word choices on the meaning and tone of the essay.

4. In the excerpt from her memoir *By Any Other Name*, Anglo Indian writer Santha Rama Rau describes a memory of her education, "Accordingly, I followed the thin, erect back of the headmistress down the veranda to my classroom feeling, at most, a passing interest in what was going to happen to me in this strange, new atmosphere of School." Compare the language of Rau's memory with that of Native American writer Kimberly M. Blaeser. Discuss how both authors share the past and make it part of their present and future.

## ✎ WRITE

EXPLANATORY: What is one metaphor or other example of figurative language Kimberly M. Blaeser uses to capture her perspective on how her mixed ancestry shapes her memory? What is the explicit and implicit meaning of this language? In your response, cite evidence as you determine how the author's language refines and shapes her ideas about the topic of memory.

# Seeing at the Speed of Sound

INFORMATIONAL TEXT
Rachel Kolb
2013

## Introduction

Born and raised in Albuquerque, New Mexico, Rachel Kolb is a writer and activist whose work explores issues and experiences within the Deaf community. Despite profound bilateral hearing loss, Rachel Kolb has pursued advanced education in literature at the world's most prestigious universities; she attended Stanford University and was a Rhodes Scholar at Oxford. In this autobiographical essay, Kolb narrates the various challenges and triumphs she has encountered when lipreading.

# "Sometimes I feel guilty that I lipread at all."

**Skill:
Media**

*Kolb gives an example
of when she struggled
to lipread and
comments on her
frustration. Because of
the video, I can feel
what it is like to
attempt to lipread but
not understand what
the person is saying.*

**Skill: Connotation
and Denotation**

*The dictionary definition
of garbled is "reproduce
a sound in a distorted
way." Why not say
"distorted"? She calls
the sound a "mess," so a
word with a negative
connotation makes
sense.*

1   I AM SITTING in my office during a summer internship. **Absorbed** by my computer screen, I do not notice when my manager enters the room, much less when he starts talking. Only when a sudden hand taps my shoulder do I jump. He is gazing expectantly at me.

2   "I'm sorry, I didn't hear you come in," I say.

3   "Oh, right." His expression changes: to surprise, and then to caution. He proceeds to say something that looks like, "Would you graawl blub blub vhoom mwarr hreet twizzolt, please?" I haven't the faintest idea what he said. I have no excuse, for I was looking straight at him. But despite my attention, something went wrong. He spoke too fast; my eyes lost focus.

4   "Um, could you repeat that, please?" I ask.

5   His eyebrows raise, but he nods and says it again. I sit up straighter, attempt to concentrate, but again it reaches my eyes as a garbled mess.

6   "It's fine," he answers. "I'll send you an email."

7   Well, at least I understood *that* part, I think as he walks out.

8   Lipreading, on which I rely for most social interaction, is an **inherently** tenuous mode of communication. It's essentially a skill of trying to grasp with one sense the information that was intended for another. When I watch people's lips, I am trying to learn something about sound when the eyes were not meant to hear.

9   Spoken words occur in my blind spot, a vacancy of my perception. But if I watch a certain way, I can bring them into enough focus to guess what they are. The brain, crafty as it is, fills in the missing information from my store of knowledge.

10   Want an example?
---- the ---- before -------- when ------------ the house
not --- cre -------------------- even ---- m------

11 Do you recognize the opening of "The Night Before Christmas"? Perhaps so, because in American culture the poem is familiar enough for one to fill in the blanks through memory. Filling in the blanks is the essence of lipreading, but the ability to decipher often depends on factors outside of my control.

12 IT IS MY FIRST WEEK as a freshman at Stanford, and I feel lost. Instead of coasting through routine interactions with people familiar to me, I have thrown myself into a place where almost nothing is predictable. I sit down at a table of strangers. One of them, I realize, is the guy from the room next to mine. "What's your name?" I ask him.

13 He answers, but I frown.

14 "Could you say that again?" I say.

15 He does, but I still do not understand. The name starts with a B, and ends with a Y, but it is not a name I have seen before. Bobby, Barry, Buddy—none of them match what I saw on his face.

16 My neighbor, sensing my struggle, mumbles, "Just call me Ben."

17 Later that day I find out his name is Benamy.

18 EVEN THE MOST skilled lipreaders in English, I have read, can discern an average of 30 percent of what is being said. I believe this figure to be true. There are people with whom I catch almost every word—people I know well, or who take care to speak at a reasonable rate, or whose faces are just easier on the eyes (for lack of a better phrase). But there are also people whom I cannot understand at all. On average, 30 percent is a reasonable number.

19 But 30 percent is also rather unreasonable. How does one have a meaningful conversation at 30 percent? It is like functioning at 30 percent of normal oxygen, or eating 30 percent of recommended calories—possible to subsist, but difficult to feel at your best and all but impossible to excel. Often I stick with contained discussion topics because they maximize the number of words I will understand. They make the conversation feel safe. "How are you?" "How's school?" "Did you have a nice night?" Because I can anticipate that the other person will say "Fine, how are you?" or "Good," I am at lower risk for communication failure.

20 My companions could be discussing any topic in the universe: the particulate nature of matter, the child who keeps wetting the bed, the villa in Nice that they visited last summer. And, because the human mind is naturally erratic in conversation, ever distractible, ever spontaneous, this is just what will end up happening. How am I to predict the unpredictable? The infinity of the universe,

and of man's mind, strikes me as immensely beautiful—but also very frightening.

21 I don't like superficial remarks and predictable rejoinders, but staying in shallow waters is better than sinking. So long as I preserve my footing, I keep up the appearance of being able to converse—to other people and, more important, to myself.

22 "YOU KNOW, you could be a spy," David, who lives in my dorm, tells me as we are sitting at brunch.

23 "Why do you say that?" I ask.

24 "Because"—he leans in excitedly—"because you could look through binoculars and lipread and understand everything people are saying!"

25 "Oh." I smile and cross my arms.

26 "Could you understand those people over there?" David points to a couple at another table.

27 "Maybe," I say, without trying. I dare not explain that they're too far away.

28 THE TERM "LIPREADING" implies that the skill is, in a sense, exactly like reading—in which the words on the page are clear and perfectly legible. "Can you read my lips?" strangers ask when they meet me. (Never mind that the question is inherently illogical: If I couldn't lipread, how on earth could I answer?) As they ask it, I can see the other, unspoken questions reeling in their heads—What if she can't? What will I do then? *Mime?*

29 When I answer that, yes, I can lipread, they relax. Then they prattle on as if all preconditions are off. Because I can "read" their lips, I must therefore be able to "read" everything they say. After all, it would be absurd for me to protest that I can sometimes read the words in a book, but sometimes not. Either you can read, or you can't. (Likewise, either you can hear perfectly—meaning hear and understand everything—or you can't hear at all. Forget hearing aids and microphones and other assistive devices.)

30 "How did you learn to lipread?" is another common query. I do not have a satisfactory answer. The truth is, I can't explain it. No more than I could explain how I learned to walk, or than anyone else could explain how she learned to hear and understand language. "Practice," I usually answer. Since I entered a mainstreamed public school in first grade, there have been no other deaf people **occupying** center stage in my life. My world is primarily a hearing one, and I learned to deal with this reality at a very young age. There was no reason to sign with anyone besides close friends and family, no reason to

expect anyone to communicate on my terms. Surrounded by hearing people all the time, my only option has been to adapt, and lipreading is the skill that I have practiced most.

31 But this answer is too simple. The foundation for my success with communication was laid in my earliest years, at a deaf preschool. That was perhaps the only time in my life when I experienced full communication access each day. Everyone—students, teachers, speech therapists, parents, siblings—signed. From ages 2 to 5, I lived, breathed and conversed with people like me—at least, as alike as a young child understands. There was no reason for me to doubt myself or my abilities, so I grew fluent and confident with language. I learned its nuances, its facial and emotional expressions. I learned that it was not inaccessible, as it would sometimes later seem.

32 Self-confidence fuels the desire to practice and protects against the degradation of communication breakdown; but my ability to lipread is attributable not only to my own efforts, but also to the contributions of others. When I was less than a year old, my parents started me in speech therapy, which I continued for 18 years. There, I encountered the visual and physical fragments of the sound that was so absent from my world. This sound was mysterious to me. I could not grasp it—even with hearing aids—but I could see it. Under the tutelage of a succession of speech therapists, with support from my family, I became a student of its aftereffects.

33 In teaching me how to make sound's shapes with my own mouth, they taught me how to focus on their faces with the deepest intensity. Like a detective-in-training, I learned to recognize consonantal stops, the subtle visual differences between a "d" and a "g." (On the other hand, "p" and "b" are all but impossible to distinguish by lipreading alone, because their only difference is that one is voiced and one is not.) I learned how to zone in on the minutest changes in the muscles of the face. Over many years of drills and refinement, I learned how to construct the appearance of functioning like a hearing person. But I did not hear: I saw.

34 IT IS THE FIRST WEEK of first grade, and the teacher has instructed us to line up by the door so we can follow her, duckling-like, to lunch. I do not know that she has asked us to line up in alphabetical order. My interpreter, who is usually around, seems to have disappeared. Satisfied to follow the other children, I take a spot in line and wait. Only then do I realize that my peers are talking, that they are rearranging themselves. I frown when the girl in front of me says something.

35 "Uh, what?" I say, not understanding her.

36 She says it again, to no avail.

NOTES

37    "What?" I repeat, frustrated at the way the words brush off her lips and fly away.

38    She repeats herself. This time I understand that it is a question. Well, most questions are easily answerable with "yes" or "no."

39    I decide fast, "Yes." Surely a positive response will make the girl happy.

40    Instead, she frowns, and I realize I have said the wrong thing. Panicking, I tell her, "No," then, "Um, I don't know."

41    She giggles, as if I have said something funny, and whispers to a friend. Then she says it again—and everything clears in a rush. "What's your last name?"

42    As I answer, a cold surge rises in my chest. Without knowing it, I have made myself look too dumb to say my own name.

43    SOMETIMES I FEEL GUILTY that I lipread at all. I fear that I am betraying myself by accepting the conventions of the hearing world. I fear that I lack balance—that I am abandoning the communication tactics that work for me, in order to throw myself headlong at a system that does not care about my needs. When I attempt to function like a hearing person, am I not sacrificing my integrity to a game that I lack the tools to tackle, a game that in the end makes me look slow or stupid?

44    Deaf people—meaning Deaf people who live solely in the Deaf community, and hold on to an inherent pride in their Deafness—often speak of communicating as they please and letting the hearing world "deal with it." They believe in the beauty and, dare I say it, the superiority of sign language. Spoken language, compared with the visual nuances of signing, might as well be caveman guttural grunts.

45    When I lipread, I leave the clarity of sign language behind. I attempt to communicate with hearing people on their terms, with no expectation that they will return the favor. The standards I am striving for seem ridiculous: I am trying singlehandedly to cross the chasm of disability. Might not my stubbornness be of more harm than good?

46    I struggle with this. Some days I wonder what it would be like if I refused to speak. I could roll out of bed one morning, decide to take control of my communication on my terms, and make everyone write it down or sign, as other Deaf people do. Some days I resent myself. I wonder if I am weak, ashamed or overly anxious to please.

47   I AM 12 and at a summer camp for the deaf. The entire group has just gone whitewater rafting and is stopping to get ice cream. My peers line up by the counter, signing to each other about the flavors they want. I smile and join, finding the conversation perfectly normal. But when the clerk speaks to us, the other kids freeze like mice after the shadow of a hawk has swooped over the grass.

48   With a jolt, I realize that they have no means with which to understand this hearing woman. Most do not speak, go to deaf schools, have never had reason to learn to lipread. Their barrier is the same as mine, but completely— instead of partially—insurmountable.

49   "What did you say?" I ask the store attendant, looking her in the eye. My voice feels thick from disuse, but still I am aware of its clarity. The other kids stare at me, their hands slack.

50   "I said, would you like a free sample?" the attendant says. I understand her and sign the message to the others. They nod, and sign which flavors they want to taste. I repeat, speaking, to the attendant.

51   After the ordering, when I finally sit down, my own ice cream in hand, I feel strangely lightheaded. This—being able to endow spoken words with meaning, rather than having them translated by somebody else—is new for me. Because I have so often felt powerless, I have never realized the power that I possess.

52   What would I do, I wonder, if I could not lipread? How could I ever stand it?

53   SOME PEOPLE ARE all but impossible for me to lipread. People with thin lips; people who mumble; people who speak from the back of their throats; people with dead-fish, unexpressive faces; people who talk too fast; people who laugh a lot; tired people who slur their words; children with high, babyish voices; men with moustaches or beards; people with any sort of accent.

54   Accents are a visible tang on people's lips. Witnessing someone with an accent is like taking a sip of clear water only to find it tainted with something else. I startle and leap to attention. As I explore the strange taste, my brain puzzles itself trying to pinpoint exactly what it is and how I should respond. I dive into the unfamiliar contortions of the lips, trying to push my way to some intelligible meaning. Accented words pull against the gravity of my experience; like slime-glossed fish, they wriggle and leap out of my hands. Staring down at my fingers' muddy residue, my only choice is to shrug and cast out my line again.

55    Some people, though not inherently difficult to understand, make themselves that way. By viewing lipreading as a mysterious and complicated thing, they make the process harder. They over-enunciate, which distorts the lips like a funhouse mirror. Lips are naturally beautiful, especially when words float from them without thought; they ought never be contorted in this way. There are other signs, too: nervous gestures and exaggerated expressions, improvised sign language, a tic-like degree of smiling and nodding.

56    I sense that such people are terrified of not being understood. What they do not realize is that, when they are not at ease, I cannot be either. I am used to asking for repetition when I miss something, but if I do, such people will only freeze. In their minds, they have not tried hard enough. They turn this into a failing—instead of an unfortunate circumstance.

57    Encountering people who are nervous about lipreading gives me a strange **complex.** I wish only for them to be comfortable, not agitated or guilty. I want them to perceive me as more skilled, more normal, more approachable than they first thought. I do not want them to see me struggle. If I detect nervousness in a companion, I do my best to gloss it over—and present a semblance of normalcy, not the chaos I feel inside.

58    But despite its frustrations and misunderstandings, lipreading is sustenance for me. I once heard that prominent deaf educator Madan Vasishta said that he would rather have an incomplete conversation with a hearing person, one on one, than a conversation using a sign-language interpreter in which he understood everything. I take his point: The rawness of unfiltered contact surpasses even the reassurance provided by translation.

59    When the connection clicks, when I can read the curve and flow of a person's face, my **ebullience** soars. Our exchange is less like taking wild guesses at my own risk, and more like using the deftness of strategy and skill. I interact with hearing people as if I am one of their own. That they don't notice, don't remember that I am deaf! However unconscious, that is the greatest compliment of all.

60    DANIEL IS FROM Singapore. He speaks English, but his accent makes his syllables march in dizzying formations. To my eyes, his every utterance is bewildering.

61    Most people, once they figure out that I have such difficulty understanding them, stop trying. They feel the breakdown in the air, as I do, and they cannot tolerate its weight. But not Daniel. One day, he walks into my dorm room, says hi, and looks down to type on his cell phone. Thinking him sidetracked, I look out the window and wait. But soon he comes closer and shows me the screen.

62   *How are you today?* it says.

63   I grin. I want to leap up and hug him. "I'm fine," I announce. "How are you?"

64   He types: *I'm pretty good. Sorry about my accent. I know it makes it hard.*

65   "It's all right," I say. "I really wish I could understand you."

66   Daniel shrugs and smiles. *How are your classes? Have you written anything new lately?*

67   Anyone passing by in the hallway, hearing only my voice, would find this an odd, one-sided conversation. But, for me, it is perfect clarity.

68   EVERYONE HAS an Achilles heel,[1] something that exposes her weaknesses. Mine is darkness. When it is dark, my appearance of communicative normalcy no longer stands. No speaker, no understanding can reach me. There is no way for me to penetrate any mind but my own, or to grasp whatever words other minds might exchange.

69   That sounds bleak, but it isn't really. With utter darkness comes resignation, a kind of peace. When it is completely dark, the responsibility for communication is no longer mine. Lipreading, writing, seeing: There is nothing more that I can do. I am free to retreat into the solace of my thoughts—which, in the end, is where I can feel most comfortable.

70   It's dim lighting, or bad visual aesthetics, that is a torment. When there is even the slightest sliver of light, there is still a chance. When lighting conditions are impractical or when I cannot squarely see the person who is talking, I still try. More often than not, I frustrate myself in the effort.

71   With lipreading, each day brings a moment in which I literally cannot do it anymore. I grow too tired of the guessing game that I can never quite win. The muscles behind my eyes ache from the strain. (Hearing is very different from sight, in that it does not involve muscular tension. I think of ears as very passive, whereas eyes are continuously moving to focus and see.) Often my corneas go dry; my vision gets blurry. The words on people's lips melt away, sliding down their faces like condensation on glass. I am back in the blind spot again.

72   THE AUDIOLOGIST sits in the booth, where I see her face from my seat in a soundproof testing room. It is time for the tests I take every few years to monitor the ongoing status of my hearing, sometimes for official disability

---

1. **Achilles heel** in Greek mythology, the warrior Achilles was invincible except for a small area of his heel; in modern usage, it refers to a person's weakest or most vulnerable trait

documentation. We have just finished a tone-recognition test, and now she will ask me to repeat back the sentences she reads. It is, of course, pointless to say that I will not be able to do it.

73    She places a piece of paper over her mouth, and I hear her voice as garbled noise, individual units barely distinguishable. I sit helpless, but once in a while take a guess. At most, I catch a word, or two. After nearly 40 sentences, I struggle to remain composed. This, such a simple exercise for anyone else, but for me —

74    I see her lower the paper from her face. My eyes latch onto her clear, articulate lips. "The bag of candy was on the shelf," she says.

75    "The bag of candy was on the shelf," I say, instantly smiling.

76    "The rabbit ran into the hole," she says.

77    "The rabbit ran into the hole."

78    We continue, then she wags her eyebrows and turns off her microphone. A new trick! "The mouse stole the cheese," she says, soundlessly. Any hearing person would spin into murkiness, but I can see, and that is enough.

79    "The mouse stole the cheese," I say, wanting to laugh.

80    Several more, almost perfectly, before she lays down her pencil. We gaze at each other. "You're amazing, you know that?" she says, and I glance down, letting my eyes take a rest. I smile and I smile.

# First Read

Read "Seeing at the Speed of Sound." After you read, complete the Think Questions below.

## ☁ THINK QUESTIONS

1. At summer camp, what does the author learn about her ability to read lips? Use evidence from the text to support your answer.

2. The author writes "Spoken language, compared with the visual nuances of signing, might as well be caveman guttural grunts." How does the video "Can You Read My Lips?" illustrate this claim? Cite specific details from the video to support your answer.

3. What does the author say is her "Achilles heel"? How does she go on to describe what this is like? Use evidence from the text to support your answer.

4. What is the meaning of the word **inherently** as it is used in the text? Write your best definition, along with a brief explanation of how you arrived at its meaning.

5. Use context clues to determine the meaning of the word **complex** as it is used in "Seeing at the Speed of Sound." Write your definition of *complex*, along with those words or phrases from the text that helped most. Then check a dictionary to confirm your understanding.

Please note that excerpts and passages in the StudySync® library and this workbook are intended as touchstones to generate interest in an author's work. The excerpts and passages do not substitute for the reading of entire texts, and StudySync® strongly recommends that students seek out and purchase the whole literary or informational work in order to experience it as the author intended. Links to online resellers are available in our digital library. In addition, complete works may be ordered through an authorized reseller by filling out and returning to StudySync® the order form enclosed in this workbook.

Reading & Writing Companion    **371**

# Skill:
# Connotation and Denotation

Use the Checklist to analyze Connotation and Denotation in "Seeing at the Speed of Sound." Refer to the sample student annotation about Connotation and Denotation in the text.

## ••• CHECKLIST FOR CONNOTATION AND DENOTATION

In order to identify the denotative meanings of words, use the following steps:

✓ First, note unfamiliar words and phrases, key words used to describe important individuals, events, or ideas, or words that inspire an emotional reaction.

✓ Next, determine and note the denotative meaning of words by consulting a reference material such as a dictionary, glossary, or thesaurus.

✓ Finally, analyze nuances, or subtle distinctions, in the meanings of words with similar denotations.

To better understand the meaning of words and phrases as they are used in a text, including connotative meanings, use the following questions as a guide:

✓ What is the genre or subject of the text? Based on context, what do you think the meaning of the word is intended to be?

✓ Is your inference the same or different from the dictionary definition?

✓ Does the word create a positive, negative, or neutral emotion?

✓ What synonyms or alternative phrasing help you describe the connotative meaning of the word?

✓ For what reason might the author have chosen this word over another word with the same denotation?

To determine the meaning of words and phrases as they are used in a text, including connotative meanings, use the following questions as a guide:

✓ What is the denotative meaning of the word? Is that denotative meaning correct in context?

✓ What possible positive, neutral, or negative connotations might the word have, depending on context?

✓ What textual details signal a particular connotation for the word?

# Skill:
# Connotation and Denotation

Reread paragraph 69 of "Seeing at the Speed of Sound." Then, using the Checklist on the previous page, answer the multiple-choice questions below.

## ↻ YOUR TURN

1. This question has two parts. First, answer Part A. Then, answer Part B.

   **Part A:** What is the denotative meaning of the word *resignation* as it is used in this sentence?

   ○ A.  sighting something again

   ○ B.  accepting something unacceptable but inevitable

   ○ C.  the act of retiring from a job

   ○ D.  a document conveying someone's intention of retiring from a job

   **Part B:** Which context clue BEST supports the specific meaning of the word *resignation* from Part A?

   ○ A.  "I can feel most comfortable"

   ○ B.  "That sounds bleak, but it isn't really"

   ○ C.  "There is nothing more that I can do"

   ○ D.  "I am free to retreat into the solace of my thoughts"

2. Which context clue best supports the idea that *resigned* has a positive connotation?

   ○ A.  "That sounds bleak"

   ○ B.  "Lipreading, writing, seeing"

   ○ C.  "a kind of peace"

   ○ D.  "the responsibility for communication is no longer mine"

# Skill:
# Media

Use the Checklist to analyze Media in "Seeing at the Speed of Sound." Refer to the sample student annotation about Media in the text.

Copyright © Bookheaded Learning, LLC

## ••• CHECKLIST FOR MEDIA

In order to identify various accounts of a subject told in different mediums, note the following:

- ✓ the similarities and differences between various accounts of a subject

- ✓ the features of each medium, such as a person's life story in both print and multimedia, including strengths and weaknesses

- ✓ how each medium presents an account of a subject

- ✓ what details are emphasized in each account and what are removed

- ✓ how credible and accurate each source is, whatever the media format

- ✓ how to integrate the multiple sources to gain the most from the information presented

To analyze various accounts of a subject told in different mediums, determining which details are emphasized in each account, consider the following questions:

- ✓ How does each medium present an account of a subject?

- ✓ Which details are emphasized in each account? What is included?

- ✓ What has been left out of each account, and why?

- ✓ How credible and accurate is each media source? How do you know?

# Skill:
# Media

Reread paragraphs 18 and 19 of "Seeing at the Speed of Sound" and watch the video clip in the digital lesson. Then, using the Checklist on the previous page, answer the multiple-choice questions below.

## ↻ YOUR TURN

1. Which statement best expresses the main emphasis of the text passage?

   ○ A. Lipreaders comprehend an average of 30 percent of what is being said, but this is not enough to communicate successfully.

   ○ B. Most people only comprehend 30 percent of the average conversation, but often miss important information.

   ○ C. Kolb can, on average, comprehend 30 percent of any conversation, so she gets by.

   ○ D. Kolb uses analogies to explain how much 30 percent of anything really is.

2. Which statement best expresses the emphasis of the video clip?

   ○ A. Kolb describes what she is attempting to do when she lipreads.

   ○ B. Kolb motivates other people to learn how to lipread.

   ○ C. Kolb teaches other people how to lipread.

   ○ D. Kolb explains how she lost her hearing.

3. What is emphasized more strongly in the video clip than in the passage?

   ○ A. In the video clip, Kolb translates lipreading into spoken language, which is not in the passage.

   ○ B. The video clip explains how people use lipreading to successfully communicate, which the passage omits.

   ○ C. The video clip demonstrates, more specifically than the passage, how much Kolb might miss as she tries to piece together information though lipreading.

   ○ D. The video clip presents analogies to show what a lipreader can miss when trying to follow a conversation, more than the passage does.

SEEING AT THE
SPEED OF SOUND

# Close Read

Reread "Seeing at the Speed of Sound." As you reread, complete the Skills Focus questions below. Then use your answers and annotations from the questions to help you complete the Write activity.

## ◎ SKILLS FOCUS

1. Explain the author's use of the word *lipreading* in paragraph 28 as it applies to that skill. Explain both the connotative and denotative meanings of this word in the passage.

2. In comparing the video of Rachel Kolb with her essay, "Seeing at the Speed of Sound," discuss what each medium brings to the subject, as well as what one medium can do that the other cannot. Cite specific examples from each medium in your response.

3. Discuss how Rachel Kolb uses the sections of her text, defined by words in all capital letters, to develop and shape the key ideas in her essay.

4. Evaluate Kolb's point of view as it is expressed in the essay and video. Discuss Kolb's reasoning, style of rhetoric, and use of evidence in your response.

5. Explain how Kolb's past understanding of the deaf world and lipreading inform her life going forward. Cite evidence from the essay and video in your response.

## ✏ WRITE

ARGUMENTATIVE: In your opinion, which medium—the essay or the video—is a more effective medium for conveying the challenges and triumphs Kolb has encountered while lipreading? Use evidence from the essay and video, as well as original analysis, to support your claim.

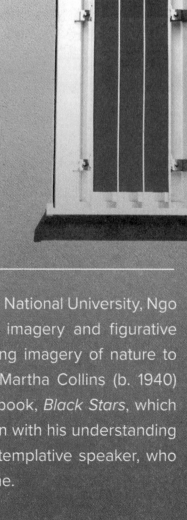

# From Behind A Covered Window

POETRY

Ngo Tu Lap
(translated by Martha Collins)
2007

## Introduction

As a professor of film theory and criticism at Vietnam National University, Ngo Tu Lap (b. 1962) places particular emphasis on imagery and figurative language. His poetry paints stunning visuals, using imagery of nature to express complex human emotions. Poet and translator Martha Collins (b. 1940) translated "From Behind a Covered Window" from Lap's book, *Black Stars*, which places his childhood after the Vietnam War in conversation with his understanding of life across the world. In this poem, Lap depicts a contemplative speaker, who questions both the meaning of self and the meaning of time.

# "Is there only myself?"

1   Is there, out there, a sky
2   Sunny or windy or **humid** with autumn
3   A sky at dawn, or a sunset sky?

4   Are there, out there, human faces
5   Strange or familiar
6   Happy or hurting
7   Friendly faces, or faces like beasts'?

8   Is there, out there, a nothingness
9   With no future, and no past?
10  Was it I who drew the curtains across the window?

11  Is there, out there, dark earth
12  That buries all **flesh** that once was beauty
13  That buries all **glances**, all shut lips?

14  Is there only this place?
15  Is there only this late afternoon?
16  Is there only myself?

From Black Stars by Ngo Tu Lap, translated by Martha Collins (Minneapolis: Milkweed Editions, 2013). Copyright © 2013 by Ngo Tu Lap and Martha Collins. Reprinted with permission from Milkweed Editions. milkweed.org

## WRITE

NARRATIVE:  In this poem, the speaker questions the nature of existence. Write a narrative involving a narrator or character who is a questioner, not unlike Socrates in Plato's *Republic*. Use dialogue and descriptive details to bring this narrator or character to life for the reader.

# Love Is Not All

POETRY
Edna St. Vincent Millay
1931

## Introduction

Edna St. Vincent Millay (1892–1950) was one of the most famous American poets of her time, winning the Pulitzer Prize for Poetry in 1923. Millay's unconventional and bohemian lifestyle was representative of the liberated, modern woman of the Jazz era, and her frank commentary on taboo topics like feminism and sexuality earned her fans and critics alike. She was well known for dramatic and captivating live readings of her work. In "Love Is Not All," Millay contemplates the importance of love.

# "I might be driven to sell your love for peace,"

**Skill: Poetic Elements and Structure**

This 14-line poem has aspects of a Shakespearean sonnet, with rhyme and 10 syllables per line. Also, the words *not* and *nor* repeat. The structure emphasizes the speaker's certainty that love is not essential.

**Skill: Connotation and Denotation**

The denotative meaning of *thick* is "dense or heavy mass," so the idea is of a lung "thickened," without breath. This creates a strong image, almost like "suffocated," but "thickened" sounds worse, harder.

1   Love is not all: it is not meat nor drink
2   Nor **slumber** nor a roof against the rain;
3   Nor yet a floating **spar** to men that sink
4   And rise and sink and rise and sink again;
5   Love can not fill the thickened lung with breath,
6   Nor clean the blood, nor set the **fractured** bone;
7   Yet many a man is making friends with death
8   Even as I speak, for lack of love alone.
9   It well may be that in a difficult hour,
10  Pinned down by pain and moaning for **release**,
11  Or nagged by want past **resolution's** power,
12  I might be driven to sell your love for peace,
13  Or trade the memory of this night for food.
14  It well may be. I do not think I would.

---

# First Read

Read "Love Is Not All." After you read, complete the Think Questions below.

## ☁ THINK QUESTIONS

1. Refer to one or more details from the text to support your understanding of the poem's title and how it relates to the content of the sonnet.

2. How might you describe the poet's reasons or purpose for writing this poem? Use details from the text to develop and support your answer.

3. What do the final lines of the poem tell you about the speaker? Support your answer with textual evidence.

4. Use context clues to determine the meaning of the word **fractured** as it is used in line 6. Write your definition of *fractured* and tell how you found and verified it.

5. Read the following dictionary entry:

**resolution**
res•o•lu•tion *noun*

1. Clarity in a picture or screen
2. The end of a conflict
3. The decision to continue doing something

Which definition most closely matches the meaning of **resolution** in line 11? Write the correct definition of *resolution* and explain how you figured it out.

Please note that excerpts and passages in the StudySync® library and this workbook are intended as touchstones to generate interest in an author's work. The excerpts and passages do not substitute for the reading of entire texts, and StudySync® strongly recommends that students seek out and purchase the whole literary or informational work in order to experience it as the author intended. Links to online resellers are available in our digital library. In addition, complete works may be ordered through an authorized reseller by filling out and returning to StudySync® the order form enclosed in this workbook.

Reading & Writing Companion  381

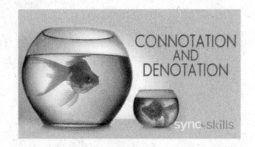

# Skill:
# Connotation and Denotation

Use the Checklist to analyze Connotation and Denotation in "Love Is Not All." Refer to the sample student annotation about Connotation and Denotation in the text.

## ••• CHECKLIST FOR CONNOTATION AND DENOTATION

In order to identify the denotative meanings of words, use the following steps:

✓ First, note unfamiliar words and phrases, key words used to describe important characters, events, and ideas, or words that inspire an emotional reaction.

✓ Next, determine and note the denotative meaning of words by consulting a reference material such as a dictionary, glossary, or thesaurus.

✓ Finally, analyze nuances in the meaning of words with similar denotations.

To better understand the meaning of words and phrases as they are used in a text, including connotative meanings, use the following questions as a guide:

✓ What is the genre or subject of the text? Based on context, what do you think the meaning of the word is intended to be?

✓ Is your inference the same or different from the dictionary definition?

✓ Does the word create a positive, negative, or neutral emotion?

✓ What synonyms or alternative phrasing help you describe the connotative meaning of the word?

To determine the meaning of words and phrases as they are used in a text, including connotative meanings, use the following questions as a guide:

✓ What is the denotative meaning of the word? Is that denotative meaning correct in context?

✓ What possible positive, neutral, or negative connotations might the word have, depending on context?

✓ What textual details signal a particular connotation for the word?

✓ Why did the author or poet choose this word over another?

# Skill:
# Connotation and Denotation

Reread lines 12–14 of "Love Is Not All." Then, using the Checklist on the previous page, answer the multiple-choice questions below.

## ↻ YOUR TURN

1.  The denotative meaning of *driven* is "resolutely or willfully determined." Which context clue best supports the idea that *driven* has a negative connotation in line 12 of the poem?

    ○ A. "I might be"
    ○ B. "to sell your love"
    ○ C. "for peace"
    ○ D. "I would"

2.  The denotative meaning of *memory* is "something remembered." Which context clue from lines 13–14 best supports the idea that *memory* has a positive connotation in line 13?

    ○ A. "It well may be"
    ○ B. "this night for food"
    ○ C. "I do not think I would"
    ○ D. "Or trade"

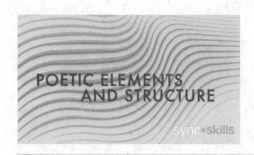

# Skill:
# Poetic Elements and Structure

Use the Checklist to analyze Poetic Elements and Structure in "Love Is Not All." Refer to the sample student annotation about Poetic Elements and Structure in the text.

## ••• CHECKLIST FOR POETIC ELEMENTS AND STRUCTURE

In order to identify a poet's choices concerning how to structure a poem, order events within it, and manipulate time, note the following:

- ✓ the form of the poem, such as a lyric poem or sonnet
- ✓ rhyme, rhythm, and meter, if present
- ✓ line lengths, use of punctuation, and inclusion (or not) of stanzas in the poem
- ✓ sections of the poem that generate emotional responses, such as surprise
- ✓ events, if present, and how they are ordered

In order to identify poetic elements in a poem, note the following:

- ✓ repetition of words or phrases for emphasis
- ✓ sound elements, including
  - • alliteration: the repetition of initial consonant sounds in words
  - • consonance: the repetition of consonant sounds within words
  - • assonance: the repetition of similar vowel sounds
  - • onomatopoeia: words that mimic sound, e.g., "meow."

To analyze how a poet's choices concerning how to structure a poem, order events within it, and manipulate time create such effects as mystery, tension, or surprise, consider the following questions:

- ✓ How does the poet structure his or her poem? How does he or she order events within the poem? How does he or she manipulate time?

- ✓ What effects, such as mystery, tension, or surprise, does the poet create through his or her choices?

- ✓ How does the poet's choice of form or structure affect the overall meaning of the poem?

- ✓ How do the elements a poet uses affect the poem?

# Skill:
# Poetic Elements and Structure

Reread lines 5–8 of "Love Is Not All." Then, using the Checklist on the previous page, answer the multiple-choice questions below.

## ⟳ YOUR TURN

1. Which of the following correctly analyzes the structure of this section of the sonnet?

   ○ A. The poet uses a regular meter of iambic pentameter throughout the stanza, alternating unstressed and stressed syllables, and there is a regular rhyme scheme.

   ○ B. The poet uses an irregular meter throughout the stanza because there is no consistent pattern of unstressed and stressed syllables, but there is a regular rhyme scheme.

   ○ C. The poet uses an irregular meter in lines 5–6 and a regular meter of iambic pentameter in lines 7–8, but there is no regular rhyme scheme

   ○ D. The poet uses a regular meter of iambic pentameter in lines 5–6 and an irregular meter in lines 7–8, and there is a regular rhyme scheme.

2. What is the effect of the structure on the poem's meaning?

   ○ A. It creates a steady, rhythmic quality, which emphasizes the traditional format of the sonnet, suggesting the speaker is unconcerned about love.

   ○ B. It mimics the image of a lung breathing air in and out, as described in line 5, suggesting love's ease.

   ○ C. It signals a shift in meaning between lines 5–6 and lines 7–8, suggesting some kind of emotional response to love that the speaker wants to express.

   ○ D. It emphasizes the words *fill* and *lung* and takes emphasis away from the words *lack* and *love*, showing that love is a physical experience rather than an emotional one.

LOVE IS NOT ALL

# Close Read

Reread "Love Is Not All." As you reread, complete the Skills Focus questions below. Then use your answers and annotations from the questions to help you complete the Write activity.

## ⊚ SKILLS FOCUS

1. Identify word choices in the poem that denote or connote the idea of suffering. Explain how this choice of language contributes to the speaker's message about love.

2. A slant rhyme occurs when words have similar end sounds but not an exact rhyme. Identify the only slant rhyme in the poem and explain how it emphasizes the speaker's uncertain or conflicted attitude toward love.

3. In "From Behind a Covered Window" the speaker says:

   *Is there, out there, a nothingness*
   *With no future, and no past?*
   *Was it I who drew the curtains across*
   *the window?*

Compare and contrast the cumulative effects of repetition and negative word choices in Edna St. Vincent Millay's sonnet "Love Is Not All" and Ngo Tu Lap's free verse poem "From Behind a Covered Window."

4. *Explicit* means "stated clearly and in detail," and *implicit* means "implied but not stated directly." Explain what the speaker of "Love Is Not All" says, both explicitly and implicitly, about the effect of past love on a person's future.

## ✎ WRITE

LITERARY ANALYSIS: Both Edna St. Vincent Millay and Ngo Tu Lap express uncertainty in their poems. However, they do so across time and culture and through different poetic forms. Whereas Millay uses the tightly structured form of a sonnet, Ngo Tu Lap uses the more open format of free verse. Compare and contrast each poet's message about uncertainty. As part of your response, analyze an extract from each poem to show how each poet uses rhyme and other poetic conventions to communicate his or her message.

Facial expressions
—including fear—
may not be as universal
as we thought

INFORMATIONAL TEXT
Michael Price
2016

## Introduction

Michael Price is a science writer based in San Diego, California. He frequently writes about animals, genetics, technology, and the history of science. In this piece, he explores whether facial expressions are "universal"—that is, whether people all over the world use the same expressions to express the same emotions.

# "... these facial behaviors are not pancultural, but are instead culturally specific."

1   When you're smiling, it may feel like the whole world is smiling with you, but a new study suggests that some facial expressions may not be so universal. In fact, several expressions commonly understood in the West—including one for fear—have very different meanings to one indigenous, isolated society in Papua New Guinea.[1] The new findings call into question some widely held tenets of emotional theory, and they may undercut emerging technologies, like robots and artificial intelligence programs tasked with reading people's emotions.

2   For more than a century, scientists have wondered whether all humans experience the same basic range of emotions—and if they do, whether they express them in the same way. In the 1870s, it was the central question Charles Darwin explored in *The Expression of the Emotions in Man and Animals*. By the 1960s, emeritus psychologist Paul Ekman, then at the University of California (UC) in San Francisco, had come up with an accepted **methodology** to explore this question. He showed pictures of Westerners with different facial expressions to people living in isolated cultures, including in Papua New Guinea, and then asked them what emotion was being conveyed. Ekman's early experiments appeared conclusive. From anger to happiness to sadness to surprise, facial expressions seemed to be universally understood around the world, a biologically innate response to emotion.

3   That conclusion went virtually unchallenged for 50 years, and it still features **prominently** in many psychology and anthropology textbooks, says James Russell, a psychologist at Boston College and corresponding author of the recent study. But over the last few decades, scientists have begun questioning the methodologies and assumptions of the earlier studies.

4   Psychologist Carlos Crivelli was one of them. In 2011, he was working with his colleague, psychologist José-Miguel Fernández-Dols, at the Autonomous University of Madrid. Together, they came up with a plan to investigate Ekman's initial research in Papua New Guinea. Crivelli and longtime friend and research partner, Sergio Jarillo, an anthropologist at the American

NOTES

Skill: Central or Main Idea

*The topic is how we read facial expressions. The main idea seems to be explicitly stated in the title of the article and in the opening sentence. I can check to see if all the details support and build on this.*

---

1. **Papua New Guinea**  a heavily rural island nation north of Australia

Museum of Natural History in New York City, traveled to the Trobriand Islands off Papua New Guinea's east coast, where about 60,000 indigenous Trobrianders live. These horticulturists and fishermen have been historically isolated from both mainland Papua New Guinea and the outside world. To learn all that they could, Crivelli and Jarillo embedded themselves in the local culture. They were adopted by host families and took clan names; Crivelli became "*Kelakasi*" and Jarillo, "*Tonogwa*." They spent many months learning the local language, Kilivila.

5   When it came time to begin the study, they didn't need translators or local guides. They simply showed 72 young people between the ages of 9 and 15 from different villages photos from an established set of faces used in psychological research. The researchers asked half the Trobrianders to link each of the faces to an emotion from a list: happiness, sadness, anger, fear, disgust, or hunger. The other half was given a different task.

6   Crivelli found that they matched smiling with happiness almost every time. Results for the other combinations were mixed, though. For example, the Trobrianders just couldn't widely agree on which emotion a scowling face corresponded with. Some said this and some said that. It was the same with the nose-scrunching, pouting, and a neutral expression. There was one facial expression, though, that many of them did agree on: a wide-eyed, lips-parted gasping face (similar to above) that Western cultures almost universally associate with fear and submission. The Trobrianders said it looked "angry."

7   Surprised, Crivelli showed a different set of Trobrianders the same faces, but he couched his questions in stories—e.g., "Which of these people would like to start a fight?"—to draw out more context. They, too, associated the gasp face with threatening behavior, Crivelli reports today in the Proceedings of the National Academy of Sciences. "The **implications** here are really big," he says. "It strongly suggests that at least these facial behaviors are not pancultural, but are instead culturally specific."

A young Trobriander from the village of Kaulaka points to a gasping face, indicating that he recognizes it as a threat display. CARLOS CRIVELLI AND SERGIO JARILLO

**Skill: Summarizing**

*Summary: The Trobrianders always matched smiling faces to happiness but couldn't agree on what some other expressions meant, including a scowling face. They associated the expression with both fear and anger.*

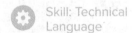

**Skill: Technical Language**

*According to the dictionary, pancultural means "relevant to all cultures." In this context, Crivelli is saying that facial expressions do not have the same meaning across cultures, which is different from earlier findings.*

8   That's not to say that emotions don't elicit natural physiological reactions, Russell explains, but the study suggests that reactions and interpretations can vary from culture to culture. With the gasp face, for example, Russell speculates that the expression could be a natural response to urgent, distressing situations. Whereas Western culture has tied that expression to *feeling* fear, it might be that the Trobrianders associate the expression with *instilling* it. Crivelli agrees, and points to another culture whose ritualized dances feature a similar expression in a threatening fashion: the Māori of New Zealand.

9   Based on his research, Russell champions an idea he calls **"minimal universality."** In it, the finite number of ways that facial muscles can move creates a basic template of expressions that are then filtered through culture to gain meaning. If this is indeed the case, such cultural diversity in facial expressions will prove challenging to emerging technologies that aspire to decode and react to human emotion, he says, such as emotion recognition software being designed to recognize when people are lying or plotting violence.

10  "This is novel work and an interesting challenge to a tenet of the so-called universality thesis," writes Disa Sauter, a psychologist at the University of Amsterdam, in an email. She adds that she'd like to see the research replicated with adult participants, as well as with experiments that ask people to produce a threatening or angry face, not just interpret photos of expressions. "It will be crucial to test whether this pattern of 'fear' expressions being associated with anger/threat is found in the production of facial expressions, since the universality thesis is primarily focused on production rather than perception."

11  Social psychologist Alan Fridlund at UC in Santa Barbara, says the researchers' level of immersion in the Trobrianders' culture gives them a unique perspective on threat displays, and not relying on translators improves the study's accuracy. "I think the real strength of this paper is that it knows its participants so well," he says.

12  But he adds that the snapshot method may not be the best way to analyze how people view different facial expressions—after all, in everyday life, people see facial expressions in the context of what's going on around them, he says. Another problem has to do with the study design—"happiness" was the only positive emotion that Trobrianders were given as an option, Fridlund says, which may have biased the results. For example, if the researchers had included "amusement" or "contentment" as answers, the apparent agreement over smiling might have disappeared.

13  Despite agreeing broadly with the study's conclusions, Fridlund doubts it will sway hardliners convinced that emotions bubble forth from a common fount.

Skill: Technical Language

*Words and phrases like these are academic terms related to the study. The cumulative effect of all these terms gives the article a feeling of authority.*

Ekman's school of thought, for example, arose in the post-World War II era when people were seeking ideas that reinforced our common humanity, Fridlund says. "I think it will not change people's minds. People have very deep reasons for adhering to either universality or cultural diversity."

Republished with permission of the American Association for the Advancement of Science. From *Science*, Michael Price, October 17, 2016; permission conveyed through Copyright Clearance Center, Inc.

FACIAL
EXPRESSIONS—
INCLUDING FEAR—MAY
NOT BE AS UNIVERSAL
AS WE THOUGHT

# First Read

Read "Facial expressions—including fear—may not be as universal as we thought." After you read, complete the Think Questions below.

## ☁ THINK QUESTIONS

1. Describe the studies conducted by psychologist Paul Ekman on facial expression and the conclusions he reached. How did his studies affect the fields of psychology and anthropology? Cite evidence from the text in your answer.

2. How did work by psychologist Carlos Crivelli counter Paul Ekman's conclusions? Use evidence from the text to explain your answer.

3. What problems still prevent a definitive conclusion about the universality of facial expressions? Cite evidence from the text in your answer.

4. Use context clues to determine the meaning of the word **prominently** as it is used in the text. Write your best definition of *prominently*, along with a brief explanation of how you arrived at its meaning.

5. Keeping in mind that the Latin word *minimus* means "small," determine the meaning of the word **minimal** as it is used in the text. Write your definition of *minimal*, and explain which clues helped you figure it out.

Please note that excerpts and passages in the StudySync® library and this workbook are intended as touchstones to generate interest in an author's work. The excerpts and passages do not substitute for the reading of entire texts, and StudySync® strongly recommends that students seek out and purchase the whole literary or informational work in order to experience it as the author intended. Links to online resellers are available in our digital library. In addition, complete works may be ordered through an authorized reseller by filling out and returning to StudySync® the order form enclosed in this workbook.

Reading & Writing Companion

393

# Skill:
# Central or Main Idea

Use the Checklist to analyze Central or Main Idea in "Facial expressions—including fear—may not be as universal as we thought." Refer to the sample student annotation about Central or Main Idea in the text.

## ••• CHECKLIST FOR CENTRAL OR MAIN IDEA

In order to determine a central idea of a text, note the following:

✓ the topic or subject of the text

✓ the central or main idea, if it is explicitly stated

✓ key details and supporting ideas that shape and refine the author's point or message

✓ ways in which supporting ideas relate to the central idea

✓ details that shape, refine, or otherwise contribute to the central idea

✓ ways that the author builds on ideas to communicate a message

To determine a central idea of a text and analyze its development over the course of the text, including its relationship to supporting ideas, consider the following questions:

✓ What is the topic of the text? How do you know?

✓ Is there a place where the author explicitly states the central idea?

✓ What main idea(s) do the details in each paragraph explain or describe?

✓ What bigger idea do all the paragraphs support?

✓ What is the best way to state the central idea?

✓ How do the supporting ideas and details help develop the central idea over the course of the text?

✓ How might you summarize the text's message? What details would you include?

Copyright © BookheadEd Learning, LLC

# Skill:
# Central or Main Idea

Reread paragraphs 10–12 of "Facial expressions—including fear—may not be as universal as we thought." Then, using the Checklist on the previous page, answer the multiple-choice questions below.

## ⟳ YOUR TURN

1. This question has two parts. First, answer Part A. Then, answer Part B.

   **Part A:** What of the following most clearly states the central idea of these paragraphs?

   ○ A. Happiness is not the only positive emotion people have.

   ○ B. While the study has many strengths, further research is needed to build a stronger case.

   ○ C. The initial research only included children, and adults need to be included as well.

   ○ D. The study is completely false in its conclusions.

   **Part B:** Which of the following statements BEST supports the central idea in Part A?

   ○ A. "Another problem has to do with the study design—'happiness' was the only positive emotion that Trobrianders were given as an option."

   ○ B. "Immersion in the Trobrianders' culture gives them a unique perspective on threat displays, and not relying on translators improves the study's accuracy."

   ○ C. "'I think the real strength of this paper is that it knows its participants so well,' he says. But he adds that the snapshot method may not be the best way."

   ○ D. "She adds that she'd like to see the research replicated with adult participants, as well as with experiments that ask people to produce a threatening or angry face, not just interpret photos of expressions."

Please note that excerpts and passages in the StudySync® library and this workbook are intended as touchstones to generate interest in an author's work. The excerpts and passages do not substitute for the reading of entire texts, and StudySync® strongly recommends that students seek out and purchase the whole literary or informational work in order to experience it as the author intended. Links to online resellers are available in our digital library. In addition, complete works may be ordered through an authorized reseller by filling out and returning to StudySync® the order form enclosed in this workbook.

Reading & Writing
Companion

395

# Skill:
# Summarizing

Use the Checklist to analyze Summarizing in "Facial expressions—including fear—may not be as universal as we thought." Refer to the sample student annotation about Summarizing in the text.

## ••• CHECKLIST FOR SUMMARIZING

In order to determine how to write an objective summary of a text, note the following:

✓ answers to the basic questions *who, what, where, when, why,* and *how*

✓ in literature or nonfiction, how the theme or central idea is developed over the course of the text, and how it is shaped and then refined by specific details

✓ any personal thoughts, judgments, or opinions in the summary that need to be eliminated for objectivity

To provide an objective summary of a text, consider the following questions:

✓ What are the answers to basic *who, what, where, when, why,* and *how* questions in literature and works of nonfiction?

✓ Does my summary include how the theme or central idea is developed over the course of the text and how it is shaped and refined by specific details?

✓ Have I included only details that are key to understanding the text?

✓ Is my summary objective, or have I added my own thoughts, judgments, and personal opinions?

# Skill:
# Summarizing

Reread paragraphs 8 and 9 of "Facial expressions—including fear—may not be as universal as we thought." Then, using the Checklist on the previous page, answer the multiple-choice questions below.

## ↻ YOUR TURN

1. Which detail from paragraph 8 is the most important to highlight for a summary?

   ○ A. "That's not to say that emotions don't elicit natural physiological reactions."
   ○ B. "The study suggests that reactions and interpretations can vary from culture to culture."
   ○ C. "Crivelli agrees."
   ○ D. "Russell speculates that the expression could be a natural response to urgent, distressing situations."

2. What is the best summary of the information in paragraph 9?

   ○ A. There are a finite number of facial expressions because there are only so many ways that the muscles in the human face can move.
   ○ B. Emotion recognition is a fantastic technology that is being hindered by different cultures interpretations of facial expressions.
   ○ C. "Minimal universality" is an idea which states that there are a finite number of facial expressions, but different cultures can assign different meanings to them posing a problem to emotion decoding technologies.
   ○ D. "Minimal universality" is the idea that there are a finite number of facial expressions.

# Skill:
# Technical Language

Use the Checklist to analyze Technical Language in "Facial expressions—including fear—may not be as universal as we thought." Refer to the sample student annotations about Technical Language in the text.

## ••• CHECKLIST FOR TECHNICAL LANGUAGE

In order to determine the meaning of words and phrases as they are used in a text, note the following:

- ✓ the subject of the book or article

- ✓ any unfamiliar words that you think might be terms related to a specific field of study

- ✓ words that have multiple meanings that change when used with a specific subject

- ✓ the possible contextual meaning of a word, or the definition from a dictionary

To determine the meaning of words and phrases as they are used in a text, including technical meanings, consider the following questions:

- ✓ What is the subject of the informational text?

- ✓ How does the use of subject-specific, technical language help establish the author as an authority on the subject?

- ✓ Are there any technical words that have an impact on the meaning and tone of the book or article?

- ✓ Does the cumulative, or increasing use of technical language—such as the kind you might find in a government document—have an effect on meaning, tone, and readability?

# Skill:
# Technical Language

Reread the following excerpt from paragraph 4 from "Facial expressions—including fear—may not be as universal as we thought" and the dictionary entry. Then, using the Checklist on the previous page, answer the multiple-choice questions below.

## ⟳ YOUR TURN

From "Facial expressions—including fear—may not be as universal as we thought" by Michael Price

Together, they came up with a plan to investigate Ekman's initial research in Papua New Guinea. Crivelli and longtime friend and research partner, Sergio Jarillo, an **anthropologist** at the American Museum of Natural History in New York City, traveled to the Trobriand Islands off Papua New Guinea's east coast, where about 60,000 **indigenous** Trobrianders live.

**anthropologist**
*noun*
a person who studies all aspects of the past and present of human beings

**indigenous**
*adjective*

1. innate
2. inherent
3. natural
4. native

1. Read the dictionary entry for *anthropologist*. Which statement validates the meaning of *anthropologist* as it is used in the text?

   ○ A. Sergio Jarillo researches how and why humans interact and behave the way they do.
   ○ B. Sergio Jarillo examines how plants and animals interact on isolated islands like the Trobriand Islands.
   ○ C. Sergio Jarillo administers mental health advice to human beings.
   ○ D. Sergio Jarillo explores the history of lands around the world.

2. Read the dictionary entry for *indigenous*. Which definition clarifies the meaning of *indigenous* as it is used in the text?

   ○ A.  1. innate
   ○ B.  2. inherent
   ○ C.  3. natural
   ○ D.  4. native

3. What is the cumulative effect of the technical terms used in the paragraph on the meaning of the text?

   ○ A.  The terms give the text a tone of authority.
   ○ B.  The terms demonstrate the seriousness of the study.
   ○ C.  The terms identify the locations where the study will take place.
   ○ D.  The terms clarify the roles of the people involved in the research study.

FACIAL
EXPRESSIONS—
INCLUDING FEAR—MAY
NOT BE AS UNIVERSAL
AS WE THOUGHT

# Close Read

Reread "Facial expressions—including fear—may not be as universal as we thought." As you reread, complete the Skills Focus questions below. Then use your answers and annotations from the questions to help you complete the Write activity.

## ◎ SKILLS FOCUS

1. State the central idea of the article. Explain how the author uses research, details, and other evidence to develop this idea throughout the article.

2. The author identifies several researchers in the article using titles that represent their fields of work and study. Discuss the impact those terms have on the meaning and tone of the article.

3. Write a brief, objective summary of the article, using only those details that are needed to develop or explain the central idea.

4. Discuss how the use of the photo and caption contributes to the information in the article.

5. Think about the role that perception plays in humans' understanding of themselves, according to the article. Explain how this research could change future interactions of humans across cultures.

## ✏ WRITE

EXPLANATORY: Analyze how the author uses evidence, details, examples, and technical language to communicate a thesis or central idea about changes in emotional theory. Discuss how the author develops this central idea over the course of the texts, including how it is shaped and refined by specific details.

# Dream Psychology:
## Psychoanalysis for Beginners

**INFORMATIONAL TEXT**
Sigmund Freud
1920

## Introduction

Psychoanalysis—a set of theories and techniques surrounding human development, personality and behavior—was popularized around the turn of the 20th century by Austrian neurologist Sigmund Freud (1856–1939). Initially, Freud's theories on the conscious and unconscious mind were viewed with a heavy skepticism by the medical community, but his work ultimately proved to be highly influential, and today he is considered the founding father of an entire field of study. In this excerpt from *Dream Psychology*, Freud discusses the relevance of dreams according to his hypothesis, and offers up a dream of his own as a case study.

# "I perceive that it is wrong to regard the dream as psychically unimportant."

from Chapter I: Dreams Have a Meaning

1   In what we may term "prescientific days" people were in no uncertainty about the **interpretation** of dreams. When they were recalled after awakening they were regarded as either the friendly or hostile manifestation of some higher powers, demoniacal and Divine. With the rise of scientific thought the whole of this expressive mythology was transferred to psychology; today there is but a small minority among educated persons who doubt that the dream is the dreamer's own psychical act.

Freud's iceberg theory of the mind held that the majority of human thought is beneath the surface.

2   But since the downfall of the mythological hypothesis an interpretation of the dream has been wanting. The **conditions** of its origin; its relationship to our psychical life when we are awake; its independence of disturbances which, during the state of sleep, seem to compel notice; its many peculiarities repugnant to our waking thought; the **incongruence** between its images and the feelings they engender; then the dream's evanescence, the way in which, on awakening, our thoughts thrust it aside as something bizarre, and our reminiscences mutilating or rejecting it—all these and many other problems have for many hundred years demanded answers which up till now could never have been satisfactory. Before all there is the question as to the meaning of the dream, a question which is in itself double-sided. There is, firstly, the psychical significance of the dream, its position with regard to the psychical processes, as to a possible biological function; secondly, has the dream a meaning—can sense be made of each single dream as of other mental **syntheses**?

3   Three tendencies can be observed in the estimation of dreams. Many philosophers have given currency to one of these tendencies, one which at the same time preserves something of the dream's former over-valuation.

The foundation of dream life is for them a peculiar state of psychical activity, which they even celebrate as elevation to some higher state. Schubert, for instance, claims: "The dream is the liberation of the spirit from the pressure of external nature, a detachment of the soul from the fetters of matter." Not all go so far as this, but many maintain that dreams have their origin in real spiritual excitations, and are the outward manifestations of spiritual powers whose free movements have been hampered during the day ("Dream Phantasies," Scherner, Volkelt). A large number of observers acknowledge that dream life is capable of extraordinary achievements—at any rate, in certain fields ("Memory").

4    In striking contradiction with this the majority of medical writers hardly admit that the dream is a psychical phenomenon at all. According to them dreams are provoked and initiated exclusively by stimuli proceeding from the senses or the body, which either reach the sleeper from without or are accidental disturbances of his internal organs. The dream has no greater claim to meaning and importance than the sound called forth by the ten fingers of a person quite unacquainted with music running his fingers over the keys of an instrument. The dream is to be regarded, says Binz, "as a physical process always useless, frequently morbid." All the peculiarities of dream life are explicable as the incoherent effort, due to some physiological stimulus, of certain organs, or of the cortical elements of a brain otherwise asleep.

5    But slightly affected by scientific opinion and untroubled as to the origin of dreams, the popular view holds firmly to the belief that dreams really have got a meaning, in some way they do foretell the future, whilst the meaning can be unravelled in some way or other from its oft bizarre and enigmatical content. The reading of dreams consists in replacing the events of the dream, so far as remembered, by other events. This is done either scene by scene, *according to some rigid key*, or the dream as a whole is replaced by something else of which it was a *symbol*. Serious-minded persons laugh at these efforts—"Dreams are but sea-foam!"

6    One day I discovered to my amazement that the popular view grounded in superstition, and not the medical one, comes nearer to the truth about dreams. I arrived at new conclusions about dreams by the use of a new method of psychological investigation, one which had rendered me good service in the investigation of phobias, obsessions, illusions, and the like, and which, under the name "psycho-analysis," had found acceptance by a whole school of investigators. The manifold **analogies** of dream life with the most diverse conditions of psychical disease in the waking state have been rightly insisted upon by a number of medical observers. It seemed, therefore, *a priori,*[1] hopeful to apply to the interpretation of dreams methods of investigation

1.  *a priori* (Latin) "what comes first," a term denoting reasoning or knowledge that comes before observation or analysis, or is self-evident

which had been tested in psychopathological processes. Obsessions and those peculiar sensations of haunting dread remain as strange to normal consciousness as do dreams to our waking consciousness; their origin is as unknown to consciousness as is that of dreams. It was practical ends that impelled us, in these diseases, to fathom their origin and formation. Experience had shown us that a cure and a consequent mastery of the obsessing ideas did result when once those thoughts, the connecting links between the morbid ideas and the rest of the psychical content, were revealed which were heretofore veiled from consciousness. The procedure I employed for the interpretation of dreams thus arose from psychotherapy.[2]

. . .

7   I will now point out where this method leads when I apply it to the examination of dreams. Any dream could be made use of in this way. From certain motives I, however, choose a dream of my own, which appears confused and meaningless to my memory, and one which has the advantage of brevity. Probably my dream of last night satisfies the requirements. Its content, fixed immediately after awakening, runs as follows:

8   *"Company; at table or table d'hôte. . . . Spinach is served. Mrs. E.L., sitting next to me, gives me her undivided attention, and places her hand familiarly upon my knee. In defence I remove her hand. Then she says: 'But you have always had such beautiful eyes.'. . . . I then distinctly see something like two eyes as a sketch or as the contour of a spectacle lens. . . ."*

9   This is the whole dream, or, at all events, all that I can remember. It appears to me not only obscure and meaningless, but more especially odd. Mrs. E.L. is a person with whom I am scarcely on visiting terms, nor to my knowledge have I ever desired any more cordial relationship. I have not seen her for a long time, and do not think there was any mention of her recently. No emotion whatever accompanied the dream process.

10   Reflecting upon this dream does not make it a bit clearer to my mind. I will now, however, present the ideas, without premeditation and without criticism, which **introspection** yielded. I soon notice that it is an advantage to break up the dream into its elements, and to search out the ideas which link themselves to each fragment.

11   *Company; at table or table d'hôte.* The recollection of the slight event with which the evening of yesterday ended is at once called up. I left a small party in the company of a friend, who offered to drive me home in his cab. "I prefer

2. **psychotherapy**   a practice in which mental health disorders are treated using psychological means, often with the guidance of a counselor or therapist

a taxi," he said; "that gives one such a pleasant occupation; there is always something to look at." When we were in the cab, and the cab-driver turned the disc so that the first sixty hellers were visible, I continued the jest. "We have hardly got in and we already owe sixty hellers. The taxi always reminds me of the table d'hôte. It makes me avaricious and selfish by continuously reminding me of my debt. It seems to me to mount up too quickly, and I am always afraid that I shall be at a disadvantage, just as I cannot resist at table d'hôte the comical fear that I am getting too little, that I must look after myself." In far-fetched connection with this I quote:

12     "To earth, this weary earth, ye bring us,
To guilt ye let us heedless go."

13     Another idea about the table d'hôte. A few weeks ago I was very cross with my dear wife at the dinner-table at a Tyrolese health resort, because she was not sufficiently reserved with some neighbors with whom I wished to have absolutely nothing to do. I begged her to occupy herself rather with me than with the strangers. That is just as if I had *been at a disadvantage at the table d'hôte*. The contrast between the behavior of my wife at the table and that of Mrs. E.L. in the dream now strikes me: *"Addresses herself entirely to me."*

14     Further, I now notice that the dream is the reproduction of a little scene which transpired between my wife and myself when I was secretly courting her. The caressing under cover of the tablecloth was an answer to a wooer's passionate letter. In the dream, however, my wife is replaced by the unfamiliar E.L.

15     Mrs. E.L. is the daughter of a man to whom I *owed money*! I cannot help noticing that here there is revealed an unsuspected connection between the dream content and my thoughts. If the chain of associations be followed up which proceeds from one element of the dream one is soon led back to another of its elements. The thoughts evoked by the dream stir up associations which were not noticeable in the dream itself.

16     Is it not customary, when some one expects others to look after his interests without any advantage to themselves, to ask the innocent question satirically: "Do you think this will be done *for the sake of your beautiful eyes*?" Hence Mrs. E.L.'s speech in the dream. "You have always had such beautiful eyes," means nothing but "people always do everything to you for love of you; you have had *everything for nothing*." The contrary is, of course, the truth; I have always paid dearly for whatever kindness others have shown me. Still, the fact that I *had a ride for nothing* yesterday when my friend drove me home in his cab must have made an impression upon me.

17     In any case, the friend whose guests we were yesterday has often made me his debtor. Recently I allowed an opportunity of requiting him to go by. He has

NOTES

had only one present from me, an antique shawl, upon which eyes are painted all round, a so-called Occhiale, as a *charm* against the *Malocchio*. Moreover, he is an *eye specialist*. That same evening I had asked him after a patient whom I had sent to him for *glasses*.

18  As I remarked, nearly all parts of the dream have been brought into this new connection. I still might ask why in the dream it was *spinach* that was served up. Because spinach called up a little scene which recently occurred at our table. A child, whose *beautiful eyes* are really deserving of praise, refused to eat spinach. As a child I was just the same; for a long time I loathed *spinach*, until in later life my tastes altered, and it became one of my favorite dishes. The mention of this dish brings my own childhood and that of my child's near together. "You should be glad that you have some spinach," his mother had said to the little gourmet. "Some children would be very glad to get spinach." Thus I am reminded of the parents' duties towards their children. Goethe's words—

19  "To earth, this weary earth, ye bring us,
To guilt ye let us heedless go"—

20  take on another meaning in this connection.

21  Here I will stop in order that I may recapitulate the results of the analysis of the dream. By following the associations which were linked to the single elements of the dream torn from their context, I have been led to a series of thoughts and reminiscences where I am bound to recognize interesting expressions of my psychical life. The matter yielded by an analysis of the dream stands in intimate relationship with the dream content, but this relationship is so special that I should never have been able to have inferred the new discoveries directly from the dream itself. The dream was passionless, disconnected, and **unintelligible**. During the time that I am unfolding the thoughts at the back of the dream I feel intense and well-grounded emotions. The thoughts themselves fit beautifully together into chains logically bound together with certain central ideas which ever repeat themselves. Such ideas not represented in the dream itself are in this instance the antitheses *selfish, unselfish, to be indebted, to work for nothing*. I could draw closer the threads of the web which analysis has disclosed, and would then be able to show how they all run together into a single knot; I am debarred from making this work public by considerations of a private, not of a scientific, nature. After having cleared up many things which I do not willingly acknowledge as mine, I should have much to reveal which had better remain my secret. Why, then, do not I choose another dream whose analysis would be more suitable for publication, so that I could awaken a fairer conviction of the sense and cohesion of the results disclosed by analysis? The answer is, because every dream which I investigate leads to the same difficulties and places me under the same need of discretion; nor should

I forgo this difficulty any the more were I to analyze the dream of someone else. That could only be done when opportunity allowed all concealment to be dropped without injury to those who trusted me.

22 The conclusion which is now forced upon me is that the dream is a *sort of substitution* for those emotional and intellectual trains of thought which I attained after complete analysis. I do not yet know the process by which the dream arose from those thoughts, but I perceive that it is wrong to regard the dream as psychically unimportant, a purely physical process which has arisen from the activity of isolated cortical elements awakened out of sleep.

23 I must further remark that the dream is far shorter than the thoughts which I hold it replaces; whilst analysis discovered that the dream was provoked by an unimportant occurrence the evening before the dream.

## ✎ WRITE

EXPLANATORY: Using Freud's method of dream analysis in this excerpt as a model, conduct an analysis of a dream of your own. Begin by briefly describing the dream you will be analyzing, and then discuss the particular thoughts or images in the dream, and what insights they may yield. You should follow Freud's basic process of analysis and use textual evidence to ground your analysis in his methods. However, your dream—as well as the conclusions you draw—must be your own.

# The Secret Life of Salvador Dalí

INFORMATIONAL TEXT
Salvador Dalí
1942

## Introduction

Salvador Dalí (1904–1989) was a world-famous artist from Catalonia, Spain. Highly influenced by the writing of Sigmund Freud—in particular, Freud's work on the significance of the subconscious—Dalí's art helped to define an avant garde 20th-century artistic movement known as Surrealism. Like other Surrealists, Dalí believed that the subconscious world held a greater importance than the world of the conscious mind. In this excerpt from his autobiography, he talks about attending the local communal school led by the eccentric Señor Traite, a person of "mythical prestige." He also recalls the ways in which, early on, he felt separate from other "typical" children, exploring his mind as a child and the powerful ways in which "revery and myth began to mingle."

# "One single thing, and this I did with desperate eagerness: I fabricated 'false memories.'"

**Chapter Four**

**False Childhood Memories**

1   Why had my parents chosen a school with so sensational a master as Señor Traite? My father, who was a free-thinker, and who had sprung from sentimental Barcelona, the Barcelona of "Clavé choirs[1]," the anarchists and the Ferrer trial[2], made it a matter of principle not to put me into the Christian schools or those of the Marist brothers[3], which would have been **appropriate** for people of our rank, my father being a notary and one of the most esteemed men of the town. In spite of this he was absolutely determined to put me into the communal school—Señor Traite's school. This attitude was regarded as a real eccentricity, only partly justified by the mythical prestige of Señor Traite, of whose pedagogical[4] gifts none of my parents' acquaintances had the slightest personal experience, since they had all raised their children elsewhere.

2   I therefore spent my first school year living with the poorest children of the town, which was very important, I think, for the development of my natural tendencies to megalomania. Indeed I became more and more used to considering myself, a rich child, as something precious, delicate, and absolutely different from all the ragged children who surrounded me. I was the only one to bring hot milk and cocoa put up in a magnificent thermos bottle wrapped in a cloth embroidered with my initials. I alone had an **immaculate** bandage put on the slightest scratch, I alone wore a sailor suit with insignia embroidered in thick gold on the sleeves, and stars on my cap, I alone had hair that was combed a thousand times and that smelt good of a perfume that must have seemed so troubling to the other children who would take turns coming up to me to get a better sniff of my privileged head. I was the only one, moreover, who wore well-shined shoes with silver buttons. These became, each time one of them got torn off, the occasion of a tussle

---

1. **Clavé choirs** popular choral groups tracing back to northern Spain in the 19th century
2. **the Ferrer trial** Francisco Ferrer was a Spanish educator who advocated for freedom of thought and was executed in 1909 by a military tribunal
3. **Marist brothers** a Catholic organization devoted to the education of young people
4. **pedagogical** relating to the theories and practice of education

for its possession among my schoolmates who in spite of the winter went barefoot or half shod with the gaping remnants of foul, unmatched and ill-fitted *espadrilles*[5]. Moreover, and especially, I was the only one who never would play, who never would talk with anyone. For that matter my schoolmates, too, considered me so much apart that they would only come near me with some misgivings in order to admire at close range a lace handkerchief that bloomed from my pocket, or my slender and flexible new bamboo cane adorned with a silver dog's head by way of a handle.

3    What, then, did I do during a whole year in this wretched state school? Around my solitary silence the other children disported themselves, possessed by a frenzy of continual turbulence. This spectacle appeared to me wholly incomprehensible. They shouted, played, fought, cried, laughed, hastening with all the obscure avidity of being to tear out pieces of living flesh with their teeth and nails, displaying that common and ancestral dementia which slumbers within every healthy biological specimen and which is the normal nourishment, appropriate to the practical and animal development of the "principal of action." How far was I from this development of the "practical principle of action—at the other pole, in fact! I was headed, rather, in the opposite direction: each day I knew less well how to do each thing! I admired the ingenuity of all those little beings possessed by the demon of all the wiles and capable of skillfully repairing their broken pencil-boxes with the use of small nails! And the complicated figures they could make by folding a piece of paper! With what dexterity and rapidity they would undo the most stubborn laces of their *espadrilles*, whereas I was capable of remaining locked up in a room a whole afternoon, not knowing how to turn the door-handle to get out; I would get lost as soon as I got into any house, even those I was most familiar with; I couldn't even manage by myself to take off my sailor blouse which slipped over the head, a few experiments in this exercise having **convinced** me of the danger of dying of suffocation. "Practical activity" was my enemy and the objects of the external world became beings that were daily more terrifying.

4    Señor Traite, too, seated on the height of his wooden platform, wove his chain of slumbers with a consciousness more and more akin to the vegetable, and if at times his dreams seemed to rock him with the gentleness of reeds bowing in the wind, at other moments he became as heavy as a tree-trunk. He would take advantage of his brief awakenings to reach for a pinch of snuff and to **chastise**, by pulling their ears till they bled, those going beyond the limit of the usual uproar who either by an adroitly aimed wad of spittle or by a fire kindled with books to roast chestnuts managed to anticipate his normal awakening with a disagreeable jolt.

5    What, I repeat, did I do during a whole year in this wretched school? One single thing, and this I did with desperate eagerness: I fabricated "false

5. *espadrilles* casual, flat shoes

memories." The difference between false memories and true ones is the same as for jewels: it is always the false ones that look most real, the most brilliant. Already at this period I remembered a scene which, by its improbability, must be considered as my first false memory. I was looking at a naked child who was being washed; I do not remember the child's sex, but I observed on one of its buttocks a horrible swarming mass of ants which seemed to be stationary in a hole the size of an orange. In the midst of the ablutions the child was turned round with its belly upward and I then thought that the ants would be crushed and that the hole would hurt it. The child was once more put back into its original position. My curiosity to see the ants again was **enormous**, but I was surprised that they were no longer there, just as there was no longer a trace of a hole. This false memory is very clear, although I cannot localize it in time.

6   On the other hand, I am perfectly sure that it was between the ages of seven and eight while I was at Señor Traite's school, forgetting the letters of the alphabet and the way to spell my name, that the growing and all-powerful sway of revery and myth began to mingle in such a continuous and imperious way with the life of every moment that later it has often become impossible for me to know where reality begins and the imaginary ends.

7   My memory has welded the whole into such a homogenous and indestructible mass that only a critically objective examination of certain events that are too absurd or clearly impossible obliges me to consider them as authentic false memories. For instance, when one of my memories pertains to events happening in Russia I am after all forced to catalogue it as false, since I have never been in that country in my life. And it is indeed to Russia that certain false memories go back.

Excerpted from *The Secret Life of Salvador Dalí* by Salvador Dalí, published by Dover Publications.

✏ WRITE

EXPLANATORY: This excerpt from Dalí's autobiography provides a glimpse into the childhood mind of an influential artist. Explain the role that imagination played in Dalí's childhood, using textual evidence and original commentary. Then, consider your opinion on the value of imagination for adults. Based on what you read and your own experience, is imagination a form of child's play, or is it a brainpower that can benefit adults too? Explain your thinking.

# Rock, Ghost, Willow, Deer:
## A Story of Survival

INFORMATIONAL TEXT
Allison Adelle Hedge Coke
2004

## Introduction

The editor, poet and educator Allison Adelle Hedge Coke (b. 1958) writes of growing up as a "mixed-blood woman." A descendant of the Cherokee, Huron and Metis tribes, Hedge Coke's educational and written work focuses on the Native American experience, often with at-risk communities. These opening pages from her memoir, *Rock, Ghost, Willow, Deer: A Story of Survival*, find their power in themes common to her writing—identity, storytelling, and memory.

# "All my names are good names, and I am thankful for them."

1   I descend from mobile and village peoples, interracial, **ingenious**, adventurous, and bold. None famous, none of any more than humble means, though in this great ancestral river thoroughly bloodstreamed true, I am born from those so **devoted** to their beliefs and way of living they would eagerly choose to be **memorialized** through songs or stories of honorable doings, or maybe through sharing a bit of tobacco on special occasions, rather than by accumulating material legacies in life.

2   Before me and around me were warriors, fighters, hunters, fishers, gatherers, growers, traders, midwives, runners, avid horse people, weavers, seamstresses, artists, craftspeople, musicians, storytellers, singers, linguists, dreamers, philosophers; they were Huron, Tsa la gi (Cherokee), Muscogee, French-Canadian, Portuguese, English, Alsace-Lorraine, Irish, Welsh; and there was the insane.

3   I understood all of this by the age of three.

4   When I was a tiny child, my father would sit me up at the hardwood kitchen table near my older sister, Pumpkin, and give us seed and pony beads to string. I could barely reach the surface of what seemed then to be an **enormous** gate-leg table to work, so I propped myself up higher by sitting with my feet and knees tucked under me on the light-brown vinyl chair seat. Being included made me feel like a big girl, so I worked hard.

5   As I remember, this table was off to the side of our kitchen on the north side of the house. We lived on an unfinished road, speckled with small clusters of mixed-blood and Indian families, on East Eleventh Street in Amarillo, Texas. My family had settled there temporarily because of my father's work in the Department of Agriculture. Amarillo is supposed to be a dry place, but when I was young, sometimes in spring, the smell of rain would hang in the air for days. Mint lined our front porch; a mud puppy we called Sam and a box turtle the size of a small shaker lived under it. The grasshoppers were so fat back then we would hull them out and eat their meat for snacks, imitating my father's Depression stories, just to make an impression on other kids.

6    I was born August 4, 1958, just north of the area. Named Allison Adele, my first name **acknowledging** a character in a book who, though slightly crippled herself, helped people who had special needs, the second honoring my mother's aunt Ivy Adele. I was told that the two names together mean "back foot soldier (rear or tail fighter) for truth (honor)." My birth certificate reads "Hedge Coke," as two words, and this is how I spell my last name. My sister's certificate reads "Hedgecoke" as one word. It varies throughout my family. My father says the name was closer to Crow (male), or Bird in the Bush, or Bush Crow originally, and we think of it in that way today still. I have other names, but they are personal—mostly unspoken. All my names are good names, and I am thankful for them. A name creates life patterns, which form and shape a life; my life, like my name, must have been formed many times over then handed to me to realize.

7    My dad has a good sense of humor, so when the nicknames come, they are from him. My toddler nickname was Baby No. The movie *Doctor No* was released locally while I was beginning to get mobile. I was into everything. My dad says he couldn't resist. He calls my sister Pumpkin Head since her face is round and full. She smiles wide, too. These are the first names we knew each other by. We see Baby No and Pumpkin Head in each other's eyes still today.

8    Each time my father starts us beading, I try my best to get my stubby fingers to shape long, bright necklaces with corn and flower patterns. He sits across from us and works on nine- and twelve-row patterns of his own. I am still young enough to be limited to stringing ponies; I finish a pattern that actually resembles my intention. My father looks it over carefully, nods, and, without saying anything about the beadwork, smiles and says my face is beaming.

9    I ask him what a beam is, and he tells me it is the stroke of sunlight pouring through a clearing in the clouds.

10   I didn't know my face could do such a thing.

11   In that kitchen my first clear memories begin. We are surrounded by cabinets, far above my reach, filled partially with flour, cornmeal, cereal, and macaroni and cheese, just as in every other house nearby. The windows are all open. Crossing the ceiling corners are cobwebs that my father saves for blood **coagulants** in case we get cut or step on nails barefoot. If a spider happens out onto the linoleum floor, he scoops it up with his bare hands and carries it outside, allowing it to be free to make webs elsewhere. He says the spider brought both pottery and weaving to The People and we should respect her for doing so.

Excerpted from *Rock, Ghost, Willow, Deer: A Story of Survival* by Allison Adelle Hedge Coke, published by University of Nebraska Press.

**WRITE**

PERSONAL ESSAY: In this excerpt from her memoir *Rock, Ghost, Willow, Deer: A Story of Survival*, Allison Hedge Coke traces her understanding of who she is back to the moment at which her "first clear memories" began. Mimicking the style of her memoir, write your own personal essay recounting your first clear memory.

# The God of Small Things

FICTION
Arundhati Roy
1997

# Introduction

S et in India at the end of the 20th century, *The God of Small Things* by Arundhati Roy (b. 1961) presents India's complex social and historical identity in an intricate narrative about a family and a community. Rahel and Estha, twin sister and brother, live in a small town in southern India with their mother, Ammu, their uncle, Chacko, and their grandmother, Mammachi. Chacko, educated at Oxford, is a "self-proclaimed Marxist" and the inept manager of the family's pickle factory. In this excerpt, Chacko uses the example of his late father, Pappachi, to teach the twins about India's colonial heritage.

# "A war that we have won and lost. The very worst sort of war."

NOTES

1 Chacko said that the correct word for people like Pappachi was Anglophile. He made Rahel and Estha look up Anglophile in the Reader's Digest Great Encyclopaedic Dictionary. It said: Person well **disposed** to the English. Then Estha and Rahel had to look up dispose.

2 It said:

(1) *Place suitably in particular order.*
(2) *Bring mind into certain state.*
(3) *Do what one will with, get off one's hands, stow away, demolish, finish, settle, consume (food), kill, sell.*

3 Chacko said that in Pappachi's case it meant (2) *Bring mind into certain state*. Which, Chacko said, meant that Pappachi's mind had been *brought into a state* which made him like the English.

4 Chacko told the twins that, though he hated to admit it, they were all Anglophiles. They were a *family* of Anglophiles. Pointed in the wrong direction, trapped outside their own history and unable to retrace their steps because their footprints had been swept away. He explained to them that history was like an old house at night. With all the lamps lit. And ancestors whispering inside.

5 "To understand history," Chacko said, "we have to go inside and listen to what they're saying. And look at the books and the pictures on the wall. And smell the smells."

6 Estha and Rahel had no doubt that the house Chacko meant was the house on the other side of the river, in the middle of the **abandoned** rubber estate where they had never been. Kari Saipu's house. The Black Sahib. The Englishman who had "gone native." Who spoke Malayalam and wore mundus. Ayemenem's own Kurtz. Ayemenem his private Heart of Darkness. He had shot himself through the head ten years ago, when his young lover's parents had taken the boy away from him and sent him to school. After the suicide, the property had become the subject of extensive **litigation** between Kari

Saipu's cook and his secretary. The house had lain empty for years. Very few people had seen it. But the twins could picture it.

7   The History House.

8   With cool stone floors and dim walls and billowing ship-shaped shadows. Plump, translucent lizards lived behind old pictures, and waxy, crumbling ancestors with tough toe-nails and breath that smelled of yellow maps gossiped in sibilant, papery whispers.

9   "But we can't go in," Chacko explained, "because we've been locked out. And when we look in through the windows, all we see are shadows. And when we try and listen, all we hear is a whispering. And we cannot understand the whispering, because our minds have been invaded by a war. A war that we have won and lost. The very worst sort of war. A war that captures dreams and re-dreams them. A war that has made us adore our conquerors and despise ourselves."

10  "*Marry* our conquerors, is more like it," Ammu said dryly, referring to Margaret Kochamma. Chacko ignored her. He made the twins look up Despise. It said: *To look down upon; to view with contempt; to scorn or disdain.*

11  Chacko said that in the context of the war he was talking about –the War of Dreams –*Despise* meant all those things.

12  "We're Prisoners of War," Chacko said. "Our dreams have been doctored. We belong nowhere. We sail unanchored on troubled seas. We may never be allowed ashore. Our sorrows will never be sad enough. Our joys never happy enough. Our dreams never big enough. Our lives never important enough. To matter."

13  Then, to give Estha and Rahel a sense of Historical **Perspective** (though Perspective was something which, in the weeks to follow, Chacko himself would sorely lack), he told them about the Earth Woman. He made them imagine that the earth –four thousand six hundred million years old –was a forty-six-year-old woman –as old, say, as Aleyamma Teacher, who gave them Malayalam lessons. It had taken the whole of the Earth Woman's life for the earth to become what it was. For the oceans to part. For the mountains to rise. The Earth Woman was eleven years old, Chacko said, when the first single-celled organisms appeared. The first animals, creatures like worms and jellyfish, appeared only when she was forty. She was over forty-five –just eight months ago—when dinosaurs roamed the earth.

Please note that excerpts and passages in the StudySync® library and this workbook are intended as touchstones to generate interest in an author's work. The excerpts and passages do not substitute for the reading of entire texts, and StudySync® strongly recommends that students seek out and purchase the whole literary or informational work in order to experience it as the author intended. Links to online resellers are available in our digital library. In addition, complete works may be ordered through an authorized reseller by filling out and returning to StudySync® the order form enclosed in this workbook.

Reading & Writing Companion   419

14 "The whole of human civilization as we know it," Chacko told the twins, "began only *two hours* ago in the Earth Woman's life. As long as it takes us to drive from Ayemenem to Cochin."

15 It was an awe-inspiring and humbling thought, Chacko said (Humbling was a nice word, Rahel thought. *Humbling along without a care in the world* ), that the whole of **contemporary** history, the World Wars, the War of Dreams, the Man on the Moon, science, literature, philosophy, the pursuit of knowledge —was no more than a blink of the Earth Woman's eye.

16 "And we, my dears, everything we are and ever will be are just a twinkle in her eye," Chacko said grandly, lying on his bed, staring at the ceiling.

17 When he was in this sort of mood, Chacko used his Reading Aloud voice. His room had a church-feeling. He didn't care whether anyone was listening to him or not. And if they were, he didn't care whether or not they had understood what he was saying. Ammu called them his Oxford Moods.

*Excerpted from* The God of Small Things *by Arundhati Roy, published by HarperCollins Publishers.*

## ✎ WRITE

DISCUSSION: In the novel excerpt from *The God of Small Things*, the narrator alludes to Conrad's *Heart of Darkness* as the uncle of the twins, Chacko, instructs them about India's colonial history. Chacko explains that to understand history, "we have to go inside and listen to what they're saying. And look at the books and the pictures on the wall. And smell the smells." How does "going inside" history help the family—and by extension, anyone—understand who they are and where they are going? Prepare for a discussion with your peers by writing down the meaning of the allusion, your stance about this claim, your reasoning, and evidence to support your position.

# Persepolis

INFORMATIONAL TEXT
Marjane Satrapi
2000

## Introduction

First published in 2000, the critically acclaimed graphic novel *Persepolis* is based on the childhood experiences of Marjane Satrapi (b. 1969), who grew up in Iran during the Islamic Revolution. The title is a reference to the ancient capital of the Persian Empire. In the chapter presented here, entitled "The Shabbat," rumors have begun to spread that Iraq is on the verge of using ballistic missiles against the people of Iran. The Iran–Iraq War began on September 22, 1980, when Iraq invaded Iran following a long history of border disputes. Iraq planned to annex the oil-rich Khuzestan Province and the east bank of the Shatt al-Arab, a river formed by the union of the Tigris and Euphrates Rivers. Initially, Satrapi's family is skeptical. But when the rumors turn out to be true, no place is safe. And when a missile explodes in Satrapi's neighborhood, her life is changed forever.

"When the sirens went on, it meant we had three minutes to know if the end had come."

Skill:
Character

As the characters discuss their worries over the war, I notice they seem both worldly and close-knit. They drink tea as they discuss their feelings openly and honestly. The drawing shows their reactions, too.

Page 133

**Page 134**

Skill:
Character

All three characters look worried about the war and the possibility of being hit by a missile. But Marji looks trusting as she asks her parents about what to do. Marji's fear and trust show her to be a complex character.

Skill:
Media

With the pictures, I can see the buildings being bombed and the look of terror on the family's face. The pictures emphasize the feeling of a sudden explosion. Through the text I learn about the family's responses.

'Please note that excerpts and passages in the StudySync® library and this workbook are intended as touchstones to generate interest in an author's work. The excerpts and passages do not substitute for the reading of entire texts, and StudySync® strongly recommends that students seek out and purchase the whole literary or informational work in order to experience it as the author intended. Links to online resellers are available in our digital library. In addition, complete works may be ordered through an authorized reseller by filling out and returning to StudySync® the order form enclosed in this workbook.

Reading & Writing Companion 423

Skill:
Story Structure

I see the parallel plots of Marji's childhood, her friend Neda's childhood, and the war. The large panel slows down the story. This time to focus on them gives me time to feel scared for these young girls.

**Page 135**

NOW THAT TEHRAN WAS UNDER ATTACK, MANY FLED. THE CITY WAS DESERTED. AS FOR US, WE STAYED. NOT JUST OUT OF FATALISM. IF THERE WAS TO BE A FUTURE, IN MY PARENTS' EYES, THAT FUTURE WAS LINKED TO MY FRENCH EDUCATION. AND TEHRAN WAS THE ONLY PLACE I COULD GET IT.

SOME PEOPLE, MORE CIRCUMSPECT, TOOK SHELTER IN THE BASEMENTS OF BIG HOTELS, WELL-KNOWN FOR THEIR SAFETY. APPARENTLY, THEIR REINFORCED CONCRETE STRUCTURES WERE BOMBPROOF.

ONE EXAMPLE WAS OUR NEIGHBORS, THE BABA-LEVYS. THEY WERE AMONG THE FEW JEWISH FAMILIES THAT HAD STAYED AFTER THE REVOLUTION. MR. BABA-LEVY SAID THEIR ANCESTORS HAD COME THREE THOUSAND YEARS AGO, AND IRAN WAS THEIR HOME.

...THEIR DAUGHTER NEDA WAS A QUIET GIRL WHO DIDN'T PLAY MUCH, BUT WE WOULD TALK ABOUT ROMANCE FROM TIME TO TIME.

...ONE DAY A BLOND PRINCE WITH BLUE EYES WILL COME AND TAKE ME TO HIS CASTLE...

OH YEAH! ME TOO!

SO LIFE WENT ON...

Persepolis

**Page 136**

NOTES

Skill: Character

Here Marji undergoes a transformation. The character of the "typical" teenager who enjoys shopping is shattered by a missile. Leaving the jeans may symbolize that Marji has undergone a loss of innocence.

Skill: Story Structure

The use of nine panels of the same size packs the page with events: Marji with her mom, information about money, everyday shopping, and the shock of a bomb and its aftermath. The last panel is full of suspense.

NOTES

**Page 137**

**Page 138**

Skill:
Media

In the top panel, the emphasis is on the bombed-out windows of the buildings and the slumped form of Marji as she walks to see if her mother is alive. The text tells me what Marji is thinking.

Persepolis

NOTES

**Page 139**

**428** Reading & Writing Companion

Copyright © BookheadEd Learning, LLC

**Page 140**

"The Shabbat" from PERSEPOLIS: THE STORY OF A CHILDHOOD by Marjane Satrapi, translation copyright © 2003 by L'Association, Paris, France. Used by permission of Pantheon Books, an imprint of the Knopf Doubleday Publishing Group, a division of Penguin Random House LLC. All rights reserved.

Please note that excerpts and passages in the StudySync® library and this workbook are intended as touchstones to generate interest in an author's work. The excerpts and passages do not substitute for the reading of entire texts, and StudySync® strongly recommends that students seek out and purchase the whole literary or informational work in order to experience it as the author intended. Links to online resellers are available in our digital library. In addition, complete works may be ordered through an authorized reseller by filling out and returning to StudySync® the order form enclosed in this workbook.

Reading & Writing Companion   **429**

# First Read

Read *Persepolis*. After you read, complete the Think Questions below.

---

1. Why is Marji's mother shocked at the price of jeans? Cite evidence from the text to support your answer.

2. After the missile attacks start, why does Marji's family remain in Tehran? Support your answer using evidence from the text.

3. When Marji learns that the missile destroyed their neighbor's house, why does her mother try to change the subject? Cite evidence from the text to support your answer.

4. Given that *circum* is a Latin root meaning "around" and *spect* is a Latin root meaning "to see," write your best definition of **circumspect**. Then use an online or print dictionary to verify the meaning.

5. Using context clues, write your best defintion of the word **euphoria** as it is used in the text. Then describe which clues helped you figure it out.

# Skill: Character

Use the Checklist to analyze Character in *Persepolis*. Refer to the sample student annotations about Character in the text.

## ••• CHECKLIST FOR CHARACTER

In order to determine how complex characters develop and interact with other characters in a text, note the following:

✓ look for complex characters in the text, such as a character that

- has conflicting emotions and motivations

- develops and changes over the course of a story or drama

- advances the events of the plot

- develops the central idea, or theme, through his or her actions

✓ the ways that characters respond, react, or change as the events of the plot unfold and how they interact with other characters in the story

✓ how the reactions and responses of complex characters help to advance the plot and develop the theme

✓ the resolution of the conflict in the plot and the ways it affects the characters

To analyze how complex characters develop over the course of a text and interact with other characters, consider the following questions:

✓ Which characters in the text could be considered complex?

✓ How do the characters change as the plot unfolds? When do they begin to change? Which events cause them to change? How do these changes advance the plot and develop the theme?

✓ How do the complex characters interact with other characters?

✓ How does the resolution affect the characters?

# Skill:
# Character

Reread pages 94 and 95 of *Persepolis*. Then, using the Checklist on the previous page, answer the multiple-choice questions below.

## ↻ YOUR TURN

1.  Which of the following best explains how the author uses the plot events of the Iran-Iraq war to develop the complex characters of members of Iranian society?

    ○ A. Iranians are too scared to help each other, reflecting a fearful society.

    ○ B. Iranians are inclined to hide, reflecting the damages of war.

    ○ C. The taxi driver calling for his money reflects Iran's poverty.

    ○ D. Iranians have differing responses to war, reflecting the society at a human level.

2.  On page 95, how does the author develop Marji's mother as a complex character through her reaction to the key event of the bombing?

    ○ A. Marji's mother is an aggressive character because she, despite Marji's wishes, forces Marji to face violence with courage.

    ○ B. Marji's mother is a protective character because she shields Marji from the violent aftermath of the missile.

    ○ C. Marji's mother is an innocent character because she does not understand that Marji's friend has died in the bombing.

    ○ D. Marji's mother is a villainous character because she opposes Marji's attempt to see what lies in the wreckage.

# Skill:
# Story Structure

Use the Checklist to analyze Story Structure in *Persepolis*. Refer to the sample student annotations about Story Structure in the text.

## ••• CHECKLIST FOR STORY STRUCTURE

In order to determine how an author's choices concerning how to structure a text, order events within it, and manipulate time create such effects as mystery, tension, or surprise, note the following:

✓ the pattern an author uses to organize the events in a story:

- chronological, or in time order

- nonlinear, or events out of time order

✓ the author's use of description, dialogue, and narration to develop the plot

✓ any devices the author uses to manipulate time, such as the following:

- foreshadowing: hinting at events to come later

- flashback: shifting to an event that happened in the past

- pacing: increasing or decreasing the speed of the events

✓ parallel plots, or two or more plots in a story that are usually linked by a common character and a similar theme

To analyze how an author's choices concerning how to structure a text, order events within it, and manipulate time create such effects as mystery, tension, or surprise, consider the following questions:

✓ How do the author's choices about the structure create effects as mystery, tension, or surprise?

✓ How does the pace in which events take place affect the story?

✓ Are there parallel plots in the story? How do they work together?

✓ How does the author manipulate time in the story? What effect(s) does this create?

✓ How does the author use flashbacks or foreshadowing create an effect, such as tension?

# Skill:
# Story Structure

Reread page 95 of *Persepolis*. Then, using the Checklist on the previous page, answer the multiple-choice questions below.

## ↻ YOUR TURN

1. How do the parallel plots of Marji's childhood, her friend Neda's life, and the Iran-Iraq War build to a climax, or high point of emotion, on this page?

   ○ A. The last panel, where we see nothing, creates a feeling of hopelessness that is the climax of the scene on this page.

   ○ B. The third panel, where we see Marji's realization of the effects of war, is the climax of the scene on this page.

   ○ C. The fourth panel, where we see Marji's covering her eyes to avoid the truth, is the climax of the scene on this page.

   ○ D. The second panel, where Marji's mother pulls her away, is the climax of the scene on this page.

2. What is the common theme that connects the parallel plot lines of Marji's childhood, her friend Neda, and the Iran-Iraq war?

   ○ A. There is a common theme of hope during dark times.

   ○ B. There is a common theme of growth through struggle.

   ○ C. There is a common theme of destruction of innocence.

   ○ D. There is a common theme of hatred of the other.

# Skill:
# Media

Use the Checklist to analyze Media in *Persepolis*. Refer to the sample student annotations about Media in the text.

## ••• CHECKLIST FOR MEDIA

In order to determine the representation of a subject or a key scene in two different artistic mediums, do the following:

- ✓ note the artistic medium and its features

- ✓ identify what is emphasized or absent in each treatment of a subject or a key scene

- ✓ examine why the same subject receives completely different treatments in different media

- ✓ consider sources, as a story about a historical event might refer, directly or indirectly, to letters, paintings, plays, or photographs from the same place and time as the events that took place

To analyze the representation of a subject or a key scene in two different artistic mediums, including what is emphasized or absent in each treatment, consider the following questions:

- ✓ Is the content informational or fictional? How does this affect the treatment of the key scene or subject?

- ✓ What are the strengths and weaknesses of each artistic medium? How does this affect the treatment of the key scene or subject?

- ✓ What is emphasized and what is absent, or left out of each medium's version of events?

Skill:
Media

Reread page 95 of *Persepolis*. Then, using the Checklist on the previous page, answer the multiple-choice questions below.

## ⟳ YOUR TURN

1. What does the illustration of the Baba-Levys' house add to the text description of the destruction?

   ○ A. The illustration helps us understand that the destruction of the building is not as bad as the words make it sound.

   ○ B. The words say that the house was "completely destroyed," but the image helps us see just how bad the destruction was.

   ○ C. Even though the text says the building was "completely destroyed," the illustration gives us hope that the Baba-Levys are alive.

   ○ D. The illustration does not add to the description.

2. How does the last panel of the story emphasize the text in conveying Marji's emotions?

   ○ A. The image lets us know that the narrator does not want us to see her screaming.

   ○ B. The image does not add to the text, but instead detracts because we are unable to see anything.

   ○ C. The words tell us what she is feeling, but the black panel helps to convey the depth of the darkness of those emotions.

   ○ D. The black panel shows us that the emotions are not important enough to illustrate.

# PERSEPOLIS

# Close Read

Reread *Persepolis*. As you reread, complete the Skills Focus questions below. Then use your answers and annotations from the questions to help you complete the Write activity.

## ◎ SKILLS FOCUS

1. Analyze how the the narrator, Marji, develops over the course of the excerpt, including how her interactions with other characters shape her development.

2. Reading the text by itself without the pictures, explain how *Persepolis* changes in terms of both narrative and emotional content.

3. Think about the parallel events of *Persepolis*, including the war from the outside world vs. the day-to-day life of an ordinary Iranian family, as well as the single moment of flashback, where Marji dreams of a prince with her friend Neda Baba-Levy. Analyze how Satrapi's story structure creates emotional effects such as tension and empathy.

4. In *Rock,Ghost, Willow, Deer: A Story of Survival*, author Coke says, "My dad has a good sense of humor, so when the nicknames come, they are from him. My toddler nickname was Baby No," a joke connected to the James Bond film *Doctor No*, implying that she was often told "no." Identify how the author of *Persepolis* uses the specific culture of Marji's family to reveal their humor.

5. Discuss how, in creating *Persepolis*, Marjane Satrapi's past changed her future.

## ✎ WRITE

LITERARY ANALYSIS: In *The God of Small Things*, Chacko says of Anglo-Indian history, "And we cannot understand the whispering, because our minds have been invaded by a war. A war that we have won and lost. The very worst sort of war. A war that captures dreams and re-dreams them." Explain how this quotation connects to the unique and shared experiences of the people or characters depicted in the graphic novel *Persepolis*, the memoir *Rock,Ghost, Willow, Deer: A Story of Survival*, and the novel *The God of Small Things*. Select ideas or evidence from the various texts to support your response.

Please note that excerpts and passages in the StudySync® library and this workbook are intended as touchstones to generate interest in an author's work. The excerpts and passages do not substitute for the reading of entire texts, and StudySync® strongly recommends that students seek out and purchase the whole literary or informational work in order to experience it as the author intended. Links to online resellers are available in our digital library. In addition, complete works may be ordered through an authorized reseller by filling out and returning to StudySync® the order form enclosed in this workbook.

Reading & Writing
Companion

437

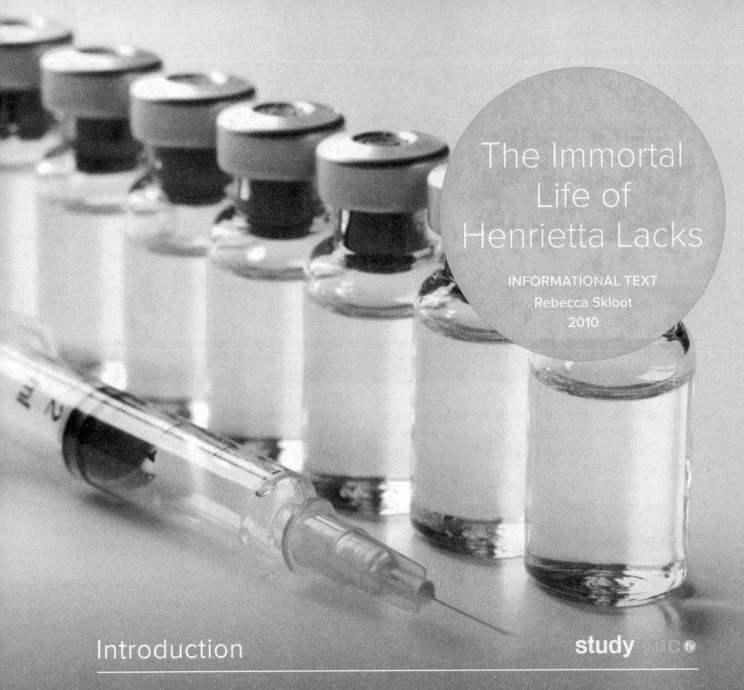

# The Immortal Life of Henrietta Lacks

INFORMATIONAL TEXT
Rebecca Skloot
2010

## Introduction

**study**sync ᴛᴠ

Author Rebecca Skloot (b. 1972) was a freshman biology student when she learned of a unique and moving human story. It was a tale of medical discoveries, ethics, race, and big business—and the struggles of an underprivileged family in East Baltimore. Though scientists worldwide know her as HeLa, at the center of this controversy is Henrietta Lacks. She was a poor black tobacco farmer whose cells were removed without her consent as she lay dying of cervical cancer in 1951. The years Skloot spent researching Henrietta exposed the truth—those cells taken from Lacks and kept alive have contributed to great medical breakthroughs including the polio vaccine, cloning, and much more, yet Lacks had remained unknown and her family was never compensated. The world has benefited and many people have profited from Henrietta without even knowing she existed.

# "Like guinea pigs and mice, Henrietta's cells have become the standard laboratory workhorse."

Excerpt from Prologue

## THE WOMAN IN THE PHOTOGRAPH

1. There's a photo on my wall of a woman I've never met, its left corner torn and patched together with tape. She looks straight into the camera and smiles, hands on hips, dress suit neatly pressed, lips painted deep red. It's the late 1940s and she hasn't yet reached the age of thirty. Her light brown skin is smooth, her eyes still young and playful, **oblivious** to the tumor growing inside her—a tumor that would leave her five children motherless and change the future of medicine. Beneath the photo, a caption says her name is "Henrietta Lacks, Helen Lane or Helen Larson."

2. No one knows who took that picture, but it's appeared hundreds of times in magazines and science textbooks, on blogs and laboratory walls. She's usually identified as Helen Lane, but often she has no name at all. She's simply called HeLa, the code name given to the world's first immortal human cells—*her* cells, cut from her cervix just months before she died.

3. Her real name is Henrietta Lacks.

4. I've spent years staring at that photo, wondering what kind of life she led, what happened to her children, and what she'd think about cells from her cervix living on forever—bought, sold, packaged, and shipped by the trillions to laboratories around the world. I've tried to imagine how she'd feel knowing that her cells went up in the first space missions to see what would happen to human cells in zero gravity, or that they helped with some of the most important advances in medicine: the polio vaccine, chemotherapy, cloning, gene mapping, in vitro fertilization. I'm pretty sure that she—like most of us— would be shocked to hear that there are trillions more of her cells growing in laboratories now than there ever were in her body.

5. There's no way of knowing exactly how many of Henrietta's cells are alive today. One scientist estimates that if you could pile all HeLa cells ever grown onto a scale, they'd weigh more than 50 million metric tons—an inconceivable

Please note that excerpts and passages in the StudySync® library and this workbook are intended as touchstones to generate interest in an author's work. The excerpts and passages do not substitute for the reading of entire texts, and StudySync® strongly recommends that students seek out and purchase the whole literary or informational work in order to experience it as the author intended. Links to online resellers are available in our digital library. In addition, complete works may be ordered through an authorized reseller by filling out and returning to StudySync® the order form enclosed in this workbook.

Reading & Writing Companion   439

number, given that an individual cell weighs almost nothing. Another scientist calculated that if you could lay all HeLa cells ever grown end-to-end, they'd wrap around the Earth at least three times, spanning more than 350 million feet. In her prime, Henrietta herself stood only a bit over five feet tall.

6   I first learned about HeLa cells and the woman behind them in 1988, thirty-seven years after her death, when I was sixteen and sitting in a community college biology class. My instructor, Donald Defler, a gnomish balding man, paced at the front of the lecture hall and flipped on an overhead projector. He pointed to two diagrams that appeared on the wall behind him. They were schematics of the cell reproduction cycle, but to me they just looked like a neon-colored mess of arrows, squares, and circles with words I didn't understand, like "MPF Triggering a Chain Reaction of Protein Activations."

7   I was a kid who'd failed freshman year at the regular public high school because she never showed up. I'd transferred to an alternative school that offered dream studies instead of biology, so I was taking Defler's class for high-school credit, which meant that I was sitting in a college lecture hall at sixteen with words like *mitosis* and *kinase inhibitors* flying around. I was completely lost.

8   "Do we have to memorize everything on those diagrams?" one student yelled.

9   Yes, Defler said, we had to memorize the diagrams, and yes, they'd be on the test, but that didn't matter right then. What he wanted us to understand was that cells are amazing things: There are about one hundred trillion of them in our bodies, each so small that several thousand could fit on the period at the end of this sentence. They make up all our tissues—muscle, bone, blood— which in turn make up our organs.

10  Under the microscope, a cell looks a lot like a fried egg: It has a white (the *cytoplasm*) that's full of water and proteins to keep it fed, and a yolk (the *nucleus*) that holds all the genetic information that makes you *you*. The cytoplasm buzzes like a New York City street. It's crammed full of molecules and vessels endlessly shuttling **enzymes** and sugars from one part of the cell to another, pumping water, nutrients, and oxygen in and out of the cell. All the while, little cytoplasmic factories work 24/7, cranking out sugars, fats, proteins, and energy to keep the whole thing running and feed the nucleus—the brains of the operation. Inside every nucleus within each cell in your body, there's an identical copy of your entire **genome**. That genome tells cells when to grow and divide and makes sure they do their jobs, whether that's controlling your heartbeat or helping your brain understand the words on this page.

11   Defler paced the front of the classroom telling us how mitosis—the process of cell division—makes it possible for embryos to grow into babies, and for our bodies to create new cells for healing wounds or replenishing blood we've lost. It was beautiful, he said, like a perfectly choreographed dance.

12   All it takes is one small mistake anywhere in the division process for cells to start growing out of control, he told us. Just *one* enzyme misfiring, just *one* wrong protein activation, and you could have cancer. Mitosis goes **haywire**, which is how it spreads.

13   "We learned that by studying cancer cells in culture," Defler said. He grinned and spun to face the board, where he wrote two words in enormous print: HENRIETTA LACKS.

14   Henrietta died in 1951 from a vicious case of cervical cancer, he told us. But before she died, a surgeon took samples of her tumor and put them in a petri dish. Scientists had been trying to keep human cells alive in culture for decades, but they all eventually died. Henrietta's were different: they reproduced an entire generation every twenty-four hours, and they never stopped. They became the first immortal human cells ever grown in a laboratory.

15   "Henrietta's cells have now been living outside her body far longer than they ever lived inside it," Defler said. If we went to almost any cell culture lab in the world and opened its freezers, he told us, we'd probably find millions—if not billions—of Henrietta's cells in small vials on ice.

16   Her cells were part of research into the genes that cause cancer and those that suppress it; they helped develop drugs for treating herpes, leukemia, influenza, hemophilia, and Parkinson's disease; and they've been used to study lactose digestion, sexually transmitted diseases, appendicitis, human longevity, mosquito mating, and the negative cellular effects of working in sewers. Their **chromosomes** and proteins have been studied with such detail and precision that scientists know their every quirk. Like guinea pigs and mice, Henrietta's cells have become the standard laboratory workhorse.

17   "HeLa cells were one of the most important things that happened to medicine in the last hundred years," Defler said.

18   Then, matter-of-factly, almost as an afterthought, he said, "She was a black woman." He erased her name in one fast swipe and blew the chalk from his hands. Class was over.

19   As the other students filed out of the room, I sat thinking, *That's it? That's all we get? There has to be more to the story.*

Please note that excerpts and passages in the StudySync® library and this workbook are intended as touchstones to generate interest in an author's work. The excerpts and passages do not substitute for the reading of entire texts, and StudySync® strongly recommends that students seek out and purchase the whole literary or informational work in order to experience it as the author intended. Links to online resellers are available in our digital library. In addition, complete works may be ordered through an authorized reseller by filling out and returning to StudySync® the order form enclosed in this workbook.

Reading & Writing
Companion

441

20  I followed Defler to his office.

21  "Where was she from?" I asked. "Did she know how important her cells were? Did she have any children?"

22  "I wish I could tell you," he said, "but no one knows anything about her."

23  After class, I ran home and threw myself onto my bed with my biology textbook. I looked up "cell culture" in the index, and there she was, a small parenthetical:

24    In culture, cancer cells can go on dividing indefinitely, if they have a continual supply of nutrients, and thus are said to be "immortal." A striking example is a cell line that has been reproducing in culture since 1951. (Cells of this line are called HeLa cells because their original source was a tumor removed from a woman named Henrietta Lacks.)

25  That was it. I looked up HeLa in my parents' encyclopedia, then my dictionary: No Henrietta.

26  As I graduated from high school and worked my way through college toward a biology degree, HeLa cells were omnipresent. I heard about them in histology, neurology, pathology; I used them in experiments on how neighboring cells communicate. But after Mr. Defler, no one mentioned Henrietta.

27  When I got my first computer in the mid-nineties and started using the Internet, I searched for information about her, but found only confused snippets: most sites said her name was Helen Lane; some said she died in the thirties; others said the forties, fifties, or even sixties. Some said ovarian cancer killed her, others said breast or cervical cancer.

28  Eventually I tracked down a few magazine articles about her from the seventies. *Ebony* quoted Henrietta's husband saying, "All I remember is that she had this disease, and right after she died they called me in the office wanting to get my permission to take a sample of some kind. I decided not to let them." *Jet* said the family was angry—angry that Henrietta's cells were being sold for twenty-five dollars a vial, and angry that articles had been published about the cells without their knowledge. It said, "Pounding in the back of their heads was a gnawing feeling that science and the press had taken advantage of them."

29  The articles all ran photos of Henrietta's family: her oldest son sitting at his dining room table in Baltimore, looking at a genetics textbook. Her middle son in military uniform, smiling and holding a baby. But one picture stood out

more than any other: in it, Henrietta's daughter, Deborah Lacks, is surrounded by family, everyone smiling, arms around each other, eyes bright and excited. Except Deborah. She stands in the foreground looking alone, almost as if someone pasted her into the photo after the fact. She's twenty-six years old and beautiful, with short brown hair and catlike eyes. But those eyes glare at the camera, hard and serious. The caption said the family had found out just a few months earlier that Henrietta's cells were still alive, yet at that point she'd been dead for twenty-five years.

30  All of the stories mentioned that scientists had begun doing research on Henrietta's children, but the Lackses didn't seem to know what that research was for. They said they were being tested to see if they had the cancer that killed Henrietta, but according to the reporters, scientists were studying the Lacks family to learn more about Henrietta's cells. The stories quoted her son Lawrence, who wanted to know if the immortality of his mother's cells meant that he might live forever too. But one member of the family remained voiceless: Henrietta's daughter, Deborah.

31  As I worked my way through graduate school studying writing, I became fixated on the idea of someday telling Henrietta's story. At one point I even called directory assistance in Baltimore looking for Henrietta's husband, David Lacks, but he wasn't listed. I had the idea that I'd write a book that was a biography of both the cells and the woman they came from—someone's daughter, wife, and mother.

32  I couldn't have imagined it then, but that phone call would mark the beginning of a decadelong adventure through scientific laboratories, hospitals, and mental institutions, with a cast of characters that would include Nobel laureates, grocery store clerks, convicted felons, and a professional con artist. While trying to make sense of the history of cell culture and the complicated ethical debate surrounding the use of human tissues in research, I'd be accused of conspiracy and slammed into a wall both physically and metaphorically, and I'd eventually find myself on the receiving end of something that looked a lot like an exorcism. I did eventually meet Deborah, who would turn out to be one of the strongest and most resilient women I'd ever known. We'd form a deep personal bond, and slowly, without realizing it, I'd become a character in her story, and she in mine.

33  Deborah and I came from very different cultures: I grew up white and agnostic in the Pacific Northwest, my roots half New York Jew and half Midwestern Protestant; Deborah was a deeply religious black Christian from the South. I tended to leave the room when religion came up in conversation because it made me uncomfortable; Deborah's family tended toward preaching, faith healings, and sometimes voodoo. She grew up in a black neighborhood that was one of the poorest and most dangerous in the country; I grew up in a

safe, quiet middle-class neighborhood in a predominantly white city and went to high school with a total of two black students. I was a science journalist who referred to all things supernatural as "woo-woo stuff"; Deborah believed Henrietta's spirit lived on in her cells, controlling the life of anyone who crossed its path. Including me.

34 "How else do you explain why your science teacher knew her real name when everyone else called her Helen Lane?" Deborah would say. "She was trying to get your attention." This thinking would apply to everything in my life: when I married while writing this book, it was because Henrietta wanted someone to take care of me while I worked. When I divorced, it was because she'd decided he was getting in the way of the book. When an editor who insisted I take the Lacks family out of the book was injured in a mysterious accident, Deborah said that's what happens when you piss Henrietta off.

35 The Lackses challenged everything I thought I knew about faith, science, journalism, and race. Ultimately, this book is the result. It's not only the story of HeLa cells and Henrietta Lacks, but of Henrietta's family—particularly Deborah—and their lifelong struggle to make peace with the existence of those cells, and the science that made them possible.

Excerpted from THE IMMORTAL LIFE OF HENRIETTA LACKS by Rebecca Skloot, copyright © 2010, 2011 by Rebecca Skloot. Used by permission of Crown Books, an imprint of the Crown Publishing Group, a division of Random House LLC. All rights reserved.

 WRITE

EXPLANATORY: In this excerpt from the prologue of *The Immortal Life of Henrietta Lacks*, Rebecca Skloot establishes her purpose for writing. How does the author use informational text structure, including a thesis or claim and sentences or paragraphs that refine her ideas, to help the reader understand the purpose of the book she has written about Lacks?

Extended Writing Project and Grammar

EXTENDED WRITING PROJECT

NARRATIVE WRITING

# Narrative Writing Process: Plan

| PLAN | DRAFT | REVISE | EDIT AND PUBLISH |

"Those who cannot remember the past are condemned to repeat it," wrote the Spanish American philosopher George Santayana. This quotation is often used as a reminder about the importance of memory. What we remember about our lives and about our history—as well as what we forget—influences the choices we make in the future.

## WRITING PROMPT

**How can memories change our future?**

From this unit or any other unit, reflect on texts that deal with the memories and dreams of individuals. Create an original narrative in which the protagonist is driven to action by the recurrence of a significant memory. Use what you have learned from these texts and your own prior knowledge to inform your writing. You may choose to write about an imagined character or you may write a personal narrative reflecting your own experiences. Be sure to describe the memory and to make the connection between this memory and the primary conflict of your narrative. Remember to include the following:

- a well-developed protagonist and other characters
- a plot that includes pivotal moments
- a distinct conflict and resolution
- a clear setting
- dialogue and descriptive details
- a thoughtful theme or reflection connected to the prompt

## Introduction to Narrative Writing

Narrative writing tells a story of experiences or events that have been imagined by a writer or that have happened in real life. Good narrative writing effectively uses genre characteristics and craft such as relevant descriptive details and a purposeful structure with a series of events that contain a beginning, middle, and end. The characteristics of fiction writing include:

- setting
- characters
- plot
- theme/reflection
- point of view

In addition to these characteristics, narrative writers also carefully craft their work through their use of dialogue, details, word choice, and figurative language. These choices help to shape the tone, mood, and overall style of the text. Effective narratives combine these genre characteristics and craft to engage the reader.

As you continue with this Extended Writing Project, you'll receive more instruction and practice at crafting each of the characteristics of fiction writing to create your own narrative.

Please note that excerpts and passages in the StudySync® library and this workbook are intended as touchstones to generate interest in an author's work. The excerpts and passages do not substitute for the reading of entire texts, and StudySync® strongly recommends that students seek out and purchase the whole literary or informational work in order to experience it as the author intended. Links to online resellers are available in our digital library. In addition, complete works may be ordered through an authorized reseller by filling out and returning to StudySync® the order form enclosed in this workbook.

Reading & Writing Companion    **447**

Before you get started on your own narrative, read this narrative that one student, Monica, wrote in response to the writing prompt. As you read the Model, highlight and annotate the features of narrative writing that Monica included in her narrative.

 NOTES

## ☰ STUDENT MODEL

### "Help Me! I'm Lost (Again)!"

1   Okay, I'm lost in the woods, and nobody knows where I am. Great. It's getting dark, and my phone is almost dead, and I don't have any food or water. Was that a raindrop I felt? Sigh. It's not like I didn't expect this to happen. I knew it was a bad idea to agree to go on this hike, but Nola told me that I needed to get over my fear of getting lost, which it turns out is not so much a fear as a prediction.

2   Ever since I was a kid, I have had a terrible sense of direction. Give me a map, a compass, a smart phone with GPS, it doesn't matter—I always get lost. The memory of the first time I ever got lost is forever imprinted on my mind. I was four or five, and Dad had taken me to one of those big box hardware stores. It was around Halloween. I drove Dad crazy talking about the princess-pirate-astronaut-cowgirl costume I wanted to wear. Dad was asking an employee for help with finding something when I heard this weird laughing sound: *harharharharhar*. Curious, I wandered around a corner and I came face-to-face with the Halloween display—a whole warehouse wall of life-sized animatronic ghouls and skeletons. The one making all the noise was a spooky-eyed skeleton whose jaw moved as it cackled. A huge hairy spider bounced around in its rib cage for that extra creepy special effect. Naturally, I screamed, and then I ran. I ran up and down every aisle in the store in search of my dad, wailing my head off. My dad, the store employee, and several concerned customers finally found me curled up and sobbing in the rug department.

3   Twelve years later, here I am stranded in the woods. How did this happen? Let's see . . . Nola and I were walking along the Yellow Trail—it was supposed to be the easiest—and then we both said, "Oh, look at that!" at the exact same second. I thought we were both talking about the same thing. I snapped my picture with my phone and when I looked up, Nola was gone. Gone!

4   I take a deep breath and try to push away the feeling of panic that is rising like flood waters around me. Dad told me what to do if I got lost. I think hard until I remember. "Don't panic" was number one. Check, sort of. "Stay on the path." I look down at the rocky path beneath my feet. Check. "Don't wander off." Well, too late on that one. "Use the whistle." The whistle! I pull out from my pocket the cheap yellow plastic whistle that I won at the spring fling carnival. I raise it to my lips and blast it hard. Tweeeee!

5   Miraculously, I hear Nola's voice. "Monica?" I turn to see her startled face. "There you are! I stopped to take a picture of that butterfly. When I turned around you were gone. Where did you go?"

6   Butterfly? I didn't see a butterfly. I saw a . . . ?—No way!—I pull out my phone, click open my photo app, and gasp at what I see before handing it over to my friend.

7   "Wow, Monica. That's a *really* big spider," Nola says. She sounds impressed. I'm impressed too. Since my encounter with the rib cage spider all those years ago, I haven't been too crazy about spiders either.

8   "I wonder if maybe after you took the picture of this spider you freaked out a little bit, like when you were little. You must have taken off down the trail. You weren't that far ahead of me. Just around the bend," Nola says.

9   "Really? I felt completely lost," I say.

10   Nola smiles kindly at me. She says, "Well, we picked the easy trail for you, remember. It's just a big circle. If you had kept going, you would have ended up at the ranger station by the parking lot. You weren't too lost." Then she adds, "Besides, I put a tracker tile in your jacket pocket just in case. Your dad gave it to me to use. He says he has a drawer full of them just for you."

11   For some reason, I start to giggle. I feel a little embarrassed, but mostly I feel relieved. I may never develop a reliable sense of direction, but I know two things now. One is that you can conquer your fears—I have a picture of a humongous, hairy spider to prove that. The other is that it doesn't matter if I can't navigate my way out of a paper bag as long as I have good friends like Nola—and tracker tiles!

# WRITE

Writers often take notes about story ideas before they sit down to write. Think about what you've learned so far about organizing narrative writing to help you begin prewriting.

- **Purpose**: What kind of memory do you want to write about? Will it be one you yourself have experienced, or will you invent one? What is its impact?

- **Audience**: Who is your audience and what message do you want to express to your audience?

- **Setting**: Where and when will your story take place? How might the setting of your story affect the characters and the conflict?

- **Characters**: What types of characters will you write about? Will you be the protagonist of your story or will you make up a character?

- **Plot**: What challenges might the characters face? What events will lead to the resolution of the conflict while keeping a reader engaged?

- **Theme/reflection**: If you are writing an imagined narrative, what general message about life do you want to express? If you are writing a real narrative, what careful thoughts about the significance of your experience will you include?

- **Point of view**: From which point of view should your story be told, and why?

## Response Instructions

Use the questions in the bulleted list to write a one-paragraph summary. Your summary should describe what will happen in your narrative like the one above.

Don't worry about including all of the details now; focus only on the most essential and important elements. You will refer back to this short summary as you continue through the steps of the writing process.

# Skill:
# Organizing Narrative Writing

## ••• CHECKLIST FOR ORGANIZING NARRATIVE WRITING

As you consider how to organize your writing for your narrative, use the following questions as a guide:

- Who is the narrator and who are the characters (or individuals) in the narrative?
- Will the story be told from one or multiple points of view?
- Where will (or did) the story take place?
- What conflict or problem will the characters (or individuals) involved have to resolve?
- Have I created a smooth progression of experiences or plot events?

Here are some strategies to help you create a smooth progression of experiences or events in your narrative:

- Establish a context

  > choose a setting and a situation, problem, or observation that characters will have to face and resolve

  > use cause-and-effect relationships or a sequential structure to create a smooth progression of experiences or events

  > decide how the conflict will be be resolved

    o the problem often builds to a climax, when the characters are forced to take action

- Introduce a narrator and/or characters

  > characters (or individuals) can be introduced all at once or over the course of the narrative

  > choose the role each character will play in the story

  > choose one or multiple points of view, either first or third person

    o a first-person narrator can be a participant or character in the story

    o a third-person narrator tells the story as an outside observer

YOUR TURN

Complete the chart below by matching each event to its correct place in the narrative sequence.

| Events | |
|---|---|
| A | She realizes that this old memory makes her feel good and recalls more of her earliest childhood. |
| B | She vows to go home and come back with her mom and dad and revisit her past. |
| C | The main character gets lost driving through an unfamiliar neighborhood. |
| D | She suddenly sees a home she has only previously seen in old family pictures. She realizes it was her parents' home when she was a baby and somehow she remembered it. |
| E | She starts to recognize landmarks, although she doesn't remember ever being there before. |

| Narrative Sequence | Event |
|---|---|
| Exposition | |
| Rising Action | |
| Climax | |
| Falling Action | |
| Resolution | |

## ↻ YOUR TURN

Complete the chart below by writing a short summary of what will happen in each section of your narrative.

| Outline | Summary |
|---|---|
| Exposition | |
| Rising Action | |
| Climax | |
| Falling Action | |
| Resolution | |

Please note that excerpts and passages in the StudySync® library and this workbook are intended as touchstones to generate interest in an author's work. The excerpts and passages do not substitute for the reading of entire texts, and StudySync® strongly recommends that students seek out and purchase the whole literary or informational work in order to experience it as the author intended. Links to online resellers are available in our digital library. In addition, complete works may be ordered through an authorized reseller by filling out and returning to StudySync® the order form enclosed in this workbook.

Reading & Writing
Companion

453

# Skill:
# Story Beginnings

Copyright © BookheadEd Learning, LLC

## ••• CHECKLIST FOR STORY BEGINNINGS

Before you write the beginning of your narrative, ask yourself the following questions:

- What kind of a story am I writing? Is it serious or humorous, formal or informal?

- What does the reader need to know about the narrator, main character, setting, and conflict?

- What will happen to my character in the story?

- Who is the narrator of my story? Should I establish either a singular narrator or multiple points of view?

Here are some methods to help you set out a problem, situation, or observation; establish one or multiple point(s) of view; and introduce a narrator and/or characters:

- Action

  > What action could help reveal information about my character or conflict?

  > How might an exciting moment grab my reader's attention?

  > How could a character's reaction or observation help set the mood?

- Description

  > Does my story take place in a special location or specific time period?

  > How can describing a location or character grab my readers' attention? What powerful emotions can I use?

- Dialogue

  > What dialogue would help my reader understand the setting or the conflict?

  > How could a character's internal thoughts provide information for my reader?

- Information

  > Would a surprising statement grab readers' attention?

  > What details will help my reader understand the character, conflict, or setting?

- Point of view

  > one point of view: first person, third person, third-person omniscient, or third-person limited

  > multiple points of view: introducing more than one narrator or character to tell the story

YOUR TURN

Choose the best answer to each question.

1. Below is a section from another revision of Monica's opening. Which sentence below, if added, would change the whole tone or mood of the narrative?

Okay, I'm lost in the woods, and nobody knows where I am. Great. It's getting dark, and my phone is almost dead, and I don't have any food or water. Was that a raindrop I felt? Sigh. It's not like I didn't expect this to happen. I knew it was a bad idea to agree to go on this hike, but Nola told me that I needed to get over my fear of getting lost, which it turns out is not so much a fear as a prediction.

- A. I'm afraid of the dark and I really hate being out of contact with civilization.
- B. Of the many adventures I have had during my life, perhaps a hike I took in the woods was the most revealing.
- C. I have a list of terrible things that happen to me on hikes.
- D. I really don't enjoy hiking, but Nola was sure I would change my mind.

2. Monica wants to improve the beginning of a previous draft of her story. Which sentence could reasonably be added to give more expository information about the narrator if inserted after the underlined sentence?

Okay, I'm lost in the woods, and nobody knows where I am. Great. It's getting dark, and my phone is almost dead, and I don't have any food or water. Was that a raindrop I felt? Sigh. <u>It's not like I didn't expect this to happen.</u>

- A. I saw that a course in nature survival is offered by the park service.
- B. Park rangers around the world know that hikers often fail to plan for the weather.
- C. Weather this time of year is often unpredictable.
- D. I'd listened to the weather report before we left, but I ignored it, of course.

 WRITE

Use the questions in the checklist section to revise the beginning of your narrative.

# Narrative Writing Process: Draft

| PLAN | DRAFT | REVISE | EDIT AND PUBLISH |
|---|---|---|---|

You have already made progress toward writing your real or imagined narrative. Now it is time to draft your real or imagined narrative.

## ✏ WRITE

Use your plan and other responses in your Binder to draft your narrative. You may also have new ideas as you begin drafting. Feel free to explore those new ideas as you have them. You can also ask yourself these questions to ensure that your writing is focused, organized, and developed:

**Draft Checklist:**

☐ **Focused**: Have I made the conflict and its cause clear to readers? Have I included only relevant details and nothing extraneous that might confuse my readers?

☐ **Organized**: Does the sequence of events in my narrative make sense? Do I want to start with the significant memory or treat it as a flashback? Will readers be engaged by the sequence of events and keep reading to find out what happens next?

☐ **Developed**: Does my writing flow together naturally, or is it choppy? Will my readers be able to easily follow and understand descriptions of the characters, settings, and events?

Before you submit your draft, read it over carefully. You want to be sure that you've responded to all aspects of the prompt.

Here is Monica's first draft. As you read, notice how Monica develops her draft to be focused, structured, and coherent. As she continues to revise and edit her narrative, she will find and improve weak spots in her writing, as well as correct any language or punctuation mistakes.

## ☰ STUDENT MODEL: FIRST DRAFT

### "Help Me! I'm Lost (Again)!"

It's getting dark, and my phone is almost dead, and I don't have any food or water. Was that a raindrop I felt? Sigh. It's not like I didn't expect this to hapen. I knew it was a bad idea to agree to go on this hike.

~~Every since I was a kid, I have had a terible sense of direction. Give me a map, a compass, a smart phone with GPS, it doesn't matter, I always get lost. The first time I ever got lost is stuck in my mind, I was four or five, and Dad had taken us to the hardware store. It was around Halloween. Dad was asking for help finding something when I heard this wierd sound. Curious, I went around a corner and I came face-to-face with the Halloween display. The one making all the noise was a skeleton whose jaw moved as they laughed. A spider bounced around in their rib cage. I totally lost it. I ran and ran up and down every ailse in the store. My dad found me in the rug department.~~

Ever since I was a kid, I have had a terrible sense of direction. Give me a map, a compass, a smart phone with GPS, it doesn't matter—I always get lost. The memory of the first time I ever got lost is forever imprinted on my mind. I was four or five, and Dad had taken me to one of those big box hardware stores. It was around Halloween. I drove Dad crazy talking about the princess-pirate-astronaut-cowgirl costume I wanted to wear. Dad was asking an employee for help with finding something when I heard this weird laughing sound: *harharharharhar*. Curious, I wandered around a corner and I came face-to-face with the Halloween display—a whole warehouse wall of life-sized animatronic ghouls and skeletons. The one making all the noise was a spooky-eyed skeleton whose jaw moved as it cackled. A huge hairy spider bounced around in its rib cage for that extra creepy special effect. Naturally, I screamed, and then I ran. I ran up and down every aisle in the store in search of my dad, wailing my head off. My dad, the store employee, and several concerned

**Skill:**
**Descriptive Details**

*Monica uses exact language and sensory details to help readers imagine the setting and focus on the action. She replaces "stuck in my mind" with "forever imprinted on my mind." She adds a sound detail ("harharharharhar") and a vivid verb ("cackled") to help readers imagine what she heard in the hardware store.*

### Skill:
### Transitions

Monica adds a time transition, "Twelve years later," to show that the flashback story she told about being with her father and being scared by a display spider happened in the past, when she also got lost. She then adds other transitional phrases to show shifts in time ("at the exact same second") and sudden jumps in thought ("when I looked up") that clarify the order of events.

### Skill:
### Narrative Techniques

Monica includes some dialogue to help show her thought process as the narrative approaches its climax. In addition, she wants to add more sensory language to slow down the pace of the narrative and create a more suspenseful tone around the climax.

customers finally found me curled up and sobbing in the rug department.

~~I am stranded in the woods. How did this happen? Nola and I were walking along the Yellow Trail and then we both said, "Oh, look at that!" I snapped my picture with my phone. I looked up. Where was Nola?~~

Twelve years later, here I am stranded in the woods. How did this happen? Let's see . . . Nola and I were walking along the Yellow Trail—it was supposed to be the easiest—and then we both said, "Oh, look at that!" at the exact same second. I thought we were both talking about the same thing. I snapped my picture with my phone and when I looked up, Nola was gone. Gone!

~~I take a deep breath and try to push away a feeling of panic Dad gave me advice for if I got lost. I think hard until I remember. That's right! He said not to panic, stay on the path, don't wander off, and use the whisle. I pull the whislte out from my pocket. I raise them to my lips and blast them hard. It makes a loud noise in the quiet woods.~~

I take a deep breath and try to push away the feeling of panic that is rising like flood waters around me. Dad told me what to do if I got lost. I think hard until I remember. "Don't panic" was number one. Check, sort of. "Stay on the path." I look down at the rocky path beneath my feet. Check. "Don't wander off." Well, too late on that one. "Use the whistle." The whistle! I pull out from my pocket the cheap yellow plastic whistle that I won at the spring fling carnival. I raise it to my lips and blast it hard. Tweeeee!

I hear Nola's voice. "Monica?" I turn to see her face. "There you are! I stopped to take a picture of that butterfly. When I turned around you were gone. Where did you go?"

Butterfly? I didn't see a butterfly. I saw a . . . ? No way! I pull out my phone, click open my photo ap, and gasp at what I see. Before I handed it over to my freind for how Nola would react.

"Wow, Monica. That's a *really* big spider," Nola says. She had sounded impressed. I'm impressed too since my enconter with the rib cage spider all those years ago, I haven't been too crazy about them either.

"I wonder if maybe after you took the picture of this spider you freaked out a little bit, like when you were little. You must have taken off down the trail. You weren't that far ahead of me. Just around the bend."

"Really? I felt compleatly lost"

She says, "Well, we picked the easy trail for you, remember. Its just a big circle. If you had kept going, you would have ended up at the ranger station. You weren't to lost." Nola smiles kindly at me. Then she adds, "Besides, I put a tracker tile in your pocket just in case. Your dad gave it to me."

~~I feel releived. I may never develop a reliable sense of direction. I know two things now. One is that you can conquer your fears. The other is that it doesn't matter if I can't navigate. I have good friends like Nola—and tracker tiles!~~

For some reason, I start to giggle. I feel a little embarrassed, but mostly I feel relieved. I may never develop a reliable sense of direction, but I know two things now. One is that you can conquer your fears—I have a picture of a humongous spider to prove that. The other is that it doesn't matter if I can't navigate my way out of a paper bag as long as I have good friends like Nola—and tracker tiles!

Skill:
Conclusions

*The details she added, such as "I start to giggle" and "I feel a little embarrassed," show that Monica can laugh at herself. The addition of other humorous details gives her narrative deeper emotions while also maintaining the original humor, making a stronger conclusion.*

# Skill:
# Narrative Techniques

## ••• CHECKLIST FOR NARRATIVE TECHNIQUES

As you begin to develop the techniques you will use in your narrative, ask yourself the following questions:

- Is it clear which character is talking in a dialogue?
- Is the pacing of events suitable and effective?
- Which literary devices can strengthen descriptions of the characters or plot events? How can I use personal reflection to develop my narrative?
- What additional characters and/or events might help to develop the narrative?

Here are some methods that can help you write dialogue, pacing, description, reflection, and multiple plot lines, to develop experiences, events, and/or characters in your narrative:

- use character dialogue to explain events or actions

  > use quotation marks correctly

  > include identifying names as needed before or after quotation marks

- use description so the reader can visualize the characters, setting, and other elements

  > descriptions should contribute to the reader's understanding of the element being described

- use pacing effectively

  > for a quick pace, use limited description, short paragraphs, brief dialogue, and simpler sentences

  > for a slower pace, use detailed description, longer paragraphs, and complex sentence structures

- use reflection to comment on the overall message

  > include character or personal inner thoughts or personal insight

- create multiple plot lines that further develop the narrative's message

  > include characters, events, or other elements that will further develop the plot

- use any combination of the techniques above

## ↻ YOUR TURN

Choose the best answer to each question.

1. Monica wants to improve the ending of a previous draft of her narrative. Which sentence could she add to provide more reflection about the significance of her experience?

> I feel a little silly because I wasn't actually lost. I guess a sense of direction is something you are born with, and I just didn't get one. This experience taught me something important.

- ○ A. After all, what else can I really do?
- ○ B. I'll never get used to getting lost.
- ○ C. Next time I'll remember to bring a map.
- ○ D. Every day is an opportunity for an adventure.

2. Monica wants to increase suspense in the plot by adding dialogue. Which is the best piece of dialogue to add to the second paragraph in Monica's draft and where best to add it?

> Curious, I went around a corner and I came face-to-face with the Halloween display. (1) The one making all the noise was a skeleton whose jaw moved as they laughed. (2) A spider bounced around in their rib cage. I totally lost it. I ran and ran up and down every ailse in the store. (3) My dad found me in the rug department. (4)

- ○ A. (1) "Can I help you, miss?" a store clerk asked.
- ○ B. (2) "Mwa ha ha ha," it said.
- ○ C. (3) "Dad! Dad! Where are you? I can't find you," I shouted.
- ○ D. (4) "I'm here, honey. What's wrong?" he asked, with an arm around my shoulder.

## ✎ WRITE

Use the questions in the checklist to revise a section of your fictional or personal narrative.

# Skill:
# Transitions

Copyright © BookheadEd Learning, LLC

---

## ••• CHECKLIST FOR TRANSITIONS

Before you revise your current draft to include transitions, think about:

- the order of events including the rising action, climax, falling action, and resolution
- moments where the time or setting changes
- how events build on previous events and create a unified story

Next, reread your current draft and note areas in your essay where:

- the order of events is unclear or illogical
- changes in time or setting are confusing or unclear. Look for:

  > sudden jumps

  > missing or illogical plot events or character experiences

  > places where you could add more context or exposition, such as important background information about the narrator, setting, characters, and conflict

Revise your draft to use a variety of techniques to sequence events so that they build on one another to create a coherent whole, using the following questions as a guide:

- Do the events of the rising action, climax, falling action, and resolution flow smoothly?
- What other techniques could I use so that events in my story build on one another, creating a coherent whole?
- Are there better transitional words, phrases, or clauses that I can use to show shifts in time, setting, and relationships between experiences and events?

  > transitions such as *moreover*, *likewise*, and *by the same token* show relationships between experiences and events

  > transitions such as *simultaneously* or *afterward* signal shifts in time and settings

## ↻ YOUR TURN

Read the transitions below. Then, complete the chart by matching each transition to the correct place in the outline so the plot of this narrative story is represented in a clear and logical order.

| | Transition Options |
|---|---|
| A | As I was cleaning out the garage, I came across a box inside a box inside another box. That's it! I suddenly remembered. |
| B | I had hid a valuable ring my grandmother gave me but I couldn't remember where I put it and I was just sick about it. |
| C | I ran back to my bedroom and dug out a large plastic Easter egg. Inside was another egg, and another, and then, grandma's ring! |
| D | I swore I would either wear that ring or keep it tied to my bedpost so I would never lose it again. |
| E | This is a true story that began ten years ago. |

| Outline | Transition |
|---|---|
| Exposition | |
| Rising Action | |
| Climax | |
| Falling Action | |
| Resolution | |

YOUR TURN

Complete the chart by writing transitions that you will use to establish order and guide the reader through each part of the plot of your narrative.

| Outline | Transition |
|---|---|
| Exposition | |
| Rising Action | |
| Climax | |
| Falling Action | |
| Resolution | |

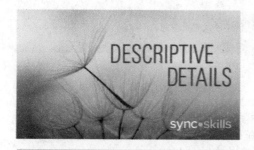

# Skill:
# Descriptive Details

First, reread the draft of your narrative and identify the following:

- where descriptive details are needed to convey experiences and events
- vague, general, or overused words and phrases
- places where you want to tell how something looks, sounds, feels, smells, or tastes, such as:

> experiences

> events

> settings

> characters

Use precise words and phrases, telling details, and sensory language to convey a vivid picture of the experiences, events, setting, and/or characters, using the following questions as a guide:

- What experiences and events do I want to convey in my writing?
- Have I included telling details that help reveal the experiences and events in the story?
- How do I want the characters and setting portrayed?
- How can I use sensory language, or words that describe sights, sounds, feels, smells, or tastes, so that readers can clearly visualize the experiences, events, setting, and/or characters in my story?
- What can I refine or revise in my word choice to make sure that the reader can picture what is taking place?

Please note that excerpts and passages in the StudySync® library and this workbook are intended as touchstones to generate interest in an author's work. The excerpts and passages do not substitute for the reading of entire texts, and StudySync® strongly recommends that students seek out and purchase the whole literary or informational work in order to experience it as the author intended. Links to online resellers are available in our digital library. In addition, complete works may be ordered through an authorized reseller by filling out and returning to StudySync® the order form enclosed in this workbook.

Reading & Writing Companion **465**

**YOUR TURN**

Choose the best answer to each question.

1. Below is a section from a previous draft of Monica's story. Monica wants to add touch and sight details to the underlined sentence. Which sentence best adds those details?

> I ran and ran up and down every aisle in the store looking for my dad. Finally, Dad found me. <u>I was sobbing in the rug department.</u>

- ○ A. I was sobbing on a rough, brown carpet in the rug department.
- ○ B. I was wailing loudly in the rug department.
- ○ C. I was sobbing on a big rug in the rug department.
- ○ D. I was crying my eyes out by myself in the rug department wondering where my dad was.

2. Below is a section from a previous draft of Monica's story. Monica wants to revise the underlined sentence to include a more precise and accurate action verb. Which sentence best accomplishes this goal?

> <u>Curious, I walked around the corner.</u> There I saw the Halloween display. I screamed and started running.

- ○ A. Curious, I was around the corner.
- ○ B. Curious, I looked around the corner.
- ○ C. Curious, I strode around the corner.
- ○ D. Curious, I went around the corner.

 **WRITE**

Use the questions in the checklist to revise a section of your fictional or personal narrative. While revising, be sure to develop the ideas of your narrative with effective use of descriptive details in order to focus your reader's attention on important aspects of character, setting, or plot.

# Skill:
# Conclusions

## ••• CHECKLIST FOR CONCLUSIONS

Before you write your conclusion, ask yourself the following questions:

- What important details should I include in the summary in my conclusion?
- What other thoughts and feelings could the characters share with readers in the conclusion?
- Should I express the importance of the events in my narrative through dialogue or a character's actions?

Below are two strategies to help you provide a conclusion that follows from and reflects on what is experienced, observed, or resolved over the course of the narrative:

- Peer Discussion
  - > talk with a partner about possible endings for your narrative, writing notes about your discussion
  - > review your notes and think about how you want to end your story
  - > briefly summarize the events in the narrative through the narrator or one of the characters
  - > describe the narrator's observations about the events they experienced
  - > reveal to readers why the experiences in the narrative matter through a character's reflections or resolutions
  - > write your conclusion

- Freewriting
  - > freewrite for 10 minutes to develop a conclusion, without concern for grammar or punctuation
  - > review your notes and think about how you want to end your story
  - > briefly summarize the events in the narrative through the narrator or one of the characters
  - > describe the narrator's observations about the events they experienced
  - > reveal to readers why the experiences in the narrative matter through a character's reflections or resolutions
  - > write your conclusion

**YOUR TURN**

Choose the best answer to each question.

1. Below is part of the conclusion from the final version of Monica's story. Which section of dialogue best reveals Monica's realization that the situation was not what it seemed?

> "I wonder if maybe after you took the picture of this spider you freaked out a little bit, like when you were little. You must have taken off down the trail. You weren't that far ahead of me. Just around the bend," Nola says.
>
> "Really? I felt completely lost," I say.
>
> Nola smiles kindly at me. She says, "Well, we picked the easy trail for you, remember."

- ○ A. "I wonder if maybe after you took the picture of this spider you freaked out a little bit, like when you were little."
- ○ B. "Really? I felt completely lost," I say.
- ○ C. "You weren't that far ahead of me."
- ○ D. "Well, we picked the easy trail for you, remember."

2. Read the conclusion from Monica's final version below. Which section is used to emphasize the change that has taken place in the narrator?

> For some reason, I start to giggle. I feel a little embarrassed, but mostly I feel relieved. I may never develop a reliable sense of direction, but I know two things now. One is that you can conquer your fears—I have a picture of a humongous, hairy spider to prove that. The other is that it doesn't matter if I can't navigate my way out of a paper bag as long as I have good friends like Nola—and tracker tiles!

- ○ A. For some reason, I start to giggle. I feel a little embarrassed, but mostly I feel relieved.
- ○ B. One is that you can conquer your fears—I have a picture of a humongous, hairy spider to prove that.
- ○ C. The other is that it doesn't matter if I can't navigate my way out of a paper bag as long as I have good friends like Nola—and tracker tiles!
- ○ D. I may never develop a reliable sense of direction, but I know two things now.

 **WRITE**

Use the questions in the checklist section to revise the conclusion of your narrative so that it follows logically from the events of the plot and what the characters have experienced.

# Narrative Writing Process: Revise

| PLAN | DRAFT | REVISE | EDIT AND PUBLISH |
|------|-------|--------|------------------|

You have written a draft of your real or imagined narrative. You have also received input from your peers about how to improve it. Now you are going to revise your draft.

## ← REVISION GUIDE

Examine your draft to find areas for revision. Keep in mind your purpose and audience as you revise for clarity, development, organization, and style. Use the guide below to help you review:

| Review | Revise | Example |
|--------|--------|---------|
| **Clarity** | | |
| Label each piece of dialogue so you know who is speaking. Annotate any places where it is unclear who is speaking. | Use the character's name to show who is speaking, or add description about the speaker. | "I wonder if maybe after you took the picture of this spider you freaked out a little bit, like when you were little. You must have taken off down the trail. You weren't that far ahead of me. Just around the bend.", " **Nola says.** "Really? I felt compleatly lost." ," **I say.** |

| Review | Revise | Example |
|---|---|---|
| **Development** | | |
| Identify key moments exploring the conflict or leading up to the climax. Annotate content that doesn't help you move the narrative toward the climax or the resolution. | Focus on a single event and think carefully about whether it drives the story forward or keeps it standing still. If it doesn't move the narrative forward, you might consider adding or deleting details to make it more important to the plot. | Twelve years later, here I am stranded in the woods. How did this happen? Let's see . . . Nola and I were walking along the Yellow Trail—it was supposed to be the easiest—and then we both said, "Oh, look at that!" at the exact same second. I thought we were both talking about the same thing. I snapped my picture with my phone. I looked up. Where was Nola? and when I looked up, Nola was gone. Gone! |
| **Organization** | | |
| Explain your story in one or two sentences. Reread and annotate any places that don't match your explanation. | Rewrite the events in the correct sequence. Delete events that are not essential to the story and include details that are essential. | Nola smiles kindly at me. She says, "Well, we picked the easy trail for you, remember. Its just a big circle. If you had kept going, you would have ended up at the ranger station by the parking lot. You weren't to lost." Nola smiles kindly at me. |
| **Style: Word Choice** | | |
| Find places where the use of precise or sensory language could help readers visualize the characters, setting, or action. | Select sentences to rewrite using specific nouns and action verbs or sensory language. | Miraculously, I hear Nola's voice. "Monica?" I turn to see her startled face. "There you are! I stopped to take a picture of that butterfly. When I turned around you were gone. Where did you go?" |

| Review | Revise | Example |
|---|---|---|
| **Style: Sentence Effectiveness** | | |
| Think about a key event where you want your reader to feel a specific emotion. Long sentences can draw out a moment and make a reader think; short sentences can show urgent actions or danger. | Rewrite a key event making your sentences longer or shorter to achieve the emotion you want your reader to feel. | For some reason, I start to giggle. I feel a little embarrassed. Mostly, but mostly I feel releived relieved. I may never develop a reliable sense of direction, but I know two things now. One is that you can conquer your fears.—I have a picture of a humongous, hairy spider to prove that. The other is that it doesn't matter if I can't navigate when my way out of a paper bag as long as. I have good friends like Nola—and tracker tiles! |

## ✏ WRITE

Use the guide above, as well as your peer reviews, to help you evaluate your narrative to determine areas that should be revised.

Please note that excerpts and passages in the StudySync® library and this workbook are intended as touchstones to generate interest in an author's work. The excerpts and passages do not substitute for the reading of entire texts, and StudySync® strongly recommends that students seek out and purchase the whole literary or informational work in order to experience it as the author intended. Links to online resellers are available in our digital library. In addition, complete works may be ordered through an authorized reseller by filling out and returning to StudySync® the order form enclosed in this workbook.

Reading & Writing Companion  **471**

# Grammar: Participles and Participial Phrases

## Participles

A participle is a verb form. Participles can be either past or present. Present participles always end with *-ing*. Past participles for regular verbs end in *-ed*. Participles for irregular verbs take different endings, for example, *-en* as in *broken*.

Participles can also function as adjectives modifying a noun or pronoun.

| Text | Explanation |
|---|---|
| When the men's high jump finalists were introduced, broadcasters announced a **laser-focused** Holm as the favorite.<br><br>The Sports Gene | The past participle *laser-focused* modifies the proper noun *Holm*. |
| People observe the colors of a day only at its beginnings and ends, but to me it's quite clear that a day merges through a multitude of shades and intonations, with each **passing** moment.<br><br>The Book Thief | The present participle *passing* modifies the noun *moment*. |

## Participial Phrases

A participial phrase consists of a past or present participle and other words that complete its meaning. Like participles, participial phrases can function as adjectives. They should appear as close as possible to the nouns or pronouns they modify.

| Text | Explanation |
|---|---|
| Only some do—the **innately talented** ones.<br><br>Outliers | The participial phrase *innately talented* modifies the pronoun *ones*. |
| I recalled a short story Tolstoy had written about a man **sleeping in the forest**.<br><br>Iraq War Blog | The participial phrase *sleeping in the forest* modifies the noun *man*. |

## ⟳ YOUR TURN

1. Which revision is the best replacement for the text in bold?

> The child watched the top **that was going around and around and around**.

- ○ A. Insert the participle **spinned** in front of the noun **top**.
- ○ B. Insert the participle **spinning** in front of the noun **top**.
- ○ C. Insert the participle **spinning** in front of the noun **child**.
- ○ D. The adjective is a correct participle or participial phrase.

2. Which revision is the best replacement for the text in bold?

> Valerie finds her after-school job very difficult to do **given her lack of experience**.

- ○ A. Replace the participial phrase with **given her lacking of experience**.
- ○ B. Replace the participial phrase with **giving her lack of experience**.
- ○ C. Move the participial phrase to the beginning of the sentence, and follow it with a comma.
- ○ D. The text is a correctly placed participial phrase.

3. Which revision is the best replacement for the text in bold?

> **Had misplaced my keys**, I could not get into my house.

- ○ A. Change the participial phrase to **Having misplaced my keys**.
- ○ B. Change the participial phrase to **Had misplacing my keys**.
- ○ C. Change the participial phrase to **Misplacing my keys**.
- ○ D. The participial phrase is used correctly.

4. Which revision is the best replacement for the text in bold?

> The runners, **tired from the race**, rested on the nearby beach.

- ○ A. Replace the participial phrase with **tiring**.
- ○ B. Replace the participial phrase with **tiring from the race**.
- ○ C. Move the phrase to the end of the sentence, after the word **beach**.
- ○ D. The participial phrase is used correctly.

# Grammar:
# Verb Phrases

A verb phrase consists of a main verb and all its auxiliary verbs. The most common auxiliary verbs are the forms of *be* and *have*. They can also be combined with other auxiliary verbs.

We **are** playing. We **have** played. We **had been** playing.

## AUXILIARY VERBS

Forms of *be*:           *am, is, are, was, were, being, been*
Forms of *have*:       *has, have, had, having*
Other helping verbs:   *can, could, do, does, did, may, might, must, shall, should, will, would*

| Rule | Text |
|---|---|
| Helping verbs are combined with main verbs to form verb phrases. | He **might have spoken**, but I **did** not **hear**; one hand was stretched out, seemingly to detain me, but I escaped and rushed downstairs. <br><br> Frankenstein |
| Forms of the helping verb *be* are used with the present participle. | The Challenger crew **was pulling** us into the future, and we'll continue to follow them. <br><br> Address to the Nation on the Explosion of the Space Shuttle Challenger |
| Forms of the helping verb *have* are used with the past participle of a main verb. | I understand that Germany **has** actually **stopped** the sale of uranium from the Czechoslovakian mines which she **has taken** over. <br><br> Einstein's Letter to the President |
| Other auxiliary verbs can be used to add further meaning to the main verb. | "At last! In this I **can carry** fire, and the children of men **shall have** the great gift in spite of Jupiter." <br><br> Prometheus: The Friend of Man |
| As many as three auxiliary verbs can be combined to help the main verb. | He **couldn't have been gone** for long, though, when he was violently awakened again. <br><br> Civil Peace |

## ↻ YOUR TURN

1. How should this sentence be changed to include a **verb phrase** using the indicated verb?

> Irene and Ben _____ us along the parade route. (meet)

- ○ A. Irene and Ben will meet us along the parade route.
- ○ B. Irene and Ben met us along the parade route.
- ○ C. Irene and Ben already met us along the parade route.
- ○ D. None of the above.

2. How should this sentence be changed to include a **verb phrase** using the indicated verb?

> Charlie _____ patience from his grandfather. (learn)

- ○ A. Charlie learned patience from his grandfather.
- ○ B. Charlie is learning patience from his grandfather.
- ○ C. Charlie learns patience from his grandfather.
- ○ D. None of the above.

3. How should this sentence be changed to include a **verb phrase** using the indicated verb?

> Dr. Carmichael _____ a survey on sleep habits. (conduct)

- ○ A. Dr. Carmichael is conducting a survey on sleep habits.
- ○ B. Dr. Carmichael conducts a survey on sleep habits.
- ○ C. Dr. Carmichael conducted a survey on sleep habits.
- ○ D. None of the above.

4. How should this sentence be changed to include a **verb phrase** using the indicated verb?

> The history museum _____ a collection of Civil War clothing. (acquire)

- ○ A. The history museum already acquired a collection of Civil War clothing.
- ○ B. The history museum acquired a collection of Civil War clothing.
- ○ C. The history museum might acquire a collection of Civil War clothing.
- ○ D. None of the above.

# Grammar: Noun Clauses

A clause is a group of words that contains both a subject and a verb. A noun clause is a subordinate clause that acts as a noun in a sentence. A noun clause usually begins with one of these words: *how*, *that*, *what*, *whatever*, *when*, *where*, *which*, *whichever*, *who*, *whom*, *whoever*, *whose*, or *why*.

| Noun Phrase as Subject | Noun Clause as Subject |
| --- | --- |
| **Our next family road trip** will be a great adventure. | **Wherever the road takes us** will be a great adventure. |

In most sentences containing noun clauses, you can replace the noun clause with a pronoun such as *he* or *it*, and the sentence will still make sense. You can use a noun clause in the same ways you use a noun—as a subject, a direct object, an indirect object, an object of a preposition, and a predicate noun.

| Function of Clause | Text |
| --- | --- |
| Direct Object | Carlos Mattis, Lindenwood's top high jumper, had enough of Thomas' lip and bet him **that he could not clear 6'6" in a high jump competition**.<br><br>The Sports Gene |
| Subject | **That Thomas could not clear 6'6" in the high jump competition** was the focus of Mattis' bet. |
| Object of a Preposition | Mattis made a bet about **how high Thomas could jump**. |
| Predicate Noun | The focus of Mattis' bet was **that Thomas would not clear 6'6" in a high jump competition**. |

## ↻ YOUR TURN

1. Choose the revision that uses a noun clause as a **predicate noun**.

> The principal announced that Friday would be an in-service day.

- ○ A. Whether Friday would be an in-service day or not was announced that morning.
- ○ B. Everyone discussed why the principal chose Friday for the in-service day.
- ○ C. The principal's announcement about an in-service day was what we expected.
- ○ D. No change needs to be made to this sentence.

2. Choose the revision that uses a noun clause as the **object of a preposition**.

> Krista asked why the classroom door was locked.

- ○ A. Krista asked about why the classroom door was locked.
- ○ B. Why the classroom door was locked was a question Krista had.
- ○ C. The question was why the classroom door was locked.
- ○ D. No change needs to be made to this sentence.

3. Choose the revision that uses a noun clause as the **direct object**.

> That the chemical we added turned this blue mixture to pink is a problem.

- ○ A. The issue is that the chemical we added turned this blue mixture to pink.
- ○ B. We need to recognize that the chemical we added turned this blue mixture to pink.
- ○ C. I have a simple answer for why the chemical we added turned this blue mixture to pink.
- ○ D. No change needs to be made to this sentence.

4. Choose the revision that uses a noun clause as the **subject**.

> Do you understand how I feel?

- ○ A. One thing you should understand is how I feel.
- ○ B. How I feel is something you don't understand.
- ○ C. You hardly think about how I feel.
- ○ D. No change needs to be made to this sentence.

# Grammar: Basic Spelling Rules II

| Rule | Text |
|---|---|
| When adding *-ed* to a word that ends in a single consonant following one vowel, double the final consonant if the word is one syllable. | Suddenly he **slipped** and it seemed certain that they had him.<br><br>Animal Farm |
| When adding *-ly* to a word that ends in a single *l*, keep the *l*. | Two days after McCandless set up camp beside Lake Mead, an **unusually** robust wall of thunderheads reared up in the afternoon sky . . .<br><br>Into the Wild |
| When forming compound words, keep the original spelling of both words. | He knew that when he returned to the **firehouse**, he might wink at himself, a minstrel man, burnt-corked, in the mirror.<br><br>Fahrenheit 451 |
| Although the *sēd* sound is usually spelled *cede*, there are four exceptions: *supersede*, *exceed*, *proceed*, and *succeed*. | He bounded over the crevices in the ice, among which I had walked with caution; his stature, also, as he approached, seemed to **exceed** that of man.<br><br>Frankenstein |

## ⟳ YOUR TURN

1. How should this sentence be changed?

> They could have seen an action movie, but they preferred to go to a criticaly acclaimed film at the arts cinema.

- ○ A. Change **preferred** to **prefered**.
- ○ B. Change **criticaly** to **critically**.
- ○ C. Change **acclaimed** to **acclaimmed**.
- ○ D. No change needs to be made to this sentence.

2. How should this sentence be changed?

> I was compelled to read the self-help book after being reminded that the slightest change could improve my life drastically.

- ○ A. Change **reminded** to **remindded**.
- ○ B. Change **drastically** to **drasticaly**.
- ○ C. Change **compelled** to **compeled**.
- ○ D. No change needs to be made to this sentence.

3. How should this sentence be changed?

> By constantly discussing their shared dream, Ryne and Lennie inspire themselves to work toward an incredibally difficult goal.

- ○ A. Change **constantly** to **constanly**.
- ○ B. Change **discussing** to **discusing**.
- ○ C. Change **incredibally** to **incredibly**.
- ○ D. No change needs to be made to this sentence.

4. How should this sentence be changed?

> The characters in the movie succede in finding closeness before ultimately being driven apart by a misunderstanding.

- ○ A. Change **succede** to **succeed**.
- ○ B. Change **closeness** to **closness**.
- ○ C. Change **ultimately** to **ultimatly**.
- ○ D. No change needs to be made to this sentence.

# Narrative Writing Process: Edit and Publish

| PLAN | DRAFT | REVISE | EDIT AND PUBLISH |
|---|---|---|---|

You have revised your real or imagined narrative based on your peer feedback and your own examination.

Now, it is time to edit your narrative. When you revised, you focused on the content of your narrative. You probably looked at your story's narrative techniques, transitions, descriptive details, and conclusion. When you edit, you focus on the mechanics of your story, paying close attention to things like grammar and punctuation.

## Use the checklist below to guide you as you edit:

☐ Have I followed the rules for using participles and participial phrases?

☐ Have I used verb phrases correctly?

☐ Have I used noun clauses effectively?

☐ Do I have any sentence fragments or run-on sentences?

☐ Have I spelled everything correctly?

## Notice some edits Monica has made:

- Added dashes to set off an interruption.

- Revised sentence structure using a participial phrase.

- Removed a misused and unnecessary prepositional phrase (with a noun clause as the object).

- Changed an incorrect verb phrase to the correct verb form in the correct tense.

- Fixed a run-on sentence by adding a dependent clause.

- Replaced a pronoun that had an unclear antecedent.

- Corrected misspelled words.

Butterfly? I didn't see a butterfly. I saw a . . . ?—No way!— I pull out my phone, click open my photo ~~ap~~ **app**, and gasp at what I see. ~~Before~~ **before** ~~I handed~~ **handing** it over to my ~~freind~~ **friend** ~~for how Nora would react~~.

"Wow, Monica. That's a *really* big spider," Nola says. She ~~had sounded~~ **sounds** impressed. I'm impressed ~~too since~~ **too. Since** my ~~enconter~~ **encounter** with the rib cage spider all those years ago, I haven't been too crazy about ~~them~~ **spiders** either.

---

## ✏ WRITE

Use the questions above, as well as your peer reviews, to help you evaluate your real or imagined narrative to determine areas that need editing. Then edit your narrative to correct those errors.

Once you have made all your corrections, you are ready to publish your work. You can distribute your writing to family and friends, hang it on a bulletin board, or post it on your blog. If you publish online, share the link with your family, friends, and classmates.

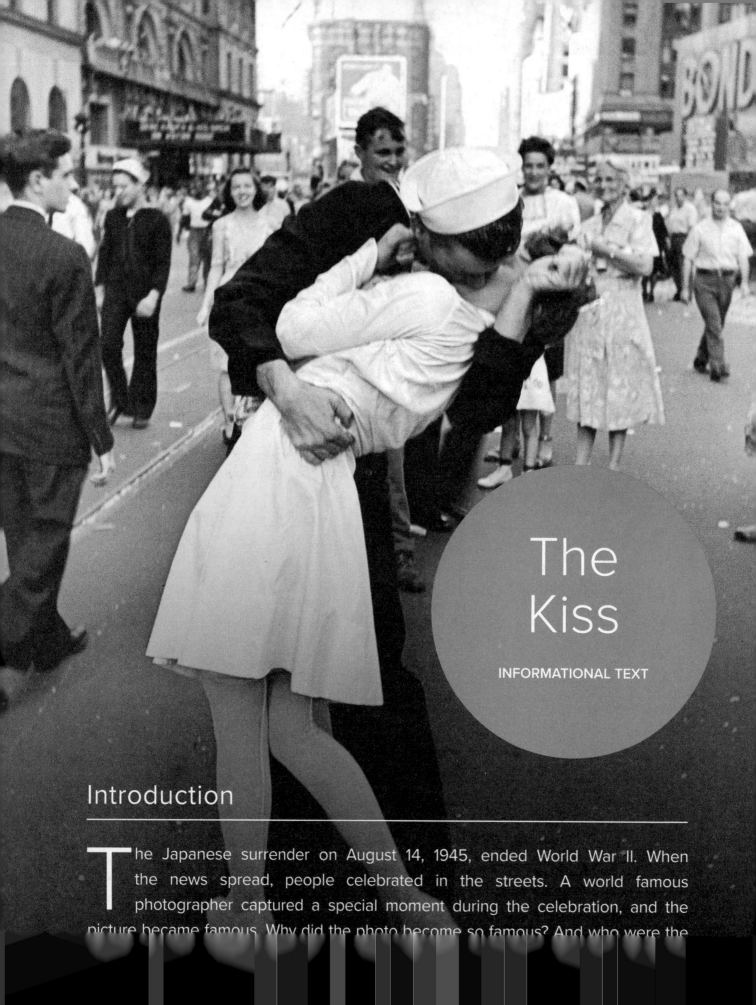

# The Kiss

INFORMATIONAL TEXT

## Introduction

The Japanese surrender on August 14, 1945, ended World War II. When the news spread, people celebrated in the streets. A world famous photographer captured a special moment during the celebration, and the picture became famous. Why did the photo become so famous? And who were the

## V VOCABULARY

**maintain**

to keep or continue

**precise**

clearly defined and accurate

**elation**

a feeling of great joy and happiness

**version**

a variation or revision of an earlier form of something

**impulsively**

suddenly and without serious thought

## ☰ READ

NOTES

1   During World War II, the United States was involved in two "theaters," or geographical areas—Europe and the Pacific. America joined the Allied forces to end the war in Europe victoriously on V-E Day (Victory in Europe Day), May 8, 1945. Battles in the Pacific continued. Many people thought that the Japanese would **maintain** their fierce resistance and never surrender to the enemy. However, on August 14, 1945, the Japanese government surrendered. When news reached the United States, people cheerfully celebrated. The most remembered celebration occurred in Times Square in New York City. A photograph called "The Kiss" recorded that moment.

2   When news of the Japanese surrender reached New York, people ran into the streets. They were randomly hugging one another, laughing, and singing. In Times Square, the conventional formal manner of strangers changed. Sailors climbed lampposts to erect American flags. Strings of paper and confetti rained down from windows. **Elation** spread like giggles in a first-grade classroom.

Please note that excerpts and passages in the StudySync® library and this workbook are intended as touchstones to generate interest in an author's work. The excerpts and passages do not substitute for the reading of entire texts, and StudySync® strongly recommends that students seek out and purchase the whole literary or informational work in order to experience it as the author intended. Links to online resellers are available in our digital library. In addition, complete works may be ordered through an authorized reseller by filling out and returning to StudySync® the order form enclosed in this workbook.

3   In the midst of this, world-famous photographer Alfred Eisenstaedt began taking photos of the people expressing their relief and joy. Because of his expertise, he did not need time to set up a memorable picture. Methodical process turned into unplanned work. His purpose was to capture human emotion. One picture, snapped by Eisenstaedt, was that of a sailor kissing a nurse.

4   In the confusion and celebration, Eisenstaedt never got the names and addresses of the couple he photographed. Two weeks later, the photo appeared on the cover of *Life* magazine. It became the most famous kiss in American history. The main idea was to express both love and joy. The photo has become part of American culture to this day. It appears on everything from coffee mugs to calendars. People wanted to know the identity of the couple, so the search began. In 1979, Eisenstaedt believed he had found the nurse, but the sailor's identity was unknown. Had he actually found the nurse?

5   The mystery continued over the years. The question was always the same: who were these two individuals? Their faces were almost totally hidden in the photo. Many people have claimed to be the couple. Different stories have commonly appeared in articles and books. Couples, observers, and even a forensic artist confirmed those accounts. Then *The Kissing Sailor*, a book published in 2012, identified the two, who were then in their nineties. The young sailor had **impulsively** grabbed a dental assistant and kissed her. The time, according to them, was about two o'clock.

6   An online discussion, however, suggested the time was around 7:03 p.m., about the time that President Truman announced the surrender of Japan. Another person claiming to have witnessed the kiss insists it was around 6 p.m. A physicist and his team then joined the discussion. They carefully studied maps of Times Square made at the time, archival photos, and building blueprints. They believed that observing the shadows cast by the buildings in the picture itself would indicate the **precise** time of the picture. The physicist and his team insisted that the time was actually 5:51 p.m. This, of course, did not identify the pair and might dismiss the claim of the elderly couple mentioned in the book. Nonetheless, the information provided another clue about the photo.

7   By now, many observers and perhaps even the couple themselves have died, but the photograph remains an important part of American culture. In 2005, to celebrate the sixtieth anniversary of V-J Day (Victory over Japan Day), a sculptor created a 25-foot-tall **version** of the familiar kiss. The statue is called *Embracing Peace*. It was placed in Times Square for the 2015 "Kiss-In" event.

# First Read

Read "The Kiss." After you read, complete the Think Questions below.

## ☁ THINK QUESTIONS

1. Why were Americans celebrating on August 14, 1945?

   Americans celebrated because _____.

2. Who took the famous photograph of a sailor kissing a stranger?

   The famous photograph was taken by _____.

3. What did one artist create to celebrate the sixtieth anniversary of V-J Day?

   One artist created _____.

4. Use context to confirm the meaning of the word *precise* as it is used in "The Kiss." Write your definition of *precise* here.

   *Precise* means _____.

   A context clue is _____.

5. What is another way to say that new parents feel *elation*?

   The new parents feel _____.

Please note that excerpts and passages in the StudySync® library and this workbook are intended as touchstones to generate interest in an author's work. The excerpts and passages do not substitute for the reading of entire texts, and StudySync® strongly recommends that students seek out and purchase the whole literary or informational work in order to experience it as the author intended. Links to online resellers are available in our digital library. In addition, complete works may be ordered through an authorized reseller by filling out and returning to StudySync® the order form enclosed in this workbook.

Reading & Writing
Companion

485

# Skill:
# Analyzing Expressions

 ## ★ DEFINE

When you read, you may find English expressions that you do not know. An **expression** is a group of words that communicates an idea. Three types of expressions are idioms, sayings, and figurative language. They can be difficult to understand because the meanings of the words are different from their **literal**, or usual, meanings.

An **idiom** is an expression that is commonly known among a group of people. For example, "It's raining cats and dogs" means it is raining heavily. **Sayings** are short expressions that contain advice or wisdom. For instance, "Don't count your chickens before they hatch" means do not plan on something good happening before it happens. **Figurative** language is when you describe something by comparing it with something else, either directly (using the words *like* or *as*) or indirectly. For example, "I'm as hungry as a horse" means I'm very hungry. None of the expressions are about actual animals.

## ••• CHECKLIST FOR ANALYZING EXPRESSIONS

To determine the meaning of an expression, remember the following:

✓ If you find a confusing group of words, it may be an expression. The meaning of words in expressions may not be their literal meaning.

- Ask yourself: Is this confusing because the words are new? Or because the words do not make sense together?

✓ Determining the overall meaning may require that you use one or more of the following:

- context clues

- a dictionary or other resource

- teacher or peer support

✓ Highlight important information before and after the expression to look for clues.

## ⟳ YOUR TURN

Read the excerpts and literal meaning of each expression below. Then, complete the chart by matching correctly the meaning of the expression as it is used in the text.

| Expression Meanings | |
|---|---|
| **A** | People shared their joy from person to person so that everyone felt happy. |
| **B** | He took a photograph that shows how people felt that day. |

| Excerpt | Literal Meaning | Meaning in the Text |
|---|---|---|
| His purpose was to **capture human emotion**. One picture, snapped by Eisenstaedt, was that of a sailor kissing a nurse. | catch feelings, like in your hand or in a container | |
| Sailors climbed lampposts to erect American flags. Strings of paper and confetti rained down from windows. **Elation spread like giggles in a first-grade classroom.** | joy spread like a sound spreads through the air | |

# Skill:
# Developing Background Knowledge

## ★ DEFINE

**Developing background knowledge** is the process of gaining information about different topics. By developing your background knowledge, you will be able to better understand a wider variety of texts.

First, preview the text to determine what the text is about. To **preview** the text, read the title, headers, and other text features and look at any images or graphics. As you are previewing, identify anything that is unfamiliar to you and that seems important.

While you are reading, you can look for clues that will help you learn more about any unfamiliar words, phrases, or topics. You can also look up information in another resource to increase your background knowledge.

## ••• CHECKLIST FOR DEVELOPING BACKGROUND KNOWLEDGE

To develop your background knowledge, do the following:

- ✓ Preview the text. Read the title, headers, and other features. Look at any images and graphics.

- ✓ Identify any words, phrases, or topics that you do not know a lot about.

- ✓ As you are reading, try to find clues in the text that give you information about any unfamiliar words, phrases, or topics.

- ✓ If necessary, look up information in other sources to learn more about any unfamiliar words, phrases, or topics. You can also ask a peer or teacher for information or support.

- ✓ Think about how the background knowledge you have gained helps you better understand the text.

## ♻ YOUR TURN

Read each quotation from "The Kiss" below. Then, complete the chart by identifying the background knowledge that helps you understand each quotation.

| Background Knowledge Options | |
|---|---|
| A | In the 1940s, it was common for the president to announce important news to the public over the radio. |
| B | Times Square is a busy intersection in New York City. |
| C | At midday, shadows are short because the sun is directly overhead. Later in the day, shadows appear longer. |

| Quotation | Background Knowledge |
|---|---|
| "In Times Square, the conventional formal manner of strangers changed. Sailors climbed lampposts to erect American flags." | |
| "An online discussion, however, suggested the time was around 7:03 p.m., about the time that President Truman announced the surrender of Japan." | |
| "They believed that observing the shadows cast by the buildings in the picture itself would indicate the precise time of the picture." | |

Please note that excerpts and passages in the StudySync® library and this workbook are intended as touchstones to generate interest in an author's work. The excerpts and passages do not substitute for the reading of entire texts, and StudySync® strongly recommends that students seek out and purchase the whole literary or informational work in order to experience it as the author intended. Links to online resellers are available in our digital library. In addition, complete works may be ordered through an authorized reseller by filling out and returning to StudySync® the order form enclosed in this workbook.

Reading & Writing Companion 489

# Close Read

## ✏ WRITE

NARRATIVE: Write a story based on the text "The Kiss" and Alfred Eisenstaedt's famous photograph from V-J Day. The two main characters are the sailor and the dental assistant. Use the background knowledge and recount details from the text to write your story. Pay attention to and edit for pronouns and antecedents.

**Use the checklist below to guide you as you write.**

☐ Where do the main characters meet?

☐ How do the main characters feel?

☐ What do the main characters say?

**Use the sentence frames to organize and write your narrative.**

A young _____ named Ella walked through Times Square.

All around her, people celebrated _____.

A young _____ named George caught Ella's eye.

They ran toward each other and _____ in the middle of Times Square.

The two young people did not notice that a man had taken their _____.

# Welcome To America, Mr. Harris

NONFICTION

## Introduction

When you introduce yourself to someone, you are telling this person more than what people call you. Your name can have special meaning, and for many, a name can tell a story of culture, identity, and immigration. In the 19th and 20th centuries, people from many nations moved to America to start a new life. However, they might not have expected their names to be new as well. It is believed that some immigrants' names were changed when they became American, and others wanted to change their names to fit into their new society. Today, we celebrate Americans' differences, starting by celebrating their names.

##  VOCABULARY

### identify

to indicate who or what
someone or something is

### progress

to move forward toward a better
outcome

### myth

a traditional story, usually
explaining an event in history,
that hasn't been proven true

### official

a person of authority

---

**NOTES**

## ≡ READ

1   Everyone has a name. We may use our names hundreds of times in a single week. We say them. We read them. We write them. We often take our names for granted. Having a name is just a simple, unremarkable fact. But is it really? What would life be like without the name you grew up with?

2   Over time, we come to **identify** ourselves by our names. They often reflect our family and culture. They are a source of pride and identity. Many immigrants coming to the U.S. during the 19th and early 20th centuries had to change their names. Today that practice has almost completely stopped, and the trend has turned around. In fact, many immigrants who chose to give up their names during the last century are reclaiming them now. It may not sound like a big deal, but, in reality, it marks an important moment in American history. Today, we recognize and celebrate immigrants' contributions to building our nation.

Remembering the past to understand the present

3   From 1892 to 1954, Ellis Island in New York was one of the busiest inspection centers in the U.S. for processing immigrants. Today, almost 40% of U.S.

NOTES

citizens have at least one relative who arrived at Ellis Island. Over 12 million people passed through the facility. During peak times, Ellis Island **officials** could interview 5,000 people per day. For a number of the immigrants, it was a tense process. People were tired, nervous, and unsure about the future.

4 As the years passed, an urban **myth** developed. The myth told how Ellis Island officials changed immigrants' names on documents without getting permission. According to the myth, the immigrant might say "My name is Hirsch." Then the official might make the name more Anglo-American on the paperwork, saying "Welcome to America, Mr. Harris." The truth is that the vast majority of immigrants passed through Ellis Island without officials changing their names. However, the very fact that this myth developed points to just how much we identify with our names.

5 One truth that may underlie that urban myth is that many immigrants did change their names. During that time in American history, immigrants often faced harsh discrimination. This discrimination made it more difficult to find work. It was not unusual to see advertisements for jobs with hurtful disclaimers like "No Irish Need Apply" or "Italians Need Not Apply." At the time, it was legal for employers to discriminate against immigrants. This practice forced many immigrants to change their names. Some anglicized their names. Others dropped their names completely and took Anglo-American names. With new names, immigrants hoped to find jobs and to prevent their children from facing the same discrimination in order to have a better life.

## Changing attitudes, not names

6 It's a different world today. Over the years, the majority of Americans' attitudes towards newcomers has **progressed**. Now immigrants to the U.S. rarely change their names. Some examples of famous Americans who more recently immigrated to the US and kept their names include Arnold Schwarzenegger (governor and actor), Gloria Estefan (singer), Mila Kunis (actor), Salma Hayek (producer and actor), and Dikembe Mutombo (athlete and humanitarian).

7 Why do we need to recognize and celebrate this fact? It shows that the U.S. is truly multicultural. Many Americans embrace national and cultural diversity. To protect diversity, the U.S. even ended up passing an anti-discrimination law on July 2, 1964. The Civil Rights Act prohibits discrimination in employment on the basis of race, color, sex, or ethnic origin.

8 Having to change your name because you are a new immigrant to the U.S. may seem unusual today. However, only a few generations ago, many immigrants had no other choice. They had to blend in to get work and stay safe. In the 21st century, our nation celebrates its rich cultural history. As a nation of immigrants, people who now come to the U.S. are less likely to change their names. Even with globally diverse names we can still celebrate shared values.

# First Read

Read "Welcome to America, Mr. Harris." After you read, complete the Think Questions below.

## ☁ THINK QUESTIONS

1. What popular myth developed about immigrants' names?

   The myth about immigrants' names _____.

2. According to the text, why did some immigrants change their names?

   Some immigrants changed their names _____.

3. What was the purpose of the Civil Rights Act of 1964?

   The Civil Rights Act _____.

4. Use context to confirm the meaning of the word *identify* as it is used in "Welcome to America, Mr. Harris." Write your definition of *identify* here.

   *Identify* means _____.

   A context clue is _____.

5. What is another way to say that someone's opinion has *progressed*?

   The person's opinion has _____.

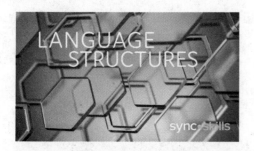

# Skill:
# Language Structures

---

## ★ DEFINE

In every language, there are rules that tell how to **structure** sentences. These rules define the correct order of words. In the English language, for example, a **basic** structure for sentences is subject, verb, and object. Some sentences have more **complicated** structures.

You will encounter both basic and complicated **language structures** in the classroom materials you read. Being familiar with language structures will help you better understand the text.

---

## ••• CHECKLIST FOR LANGUAGE STRUCTURES

To improve your comprehension of language structures, do the following:

✓ Monitor your understanding.

- Ask yourself: Why do I not understand this sentence? Is it because I do not understand some of the words? Or is it because I do not understand the way the words are ordered in the sentence?

✓ Pay attention to verbs followed by prepositions.

- A **verb** names an action.

  > Example: I **sit** on my chair.

  > This tells the reader what the subject of the sentence is doing (sitting).

- A **preposition** defines the relationship between two or more nouns or verbs in a sentence.

  > Example: I sit **on** my chair.

  > This tells the reader where the subject is doing the action (on a chair).

---

- Sometimes the preposition comes directly after the verb, but it can also be separated by another word.

  > Example: I **took** it **to** school with me.

- Sometimes the preposition changes the meaning of the verb. This is called a **phrasal verb**.

  > Example: The teacher liked to **call on** the students in the front of the class.

  > The phrasal verb *call on* means "to select someone to share information."

✓ Break down the sentence into its parts.

- Ask yourself: What words make up the verbs in this sentence? Is the verb followed by a preposition? How does this affect the meaning of the sentence?

✓ Confirm your understanding with a peer or teacher.

**YOUR TURN**

Read paragraph 7 from "Welcome to America, Mr. Harris." Then, answer the multiple-choice questions below.

---

from **"Welcome to America, Mr. Harris"**

(1) Why do we need to recognize and celebrate this fact? (2) It shows that the U.S. is truly multicultural. (3) Many Americans embrace national and cultural diversity. (4) To protect diversity, the U.S. even ended up passing an anti-discrimination law on July 2, 1964. (5) The Civil Rights Act prohibits discrimination in employment on the basis of race, color, sex, or ethnic origin.

---

1. In sentence 1, the phrasal verb *need to* means—

   ○ A. be attached to

   ○ B. look forward to

   ○ C. take to

   ○ D. be obligated to

2. In sentence 4, the phrasal verb *ended up* means—

   ○ A. arrived at a certain location

   ○ B. happened as a result

   ○ C. turned upside down

   ○ D. happened recently

3. Which phrasal verb could replace the word *celebrate* in sentence 1?

   ○ A. let loose

   ○ B. live up to

   ○ C. think highly of

   ○ D. turn up

4. Which phrasal verb could replace the word *embrace* in sentence 3?

   ○ A. agree with

   ○ B. call up

   ○ C. pull over

   ○ D. give away

Please note that excerpts and passages in the StudySync® library and this workbook are intended as touchstones to generate interest in an author's work. The excerpts and passages do not substitute for the reading of entire texts, and StudySync® strongly recommends that students seek out and purchase the whole literary or informational work in order to experience it as the author intended. Links to online resellers are available in our digital library. In addition, complete works may be ordered through an authorized reseller by filling out and returning to StudySync® the order form enclosed in this workbook.

Reading & Writing Companion 497

# Skill:
# Main Ideas and Details

## ★ DEFINE

The **main ideas** are the most important ideas of a paragraph, a section, or an entire text. The **supporting details** are details that describe or explain the main ideas.

To **distinguish** between the main ideas and the supporting details, you will need to decide what information is the most important and supports or explains the main ideas.

## ••• CHECKLIST FOR MAIN IDEAS AND DETAILS

In order to distinguish between main ideas and supporting details, do the following:

✓ Preview the text. Look at headings, topic sentences, and boldface vocabulary.

  • Ask yourself: What seem to be the main ideas in this text?

✓ Read the text.

  • Ask yourself: What are the most important ideas? What details support or explain the most important ideas?

✓ Take notes or use a graphic organizer to distinguish between main ideas and supporting details.

YOUR TURN

Read paragraphs 6 and 7 from "Welcome to America, Mr. Harris." Then, answer the multiple-choice questions below.

---

from **"Welcome to America, Mr. Harris"**

It's a different world today. Over the years, the majority of Americans' attitudes towards newcomers has progressed. Now immigrants to the U.S. rarely change their names. Some examples of famous Americans who more recently immigrated to the US and kept their names include Arnold Schwarzenegger (governor and actor), Gloria Estefan (singer), Mila Kunis (actor), Salma Hayek (producer and actor), and Dikembe Mutombo (athlete and humanitarian).

Why do we need to recognize and celebrate this fact? It shows that the U.S. is truly multicultural. Many Americans embrace national and cultural diversity. To protect diversity, the U.S. even ended up passing an anti-discrimination law on July 2, 1964. The Civil Rights Act prohibits discrimination in employment on the basis of race, color, sex, or ethnic origin.

---

1.  The main idea of paragraph 6 is—

   O  A.  Arnold Schwarzenegger did not change his name when he moved to the United States.
   O  B.  Some names can be hard to pronounce.
   O  C.  Many Americans welcome immigrants, and it is no longer necessary to have an Anglo-American name.
   O  D.  Even though there has been a lot of progress for immigrants to the United States, many people still feel pressure to change their names.

2.  The main idea of paragraph 7 is—

   O  A.  The U.S. changed immigration policy after 1964.
   O  B.  The U.S. is a diverse nation that protects individual rights.
   O  C.  The Civil Rights Act is an important piece of legislation.
   O  D.  There are many different kinds of discrimination.

3.  A detail that best supports the main idea of paragraph 7 is—

   O  A.  "we need to recognize and celebrate this fact"
   O  B.  "the U.S. is truly multicultural"
   O  C.  "the U.S. even ended up passing an anti-discrimination law"
   O  D.  "immigrants to the U.S. rarely change their names"

# Close Read

---

### ✏ WRITE

PERSONAL RESPONSE: Think about how your name has shaped who you are. What does your name mean to you? To what extent have your feelings about your name changed over time? Write a paragraph that answers these questions. Give details about your personal experience to support your main ideas. Pay attention to and edit for doubling final consonants when adding suffixes.

**Use the checklist below to guide you as you write.**

☐ What does your name mean to you?

☐ How does your name connect you to your family or culture?

☐ How have your feelings about your name changed over time?

**Use the sentence frames to organize and write your personal response.**

My name is _____. My name means _____.

I _____ my name. The reason for this is _____.

When I was younger, _____.

The reason for this is _____.

For example, _____.

---

# studysync®

studysync®

ASSIGNMENTS    BINDER    LIBRARY

## The Ties That Bind

UNIT 4

# The Ties That Bind

## What brings us back to one another?

Genre Focus: **DRAMA**

## Texts

# Extended Oral Project and Grammar

## What brings us back to one another?

### GLORIA ANZALDÚA

Gloria Anzaldúa (1942–2004) drew from her upbringing on a ranch settlement in the Rio Grande Valley of southern Texas to develop her concept of the borderland and marginal identity. One of the first openly lesbian Chicana writers, Anzaldúa played a formative role in the development of feminist theory and united feminist concerns with issues of race and class. For Anzaldúa, personal experiences can be "a lens with which to reread and rewrite the cultural stories into which we are born."

### DANIEL CHACÓN

Voicing his belief that there is a degree of cultural specificity to how people view reality, Texas-based Latino writer Daniel Chacón (b. 1962) said in an interview, "The movement of poetry and the movement of fiction are like walking into a landscape." His stories offer intimate portrayals of characters struggling with the difficulty of constructing their own identities while resisting the pressure to conform to social norms.

### ALICE DUNBAR-NELSON

As a writer and political activist, Alice Dunbar-Nelson (1875–1935) was a committed advocate for marginalized communities, especially the close-knit Creole families of her native New Orleans. Though she moved to New York City around 1895 and eventually became a central figure of the Harlem Renaissance literary movement, her work would continue to explore her African American, Anglo, Native American, and Creole heritage, and the social dynamics that contributed to racial oppression in the South.

### TERRY GEORGE

Irish screenwriter and director Terry George (b. 1952) was already an Academy Award-winning screenwriter when Keir Pearson approached him about directing what would become the film Hotel *Rwanda*. Much of George's previous work had focused on political strife in Northern Ireland, and when he met with Pearson, he was interested in telling a story about Africa. George signed on to co-write, produce, and direct the film, for which he and Pearson won the Academy Award for Best Original Screenplay—George's second.

### RONI JACOBSON

Describing what compelled her to refuse to give up her seat on a public bus to a white passenger, civil rights activist Claudette Colvin said, "History had me glued to the seat." Journalist Roni Jacobson's interview with Colvin, whose protest preceded that of Rosa Parks by nine months, sheds light on the lesser-known activist, one of countless individuals whose actions, though they often went undocumented, were essential to the success of the civil rights movement.

### NAOMI SHIHAB NYE

Born in St. Louis, Missouri, Naomi Shihab Nye (b. 1952) has also lived in Palestine, Jerusalem, and San Antonio, Texas. Her numerous poetry collections addressing cultural differences, local life, and the everyday are often based on her travels and the people she encounters in her day-to-day life. "Kindness," one of her most beloved poems, for instance, is based on an experience she had while traveling through South America when a stranger extended a kind gesture to her in a moment of vulnerability.

### KEIR PEARSON

When screenwriter Keir Pearson (b. 1966) set out to write the screenplay for the film that would become *Hotel Rwanda* (2004), he decided to focus his account of the Rwandan Civil War on the true story of Paul Rusesabagina, a hotel manager who sheltered over 1,200 Tutsis from being massacred by Hutu soldiers who belonged to an opposing ethnic group. *Hotel Rwanda* was Pearson's first screenplay, which won him and co-writer Terry George the Academy Award for Best Original Screenplay in 2004.

### WILLIAM SHAKESPEARE

English poet John Keats famously observed of William Shakespeare (1564–1616) that he possessed the power of "negative capability," or the ability to accept "uncertainties, mysteries, doubts" without "reaching after fact and reason." This ability is made manifest in Shakespeare's plays through the depth and complexity of his characters and the moral ambiguity audiences feel as a result. The tragedies in particular blur the line between hero and villain in their portrayals of human behavior and emotion.

### MICHELANGELO DI LODOVICO BUONARROTI SIMONI

In 1508, Italian Renaissance artist Michelangelo Buonarroti (1475–1564) was commissioned to paint the Sistine Chapel of St. Peter's Basilica in Vatican City. The original cathedral, built between 320 and 327 CE, had fallen into disrepair. The style of art and architecture in the expanded, renovated cathedral reflects the papacy's renewed interest in classical antiquity and humanist ideals at the time. Michelangelo's ceiling frescoes depicting biblical scenes including, famously, *The Creation of Adam,* set a new standard for portrayals of the human figure in art.

### FIROOZEH DUMAS

Having moved from Iran to Southern California at a young age, Firoozeh Dumas (b. 1965) wrote her first book, *Funny in Farsi: A Memoir of Growing Up Iranian in America* (2003), with the intent of showing her children that the commonalities between Iranian and American cultures far outweigh the differences. A humorous account of her experience as an immigrant, the memoir offers a wry take on some of the more absurd aspects of American culture.

### LARISSA FASTHORSE

In an interview, playwright, director, and choreographer Larissa FastHorse translates the Lakota term *hunka* as "the making of relatives." FastHorse believes that chosen family is a rare blessing that, if found, should be prized above one's biological family. One of her first plays, *Cherokee Family Reunion* (2012), is about the marriage of a Cherokee man and a white woman, and their respective families' efforts to overcome cultural differences. Originally from South Dakota, she is a member of the Rosebud Sioux Tribe, Sicangu Lakota Nation.

# LITERARY FOCUS:
## The Renaissance

## Introduction

This introduction provides readers with social and cultural context for the period of European history called the Renaissance and the literature that came out of it. The Renaissance and the invention of the printing press took control of literature largely out of the hands of the church. As individuals were given more access and creativity, they drew inspiration from older texts and forms but wrote literature for far wider audiences. Renaissance authors and artists such as Leonardo da Vinci and Geoffrey Chaucer chose to portray human beings as they were, in all of their glory and their vice. Discover what made widely recognized masters in their fields such as Shakespeare and Michelangelo so different than those who had come before them.

# "They prized rational thought over religious feeling."

1   Have you ever heard someone referred to as a Renaissance man or woman? This person is a genius with many talents and overlapping interests, who seems to do everything well. For example, he might be a doctor who is also a classical pianist and a cook. She might be an architect who also is a marathon runner and speaks four languages. The Renaissance was an intellectual, artistic, and cultural movement that lasted from the 14th to 17th centuries in Europe, but its impact on life throughout the world—on the arts, government, religion, and social structures—was tremendous then and is still felt today.

**A Rebirth of Learning and the Rise of Humanism**

2   The word *renaissance*, from the Latin root *renāscī*, is French for "rebirth." It refers to the early 1400s, when Europeans woke up from a long period of intellectual slumber. That the word comes from Latin is appropriate, as Italy was the birthplace of the Renaissance. Around the 13th century, Europeans rediscovered many classical texts and arts that had all but disappeared during the Middle Ages. Medieval scholarship and arts had confined themselves to topics related to religious faith. In fact, the average person's life was dictated by the king and the Catholic church. Those who were educated spoke Latin, not the local language, and the Bible was the only book people who could read ever read. As new ideas spread, medieval ideas were replaced. Renaissance scholars, artists, and writers used elements of classical texts and art—including emphasis on reason, human morality, and the genres of tragedy and comedy—to transform fields such as philosophy, painting, storytelling, and theater.

3   With their emphasis on human experiences in a mostly pre-Christian era, Classical texts and art led to the rise of **humanism**, a school of thought that prioritized the human experience over the **sacred**, or divine. Humanists believed that people could rely on their intellects and physical abilities rather than God's grace to solve their problems. Most Renaissance artists were humanists, who believed human beings were **rational** yet deeply flawed. At the same time, Renaissance writers rejected Latin as their primary language and began to write in their **vernacular** languages. For the first time, Italian,

French, Spanish, Portuguese, and English poets began expressing themselves in their local dialects.

4    The rise of humanism did not eclipse the Church, which was still a powerful force in daily life. Church leaders harnessed the talents of Renaissance artists, such as Michelangelo, Raphael, and Leonardo da Vinci, to create artworks to adorn Rome's churches. These artists continued to mine the Bible for material, but the resulting artworks blended sacred and **profane** elements in a new way. They recreated biblical characters as real, physical, human-looking figures rather than as the one-dimensional icons that characterized religious art in the Middle Ages.

*The Virgin of the Rocks* by Leonardo da Vinci

**The Spread of Learning and the Arts Across Europe**

5    The introduction of the metal movable-type printing press in Europe in the 1450s by a German named Johannes Gutenberg accelerated the pace of learning during the Renaissance. Until the printing press, books were written and copied by hand, a long and arduous process. The printing press made it possible for many copies to be made quickly. This new technology promoted the spread of reading and created a demand for new texts written in people's native languages.

6    During the Renaissance, poetry and drama flourished. Renaissance poets and playwrights borrowed structures from classical works and used them in new ways. Renowned Italian writers include Francesco Petrarch, who invented the Italian sonnet form; Dante Alighieri, whose epic masterpiece *The Divine Comedy* describes a poet's journey through hell; and Giovanni Boccaccio, whose *The Decameron*, a series of tales about a group of nobles escaping the plague, inspired Geoffrey Chaucer's *The Canterbury Tales*. In their works, these writers explored humanist themes while respecting classical poetic forms. They employed sensory and vernacular language to convey life in the real world. One example of this blend is Michelangelo's "On the Painting of

the Sistine Chapel," which uses the traditional sonnet form—with a strict rhyme scheme and meter—to tell about a humorous topic using vernacular language that is often vulgar and grotesque.

7   The Italian artists and writers influenced writers in northern Europe, such as Edmund Spenser, William Shakespeare, and Christopher Marlowe in England, and Francois Rabelais in France. Shakespeare's poetry incorporates classical structures as it explores intense human emotions, such as love, ambition, rage, and fear. As a playwright, Shakespeare created characters that were truly human, not idealized or one-dimensional. In plays like *Henry V*, *Macbeth*, and *Julius Caesar*, Shakespeare was not afraid to give his monarchs flaws and faults. All of his characters—lovers, soldiers, priests, kings, and fools— were psychologically complex and multidimensional.

*The School of Athens*, a fresco by Raphael.

8   **Major Concepts**

- **Rediscovery of ancient and classical literature, art, and ideas**—With the reemergence of ancient and classical texts, Renaissance scholars, artists and writers rediscovered ideas and learning that had been lost for centuries. They reconnected with learning that predated and often contradicted the Christian church and its teaching on the role of humanity in the world. Renaissance literature often addresses ancient and classical ideas, such as an emphasis on reason, human morality, and the genres of tragedy and comedy.

- **Influence of Humanist philosophy**—Renaissance scholars, artists, and writers considered the human experience, not God and the Bible, to be at the center of the world. They prized rational thought over religious feeling. Humanists trusted that individuals could, through **self-actualization,** achieve intellectual and artistic greatness. They celebrated human achievements and intellect, accepted human frailties and flaws in their art, and depicted humans as real beings, not ideals.

NOTES

### Style and Form

9   **Making Old Forms New**

- Renaissance artists and writers borrowed from ancient works in a way that felt new and progressive. For example, artists painted people as real human beings. Poets borrowed poetic structures and devices from classical texts to explore human experience using modern language.

- Writers employed sensory language to convey real human experiences and vernacular language instead of Latin to reflect real people's experiences.

10  **Blending of Sacred and Profane Elements**

- The Church and the Bible still influenced art and literature during the Renaissance, but now artists represented biblical figures as real human beings, not one-dimensional or idealized figures. Characters in literature were complex, flawed, and multidimensional.

11  The second half of the Renaissance overlapped with the Reformation, a religious movement that started in 1517 in northern Europe to reform the excesses of the Catholic church. This movement was influenced by the Renaissance, with its emphasis on humanism and literacy. Reformers defied Catholic leaders by translating the Bible into vernacular languages and using the printing press to make biblical texts available to everyone, not just the clergy. Centuries later, the art and literature of the Renaissance continue to be celebrated in museums, read in schools, and performed on the world's stages. Where do you notice the influence of the Renaissance on the modern world?

# Literary Focus

Read "Literary Focus: The Renaissance." After you read, complete the Think Questions below.

## ☁ THINK QUESTIONS

1. Explain how the rediscovery of classical texts and art led to the rise of a humanist philosophy during the Renaissance. Be sure to cite evidence directly from the text.

2. How did Renaissance artists blend sacred and profane elements? How did Renaissance poets and playwrights do something similar by mixing classical forms and new ideas? Explain, citing evidence from the text to support your response.

3. What effect did the introduction of the printing press have on literature and literacy during the Renaissance? Cite evidence from the text to support your explanations.

4. The word **vernacular** has its root in the Latin *vernaculus,* meaning "native." With this information in mind, write your best definition of the word *vernacular* as it used in this text. Cite any words or phrases that were particularly helpful in coming to your conclusion.

5. Use context clues to determine the meaning of the word **profane**. Write your best definition, along with the words and phrases that were most helpful in determining the word's meaning. Then, check a dictionary to confirm your understanding.

Please note that excerpts and passages in the StudySync® library and this workbook are intended as touchstones to generate interest in an author's work. The excerpts and passages do not substitute for the reading of entire texts, and StudySync® strongly recommends that students seek out and purchase the whole literary or informational work in order to experience it as the author intended. Links to online resellers are available in our digital library. In addition, complete works may be ordered through an authorized reseller by filling out and returning to StudySync® the order form enclosed in this workbook.

Reading & Writing Companion 511

# As You Like It
## (Act II, Scene vii)

DRAMA
William Shakespeare
1599

## Introduction

*A*s *You Like It* is a pastoral comedy by William Shakespeare (1564–1616) about finding love in the Forest of Arden. Rosalind, the daughter of Duke Senior, is banished by her uncle Frederick after he takes over his brother's territory. With her best friend Celia, she flees to the Forest of Arden, disguising herself as the young man Ganymede to avoid detection. The following speech is among the Bard's most memorable and oft-quoted lines, delivered before Duke Senior by the melancholy Jaques, one of the denizens of the forest.

# "And so he plays his part."

1  All the world's a stage,
2  And all the men and women merely players;
3  They have their exits and their entrances,
4  And one man in his time plays many parts,
5  His acts being seven ages. At first, the infant,
6  **Mewling** and puking in the nurse's arms.
7  Then the whining schoolboy, with his satchel
8  And shining morning face, creeping like snail
9  Unwillingly to school. And then the lover,
10  Sighing like furnace, with a woeful ballad
11  Made to his mistress' eyebrow. Then a soldier,
12  Full of strange oaths and bearded like the pard,[1]
13  Jealous in honor, sudden and quick in **quarrel**,
14  Seeking the bubble reputation
15  Even in the cannon's mouth. And then the justice,
16  In fair round belly with good capon lined,
17  With eyes **severe** and beard of formal cut,
18  Full of wise saws and modern instances;
19  And so he plays his part. The sixth age shifts
20  Into the lean and slippered pantaloon,[2]
21  With spectacles on nose and pouch on side;
22  His youthful hose, well saved, a world too wide
23  For his shrunk **shank**, and his big manly voice,
24  Turning again toward childish treble, pipes
25  And whistles in his sound. Last scene of all,
26  That ends this strange eventful history,
27  Is second childishness and mere **oblivion**,
28  Sans teeth, sans eyes, sans taste, sans everything.

1. **pard** leopard
2. **pantaloon** trousers

**WRITE**

PERSONAL RESPONSE: In this speech, Shakespeare shows a character who sums up life in "seven ages," or acts. For you, based on your experiences, culture, and observations, what are your seven ages of life? You don't have to write about them in iambic pentameter, but give each "age" on your list a few descriptive details to explain it, from being a child to being an adult. After you compose your list, explain how your seven acts or ages compare to Shakespeare's.

# Macbeth
## (Act I, Scene iii)

DRAMA
William Shakespeare
1606

# Introduction

I n Act I, Scene iii of William Shakespeare's *Macbeth*, Macbeth and his friend Banquo have just finished a bloody battle to quell a rebellion against King Duncan. On their way home, they encounter three witches eager to make predictions about both of their futures. The effect of these prophecies on Macbeth are immediate and will have far-reaching consequences in Shakespeare's great tragedy.

# "If chance will have me king, why, chance may crown me, Without my stir."

Act I, Scene iii

1   A heath near Forres.
2   *[Thunder. Enter three Witches]*

3   FIRST WITCH: Where hast thou been, sister?

4   SECOND WITCH: Killing swine.

5   THIRD WITCH: Sister, where thou?

6   FIRST WITCH: A sailor's wife had chestnuts in her lap,
7   And munch'd, and munch'd, and munch'd:—
8   'Give me,' quoth I:
9   'Aroint thee, witch!' the rump-fed ronyon cries.
10  Her husband's to Aleppo gone, master o' the Tiger:
11  But in a sieve I'll thither sail,
12  And, like a rat without a tail,
13  I'll do, I'll do, and I'll do.

14  SECOND WITCH: I'll give thee a wind.

15  FIRST WITCH: Thou'rt kind.

16  THIRD WITCH: And I another.

17  FIRST WITCH: I myself have all the other,
18  And the very ports they blow,
19  All the quarters that they know
20  I' the shipman's card.
21  I will drain him dry as hay:
22  Sleep shall neither night nor day
23  Hang upon his pent-house lid;
24  He shall live a man forbid:
25  Weary se'nnights nine times nine

**Skill:
Character**

The first witch is angry because a woman wouldn't share her chestnuts. She decides to follow her husband out to sea and torture him. Her sister witches offer help. They make sport of people's lives and are vengeful as well as close.

26  Shall he dwindle, peak and pine:

27  Though his bark cannot be lost,

28  Yet it shall be tempest-tost.

29  Look what I have.

30  SECOND WITCH: Show me, show me.

31  FIRST WITCH: Here I have a pilot's thumb,

32  Wreck'd as homeward he did come.

33  *[Drum within]*

34  THIRD WITCH: A drum, a drum!

35  Macbeth doth come.

36  ALL: The weird sisters, hand in hand,

37  Posters of the sea and land,

38  Thus do go about, about:

39  Thrice to thine and thrice to mine

40  And thrice again, to make up nine.

41  Peace! the charm's wound up.

42  *[Enter MACBETH and BANQUO]*

43  MACBETH: So foul and fair a day I have not seen.

44  BANQUO: How far is't call'd to Forres? What are these

45  So wither'd and so wild in their attire,

46  That look not like the inhabitants o' the earth,

47  And yet are on't? Live you? or are you aught

48  That man may question? You seem to understand me,

49  By each at once her chappy finger laying

50  Upon her skinny lips: you should be women,

51  And yet your beards forbid me to interpret

52  That you are so.

53  MACBETH: Speak, if you can: what are you?

54  FIRST WITCH: All hail, Macbeth! hail to thee, thane[1] of Glamis!

55  SECOND WITCH: All hail, Macbeth, hail to thee, thane of Cawdor!

**Skill:**
**Summarizing**

*I restate what I highlighted so it makes sense:*

*The witch has control of the winds.*

*She will drain the life out of him.*

*He won't be able to sleep.*

*For 81 weeks he will be lost.*

*His ship can't be sunk, but she makes storms to toss it.*

Macbeth and Banquo encountering the three witches, depicted in an illustration for an edition of Shakespeare's works published in London in 1858

---

1. **thane** a member of the aristocracy in Anglo-Saxon times

NOTES

Skill:
Character

*Banquo here asks
Macbeth why he's
acting scared and then
confronts the witches,
commands them to tell
him more about his
future, and tells them
he's not afraid of them.
He seems brave to me.*

Skill:
Media

*I notice that in the
video the men wear the
clothing of modern
warfare, not the
medieval clothing I
expected. That,
combined with the
modern and sparse set,
transports the play to
an unspecified modern
time.*

56  THIRD WITCH: All hail, Macbeth, thou shalt be king hereafter!

57  BANQUO: Good sir, why do you start; and seem to fear
58  Things that do sound so fair? I' the name of truth,
59  Are ye fantastical, or that indeed
60  Which outwardly ye show? My noble partner
61  You greet with present grace and great prediction
62  Of noble having and of royal hope,
63  That he seems **rapt** withal: to me you speak not.
64  If you can look into the seeds of time,
65  And say which grain will grow and which will not,
66  Speak then to me, who neither beg nor fear
67  Your favours nor your hate.

68  FIRST WITCH: Hail!

69  SECOND WITCH: Hail!

70  THIRD WITCH: Hail!

71  FIRST WITCH: Lesser than Macbeth, and greater.

72  SECOND WITCH: Not so happy, yet much happier.

73  THIRD WITCH: Thou shalt get kings, though thou be none:
74  So all hail, Macbeth and Banquo!

75  FIRST WITCH: Banquo and Macbeth, all hail!

76  MACBETH: Stay, you imperfect speakers, tell me more:
77  By Sinel's death I know I am thane of Glamis;
78  But how of Cawdor? the thane of Cawdor lives,
79  A prosperous gentleman; and to be king
80  Stands not within the **prospect** of belief,
81  No more than to be Cawdor. Say from whence
82  You owe this strange intelligence, or why
83  Upon this blasted heath you stop our way
84  With such prophetic greeting? Speak, I charge you.

85  *[Witches vanish]*

86  BANQUO: The earth hath bubbles, as the water has,
87  And these are of them. Whither are they vanish'd?

88  MACBETH: Into the air; and what seem'd corporal melted
89  As breath into the wind. Would they had stay'd!

90 BANQUO: Were such things here as we do speak about?
91 Or have we eaten on the insane root
92 That takes the reason prisoner?

93 MACBETH: Your children shall be kings.

94 BANQUO: You shall be king.

95 MACBETH: And thane of Cawdor too: went it not so?

96 BANQUO: To the selfsame tune and words. Who's here?

97 *[Enter ROSS and ANGUS]*

98 ROSS: The king hath happily received, Macbeth,
99 The news of thy success; and when he reads
100 Thy personal venture in the rebels' fight,
101 His wonders and his praises do contend
102 Which should be thine or his: silenced with that,
103 In viewing o'er the rest o' the selfsame day,
104 He finds thee in the stout Norweyan ranks,
105 Nothing afeard of what thyself didst make,
106 Strange images of death. As thick as hail
107 Came post with post; and every one did bear
108 Thy praises in his kingdom's great defence,
109 And pour'd them down before him.

110 ANGUS: We are sent
111 To give thee from our royal master thanks;
112 Only to herald thee into his sight,
113 Not pay thee.

114 ROSS: And, for an earnest of a greater honour,
115 He bade me, from him, call thee thane of Cawdor:
116 In which addition, hail, most worthy thane!
117 For it is thine.

118 BANQUO: What, can the devil speak true?

119 MACBETH: The thane of Cawdor lives: why do you dress me
120 In borrow'd robes?

121 ANGUS: Who was the thane lives yet;
122 But under heavy judgment bears that life
123 Which he deserves to lose. Whether he was combined
124 With those of Norway, or did line the rebel

NOTES

125 With hidden help and vantage, or that with both
126 He labour'd in his country's wreck, I know not;
127 But treasons capital, confess'd and proved,
128 Have overthrown him.

129 MACBETH: [*Aside*] Glamis, and thane of Cawdor! The greatest is behind.
130 [*To ROSS and ANGUS*]
131 Thanks for your **pains**.
132 [*To BANQUO*]
133 Do you not hope your children shall be kings,
134 When those that gave the thane of Cawdor to me
135 Promised no less to them?

136 BANQUO: That trusted home
137 Might yet enkindle you unto the crown,
138 Besides the thane of Cawdor. But 'tis strange:
139 And oftentimes, to win us to our harm,
140 The instruments of darkness tell us truths,
141 Win us with honest trifles, to betray's
142 In deepest consequence.
143 Cousins, a word, I pray you.

144 MACBETH: [*Aside*] Two truths are told,
145 As happy **prologues** to the swelling act
146 Of the imperial theme.—I thank you, gentlemen.
147 [*Aside*]
148 Cannot be ill, cannot be good: if ill,
149 Why hath it given me earnest of success,
150 **Commencing** in a truth? I am thane of Cawdor:
151 If good, why do I yield to that suggestion
152 Whose horrid image doth unfix my hair
153 And make my seated heart knock at my ribs,
154 Against the use of nature? Present fears
155 Are less than horrible imaginings:
156 My thought, whose murder yet is but fantastical,
157 Shakes so my single state of man that function
158 Is smother'd in surmise, and nothing is
159 But what is not.

160 BANQUO: Look, how our partner's rapt.

161 MACBETH: [*Aside*] If chance will have me king, why, chance may crown me,
162 Without my stir.

NOTES

163   BANQUO: New honors come upon him,
164   Like our strange garments, cleave not to their mould
165   But with the aid of use.

166   MACBETH: *[Aside]* Come what come may,
167   Time and the hour runs through the roughest day.

168   BANQUO: Worthy Macbeth, we stay upon your leisure.

169   MACBETH: Give me your favour: my dull brain was wrought
170   With things forgotten. Kind gentlemen, your pains
171   Are register'd where every day I turn
172   The leaf to read them. Let us toward the king.
173   Think upon what hath chanced, and, at more time,
174   The interim having weigh'd it, let us speak
175   Our free hearts each to other.

176   BANQUO: Very gladly.

177   MACBETH: Till then, enough. Come, friends.

178   *[Exeunt]*

# First Read

Read *Macbeth*. After you read, complete the Think Questions below.

## ☁ THINK QUESTIONS

1. Why do you think Shakespeare uses the prophecy of the witches to set Macbeth's rise to power in motion? Support your answer with evidence from the text.

2. What can you tell about Macbeth and Banquo from the way each reacts to the witches' prophecy? Support your answer with evidence from the text.

3. What does *Macbeth's* use of paradox in line 148—"cannot be ill, cannot be good"—indicate about his frame of mind?

4. Explain how you can use your knowledge of Greek prefix *pro-*, meaning "prior to," as well as context clues to determine the meaning of the word **prologues** as it is used in this passage.

5. Use context clues to determine the meaning of the word **pains** as it is used in this passage from *Macbeth*. Write your definition of *pains* and explain how you arrived at it.

# Skill:
# Character

Use the Checklist to analyze Character in *Macbeth*. Refer to the sample student annotations about Character in the text.

## ••• CHECKLIST FOR CHARACTER

In order to determine how complex characters develop and interact with other characters in a text, note the following:

- ✓ look for complex characters in the text, such as a character that
    - has conflicting emotions and motivations
    - develops and changes over the course of a story or drama
    - advances the events of the plot
    - develops the central idea, or theme, through his or her actions
- ✓ the ways that characters respond, react, or change as the events of the plot unfold and how they interact with other characters in the story
- ✓ how the reactions and responses of complex characters help to advance the plot and develop the theme
- ✓ the resolution of the conflict in the plot and the ways it affects the characters

To analyze how complex characters develop over the course of a text and interact with other characters, consider the following questions:

- ✓ Which characters in the text could be considered complex?
- ✓ How do the characters change as the plot unfolds? When do they begin to change? Which events cause them to change? How do these changes advance the plot and develop the theme?
- ✓ How do the complex characters interact with other characters?
- ✓ How does the resolution affect the characters?

Please note that excerpts and passages in the StudySync® library and this workbook are intended as touchstones to generate interest in an author's work. The excerpts and passages do not substitute for the reading of entire texts, and StudySync® strongly recommends that students seek out and purchase the whole literary or informational work in order to experience it as the author intended. Links to online resellers are available in our digital library. In addition, complete works may be ordered through an authorized reseller by filling out and returning to StudySync® the order form enclosed in this workbook.

Reading & Writing Companion     523

# Skill:
# Character

Reread lines 136–159 of *Macbeth*. Then, using the Checklist on the previous page, answer the multiple-choice questions below.

## ↻ YOUR TURN

1. In lines 136–143, Banquo suggests that while the witches win their confidence with some correct or semi-correct predictions, he or Macbeth may use these truths to lead to something of consequence. What do these lines reveal about Banquo's character?

   ○ A. He is power hungry because he wants Macbeth to stop at nothing to follow what the witches say.
   ○ B. He is cautious because he is telling Macbeth that the witches' prophecy might be leading him into danger.
   ○ C. He is jealous because he wishes that he were receiving the same prophecy as Macbeth.
   ○ D. He is a worrier because he is concerned the prophecy will not come true for either of them.

2. The witches have prophesied that Macbeth will be king one day. Which line from the passage tells us that there might be dark side to Macbeth's character?

   ○ A. Cannot be ill, cannot be good: if ill,
       Why hath it given me earnest of success,
       Commencing in a truth?
   ○ B. Two truths are told,
       As happy prologues to the swelling act
       Of the imperial theme.
   ○ C. If good, why do I yield to that suggestion
       Whose horrid image doth unfix my hair . . .
   ○ D. Present fears
       Are less than horrible imaginings: . . .

# Skill:
# Summarizing

Use the Checklist to analyze Summarizing in *Macbeth*. Refer to the sample student annotation about Summarizing in the text.

In order to determine how to write an objective summary of a text, note the following:

✓ in literature or nonfiction, note how the theme or central idea is developed over the course of the text, and how it is shaped and then refined by specific details

✓ answers to the basic questions *who*, *what*, *where*, *when*, *why*, and *how*

✓ avoidance of words or phrases that include your own personal thoughts, judgments, or opinions

To provide an objective summary of a text, consider the following questions:

✓ What are the answers to basic *who*, *what*, *where*, *when*, *why*, and *how* questions in literature and works of nonfiction?

✓ Does my summary include how the theme or central idea is developed over the course of the text and how it is shaped and refined by specific details in my summary?

✓ Is my summary objective, or have I added my own thoughts, judgments, and personal opinions?

Please note that excerpts and passages in the StudySync® library and this workbook are intended as touchstones to generate interest in an author's work. The excerpts and passages do not substitute for the reading of entire texts, and StudySync® strongly recommends that students seek out and purchase the whole literary or informational work in order to experience it as the author intended. Links to online resellers are available in our digital library. In addition, complete works may be ordered through an authorized reseller by filling out and returning to StudySync® the order form enclosed in this workbook.

Reading & Writing
Companion

**525**

# Skill:
# Summarizing

Reread lines 110–128 of *Macbeth*. Then, using the Checklist on the previous page, answer the multiple-choice questions below.

## ↻ YOUR TURN

1. Which detail from the text is the most important one to include in the summary?

   ○ A. The king is amazed that Macbeth fought the rebels and the army of Norway in the same day.

   ○ B. Macbeth was not afraid in battle.

   ○ C. Macbeth has been named thane of Cawdor.

   ○ D. The king wants Macbeth to come to him.

2. What is the best summary of the events that occur in this section?

   ○ A. Macbeth and Banquo run into three witches on their way home from battle. The witches predict their future telling Macbeth that he will be thane of Cawdor and then king. They tell Banquo that he will not be king, but that his sons will. They vanish when Macbeth tries to question them further.

   ○ B. Angus and Ross are sent by the king to tell Macbeth how happy the king is with Macbeth's performance in battle. He wants them to tell him that he is now thane of Cawdor because the man that was thane of Cawdor has been sentenced to death for treason.

   ○ C. Angus and Ross are sent by the king to tell Macbeth how happy the king is with Macbeth's performance in battle. He wants them to tell him that he is now thane of Cawdor because the man that was thane of Cawdor has been killed in battle.

   ○ D. Angus and Ross are sent by the king to tell Macbeth how happy the king is with Macbeth's performance in battle. He also wants them to tell him that he is now thane of Cawdor because the man that was thane of Cawdor has been sentenced to death for treason. I think this is great news for Macbeth because the fact that part of the prophecy came true means he will soon be king.

# Skill:
# Media

Use the Checklist to analyze Media in *Macbeth*. Refer to the sample student annotation about Media in the text.

## ••• CHECKLIST FOR MEDIA

In order to determine the representation of a subject or a key scene in two different artistic mediums, do the following:

- ✓ note the artistic medium and its features

- ✓ identify what is emphasized or absent in each treatment of a subject or a key scene

- ✓ examine why the same subject receives completely different treatments in different media

- ✓ consider sources, as a story about a historical event might refer, directly or indirectly, to letters, paintings, plays, or photographs from the same place and time as the events that took place

To analyze the representation of a subject or a key scene in two different artistic mediums, including what is emphasized or absent in each treatment, consider the following questions:

- ✓ What are the two mediums in which the subject or key scene is presented?

- ✓ Is the content informational or fictional? How does this affect the treatment of the key scene or subject?

- ✓ What are the strengths and weaknesses of each artistic medium? How does this affect the treatment of the key scene or subject?

- ✓ What is emphasized and what is absent, or left out of each medium's version of events?

Please note that excerpts and passages in the StudySync® library and this workbook are intended as touchstones to generate interest in an author's work. The excerpts and passages do not substitute for the reading of entire texts, and StudySync® strongly recommends that students seek out and purchase the whole literary or informational work in order to experience it as the author intended. Links to online resellers are available in our digital library. In addition, complete works may be ordered through an authorized reseller by filling out and returning to StudySync® the order form enclosed in this workbook.

Reading & Writing Companion    **527**

# Skill:
# Media

Reread lines 44–52 of *Macbeth* and watch the StudySyncTV episode. Then, using the Checklist on the previous page, answer the multiple-choice questions below.

## 🔁 YOUR TURN

1. What is the difference between the way the three witches are represented in the original play and the way the three witches are represented in the video?

   ○ A. The witches in the original play are mean and unfriendly while the witches in the video are gentle and kind.

   ○ B. The witches in the original play are described as old, wild women while the witches in the video are portrayed as children.

   ○ C. The witches in the original play are distinct characters, while the witches in the video speak all the lines together.

   ○ D. There is no difference to call out, since the witches in the original play are not described as looking any particular way.

2. What effect does the casting of the witches have on the scene?

   ○ A. The casting is unexpected and adds a humorous tone to the scene.

   ○ B. The casting is expected and emphasizes a humorous tone in the scene.

   ○ C. The casting gives the scene an unsettling and supernatural quality that emphasizes the strangeness of the witches.

   ○ D. The casting suggests the witches are really powerless and only playing a joke on Banquo and Macbeth.

# Close Read

Reread *Macbeth*. As you reread, complete the Skills Focus questions below. Then use your answers and annotations from the questions to help you complete the Write activity.

## ◎ SKILLS FOCUS

1. Summarize the events and key ideas that emerge in Act I, Scene iii of *Macbeth*. Also include any themes revealed in the scene.

2. After the Third Witch says of Macbeth, "thou shalt be king hereafter," Banquo responds. Analyze what Banquo's response reveals about Macbeth's character.

3. Explain the cumulative impact of the words in the witches' incantations and comment on their effect on the meaning and tone of this scene of *Macbeth*.

4. Explain how the production from the Royal Shakespeare Company demonstrates ways that *Macbeth* or any classic play can be reinterpreted an reimagined in performance.

5. As Macbeth and Banquo return from battle, they encounter three witches who give a prophecy about their futures. Discuss how this prophecy intertwines the lives of Macbeth and Banquo.

## ✎ WRITE

LITERARY ANALYSIS: The character of Jaques, who speaks the "Seven Ages of Man" monologue from Shakespeare's *As You Like It*, sees life as something with a predictable future. In this scene from *Macbeth*, Macbeth and his friend Banquo encounter three witches who offer unusual predictions for each of the men's futures. Based on Jaques's speech and the details of this scene, including the traits of the characters and the events, what concerns should Macbeth and Banquo have about the prophecy of the witches? Use textual evidence and your own ideas to explain your analysis.

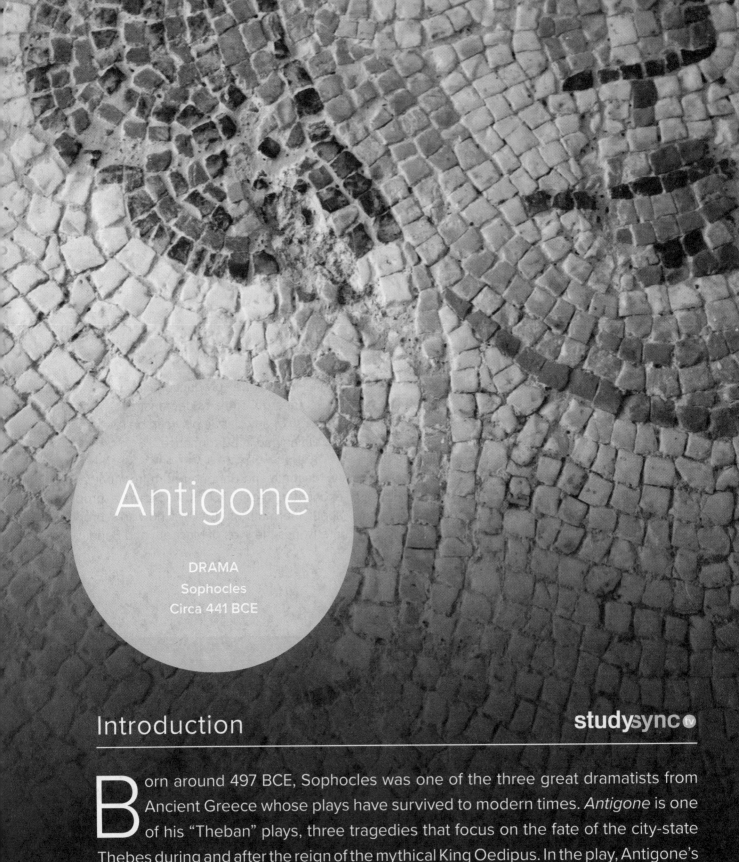

# Antigone

DRAMA
Sophocles
Circa 441 BCE

## Introduction

studysync ᴛᴠ

**B**orn around 497 BCE, Sophocles was one of the three great dramatists from Ancient Greece whose plays have survived to modern times. *Antigone* is one of his "Theban" plays, three tragedies that focus on the fate of the city-state Thebes during and after the reign of the mythical King Oedipus. In the play, Antigone's two brothers have killed each other in battle. Antigone wants to honor each of them, but her uncle, Creon, the new king, has forbidden it. In this excerpt, she asks her

# "What is it? Some dark secret stirs thy breast."

## DRAMATIS PERSONAE

*ANTIGONE and ISMENE—daughters of Oedipus[1] and sisters of Polyneices and Eteocles.*
*CREON, King of Thebes.*
*HAEMON, Son of Creon, betrothed to Antigone.*
*EURYDICE, wife of Creon.*
*TEIRESIAS, the prophet.*
*CHORUS, of Theban elders.*
*A WATCHMAN*
*A MESSENGER*
*A SECOND MESSENGER*

1 [ANTIGONE *and* ISMENE *before the Palace gates.*]

2 ANTIGONE: Ismene, sister of my blood and heart,
3 See'st thou how Zeus[2] would in our lives fulfill
4 The weird of Oedipus, a world of woes!
5 For what of pain, affliction, outrage, shame,
6 Is lacking in our fortunes, thine and mine?
7 What can its purport be? Didst hear and heed,
8 Or art thou deaf when friends are banned as foes?

9 ISMENE: To me, Antigone, no word of friends
10 Has come, or glad or **grievous**, since we twain
11 Were reft of our two brethren in one day
12 By double fratricide; and since i' the night
13 Our Argive leaguers fled, no later news
14 Has reached me, to inspirit or deject.

15 ANTIGONE: I know 'twas so, and therefore summoned thee
16 Beyond the gates to breathe it in thine ear.

Skill:
Figurative
Language

I know from research
that Oedipus killed his
dad and married his
mom. Antigone says
Zeus is fulfilling "the
weird of Oedipus,"
which is another way of
saying his "fate." Zeus
is punishing the family
for Oedipus's sin.

---

1. **Oedipus** a Greek mythological king, most famous for unknowingly fulfilling a prophecy saying he would murder his father and marry his mother
2. **Zeus** in Greek mythology, the God of Gods, highest of all deities

**Skill: Dramatic Elements and Structure**

Sophocles uses a dialogue between Ismene and Antigone to reveal exposition: their two brothers are dead and only one will receive a funeral. No one can even say a word for Polyneices. Creon is the cause of a tragic conflict.

17  ISMENE: What is it? Some dark secret stirs thy breast.

18  ANTIGONE: What but the thought of our two brothers dead,
19  The one by Creon graced with funeral rites,
20  The other disappointed? Eteocles
21  He hath consigned to earth (as fame reports)
22  With obsequies that use and wont ordain,
23  So gracing him among the dead below.
24  But Polyneices, a dishonored corse,
25  (So by report the royal edict runs)
26  No man may bury him or make lament—
27  Must leave him tombless and unwept, a feast
28  For kites to scent afar and swoop upon.
29  Such is the edict (if report speak true)
30  Of Creon, our most noble Creon, aimed
31  At thee and me, aye me too; and anon
32  He will be here to promulgate, for such
33  As have not heard, his mandate; 'tis in sooth
34  No passing humor, for the edict says
35  Whoe'er transgresses shall be stoned to death.
36  So stands it with us; now 'tis thine to show
37  If thou art worthy of thy blood or **base**.

38  ISMENE: But how, my rash, fond sister, in such case
39  Can I do anything to make or mar?

40  ANTIGONE: Say, wilt thou aid me and abet? Decide.

41  ISMENE: In what bold venture? What is in thy thought?

42  ANTIGONE: Lend me a hand to bear the corpse away.

43  ISMENE: What, bury him despite the interdict?

44  ANTIGONE: My brother, and, though thou deny him, thine.
45  No man shall say that I betrayed a brother.

46  ISMENE: Wilt thou persist, though Creon has forbid?

47  ANTIGONE: What right has he to keep me from my own?

48  ISMENE: Bethink thee, sister, of our father's fate,
49  Abhorred, dishonored, self-convinced of sin,
50  Blinded, himself his executioner.

Antigone with Ismene.

51  Think of his mother-wife (ill sorted names)
52  Done by a noose herself had twined to death;
53  And last, our **hapless** brethren in one day,
54  Both in a mutual destiny involved,
55  Self-slaughtered, both the slayer and the slain.
56  Bethink thee, sister, we are left alone;
57  Shall we not perish wretchedest of all,
58  If in defiance of the law we cross
59  A monarch's will? —Weak women, think of that,
60  Not framed by nature to contend with men.
61  Remember this too that the stronger rules;
62  We must obey his orders, these or worse.
63  Therefore I plead compulsion and entreat
64  The dead to pardon. I perforce obey
65  The powers that be. 'Tis foolishness, I ween,
66  To overstep in aught the golden mean.

67  ANTIGONE: I urge no more; nay, wert thou willing still,
68  I would not welcome such a fellowship.
69  Go thine own way; myself will bury him.
70  How sweet to die in such employ, to rest—
71  Sister and brother linked in love's embrace—
72  A sinless sinner, banned awhile on earth,
73  But by the dead commended; and with them
74  I shall abide for ever. As for thee,
75  Scorn, if thou wilt, the eternal laws of Heaven.

76  ISMENE: I scorn them not, but to defy the State[3]
77  Or break her ordinance I have no skill.

78  ANTIGONE: A specious pretext. I will go alone
79  To lap my dearest brother in the grave.

80  ISMENE: My poor, fond sister, how I fear for thee!

81  ANTIGONE: O waste no fears on me; look to thyself.

82  ISMENE: At least let no man know of thine intent,
83  But keep it close and secret, as will I.

84  ANTIGONE: O tell it, sister; I shall hate thee more
85  If thou proclaim it not to all the town.

86  ISMENE: Thou hast a fiery soul for numbing work.

87  ANTIGONE: I pleasure those whom I would liefest please.

---

3. **the State** a country or a people with a shared government

NOTES

 Skill: Dramatic Elements and Structure

Ismene disagrees with Antigone, arguing that so many of their family have died in disgrace. She does not want to disobey Creon. The verse style of iambic pentameter makes her argument sound strong and also builds tension.

 Skill: Figurative Language

What does she mean by "a sinless sinner?" It's an oxymoron. She speaks of being banned on earth, but also "commended." I think she means that her actions are illegal on earth but applauded in heaven.

88  ISMENE: If thou succeed; but thou art doomed to fail.

89  ANTIGONE: When strength shall fail me, yes, but not before.

90  ISMENE: But, if the venture's hopeless, why essay?

91  ANTIGONE: Sister, forbear, or I shall hate thee soon,
92  And the dead man will hate thee too, with cause.
93  Say I am mad and give my madness rein
94  To wreck itself; the worst that can befall
95  Is but to die an honorable death.

96  ISMENE: Have thine own way then; 'tis a mad endeavor,
97  Yet to thy lovers thou art dear as ever. [*Exeunt*]

**Skill: Dramatic Elements and Structure**

Ismene dismisses Antigone's decision and leaves. I see a Chorus has entered, and the stage direction includes "Strophe 1." It sounds as if others are commenting on other parts of the story of Thebes, the setting.

CHORUS:
*(Strophe 1)*
98   Sunbeam, of all that ever dawn upon
99   Our seven-gated Thebes the brightest ray,
100  O eye of golden day,
101  How fair thy light o'er Dirce's fountain shone,
102  Speeding upon their headlong homeward course,
103  Far quicker than they came, the Argive force;
104  Putting to flight
105  The argent shields, the host with scutcheons white.
106  Against our land the proud invader came
107  To vindicate fell Polyneices' claim.
108  Like to an eagle swooping low,
109  On pinions white as new fall'n snow.
110  With clanging scream, a horsetail plume his crest,
111  The aspiring lord of Argos onward pressed.

**Skill: Point of View**

As the Chorus describes the Greek gods Ares and Zeus participating in the war, with Zeus striking the enemy with his iconic lighting bolt, I see the culture of Ancient Greece and Sophocles's view of the world.

*(Antistrophe 1)*
112  Hovering around our city walls he waits,
113  His spearmen raven at our seven gates.
114  But ere a torch our crown of towers could burn,
115  Ere they had tasted of our blood, they turn
116  Forced by the Dragon; in their rear
117  The din of Ares panic-struck they hear.
118  For Zeus who hates the braggart's boast
119  Beheld that gold-bespangled host;
120  As at the goal the paean they upraise,
121  He struck them with his forked lightning blaze.

*(Str. 2)*
122  To earth from earth rebounding, down he crashed;

123 The fire-brand from his impious hand was dashed,
124 As like a Bacchic **reveler** on he came,
125 Outbreathing hate and flame,
126 And tottered. Elsewhere in the field,
127 Here, there, great Area like a war-horse wheeled;
128 Beneath his car down thrust
129 Our foemen bit the dust.

130 Seven captains at our seven gates
131 Thundered; for each a champion waits,
132 Each left behind his armor bright,
133 Trophy for Zeus who turns the fight;
134 Save two alone, that ill-starred pair
135 One mother to one father bare,
136 Who lance in rest, one 'gainst the other
137 Drave, and both perished, brother slain by brother.

*(Ant. 2)*
138 Now Victory to Thebes returns again
139 And smiles upon her chariot-circled plain.
140 Now let feast and festal should
141 Memories of war blot out.
142 Let us to the temples throng,
143 Dance and sing the live night long.
144 God of Thebes, lead thou the round.
145 Bacchus, shaker of the ground!
146 Let us end our revels here;
147 Lo! Creon our new lord draws near,
148 Crowned by this strange chance, our king.
149 What, I marvel, pondering?
150 Why this summons? Wherefore call
151 Us, his elders, one and all,
152 Bidding us with him debate,
153 On some grave concern of State?

154 [Enter CREON]

155 CREON: Elders, the gods have righted once again
156 Our storm-tossed ship of state, now safe in port.
157 But you by special summons I **convened**
158 As my most trusted councilors; first, because
159 I knew you loyal to Laius of old;
160 Again, when Oedipus restored our State,
161 Both while he ruled and when his rule was o'er,
162 Ye still were constant to the royal line.
163 Now that his two sons perished in one day,

**Skill:**
**Point of View**

*These lines include many details that are specific to the cultural experience of Ancient Greece. Chariots and festivities filled with images of temples, dancing, and Greek gods show a world where gods are key to life.*

164  Brother by brother murderously slain,

165  By right of kinship to the Princes dead,

166  I claim and hold the throne and sovereignty.

167  Yet 'tis no easy matter to discern

168  The temper of a man, his mind and will,

169  Till he be proved by exercise of power;

170  And in my case, if one who reigns supreme

171  Swerve from the highest policy, tongue-tied

172  By fear of consequence, that man I hold,

173  And ever held, the basest of the base.

174  And I condemn the man who sets his friend

175  Before his country. For myself, I call

176  To witness Zeus, whose eyes are everywhere,

177  If I perceive some mischievous design

178  To sap the State, I will not hold my tongue;

179  Nor would I reckon as my private friend

180  A public foe, well knowing that the State

181  Is the good ship that holds our fortunes all:

182  Farewell to friendship, if she suffers wreck.

183  Such is the policy by which I seek

184  To serve the Commons and conformably

185  I have proclaimed an edict as concerns

186  The sons of Oedipus; Eteocles

187  Who in his country's battle fought and fell,

188  The foremost champion—duly bury him

189  With all observances and ceremonies

190  That are the guerdon of the heroic dead.

191  But for the miscreant exile who returned

192  Minded in flames and ashes to blot out

193  His father's city and his father's gods,

194  And glut his vengeance with his kinsmen's blood,

195  Or drag them captive at his chariot wheels—

196  For Polyneices 'tis ordained that none

197  Shall give him burial or make mourn for him,

198  But leave his corpse unburied, to be meat

199  For dogs and carrion crows, a ghastly sight.

200  So am I purposed; never by my will

201  Shall miscreants take precedence of true men,

202  But all good patriots, alive or dead,

203  Shall be by me preferred and honored.

204  CHORUS: Son of Menoeceus, thus thou will'st to deal

205  With him who loathed and him who loved our State.

206  Thy word is law; thou canst dispose of us

207  The living, as thou will'st, as of the dead.

# First Read

Read *Antigone*. After you read, complete the Think Questions below.

## ☁ THINK QUESTIONS

1. What is the relationship between Antigone and Ismene? What are they discussing as this excerpt from the play opens? Cite evidence from the text to demonstrate your understanding.

2. According to the Chorus, what happened between the brothers Eteocles and Polyneices? How do things in Thebes stand now? Cite evidence from the text to demonstrate your understanding.

3. What is Antigone's plan, and what is Ismene's response? Cite evidence from the text and explain your understanding.

4. Antigone tells her sister, "'Tis thine to show / If thou art worthy of thy blood or base." The word *or* tells you that *base* is being contrasted with *worthy of thy blood*. Given that, what do you suppose **base** means? Write your ideas.

5. Use context clues to determine the meaning of the word **reveler** as it is used in the text. Write your definition of *reveler*, and explain which clues helped you arrive at it.

Please note that excerpts and passages in the StudySync® library and this workbook are intended as touchstones to generate interest in an author's work. The excerpts and passages do not substitute for the reading of entire texts, and StudySync® strongly recommends that students seek out and purchase the whole literary or informational work in order to experience it as the author intended. Links to online resellers are available in our digital library. In addition, complete works may be ordered through an authorized reseller by filling out and returning to StudySync® the order form enclosed in this workbook.

Reading & Writing Companion

537

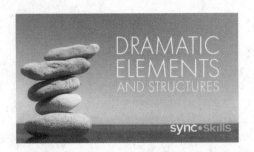

# Skill: Dramatic Elements and Structure

Use the Checklist to analyze Dramatic Elements and Structure in *Antigone*. Refer to the sample student annotations about Dramatic Elements and Structure in the text.

## ••• CHECKLIST FOR DRAMATIC ELEMENTS AND STRUCTURE

In order to identify the dramatic elements and structure in a drama, note the following:

✓ the form of the drama, such as comedy or tragedy

✓ the characters and setting(s) by act and scene

✓ the stage directions used

✓ the style of language, including verse or other formal language

✓ the order of events in the plot and how it creates mystery, tension, or surprise

✓ the overall structure of the text and what effects it creates including mystery, tension, or surprise

✓ moments when the author manipulates time to create a particular effect such as mystery, tension, or surprise

To analyze how an author's choices concerning how to structure a text, order events within it, and manipulate time create such effects as mystery, tension, or surprise, consider the following questions:

✓ How does the drama develop over the course of the text?

✓ What choices does the author make in regards to the structure of the text, the order of events, and the manipulation of time?

✓ How do the author's choices create mystery, tension, or surprise?

# Skill: Dramatic Elements and Structure

sync•Skills

Reread lines 98–137 of *Antigone*. Then, using the Checklist on the previous page, answer the multiple-choice questions below.

## ↻ YOUR TURN

1. How does playwright use the Chorus in this section of the play to manipulate time?

   ○ A. to describe the war for control of Thebes that recently ended

   ○ B. to predict the future of Thebes

   ○ C. to praise the god Zeus for saving Thebes in the present

   ○ D. to tell of the fall of Thebes in war long ago

2. How does the Chorus contribute to plot development in lines 98–111?

   ○ A. The Chorus tells of Polyneices coming to protect Thebes from invaders.

   ○ B. The Chorus makes clear that Polyneices invaded Thebes to claim the throne.

   ○ C. The Chorus describes the invading forces that came to kill Polyneices.

   ○ D. The Chorus explains that Polyneices and Eteocles invaded Thebes together.

3. How do the Strophe and Antistrophe differ in terms of the way each tells part of the story in this section of the play?

   ○ A. The Strophe section talks about events that occurred long before the war, while the Antistrophe speaks of events from just before the war started.

   ○ B. The Strophe and Antistrophe sections discuss two different sets of events.

   ○ C. The Strophe section apologizes for the events of the war, while the Antistrophe celebrates the outcome.

   ○ D. The Strophe sections talks about the war in the past tense, while the Antistrophe speaks of it in the present.

# Skill:
# Figurative Language

Use the Checklist to analyze Figurative Language in *Antigone*. Refer to the sample student annotations about Figurative Language in the text.

## ••• CHECKLIST FOR FIGURATIVE LANGUAGE

In order to determine the meaning of a figure of speech in context, note the following:

- ✓ words that mean one thing literally and suggest something else

- ✓ similes, metaphors, or personification

- ✓ figures of speech, including

  - oxymorons, or a figure of speech in which apparently contradictory terms appear in conjunction, such as

    - > a description such as "deafening silence"

    - > sayings such as "seriously funny"

  - euphemisms, or a mild or indirect word or expression substituted for one considered to be too harsh when referring to something unpleasant or embarrassing, such as

    - > saying someone has "passed away" instead of "died"

    - > using the term "correctional facility" instead of "prison"

In order to interpret a figure of speech in context and analyze its role in the text, consider the following questions:

- ✓ Where is there figurative language in the text and what seems to be the purpose of the author's use of it?

- ✓ Why does the author use a figure of speech rather than literal language?

- ✓ How do euphemisms or oxymorons affect the meaning of the text?

- ✓ How does the figurative language develop the message or theme of the literary work?

# Skill:
# Figurative Language

Reread lines 98–111 of *Antigone*. Then, using the Checklist on the previous page, answer the multiple-choice questions below.

1. Lines 98 to 105 show an example of what kind of figurative language?

   ○ A. euphemism
   ○ B. personification
   ○ C. simile
   ○ D. oxymoron

2. What is the significance of the phrase "like to an eagle swooping low?"

   ○ A. The Chorus is describing the way the sunlight illuminates the city.
   ○ B. The Chorus is comparing the invading army to an eagle.
   ○ C. The Chorus is comparing Creon to an eagle.
   ○ D. The Chorus is using an eagle to describe how majestic the invading army is.

Please note that excerpts and passages in the StudySync® library and this workbook are intended as touchstones to generate interest in an author's work. The excerpts and passages do not substitute for the reading of entire texts, and StudySync® strongly recommends that students seek out and purchase the whole literary or informational work in order to experience it as the author intended. Links to online resellers are available in our digital library. In addition, complete works may be ordered through an authorized reseller by filling out and returning to StudySync® the order form enclosed in this workbook.

Reading & Writing    541
Companion

# Skill:
# Point of View

Use the Checklist to analyze Point of View in *Antigone*. Refer to the sample student annotations about Point of View in the text.

In order to identify the point of view or cultural experience reflected in a work of literature from outside the United States, note the following:

✓ what the narrator or speaker knows and reveals

✓ the country of origin of the characters and author

✓ moments in the work that reflect a cultural experience not common in the United States by drawing on reading from world literature, such as

• a drama written by Ibsen or Chekhov or other international authors
• a story that reflects an indigenous person's experience in another country

To analyze the point of view of a cultural experience reflected in a work of literature from outside the United States, drawing on a wide reading of world literature, consider the following questions:

✓ What point of view does the author use? How does it help reflect a specific cultural experience?

✓ What is the country of origin of the author of the text? Of the characters in the text?

✓ What texts have you read previously from these nations or cultures? How does this help you analyze the point of view of this text?

✓ How does this text use point of view to present a different cultural experience than that of the United States?

✓ Is the narrator or speaker objective or are they unreliable? How does that affect the reader's understanding?

# Skill:
# Point of View

Reread lines 155–203 of *Antigone*. Then, using the Checklist on the previous page, answer the multiple-choice questions below.

## 🔄 YOUR TURN

1.  This question has two parts. First, answer Part A. Then, answer Part B.

    **Part A:** What is Creon's point of view about leadership?

    ○ A.  He believes leaders should make concessions.
    ○ B.  He believes leaders should consider friends and family as important as the state.
    ○ C.  He believes leaders should be strong and speak their minds.
    ○ D.  He believes leaders should be forgiving.

    **Part B:** Which quote BEST supports your answer from Part A?

    ○ A.  "If I perceive some mischievous design to sap the State, I will not hold my tongue."
    ○ B.  "I condemn the man who sets his friend before his country."
    ○ C.  "Nor would I reckon as my private friend a public foe."
    ○ D.  "never by my will shall miscreants take precedence of true men."

2.  This question has two parts. First, answer Part A. Then, answer Part B.

    **Part A:** What inference can be made about how the government in Ancient Greece functioned?

    ○ A.  Councilors were chosen by the people to aid the king.
    ○ B.  A royal lineage determined who would inherit the throne.
    ○ C.  Leaders were democratically elected.
    ○ D.  Governmental decisions were made by the councilors and the king coming to agreement.

    **Part B:** Which quote BEST supports your answer from Part A?

    ○ A.  "Both while he ruled and when his rule was o'er, / Ye still were constant to the royal line."
    ○ B.  "And I condemn the man who sets his friend / Before his country."
    ○ C.  "By right of kinship to the Princes dead, I claim and hold the throne and sovereignty."
    ○ D.  "But all good patriots, alive or dead, / Shall be by me preferred and honored."

# Close Read

Reread *Antigone*. As you reread, complete the Skills Focus questions below. Then use your answers and annotations from the questions to help you complete the Write activity.

## ◎ SKILLS FOCUS

1. Analyze how Sophocles structures the dialogue between Antigone and Ismene to build the tension in the relationship.

2. Explain how the references to ancient Greek beliefs, such as the references to gods, "the golden mean," and other figures of speech affect the meaning and tone of the drama.

3. Analyze how the Greek cultural experience is reflected in Antigone's central conflict.

4. Summarize this excerpt of the drama, including the theme. Discuss how the family connections heighten the conflict.

## ✏ WRITE

LITERARY ANALYSIS: In this scene from the drama *Antigone*, how does Sophocles use a historical and cultural setting to establish the conflict and develop characters? In your response, cite textual evidence and specific dramatic elements to support your analysis.

# Claudette Colvin Explains Her Role in the Civil Rights Movement

**INFORMATIONAL TEXT**
Roni Jacobson
2017

# Introduction

Although Claudette Colvin (b. 1939) has been left out of many history books, she played a critical role in early protests against segregation in 1950s America. At 15, Colvin was told to give up her bus seat for a white passenger and refused. This was months before Rosa Parks remained seated on the same public transportation system and was credited for sparking the Montgomery Bus Boycott. Colvin's subsequent testimony as a key plaintiff in the *Browder v. Gayle* case caused the first collapse of the "underpinnings of the Jim Crow South," as described by Phillip Hoose, her National Book Award-winning biographer. Here, Roni Jacobson of *Teen Vogue* interviews this essential—yet largely unknown—civil rights hero.

# "We were second class citizens. And there was no cause for it."

**Skill: Author's Purpose and Point of View**

*The title makes clear that the piece is explanatory, and the details here tie Rosa Parks to Claudette Colvin. This suggests that the author's point of view is that Colvin did not get the recognition she deserves.*

**Skill: Informational Text Elements**

*The author connects the event of Claudette refusing to give up her seat to the historical event of Rosa Parks doing the same thing months later. Linking these two events emphasizes the equal importance of both.*

1   On March 2, 1955, nine months before Rosa Parks refused to give up her seat to a white passenger on a bus in Montgomery, Alabama, Claudette Colvin, a 15-year-old black teenager, did the same thing.

2   Parks is remembered for having sparked the Montgomery Bus Boycott,[1] which Colvin helped end more than a year later when she, along with co-plaintiffs Mary Louise Smith, Aurelia Browder and Susie McDonald, served as witnesses in *Browder v. Gayle*, a case that ended segregation in public transportation not just in Alabama, but eventually all across the United States when the Supreme Court affirmed the ruling.

3   Parks became an icon of resistance. Meanwhile, Colvin became an outcast, branded a troublemaker within her community after her **initial** arrest and conviction. She was abandoned by civil rights leaders when she became pregnant at 16. Although she has gained recognition in recent years — a book about her life won the National Book Award in 2009 — Colvin is still largely glossed over by history and her immense contribution and sacrifice has never been officially recognized by the U.S. government, as Parks' was.

4   *Teen Vogue* spoke with Colvin, now 78 years old, at her home in New York and by phone about her experiences. The following is a condensed and edited version of those conversations.

1. **Montgomery Bus Boycott** a protest, largely inspired by the resistance of Rosa Parks, that objected to the segregation of city buses

5 **_Teen Vogue:_** Tell us about the day of your protest.

6 **Claudette Colvin:** I was in 11th grade.

Skill:
Informational
Text Elements

*The author switches to an interview format and we are able to hear directly from Claudette. Hearing Colvin retell the events and describe her motivations helps us form a connection with this woman and her cause.*

7 It started out a normal day. We got out early and 13 of us students walked to downtown Montgomery and boarded a city bus on Dexter Avenue, exactly across the street from Dr. Martin Luther King's church. As the bus proceeded down Court Square, more white passengers got on the bus. In order for this white lady to have a seat, four students would have to vacate because a white person wasn't allowed to sit across from a colored person. So the bus driver asked for the four seats and three of the students got up. I remained seated.

8 History had me glued to the seat. Harriet Tubman's[2] hands were pushing down on one shoulder and Sojourner Truth's[3] hands were pushing down on the other shoulder. I was paralyzed between these two women; I couldn't move.

9 February was, at that time, only Negro History Week, not history month. But the faculty members at my school said we were gonna do it the whole month because African Americans — at that time we were called "negroes" — were deliberately kept out of American history. The boys liked to talk about Jackie Robinson, breaking the baseball barrier. My instructor talked about Sojourner Truth and Harriet Tubman. We started talking about the injustice and how we were discriminated against locally. That's why I was so fired up and so angry when the bus driver asked me to get up. It was more than myself.

10 Some white students [on the bus] were yelling: "You have to get up, you have to get up." And a colored girl, one of the students said, "Well she don't have to do nothing but stay black and die."

11 We were still on our best behavior taking all of the insults from the white passengers. The bus driver knew that I wasn't breaking the law, because these seats were already for colored people. Under Jim Crow law,[4] the bus driver could ask you to give up your seat at any time but the problem was that [the number of seats for black and white people had to be even]. He drove the bus about four stops, and when we stopped, traffic patrol got on the bus and asked me to get up. I told him I paid my fare and said, "It's my constitutional right!" The patrol officer yelled to the bus driver that he didn't have any **jurisdiction** here.

12 **_Teen Vogue_**: *What happened after that?*

---

2. **Harriet Tubman** a famous American activist who escaped from slavery and founded the Underground Railroad, which helped to help free more than seventy enslaved persons
3. **Sojourner Truth** a woman born into slavery who escaped with her daughter, then made history by being the first black woman to win a lawsuit against a white man when she sued him for custody of her enslaved son
4. **Jim Crow law** any law created, primarily in the southern United States, to enforce racial segregation following Reconstruction until the civil rights movement

Skill:
Media

The video and article both portray Claudette's arrest. The video shows a striking visual representation of Claudette dragged off the bus and sitting in jail. The article allows us to hear the emotions she was feeling at the time.

13  **Claudette Colvin:** We thought it was all over with, because the white woman remained standing and I remained seated. I knew she wasn't going to sit opposite me. He drove one block and that's when the policemen from the squad car came in and asked me the same thing, and I was even more defiant.

14  I don't know how I got off that bus. All the students said they manhandled me off the bus and into the squad car. They handcuffed me, booked me, and then instead of taking me to a **juvenile** detention center, they took me to city jail. That's when terror came down. I became very frightened. They didn't allow me to have a phone call, and I didn't know that the students were gonna go and tell my parents.

15  My mother and my pastor came down and bailed me out. I had three charges: disorderly conduct, violating segregation law, and assault and **battery**. They dropped two charges and just kept the one, assault and battery. They said I scratched the policeman because I didn't get up and walk, but I don't recall scratching him.

16  *Teen Vogue: So you were convicted of assault and battery of a police officer, a felony? Is that still on your record?*

17  **Claudette Colvin:** Yes. I was put on indefinite probation.

18  *Teen Vogue: How has that **impacted** your life?*

19  **Claudette Colvin:** That arrest changed my whole life. I was **ostracized** by people in my community and professional people also. I wanted to be an attorney. My mother would say I never stopped talking. I always had a lot of questions to ask, and I was never satisfied with the answer. A lot of things I wasn't satisfied by.

20  *Teen Vogue: What was your relationship with Rosa Parks?*

21  **Claudette Colvin:** I first met her maybe two weeks after I got arrested. Mrs. Parks got in touch with my parents. She had a youth group and said that the youth group would like to hear my story. That summer I became secretary of the youth group, and in the fall I took over when the person in charge left for college. We would meet every Sunday afternoon. Rosa would discuss discrimination in Montgomery.

22  *Teen Vogue: You were dropped by the movement after the trial as a young single mother. Do you ever feel like you don't get enough credit? For instance, the Smithsonian National Museum of African American History refers to your contribution in passing as a "test case," when in fact you played a **pivotal** role in the case that helped crumble segregation.*

23 **Claudette Colvin:** I was glad that Rosa did it and that people were at last going to stand out. It was important to have Rosa as a face that they could rally around.

24 All four of us didn't get enough credit. Mary Louise Smith,[5] who was 18, was arrested too. I was a little disappointed [at being left out], because the whole movement was about young people, saying we want more from America. We want to stand up and be first class citizens. The discrimination that's going on, whether gender or racial or whatever, religious. We want it to be brought out and defeated.

25 **Teen Vogue:** *Can you tell me more about the period after your arrest and conviction? How did people in the community react?*

26 **Claudette Colvin:** Some people, the students, were sympathetic at first. They knew my mindset and what I was thinking, but their parents persuaded them not to be involved with me because I was a troublemaker and "this wasn't the right thing to do." They already thought I was crazy. Before then, in the 10th grade, I had stopped straightening my hair. I was wearing my hair naturally and they started saying I was crazy for doing that. They didn't know I would go to the extreme and disobey the bus driver.

27 **Teen Vogue:** *This was in the 1950s. That's so ahead of its time, especially considering natural hair is still labeled unprofessional today.*

28 **Claudette Colvin:** Everybody was really really upset if their hair wasn't straight. A lot of African American women wanted to emulate white women. But I said in my mind, rationally thinking, there is no way you are going to get your hair that straight, especially in the summer. By the time I straightened it I wanted to go out and play and run it would go back anyway.

29 I lost a lot of friends because of that. Because their mothers and fathers, the only work they had was working for white people, and they didn't want to lose their jobs. That's the main thing.

30 I didn't know about depression, but I became a little depressed. I lost all my friends and really needed someone. I got pregnant in July and I went back to school in September. I began showing around four months after I was pregnant. I was expelled from school around the Christmas holiday. My principal told me not to come back.

31 **Teen Vogue:** *So Browder v. Gayle. Tell me about your role in the case. You were the star witness. What was going through your mind when you were on the witness stand? Were you nervous? Did you rehearse what you would say beforehand?*

---

5. **Mary Louise Smith** another woman who, like Rosa Parks, refused to give up her seat on a segregated city bus

Copyright © BookheadEd Learning, LLC

32 **Claudette Colvin:** I was afraid, but as I got on the stand and started to look around, I realized that I might as well get involved. I gained strength from the audience when I was testifying. [Attorney Fred Grey, the young civil rights lawyer representing Claudette] didn't go over the questions beforehand. I didn't rehearse. I just wanted to expose to white people what I was going through, and how African Americans were treated. We were second class citizens. And there was no cause for it. Just because they think that they are superior.

33 [Afterwards], people were congratulating me and I wondered what they were congratulating me about. I hoped that I did some good.

Roni Jacobson, *Teen Vogue* © Conde Nast

# First Read

Read "Claudette Colvin Explains Her Role in the Civil Rights Movement." After you read, complete the Think Questions below.

## THINK QUESTIONS

1. Why do you think civil rights leaders abandoned Colvin when she got pregnant? Cite evidence from the text to support your inference.

2. Why did Colvin's teachers consider Negro History Week unjust? How did they respond?

3. According to Colvin, how did her physical identity contribute to her being labeled a troublemaker by her own community?

4. The Latin word *jur* means "law," and the Latin *dictio* is derived from *dicere*, meaning "to say." Keeping this in mind and using context clues from the text, what do you think the word **jurisdiction** means? Write your best answer.

5. What is the meaning of the word **ostracized** as it is used in the text? Write your best definition, along with a brief explanation of the context clues that helped you arrive at the definition.

Please note that excerpts and passages in the StudySync® library and this workbook are intended as touchstones to generate interest in an author's work. The excerpts and passages do not substitute for the reading of entire texts, and StudySync® strongly recommends that students seek out and purchase the whole literary or informational work in order to experience it as the author intended. Links to online resellers are available in our digital library. In addition, complete works may be ordered through an authorized reseller by filling out and returning to StudySync® the order form enclosed in this workbook.

Reading & Writing Companion 551

# Skill: Author's Purpose and Point of View

Use the Checklist to analyze Author's Purpose and Point of View in "Claudette Colvin Explains Her Role in the Civil Rights Movement." Refer to the sample student annotation about Author's Purpose and Point of View in the text.

## ••• CHECKLIST FOR AUTHOR'S PURPOSE AND POINT OF VIEW

In order to identify author's purpose and point of view, note the following:

- ✓ facts, statistics, and graphic aids as these indicate that an author is writing to inform

- ✓ descriptions that present a complicated process in plain language, which may indicate that an author is writing to explain

- ✓ whether the author uses figurative language or other descriptive words in order to intensify an emotion

- ✓ the author's use of rhetoric, or the art of speaking and writing persuasively, such as using repetition to drive home a point

To determine the author's purpose and point of view, consider the following questions:

- ✓ How does the author convey, or communicate, information in the text?

- ✓ Does the author use figurative or emotional language? What effect does it have on the author's point of view?

- ✓ Are charts, graphs, maps, and other graphic aids included in the text? For what purpose?

- ✓ How does the author use rhetoric to try and persuade readers to accept a specific point of view or opinion? Is the use of rhetoric successful? Why or why not?

# Skill: Author's Purpose and Point of View

Reread paragraphs 3–7 of "Claudette Colvin Explains Her Role in the Civil Rights Movement." Then, using the Checklist on the previous page, answer the multiple-choice questions below.

## ⟳ YOUR TURN

1. This question has two parts. First, answer Part A. Then, answer Part B.

   **Part A:** What claim does the author imply about Colvin in this section of text that reveals the author's point of view?

   ○ A.  The author implies that Colvin should be recognized in the same way Parks is.

   ○ B.  The author implies that Colvin was a troublemaker and should be forgotten.

   ○ C.  The author implies that Colvin should be viewed as an acclaimed author.

   ○ D.  The author implies that Colvin was viewed as an icon of resistance.

   **Part B:** Which of the following quotes BEST supports your response to Part A?

   ○ A.  "Parks became an icon of resistance."

   ○ B.  "Meanwhile, Colvin became an outcast."

   ○ C.  "She was abandoned by civil rights leaders when she became pregnant at 16."

   ○ D.  "her immense contribution and sacrifice has never been officially recognized by the U.S. government, as Parks' was"

Please note that excerpts and passages in the StudySync® library and this workbook are intended as touchstones to generate interest in an author's work. The excerpts and passages do not substitute for the reading of entire texts, and StudySync® strongly recommends that students seek out and purchase the whole literary or informational work in order to experience it as the author intended. Links to online resellers are available in our digital library. In addition, complete works may be ordered through an authorized reseller by filling out and returning to StudySync® the order form enclosed in this workbook.

Reading & Writing Companion      **553**

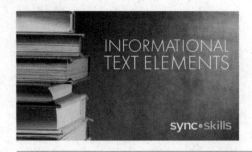

# Skill:
# Informational Text Elements

Use the Checklist to analyze Informational Text Elements in "Claudette Colvin Explains Her Role in the Civil Rights Movement." Refer to the sample student annotations about Informational Text Elements in the text.

## ••• CHECKLIST FOR INFORMATIONAL TEXT ELEMENTS

In order to determine how the author unfolds an analysis or series of ideas or events, note the following:

✓ the order in which specific points are made

✓ how the author introduces and develops ideas or events

✓ connections that are drawn between ideas and events

✓ key details in the text that describe or explain important ideas, events, or individuals

✓ other features, such as charts, maps, sidebars, and photo captions that might provide additional information outside the main text

✓ similarities and differences between types of information in a text

To analyze how the author unfolds an analysis or series of ideas or events, including the order in which the points are made, how they are introduced and developed, and the connections that are drawn between them, consider the following questions:

✓ How are the informational text elements related?

✓ In what order are the ideas or events the author presents organized?

✓ How does the order in which ideas or events are presented affect the connections between them?

✓ What other features, if any, help readers to analyze the events, ideas, or individuals in the text?

# Skill:
# Informational Text Elements

Reread paragraphs 25–30 of "Claudette Colvin Explains Her Role in the Civil Rights Movement." Then, using the Checklist on the previous page, answer the multiple-choice questions below.

## ⟳ YOUR TURN

1. This question has two parts. First, answer Part A. Then, answer Part B.

   **Part A:** Which idea most clearly connects the information in this passage?

   ○ A. A lot of African American women wanted to emulate white women during this time period.

   ○ B. Claudette lost many friends because she refused to give up her seat on the bus.

   ○ C. Some people were sympathetic at first to Claudette's arrest.

   ○ D. Claudette had to endure many hardships after she refused to give up her seat on the bus.

   **Part B:** Which of the following quotes BEST supports the message from Part A?

   ○ A. "Some people, the students, were sympathetic at first."

   ○ B. "They didn't know I would go to the extreme and disobey the bus driver."

   ○ C. "I didn't know about depression, but I became a little depressed."

   ○ D. "Everybody was really really upset if their hair wasn't straight."

2. What point is the author most likely trying to make with the following text?

   "This was in the 1950s. That's so ahead of its time, especially considering natural hair is still labeled unprofessional today."

   ○ A. Refusing to give up her seat was not the only way Claudette rebelled.

   ○ B. Claudette was not fashionable for her time.

   ○ C. Claudette should have tried to fit in.

   ○ D. Claudette was targeted by the police because of her hair.

Please note that excerpts and passages in the StudySync® library and this workbook are intended as touchstones to generate interest in an author's work. The excerpts and passages do not substitute for the reading of entire texts, and StudySync® strongly recommends that students seek out and purchase the whole literary or informational work in order to experience it as the author intended. Links to online resellers are available in our digital library. In addition, complete works may be ordered through an authorized reseller by filling out and returning to StudySync® the order form enclosed in this workbook.

Reading & Writing Companion     555

# Skill:
# Media

Use the Checklist to analyze Media in "Claudette Colvin Explains Her Role in the Civil Rights Movement." Refer to the sample student annotation about Media in the text.

## ••• CHECKLIST FOR MEDIA

In order to identify various accounts of a subject told in different mediums, note the following:

✓ the similarities and differences between various accounts of a subject

✓ the features of each medium, such as a person's life story in both print and multimedia, including strengths and weaknesses

✓ how each medium presents an account of a subject

✓ what details are emphasized in each account and what are removed

To analyze various accounts of a subject told in different mediums, determining which details are emphasized in each account, consider the following questions:

✓ How does each medium present an account of a subject?

✓ Which details are emphasized in each account? What is included?

✓ What has been left out of each account, and why?

# Skill:
# Media

Reread paragraphs 19–25 of "Claudette Colvin Explains Her Role in the Civil Rights Movement" and watch the StudySyncTV episode. Then, using the Checklist on the previous page, answer the multiple-choice questions below.

## ♻ YOUR TURN

1. This question has two parts. First, answer Part A. Then, answer Part B.

   **Part A:** The video portrays the choice to use Rosa Parks as the face of the movement as unjust. How does Claudette feel about this choice?

   ○ A.  She agrees it was wrong to choose Rosa over herself.

   ○ B.  She agrees that Rosa should have been the face of the movement.

   ○ C.  She doesn't really care one way or the other.

   ○ D.  She thinks they both should have been the face of the movement.

   **Part B:** Which quote BEST supports your answer from Part A?

   ○ A.  "It was important to have Rosa as a face that they could rally around."

   ○ B.  "All four of us didn't get enough credit."

   ○ C.  "Rosa would discuss discrimination in Montgomery."

   ○ D.  "Do you ever feel like you don't get enough credit?"

2. What information is absent from the video when compared to the information in the passage?

   ○ A.  The video does not discuss Claudette's pregnancy while this passage does.

   ○ B.  The video discusses the Claudette's meeting with Rosa Parks, which is not discussed in the passage.

   ○ C.  The video elaborates on the use of meetings and organization to assist in the work of the movement, while the passage says very little.

   ○ D.  The video does not reveal that Claudette was ostracized by her community, while the passage emphasizes this point.

Reading & Writing
Companion

# Close Read

Reread "Claudette Colvin Explains Her Role in the Civil Rights Movement." As you reread, complete the Skills Focus questions below. Then use your answers and annotations from the questions to help you complete the Write activity.

## ◎ SKILLS FOCUS

1. Explain the author's purpose for conducting this interview. Cite textual evidence, including word choice or rhetorical devices, to support your analysis.

2. Analyze how the author develops the interview with Claudette Colvin, the order in which points are made, and connections drawn between them.

3. Analyze how the information in the interview compares to the information presented in the video. Explain what is emphasized in each account as well as what is absent in each version of the account.

4. Explain why we revisit historical accounts and how these accounts help connect us to one another.

## ✏ WRITE

EXPLANATORY: One could argue that the author's purpose for writing this piece is to convey a message about the importance of remembering unsung heroes. How does the author's use of text elements help her achieve this purpose? In your response, explain several aspects of the text's format and structure that are important to the author's purpose.

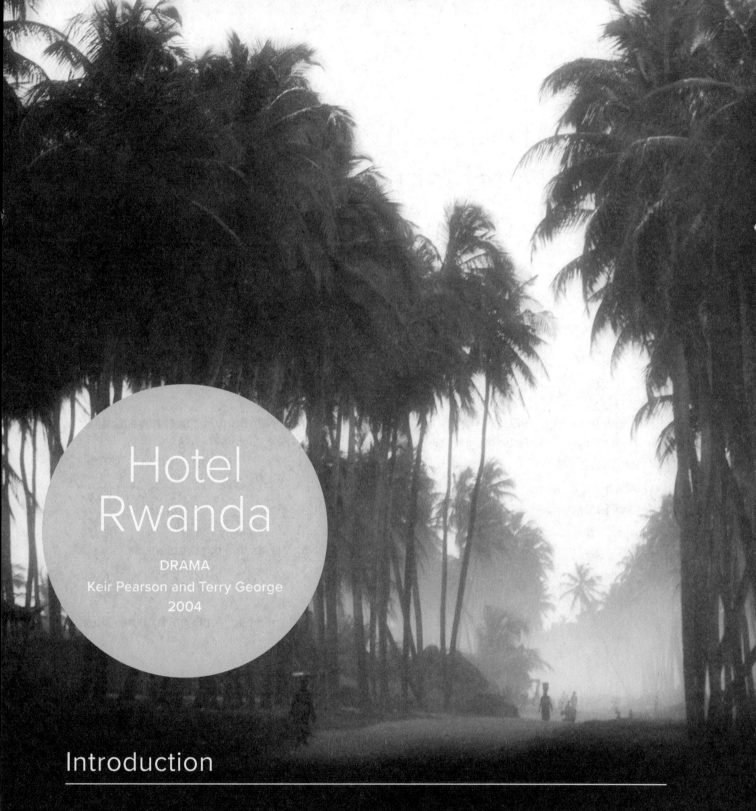

# Hotel Rwanda

DRAMA
Keir Pearson and Terry George
2004

## Introduction

Based on real-life events of the Rwandan Civil War between the Hutu and Tutsi ethnic groups, *Hotel Rwanda* dramatizes the heroic actions of Paul Rusesabagina, who is credited with hiding and saving more than a thousand people at the hotel he managed in the Rwandan capital of Kigali. In this excerpt from Keir Pearson and Terry George's screenplay, civil war has erupted, and the situation at Hotel Mille Collines is dangerous and chaotic.

# "There will be no rescue. No intervention force. We can only save ourselves."

 Skill: Dramatic Elements and Structure

*The scene is set in Belgium, but Paul calls from Kigali. This sets up the parallel plots of Tillens being safe in Europe while Paul faces danger in Rwanda. This juxtaposition increases the suspense. Will Paul and the others survive?*

INT. SABENA OFFICES – BELGIUM – TILLEN'S OFFICE – DAY

1   *The Sabena President and three VPs have an early morning meeting. The intercom buzzes.*

2   TILLENS: Yes?

3   SECRETARY (V.O. – THRU SPEAKER PHONE): Sorry, sir, but I have a call from Paul in Kigali. He says it's urgent.

4   *The President hits the speaker button.*

5   TILLENS: Paul. Are you all right?

6   PAUL (V.O. – THRU SPEAKER PHONE): We have a big problem, sir.

7   TILLENS: What?

8   PAUL (V.O. – THRU SPEAKER PHONE): The Hutu[1] Army have come. They've ordered us – all of us – out of the hotel.

9   TILLENS: Why are they doing this?

10  PAUL (V.O. – THRU SPEAKER PHONE): I think they will kill us all.

11  TILLENS (*stunned*): Kill? What do you mean . . . all? How many?

12  PAUL (V.O. – THRU SPEAKER PHONE): We have one hundred staff, and now more than eight hundred guests.

13  *Tillens can barely form words to reply.*

14  TILLENS: Eight hundred!

1. **Hutu**  a member of a people who make up the majority population of Rwanda and Burundi, historically oppressed by the Tutsi people

---

15 PAUL (V.O. – THRU SPEAKER PHONE): Yes, sir. There are now eight hundred Tutsi[2] and Hutu **refugees**. I do not have much time left, sir. I want to thank you for everything you have done for me and my family, and please thank all of my friends at Sabena.

16 *The President considers this.*

17 TILLENS: Paul, wait. I'm gonna put you on hold. Stay by the phone.

18 *He hits the hold button, looks to the other executives. They are stunned to silence by Paul's **profound** farewell.*

INT. HOTEL MILLE COLLINES – MANAGER'S OFFICE – DAY

19 *Paul sits in the office, his hand over the mouthpiece. From the lobby come soldiers' angry voices.*

20 SOLDIER (O.S.): Where are your papers?

INT. SABENA OFFICES – BELGIUM – TILLEN'S OFFICE – DAY

21 *The President gets everyone working on the phone.*

22 TILLENS: Louis, get on to the UN. Tell them what's happening. Mary, call the Prime Minister's office. Tell them I must speak with him now.

23 *The President lifts the telephone receiver and hits a button.*

24 TILLENS: Paul, are you there?

25 PAUL (V.O. – THRU SPEAKER PHONE): Yes, sir.

26 TILLENS: Who can I call to stop this?

27 *Paul thinks.*

28 PAUL (V.O. – THRU SPEAKER PHONE): The French – they supply the Hutu Army.

29 TILLENS: Do everything you can to bide time. I'll call you right back.

30 *Paul hurries from the room.*

INT. HOTEL MILLE COLLINES – LOBBY – DAY

Skill: Dramatic
Elements and
Structure

The pacing here causes a lot of suspense. The soldiers in the other room make me feel anxious. The situation is urgent, but then as I keep reading Tillens tells Paul to do what he can to bide time. There is no time! They need help now!

---

2. **Tutsi** a member of a people who make up the minority population of Rwanda and Burundi, historically the oppressors of the Hutu people

31   *Dube is at the computer, printing something. Paul walks quickly to him.*

32   PAUL: What are you doing, Dube?

33   DUBE: The Lieutenant, sir. He wants to see the guest list.

34   *Paul nervously glances at the soldiers.*

35   PAUL: Go and get these boys some more beer.

36   *Dube walks to the bar to get the beer, and Paul is on the computer, typing. A receptionist looks at the screen.*

37   RECEPTIONIST: Sir, that guest list is from two weeks ago.

38   PAUL: Shh.

39   *Paul hits the print button. The printer clicks to life.*

INT. HOTEL MILLE COLLINES – ENTRANCE – DAY

40   *Paul emerges with the printed registry. The Lieutenant marches up to Paul.*

41   HUTU LIEUTENANT: Where's the guest list?

42   *Paul hands him the print out. The Lieutenant studies it.*

43   HUTU LIEUTENANT: Anderson, Arthurs, Boulier . . . What is this?

44   PAUL: It is the guest list, sir.

45   HUTU LIEUTENANT: Are you trying to make a fool out of me?

46   PAUL: No. We stopped taking names after the President was murdered. This is the only guest list, sir.

47   HUTU LIEUTENANT: There are no Europeans left. Get me the names of all the cockroaches in there, now.

48   PAUL: That will take time.

49   HUTU LIEUTENANT: You don't have time. If I don't have the names so that I can pick out the traitors, then I'll kill everyone in there. Starting with you.

50   *The Lieutenant's radio comes to life and he turns to answer it. He listens for a moment . . .*

NOTES

51 HUTU LIEUTENANT (INTO RADIO): Yes, sir?

52 *He angrily turns to Paul and grabs him.*

53 HUTU LIEUTENANT: Who did you call?

54 PAUL: Who did I call?

55 HUTU LIEUTENANT: Don't lie to me! What is your name?

56 PAUL: Rusesabagina. Paul Rusesabagina.

57 HUTU LIEUTENANT: I'll remember you.

58 *He prods Paul's chest.*

59 HUTU LIEUTENANT (CONT'D): I'll remember you.

60 *He turns to his soldiers, gestures.*

61 HUTU LIEUTENANT (CONT'D): Let's go.

62 *They drive off.*

INT. HOTEL MILLE COLLINES – ROOF – DAY

63 *Paul emerges onto the roof. He looks around for his family, sees Tatiana, his children and the neighbors sitting huddled together.*

64 PAUL: They've gone.

65 TATIANA: Oh.

66 *Tatiana grabs him.*

67 TATIANA (CONT'D): I was so afraid for you.

68 *Dube appears.*

69 DUBE: Sir, the President of Sabena is on the phone for you.

70 *Paul strokes Tatiana's face.*

71 PAUL: I must talk with this man.

NOTES

INT. HOTEL MILLE COLLINES – MANAGER'S OFFICE – DAY

72 *Paul hits the button and lifts the telephone receiver.*

73 PAUL: Mr. Tillens.

74 TILLENS (V.O. – THRU PHONE): Paul, what's going on?

75 *Paul shakes his head in disbelief.*

76 PAUL: They left. Thank you, sir. What did you do?

INT. SABENA OFFICES – BELGIUM – TILLEN'S OFFICE – DAY

77 *The Sabena President is at his desk.*

78 TILLENS: I got through to the French President's office.

79 PAUL (V.O. – THRU SPEAKER PHONE): Well, thank you. You have saved our lives.

80 TILLENS: I pleaded with the French and the Belgians to go back and get you all. I'm afraid this is not going to happen.

81 *Silence, Tillens is ashamed, angry.*

82 TILLENS (CONT'D): They're cowards, Paul. Rwanda is not – worth a single vote to any of them. The French, the British, the Americans. I am sorry, Paul.

INT. HOTEL MILLE COLLINES – MANAGER'S OFFICE – DAY

83 *Paul is stunned.*

84 PAUL: Thank you.

INT. HOTEL MILLE COLLINES – FUNCTION ROOM – DAY

85 *The refugees are gathered, Paul addresses them.*

86 PAUL: There will be no rescue. No **intervention** force. We can only save ourselves. Many of you know influential people abroad. You must call these people.

INT. HOTEL MILLE COLLINES – MANAGER'S OFFICE – DAY

87  **MONTAGE** *of influential refugees. Odette, Benedict, Xavier call, plead, write and send faxes.*

88  *Odette sits at the desk, on the phone.*

89  PAUL (V.O.): You must tell them what will happen to us.

90  *Other refugees are on the phones.*

91  PAUL (V.O. CONT'D): Say goodbye. But when you say goodbye, say it as though you are reaching through the phone and holding their hand. Let them know that if they let go of that hand . . . you will die. We must shame them into sending help. Most importantly, this can not be a refugee camp. The Interahamwe believe that the Mille Collines is a four-star Sabena hotel. That is the only thing keeping us alive.

INT. HOTEL MILLE COLLINES – LOBBY – DAY

92  *Paul on the move, organizing, walks to the receptionist at the front desk.*

93  PAUL: Have you printed the bills?

94  *She hands him a stack of envelopes.*

95  PAUL (CONT'D): Now please erase the **registry**.

96  RECEPTIONIST: Erase it?

97  PAUL: Yes. I want no names to appear there.

98  *Dube joins him.*

99  DUBE: Boss, the carpenters are ready.

100 PAUL: Tell them to remove all of the numbers from the doors.

101 DUBE: And put what?

102 PAUL: And put nothing.

INT. HOTEL MILLE COLLINES – HALLWAY – DAY

103 *Paul goes door to door, knocking. The rooms are all packed with Tutsi refugees. A door opens. He hands an envelope to the refugee.*

104 PAUL: Good day. Here is your bill for the last week. If you cannot pay, or think you will not be able to pay, please go to the banquet room and Dube will take care of you. Thank you.

INT. HOTEL MILLE COLLINES – GROUNDS – NIGHT

105 *Refugees are clustered on the ground, in tents, as the radio voice plays over a reporter's interview of a State Department Officer.*

106 AMERICAN REPORTER (V.O. – THRU RADIO): Does the State Department have a view as to whether or not what is happening – could be genocide?

107 STATE DEPARTMENT OFFICER (V.O. – THRU RADIO): We have every reason to believe that acts of genocide have occurred.

108 *Inside his office Paul and the others listen.*

109 BRITISH REPORTER (V.O. – THRU RADIO): How many acts of genocide does it take to make genocide?

110 STATE DEPARTMENT OFFICER (V.O. – THRU RADIO): Alan, that's not a question that I'm in a position to answer.

111 BRITISH REPORTER (V.O. – THRU RADIO): Is it true that you have specific guidance not to use the word genocide in isolation, but always to preface it with this word, "acts of"?

112 STATE DEPARTMENT OFFICER (V.O. – THRU RADIO): I have guidance which I try to use as best I can. There are formulations that we are using that we are trying to be consistent in our use of.

113 *Paul is listening to all of this. Benedict turns off the radio in disgust.*

---

Pp. 71–9 from HOTEL RWANDA by TERRY GEORGE and KEIR PEARSON. Compilation copyright (c) 2005 by Newmarket Press. Used by permission of HarperCollins Publishers.

# First Read

Read *Hotel Rwanda*. After you read, complete the Think Questions below.

 **THINK QUESTIONS**

1. Use two or more details from the text to describe Paul. What details in the screenplay help you get a sense of his character?

2. Sabena's president, Mr. Tillens, attempts to secure immediate help for Paul and the eight hundred refugees. Whom does Tillens contact and what is the ultimate result for Paul and the refugees hiding in the hotel? Cite textual evidence to support your answer.

3. Why does Paul go to such elaborate measures to try and convince the Hutu lieutenant that most of the guests at the Mille Collines Hotel are Europeans? Use evidence from the text to support your answer.

4. Use context to determine the meaning of the word **intervention** as it is used in the text. Write your definition of *intervention* and tell how you found it.

5. Based on the text, what does the word **registry** mean? Explain which context clues help you arrive at a definition.

Please note that excerpts and passages in the StudySync® library and this workbook are intended as touchstones to generate interest in an author's work. The excerpts and passages do not substitute for the reading of entire texts, and StudySync® strongly recommends that students seek out and purchase the whole literary or informational work in order to experience it as the author intended. Links to online resellers are available in our digital library. In addition, complete works may be ordered through an authorized reseller by filling out and returning to StudySync® the order form enclosed in this workbook.

Reading & Writing Companion 567

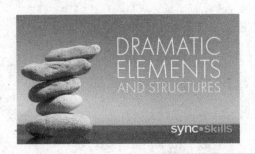

# Skill: Dramatic Elements and Structure

Use the Checklist to analyze Dramatic Elements and Structure in *Hotel Rwanda*. Refer to the sample student annotations about Dramatic Elements and Structure in the text.

## ••• CHECKLIST FOR DRAMATIC ELEMENTS AND STRUCTURE

In order to identify the dramatic elements and structure in a drama, note the following:

✓ the form of the drama, such as comedy or tragedy

✓ the characters and setting(s) by act and scene

✓ the stage directions used

✓ the style of language, including verse or other formal language

✓ the order of events in the plot and how it creates mystery, tension, or surprise

✓ the overall structure of the text and what effects it creates including mystery, tension, or surprise

✓ moments when the author manipulates time to create a particular effect such as mystery, tension, or surprise

To analyze how an author's choices concerning how to structure a text, order events within it, and manipulate time create such effects as mystery, tension, or surprise, consider the following questions:

✓ How does the drama develop over the course of the text?

✓ What choices does the author make in regards to the structure of the text, the order of events, and the manipulation of time?

✓ How does the author's choices create mystery, tension, or surprise?

# Skill: Dramatic Elements and Structure

Reread paragraphs 72–89 of *Hotel Rwanda*. Then, using the Checklist on the previous page, answer the multiple-choice questions below.

## ⟳ YOUR TURN

1. This question has two parts. First, answer Part A. Then, answer Part B.

   **Part A:** How do parallel plots interact to affect Tillens' ability to help Paul, as shown in paragraphs 72–84?

   ○ A. Tillens, who is in Belgium, is too far away from Paul to provide the help for the refugees.

   ○ B. Parallel plots do not influence Tillens's actions.

   ○ C. The parallel plots of a genocide in Rwanda and Western nations' indifference to the situation interact when Tilliens can't get help to Paul.

   ○ D. The parallel plots of historically bad relations between Rwanda and Belgium and a current genocide in Rwanda mean that Tillens will not help Paul and the refugees.

   **Part B:** Which of the following quotes BEST helps illustrate your answer from Part A?

   ○ A. "They're cowards, Paul. Rwanda is not – worth a single vote to any of them. The French, the British, the Americans. I am sorry, Paul."

   ○ B. "I pleaded with the French and the Belgians to go back and get you all. I'm afraid this is not going to happen."

   ○ C. "I got through to the French President's office."

   ○ D. "Well, thank you. You have saved our lives."

Please note that excerpts and passages in the StudySync® library and this workbook are intended as touchstones to generate interest in an author's work. The excerpts and passages do not substitute for the reading of entire texts, and StudySync® strongly recommends that students seek out and purchase the whole literary or informational work in order to experience it as the author intended. Links to online resellers are available in our digital library. In addition, complete works may be ordered through an authorized reseller by filling out and returning to StudySync® the order form enclosed in this workbook.

Reading & Writing Companion    569

# Close Read

Reread *Hotel Rwanda*. As you reread, complete the Skills Focus questions below. Then use your answers and annotations from the questions to help you complete the Write activity.

## ◎ SKILLS FOCUS

1. Analyze how the authors of the screenplay structure the events and what effects they create as a result.

2. Analyze the ways in which the characters' dialogue develops suspense in the screenplay.

3. Analyze what makes Paul a complex character, including how he develops as he interacts with other characters and responds to events in this excerpt.

4. Discuss how the threat and act of genocide defines people's relationship with their own humanity.

## ✎ WRITE

LITERARY ANALYSIS: In this excerpt from the screenplay of *Hotel Rwanda*, the language used by the characters is pivotal in creating a distinct emotional atmosphere relating to key events in the plot. Analyze how the structure of scenes and language used by the characters contribute to a tense mood in isolated scenes from *Hotel Rwanda*.

# Cherokee Family Reunion

DRAMA
Larissa Fasthorse
2013

## Introduction

Larissa FastHorse is an American playwright and choreographer. Born and raised in South Dakota, she is a member of the Lakota Nation's Rosebud Sioux Tribe. This selection from her play *Cherokee Family Reunion* introduces the Bearmeat and White families, all of whom have gathered to celebrate the wedding of the mother of the White family, Emma, to the father of the Bearmeat family, John. Members of the Bearmeat family, including Uncle Jasper, Aunt Nell, Aunt Polly, and Granny, look on as the children in both families meet each other for the first time. Christopher of the Whites and Lizzie of the Bearmeats experience an uncomfortable attraction to each other, while the other children—Morgan, Hillary, Dylan, Twodi,

# "I had a beautiful childhood in hills very like these. I want Cherokee to feel like your home."

FROM SCENE 1: THE WEDDING DAY

1  UNCLE JASPER. This is my favorite part, the reception! Take it away!

2  WEDDING SINGER. This is a little song I wrote for Emma and John's first dance.

3  *(The wedding band plays while JOHN and EMMA dance.*

   *\*Note: Recorded music can be used when UNCLE JASPER announces the first dance.)*

4  UNCLE JASPER. Everyone join in. Bearmeat family, and a White to dance with! Come on, mix it up now.

5  *(The kids awkwardly pair up and dance. CHRISTOPHER and LIZZIE spot each other and walk slowly together, it's a movie moment. Suddenly AUNT NELL and AUNT POLLY pop up between them. AUNT NELL speaks right in front of CHRISTOPHER.)*

6  AUNT NELL. We don't know anything about these kids. They could be thieves. **Hooligans**. Hare Krishnas.

7  AUNT POLLY. Oh, Nell. You're being dramatic.

8  AUNT NELL. Am I? *(Notices CHRISTOPHER.)* What do you want?

9  CHRISTOPHER. I'd love to have this dance, ma'am.

10 *(CHRISTOPHER dramatically sweeps AUNT NELL into his arms and leads her into a dance. LIZZIE and AUNT POLLY are **smitten**.*

11 *The dance ends. Whites and Bearmeats can't get away from each other fast enough.)*

12   CHRISTOPHER *(cont'd)*. If you need anything at all, just ask for Christopher. *(Joins his family.)*

13   GRANNY. Clearly a hooligan.

14   AUNT NELL. It's the smooth ones you have to watch.

15   EMMA *(to her kids)*. It's so nice of my children to celebrate my wedding in a clump like this. I had a beautiful childhood in hills very like these. I want Cherokee to feel like your home.

16   MORGAN. Hillary and I are only here for the summer, Mom.

17   DYLAN. Christopher and I only got two years of high school, then we're going back to civilization. They roasted a whole pig. It's got a face.

18   JOHN. Twodi, Meli you are the grown-ups, act like it. This is your turf so it's up to yuns to make the first move.

19   MELI. Dad, this isn't the first Thanksgiving.

20   TWODI. Well, their last name is White and they are … white.

21   JOHN. Not funny, Twodi. You want your old dad happy, right? Emma and I want you kids to have this summer together to become a family. By fall half of you will be gone to college.

22   MELI. I'm not going anywhere.

23   JOHN. I know, Meli.

24   EMMA. Can you try to mingle a little? Make like it's a party?

25   HILLARY. Sure, Mom.

26   *(EMMA goes to mingle. HILLARY gets an idea.)*

27   HILLARY. Hey guys, this is a wedding right? What dance does EVERY wedding need?

28   DYLAN. Yes! Perfect!

29   HILLARY. Get my iPod.

30   *(DYLAN goes.)*

31 JOHN. How about a Friendship Dance? To share the **culture** you are proud of with your new step siblings. Go share. Now.

32 MELI. Come on guys. Let's share. Twodi, you sing. We'll dance.

33 *(The kids gather onstage. DYLAN returns and gives JUSTIN the iPod. The White kids circle up. Bearmeats are unsure.)*

34 HILLARY *(to MELI)*. It's silly, but it's not a wedding without the "Chicken Dance," right?

35 MELI. Do you mean the Quail Dance?

36 HILLARY. What?

37 MELI. The **traditional** Cherokee Quail Dance?

38 HILLARY. Whatever. Come on, join the circle. Hit it!

39 *(JUSTIN hits the music, the "Chicken Dance." The White kids enthusiastically do the "Chicken Dance" in all its glorious, accordion stupidity.*

40 *The Bearmeats have clearly never seen anything like it. They are horrified or laughing heartily.)*

41 LIZZIE. What kind of dance is that?

42 MELI. Are they making fun of us?

43 MORGAN. It's the "Chicken Dance," it's stupid but you have to do it.

44 TWODI. No, we don't.

45 MORGAN. Oh, you're too cool for the "Chicken Dance"?

46 TWODI. Yes.

47 *(UNCLE JASPER jumps in. JUSTIN cuts the music.)*

48 UNCLE JASPER. Okie dokie. I think that's enough dancing.

49 GRANNY. Thank you for coming to celebrate my son and my new daughter-in-law, but I am sure they would like some time alone. Let's get this place cleaned up.

50 *(Everyone cleans. TWODI and MORGAN toss a couple glares at each other. CHRISTOPHER and LIZZIE bump into each other on the porch. It's instant* **chemistry**.*)*

51 CHRISTOPHER. Sorry.

52 LIZZIE. I'm a klutz. You're totally cute. *(Horrified.)* I mean it was cute what you did with Aunt Nell. You're not cute. I mean you are but—Hi.

53 CHRISTOPHER. You're cute too, roomie.

54 LIZZIE. Roomie?

55 CHRISTOPHER. We're living together now, *Brady Bunch*[1] style.

56 LIZZIE. Yeah, right. Welcome to the family.

57 *(LIZZIE flees. CHRISTOPHER smiles.)*

Excerpted from *Cherokee Family Reunion* by Larissa FastHorse, published by Dramatic Publishing Company.

---

## ✏ WRITE

DRAMA: This excerpt from *Cherokee Family Reunion* involves the blending of two families from different cultural backgrounds in a scene that depicts a range of emotions, from hope and excitement to humor and embarrassment. Highlight one moment of your life that involved a variety of emotions and dramatize it by writing a scene complete with dialogue and dramatic conventions.

---

1. **Brady Bunch** an American sitcom from the 1970s about an eight-member stepfamily and their maid, all of whom deal with typical family problems in a crowded household

# Funny in Farsi:
## A Memoir of Growing Up Iranian in America

INFORMATIONAL TEXT
Firoozeh Dumas
2003

## Introduction

The debut book by Firoozeh Dumas (b. 1965), *Funny in Farsi: A Memoir of Growing Up Iranian in America* has been described as a "warm, witty and sometimes poignant look at cross-cultural misunderstanding and family life" by *Publishers Weekly*. The often-confusing crossroads of culture and family is central to *Funny in Farsi* and other works by Dumas, who moved, along with her family, from Iran to California when she was seven years old. From welcoming the Shah in D.C. to her father's dream to compete in a game show, the book chronicles the arc of her family's story when they reach the American land where "one's tan is a legitimate topic of conversation." In this excerpt, Dumas writes of her—and her mother's—first day attending Leffingwell Elementary School.

# "It was the Promised Land. For me, it was where I could buy more outfits for Barbie."

## Chapter 1

### Leffingwell Elementary School

1   When I was seven, my parents, my fourteen-year-old brother, Farshid, and I moved from Abadan, Iran, to Whittier, California. Farid, the older of my two brothers, had been sent to Philadelphia the year before to attend high school. Like most Iranian youths, he had always dreamed of attending college abroad and, despite my mother's tears, had left us to live with my uncle and his American wife. I, too, had been sad at Farid's departure, but my sorrow soon faded—not **coincidentally,** with the receipt of a package from him. Suddenly, having my brother on a different continent seemed like a small price to pay for owning a Barbie complete with a carrying case and four outfits, including the rain gear and mini umbrella.

2   Our move to Whittier was temporary. My father, Kazem, an engineer with the National Iranian Oil Company, had been assigned to **consult** for an American firm for about two years. Having spent several years in Texas and California as a graduate student, my father often spoke about America with the eloquence and wonder normally reserved for a first love. To him, America was a place where anyone, no matter how humble his background, could become an important person. It was a kind and orderly nation full of clean bathrooms, a land where traffic laws were obeyed and where whales jumped through hoops. It was the Promised Land.[1] For me, it was where I could buy more outfits for Barbie.

3   We arrived in Whittier shortly after the start of second grade; my father enrolled me in Leffingwell Elementary School. To **facilitate** my adjustment, the principal arranged for us to meet my new teacher, Mrs. Sandberg, a few days before I started school. Since my mother and I did not speak English, the meeting consisted of a dialogue between my father and Mrs. Sandberg. My father carefully explained that I had attended a prestigious kindergarten where all the children were taught English. Eager to impress Mrs. Sandberg, he asked me to

Skill:
Word Patterns
and Relationships

*What does prestigious mean? I know prestige is respect or admiration. I see that prestigious is being used to describe the school. I can infer it is an adjective describing something that inspires respect and admiration.*

---

1. **Promised Land** a reference to the Bible, in which God promised to Abraham an idyllic and abundant land "flowing with milk and honey" in which his family would eventually settle

demonstrate my knowledge of the English language. I stood up straight and proudly recited all that I knew: "White, yellow, orange, red, purple, blue, green."

4    The following Monday, my father drove my mother and me to school. He had decided that it would be a good idea for my mother to attend school with me for a few weeks. I could not understand why two people not speaking English would be better than one, but I was seven, and my opinion didn't matter much.

**Skill:**
**Informational**
**Text Elements**

*The events are told*
*chronologically, but the*
*author takes a moment*
*to show how she sees*
*herself and her mother*
*now. Her mother seems*
*different from others in*
*the school, causing*
*embarrassment. Kids*
*can relate to this.*

5    Until my first day at Leffingwell Elementary School, I had never thought of my mother as an embarrassment, but the sight of all the kids in the school staring at us before the bell rang was enough to make me pretend I didn't know her. The bell finally rang and Mrs. Sandberg came and escorted us to class. Fortunately, she had figured out that we were precisely the kind of people who would need help finding the right classroom.

6    My mother and I sat in the back while all the children took their assigned seats. Everyone continued to stare at us. Mrs. Sandberg wrote my name on the board: F-I-R-O-O-Z-E-H. Under my name, she wrote "I-R-A-N." She then pulled down a map of the world and said something to my mom. My mom looked at me and asked me what she had said. I told her that the teacher probably wanted her to find Iran on the map.

7    The problem was that my mother, like most women of her generation, had been only briefly educated. In her era, a girl's sole purpose in life was to find a husband. Having an education ranked far below more desirable attributes such as the ability to serve tea or prepare baklava. Before her marriage, my mother, Nazireh, had dreamed of becoming a midwife. Her father, a fairly progressive man, had even refused the two earlier suitors who had come for her so that his daughter could pursue her dream. My mother planned to obtain her diploma, then go to Tabriz to learn midwifery from a teacher whom my grandfather knew. Sadly, the teacher died unexpectedly, and my mother's dreams had to be buried as well.

8    Bachelor No. 3 was my father. Like the other suitors, he had never spoken to my mother, but one of his cousins knew someone who knew my mother's sister, so that was enough. More important, my mother fit my father's physical requirements for a wife. Like most Iranians, my father preferred a fair-skinned woman with straight, light-colored hair. Having spent a year in America as a Fulbright scholar, he had returned with a photo of a woman he found attractive and asked his older sister, Sedigeh, to find someone who resembled her. Sedigeh had asked around, and that is how at age seventeen my mother officially gave up her dreams, married my father, and had a child by the end of the year.

9    As the students continued staring at us, Mrs. Sandberg gestured to my mother to come up to the board. My mother reluctantly obeyed. I cringed. Mrs. Sandberg, using a combination of hand gestures, started pointing to the map and saying, "Iran? Iran? Iran?" Clearly, Mrs. Sandberg had planned on

incorporating us into the day's lesson. I only wished she had told us that earlier so we could have stayed home.

10 After a few awkward attempts by my mother to find Iran on the map, Mrs. Sandberg finally understood that it wasn't my mother's lack of English that was causing a problem, but rather her lack of world geography. Smiling graciously, she pointed my mother back to her seat. Mrs. Sandberg then showed everyone, including my mother and me, where Iran was on the map. My mother nodded her head, acting as if she had known the location all along, but had preferred to keep it a secret. Now all the students stared at us, not just because I had come to school with my mother, not because we couldn't speak their language, but because we were stupid. I was especially mad at my mother, because she had **negated** the positive impression I had made previously by reciting the color wheel. I decided that starting the next day, she would have to stay home.

11 The bell finally rang and it was time for us to leave. Leffingwell Elementary was just a few blocks from our house and my father, grossly underestimating our ability to get lost, had assumed that my mother and I would be able to find our way home. She and I wandered aimlessly, perhaps hoping for a shooting star or a talking animal to help guide us back. None of the streets or houses looked familiar. As we stood pondering our predicament, an enthusiastic young girl came leaping out of her house and said something. Unable to understand her, we did what we had done all day: we smiled. The girl's mother joined us, then gestured for us to follow her inside. I assumed that the girl, who appeared to be the same age as I, was a student at Leffingwell Elementary; having us inside her house was probably akin to having the circus make a personal visit.

12 Her mother handed us a telephone, and my mother, who had, thankfully, memorized my father's work number, called him and explained our situation. My father then spoke to the American woman and gave her our address. This kind stranger agreed to take us back to our house.

13 Perhaps fearing that we might show up at their doorstep again, the woman and her daughter walked us all the way to our front porch and even helped my mother unlock the unfamiliar door. After making one last **futile** attempt at communication, they waved good-bye. Unable to thank them in words, we smiled even more broadly.

14 After spending an entire day in America, surrounded by Americans, I realized that my father's description of America had been correct. The bathrooms were clean and the people were very, very kind.

Excerpted from *Funny in Farsi: A Memoir of Growing Up Iranian in America* by Firoozeh Dumas, published by Random House.

Skill:
Connotation
and Denotation

*The word ponder means "think about carefully," but here it's humorous because Firoozeh and her mom have no idea what to do. She also calls it a "predicament," which sounds funnier than, say, "crisis."*

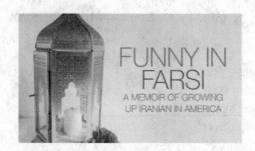

# First Read

Read *Funny in Farsi: A Memoir of Growing Up Iranian in America*. After you read, complete the Think Questions below.

## ☁ THINK QUESTIONS

1. What altered Firoozeh's sadness for her absent brother? Provide evidence from the text to support your response.

2. Why did Kazem and his family move to America? Cite evidence to support your response.

3. Why do Firoozeh and her mother need aid after they leave the elementary school? Explain, supporting your answer with evidence from the text.

4. The word **facilitate** in paragraph 3 is derived from the Latin word *facilis*, which means "easy." With this in mind and using context clues from words around it, write your best definition of *facilitate*, and explain how its Latin origins relate to the word's meaning.

5. The word **negated** comes from the Latin root *negat-*, which means "denied." Use this information to infer the meaning of *negated* as it is used in paragraph 10.

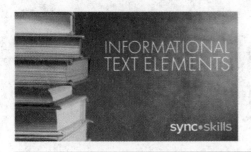

# Skill:
# Informational Text Elements

Use the Checklist to analyze Informational Text Elements in *Funny in Farsi: A Memoir of Growing Up Iranian in America*. Refer to the sample student annotation about Informational Text Elements in the text.

## ••• CHECKLIST FOR INFORMATIONAL TEXT ELEMENTS

In order to determine how the author unfolds an analysis or series of ideas or events, note the following:

- ✓ the order in which specific points are made

- ✓ how the author introduces and develops ideas or events

- ✓ connections that are drawn between ideas and events

- ✓ key details in the text that describe or explain important ideas, events, or individuals

- ✓ other features, such as charts, maps, sidebars, and photo captions that might provide additional information outside the main text

- ✓ similarities and differences between types of information in a text

To analyze how the author unfolds an analysis or series of ideas or events, including the order in which the points are made, how they are introduced and developed, and the connections that are drawn between them, consider the following questions:

- ✓ How are the informational text elements related?

- ✓ In what order are the ideas or events the author presents organized?

- ✓ How does the order in which ideas or events are presented affect the connections between them?

- ✓ What other features, if any, help readers to analyze the events, ideas, or individuals in the text?

Please note that excerpts and passages in the StudySync® library and this workbook are intended as touchstones to generate interest in an author's work. The excerpts and passages do not substitute for the reading of entire texts, and StudySync® strongly recommends that students seek out and purchase the whole literary or informational work in order to experience it as the author intended. Links to online resellers are available in our digital library. In addition, complete works may be ordered through an authorized reseller by filling out and returning to StudySync® the order form enclosed in this workbook.

Reading & Writing
Companion

581

# Skill:
# Informational Text Elements

Reread paragraphs 6–8 of *Funny in Farsi: A Memoir of Growing Up Iranian in America*. Then, using the Checklist on the previous page, answer the multiple-choice questions below.

## ↻ YOUR TURN

1. This question has two parts. First, answer Part A. Then, answer Part B.

   **Part A:** Between paragraphs 6 and 7, how does the author change the order in which she is presenting information?

   ○ A. The author begins telling her story through a flashback and then shifts to chronological order.

   ○ B. The author shifts from telling her story in chronological order to using a flashback.

   ○ C. The author shifts from making cause-and-effect connections to telling the story in chronological order.

   ○ D. The author alternates between current events and recent past to make connections between herself and her mother.

   **Part B:** Which which of the following sentence starters BEST indicates that the author is shifting to a flashback of particular events in her mother's life?

   ○ A. "The problem was . . ."

   ○ B. "Having an education . . ."

   ○ C. "In her era . . ."

   ○ D. "Before her marriage . . ."

2. How does the author develop and connect ideas in the passage?

   ○ A. The author summarizes key events in her parents' lives and key qualities of each parent.

   ○ B. The author offers a critique of her mother's choices and her father's dreams.

   ○ C. The author uses the details to show how Iranian society contrasts with American society.

   ○ D. The author connects her mother's choices to the ways that men treated her.

# Skill:
# Connotation and Denotation

Use the Checklist to analyze Connotation and Denotation in *Funny in Farsi: A Memoir of Growing Up Iranian in America*. Refer to the sample student annotation about Connotation and Denotation in the text.

## ••• CHECKLIST FOR CONNOTATION AND DENOTATION

In order to identify the denotative meanings of words, use the following steps:

✓ First, note unfamiliar words and phrases, key words used to describe important individuals, events, or ideas, or words that inspire an emotional reaction.

✓ Next, determine and note the denotative meaning of words by consulting a reference material such as a dictionary, glossary, or thesaurus.

✓ Finally, analyze nuances in the meanings of words with similar denotations.

To better understand the meaning of words and phrases as they are used in a text, including connotative meanings, use the following questions as a guide:

✓ What is the genre or subject of the text? Based on context, what do you think the meaning of the word is intended to be?

✓ Is your inference the same or different from the dictionary definition?

✓ Does the word create a positive, negative, or neutral emotion?

✓ What synonyms or alternative phrasing help you describe the connotative meaning of the word?

To determine the meaning of words and phrases as they are used in a text, including connotative meanings, use the following questions as a guide:

✓ What is the denotative meaning of the word? Is that denotative meaning correct in context?

✓ What possible positive, neutral, or negative connotations might the word have, depending on context?

✓ What textual details signal a particular connotation for the word?

# Skill:
# Connotation and Denotation

Reread paragraph 13 of *Funny in Farsi: A Memoir of Growing Up Iranian in America*. Then, using the Checklist on the previous page, answer the multiple-choice questions below.

## ↻ YOUR TURN

1. This question has two parts. First, answer Part A. Then, answer Part B.

   **Part A:** What is the connotation of the phrase "smiled even more broadly" as it is used in the sentence?

   ○ A. frustration and gratitude

   ○ B. happiness and fear

   ○ C. joy and relief

   ○ D. anger and frustration

   **Part B:** Which context clue BEST supports your answer from Part A?

   ○ A. "Perhaps fearing that we might show up at their doorstep again"

   ○ B. "the woman and her daughter walked us all the way to our front porch"

   ○ C. "they waved good-bye"

   ○ D. "Unable to thank them in words"

# Skill: Word Patterns and Relationships

Use the Checklist to analyze Word Patterns and Relationships in *Funny in Farsi: A Memoir of Growing Up Iranian in America*. Refer to the sample student annotation about Word Patterns and Relationships in the text.

## ••• CHECKLIST FOR WORD PATTERNS AND RELATIONSHIPS

In order to identify patterns of word changes to indicate different meanings or parts of speech, do the following:

✓ Determine the word's part of speech.

✓ When reading, use context clues to make a preliminary determination of the meaning of the word.

✓ When writing a response to a text, check that you understand the meaning and part of speech and that it makes sense in your sentence.

✓ Consult a dictionary to verify your preliminary determination of the meanings and parts of speech, including morphological elements such as base or root words, prefixes, and suffixes.

✓ Be sure to read all of the definitions, and then decide which definition, form, and part of speech makes sense within the context of the text.

To identify and correctly use patterns of word changes that indicate different meanings or parts of speech, consider the following questions:

✓ What is the intended meaning of the word?

✓ Do I know that this word form is the correct part of speech? Do I understand the word patterns for this particular word?

✓ When I consult a dictionary, can I confirm that the meaning I have determined for this word is correct? Do I know how to use it correctly?

Please note that excerpts and passages in the StudySync® library and this workbook are intended as touchstones to generate interest in an author's work. The excerpts and passages do not substitute for the reading of entire texts, and StudySync® strongly recommends that students seek out and purchase the whole literary or informational work in order to experience it as the author intended. Links to online resellers are available in our digital library. In addition, complete works may be ordered through an authorized reseller by filling out and returning to StudySync® the order form enclosed in this workbook.

Reading & Writing Companion    585

# Skill: Word Patterns and Relationships

Reread paragraph 10 of *Funny in Farsi: A Memoir of Growing Up Iranian in America*. Then, using the Checklist on the previous page, answer the multiple-choice questions below.

## ⟳ YOUR TURN

1. If *geography* means "the study of the physical features of the earth and its atmosphere," how does the addition of the suffix *-ical* change the meaning of the word?

   ○ A. It does not change the meaning.
   ○ B. It changes the meaning to "relating to geography."
   ○ C. It changes the meaning to "having nothing to do with geography."
   ○ D. It changes the meaning to "the place where someone is born."

2. If *gracious* means "courteous, kind, and pleasant," how does the addition of the suffix *-ly* change the meaning of the word?

   ○ A. It becomes an adjective, used to describe someone.
   ○ B. It becomes a verb, telling us what a person is doing.
   ○ C. It becomes an adverb, used to describe how someone does something.
   ○ D. It becomes a noun, telling us what something is.

# Close Read

Reread *Funny in Farsi: A Memoir of Growing Up Iranian in America*. As you reread, complete the Skills Focus questions below. Then use your answers and annotations from the questions to help you complete the Write activity.

## ◎ SKILLS FOCUS

1. Analyze how the author unfolds the series of events in this chapter of her memoir. Explain how she draws the connections between the points she makes and the events that occur.

2. Discuss the author's relationship to English and how it affected her education as she started school.

3. Discuss how the author makes humorous use of language to show the relationship between her parents.

4. Analyze the central idea of this section of the memoir, explaining how physical gestures are as important as spoken words for connecting people.

## ✎ WRITE

INFORMATIVE: The drama *Cherokee Family Reunion* and the memoir *Funny in Farsi* both address the topic of family using a tone of embarrassment. Select examples of language in each of these texts used to convey an embarrassed tone. Then, write a response in which you analyze how those examples of language contribute to the tone.

Please note that excerpts and passages in the StudySync® library and this workbook are intended as touchstones to generate interest in an author's work. The excerpts and passages do not substitute for the reading of entire texts, and StudySync® strongly recommends that students seek out and purchase the whole literary or informational work in order to experience it as the author intended. Links to online resellers are available in our digital library. In addition, complete works may be ordered through an authorized reseller by filling out and returning to StudySync® the order form enclosed in this workbook.

Reading & Writing Companion 587

# On the Painting of the Sistine Chapel

POETRY

Michelangelo di Lodovico
Buonarroti Simoni
1509

## Introduction

Michelangelo di Lodovico Buonarroti Simoni (1475–1564), or simply Michelangelo, was one of the most celebrated and well-known artists of the Italian Renaissance. His artistry took many forms: painting, sculpture, poetry, and architecture. Michelangelo's most famous work includes the statue of *David*, his painting *The Last Judgement*, and the architecture of St. Peter's Basilica in Rome. Some of his literary works lent new insights into his visual art, like this poem, which describes the crippling physical ailments that Michelangelo suffered as he painted the ceiling of the Sistine Chapel. Also included with the poem are images of a few of Michelangelo's many notable works.

# "My feet unseen move to and fro in vain."

NOTES

Michelangelo's fresco *The Last Judgment* at Sistine Chapel.

NOTES

*The Creation of Adam* by Michelangelo, painted
on the ceiling of the Sistine Chapel

1   In this hard **toil** I've such a **goiter** grown,
2   Like cats that water drink in Lombardy,
3   (Or wheresoever else the place may be)
4   That chin and belly meet perforce in one.
5   My beard doth point to heaven, my scalp its place
6   Upon my shoulder finds; my chest, you'll say,
7   A harpy's[1] is, my paintbrush all the day
8   Doth drop a rich **mosaic** on my face.
9   My **loins** have entered my paunch within,
10  My nether end my balance doth supply,
11  My feet unseen move to and fro in vain.
12  In front to **utmost** length is stretched my skin
13  And wrinkled up in folds behind, while I
14  Am bent as bowmen bend a bow in Spain.
15  No longer true or sane,
16  The judgment now doth from the mind proceed,
17  For 'tis ill shooting through a twisted reed.
18  Then thou, my picture dead,
19  Defend it, Giovan,[2] and my honour—why?
20  The place is wrong, and no painter I.
    —Michelangelo Buonarroti

✏ WRITE

RESEARCH: In this poem, Michelangelo reflects on the challenging experience of creating one of the world's most famous pieces of art. Clearly, the process of his art was not as pleasant as the product, which raises certain questions: Why was this experience so challenging? Why did he stick with the project until it was finished? Conduct brief research to answer one of these questions and then apply what you learned to your reading of the poem. In your response, write about how what you learned in your research shifted your understanding of the poem.

1. **Harpy** a mythological monster resembling a bird of prey with a woman's face
2. **Giovan** Michelangelo's friend, and the man the poem is addressing

# People Should Not Die in June in South Texas

FICTION
Gloria Anzaldúa
1993

## Introduction

"People Should Not Die in June in South Texas" is a short story by Gloria Anzaldúa (1942–2004) examining the rituals and customs surrounding the burial of a loved one. It is told from the perspective of Prieta, a young Latina girl. When her father, Urbano, dies suddenly and tragically, Prieta must put her own grief aside in order to help see her family through the hardships to come. Though Prieta bears witness to her father's wake, funeral, and burial, years pass before she can fully accept that her father is not coming back.

# "*Prieta espera al muerto.* She waits for the dead."

1   PRIETITA squeezes through the crowd of mourners and finds a place near the coffin. She stands there for hours watching relatives and friends one after the other approach the coffin, kneel beside it. They make the sign of the cross, bow slowly while backing away. Even a few Anglos come to pay their respects to Urbano, loved by all. But after two and a half days, her father has begun to smell like a cow whose carcass has been gutted by vultures. People should not die in June in south Texas.

2   Earlier that day Prietita and her mother had gone to the funeral home, where in some hidden room someone was making a two-inch incision in her father's throat. Someone was inserting a tube in his jugular vein. In some hidden room *una envenenada abuja* filled his *venas* with embalming fluid.

3   The white undertaker put his palm on the small of her mother's back and propelled her toward the more expensive coffins. Her mother couldn't stop crying. She held a handkerchief to her eyes like a blindfold, knotting and unraveling it, knotting and unraveling it. Prieta, forced to be the more practical of the two, said, "Let's take that one or this one," pointing at the coffins midrange in price. Though they would be in debt for three years, they chose *un cajón de quinientos dólares.* The undertaker had shown them the backless suits whose prices ranged from seventy to several hundred dollars. *Compraron un traje negro y una camisa blanca con encaje color de rosa.* They bought a black suit and a white shirt with pink. "Why are we buying such an expensive suit? It doesn't even have a back. And besides, it's going to rot soon," she told her mother softly. Her mother looked at her and burst out crying again. Her mother was either hysterical or very quiet and **withdrawn**, so Prieta had to swallow her own tears. They had returned in the hearse with the coffin to a house filled with relatives and friends, with tables laden with *comida* and buckets overflowing with ice and *cerveza.*

4   Prietita stands against the living room wall watching the hundreds of people slowly milling around. *"Te acompaño en el pesar," dice la tía* as she embraces her. The stench of alcohol enters her nostrils when male relatives pay their condolences to her. *Prieta se siente helada y asfixiada al mismo tiempo.* She feels cold, shocked, and suffocated. *"Qué guapa. Es la mayor y se parece mucha a su mamá,"* she hears a woman say, bursting into tears and clutching

Prietita in a desperate embrace. Faint whiffs of perfume escape from the women's hair behind their thick black mantillas. The smells of roses and carnations, *carne guisada,* sweat and body heat mingle with the sweet smell of death and fill the house in Hargill.

5  *Antes del cajón en medio de la sala auflando a la virgen su mamagrande Locha cae de rodillas persinándose.* But Prieta does not cry, she is the only one at the *velorio* who is dry-eyed. Why can't she cry? *Le dan ganas, no de florar, pero de reír a carcajadas.* Instead of crying she feels like laughing. It isn't natural. She felt the tightness in her throat give way. Her body trembled with fury. How dare he die? How dare he abandon her? How could he leave her mother all alone? Her mother was just twenty-eight. It wasn't fair. *Sale de la casa corriendo,* she runs out of the house, *Atravesó la calle,* she crosses the street, *tropezándose en las piedras,* while stumbling over rocks. *Llegó a la casa de Mamagrande Ramona en donde estaba su hermanito, Carito, el más chiquito.* She reached her grandmother's house, where her little brother was hiding out. His bewildered face asks questions she cannot answer.

6  Later Prietita slips back into the house and returns to her place by the coffin. Standing on her toes, she cocks her head over the casket. What if that sweet-**putrid** smell is perfume injected into his veins to fool them all into thinking he is dead? What if it's all a conspiracy? A lie? Under the overturned red truck someone else's face had lain broken, smashed beyond recognition. The blood on the highway had not been her father's blood.

7  For three days her father sleeps in his coffin. Her mother sits at his side every night and never sleeps. *Oliendo a muerte, Prietita duerme en su cama,* Prieta sleeps in her bed with the smell of death. *En sus sueños,* in her dreams, *su padre abre los ojos al mirarla,* her father opens his eyes. *Abre su boca a contestarle,* he opens his mouth to answer her. *Se levanta del cajón,* he rises out of the coffin. On the third day Prieta rises from her bed vacant-eyed, puts on her black blouse and skirt and black scarf, and walks to the living room. She stands before the coffin and waits for the hearse. In the car behind the hearse on the way to the church Prietita sits quietly beside her mother, sister, and brothers. Stiff-legged, she gets out of the car and walks to the hearse. She watches the pall bearers, *Tio David, Rafael, Goyo, el compadre Juan,* and others, lift the coffin out of the hearse, carry it inside the church, and set it down in the middle of the aisle.

8  *El cuerpo de su padre está tendido en medio de la iglesia.* Her father's corpse lies in the middle of the church. She watches one woman after another kneel before *la Virgen de Guadalupe* and light a candle. Soon hundreds of **votive** candles flicker their small flames and emit the smell of burning tallow.

9  "*Et Misericordia ejus a progenis timentibus eúm,*" intones the priest, flanked by altar boys on both sides. His purple gown rustles as he swings his censors

Please note that excerpts and passages in the StudySync® library and this workbook are intended as touchstones to generate interest in an author's work. The excerpts and passages do not substitute for the reading of entire texts, and StudySync® strongly recommends that students seek out and purchase the whole literary or informational work in order to experience it as the author intended. Links to online resellers are available in our digital library. In addition, complete works may be ordered through an authorized reseller by filling out and returning to StudySync® the order form enclosed in this workbook.

Reading & Writing
Companion          **593**

over her father's body and face. Clouds of frankincense cover the length of the dark shiny coffin.

10    At last the pall bearers return to the coffin. Sporting mustaches and wearing black ties, *con bigote y corbata negra,* they stand stiffly in their somber suits. She had never seen these ranchers, farmers, and farm workers in suits before. In unison they take a deep breath and with a quick movement they lift the coffin. Her mother holds Carito's hands and follows the coffin while Prieta, her sister, and brother walk behind them.

11    Outside near the cars parked in the street, Prieta watches the church slowly emptying, watches the church becoming a hollowed-out thing. In their black cotton and rayon dresses, following the coffin with faces hidden under fine-woven mantillas, the women all look like *urracas prietas,* like black crows. Her own nickname was *Urraca Prieta.*

12    From her uncle's car en route to the cemetery, Prieta watches the billows of dust rise in the wake of the hearse. Her skin feels prickly with sweat and something else. As the landscape recedes, Prietita feels as though she is traveling backwards to yesterday, to the day before yesterday, to the day she last saw her father. Prieta imagines her father as he drives the red truck filled to the brim with cotton bales. One hand suddenly leaves the wheel to clutch his chest. His body arches, then his head and chest slump over the wheel, blood streaming out through his nose and mouth, his foot lies heavy on the gas pedal. The red ten-ton truck keeps going until it gets to the second curve on the east highway going toward Edinburg. "Wake up, Papi, turn the wheel," but the truck keeps on going off the highway. It turns over, the truck turns over and over, the doors flapping open then closing and the truck keeps turning over and over until Prieta makes it stop. Her father is thrown out. The edge of the back of the truck crushes his face. Six pairs of wheels spin in the air. White cotton bales are littered around him. The article in the newspaper said that according to the autopsy report, his aorta had burst. The largest artery to the heart, ruptured.

13    She had *not* seen the crows, *las urracas prietas,* gather on the *ébano* in the backyard the night before that bright day in June. If they had not announced his death then he couldn't be dead. It was a conspiracy, a lie.

14    *Ya se acabó; ¿qué pasa? Contemplad su figura*
*la muerte le ha cubierto de pálidos azufres*
*y le ha puesto cabeza de oscuro minotauro.*

15    *Is it over? What's happening?*
*Reflect on his figure.*
*Death has covered him with pale sulfurs*
*and has given him a dark Minotaur head.*

16    The *padrinas* place the coffin under the ebony tree. People pile flower wreaths at her father's feet. Prietita shuffles over to her father lying in the coffin. Her eyes trace the jagged lines running through his forehead, cheek, and chin, where the undertaker had sewn the skin together. The broken nose, the chalky skin with the tinge of green underneath is not her father's face, *no es la cara de su papi.* No. On that bright day, June 22, someone else had been driving his truck, someone else had been wearing his khaki pants, his gold wire-rimmed glasses – someone else had his gold front tooth.

17    Mr. Leidner, her history teacher, had said that the Nazis jerked the gold teeth out of the corpses of the Jews and melted them into rings. And made their skin into lampshades. She did not want anyone to take her *papi's* gold tooth. Prieta steps back from the coffin. The blood in the highway could not be her father's blood.

18    ¡Qué no quiere verla!
*Dile a la luna que venga,*
*que no quiero ver la sangre*

19    *I don't want to see it.*
*Tell the moon to come*
*that I don't want to see the blood*

20    As she watches her father, a scream forms in her head: "No, no, no." She thinks she almost sees death creep into her father's unconscious body, kick out his soul and make his body stiff and still. She sees *la muerte's* long pale fingers take possession of her father—sees death place its hands over what had been her father's heart. A fly buzzes by, brings her back to the present. She sees a fly crawl over one of her father's hands, then land on his cheek. She wants him to raise his hand and fan the fly away. He lies unmoving. She raises her hand to crush the fly then lets it fall back to the side. Swatting the fly would mean hitting her *papi.* Death, too, lets the fly crawl over itself. Maybe the fly and death are friends. Maybe death is unaware of so inconsequential a thing as an insect. She is like that fly trying to rouse her father, *es esa mosca.*

21    She stands looking by the coffin at her own small hands—fleshy, ruddy hands—and forces herself to unclench her fists. A beat pulses in her thumb. When her hands are no longer ruddy nor pulsating she will lie like him. She will lie utterly still. Maggots will find her hands, will seek out her heart. Worms will crawl in and out of her and the world will continue as usual. That is what shocks her the most about her father's death—that people still laugh, the wind continues to blow, the sun rises in the east and sets in the west.

22    Prieta walks away from the coffin and stands at the edge of the gaping hole under the ebony tree. The hole is so deep, *el pozo tan hondo,* the earth so black, *la tierra tan prieta.* She takes great gulps of air but can't get enough into her lungs. Nausea winds its way up from the pit of her stomach, fills her

NOTES

chest and becomes a knot when it reaches her throat. Her body sways slowly back and forth. Someone gently tugs her away. *Los hombres* push a metal apparatus over the hole and *los padrinos* place the coffin over it.

23   Under the ébano, around the hole, a procession forms. The small country cemetery, with Mexicans buried on one side and a few Anglos on the other, is now bulging with hundreds of cars *y miles de gente y miles de flores.*

24   Prieta hears the whir of the machine and looks back to see it lowering her father into the hole. Someone tosses in a handful of dirt, then the next person does the same, and soon a line of people forms, waiting their turn. Prietita listens to the thuds, the slow shuffle of feet as the line winds and unwinds like a giant serpent. Her turn comes, she bends to pick up a handful of dirt. She loosens her clenched fist over the hole and hears the thud of *terremotes* hit her father's coffin. Drops fall onto the dust-covered coffin. They make little craters on the *cajón's* smooth surface. She feels as though she is standing alone near the mouth of the abyss, near the mouth slowly swallowing her father. An unknown sweetness and a familiar anguish beckon her. As she rocks back and forth near the edge, she listens to Mamagrande's litany: *"Mi hijo, mi hijo, tan bueno. Diosito mío, ¿por qué se la llevó? Ay mi hijo."*

25   Next Sunday the whole family has to go to **mass**, but Prieta doesn't want to attend. Heavily veiled women dressed in black kneel on the cement floor of the small church and recite the rosary in singsong monotones. *Llorosas rezaban el rosario,* hands moving slowly over the beads. *"Santa María, madre de Dios, ruega por nosotros . . .* Holy Mary, mother of God, pray for us now and at the hour of our death." Her mother and Mamagrande Locha dedicate Sunday masses to her father, promising *la Virgen* a mass a week for the coming year. They pay a small fee for each—all for a man who had never entered church except for the funeral mass of a friend or relative.

26   Her mother wears *luto,* vowing before a statue of *la Virgen de Guadalupe* to wear black for two years and gray for two more. In September when school resumes, her mother tells Prieta and her sister that they are to wear black for a year, then gray or brown for another two. At first her classmates stare at her. Prieta sees the curiosity and fascination in their eyes slowly turn to pity and disdain. But soon they get used to seeing her in black and drab-colored clothes and she feels invisible once more, and invincible.

27   After school and on weekends her mother shushes them when they speak loudly or laugh, forbids them to listen to the radio and covers the TV with a blanket. Prieta remembers when her father bought the TV. The other kids had been envious because hers had been the first Mexican family to have such an **extravagant** luxury. Her father had bought it for them saying it would help his *hijitos* learn to speak English without an accent. If they knew English they could get good jobs and not have to work themselves to death.

28 *Pasa mucho tiempo.* Days and weeks and years pass. *Prieta espera al muerto.* She waits for the dead. Every evening she waits for her father to walk into the house, tired after a day of hard work in the fields. She waits for him to rap his knuckles on the top of her head, the one gesture of intimacy he allowed himself with her. She waits for him to gaze at her with his green eyes. She waits for him to take off his shirt and sit bare-chested on the floor, back against the sofa watching TV, the black curly hair on the back of his head showing. Now she thinks she hears his footsteps on the front porch, and turns eagerly toward the door. For years she waits. *Four years* she waits for him to thrust open the sagging door, to return from the land of the dead. For her father is a great and good man and she is sure God will realize he has made a mistake and bring him back to them. *En el día de los muertos,* on the day of the dead, *el primero de noviembre,* on the first of November, *ella lo espera,* she waits for him. *Aunque no más viniera a visitarlos,* even if he only came to visit. *Aunque no se quedara,* even if he didn't stay—she wants to see him—*quiere verlo.* But one day, *four years* after his death, she knows that neither the One God nor her father will ever walk through her door again.

29 *pero nadie querrá mirar tus ojos*
*porque te has muerto para siempre . . .*
*como todos los muertos de la Tierra.*

30 *but no one will want to look at your eyes*
*because you have died forever . . .*
*like all the dead on Earth.*

## ✏ WRITE

LITERARY ANALYSIS: How does the author use language, character, and cultural experiences to transmit a theme about loss?

Please note that excerpts and passages in the StudySync® library and this workbook are intended as touchstones to generate interest in an author's work. The excerpts and passages do not substitute for the reading of entire texts, and StudySync® strongly recommends that students seek out and purchase the whole literary or informational work in order to experience it as the author intended. Links to online resellers are available in our digital library. In addition, complete works may be ordered through an authorized reseller by filling out and returning to StudySync® the order form enclosed in this workbook.

Reading & Writing Companion  597

# Sábado Gigante

FICTION
Daniel Chacón
2012

## Introduction

Daniel Chacón (b. 1962) is a Latino novelist and essayist. His writing, including the Hudson Prize-winning *and the shadows took him: A Novel,* typically focuses on the conflicts that arise when finding or seeking out one's identity. In this short story, the protagonist, Bruno, refuses to conform to his community's definition of masculinity. He befriends a young girl named Gracie, and together they utilize their imaginations to craft stories—as well as their own, unconventional senses of self.

# "I yelled Action! and moved the soldiers around to play out my 30-minute movie."

NOTES

1   At first, when the boys picked their teams, baseball teams, football teams, soccer teams, they assumed I would be a good player, because of my large size, and because of my name, Bruno, seriously, Bruno. My father was as large as a WWF wrestler, his muscles so bulging that the tattoos on his forearms seemed to pulse. He taught me to box when I was four years old, or tried to, but one time he left me with a bloody nose, and after that I refused to learn. Whenever he pulled out the boxing gloves and walked over to me, before he could even tie the first one on my wrist, I was **bawling** my eyes out, until my mom came over, wrapped me up in her arms and carried me away from him.

2   He told her that I was a disappointment, that maybe I should have been a girl that my name should be Hilda, which he started to call me for a time, but only around the house. He wanted my weakness to be a family secret, so he made sure I looked and talked tough in front of everyone else. They dressed me like a miniature version of him, in work boots and Ben Davis work pants, and I wore thick lumberjack flannels and buttoned them up to the neck. By the time I was in sixth grade, I was big as a gorilla. I had to look down on my teachers when they scolded me or tried to tell me I was smart and should take school subjects more seriously. Boys made assumptions about me, one of them that I was good at sports and they'd want me to play with them, but by the next game, when we chose new teams, I was the last one picked. My neighbor Carlo, a short, muscular little guy, was one of the best players in the neighborhood, a boy's boy, and he was usually a team captain, and because he was my best friend, he picked me second or third every time, even though he knew he was wasting a turn. He wanted to believe in me, wanted to believe that somewhere inside of me there was a ball player trying to get out, but he was losing his faith. One day, on the way out to the field, he reached up and grabbed my shoulders from behind and massaged me like a trainer sending his fighter into the ring. "Sábado Gigante!"[1] he said, his nickname for me. "Let's get them, Sábado," he said. Then he punched me on the arm, and although it burned like hell, I was happy to get it, because I knew it was the way he expressed **affection.**

---

1.  **Sábado Gigante**  an American Spanish-language variety show that aired from 1962 to 2015

NOTES

3   He took the game very seriously that day, screaming to his team when they messed up, yelling things at the batter when he was pitching. When a fly ball came right to me, dropping from the clouds like a slow bomb, something anyone could catch, I held up my glove and closed my eyes hoping that it would land in the cradle of my hand, but when I heard the ball thump on the ground a few feet away from me, I opened my eyes. The first thing I saw was Carlo shaking his head, disappointed in me, mouthing curses at me.

4   After that inning, as we were walking up to the batters' cage, I pretended to fall. I pretended to twist my ankle.

5   "I should sit this one out," I told him.

6   He nodded his head, patted me on the shoulder.

7   I went inside the house. My mom was home, in the bedroom reading a book. I went into my room and played with my GI Joe **figurines** and little green plastic soldiers. I pretended that they were actors and I was a giant director, literally a giant making a blockbuster movie. I yelled Action! and moved the soldiers around to play out my 30-minute movie. After a soldier was shot and killed or torn to pieces in an explosion, I yelled, Cut! And the little man wiped himself off and stood up again.

8   Later on, when I knew the ballgame was over, I went back outside, saying what a bummer it was that I couldn't play. "We could have rolled some heads," I told Carlo.

9   He was taking off his T-shirt. "Right," he said as he draped it over his shoulder.

10  One day, when the boys were off playing ball, I stepped outside and saw Gracie Gómez playing dolls on a pink blanket in her front yard. She was Carlo's sister, and I looked at her sitting on her spread-out blanket moving a doll around as if it were taking a walk. It occurred to me that since Carlo and I were best friends, Gracie was almost like family. She was like my little sister, so I went over to her. I walked over to her lawn and said "Hey," and she said "Hey."

11  Ten minutes later I was playing dolls too.

12  From that day on, I never wanted to play sports again, ever, just dolls, because you made up characters with stories and **dialogue**. You could imagine the houses they had, the jobs they did, the cities in which they lived. Gracie liked playing dolls with me, because together we imagined so much more than mommy and daddy dialogues. We were international spies, or we were young doctors in the emergency room, or we were **homicide** detectives, looking

over the murder scene, gathering clues. Our favorite dolls were Raggedy Ann and Andy, although we gave them different names for different lives, Mr. and Mrs. Martínez, Pepe and María. We also played with a bunch of other, smaller dolls, who became their family and friends, but Ann and Andy were always the stars of our little movies, which we imagined took place in places like Paris, London, Peru, Mexico City.

13   We had fun together, more fun than I ever had with Carlo, because being with him felt like work, but with her I could play, and for a time, a very short time, I was convinced that Gracie and I were best friends.

14   Her parents were from Puerto Rico, hard workers and traditional Catholics, and the only boys she was allowed to talk to were family members, including me, because our families had been neighbors for years. Unlike my mother, who worked full time and took classes at the community college, her mother stayed at home taking care of the kids and the house. Her father wanted to raise his daughter to be the same way, and she had three brothers, all of them like Carlo, boys who wanted to be men.

15   We both knew we had to hide the things we did together.

16   She never came to my door and asked for me. We came up with secret codes, and when I saw her pink blanket draped over the fence in our backyards, I knew she would be in the alley waiting for me with her dolls and accessories. Without saying anything, or else whispering, we'd tiptoe to the side of my house, where my father's 1953 Ford pickup truck had been sitting for years, all the tires flat, the windshield coated with dirt. Gracie set the pink blanket down on the bed, spreading out all her toys, and we got into the back of the truck and played.

17   One Saturday afternoon, Gracie and I were in the back of my father's truck playing dolls when I saw the boys coming around the corner down the alley. They had bats over their shoulders and baseball mitts dangling from their ends.

18   Carlo had his T-shirt off, tied around his head like an Arab, and his skin was dark brown and sweaty. Walking in the lead, all the other boys walking behind him, he looked like a soldier returning from war. I could hear them laughing like boys, talking to each other, hitting metal garbage cans with their bats, chasing away alley cats. Gracie wrapped up her dolls and their things in her blanket, and she swooped it all away and ran to the tall fence that our backyards shared, pushed a loose board and went through, and on her lawn, she spread out the blanket and hoped to look like she had been playing by herself. I jumped out of the back of the truck, uncertain whether or not Carlo had seen us. From down the throat of the alley, he squinted his eyes to get a

NOTES

better look at me. The boys got closer, and Carlo went to the gate that opened onto his backyard, slammed it open, and saw her sitting on her blanket playing dolls by herself.

19    I couldn't see her, only a blur of her colors through the slats of the fence, but he was yelling something to her in Spanish, and I saw her pink blur slide up and move across the yard toward the house, and I heard the door open and close and the blur disappeared inside.

20    "What were you doing with my sister?" Carlo asked me, walking toward me, all the boys behind him.

21    "What are you talking about?"

22    "Why was she in the truck with you?"

23    "What? No! She came over the house for some girl's thing. I think your mom wanted to tell my mom something. I don't know. So when are we going to play ball? Did I miss the game?"

24    "We're taking a break," said another boy. "You want to play next innings?"

25    "You bet!" I said. "Whose team am I on?"

26    They looked around at each other, but Carlo was still looking at me as if my face might reveal something.

27    "We were just talking," I said. "Can I play next innings? I need a glove. Someone lend me their glove."

28    The next day or so I saw Gracie playing with her dolls on a blanket on the front lawn, and seeing that no one was around, I went to join her. "Let's meet in the truck," I said.

29    She looked coldly at me and continued to play, imaging a dialogue between a mommy and a daddy. In an exaggerated deep voice, she said, "I'm going to work now, honey!"

30    "We're having spaghetti for dinner tonight," she said, in a feminine voice.

31    "Hey," I said.

32    She nodded a greeting but continued to play.

33    "I want to play," I said.

34  She started to gather her stuff in a pile. "It's not right," she said. She piled everything together, wrapped it in the blanket, twisted the top, and she walked away from me, dragging all the things behind her.

"Sábado Gigante" from "Hotel Juárez" by Daniel Chacón (©2013 Arte Público Press - University of Houston)

---

### ✏ WRITE

LITERARY ANALYSIS: How does the author's use of language contribute to and enhance the voice of the narrator in the story?

Please note that excerpts and passages in the StudySync® library and this workbook are intended as touchstones to generate interest in an author's work. The excerpts and passages do not substitute for the reading of entire texts, and StudySync® strongly recommends that students seek out and purchase the whole literary or informational work in order to experience it as the author intended. Links to online resellers are available in our digital library. In addition, complete works may be ordered through an authorized reseller by filling out and returning to StudySync® the order form enclosed in this workbook.

Reading & Writing
Companion

603

# La Juanita

FICTION
Alice Dunbar-Nelson
1899

## Introduction

American writer and political activist Alice Dunbar-Nelson (1875–1935) was one of the most influential figures of the Harlem Renaissance. In her writing she provided a voice for neglected and marginalized communities, in particular the close-knit Creole families of New Orleans. Her short story "La Juanita," which appeared in her 1899 collection *The Goodness of St. Rocque, and Other Stories,* presents the traditional biases associated with class and culture. When La Juanita, the darling of the Creole community of Mandeville, Louisiana, falls for Mercer Grangeman, a dashing young riverboat captain, her family and the entire community deem him unsuitable because of his "Americain" heritage.

# "On this particular day there was an air of suppressed excitement . . ."

1 If you never lived in Mandeville, you cannot appreciate the thrill of wholesome, satisfied joy which sweeps over its inhabitants every evening at five o'clock. It is the hour for the arrival of the "New Camelia," the happening of the day. As early as four o'clock the trailing smoke across the horizon of the **treacherous** Lake Pontchartrain appears, and Mandeville knows then that the hour for its siesta has passed, and that it must array itself in its coolest and fluffiest garments, and go down to the pier to meet this sole connection between itself and the outside world; the little, puffy, side-wheel steamer that comes daily from New Orleans and brings the mail and the news.

Alice Dunbar Nelson

Skill:
Word Meaning

*I don't know what array means; "in its coolest and fluffiest garments" makes me think it has to do with getting dressed, or clothing. It's used as a verb. I'll clarify the precise meaning using a dictionary.*

2 On this particular day there was an air of suppressed excitement about the little knot of people which gathered on the pier. To be sure, there were no outward signs to show that anything unusual had occurred. The small folks danced with the same glee over the worn boards, and peered down with daring excitement into the perilous depths of the water below. The sun, fast sinking in a gorgeous glow behind the pines of the Tchefuncta region far away, danced his mischievous rays in much the same manner that he did every other day. But there was a something in the air, a something not tangible, but mysterious, subtle. You could catch an indescribable whiff of it in your inner senses, by the half-eager, **furtive** glances that the small crowd cast at La Juanita.

3 "Gar, gar, le bateau!" said one dark-tressed mother to the wide-eyed baby. "Et, oui," she added, in an undertone to her companion. "Voila, La Juanita!"

4 La Juanita, you must know, was the pride of Mandeville, the adored, the admired of all, with her petite, half-Spanish, half-French beauty. Whether rocking in the shade of the Cherokee-rose-covered gallery of Grandpere Colomes' big house, her fair face bonnet-shaded, her dainty hands gloved to

keep the sun from too close an acquaintance, or splashing the spray from the bow of her little pirogue, or fluffing her skirts about her tiny feet on the pier, she was the pet and ward of Mandeville, as it were, La Juanita Alvarez, since Madame Alvarez was a widow, and Grandpere Colomes was strict and stern.

5   And now La Juanita had set her small foot down with a passionate stamp before Grandpere Colomes' very face, and tossed her black curls about her wilful head, and said she would go to the pier this evening to meet her Mercer. All Mandeville knew this, and cast its furtive glances alternately at La Juanita with two big pink spots in her cheeks, and at the entrance to the pier, expecting Grandpere Colomes and a scene.

6   The sun cast red glows and violet shadows over the pier, and the pines murmured a soft little vesper hymn among themselves up on the beach, as the "New Camelia" swung herself in, crabby, sidewise, like a fat old gentleman going into a small door. There was the clang of an important bell, the scream of a hoarse little whistle, and Mandeville rushed to the gang-plank to welcome the outside world. Juanita put her hand through a waiting arm, and tripped away with her Mercer, big and blond and brawny. "Un Americain, pah!" said the little mother of the black eyes. And Mandeville sighed sadly, and shook its head, and was sorry for Grandpere Colomes.

7   This was Saturday, and the big regatta would be Monday. Ah, that regatta, such a one as Mandeville had never seen! There were to be boats from Madisonville and Amite, from Lewisburg and Covington, and even far-away Nott's Point. There was to be a Class A and Class B and Class C, and the little French girls of the town flaunted their ribbons down the one oak-shaded, lake-kissed street, and dared anyone to say theirs were not the favourite colours.

8   In Class A was entered, "La Juanita,' captain Mercer Grangeman, colours pink and gold." Her name, her colours; what **impudence**!

9   Of course, not being a Mandevillian, you could not understand the shame of Grandpere Colomes at this. Was it not bad enough for his petite Juanita, his Spanish blossom, his hope of a family that had held itself proudly aloof from "dose Americain" from time immemorial, to have smiled upon this Mercer, this pale-eyed youth? Was it not bad enough for her to **demean** herself by walking upon the pier with him? But for a boat, his boat, "un bateau Americain," to be named La Juanita! Oh, the shame of it! Grandpere Colomes prayed a devout prayer to the Virgin that "La Juanita" should be capsized.

10  Monday came, clear and blue and stifling. The waves of hot air danced on the sands and adown the one street merrily. Glassily calm lay the Pontchartrain, heavily still hung the atmosphere. Madame Alvarez cast an inquiring glance

**Skill:**
**Word Meaning**

I don't know what *regatta* means, but in context it sounds like an event with boats. When I consult the dictionary, I confirm that it is "a sporting event consisting of a series of boat or yacht races."

toward the sky. Grandpere Colomes chuckled. He had not lived on the shores of the treacherous Lake Pontchartrain for nothing. He knew its every mood, its petulances and passions; he knew this glassy warmth and what it meant. Chuckling again and again, he stepped to the gallery and looked out over the lake, and at the pier, where lay the boats rocking and idly tugging at their moorings. La Juanita in her rose-scented room tied the pink ribbons on her dainty frock, and fastened cloth of gold roses at her lithe waist.

11 It was said that just before the crack of the pistol La Juanita's tiny hand lay in Mercer's, and that he bent his head, and whispered softly, so that the surrounding crowd could not hear,—

12 "Juanita mine, if I win, you will?"

13 "Oui, mon Mercere, eef you win."

14 In another instant the white wings were off scudding before the rising breeze, dipping their glossy boat-sides into the clear water, straining their cordage in their tense efforts to reach the stake boats. Mandeville indiscriminately distributed itself on piers, large and small, bath-house tops, trees, and craft of all kinds, from pirogue, dory, and pine-raft to pretentious cat-boat and shell-schooner. Mandeville cheered and strained its eyes after all the boats, but chiefly was its attention directed to "La Juanita."

15 "Ah, voila, eet is ahead!"

16 "Mais non, c'est un autre!"

17 "La Juanita! La Juanita!"

18 "Regardez Grandpere Colomes!"

19 Old Colomes on the big pier with Madame Alvarez and his granddaughter was intently straining his weather-beaten face in the direction of Nott's Point, his back resolutely turned upon the scudding white wings. A sudden chuckle of grim satisfaction caused La Petite's head to toss petulantly.

20 But only for a minute, for Grandpere Colomes' chuckle was followed by a shout of dismay from those whose glance had followed his. You must know that it is around Nott's Point that the storm king shows his wings first, for the little peninsula guards the entrance which leads into the southeast waters of the stormy Rigolets and the blustering Gulf. You would know, if you lived in Mandeville, that when the pines on Nott's Point darken and when the water shows white beyond like the teeth of a hungry wolf, it is time to steer your boat into the mouth of some one of the many calm bayous which flow silently

Skill:
Story Structure

*This dialogue reveals that La Juanita and Mercer agree to marry if he wins, even though her father disapproves. This makes the race more important to the plot. Mercer is sailing not just to win the race but to win La Juanita.*

Please note that excerpts and passages in the StudySync® library and this workbook are intended as touchstones to generate interest in an author's work. The excerpts and passages do not substitute for the reading of entire texts, and StudySync® strongly recommends that students seek out and purchase the whole literary or informational work in order to experience it as the author intended. Links to online resellers are available in our digital library. In addition, complete works may be ordered through an authorized reseller by filling out and returning to StudySync® the order form enclosed in this workbook.

Reading & Writing Companion · 607

NOTES

throughout St. Tammany parish into the lake. Small wonder that the cry of dismay went up now, for Nott's Point was black, with a lurid light overhead, and the roar of the grim southeast wind came ominously over the water.

21   La Juanita clasped her hands and strained her eyes for her namesake. The racers had rounded the second stake-boat, and the course of the triangle headed them directly for the lurid cloud.

22   You should have seen Grandpere Colomes then. He danced up and down the pier in a perfect frenzy. The thin pale lips of Madame Alvarez moved in a silent prayer; La Juanita stood coldly silent.

**Skill:**
**Story Structure**

*Here is a new and major event, when the storm hits the boats and the town with sudden force. This dramatic scene must be the climax. The words "betokened serious trouble" add to the suspense. Will the boats and the town survive?*

23   And now you could see that the advance guard of the southeast force had struck the little fleet. They dipped and scurried and rocked, and you could see the sails being reefed hurriedly, and almost hear the rigging creak and moan under the strain. Then the wind came up the lake, and struck the town with a **tumultuous** force. The waters rose and heaved in the long, sullen ground-swell, which betokened serious trouble. There was a rush of lake-craft to shelter. Heavy gray waves boomed against the breakwaters and piers, dashing their brackish spray upon the strained watchers; then with a shriek and a howl the storm burst full, with blinding sheets of rain, and a great hurricane of Gulf wind that threatened to blow the little town away.

24   La Juanita was proud. When Grandpere and Madame led her away in the storm, though her face was white, and the rose mouth pressed close, not a word did she say, and her eyes were as bright as ever before. It was foolish to hope that the frail boats could survive such a storm. There was not even the merest excuse for shelter out in the waters, and when Lake Pontchartrain grows angry, it devours without pity.

25   Your tropical storm is soon over, however, and in an hour the sun struggled through a gray and misty sky, over which the wind was sweeping great clouds. The rain-drops hung diamond-like on the thick foliage, but the long ground-swell still boomed against the breakwaters and showed white teeth, far to the south.

26   As chickens creep from under shelter after a rain, so the people of Mandeville crept out again on the piers, on the bath-houses, on the breakwater edge, and watched eagerly for the boats. Slowly upon the horizon appeared white sails, and the little craft swung into sight. One, two, three, four, five, six, seven, eight, nine, counted Mandeville. Every one coming in! Bravo! And a great cheer that swept the whole length of the town from the post-office to Black Bayou went up. Bravo! Every boat was coming in. But—was every man?

27 This was a sobering thought, and in the hush which followed it you could hear the Q. and C. train thundering over the great lake-bridge, miles away.

28 Well, they came into the pier at last, "La Juanita" in the lead; and as Captain Mercer landed, he was surrounded by a voluble, chattering, anxious throng that loaded him with questions in patois, in broken English, and in French. He was no longer "un Americain" now, he was a hero.

29 When the other eight boats came in, and Mandeville saw that no one was lost, there was another ringing bravo, and more chattering of questions.

30 We heard the truth finally. When the storm burst, Captain Mercer suddenly promoted himself to an admiralship and assumed command of his little fleet. He had led them through the teeth of the gale to a small inlet on the coast between Bayou Lacombe and Nott's Point, and there they had waited until the storm passed. Loud were the praises of the other captains for Admiral Mercer, profuse were the thanks of the sisters and sweethearts, as he was carried triumphantly on the shoulders of the sailors down the wharf to the Maison Colomes.

31 The crispness had gone from Juanita's pink frock, and the cloth of gold roses were well nigh petalless, but the hand that she slipped into his was warm and soft, and the eyes that were upturned to Mercer's blue ones were shining with admiring tears. And even Grandpere Colomes, as he brewed on the Cherokee-rose-covered gallery, a fiery punch for the heroes, was heard to admit that "some time dose Americain can mos' be lak one Frenchman."

32 And we danced at the betrothal supper the next week.

# First Read

Read "La Juanita." After you read, complete the Think Questions below.

## ☁ THINK QUESTIONS

1. What is the "New Camelia"? What is its significance to the people of Mandeville? Refer to details from the text to support your answer.

2. Why does La Juanita's family disapprove of Captain Mercer? Do you agree with their reasons for disliking him? Use evidence from the text to support your response.

3. How was Captain Mercer able to prove himself worthy of La Juanita? What more should he have done? Use evidence from the text to support your answer.

4. The Latin word *furtum* means "theft." Use this information and context clues from the text to determine the meaning of **furtive**. Write your definition of *furtive* and explain how you arrived at it.

5. Use context clues to determine the meaning of the word **impudence** as it is used in "La Juanita." Write your definition of *impudence* and explain how you figured it out.

# Skill:
# Word Meaning

Use the Checklist to analyze Word Meaning in "La Juanita." Refer to the sample student annotations about Word Meaning in the text.

## ••• CHECKLIST FOR WORD MEANING

In order to find the pronunciation of a word or determine or clarify its precise meaning or its part of speech, do the following:

- ✓ Determine the word's part of speech.
- ✓ Use context clues to make a preliminary determination of the meaning of the word.
- ✓ Consult general and specialized reference materials, both print and digital:
  - locate the word through parts of speech to understand usage
  - use the pronunciation guide and say the word aloud
- ✓ Verify the preliminary determination of the meaning of a word or phrase by reading all of the definitions, and then decide which definition makes sense within the context of the text.

In order to determine the etymology of different words, and the way in which their meanings have changed throughout history, do the following:

- ✓ Use reference materials, such as a dictionary, to determine the word origin and history.
- ✓ Consider how the historical context of the word clarifies its usage.

To determine a word's part of speech, pronunciation, precise meaning, or etymology, consider the following questions:

- ✓ What is the word describing? What inferred meanings can I make?
- ✓ How is the word being used in the phrase or sentence?
- ✓ Which definition makes sense in the sentence?
- ✓ How can the word's origin and history help me clarify its precise meaning or usage?

Please note that excerpts and passages in the StudySync® library and this workbook are intended as touchstones to generate interest in an author's work. The excerpts and passages do not substitute for the reading of entire texts, and StudySync® strongly recommends that students seek out and purchase the whole literary or informational work in order to experience it as the author intended. Links to online resellers are available in our digital library. In addition, complete works may be ordered through an authorized reseller by filling out and returning to StudySync® the order form enclosed in this workbook.

Reading & Writing
Companion

611

# Skill:
# Word Meaning

Reread paragraph 10 of "La Juanita." Then, using the Checklist on the previous page as well as the dictionary entry below, answer the multiple-choice questions.

 YOUR TURN

**moor·ing** /ˈmür · ing/

*noun*

1. the act of a person or thing that moors.
2. a place where a boat or ship is moored.
3. a device, such as cables, ropes, or anchors by or to which a boat, ship, or buoy is moored.

*verb*

4. make secure (a boat) by attaching it with cable or rope to the shore or to an anchor.
5. (of a boat) be made secure by 'mooring.

**Etymology:** first known use was in 15th century; from late Middle English: probably from the Dutch *meren*.

1. This question has two parts. First, answer Part A. Then, answer Part B.

   **Part A:** Which definition best matches the precise meaning of the content-specific word *moorings* as it is used in the paragraph?

   ○ A. make secure (a boat) by attaching it by cable or rope to the shore or to an anchor.
   ○ B. (of a boat) be made secure by mooring.
   ○ C. cables, ropes, or anchors by or to which a boat or ship is moored.
   ○ D. a place where a boat or ship is moored.

   **Part B:** Which context clue BEST supports your answer from Part A?

   ○ A. "rocking"
   ○ B. "where lay"
   ○ C. "tugging at"
   ○ D. "at the pier"

# Skill:
# Story Structure

Use the Checklist to analyze Story Structure in "La Juanita." Refer to the sample student annotations about Story Structure in the text.

## ••• CHECKLIST FOR STORY STRUCTURE

In order to determine how an author's choices concerning how to structure a text, order events within it, and manipulate time create such effects as mystery, tension, or surprise, note the following:

- ✓ the pattern an author uses to organize the events in a story

  - chronological, or in time order
  - nonlinear, or events out of time order

- ✓ the author's use of description, dialogue, and narration to convey the action of the plot

- ✓ any literary devices the author uses to manipulate time in order to create tension and suspense

  - foreshadowing: hinting at what will come later
  - flashback: shows something that happened in the past
  - pacing: how quickly or slowly the events of a story unfold

- ✓ parallel plots, or two or more plots in a story that are usually linked by a common character and a similar theme

To analyze how an author's choices concerning how to structure a text, order events within it, and manipulate time create such effects as mystery, tension, or surprise, consider the following questions:

- ✓ What is the structure of the story? How do the author's choices about the structure create effects as mystery, tension, or surprise?

- ✓ How does the speed in which events take place impact the plot?

- ✓ Are there parallel plots in the story? What do they reveal about the characters, settings, or overall theme?

- ✓ How does the author manipulate time in the story? What effects does it have on the mystery, tension, or surprise the author creates?

- ✓ How does the author use flashbacks or foreshadowing to build suspense, create mystery, or reveal a character's motivations?

Copyright © BookheadEd Learning, LLC

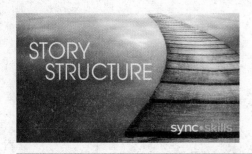

# Skill:
# Story Structure

sync skills

Reread paragraphs 26–28 of "La Juanita." Then, using the Checklist on the previous page, answer the multiple-choice questions below.

## ⟳ YOUR TURN

1. How does the scene in paragraph 26 contribute to the momentum and suspense of the story?

   ○ A. The scene reveals that the storm has caused extensive damage in the town.

   ○ B. The scene shows that the townspeople are safe, but the fate of the boats is unknown.

   ○ C. The scene reveals that all of the boats have survived, but leaves the suspense of whether or not all of the sailors have survived.

   ○ D. The scene shows the excitement that erupts after the people realize that the storm has passed and all of the sailors are okay.

2. How is the suspenseful mood continued in paragraph 28?

   ○ A. Captain Mercer has assured the people that all of the sailors are safe, but Grandpere Colomes has not yet agreed that he is a hero.

   ○ B. Captain Mercer has won the race, so he will now marry La Juanita, but Grandpere Colomes has not yet approved.

   ○ C. Captain Mercer has won the race and been accepted by the people, but why he is a hero is not yet known.

   ○ D. Captain Mercer has been accepted by the people, but it is not known if he won the race or La Juanita.

Copyright © BookheadEd Learning, LLC

# Close Read

Reread "La Juanita." As you reread, complete the Skills Focus questions below. Then use your answers and annotations from the questions to help you complete the Write activity.

## SKILLS FOCUS

1. Analyze the use of words related to the culture and explain how a dictionary helped you find a precise meaning for unknown words.

2. Analyze the character of La Juanita, including how she changes or is affected by the events of the story.

3. In "People Should Not Die in June in South Texas," the narrator begins in the present tense and uses flashbacks. In "Sábado Gigante," the first person narrator tells a series of chronological events in first person. Compare these narrative styles to the one used in "La Juanita" and discuss the effect the narrative style has on the story.

4. Discuss the personality traits of key characters and how these characters connect to each other, help drive the plot, and also bring about a satisfying resolution.

## WRITE

LITERARY ANALYSIS: The authors of "People Should Not Die in June in South Texas," "Sábado Gigante," and "La Juanita" tell stories that involve very different aspects of American experience. How do these authors use story structure and details of description, setting, and character to influence theme? In your response, be sure to compare and contrast the themes of all three short stories as well as the authors' use of setting and characterization.

Please note that excerpts and passages in the StudySync® library and this workbook are intended as touchstones to generate interest in an author's work. The excerpts and passages do not substitute for the reading of entire texts, and StudySync® strongly recommends that students seek out and purchase the whole literary or informational work in order to experience it as the author intended. Links to online resellers are available in our digital library. In addition, complete works may be ordered through an authorized reseller by filling out and returning to StudySync® the order form enclosed in this workbook.

Reading & Writing Companion 615

# Kindness

POETRY
Naomi Shihab Nye
1952

## Introduction

Naomi Shihab Nye (b. 1952) was born in St. Louis but has lived in Palestine, Jerusalem, and San Antonio, Texas. Among her many poems, "Kindness" stands out for its direct, poignant language, and it has a remarkable real-life story behind it. Nye wrote the poem during her honeymoon through South America, during which she and her husband were robbed of their money and passports, and another man on their bus was killed. Seeing the couple so sad, a kind man came up and asked what happened, and when they told him, he said, "I'm very sorry." This small, tender moment became the inspiration for one of her most beloved poems.

# "How you ride and ride thinking the bus will never stop,"

1 Before you know what kindness really is
2 you must lose things,
3 feel the future **dissolve** in a moment
4 like salt in a weakened broth.
5 What you held in your hand,
6 what you counted and carefully saved,
7 all this must go so you know
8 how **desolate** the landscape can be
9 between the **regions** of kindness.
10 How you ride and ride
11 thinking the bus will never stop,
12 the passengers eating maize and chicken
13 will stare out the window forever.

14 Before you learn the tender **gravity** of kindness,
15 you must travel where the Indian in a white poncho
16 lies dead by the side of the road.
17 You must see how this could be you,
18 how he too was someone
19 who journeyed through the night with plans
20 and the simple breath that kept him alive.

21 Before you know kindness as the deepest thing inside,
22 you must know sorrow as the other deepest thing.
23 You must wake up with sorrow.
24 You must speak to it till your voice
25 catches the thread of all sorrows
26 and you see the size of the cloth.

27 Then it is only kindness that makes sense anymore,
28 only kindness that ties your shoes
29 and sends you out into the day to mail letters and
30 **purchase** bread,
31 only kindness that raises its head
32 from the crowd of the world to say

NOTES

it is I you have been looking for,
and then goes with you everywhere
like a shadow or a friend.



## WRITE

DISCUSSION: In this poem, Naomi Shihab Nye describes the virtue of kindness as "the deepest thing inside" that allows us to positively interact with other humans. What do you think is the most important value when it comes to interacting with others? Prepare to discuss this with your peers by selecting one value and writing at least two reasons why you think it is important, as well as specific examples to support your thinking.

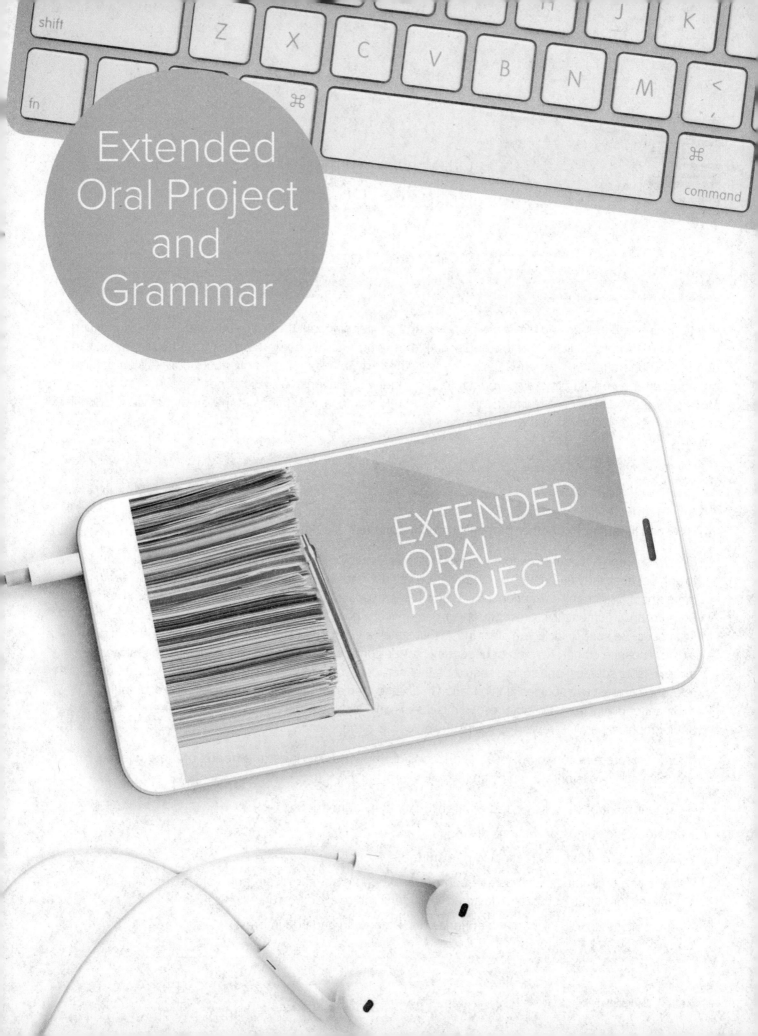

Extended
Oral Project
and
Grammar

EXTENDED
ORAL
PROJECT

ORAL
PRESENTATION
PROCESS
PLAN

# Oral Presentation Process: Plan

| PLAN | DRAFT | REVISE | EDIT AND PRESENT |
|------|-------|--------|------------------|

Relationships with friends and family are complex and challenging, but they offer advantages we cannot find on our own. When conflicts threaten our bonds, one thing that can bring us back together is seeking to understand one another's experiences. In many of the texts in this unit, an individual's ability to empathize during or after a conflict plays a powerful role in deepening relationships. As Harper Lee wrote in *To Kill A Mockingbird*, "You never really understand a person until you consider things from his point of view . . . until you climb inside of his skin and walk around in it."

## WRITING PROMPT

**How can listening to another person's story instruct us?**

Identify someone in your life whom you respect. This should be a person whose experiences stand out to you because they embody characteristics you value. Conduct an interview with this individual to learn more about his or her life experiences and how these experiences have shaped his or her values. Then, prepare an argumentative presentation to demonstrate how listening to another person's story can instruct us. Be sure to include a clear thesis that states a claim. Consider how you might include visual aids to enhance comprehension or engagement. Additionally, be sure to include evidence from at least three reliable sources; one source should be the individual you interviewed. For the others, you should reference at least two sources of information in diverse media formats, including video, audio, graphics, and print or digital texts. Possible research focuses could include historical background, current events, or biographical parallels related to your interviewee's experiences.

In order to prepare for your presentation, consider how best to meet the needs of the audience, purpose, and occasion by employing the following:

- a clear point of view supported with reasons and evidence

- rhetoric, including conventions of language

- avoidance of fallacious reasoning or distorted evidence

- speaking techniques such as eye contact, appropriate speaking rate and volume, enunciation, pauses for effect, purposeful gestures, confident and relaxed posture

- strategic use of digital media to enhance understanding and add interest

## Introduction to Oral Presentation

Argumentative oral presentations use body language, visual aids, and engaging writing to inform an audience about a topic. Good oral presentations use effective speaking techniques, relevant facts and examples, and a purposeful structure. The characteristics of argumentative oral presentations include:

- a thesis statement that tells the audience what the presentation will be about
- a claim that states an opinion or position
- counterclaims that should be addressed
- facts, evidence, details, and anecdotes that support the thesis
- an organizational structure that makes the presentation clear and easy to follow
- eye contact and clear oral communication
- gestures and visual aids that help communicate ideas and keep the audience engaged

As you continue with this Extended Oral Project, you'll receive more instruction and practice at crafting each of the characteristics of argumentative writing and speaking to create your own oral presentation.

Please note that excerpts and passages in the StudySync® library and this workbook are intended as touchstones to generate interest in an author's work. The excerpts and passages do not substitute for the reading of entire texts, and StudySync® strongly recommends that students seek out and purchase the whole literary or informational work in order to experience it as the author intended. Links to online resellers are available in our digital library. In addition, complete works may be ordered through an authorized reseller by filling out and returning to StudySync® the order form enclosed in this workbook.

Reading & Writing
Companion

**621**

Before you get started on your own argumentative oral presentation, read this presentation that one student, Dylan, wrote in response to the writing prompt. As you read the Model, highlight and annotate the features of oral presentation that Dylan included in his presentation.

## ☰ STUDENT MODEL

**One Man's Failure: The Key to Success**

### Introduction

Today I'm going to tell you about the person I respect most: Arthur Andrew Przybyla. His friends and family call him Double A, like the battery, but since he's my grandfather, I call him Poppa. I have always looked up to Poppa, but listening to his story has given me a clearer idea of what really matters and what tough times can teach us.

> # One Man's Failure: The Key to Success
>
> *based on interviews with*
>
> **Arthur Andrew "Double A" Przybyla**
> **(that's pronounced "Prezbeela")**

### Claim and Background

The life lessons shared by my grandfather demonstrate that hardship and failure can be a catalyst for success. The hardships for my grandfather began early in his life.

- Poppa was born on a farm in 1948, and as a baby boomer he has lived to see amazing events, but a certain great medical advancement had not occurred early enough. When he was five years old, Poppa contracted polio.

- According to the Centers for Disease Control and Prevention (the CDC), polio is "a crippling and potentially deadly disease." It's caused by a virus that can paralyze important muscles. Before the first polio vaccine was developed by Dr. Jonas Salk in 1955, thousands of Americans got sick with this disease every year.

- As Poppa told it, "I had a sore throat, and the next thing I knew my left leg was paralyzed. I used to be a kid who could not sit still, always climbing trees or running around in the fields." Now Poppa had to wear a leg brace and later use a cane; he had to always go slow. This big change meant he had to seek out new interests.

Salk Polio 640_master (1).mov

0:17 / 0:40

Victory Over Polio." Newsreel footage about the success of a polio vaccine.

## Evidence and Analysis #1

The disease gave Poppa an opportunity. Since he was stuck inside a lot, Poppa's mother tried to get him interested in books, including nature guides from the local library.

- After finishing her chores on the farm, they would sit and learn about birds, insects, snakes, trees, and even farming. Poppa says they spent one long winter studying those books.

- Then in the spring, Poppa went outside and looked at everything with what he called "new eyes."

- Working on the family farm would be tough for someone who could not walk or climb, but he was determined to try.

> "I felt so much joy when I knew I could name a tree just looking at the bark. Nature is remarkable and persistent. Even trees that look half dead often come back to life."
>
> — Poppa

## Evidence and Analysis #2

Though Poppa's weak leg made him feel discouraged, he still worked the family farm. Then a couple of world events happened that helped give him inspiration and direction.

- First, he was deeply impressed by the first moon walk. Poppa remembers watching the TV in "absolute awe" and made him think two things.

- One was that impossible things were possible.

- The other was that Earth was a special place. There's only one planet like it.

- I began to see a pattern here. Poppa didn't let misfortune discourage him. In fact, the challenge of it caused him to use his imagination in unexpected ways.

> "That's one small step for [a] man,
> one giant leap for mankind."
> — Astronaut Neil Armstrong
>
> NASA moon landing, July 20, 1969

Copyright © BookheadEd Learning, LLC

## Evidence and Analysis #3

The following April, Poppa read about an event called Earth Day.

- According to Earthday.org, the first Earth Day was inspired by a book, *Silent Spring*, by a scientist named Rachel Carson. Eight years later, the first Earth Day was celebrated.

- Back on the farm, Poppa sat at the dining room table with his wife, Grandma Alice, and together they came up with a plan to make a difference on the family farm: They would go organic.

---

- 1962: "The most alarming of all man's assaults upon the environment is the contamination of air, earth, rivers, and sea with dangerous and even lethal materials."
- Rachel Carson, *Silent Spring*, Chapter 2

- April 22, 1970: "20 million Americans took to the streets, parks, and auditoriums to demonstrate for a healthy, sustainable environment in massive coast-to-coast rallies."
- "The History of Earth Day," Earthday.org

---

## Counterclaim

What sounded simple at the table proved to be quite complicated.

- Some people told Poppa that he was going backward, not forward. But Poppa believed that the farming of the future would be the ways of the past. Poppa and Grandma Alice went to the library and also talked to "old timers." They learned about the ways that farmers used to farm the land. They learned about how to make compost and feed the soil.

- Because of this, Poppa told me, "I knew that we would fail. That was part of our plan." And they did fail. The first summer was too wet. The next summer there was an infestation. The third summer was too dry.

NOTES

Though they lost everything three years running, by the fourth year, they grew enough produce to set up a farm stand. After their first $50, Poppa said, "We felt like royalty." And that's how the farm got its name: Regaal Organic Farms—that's regal with two a's, as in Arthur Andrew. You can read all about the farm at Poppa's blog, because he has a blog!

## TO FARM OR NOT TO FARM ORGANICALLY

| PROS | CONS |
|------|------|
| • NO MAN-MADE FERTILIZERS | • REQUIRES KNOWLEDGE, HARD WORK |
| • NO UNNATURAL CHEMICALS; SUPPORTS HEALTHY SOIL | • HIGHLY REGULATED; HARD PROCESS TO GET CERTIFIED |
| • FOOD PRODUCED IS NUTRITIOUS, FLAVORFUL | • HIGHER COST TO PRODUCE; NO SUBSIDIES |
| • CONSUMER SATISFACTION IN HELPING FUTURE GENERATIONS | • HIGHER COST AT BEGINNING; CHALLENGING TO MARKET |

Greentumble. "Pros and Cons of Organic Farming." 20 Dec. 2015.

## Review

Here are the key points of my experience interviewing Poppa.

- Hardship and failure may be a catalyst for success. Poppa, for example, overcame polio and gained a new interest in nature.

- World events inspired Poppa to take bigger chances in his own life.

## To Recap:

- Poppa overcame polio and gained a new interest in nature.
- World events inspired Poppa: if a man could land on the moon, Poppa could start an organic farm!
- As a result of his life experience, Poppa wasn't afraid to fail in order to succeed at organic farming.

- As a result of his life experience, Poppa wasn't afraid to fail at organic farming, kept working at it, and eventually made a success of it.

## Conclusion

Being crippled at an early age and failing when he first tried organic farming made my grandfather tough and determined. His example should teach us all, as it taught me, that to succeed in life you have to have discipline and patience to survive failure and hardship. He proved that you cannot be afraid of making a mistake or attempting to do something that seems impossible just because you might have to endure pain, humiliation, or ruin. Struggle leads to success.

## Works Cited

Carson, Rachel. *Silent Spring*. Boston, Houghton Mifflin Company, 2002.

"Earth Day - April 22." Earth Day Network. www.earthday.org/earthday/.

Greentumble. "Pros and Cons of Organic Farming." 20 Dec. 2015. greentumble.com/pros-and-cons-of-organic-farming/.

"Jonas Salk Polio Vaccine Discovery." *YouTube,* uploaded by PublicDomainFootage, 26 Mar. 2011, https://www.youtube.com/watch?v=QO0E8WWAwlU.

"July 20, 1969: One Giant Leap for Mankind." NASA. https://www.nasa.gov/mission_pages/apollo/apollo11.html. 20 Jul. 2017.

Przybyla, Arthur Andrew. Personal interview. 6 Dec. 2018.

# ✏️ WRITE

When writing, it is important to consider your audience and purpose so you can write appropriately for them. Your audience consists of your teacher and peers, and your purpose is implied within the prompt. Reread the prompt to determine your purpose for writing.

To begin, review the questions below and then select a strategy, such as brainstorming, journaling, reading, or discussing, to generate ideas.

After generating ideas, begin the prewriting process by writing a summary of your writing plan. In your summary, respond to the following questions:

- **Purpose**: Who will be the focus of your presentation and what important ideas do you want to convey about this person?

- **Audience**: Who is your audience and what message do you want to express to your audience?

- **Evidence**: What facts, evidence, and details might you include? Which texts will help you support your ideas? What other research might you need to do? What anecdotes from your personal life or background knowledge are relevant to the topic of your presentation?

- **Organization**: How can you organize your presentation so that it is clear and easy to follow?

- **Clear Communication**: How will you make sure that your audience can hear and understand what you are saying?

- **Gestures and Visual Aids**: What illustrations or other visual aids could you use during your presentation? What effect will they have on your audience? What physical gestures and body language will help you communicate your ideas?

## Response Instructions

Use the questions in the bulleted list to write a one-paragraph summary. Your summary should describe what will happen in your oral presentation like the one above.

Don't worry about including all of the details now; focus only on the most essential and important elements. You will refer back to this short summary as you continue through the steps of the writing process.

# Skill:
# Evaluating Sources

## ••• CHECKLIST FOR EVALUATING SOURCES

First, reread the sources you gathered and identify the following:

- what kind of source it is, including video, audio, or text, and where the source comes from
- where information seems inaccurate, biased, or outdated
- where information seems irrelevant or tangential to your research question

In order to use advanced searches to gather relevant, credible, and accurate print and digital sources, use the following questions as a guide:

- Is the material published by a well-established source or expert author?
- Is the material up-to-date, or based on the most current information?
- Is the material factual, and can it be verified by another source?
- Are there specific terms or phrases in my research question that I can use to adjust my search?
- Can I use "and," "or," or "not" to expand or limit my search?
- Can I use quotation marks to search for exact phrases?

In order to integrate multiple sources of information presented in diverse media formats, ask the following:

- Have I included information from a variety of media?
- Am I relying too heavily on one source or source type?
- Have I varied the points at which I reference a particular source over the course of the speech or paper?
- As I listen to a presentation, am I aware of the speaker's use of sources? Where applicable, do the diverse media formats work well together?

## ⟳ YOUR TURN

Read the sentences below. Then, complete the chart by sorting them into those that show a source is credible and reliable and those that do not.

| | Sentences |
|---|---|
| A | The author is a reporter for an internationally recognized newspaper. |
| B | The article states only the author's personal opinions and leaves out other positions. |
| C | The text is objective and includes several different viewpoints. |
| D | The website is for a personal podcast. |
| E | The article includes clear arguments and counterarguments. |
| F | The text relies on loaded language or broad generalizations to persuade readers. |

| Credible and Reliable | Not Credible or Reliable |
|---|---|
| | |
| | |
| | |

**YOUR TURN**

Complete the chart below by filling in the title and author of a source you are considering using in your oral presentation and answering questions about it.

| Source Title and Author | Answer |
|---|---|
| **Source Title and Author:** Are the title and author clearly identified? What are they? | |
| **Reliability:** Has the source material been published in a well-established book, periodical, or website? | |
| **Reliability:** Is the source material up-to-date or based on the most current information? | |
| **Credibility:** Is the source material written by a recognized expert on the topic? | |
| **Credibility:** Is the source material published by a well-respected author or organization? | |
| **Bias:** Is the source material connected to persons or organizations that are objective and unbiased? | |
| **Fallacious Reasoning:** Does the source contain faulty reasoning? | |
| **Evaluation:** Should I use this source in my oral presentation? | |

# Skill: Organizing an Oral Presentation

## ••• CHECKLIST FOR ORGANIZING AN ORAL PRESENTATION

In order to present information, findings, and supporting evidence clearly, do the following:

- identify your audience in order to create your content
- choose a style for your oral presentation, either formal or informal
- make sure the information in your presentation follows a logical order and progression so your listeners can follow your line of reasoning
- determine that the development and organization of your presentation, as well as its substance and style, is appropriate for your purpose, audience, and task
- use digital media, such as textual, graphical, audio, visual, and interactive elements, to add interest and enhance your audience's understanding of the findings, reasoning, and evidence

To present information, findings, and supporting evidence clearly, consider the following questions:

- Have I chosen a style for my oral presentation, either formal or informal?
- Did I make sure that the information in my presentation follows a logical order so my listeners can follow the line of reasoning I've used?
- Have I determined that the development and organization of my presentation is appropriate for my purpose and audience?
- Has my use of digital media enhanced my audience's understanding of the information and evidence I have found, as well as the reasoning in my presentation?
- Has my use of digital media added interest to my presentation?

YOUR TURN

Read the quotations from a student's outline of her oral presentation below. Then, complete the chart by matching each quotation with its correct place in the outline.

| | Quotation Options |
|---|---|
| A | Ms. Vozhik traveled to America from Russia when she was 10 years old. Her mother died when she was 12. Still, she got straight As in school and practiced the piano for hours every night. She became good enough to get into the Juilliard School for music and traveled the world as a concert pianist before becoming a piano teacher. |
| B | I will show some of the photographs Ms. Vozhik lent me of her home in Russia and of herself as a teenager. |
| C | Ms. Vozhik said that one piece of advice from her mother that has always stuck with her is that "consistent practice is the secret to success." |
| D | I want to explain to people why my piano teacher, Anna Vozhik, is the person I most admire and respect. |
| E | According to an article from the New York Times titled "The Juilliard Effect: Ten Years Later," it can be hard "to live as a classical musician in a society that seems increasingly to be pushing classical music to the margins." |
| F | I will tell about the events in Ms. Vozhik's life in chronological order. |
| G | Anna Vozhik is not just my piano teacher, but her teaching techniques are revolutionary and should be adopted by other piano teachers everywhere. |

| Oral Presentation Component | Quotation |
|---|---|
| Overall Purpose | |
| Thesis Statement and Claim | |
| Evidence Learned During Interview | |
| Quote from Interviewee | |
| Evidence from Reliable Source Found from Online Research | |
| Text Structure | |
| Possible Visual Aids | |

**WRITE**

Use the questions in the checklist to outline your formal oral presentation. Be sure to include a clear thesis and logical progression of valid evidence from reliable sources.

# Skill: Considering Audience and Purpose

## ••• CHECKLIST FOR CONSIDERING AUDIENCE AND PURPOSE

In order to present information, findings, and supporting evidence such that listeners can follow the line of reasoning and the organization, development, substance, and style are appropriate to purpose, audience, and task, note the following:

- make sure listeners can follow your line of reasoning, or the set of reasons you have used in order to reach your conclusion

- check the development and organization of the information in your presentation to see that it is appropriate for your purpose, audience, and task

- determine that the substance, or basis of your presentation, is also appropriate for your purpose, audience, or task

- remember to adapt your speech according to your task, and if it is appropriate, use formal English and not language you would use in ordinary conversation

To better understand how to present information, findings, and supporting evidence such that listeners can follow the line of reasoning and the organization, development, substance, and style are appropriate to purpose, audience, and task, consider the following questions:

- Have I organized the information and visual aids in my presentation in a clear, logical manner, using a structure appropriate for the content?

- Are listeners able to follow the line of reasoning in my presentation?

- Have I developed and organized the information so that it is appropriate for my purpose, audience, and task?

- Is the substance and style suitable?

## ↻ YOUR TURN

Read each quotation from students' presentations below. Then, complete the chart by sorting each quotation into those that are examples of formal language and those that are examples of informal language.

| | Quotations |
|---|---|
| A | In order to mitigate the obesity epidemic, the school cafeteria should place a ban on junk food. |
| B | My experience at the opera opened my eyes to the idea that some stories are universal. |
| C | In this part of the story, all of the reader's expectations get totally flipped on their heads. |
| D | My aunt sews the most amazing dresses I've ever seen. |
| E | If you've ever been lost in the woods before, then you know how completely scary it is when it starts to get dark. |
| F | In this regard, forest fires can actually be beneficial to the land, despite the destruction they often cause. |

| Formal | Informal |
|---|---|
| | |
| | |
| | |

## ↻ YOUR TURN

Complete the chart by writing how you plan to address each aspect of audience and purpose in your oral presentation.

| Aspect | Plan |
| --- | --- |
| What are my purpose and claim, and who is my audience? | |
| Do I plan to use formal or informal language? | |
| What sort of tone, or attitude, do I want to convey? | |
| How would I describe the voice I would like to use when giving my oral presentation? | |
| How will I use language to create that particular voice? | |

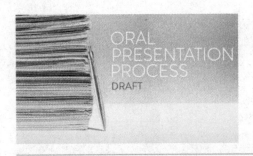

# Oral Presentation Process: Draft

| PLAN | DRAFT | REVISE | EDIT AND PRESENT |
|------|-------|--------|------------------|

You have already made progress toward writing your oral presentation. Now it is time to draft your argumentative oral presentation.

 **WRITE**

Use your plan and other responses in your Binder to draft your argumentative oral presentation. You may also have new ideas as you begin drafting. Feel free to explore those new ideas as you have them. You can also ask yourself these questions to ensure that your writing is focused, organized, and developed:

**Draft Checklist**

- **Focused**: Is the subject of my presentation clear to my audience? Have I included only relevant information and details about my subject? Have I avoided extraneous details that might confuse or distract my audience?

- **Organized:** Is the organization of ideas and events in my presentation logical? Have I reinforced this logical structure with transitional words and phrases to help my audience follow the order of ideas?

- **Developed:** Do the sentences in my presentation flow together naturally? Will the sentences sound choppy or long-winded when I deliver them orally? Do all of my details support my thesis about how listening to another person's story can shape us?

Before you submit your draft, read it over carefully. You want to be sure that you've responded to all aspects of the prompt.

Here is Dylan's draft. As you read, notice how Dylan develops his draft to be focused, organized, and developed. As he continues to revise and edit his narrative, he will find and improve weak spots in his writing, as well as correct any language or punctuation mistakes.

## ☰ STUDENT MODEL: FIRST DRAFT

### Poppa's Passion

[Use a title slide as a visual aid to preview the title of my presentation for my audience.] Today I'm gonna tell you about the person I respect most: Arthur Andrew Przybyla. Friends and family call him Double A but I call him Poppa most people respecting and admiring one's grandparents, I think Poppa is really cool. He's patient with everybody and everything, including kids, chicks, and seedlings he cares about the land he farms, and he works super hard. I have always looked up to Poppa, but listening to his story has given me a clear idea of what I want to be as an adult. The life lessons shared by my grandfather demonstrate that hardship and failure can be a catalyst for success.

 Some background: Poppa was born in 1948. That makes him a baby boomer, the generation of kids born right after the end of World War II. That means Poppa got to see some amazing events in American history, like the birth of rock and roll, the civil rights movement, the first walk on the moon, and the invention of the internet. But Poppa did not always have it easy. When he was five years old, he contracted polio according to the Centers for Disease Control and Prevention (the CDC), polio is "a crippling and potentially deadly disease." Its caused by a virus that can cause paralyze important muscles, like the ones in your legs. According to *Encyclopedia Britannica,* before the first polio vaccine was developed by Dr. Jonas Salk in 1955, thousands of Americans got sick with this disease every year. [Possibly show my audience a video about the polio vaccine.] So, Poppa went to bed with a sore throat and a fever. When he got up a few days later, he couldn't walk because the polio had paralyzed his left leg. As Poppa told it, "I used to be a kid who could not sit still. If I was awake, I was climbing trees or running around in the fields." Now Poppa had to wear a leg brace and later use a cane and always go slow. It was a big change?

Since he was stuck inside a lot, Poppa's mother tried to get him intrested in books. He tried reading stories, but he says he "always

Please note that excerpts and passages in the StudySync® library and this workbook are intended as touchstones to generate interest in an author's work. The excerpts and passages do not substitute for the reading of entire texts, and StudySync® strongly recommends that students seek out and purchase the whole literary or informational work in order to experience it as the author intended. Links to online resellers are available in our digital library. In addition, complete works may be ordered through an authorized reseller by filling out and returning to StudySync® the order form enclosed in this workbook.

Reading & Writing Companion

**639**

knew how they were going to end." Then one day when he was ten or so, his mother brought home some nature guides from the local library. She sat down with him after finishing her chores on the farm, and they studied those books. They learned about birds, insects, snakes, trees, you name it. Poppa says they spent one long winter studying those books. Then in the spring, Poppa went outside and looked at everything with what he called "new eyes." He told me about how cool it felt the first time he could name a tree just by looking at the bark. Nature, he said, "is remarkable and persistant. Even trees that look haf dead often comes back to life." He was inspired. Working on the family farm would be impossible for someone who couldn't walk or climb. Determined to try.

Then a couple of things hapened that helped give him some direction! First, he was deeply impressed by the first moon walk according to nasa's website, in July 1969, the American astronauts neil Armstrong, Buzz Aldrin, and Michael Collins landed the apollo 11 spacecraft on the moon. On July 20, Neil Armstrong was the first human being to walk on the moon's surface. Poppa remembers watching the TV. In "Absolute awe." He can still quote Armstrong's words as he stepped off the ladder onto the surface of the moon: "That's one small step for a man, one giant leap for mankind." [Project this quote for my audience to see.] Poppa knew that with his "bum leg" that he could never be an astronaut, but the moon walk made him think two things. One was that impossible things was possible. The other was that Earth was a special place. There's only one planet like it. Poppa was going to do his best to take care the little piece of land he called his own.

The following April, Poppa read about an event called Earth Day. The first Earth Day was inspired by a book, Silent Spring, by a scientist named Rachel Carson. She wrote about how polution was affecting people, and the land. On April 22, 1970 "20 million Americans took to the streets, parks, and auditoriums to demonstrate for a healthy, sustainable environment." Back on the farm, Poppa sat at the dining room table with his wife, Grandma Alice together they came up with a plan to make a difference on the family farm they would go organick. It was brilliant. My grandfather showed the world how organic crops could replace conventionally-grown produce and fruit. If my grandfather could do this, it's clear that anyone can!

The following April, Poppa read about an event called Earth Day.

- According to Earthday.org, the first Earth Day was inspired by a book, *Silent Spring*, by a scientist named Rachel Carson. Eight years later, the first Earth Day was celebrated.

- Back on the farm, Poppa sat at the dining room table with his wife, Grandma Alice, and together they came up with a plan to make a difference on the family farm: They would go organic.

It wasn't easy. All around them, neighboring farms relied on fertilizers and in order to grow big monocrops, or huge crops of the same kind of plant. Some people told Poppa that he was going backward, not forward. The same effort that Poppa put into learning about plants and animals as a kid, he applied to learning this. He told me, "I knew that we would fail. That was part of our plan." And they did fail. The first summer it was too wet. The next summer there was an infestation. The third summer it was too dry. By the fourth year, they grew more than they could eat by themselves, so they set up a farm stand at the end of the driveway. They were too busy to man it, so they left a basket for the money and a sign that said, "Eat well. Be well." At the end of the first week, they had made $50. Poppa said, "We felt like royalty." And that's how the farm got their name: Regaal Organic Farms—that's *regal* with two *a*'s, as in Arthur Andrew. As Poppa told me, "The name sounded good and almost nobody can pronounce Przybyla anyway."

Poppa, Grandma Alice, and my Uncle Sid have run Regaal Organic Farms. My parents and I visit the farm for a month. Poppa drives me and my cousins all around the fields and the orchards in his electric cart. He tells about his plans for each field. His face is full of lines from working in the sun. I know that each line represents a piece of wisdom that he is willing to share with us or anyone who asks. Poppa has his own blog. It's called "Down on the Faarm" (two *a*'s). He writes about the farm almost every day. You can click on the "Ask Me Anything" button and send him a question. Poppa always wrote back. My awesome Poppa likes "the interweb" but he loves sharing his love of the land even more. He proved that organic farming is better than other farming. His genius as a businessman showed

**Skill: Reasons and Evidence**

*Dylan's oral presentation includes exaggerations not supported by evidence. To conclude, as Dylan does, that what his grandfather did is therefore something "anyone" can do is an example of fallacious reasoning. These kinds of statements undermine Dylan's argument and are not necessary to support his point of view. Dylan revises his exaggeration by clarifying the information with facts, or by eliminating judgment words.*

Please note that excerpts and passages in the StudySync® library and this workbook are intended as touchstones to generate interest in an author's work. The excerpts and passages do not substitute for the reading of entire texts, and StudySync® strongly recommends that students seek out and purchase the whole literary or informational work in order to experience it as the author intended. Links to online resellers are available in our digital library. In addition, complete works may be ordered through an authorized reseller by filling out and returning to StudySync® the order form enclosed in this workbook.

Reading & Writing Companion    **641**

**Skill:
Communicating ideas**

*Dylan repeats important ideas toward the close of his presentation. He uses a visual aid to enhance information and add interest.*

**Skill: Sources and Citations**

*At the end of his presentation, Dylan included a Works Cited slide, providing a complete list of all the sources he used, in MLA format.*

other farmers that organics were the future and a way to make some decent money doing the right thing.

Here are the key points of my experience interviewing Poppa.

- Hardship and failure may be a catalyst for success. Poppa, for example, overcame polio and gained a new interest in nature.

- World events inspired Poppa to take bigger chances in his own life.

[Use a slide as a visual aid to recap major points.]

- As a result of his life experience, Poppa wasn't afraid to fail at organic farming, kept working at it, and eventually made a success of it.

**Sources**

- ~~Video about polio vaccine from Youtube(?)~~

- ~~Direct quotes from Poppa that I got during my interview with him~~

- ~~Quote about nature from the book *Silent Spring* by Rachel Carson~~

- ~~Quote from Neil Armstrong when he landed on the moon~~

**Works Cited**

Carson, Rachel. *Silent Spring*. Houghton Mifflin Company, 2002.

Greentumble. "Pros and Cons of Organic Farming." 20 Dec. 2015, greentumble.com/pros-and-cons-of- organic-farming/.

"The History of Earth Day." *Earth Day Network*, www.earthday.org/earthday/. Accessed 1 Oct. 2018.

"July 20, 1969: One Giant Leap for Mankind." *NASA*, 20 Jul. 2017, www.nasa.gov/mission_pages/apollo/apollo11.html.

Przybyla, Arthur Andrew. Personal interview, 6 Dec. 2018.

"Victory Over Polio." *Universal Newsreels*, Volume 28, Release No. 738, 26 Dec. 1955.

# Skill: Communicating Ideas

In order to present information, findings, and supporting evidence such that listeners can follow the line of reasoning and the organization, development, substance, and style are appropriate to purpose, audience, and task, note the following:

- present written and visual information and supporting evidence that you find in a clear, concise, and logical manner

- make sure listeners can follow your line of reasoning, or the set of reasons you have used in order to reach your conclusion

- check the development and organization of the information in your presentation to see that it is substantive and appropriate for your purpose, audience, and task

To better understand how to present information, findings, and supporting evidence such that listeners can follow the line of reasoning and the organization, development, substance, and style are appropriate to purpose, audience, and task, consider the following questions:

- Have I organized the information in my presentation in a clear, logical manner, using a structure appropriate for the content?

- Is my presentation substantive? Is my style consistent with the material?

- Are my visual aids helpful and connected to my content?

- Are listeners able to follow the line of reasoning in my presentation?

- Have I developed and organized the information so that it is appropriate for my purpose, audience, and task?

# ↻ YOUR TURN

Read the examples of students communicating their ideas below. Then, complete the chart by sorting them into those that are examples of effective communication and those that are ineffective.

| | Students' Communication |
|---|---|
| A | A student scans the room, making eye contact with individual students. |
| B | A student taps a fist against an open palm to emphasize the point she is making. |
| C | A student rushes her words to keep the presentation under five minutes. |
| D | A student slouches behind a podium in the corner of the classroom. |
| E | A student stands at ease at the front of the classroom where everyone can see him. |
| F | A student ends his formal presentation by saying, "Thank you for listening." |
| G | A student stares down at his paper or tablet as he reads aloud his presentation. |
| H | A student ends his formal presentation by saying, "Thanks guys, ttyl!" |
| I | A student grips the sides of the podium to keep from shaking. |
| J | A student speaks more slowly and loudly and with more care than in a normal conversation. |

| Category | Example of Effective Communication | Example of Ineffective (Poor) Communication |
|---|---|---|
| Posture | | |
| Eye Contact | | |
| Volume/Rate/Enunciation | | |
| Gestures | | |
| Language Conventions | | |

# ✎ WRITE

Take turns delivering your oral presentation in front of a partner.

As you present, do the following:

- Employ steady eye contact with your partner.

- Use an appropriate speaking rate, volume, pauses, and enunciation to clearly communicate with your partner.

- Use natural gestures to add interest and meaning as you speak.

- Use a comfortable, confident posture to engage your partner.

- Use language conventions appropriate for a formal presentation and avoid slang or inappropriate speech.

As you watch your partner's presentation, use the checklist to evaluate their communication of ideas.

When you finish giving your presentation, write a brief but honest reflection about your experience of communicating ideas. Did you make good eye contact? Did you speak too quickly or too softly? Did you maintain a comfortable, confident posture? Did you use appropriate conventions of language? Did you struggle to incorporate gestures that looked and felt natural? How can you better communicate your ideas in the future?

# Skill:
# Reasons and Evidence

## ••• CHECKLIST FOR REASONS AND EVIDENCE

As you begin to determine what reasons and evidence will support your claim(s) and point of view, use the following steps as a guide:

- Identify the precise claim or claims you will make in your argument.

- Identify valid reasons for your claim.

- Select evidence from credible sources to support your reasons.

- Choose or create an organizational pattern, such as compare and contrast, that will establish clear relationships among claim(s), counterclaims, reasons, and evidence.

In order to identify a speaker's reasoning and point of view, note the following:

- a statement of the speaker's argument

- the evidence that the speaker offers to support his or her point of view

- any fallacious reasoning or errors in logic that invalidate or overturn an argument, e.g., drawing a conclusion based on information that is inconclusive or questionable

- distorted or exaggerated evidence to support a point of view

- rhetorical style and what it contributes to the speaker's point of view

To evaluate a speaker's point of view, reasoning, and use of evidence and rhetoric, consider the following questions:

- Does the speaker offer any examples of fallacious reasoning? What were they, and how do they affect the speaker's point of view?

- Are there any instances of distorted or exaggerated evidence? How did it affect the speaker's argument?

- How does the speaker use rhetoric to advance his or her ideas?

## YOUR TURN

Read the examples of reasoning from a draft of Dylan's oral presentation below. Then, complete the chart by sorting them into those that are sound and those that are fallacious.

| | Dylan's Reasoning |
|---|---|
| A | He lost interest in reading short stories because so many of the ones he read became predictable. |
| B | If a person doesn't know how to identify trees by sight, it's because he is not trying, the way Poppa did. |
| C | By reading and studying books on trees, he realized he could identify a tree just by looking at the bark. |
| D | Working on the family farm would be difficult for someone who couldn't walk or climb, but he was determined to try. |
| E | Working on a family farm would be impossible for anyone who has had polio, as everyone knows. |
| F | We can always tell how a story is going to end just by reading the title. |

| Sound Reasoning | Fallacious Reasoning |
|---|---|
| | |
| | |
| | |

YOUR TURN

Read each piece of evidence in the chart below. Then, complete the chart by writing an exaggerated version of each piece of evidence. The first one has been completed for you.

| Evidence | Exaggerated or Distorted Evidence |
|---|---|
| Over time, Poppa proved that organic farming could be successful. | As a result of his hard work, Poppa has been the most successful organic farmer in the state. |
| Poppa's life story can help to teach people that they can learn something from someone who did not give up and continued until he succeeded. | |
| Poppa took inspiration from the achievements of others, such as Neil Armstrong, by walking despite polio and taking a risk on organic farming. | |

# Skill:
# Sources and Citations

## ••• CHECKLIST FOR SOURCES AND CITATIONS

In your presentation, provide citations for any information that you obtained from an outside source. This includes the following:

- direct quotations

- paraphrased information

- tables, charts, and data

- images

- videos

- audio files

Your citations should be as brief and unobtrusive as possible. Follow these general guidelines:

- The citation should include the author's last name and the page number(s) on which the information appeared, enclosed in parentheses. If the work does not have page numbers, omit them.

- If the author is not known, the citation should list the title of the work.

At the end of your presentation, include a slide with your Works Cited list, following the formatting guidelines of a standard and accepted format, such as MLA. These are the elements and the order in which they should be listed for Works Cited entries:

- author

- title of source

- container, or the title of the larger work in which the source is located

- other contributors

- version; number

- publisher; publication date; location

- for web sources: the URL (omit "http://")

Not all of these elements will apply to each citation. Include only the elements that are relevant for the source.

Please note that excerpts and passages in the StudySync® library and this workbook are intended as touchstones to generate interest in an author's work. The excerpts and passages do not substitute for the reading of entire texts, and StudySync® strongly recommends that students seek out and purchase the whole literary or informational work in order to experience it as the author intended. Links to online resellers are available in our digital library. In addition, complete works may be ordered through an authorized reseller by filling out and returning to StudySync® the order form enclosed in this workbook.

Reading & Writing Companion

649

YOUR TURN

Read the elements and examples below. Then, complete the chart by sorting them into the correct order according to MLA style for a Works Cited list.

| | Elements and Examples | | |
|---|---|---|---|
| A | "Life on a Fredericksburg Farm" | G | title of source |
| B | *Texas Monthly,* | H | 30 Jun. 2017, |
| C | author | I | container |
| D | www.texasmonthly.com/style/life-fredericksburg-farm/ | J | URL |
| E | publisher | K | Smith Ford, Lauren |
| F | publication date | L | Genesis Park, L.P., |

| Element | Example |
|---|---|
| | |
| | |
| | |
| | |
| | |
| | |

WRITE

Use the information in the checklist to create or revise your citations and Works Cited list. Make sure that each slide with researched information briefly identifies the source of the information. This will let your audience know that the information you are presenting is trustworthy. When you have completed your citations, compile a list of all your sources into a Works Cited list. Refer to the *MLA Handbook* as needed.

# Skill:
# Engaging in Discourse

## ••• CHECKLIST FOR ENGAGING IN DISCOURSE

Use the following steps and strategies to engage in meaningful and respectful discourse:

- Listen actively.

  > Pay attention by facing forward and looking directly at the speaker.

  > Avoid distractions, such as talkative neighbors.

  > Try to interpret the speaker's message.

  > Show that you are listening by nodding in agreement and maintaining an open and inviting posture.

- Respond appropriately.

  > Summarize a speaker's main points.

  > Ask questions to clarify your understanding.

  > Make comments to build upon, agree, or disagree with what someone else says.

    ○ If you disagree, be sure that you first acknowledge what the speaker says.

    ○ Use language accurately, using vocabulary appropriate to the task.

- Adjust speech and language to the context and task by asking yourself:

  > What is my purpose?

  > Who is my audience?

  > Should I use formal or informal language?

  > What is appropriate vocabulary to use for my audience and purpose?

  > What academic language or domain-specific vocabulary may need to be defined?

  > What sort of tone, or attitude, do I want to convey?

  > What word choices will help me convey that tone?

YOUR TURN

Read the examples of engaging in discourse below. Then, complete the chart by matching each example into the correct category.

| | Engaging in Discourse Examples |
|---|---|
| A | A student restates her partner's point before disagreeing with it. |
| B | A student nods in agreement as his partner speaks. |
| C | A student uses academic language to discuss the play *Antigone*. |
| D | A student sits facing her discussion partner and looks up from her smart device. |
| E | A student maintains a friendly tone even when she disagrees with her discussion partner. |
| F | A student asks a clarifying question about something he doesn't understand. |

| Listen Actively | Respond Appropriately | Adapt Speech/Language |
|---|---|---|
| | | |
| | | |

# ✏ WRITE

Read aloud the draft of your oral presentation to a partner. Then take part in a brief discussion about what you learned from each other's presentation.

As you discuss, use strategies to ensure that your discourse is meaningful and respectful:

- Pay close attention to your partner.

- Summarize or restate your partner's ideas.

- Ask clarifying questions as needed.

- Maintain an open and inviting posture.

- Respond respectfully and appropriately.

- Adapt speech to context and task and to purpose and audience.

- Use domain-specific vocabulary and academic language accurately.

When you finish, write a reflection about your experience of engaging in discourse. Did you listen actively? Restate your partner's ideas? Ask questions to clarify your understanding? Did you use speech and language appropriate to the task and context? Were you able to build on each other's comments? Did you treat each other with respect?

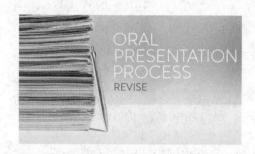

# Oral Presentation Process: Revise

| PLAN | DRAFT | REVISE | EDIT AND PRESENT |

You have written a draft of your oral presentation. You have also received input from your peers about how to improve it. Now you are going to revise your draft.

## ◂ REVISION GUIDE

Examine your draft to find areas for revision. Keep in mind your purpose and audience as you revise for clarity, development, organization, and style. Use the guide below to help you review:

| Review | Revise | Example |
|---|---|---|
| **Clarity** | | |
| Identify statements that might not be fully supported by evidence. Also identify concepts that may need defining or explaining. | Look for places where you integrate factual information but fail to identify a source. Also look for opportunities to integrate a visual aid that will help you explain concepts or add interest. | According to Earthday.org, the ~~The~~ first Earth Day was inspired by a book, *Silent Spring*, by a scientist named Rachel Carson. She wrote about how polution, particularly in the form of weed killers and pesticides used on crops, was affecting people, animals, and the land. [show a quotation from *Silent Spring* on a slide] |

Please note that excerpts and passages in the StudySync® library and this workbook are intended as touchstones to generate interest in an author's work. The excerpts and passages do not substitute for the reading of entire texts, and StudySync® strongly recommends that students seek out and purchase the whole literary or informational work in order to experience it as the author intended. Links to online resellers are available in our digital library. In addition, complete works may be ordered through an authorized reseller by filling out and returning to StudySync® the order form enclosed in this workbook.

Reading & Writing Companion **655**

| Review | Revise | Example |
|---|---|---|
| **Development** | | |
| Identify and annotate places in your presentation where your thesis is not supported by details. | Focus on a single anecdote in your presentation and add details that support your thesis about why this person embodies characteristics you value. | Some people told Poppa that he was going backward, not forward. But Poppa believed that the farming of the future would be the ways of the past. ~~The same effort that Poppa put into learning about plants and animals as a kid, he applied to learning this.~~ Poppa and Grandma Alice went to the library and also talked to "old timers." They learned about the ways that farmers used to farm the land. They learned about how to make compost and feed the soil. |
| **Organization** | | |
| Identify the major points you have made in your claim in order as you review your speech. | As you repeat important ideas toward the close of your presentation, isolate and emphasize their significance. Think about places where a visual aid might enhance a section of the presentation. | • Poppa overcame polio and gained a new interest in nature.<br><br>• World events inspired Poppa: if a man could land on the moon, Poppa could start an organic farm!<br><br>• As a result of his life experience, Poppa wasn't afraid to fail in order to succeed at organic farming. |

| Review | Revise | Example |
|---|---|---|
| **Exaggeration or Distortion** | | |
| Identify unsubstantiated, exaggerated, or distorted evidence. | Revise exaggerations or distortions by either clarifying the information with facts, or by eliminating judgment words or distorted evidence. | ~~My awesome Poppa likes "the interweb" but he loves sharing his love of the land even more.~~ You can read all about the farm at Poppa's blog, because he has a blog!~~He proved that organic farming is better than other farming. His genius as a businessman showed other farmers that organics were the future and a way to make some decent money doing the right thing.~~ |
| **Style: Word Choice** | | |
| Identify areas where word choice may be ineffective. | Revisit your presentation's title from the draft and see if it still reflects the purpose of the presentation. | ~~Poppa's Passion~~<br><br>One Man's Failure: A Key to Success |
| **Style: Sentence Effectiveness** | | |
| Look for a series of short, simple sentences. Annotate any places where a conjunction, transition, or punctuation could vary the length of sentences you use. | Shorten a section containing long sentences or join shorter sentences together using conjunctions or dependent clauses. You may also eliminate superfluous details. Think about places where a visual aid might replace text. | Then a couple of things hapened that helped give him some direction!. First, he was deeply impressed by the first moon walk. ~~according to nasa's website, in July 1969, the American astronauts neil Armstrong, Buzz Aldrin, and Michael Collins landed the apollo 11 spacecraft on the moon. On~~ According to NASA's website, on July 20, 1969, Neil Armstrong was the first human being to walk on the moon's surface. [show Armstrong's quote on a slide instead] |

# ✏ WRITE

The focus of the revision is to create a clear, credible, and effective oral presentation. In order to improve his work, Dylan is careful to integrate information from multiple sources, including the personal interview, websites, and other diverse, credible media sources. As Dylan moves toward publication of his presentation, he will continue to identify weak spots in his writing and reasoning, as well as correct errors in spelling and punctuation.

Dylan will then plan a time to practice delivering his revised oral presentation to a peer for additional feedback.

Use the guide above, as well as your peer reviews, to help you evaluate your oral presentation to determine areas that should be revised.

# Grammar: Noun Phrases

A noun **phrase** is a group of words that functions the way a single noun would in a sentence. A noun phrase may include articles, adjectives, and coordinating conjunctions.

| Text | Explanation |
|---|---|
| Ours was **the marsh country**, down by the river, within, as the river wound, twenty miles of the sea. **My first most vivid and broad impression** of the identity of things seems to me to have been gained on **a memorable raw afternoon** towards evening.<br><br>Great Expectations | The noun phrase **the marsh country** functions as a predicate nominative. The noun phrase **My first most vivid and broad impression** is the subject of the sentence. The noun phrase **a memorable raw afternoon** is the object of the preposition *on*. |
| I've got **a magic charm**<br>That I keep up my sleeve<br>I can walk **the ocean floor**<br>And never have to breathe.<br><br>Life Doesn't Frighten Me | The noun phrases **a magic charm** and **the ocean floor** function as direct objects. |

## ↻ YOUR TURN

1. Revise the sentence to include an additional noun phrase.

> The palomino horse is often seen in parades.

- ○ A. The palomino, a horse often seen in parades, is beautiful.
- ○ B. The palomino's hair is almost golden, and the horse is often seen in parades.
- ○ C. The palomino horse has almost golden hair and is often seen in parades.
- ○ D. No change is needed

2. Revise the sentence to include a noun phrase.

> Tad is treasurer and I am president.

- ○ A. Tad is the Drama Club treasurer and I am president.
- ○ B. Tad is treasurer, I am president, and Jimmy is secretary.
- ○ C. Tad, for now, is treasurer; I am president.
- ○ D. No change is needed

3. Revise the sentence to include a noun phrase.

> My father is a former trumpet player; he encouraged me to take lessons.

- ○ A. My father was a former trumpet player who encouraged me to take lessons.
- ○ B. My father was a former trumpet player, and he inspired me to take lessons.
- ○ C. A trumpet player encouraged me to take lessons.
- ○ D. No change is needed

4. Revise the sentence to include a noun phrase as the object of a preposition.

> After school we meet at Joe's.

- ○ A. Every Friday after school we meet at Joe's.
- ○ B. After school Carolee and I meet at Joe's.
- ○ C. After school we meet at Joe's on the town's west side.
- ○ D. No change is needed

# Grammar: Absolute Phrases

An **absolute phrase** consists of a noun or a pronoun that is modified by a participle or a participial phrase. In a sentence, an absolute phrase is set off by a comma. The absolute phrase stands "absolutely" by itself—it has no grammatical relation to the complete subject or the complete predicate of the sentence. However, an absolute phrase does explain something in the sentence.

| Text | Explanation |
|---|---|
| "It is demonstrable," said he, "that things cannot be otherwise than as they are; for **all being created for an end**, all is necessarily for the best end."<br><br>Candide | The absolute phrase is set off by a comma. *All* is the pronoun modified by the participial phrase *being created for an end*. It explains why "all is for the best end" but stands absolutely by itself. |
| Manufacturers report fewer typewriter sales, **computers having become common**. | The absolute phrase has a noun, *computers*. A participial phrase, *having become common*, modifies the noun. This absolute phrase is set off from the rest of the sentence by a comma because, although it explains why there are fewer typewriter sales, it has no grammatical relation to the sentence. |
| **The race over**, the runners sat in the shade to cool down.<br><br>**The race [being] over**, the runners sat in the shade to cool down. | The absolute phrase has a noun, *race*. In some absolute phrases, the participle *being* is understood rather than stated. This absolute phrase explains why the runners sat in the shade: The race was over. |

If a participial phrase does have a grammatical relationship to the rest of the sentence—for example, if it acts as the subject or modifies a noun, pronoun, or verb—it is not an absolute phrase.

| Text | Explanation |
|---|---|
| He told us that **having been chosen because of his strength**, he had been forced to place his own father's body into the furnace.<br><br>Night | This phrase is **not** an absolute phrase. It is a participial phrase modifying the pronoun *he*. |

Please note that excerpts and passages in the StudySync® library and this workbook are intended as touchstones to generate interest in an author's work. The excerpts and passages do not substitute for the reading of entire texts, and StudySync® strongly recommends that students seek out and purchase the whole literary or informational work in order to experience it as the author intended. Links to online resellers are available in our digital library. In addition, complete works may be ordered through an authorized reseller by filling out and returning to StudySync® the order form enclosed in this workbook.

Reading & Writing Companion    **661**

## ↻ YOUR TURN

1. How should this sentence be changed?

His story phoned in, the reporter prepared to enjoy the rest of the evening.

○ A. Insert **was** between **story** and **phoned**.
○ B. Insert **was** between **story** and **phoned** and change **in, the** to **in. The**.
○ C. Insert **being** between **story** and **phoned**.
○ D. No change needs to be made to this sentence.

2. How should this sentence be changed?

We fought the traffic at rush hour, the appliance store was expected to close at six o'clock.

○ A. Change **was** to **being**.
○ B. Change the comma to a semicolon.
○ C. Move **the appliance store was expected to close at six o'clock** to the beginning of the sentence and adjust the capitalization and punctuation.
○ D. No change needs to be made to this sentence.

3. How should this sentence be changed?

The trip having been strenuous and exhausting William wanted to sleep for days.

○ A. Change **having been** to **being**.
○ B. Change **having been** to **was**.
○ C. Insert a comma after **exhausting**.
○ D. No change needs to be made to this sentence.

4. How should this sentence be changed?

Nancy's salary was lower, but her take-home pay was higher than at her old job, the insurance premium being paid by her new employer.

○ A. Insert **and** between **job** and **the**, and insert **was** between **premium** and **being**.
○ B. Remove the commas after **lower** and **job**.
○ C. Remove **was** after **salary** and remove **but** after the word **lower**.
○ D. No change needs to be made to this sentence.

Reading & Writing Companion

**MODIFIERS**
ADJECTIVAL AND
ADVERBIAL PHRASES

# Grammar: Adjectival and Adverbial Phrases

Most adjectives and adverbs have three degrees: the positive, or base, form; the comparative form; and the superlative form. When a group of words modifies, or describes, a word in a sentence, it's called a phrase.

Adjectival or adjective phrases modify a noun or pronoun in a sentence. An adjectival phrase usually includes an adverb before the adjective.

| Adjective | Adjectival Phrase |
|---|---|
| Klavdiia ran off with the **youngest** <u>child</u> to Kansk, near Krasnoiarsk, where her **grown-up** <u>sister</u> Raisa lived.<br><br>The Whisperers: Private Life in Stalin's Russia | Never can there come fog too thick, never can there come mud and mire too deep, to assort with the **groping and floundering** <u>condition</u> which this High Court of Chancery, **most pestilent** of hoary <u>sinners</u>, holds this day in the sight of heaven and earth.<br><br>Bleak House |

Adverbial, or adverb, phrases modify a verb, an adjective, or another adverb in a sentence.

| Adverb | Adverbial Phrase |
|---|---|
| Two days after McCandless set up camp beside Lake Mead, an **unusually** <u>robust</u> wall of thunderheads reared up in the afternoon sky, and it began to rain, **very** <u>hard</u>, over much of the Detrital Valley<br><br>Into the Wild | But it did get the engine wet, so wet that when McCandless <u>tried</u> to start the car **soon thereafter**, the engine wouldn't catch, and in his impatience he drained the battery.<br><br>Into the Wild |

## ⟳ YOUR TURN

1. Replace the bold word with an adverbial phrase.

> It rains **often** in April.

- ○ A. regularly
- ○ B. most often
- ○ C. rarely
- ○ D. No change needs to be made to this sentence.

2. Replace the bold word with an adjectival phrase.

> The **talented** actors performed.

- ○ A. untrained
- ○ B. group of unbelievably talented
- ○ C. group of
- ○ D. No change needs to be made to this sentence.

3. Select the adjectival phrase from the sentence below.

> That old food tastes awfully bad.

- ○ A. old food
- ○ B. tastes awfully
- ○ C. awfully bad
- ○ D. This sentence does not have an adjectival phrase.

4. Select the adverbial phrase from the sentence below.

> Miguel was very badly hurt in the fall.

- ○ A. very
- ○ B. in the fall
- ○ C. very badly
- ○ D. There is no adverbial phrase in the sentence.

# Oral Presentation Process: Edit and Present

| PLAN | DRAFT | REVISE | EDIT AND PRESENT |
|------|-------|--------|------------------|

You have revised your oral presentation based on your peer feedback and your own examination.

Now, it is time to edit your argumentative oral presentation. When you revised, you focused on the content of your oral presentation. You practiced strategies for communicating your ideas and engaging in discourse. When you edit, you focus on the mechanics of your oral presentation, paying close attention to standard English conventions that can be heard by your audience while you are talking.

## Use the checklist below to guide you as you edit:

☐ Are there sentences that are too long and hard to follow?

☐ Have I used punctuation such as periods, commas, colons, and semicolons correctly to indicate pauses for effect?

☐ Have I used correct subject-verb agreement?

☐ Have I used any noun phrases, absolute phrases, adjectival phrases, and adverbial phrases correctly?

☐ Have I used any language that is too informal for my presentation?

☐ Have I added digital media strategically to enhance my presentation?

## Notice some edits Dylan has made:

- Replaced slang or informal language with formal language.

- Fixed an error in the use of absolute phrases.

- Corrected verb forms and pronoun/antecedent agreement.

- Corrected the meaning of a sentence by adding a coordinating conjunction.

- Replaced a slangy adjectival phrase with an adjective.

- Created noun phrases to add details that emphasize his subject's patience.

- Adjusted an adverbial phrase to be more formal.

[Title slide.] Today I'm ~~gonna~~ going to tell you about the person I respect most: Arthur Andrew Przybyla (that's pronounced "Prezbeela"). His friends and family call him Double A, like the battery, but since he's my grandfather, I call him Poppa. ~~most.~~ Most people ~~respecting~~ and ~~admireing~~ ~~one's~~ their grandparents, but I think Poppa is ~~really cool~~ special. ~~He's~~ is patient with everybody and everything, including little kids, baby chicks, and tiny seedlings; he cares about the land he farms, and he works ~~super~~ really hard. I have always looked up to Poppa, but listening to his story has given me a clearer idea of what really matters and what tough times can teach us. The life lessons shared by my grandfather demonstrate that hardship and failure can be a catalyst for success.

## ✏ WRITE

Use the questions above, as well as your peer reviews, to help you evaluate your oral presentation to determine areas that need editing. Then edit your presentation to correct those errors. Finally, rehearse your presentation, including both the delivery of your written work and the strategic use of digital media you plan to incorporate.

Once you have made all your corrections and rehearsed with your digital media selections, you are ready to present your work. You may present to your class or to a group of your peers. You can record your presentation to share with family and friends, or post it on your blog. If you publish online, share the link with your family, friends, and classmates.

# The Game Ritual

FICTION

## Introduction

When each player eats a peanut butter sandwich before a game, a struggling soccer team wins. The activity becomes a ritual, as do others when the team keeps winning. Soon the team members are performing three different rituals before every game. What would happen, however, if one of the rituals was accidentally skipped? Would the winning streak come to an end—or would it all prove to be just superstition?

## V VOCABULARY

**deficiency**
lack or shortage

**adept**
very skilled at something

**element**
smaller part of something bigger

**obvious**
very easy to see or to understand

**guarantee**
something that assures or promises a certain outcome

## ≡ READ

NOTES

1   The whole superstition thing with our soccer team started innocently enough. Our team captain, Rosalind, dedicated herself to improving our performance. She had read an article about good health and decided that our lackluster performance was caused by a nutritional **deficiency**. So, after practice the day before our match with Edgefield High, she instructed (some might say commanded) each of us to eat a peanut butter sandwich on the morning of the game for the protein. The next day, our team scored a one-point win over Edgefield. It was the first time we had ever done that well.

2   Before the next game, we all enjoyed the peanut butter sandwich breakfast again. Although the final score was close, we won again! This is where things got interesting. As we gathered in the locker room before our next game, Gabriella announced that she had written a team poem.

3   Of course, we all wanted to hear it. Although it lacked a lot in terms of poetic beauty, it did fire up the team. We won with a last minute goal. So now our

success was attributed to peanut butter and poetry, an interesting combination to say the least. But it didn't stop there.

4   The following Saturday, we put uniforms and pads on while listening to "our poem." Then Debbie, the most cheerful member of the team, added another **element** to the pregame ritual.

5   "I'm so sure we're going to win," she chattered. "I'm going to do my victory dance now!" She did, and we all joined in. The score was three to two; we won again.

6   Could we continue to add more and more things to do before a game to **guarantee** a win? After all, professional athletes thump helmets, wear special socks, or bounce the basketball exactly seven times before taking a free shot. Whatever the cause, we were doing well, until the game that would take us into the playoffs. We lost that one. It was my fault.

7   I knew our team had become much more **adept**. But I was really nervous about this game. I slept badly that night as a result. When the alarm went off, I hit the snooze button. When Mom finally came in to wake me, I got up in a panic. I was going to be late for the game! I threw on jeans and a shirt and grabbed my bag. As I headed to the door, Mom handed me a peanut butter protein bar. I did not have the peanut butter sandwich for breakfast.

8   All the way to school, my head was spinning like a wayward top. I wondered, fearfully, if what I had done would make a difference. But how could eating a peanut butter sandwich actually change anything? I had a protein bar made out of the same ingredient, though I could hardly swallow it.

9   As we suited up, I could feel that bar knocking against the sides of my stomach like a plank in a rough sea. Gabriella read her poem. Debbie led her dance. I pretended all was well. I was terrified of what might happen if the team knew I hadn't followed part of the ritual.

10  During the game, I fell a few times just running down the field. I was an awkward duck trying to fly. Then, horribly, the other team took the ball down the field right past me and scored in the final minute of the game! We were not going to the playoffs.

11  I never told anyone about the sandwich, and I quit the team before the next season. That was a long time ago. Truthfully, I've never quite answered the **obvious** question: did we lose because I was exhausted and nervous? Or did we lose because I failed to eat a peanut butter sandwich?

Please note that excerpts and passages in the StudySync® library and this workbook are intended as touchstones to generate interest in an author's work. The excerpts and passages do not substitute for the reading of entire texts, and StudySync® strongly recommends that students seek out and purchase the whole literary or informational work in order to experience it as the author intended. Links to online resellers are available in our digital library. In addition, complete works may be ordered through an authorized reseller by filling out and returning to StudySync® the order form enclosed in this workbook.

Reading & Writing Companion   **669**

# First Read

Read "The Game Ritual." After you read, complete the Think Questions below.

## ☁ THINK QUESTIONS

1. Who is the narrator?

   The narrator is _____

   _____.

2. Why does the team decide to eat peanut butter sandwiches before each game?

   The team eats peanut butter sandwiches because _____

   _____.

3. What happens after the narrator eats a protein bar instead of a peanut butter sandwich before a game?

   After the narrator eats a protein bar _____

   _____.

4. Use context to confirm the meaning of the word *element* as it is used in "The Game Ritual." Write your definition of *element* here.

   *Element* means _____.

   A context clue is _____.

5. What is another way to say that you *guarantee* something will happen?

   You _____

   _____.

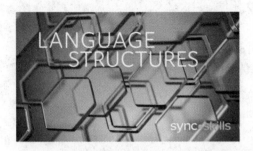

# Skill:
# Language Structures

## ★ DEFINE

In every language, there are rules that tell how to **structure** sentences. These rules define the correct order of words. In the English language, for example, a **basic** structure for sentences is subject, verb, and object. Some sentences have more **complicated** structures.

You will encounter both basic and complicated **language structures** in the classroom materials you read. Being familiar with language structures will help you better understand the text.

## ••• CHECKLIST FOR LANGUAGE STRUCTURES

To improve your comprehension of language structures, do the following:

✓ Monitor your understanding.

- Ask yourself: Why do I not understand this sentence? Is it because I do not understand some of the words? Or is it because I do not understand the way the words are ordered in the sentence?

✓ Pay attention to **perfect tenses** as you read. There are three perfect tenses in the English language: the present perfect, past perfect, and future perfect. The word *perfect* means "completed." These tenses describe actions that are completed or finished.

- **Present perfect tense** expresses an action that occurred at some indefinite time in the past.

  > Combine *have* or *has* with the past participle of the main verb.

    Example: I **have played** basketball for three years.

- **Past perfect tense** describes an action that happened before another action or event in the past.

  > Combine *had* with the past participle of the main verb.

    Example: I **had learned** how to dribble a ball before I could walk!

Please note that excerpts and passages in the StudySync® library and this workbook are intended as touchstones to generate interest in an author's work. The excerpts and passages do not substitute for the reading of entire texts, and StudySync® strongly recommends that students seek out and purchase the whole literary or informational work in order to experience it as the author intended. Links to online resellers are available in our digital library. In addition, complete works may be ordered through an authorized reseller by filling out and returning to StudySync® the order form enclosed in this workbook.

Reading & Writing
Companion

671

- **Future perfect tense** expresses one future action that will begin and end before another future event begins.

  > Use *will have* or *shall have* with the past participle of a verb.

  Example: Before the end of the year, I **will have** played more than 100 games!

✓ Break down the sentence into its parts.

- Ask yourself: What actions are expressed in this sentence? Are they completed or are they ongoing? What words give me clues about when an action is taking place?

✓ Confirm your understanding with a peer or teacher.

YOUR TURN

Read each sentence below and notice the perfect tense used in each one. Then, complete the chart by writing the letter of the sentence in the correct column.

| | Sentence Options |
|---|---|
| A | Our team had succeeded two years in a row. |
| B | Before the game, I will have practiced my soccer skills dozens of times. |
| C | I have practiced my soccer skills. |
| D | Our team will have succeeded three years in a row if we win tonight. |
| E | Our team has succeeded. |
| F | I had practiced my soccer skills for several weeks before I noticed improvements. |

| Present Perfect | Past Perfect | Future Perfect |
|---|---|---|
| | | |
| | | |

# Skill:
# Drawing Inferences and Conclusions

## ★ DEFINE

Making **inferences** means connecting your experiences with what you read. Authors do not always tell readers directly everything that takes place in a story or text. You need to use clues to infer, or make a guess, about what is happening. To make an inference, first find facts, details, and examples in the text. Then think about what you already know. Combine the **textual evidence** with your **prior knowledge** to draw a **conclusion** about what the author is trying to communicate.

Making inferences and drawing conclusions can help you better understand what you are reading. It may also help you search for and find the author's message in the text.

## ••• CHECKLIST FOR DRAWING INFERENCES AND CONCLUSIONS

In order to make inferences and draw conclusions, do the following:

✓ Look for information that is missing from the text or that is not directly stated.

- Ask yourself: What is confusing? What is missing?

✓ Think about what you already know about the topic.

- Ask yourself: Have I had a similar experience in my life? Have I learned about this subject in another class?

✓ Combine clues from the text with prior knowledge to make an inference and draw a conclusion.

- Think: I can conclude _____,

    because the text says _____

    and I know that _____.

✓ Use textual evidence to support your inference and make sure that it is valid.

Copyright © BookheadEd Learning, LLC

**674**  Reading & Writing Companion

Please note that excerpts and passages in the StudySync® library and this workbook are intended as touchstones to generate interest in an author's work. The excerpts and passages do not substitute for the reading of entire texts, and StudySync® strongly recommends that students seek out and purchase the whole literary or informational work in order to experience it as the author intended. Links to online resellers are available in our digital library. In addition, complete works may be ordered through an authorized reseller by filling out and returning to StudySync® the order form enclosed in this workbook.

**YOUR TURN**

Read paragraphs 10 and 11 of "The Game Ritual." Then, complete the multiple-choice questions below.

---

from **"The Game Ritual"**

During the game, I fell a few times just running down the field. I was an awkward duck trying to fly. Then, horribly, the other team took the ball down the field right past me and scored in the final minute of the game! We were not going to the playoffs.

I never told anyone about the sandwich, and I quit the team before the next season. That was a long time ago. Truthfully, I've never quite answered the obvious question: did we lose because I was exhausted and nervous? Or did we lose because I failed to eat a peanut butter sandwich?

---

1. Based on this excerpt, the reader can infer that—

   ○ A. the narrator wanted to keep her teammates from finding out about her breakfast.

   ○ B. the narrator did not want to play that day because she had a painful ankle injury.

   ○ C. the narrator wishes that she had suggested a different set of pregame rituals.

   ○ D. the narrator might have an injury from falling down on the field so many times.

2. A detail that best supports this inference is—

   ○ A. "During the game, I fell a few times just running down the field. I was an awkward duck. . ."

   ○ B. ". . .the other team took the ball down the field right past me and scored in the final minute of the game!"

   ○ C. "I never told anyone about the sandwich, and I quit the team before the next season."

   ○ D. "I've never quite answered the obvious question: did we lose because I was exhausted and nervous?"

Please note that excerpts and passages in the StudySync® library and this workbook are intended as touchstones to generate interest in an author's work. The excerpts and passages do not substitute for the reading of entire texts, and StudySync® strongly recommends that students seek out and purchase the whole literary or informational work in order to experience it as the author intended. Links to online resellers are available in our digital library. In addition, complete works may be ordered through an authorized reseller by filling out and returning to StudySync® the order form enclosed in this workbook.

Reading & Writing Companion   **675**

# Close Read

---

### ✏ WRITE

PERSONAL RESPONSE: At the end of "The Game Ritual," the narrator wonders if her team lost because she was exhausted or because she didn't eat a peanut butter sandwich. Draw inferences and conclusions from what you read to write an answer to her question. Use details and examples from the text to support your answer. Pay attention to and edit for the possessive case.

**Use the checklist below to guide you as you write.**

☐ How does the team feel about its ritual?

☐ What are two possible reasons for the team's loss?

☐ Which reason do you find more likely? Why?

**Use the sentence frames to organize and write your personal response.**

The team feels _____ about its ritual.

The narrator of "The Game Ritual" wonders if _____

or _____ made her team lose.

If her teammates knew that she had not followed the ritual, they might _____,

because _____.

Based on my experience, I believe that the team lost because _____

I think that _____

# Twisted Texting

**DRAMA**

## Introduction

Written as a series of text messages between the four main characters, this text explores complications related to dating in the 21st century. After an invitation for a date falls into the wrong hands, a group of friends scrambles to find a solution that won't hurt anyone's feelings, and they just might find love along the way.

## V VOCABULARY

### magnetism

the power in a magnet that attracts certain metals; also used to refer to a person's ability to attract other people

### ensued

followed; happened as a result of something else

### reminiscing

remembering or talking about events that happened in the past

### gawking

staring at a person in a rude way

### calamity

disaster; an event that causes great harm

NOTES

## ☰ READ

**Today, 8:22 AM**

1  GIA: OMG!!!! You'll never believe what happened!!!

2  ANGIE: What

3  GIA: I opened my locker and I found a note from LEX!!! That senior I've had a crush on for literally EVER!!! He saw me at the dance on Friday and thought I was gorgeous. He wants to meet up to talk about **magnetism** b/c he can't help but be attracted to me. that part was weird b/c I don't remember talking to him on Friday, but we did sit next to each other in physics last year, so maybe he's **reminiscing**? I dunno but HE WANTS TO HANG OUT WITH MEEEEE!!!! Can you believe it?

4  ANGIE: Whoa i totally believe he'd be into you. Did you see yourself on Friday? You were a knockout. But i gotta go. world history. :-/

**Today, 8:24 AM**

5   ANGIE: i'm in trouble. Remember Friday when you me and Lex were talking at the dance? I think he liked me and wants to ask me out bc he tried to put a note in my locker saying so. but **CALAMITY ensued** because he put it in Gia's locker. What do i do?!?!?!??!

6   JEFF: Why would he think Gia's locker was your locker?

7   ANGIE: They're next to each other. Easy mistake

8   ANGIE: But seriously what am i gonna do?!?!?!?!? Can you talk to him for me

9   JEFF: I'll take care of it. Don't worry.

10  ANGIE: Thanks

11  JEFF: Do you want to say yes?

12  ANGIE: I dunno. He's cute and funny, but Gia has liked him since freshman year. I can't do that to her

13  JEFF: You're a good friend. That's why you're so great.

14  ANGIE: :-D

**Today, 8:31 AM**

15  JEFF: Did you ask out Gia?

16  LEX: Who?

17  JEFF: Gia Miller. She sat next to us in physics last year. She has glasses and long curly hair.

18  LEX: Yeah, I know her. She's cute, but no i didn't ask her out. why?

Please note that excerpts and passages in the StudySync® library and this workbook are intended as touchstones to generate interest in an author's work. The excerpts and passages do not substitute for the reading of entire texts, and StudySync® strongly recommends that students seek out and purchase the whole literary or informational work in order to experience it as the author intended. Links to online resellers are available in our digital library. In addition, complete works may be ordered through an authorized reseller by filling out and returning to StudySync® the order form enclosed in this workbook.

Reading & Writing Companion     679

19  JEFF: She found a note in her locker.

20  LEX: Where's her locker?

21  JEFF: Next to Mr. Edwards' classroom.

22  LEX: Oh no. The note was for Angie. I must have put it in the wrong locker? Can you help?

23  JEFF: I'll take care of it.

24  LEX: Thanks man

25  JEFF: Just be at Dino's Pizza tonight @ 7.

**Today, 9:37 AM**

26  JEFF: I hear you have a date with Lex. Are you nervous?

27  GIA: A little. The guy looks like he should be on the cover of a fitness magazine.

28  JEFF: Would you feel better if Angie came too? Like as your wingman? I could pretend to be her date.

29  GIA: OMG. YES. That would be great. Can you set it up with A? I gotta run into econ.

30  JEFF: Set up a date with Angie? I'd love to. Just be at Dino's tonight @ 7.

**Today, 9:40 AM**

31  JEFF: Problem solved. We'll all go out. Gia will never know the note was for you.

32  ANGIE: You're my hero, J

33  JEFF: See you tonight. Dino's @ 7:00.

**Today, 7:04 PM**

34  GIA: OMG OMG OMG I CANNOT BELIEVE THIS IS HAPPENING

35  ANGIE: Chill girl. He's gonna love you. Just be yourself

**Today, 7:04 PM**

36  LEX: Thanks for taking care of this. Angie looks incredible. But why is Gia here too?

37  JEFF: Girls do everything together.

**Today, 7:05 PM**

38  ANGIE: Can't believe we're pulling this off. Great job J

39  JEFF: Anything for you.

**Today, 7:25 PM**

40  GIA: Why does L keep **gawking** at you?

41  ANGIE: I dunno

42  GIA: Take J and go look at the jukebox

**Today, 7:32 PM**

43  LEX: Dude where did you go? how did i end up on your date?

**Today, 7:35 PM**

44  LEX: Seriously where are you

**Today, 7:45 PM**

45  LEX: Nevermind. Gia is super cool. I think I want to go out with her again. can't believe I didn't realize it before.

**Today, 7:47 PM**

46  ANGIE: OMG You'll never believe this. J confessed that he likes me and i think i have feelings for him too. You and L look cozy, so we're gonna take off.

47  GIA: Looks like we are all in <3 Can you believe it?

# First Read

Read "Twisted Texting." After you read, complete the Think Questions below.

☁ **THINK QUESTIONS**

1. In whose locker did Lex put a note? In whose locker did he mean to put a note?

   Lex put a note in _____.

   He meant to put a note in _____.

2. Where and when will all four characters meet tonight?

   The four characters will meet at _____.

3. Who ends up with whom at the end of the play?

   At the end of the play, _____ ends up with _____ and

   _____ ends up with _____.

4. Use context to confirm the meaning of the word *gawking* as it is used in "Twisted Texting." Write your definition of *gawking* here.

   *Gawking* means _____.

   A context clue is _____.

5. What is another way to say that an event is a *calamity*?

   An event is _____.

# Skill:
# Analyzing Expressions

## ★ DEFINE

When you read, you may find English expressions that you do not know. An **expression** is a group of words that communicates an idea. Three types of expressions are idioms, sayings, and figurative language. They can be difficult to understand because the meanings of the words are different from their **literal**, or usual, meanings.

An **idiom** is an expression that is commonly known among a group of people. For example, "It's raining cats and dogs" means it is raining heavily. **Sayings** are short expressions that contain advice or wisdom. For instance, "Don't count your chickens before they hatch" means do not plan on something good happening before it happens. **Figurative** language is when you describe something by comparing it with something else, either directly (using the words *like* or *as*) or indirectly. For example, "I'm as hungry as a horse" means I'm very hungry. None of the expressions are about actual animals.

## ••• CHECKLIST FOR ANALYZING EXPRESSIONS

To determine the meaning of an expression, remember the following:

✓ If you find a confusing group of words, it may be an expression. The meaning of words in expressions may not be their literal meaning.

  • Ask yourself: Is this confusing because the words are new? Or because the words do not make sense together?

✓ Determining the overall meaning may require that you use one or more of the following:

  • context clues

  • a dictionary or other resource

  • teacher or peer support

✓ Highlight important information before and after the expression to look for clues.

## ⟳ YOUR TURN

Read the excerpts and literal meaning of each expression below. Then, complete the chart by correctly matching the meaning of the expression as it is used in the text.

| Meaning Options | |
|---|---|
| A | arrange a plan |
| B | very attractive |
| C | succeeding at this difficult task |

| Excerpt | Literal Meaning | Meaning in the Text |
|---|---|---|
| You were a **knockout**. | a strong hit, such as in boxing | |
| Can you **set it up** with A? | put something together, such as a board game | |
| Can't believe we're **pulling this off**. | removing something, such as a bandage | |

# Skill: Visual and Contextual Support

---

 ## ★ DEFINE

**Visual support** is an image or an object that helps you understand a text. **Contextual support** is a **feature** that helps you understand a text. By using visual and contextual supports, you can develop your vocabulary so you can better understand a variety of texts.

First, preview the text to identify any visual supports. These might include illustrations, graphics, charts, or other objects in a text. Then, identify any contextual supports. Examples of contextual supports are titles, headers, captions, and boldface terms. Write down your **observations**.

Then, write down what those visual and contextual supports tell you about the meaning of the text. Note any new vocabulary that you see in those supports. Ask your peers and your teacher to **confirm** your understanding of the text.

## ••• CHECKLIST FOR VISUAL AND CONTEXTUAL SUPPORT

To use visual and contextual support to understand texts, do the following:

- ✓ Preview the text. Read the title, headers, and other features. Look at any images and graphics.

- ✓ Write down the visual and contextual supports in the text.

- ✓ Write down what those supports tell you about the text.

- ✓ Note any new vocabulary that you see in those supports.

- ✓ Create an illustration for the reading and write a descriptive caption.

- ✓ Confirm your observations with your peers and teacher.

## ↻ YOUR TURN

Read lines 5 and 6 of "Twisted Texting." Then, complete the multiple-choice questions below.

---

from **"Twisted Texting"**

Today, 8:24 AM

ANGIE: i'm in trouble. Remember Friday when you me and Lex were talking at the dance? I think he liked me and wants to ask me out bc he tried to put a note in my locker saying so. but CALAMITY ensued because he put it in Gia's locker. What do i do?!?!?!??!

JEFF: Why would he think Gia's locker was your locker?

---

1. The texts here are between—

   ○ A. Angie and Gia.
   ○ B. Angie and Jeff.
   ○ C. Jeff and Lex.
   ○ D. Gia and Jeff.

2. The heading at the top of the scene tells—

   ○ A. who is speaking to whom.
   ○ B. what the actors should do.
   ○ C. where the scene happens.
   ○ D. when the scene happens.

3. Why does Angie capitalize "CALAMITY"?

   ○ A. to show Jeff how important her ideas are
   ○ B. to indicate an important vocabulary word
   ○ C. to emphasize this terrible problem
   ○ D. to remind the reader of a character's name

4. How do the illustrations in the story help the reader understand the informal punctuation in the dialogue?

   ○ A. They remind the reader that teenagers might use informal language when texting.
   ○ B. They explain that conversations are often quite personal.
   ○ C. They show the characters being clumsy with their phones.
   ○ D. They indicate that very young children wrote this dialogue.

# Close Read

---

## ✏ WRITE

LITERARY ANALYSIS: Explain how "Twisted Texting" shows that traditional messages and electronic messages can complicate and clarify situations. Include information about the format and language of each type of message to compare and contrast them. Pay attention to and edit for suffixes and silent E and final Y.

**Use the checklist below to guide you as you write:**

☐ How do traditional messages and electronic messages complicate the characters' lives?

☐ How do traditional messages and electronic messages make the characters' lives better?

☐ How are these two methods of communication different in this play?

**Use the sentence frames to organize and write your literary analysis.**

The play "Twisted Texting" shows that traditional messages can create _____

and electronic messages can help _____.

Lex writes his feelings clearly in his note, but he causes confusion by giving the note to _____.

Then, Jeff solves the problem by inviting _____ to a pizza

date. Lex thinks he is going to meet Angie, but then he _____.

Jeff's text messages are short so they (do/don't) provide information about how the friends would be paired up on the date.

# Chopped, Stirred, and Blended

ASSIGNMENTS    BINDER    LIBRARY

**UNIT 5**

# Chopped, Stirred, and Blended

What are the ingredients of culture?

Genre Focus: **POETRY**

## Texts

Paired Readings

# Extended Writing Project and Grammar

# Unit 5: Chopped, Stirred, and Blended

## What are the ingredients of culture?

### MATSUO BASHŌ

Matsuo Bashō (1644–1694) was born the son of a samurai in Kyoto, Japan. A master of the seventeen-syllable haiku form of poetry, Bashō also invented *haibun,* a combination of prose and haiku that traces a journey. Written over five months and twelve hundred miles, his most well-known haibun, *Oku no Hosomichi,* or *Narrow Road to the Interior,* incorporates encounters and conversations he had throughout his journey with his own observations and reflections.

### JUDITH ORTIZ COFER

Judith Ortiz Cofer (1952–2016) was born in Hormigueros, a small town in Puerto Rico, and moved with her family to Augusta, Georgia, at the age of fifteen. Writing across poetry, short stories, essays, and autobiography, Cofer often draws from personal experience to explore the disparities between cultures and the immigrant experience. Her poem "The Latin Deli: An Ars Poetica" (1993) focuses on the titular establishment as a haven for those struggling to adapt to life away from their native country.

### LIZZIE COLLINGHAM

Food historian Lizzie Collingham (b. 1947) has written books on a range of subjects from the way British imperialism affected diet and physique to innovations in food science during World War II. In *Curry: A Tale of Cooks and Conquerors* (2007), she delves into the history of Indian cuisine as it developed in tandem with social, political, and economic forces like colonialism and the expansion of global trade networks.

### RITA DOVE

Born in Akron, Ohio, poet and essayist Rita Dove (b. 1952) is celebrated for the way she addresses a range of cultural, political, and historical themes in her work without foregoing detail. Her poem "Parsley" (1983), for instance, takes as its starting point the 1937 massacre of up to 20,000 Haitians living in the Dominican Republic. Dictator Rafael Trujillo ordered his soldiers to use the Spanish word for *parsley, perejil,* to distinguish ethnic Haitians from native Dominicans based on differences in how the two groups commonly pronounce the *r* sound.

### CHEN JITONG

Writer and diplomat Chen Jitong (1851–1907) wrote several books in French on Chinese culture and society while serving as a military attaché at the Chinese Embassy in Paris in the 1880s. He was also a skilled speaker and, after returning to China later in life, became a reformer and newspaper editor. His 1878 text "Chinese Cooking" refutes popular misconceptions the French held about Chinese cuisine.

### AUDRE LORDE

Audre Lorde (1934–1992) was born in New York City to parents of Caribbean ancestry. One of the most influential black feminist writers and activists of the 20th century, Lorde was dedicated to addressing social injustice. Critical of Second Wave Feminism's disregard for considerations of gender, race, and class, much of her work argued for the necessity of recognizing difference in order to effect social and political change. Lorde published numerous collections of poetry and essays in her life, including the now-canonical *Sister Outsider* (1984).

## V. S. NAIPAUL

A Caribbean novelist of Indian descent born in Trinidad and educated at Oxford University, V. S. Naipaul (1932–2018) wrote about the difficulty of finding one's subject as a writer, noting that at first, he didn't know where to focus, since he'd had such varied experiences in his life. He found inspiration in a childhood memory of a neighbor in Trinidad, who became a main character in Naipaul's short story collection, *Miguel Street* (1959). This formally innovative collection combines observation, folklore, newspaper cuttings, and personal memory.

## WILLIAM WORDSWORTH

Along with Samuel Taylor Coleridge, English poet William Wordsworth (1770–1850) is credited with initiating what would come to be known as the Romantic movement in English literature. Romanticism diverged from 18th-century rationalism in that it placed greater emphasis on nature, individual thought, and personal feeling. Wordsworth's concern with the relationship between humans and nature was in large part a response to the cultural shifts brought about by the Industrial Revolution.

## DIANE BURNS

The daughter of a Chemehuevi father and an Anishinabe mother, poet Diane Burns (1956–2006) grew up in both Kansas and California. She is known for her poetry exploring Native American identity and customs, and for her role in New York City's Lower East Side poetry community during the 1980s. "Maple Sugaring (In Aunt Alberta's Backyard)" from her 1981 poetry collection, *Riding the One-Eyed Ford,* describes how the tradition of maple sugaring brings family members together.

## CARY FUNK AND BRIAN KENNEDY

Cary Funk is the director of research on science and society at the Pew Research Center. Her research focuses on public opinion about issues around climate, energy, and agriculture, among others. Brian Kennedy is a research associate at the Pew Research Center, whose research also focuses on science and society. In 2016, Funk and Kennedy co-wrote an article about Americans' differing views on the benefits and risks of organic and genetically modified foods.

## PEGGY SIAS LANTZ

Nature enthusiast Peggy Sias Lantz lives on the same lake in central Florida where her grandfather settled in 1914. A former editor of publications for the Florida Native Plant Society and the Florida Audubon Society, Lantz has written four books and numerous articles on Florida plants and wildlife. Her 2014 compendium *Florida's Edible Wild Plants: A Guide to Collecting and Cooking* combines practical knowledge on locating and identifying wild plants with personal anecdotes and recipes.

## Introduction

This informational text offers background information about the emergence of cross-cultural literature. From travel writing and memoir to fiction and poetry, cross-cultural texts comprise many genres and explore what it means to navigate multiple cultures. "Literary Focus: Cross-Cultural Texts" explores how this larger body of work reveals negative and positive aspects of having a cross-cultural identity and attempts to cultivate a better understanding in its readers.

# "Cross-culturalism is an old concept."

1   Can you remember the first time you were in a place that was strange and new—for example, a time you started at a new school or visited another state or country? How did you feel at first? Maybe you were a little disoriented because the routines and the rules were different. Maybe you experienced homesickness for familiar faces and places. If you were in a place where people spoke a different language, maybe you felt proud or maybe unsteady the first time you tried to express familiar ideas using new words. Experiences and emotions like these are often explored in cross-cultural literature.

**Cross-Cultural Literature**

2   Cross-culturalism is an old **concept**. Since the first civilizations formed, there have been people who chose or were forced to leave their communities to live among people of different cultures. Unlike multiculturalism, which celebrates the different cultures of the people living in the same community, cross-culturalism reflects the complicated and conflicting feelings people experience when they immerse themselves in a new culture.

3   Although cross-cultural exchange has been occurring for as long as civilizations have been interacting, the term cross-culturalism was first used in the 1940s to describe cultural **hybridity**, or the joining or mixing of different cultures. Cuban anthropologist Fernando Ortiz used the word to describe the blending of aspects of African and Hispanic cultures that he observed in Latin America, such as cooking styles, music, dance, and religions. The development of cross-culturalism as a literary form has largely coincided with the postmodern era (which you learned about in *The Power of Communication* unit), and thus it's no coincidence that cross-cultural literature shares many traits with other postmodern forms.

**Genres**

4   **Cross-cultural** literature highlights and explains similarities and differences between and among cultures. In many cases, the literature promotes understanding across cultures. Cross-cultural literature includes the genres of travel and food writing as well as fiction, poetry, and memoir. The works are

written for an audience that might not be familiar with the cultures involved, and the writer, an expert on both cultures, serves as a translator for readers. At the same time, readers become active participants. As they read, they begin to make connections between their own culture and the ones they are reading about.

5   Travel and food writing are genres that tend to focus on the positive aspects of cross-culturalism. Their writers want readers to engage with a new culture in a positive way. For example, Judith Ortiz Cofer's poem "The Latin Deli: An Ars Poetica" lovingly describes her local Latin deli, a refuge for Latin immigrants hungry for a taste of home. In *Curry: A Tale of Cooks and Conquerors,* Lizzy Collingham explains how curry is a staple food that serves as a cultural bond. Some writers in these genres acknowledge that misunderstandings between cultures exist and try to prod readers to overcome them. In *Chinese Cooking,* Chen Jitong diplomatically assures a French woman that Chinese people "had [no] appetite for dog meat" and posed no threat to her little dogs.

**Cross-Cultural Topics and Themes**

6   Often, the authors of cross-cultural works explore topics related to cultural exchange, such as immigration, communication through multiple languages, global travel, and prejudice. They often know multiple cultures and languages, and their work frequently explores what it means to experience new foods, music, and art, along with new people and landscapes. In addition, texts explore a range of themes from alienation and culture shock to acceptance and appreciation. Authors and characters in cross-cultural literature are frequently navigating multiple cultures, and the texts express a range of feelings toward the cultures they bridge in their writing, including humor, bewilderment, and reflection. Themes around navigating multiple cultures can also be seen in cross-cultural art. Ethiopian-American artist Julie Mehretu layers paint and other artistic mediums to create her paintings, which are known for their abstract and colorful representation of global maps and landscapes.

A mural by Julie Mehretu inside the new world headquarters for Goldman Sachs at 200 West Street in Manhattan.

7   Like other postmodern literary movements of the twentieth and twenty-first centuries, cross-cultural texts often have a postmodern feel. The works often incorporate **intertextuality** by quoting, referencing, or making allusions to other texts from other cultures, languages, or traditions. The works also often include an array of different voices and languages. Rita Dove's poem "Parsley" is filled with the voices of the Dominican general, his mother, his mother's parrot, and the Haitians who have difficulty pronouncing the Spanish word for *parsley*. V.S. Naipaul's story "B. Wordsworth" uses dialect to show cultural differences between the characters. Cross-cultural texts also tend to blend genres and appropriate forms. For example, Judith Ortiz Cofer's poem "The Latin Deli: An Ars Poetica" takes its title and theme from the ancient Greek poem "Ars Poetica," which was the first recorded reflection on the purpose of poetry. Instead, Cofer's poem explores the meaning and value of a local specialty grocery store. Similarly, cross-cultural art often has a postmodern feel. For instance, Turkish Artist Fahrelnissa Zeid used a multiplicity of colors and an abstract pattern in the painting *Towards a Sky* to reflect the international influences of her work.

*Towards a Sky* by Fahrelnissa Zeid, 1953.

8 **Major Concepts**

- **Navigating Multiple Cultures:** Cross-cultural texts explore exchanges between and among cultural groups and the range of themes and emotions that can accompany such interactions. By doing so, these texts shed light on the complex process of making sense of one's own cultural identity and that of others.

- **Purpose and Themes:** Cross-cultural texts focus points of contact between different cultures that result in tension or harmony—or in some cases both of these at once. By writing about war, immigration, and chance encounters between people of different cultures, cross-cultural writers examine, probe, criticize, or celebrate cultural differences and similarities. They draw attention to aspects of cultures that might not have been previously celebrated or widely known.

9 **Style and Form**

- **Postmodern Form:** Cross-cultural literature uses many of the same techniques as other postmodern literature from the twentieth and twenty-first centuries. It includes multiple languages and voices, and it often blends and borrows from other genres. For example, *Curry: A Tale of Cooks and Conquerors* is a blend of food writing and history, written by a British author whose topic is Indian cuisine. Cross-cultural texts use intertextuality, or allusions to texts from different cultures and may explore themes involving disorientation, culture shock, longing, foreignness, and escape.

10 In the twenty-first century, the world has become a global village. International borders can be crossed and cultures can be explored with the tap of a browser button, yet we don't always understand what we see. The writers of cross-cultural literature help explain a complicated world by writing about their experiences of living in multiple cultures. How does cross-cultural literature reflect life and the world today?

# Literary Focus

Read "Literary Focus: Cross-Cultural Texts." After you read, complete the Think Questions below.

## ☁ THINK QUESTIONS

1. Which genres are associated with cross-cultural literature and why do these genres suit the literary focus? Provide examples. Be sure to cite evidence directly from the text.

2. What themes and topics do cross-cultural texts address? Explain, citing evidence from the text to support your response.

3. What techniques do cross-cultural writers use to convey their experiences of living at the intersection of two or more cultures? Cite evidence from the text to support your explanations.

4. Use context clues to determine the meaning of the word **hybridity**. Write your best definition, along with the words and phrases that were most helpful in determining the word's meaning. Then, check a dictionary to confirm your understanding.

5. The word *intertextuality* combines the Latin root word *textual*, which means "related to a printed work," with the prefix *inter*, meaning "between" and the suffix *–ity*. With this information in mind, write your best definition of the word **intertextuality** as it used in this text. Cite any words or phrases that were particularly helpful in coming to your conclusion.

# Melons

POETRY
Matsuo Basho
1689, 1694, 1690

## Introduction

Matsuo Bashō ( (1644–1694) was born near Kyoto, Japan. As a young man, Bashō studied Taoism and Chinese poetry and later became a revered teacher and master of the haiku form. A haiku is composed of 17 syllables; in Japanese it is composed as one line, while in English it is typically written in three lines with a 5-7-5 syllabic structure, though this can depend on the translator. Because haiku are so short, diction, or word choice, is very important, with each word contributing to the meaning and tone of the poem. The heart of a haiku is one or two concrete images that illustrate the essence of a specific moment in time. Like many Japanese poems, haiku are often linked to specific seasons. The three Bashō haiku in this selection center on the image of a melon, a highly prized summer fruit.

# "don't be like me"

NOTES

1 562.
2 the first melon
3 shall it be cut **crosswise**
4 or into round slices?

5 956.
6 morning **dew**
7 the muddy melon **stained**
8 with coolness

9 659.
10 don't be like me
11 even though we're like the melon
12 split in two

---

✏️ **WRITE**

POETRY: Matsuo Bashō uses the poetic form of the haiku—a Japanese verse of three lines—to describe melons. Select one food item you associate with a season of the year. Then, compose two haiku, each of which expresses a different idea about this food. Be sure that your poems are each three lines. To satisfy the structure of a haiku, the first line should have five syllables, the second line should have seven syllables, and the third line should have five syllables.

Please note that excerpts and passages in the StudySync® library and this workbook are intended as touchstones to generate interest in an author's work. The excerpts and passages do not substitute for the reading of entire texts, and StudySync® strongly recommends that students seek out and purchase the whole literary or informational work in order to experience it as the author intended. Links to online resellers are available in our digital library. In addition, complete works may be ordered through an authorized reseller by filling out and returning to StudySync® the order form enclosed in this workbook.

Reading & Writing
Companion

701

# Parsley

POETRY
Rita Dove
1983

## Introduction

Renowned poet and essayist Rita Dove (b. 1952) was born and raised in Akron, Ohio. In addition to being a Pulitzer Prize recipient, Dove became the first African American (not to mention the youngest ever) to be selected as American Poet Laureate. The breadth and scope of Dove's work is celebrated for its lyricism, compassion and insight, as well as its forays into a wide range of cultural, political, and historical landscapes. One of her most noted works is 1983's "Parsley," a meditation on a real-world incident known to history as *La Masacre del Perejil* (the Parsley Massacre). In 1937, dictator Rafael Trujillo ordered the execution of all Haitians living in the Dominican Republic by using the Spanish word for "parsley" —*perejil*—to distinguish ethnic Haitians from native Dominicans based on differences in how the two linguistic groups commonly pronounced the *r* sound. His order resulted in the deaths of up to 20,000 people.

# "El General has found his word: *perejil.* / Who says it, lives."

The Dominican Republic and Haiti, which share a border.

*1. The Cane Fields[1]*

1 There is a parrot imitating spring
2 in the palace, its feathers parsley green.
3 Out of the swamp the cane appears

4 to haunt us, and we cut it down. El General[2]
5 searches for a word; he is all the world
6 there is. Like a parrot imitating spring,

7 we lie down screaming as rain punches through
8 and we come up green. We cannot speak an R—
9 out of the swamp, the cane appears

10 and then the mountain we call in whispers *Katalina.*
11 The children gnaw their teeth to arrowheads.
12 There is a parrot imitating spring.

Skill:
Textual Evidence

*The parrot may symbolize false hope or the contrast between lies and reality. The line that the bird is "imitating" spring is repeated, but in reality life here is awful. The people work in a swamp cutting sugar cane.*

---

1. **Cane Fields** sugarcane, an East Asian food crop, was introduced to Hispaniola (the island comprising Haiti and the Dominican Republic) by Cristoforo Colombo, or Columbus
2. **El General** Rafael Trujillo (1891–1961), military dictator of the Dominican Republic

**Skill: Connotation and Denotation**

Both definitions of *shining* have a positive connotation. Here the word feels darker. The word refers to his teeth and is followed by the phrase "out of the swamp." Shining teeth and swamps remind me of alligators.

**Skill: Connotation and Denotation**

The poet has chosen the word *kill*, a far less complex word than, say, *massacre*. In context, with words like *stomps* and *screams*, the choice of *kill* makes sense: the general is like a baby having a terrible tantrum.

13  El General has found his word: *perejil*[3].
14  Who says it, lives. He laughs, teeth shining
15  out of the swamp. The cane appears

16  in our dreams, **lashed** by wind and streaming.
17  And we lie down. For every drop of blood
18  there is a parrot imitating spring.
19  Out of the swamp the cane appears.

*2. The Palace*

20  The word the general's chosen is parsley.
21  It is fall, when thoughts turn
22  to love and death; the general thinks
23  of his mother, how she died in the fall
24  and he planted her walking cane at the grave
25  and it flowered, each spring **stolidly** forming
26  four-star blossoms. The general

27  pulls on his boots, he stomps to
28  her room in the palace, the one without
29  curtains, the one with a parrot
30  in a brass ring. As he paces he wonders
31  Who can I kill today. And for a moment
32  the little knot of screams
33  is still. The parrot, who has traveled

34  all the way from Australia in an ivory
35  cage, is, **coy** as a widow, practising
36  spring. Ever since the morning
37  his mother collapsed in the kitchen
38  while baking skull-shaped candies
39  for the Day of the Dead[4], the general
40  has hated sweets. He orders pastries
41  brought up for the bird; they arrive

42  dusted with sugar on a bed of lace.
43  The knot in his throat starts to twitch;
44  he sees his boots the first day in battle
45  splashed with mud and urine
46  as a soldier falls at his feet amazed—
47  how stupid he looked!— at the sound
48  of **artillery.** *I never thought it would sing*

---

3. *Perejil* (Spanish) parsley
4. **Day of the Dead** an annual festival of Mexican origin honoring the dead

---

49  the soldier said, and died. Now

50  the general sees the fields of sugar
51  cane, lashed by rain and streaming.
52  He sees his mother's smile, the teeth
53  gnawed to arrowheads. He hears
54  the Haitians sing without R's
55  as they swing the great machetes:
56  *Katalina,* they sing, *Katalina,*

57  *mi madle, mi amol en muelte.* God knows
58  his mother was no stupid woman; she
59  could roll an R like a queen. Even
60  a parrot can roll an R! In the bare room
61  the bright feathers arch in a **parody**
62  of greenery, as the last pale crumbs
63  disappear under the blackened tongue. Someone

64  calls out his name in a voice
65  so like his mother's, a startled tear
66  splashes the tip of his right boot.
67  *My mother, my love in death.*
68  The general remembers the tiny green sprigs
69  men of his village wore in their capes
70  to honor the birth of a son. He will
71  order many, this time, to be killed

72  for a single, beautiful word.

From *Museum* by Rita Dove, Carnegie-Mellon University Press, 1983.
Reprinted by permission of the author.

Please note that excerpts and passages in the StudySync® library and this workbook are intended as touchstones to generate interest in an author's work. The excerpts and passages do not substitute for the reading of entire texts, and StudySync® strongly recommends that students seek out and purchase the whole literary or informational work in order to experience it as the author intended. Links to online resellers are available in our digital library. In addition, complete works may be ordered through an authorized reseller by filling out and returning to StudySync® the order form enclosed in this workbook.

Reading & Writing
Companion

**705**

# First Read

Read "Parsley." After you read, complete the Think Questions below.

## ☁ THINK QUESTIONS

1. In two or three sentences, explain the significance of the poem's title. Illustrate your answer using details from the text.

2. Who is the speaker of the poem? Support your inferences using ideas from the text that are directly stated or implied.

3. What evidence can you find in the poem that indicates the general's mother used to work in the cane fields? Be sure to reference specific lines from the text in your answer.

4. Use context clues to determine the meaning of the word **coy** as it is used in the text. Write your definition of *coy* and explain how you figured it out.

5. Keeping in mind that the prefix *par* can mean "contrary to" or "wrong" (*paranoid*, for example) use your knowledge of the prefix and context clues in the passage to determine the meaning of **parody**. Write your definition of *parody*. Then check your inferred meaning in a print or digital dictionary.

# Skill:
# Textual Evidence

Use the Checklist to analyze Textual Evidence in "Parsley." Refer to the sample student annotation about Textual Evidence in the text.

## ••• CHECKLIST FOR TEXTUAL EVIDENCE

In order to support an analysis by citing evidence that is explicitly stated in the text, do the following:

- ✓ Read the text closely and critically.

- ✓ Identify what the text says explicitly.

- ✓ Find the most relevant textual evidence that supports your analysis.

- ✓ Consider why an author explicitly states specific details.

- ✓ Cite the specific words, phrases, lines, or stanzas from the text that support your analysis.

In order to interpret implicit meanings in a text by making inferences, do the following:

- ✓ Combine information directly stated in the text with your own knowledge, experiences, and observations.

- ✓ Cite the specific words, phrases, sentences, or paragraphs from the text that led to and support this inference.

In order to cite textual evidence to support an analysis of what the text says explicitly as well as inferences drawn from the text, consider the following questions:

- ✓ Have I read the text closely and critically?

- ✓ What inferences am I making about the text?

- ✓ What textual evidence am I using to support these inferences?

- ✓ Am I quoting the evidence from the text correctly?

- ✓ Does my textual evidence logically relate to my analysis or the inference I am making?

Please note that excerpts and passages in the StudySync® library and this workbook are intended as touchstones to generate interest in an author's work. The excerpts and passages do not substitute for the reading of entire texts, and StudySync® strongly recommends that students seek out and purchase the whole literary or informational work in order to experience it as the author intended. Links to online resellers are available in our digital library. In addition, complete works may be ordered through an authorized reseller by filling out and returning to StudySync® the order form enclosed in this workbook.

Reading & Writing Companion    707

# Skill:
# Textual Evidence

Reread lines 8–19 of "Parsley." Then, using the Checklist on the previous page, answer the multiple-choice questions below.

## ↻ YOUR TURN

1. This question has two parts. First, answer Part A. Then, answer Part B.

   **Part A:** Which of the following best describes what the cane symbolizes in lines 8–19?

   ○ A. It symbolizes hope.

   ○ B. It symbolizes oppression.

   ○ C. It symbolizes the inability to pronounce *R*.

   ○ D. It symbolizes the dangerous side of nature.

   **Part B:** Which piece of textual evidence BEST supports your answer from Part A?

   ○ A. "He laughs, teeth shining."

   ○ B. "There is a parrot imitating spring."

   ○ C. "El General has found his word: *perejil*."

   ○ D. "The cane appears/in our dreams, lashed by wind and streaming."

# Skill:
# Connotation and Denotation

Use the Checklist to analyze Connotation and Denotation in "Parsley." Refer to the sample student annotations about Connotation and Denotation in the text.

## ••• CHECKLIST FOR CONNOTATION AND DENOTATION

In order to identify the denotative meanings of words, use the following steps:

✓ First, note unfamiliar words and phrases, key words used to describe important characters, events, and ideas, or words that inspire an emotional reaction.

✓ Next, determine and note the denotative meaning of words by consulting a reference material such as a dictionary, glossary, or thesaurus.

✓ Finally, analyze nuances in the meaning of words with similar denotations.

To better understand the meaning of words and phrases as they are used in a text, including connotative meanings, use the following questions as a guide:

✓ What is the genre or subject of the text? Based on context, what do you think the meaning of the word is intended to be?

✓ Is your inference the same as or different from the dictionary definition?

✓ Does the word create a positive, negative, or neutral emotion?

✓ What synonyms or alternative phrasing help you describe the connotative meaning of the word?

To determine the meaning of words and phrases as they are used in a text, including connotative meanings, use the following questions as a guide:

✓ What is the denotative meaning of the word? Is that denotative meaning correct in context?

✓ What possible positive, neutral, or negative connotations might the word have, depending on context?

✓ What textual details signal a particular connotation for the word?

# Skill:
# Connotation and Denotation

Reread lines 65–72 of "Parsley." Then, using the Checklist on the previous page, answer the multiple-choice questions below.

## ♻ YOUR TURN

1. This question has two parts. First, answer Part A. Then, answer Part B.

   **Part A:** How does the connotative meaning of the phrase "tiny green sprigs" change over the course of this section of the poem?

   ○ A.  The connotative meaning changes from distressed to soothing.
   ○ B.  The connotative meaning changes from joyous to horrifying.
   ○ C.  The connotative meaning changes from pleasant to unhappy.
   ○ D.  The connotative meaning changes from playful to indifferent.

   **Part B:** Which of the following lines BEST supports your response to Part A?

   ○ A.  "My mother, my love in death."
   ○ B.  "men of his village wore in their capes"
   ○ C.  "to honor the birth of a son. He will / order many, this time, to be killed"
   ○ D.  "for a single, beautiful word"

# Close Read

Reread "Parsley." As you reread, complete the Skills Focus questions below. Then use your answers and annotations from the questions to help you complete the Write activity.

## ◎ SKILLS FOCUS

1. Identify a portion of the poem in which the speaker uses the pronoun *we*. Explain how the poet's use of this pronoun impacts the tone of the poem.

2. Explain the implicit meaning of part 1 of the poem. In your response, discuss how the poem's imagery helps to convey an essential truth about the Haitian laborers' experience.

3. Compare the two parts of the poem, "The Cane Fields" and "The Palace." Explain how the contrast between the points of view of the general and the Haitian laborers in these parts strengthens the poem's theme.

4. Highlight the following lines of the poem: "In the bare room / the bright feathers arch in a parody / of greenery, as the last pale crumbs / disappear under the blackened tongue." Discuss the author's language in these lines and explain the tone the language creates. As you analyze the author's word choice, think of both denotative and connotative word meanings.

5. Thinking of sugar cane as an ingredient of culture, use evidence from the poem to analyze the cost of this resource to the people depicted in the poem.

## ✏ WRITE

LITERARY ANALYSIS: In this political poem, Dove uses symbolism to convey themes about inequality, prejudice, violence, and family. Remembering that a symbol is often a material item that stands for something else, such as a flag for patriotism, choose one symbol that is central to the poem's meaning. Write a literary analysis in which you interpret the meaning of this symbol and explain how the poet uses it to develop a specific theme.

Please note that excerpts and passages in the StudySync® library and this workbook are intended as touchstones to generate interest in an author's work. The excerpts and passages do not substitute for the reading of entire texts, and StudySync® strongly recommends that students seek out and purchase the whole literary or informational work in order to experience it as the author intended. Links to online resellers are available in our digital library. In addition, complete works may be ordered through an authorized reseller by filling out and returning to StudySync® the order form enclosed in this workbook.

Reading & Writing Companion 711

# The Latin Deli: An Ars Poetica

POETRY
Judith Ortiz Cofer
1993

## Introduction

Acclaimed author Judith Ortiz Cofer (1952–2016) was born in Puerto Rico but spent most of her childhood in Paterson, New Jersey, before moving to Georgia as a teenager. Writing in a variety of literary genres, including poetry, short stories, essays and autobiography, Ortiz Cofer's work draws from personal experience to explore cultural conflicts, women's issues, and the American South. As is often true in her work, "The Latin Deli: An Ars Poetica" captures the intimate, poignant struggles of people transplanted to a new culture and way of life.

# "she is the Patroness of Exiles, a woman of no-age who was never pretty"

1 Presiding over a formica counter,
2 Plastic Mother and Child magnetized
3 to the top of an ancient register,
4 the heady mix of smells from the open bins
5 of dried codfish, the green plantains
6 hanging in stalks like **votive** offerings,
7 she is the **Patroness** of **Exiles**,
8 a woman of no-age who was never pretty,
9 who spends her days selling canned memories
10 while listening to the Puerto Ricans complain
11 that it would be cheaper to fly to San Juan
12 than to buy a pound of Bustelo coffee[1] here,
13 and to the Cubans perfecting their speech
14 of a "glorious return" to Havana—where no one
15 has been allowed to die and nothing to change until then;
16 to Mexicans who pass through, talking **lyrically**
17 of dólares[2] to be made in El Norte—

18 all wanting the comfort
19 of spoken Spanish, to gaze upon the family portrait
20 of her plain wide face, her ample bosom
21 resting on her plump arms, her look of **maternal** interest
22 as they speak to her and each other
23 of their dreams and their **disillusions**—
24 how she smiles understanding,
25 when they walk down the narrow aisles of her store
26 reading the labels of the packages aloud, as if
27 they were the names of lost lovers: Suspiros[3],
28 Merengues, the stale candy of everyone's childhood.

 Skill: Figurative Language

*The simile comparing the food to votives, as in church, develops a sense of the deli as a sacred place.
"Patroness of Exiles" alludes to a phrase, "Mother of Exiles," in a poem about the Statue of Liberty.*

---

1. **Bustelo coffee** Café Bustelo, a brand of coffee founded in New York City preferred by many Cuban immigrants
2. **dólares** (Spanish) dollars
3. **Suspiros** a Mexican bakery chain

29  She spends her days
30  Slicing *jamón y queso*⁴ and wrapping it in wax paper
31  tied with string: plain ham and cheese
32  that would cost less at the A&P⁵, but it would not satisfy
33  the hunger of the fragile old man lost in the folds
34  of his winter coat, who brings her lists of items
35  that he reads to her like poetry, or the others,
36  whose needs she must **divine**, conjuring up products
37  from places that now exist only in their hearts—
38  closed ports she must trade with.

Skill: Figurative Language

The metaphor compares the customers' hearts to "closed ports." Ports are where ships load and unload; their port is empty. The customers are cut off from their homelands, and the owner "trades," or sells the items they miss.

"The Latin Deli: An Ars Poetica" is reprinted with permission from the publisher of "America's Review" by Judith Ortiz Cofer (©1992 Arte Publico Press - University of Houston)

4. **jamón y queso**  (Spanish) ham and cheese
5. **A&P**  an American grocery store chain that operated from 1859 to 2015

# First Read

Read "The Latin Deli: An Ars Poetica." After you read, complete the Think Questions below.

 **THINK QUESTIONS**

1. Refer to one or more details from the text to describe the physical setting of this poem in both objective and subjective terms. Which of the five senses does the poet write about in her description?

2. Use details from the text to write two or three sentences that explore the poet's frequent references to speech and language in the poem. From these, what inferences can you make about the shopkeeper's attitude toward her clients?

3. Why do you think the Latin deli attracts so many customers despite its high prices? Support your response with evidence from the text.

4. Use context to determine the meaning and part of speech of the word **lyrically**. Write your definition of the word. Briefly explain how the multiple meanings of the base word *lyric* might have influenced Ortiz Cofer's decision to include this particular word in her poem.

5. Remembering that the Latin word *mater* means "mother," use the context clues provided in the passage to determine the meaning of **maternal**. Write your definition of *maternal* and explain how other context clues in the poem help you verify that definition.

Please note that excerpts and passages in the StudySync® library and this workbook are intended as touchstones to generate interest in an author's work. The excerpts and passages do not substitute for the reading of entire texts, and StudySync® strongly recommends that students seek out and purchase the whole literary or informational work in order to experience it as the author intended. Links to online resellers are available in our digital library. In addition, complete works may be ordered through an authorized reseller by filling out and returning to StudySync® the order form enclosed in this workbook.

Reading & Writing Companion   **715**

# Skill:
# Figurative Language

Use the Checklist to analyze Figurative Language in "The Latin Deli: An Ars Poetica." Refer to the sample student annotations about Figurative Language in the text.

## ••• CHECKLIST FOR FIGURATIVE LANGUAGE

In order to determine the meaning of a figure of speech in context, note the following:

✓ words that mean one thing literally and suggest something else

✓ similes, metaphors, or personification

✓ figures of speech, including

- allusions, or indirect references to works of literature, historical events, or other well-known subjects (e.g., "a Scrooge" for a stingy person, alluding to *A Christmas Carol*)

- oxymorons, or a figure of speech in which apparently contradictory terms appear in conjunction, such as

  > a description such as "deafening silence"

  > sayings such as "seriously funny"

- euphemisms, or a mild or indirect word or expression substituted for one considered to be too harsh when referring to something unpleasant or embarrassing, such as

  > saying someone has "passed away" instead of "died"

  > using the term "correctional facility" instead of "prison"

In order to interpret a figure of speech in context and analyze its role in the text, consider the following questions:

✓ Where is there figurative language language in the text and what seems to be the purpose of the author's use of it?

✓ Why does the author use a figure of speech rather than literal language?

✓ How do allusions, euphemisms, or oxymorons affect the meaning of the text?

✓ How does the figurative language develop the message or theme of the literary work?

## Skill:
## Figurative Language

Reread lines 18–28 of "The Latin Deli: An Ars Poetica." Then, using the Checklist on the previous page, answer the multiple-choice questions below.

### ⟳ YOUR TURN

1. How does the use of the figure of speech "the family portrait" describe the feelings of the customers for the shopkeeper?

   ○ A. It shows that the customers see the shopkeeper as an overprotective mother.

   ○ B. It implies that the customers look upon the shopkeeper with disdain and anger.

   ○ C. It shows that the customers look upon the shopkeeper with a familial warmth and kindness.

   ○ D. It suggests that the customers see the shopkeeper as someone who can teach them how to grow up.

2. The poet's use of metaphor in lines 26 and 27 has the effect of—

   ○ A. emphasizing the customers' appreciation for the shopkeeper.

   ○ B. highlighting the customers' feelings of homesickness.

   ○ C. drawing attention to the customers' hopefulness.

   ○ D. introducing a theme about the need for romantic love.

# Close Read

Reread "The Latin Deli: An Ars Poetica." As you reread, complete the Skills Focus questions below. Then use your answers and annotations from the questions to help you complete the Write activity.

## ◎ SKILLS FOCUS

1. Identify one example in the poem of how Ortiz Cofer uses food in a figurative way. Analyze the role of this figurative language in the poem.

2. Identify a theme of the poem and explain its development, including how it emerges and is refined by specific details and figurative language.

3. Analyze the poet's choices concerning the structure and style of the poem, and explain the emotional effects she creates.

4. Though Ortiz Cofer was an American poet, her speaker discusses Cubans as well as Puerto Ricans (who are American citizens) throughout the poem. Analyze the ways in which the speaker reveals a particular point of view about culture from outside the United States.

## ✏ WRITE

ARGUMENTATIVE: When you think of art, you may picture a fancy museum with an admission fee and beautiful works framed on the walls. "The Latin Deli: An Ars Poetica" gives a different and less obvious interpretation of what constitutes art. In what ways is the owner of the deli an artist? Make a claim and support it with evidence from the poem.

# Curry:
## A Tale of Cooks and Conquerors

INFORMATIONAL TEXT
Lizzie Collingham
2007

## Introduction

In *Curry: A Tale of Cooks and Conquerors*, food historian Lizzie Collingham explores the historical mixing of cultures from which numerous Indian cuisines are derived. Through colonization, invasion, and trade, the ingredients and practices of contemporary Indian dining—including spices, vinegars and cooking preferences—began to coalesce. Collingham also considers the role Indian food plays worldwide, traveling from the subcontinent to Europe, the Americas, and East Asia. In this excerpt, Collingham uses chicken tikka masala to argue that the concept of "authenticity" is often overvalued.

# "What does authenticity really mean?"

### Chapter 1: Chicken Tikka Masala: The Quest for an Authentic Indian Meal

1 The area in Manhattan where 1st Avenue intersects with East 6th Street is so overcrowded with Indian restaurants that it is known as "Curry Row." Here you can order a lamb vindaloo, a seafood biryani, a sweet yellow dhansak, or a mild and creamy beef korma with side dishes of aloo gobi and naan bread. This catalogue of dishes conjures up the aroma of fried onions; windows adorned with bright red fairy lights, white tablecloths, patchy service, Indian music humming in the background, and a two-course meal for under $20.

2 Further uptown at Utsav on 6th Avenue the cheerful but **utilitarian** atmosphere of gaudy lights and bright colors have been exchanged for pale peach walls and plush carpeting. Utsav is an example of a new breed of Indian restaurant. The fountain in the entrance gives the place a touch of class; high ceilings, large airy windows, and comfortable banquettes add a luxurious feel to the dining room. The menu too, is different from the standard Indian restaurant. The choice of any familiar curry with chicken, lamb, or beef has been replaced by more specialized regional dishes, ranging from Kashmiri-style shrimp curry to Goan chicken xacutti and Konkan coconut-flavored fish. Utsav places great emphasis on authenticity of flavor and the higher prices match this attention to detail and quality.

3 Utsav is an example of one of the many new-style Indian restaurants that have begun opening in both America and Britain. In London restaurants such as Veeraswamy's and Zaika are examples of this new trend, the results of a new breed of Indian chefs making a bid to elevate Indian food from its status as cheap nosh to an elegant cuisine, every bit as sophisticated as French cookery. On both sides of the Atlantic, these high-class restaurants place great value on the authenticity of their food. The chefs are often specially trained in India and cook only dishes from their home region. Even the more traditional restaurants are beginning to follow this trend and advertise their dishes as "authentic." Supermarkets, too, offer an "authentic" Indian experience with every ready-prepared Indian meal. But what does authenticity really mean? And is authenticity really the right yardstick by which to judge an Indian meal?

4    In Britain this debate was brought to a head in 2001 when the then foreign minister Robin Cook announced chicken tikka masala as the new national dish of Great Britain. Food critics immediately responded by condemning it as a British invention. Chicken tikka masala, they sneered, was not a shining example of British multiculturalism[1] but a demonstration of the British **facility** for reducing foreign foods to their most unappetizing and inedible forms. Rather than the inspired invention of an enterprising Indian chef, this offensive dish was dismissed as the result of an ignorant customer's complaint that his chicken tikka was too dry. When the chef whipped together a can of Campbell's tomato soup, some cream, and a few spices to provide a gravy for the offending chicken, he produced a **mongrel** dish of which, to their shame, Britons now eat at least 18 tons a week. Chicken tikka masala's most **heinous** crime, according to its critics, is not so much that it tastes horrid but that it is not authentic. In fact, journalists in Britain and America report with glee that none of the curries we eat in old-style curry houses are authentic, not to mention the fact that the "Indian" food they serve is cooked by Bangladeshis.

5    The majority of Indian restaurant owners in Britain, and most of the proprietors of New York's East 6th Street establishments, do indeed come from Bangladesh. However, for much of the period that this book covers, Bangladesh, like Pakistan and Sri Lanka, belonged to a broader food world that can be termed Indian. It was not until 1947 that Pakistan became a nation. Sri Lanka followed in 1948. And Bangladesh split from Pakistan in 1971. Food on the Indian subcontinent does not divide into different culinary styles and dishes along these relatively new national boundaries so much as along much older regional boundaries. The food of Bangladesh belongs to the culinary world of Bengal. Punjabis share a food culture although their region was split in two with the creation of Pakistan. These are just two of the many culinary regions on the Indian subcontinent.

6    In fact, the food of people from one region of India is sometimes unrecognizable as Indian food to someone from another. Satya, a villager from the Punjab, arrived in Delhi in the 1950s. She had never traveled outside the Punjab before and she found the customs of the other people living in her apartment building strange and fascinating. She noted with astonishment that the Madrassi family "preferred rice with their food, not chapaties like our Punjab folk. Whatever vegetables they prepare—lentils, aubergines, tomatoes—they must have rice to go with them. Then they scrape it all up in balls with their fingers so that the juice runs down their forearms, not neatly with a piece of chapati or a spoon. So one day I said... 'Look, why don't you eat like we do? After all, you are people of good family. Surely where you come from people

---

1. **multiculturalism** the respect and honoring of traits and aspects of various component cultures of a polyglot society; in contrast to the idea of the "melting pot"

don't eat like that?'" The neighbor "was very offended and abused me roundly, when I had only meant to tell her nicely that we didn't like to watch such messy eating." The outraged Madrassi might well have retorted that while her food might be sloppy and messy to eat, at least it wasn't heavy and greasy like the Punjabi food Satya and her family ate. If the women ever recovered their friendship, they might well have united in condemning their Gujarati neighbors for their penchant for sickly sweet food, their Bengali neighbors for filling the place with the reek of mustard oil, and their Telugu neighbors for producing meals that were unbearably hot.

7  The differences in regional tastes are so pronounced that they translate into foods from other culinary cultures. In Bombay, a Maratha Hindu street vendor serves "Chinese" lunches to office workers on Narima Point. But before preparing the food he assesses the regional origin of his customer and adjusts the flavor accordingly. For Gujaratis he adds some extra sauce to sweeten it; for Punjabis he adds extra chilli.

8  The range of culinary styles within India means that authenticity is more accurately tied to a region. But the regional subdivisions of Indian food are complicated by local patterns of consumption, as Francis Buchanan discovered when he was traveling across southern India in the early nineteenth century. He was observant of the **minutiae** of everyday life and noticed that in each locality the people relied on a different grain (rice, wheat, millet, sorghum) as the mainstay of their diet. "Habit," he wrote, "seems to be able to render every kind of grain sufficiently wholesome." But the peasants were unable to adapt to a different grain and when "compelled or induced to try another" their digestions became disordered. This was brought home to him by his servants, all suffering miserably from stomach complaints due to the constant changes in the staple grain as they traveled. Buchanan was surrounded by gloomy Indians homesick for their customary foods.

9  The staple food of each locality still ties people to their land and their community today. Indians from Bangladesh to Tamil Nadu believe that the local qualities of the soil and water are absorbed into the grain crop. When the grain is consumed it imparts these qualities to the population, giving them their strength. In Bangladesh, rice grown on village land is valued as more nutritious and more filling than rice bought at the market. Eating local-grown rice fills the villagers with the nature of their home and binds them to their community. Before setting out on a journey a traveler is required to eat large amounts of village-grown rice, to fill him with the essences of home.

*Excerpted from Curry: A Tale of Cooks and Conquerors by Lizzie Collingham, published by Oxford University Press.*

Copyright © Bookheaded Learning, LLC

## ✏ WRITE

DISCUSSION: To what extent does food serve as a metaphor for culture? Synthesize evidence from this text and at least one other text from the unit to support your opinion. Prepare to discuss with your peers by writing down your thoughts on this question, as well as your reasoning and examples from the texts you chose to support your thinking.

# Chinese Cooking

INFORMATIONAL TEXT
Chen Jitong
1878

## Introduction

Chen Jitong (1851–1907) was a diplomat and scholar who endeavored to represent the culture of the late Qing dynasty to international audiences. In "Chinese Cooking," Jitong recounts firsthand experiences of his time as a Chinese ambassador in 19th-century Paris, especially those experiences that left him questioning Europeans' judgment of his Chinese heritage—in particular, the country's food. A celebrity in Parisian culture, Jitong's writing in French (which he learned as an adult) aims to disabuse Europeans of uninformed prejudices about Chinese food.

# "But never are disgusting or even curious dishes seen on our tables."

1   Once a Berlin lady, after having found that our cooking was delicious, asked the name of each of the dishes of one of our interpreters, who, not knowing the exact translation of the technical expression, "seaslug," answered that the dish in question was "sea hedgehog," or "*seeigel*" in German. This was enough to disgust our **amiable** guest, who refused to continue her dinner. I was sitting next to her, and she told me that she could feel it crawling in her throat still, which shows how great is the force of imagination.

2   Marquis d'Hervey de Saint-Denys[1] gave a Chinese dinner during the Exhibition of 1867[2], and Cham, the famous caricaturist, drew the menu. There were some abominable things in this bill of fare, and the faces of the guests after they had glanced at it was a sight to be seen. It took the marquis all his eloquence to reassure them. I will not deny that there are people in China who eat

Bird's-eye view of the International Exposition of 1867 in Paris.

these extraordinary dishes, but these are the exceptions to the rule. I repeat here, that never in my life have I seen or heard of anyone who ate cat or dog, a practice which only quite recently a writer in the *Figaro*[3] accused us of.

3   Apropos of this, I must relate a very **curious** thing that befell us, when, in the spring of 1878, our **legation** first settled in Paris. One day I received a call from a footman[4] in livery[5], who desired to speak to me in the name of his mistress, a Polish countess of very high position. This lady had among her pets twelve

---

1. **Marquis d'Hervey de Saint-Denys** French sinologist (student of China) 1822–1892 who introduced many Chinese fruits, vegetables, and herbs to the West and is known as the father of 'lucid dreaming'
2. **Exhibition of 1867** the Universal Exposition of Art and Industry was the second World's Fair hosted in Paris, with exhibits from 42 countries
3. *Figaro* the national newspaper of France, published daily in Paris since 1826
4. **footman** a house servant who attends to guests, as a porter might in a hotel
5. **livery** the uniform of a servant or official

little Chinese dogs, those hairless little bow-wows that everybody has seen. She loved them dearly, and being frightened lest the Chinese colony might eat up her darlings, sent me word, considering us apparently as wild beasts or savages, to the effect that if one of her pets should disappear, she would set fire to the embassy building. I reassured the good old lady, and sent her word that none of my countrymen had an appetite for dog meat, and that should she miss one of her pets one day, it would be much wiser on her part, before committing the crime of arson with premeditation, to go round to the police station or to the dogs' home.

4    In short, we eat very much as you do, with rather more variety, thanks to the productiveness of our country and of our sea. But never are disgusting or even curious dishes seen on our tables. It is true that we prepare our dishes in a different manner. For instance, we cut the food up into very little pieces, in consequence of which the nature of the dish is not to be recognized, but our dishes are nonetheless delicious on that account. I could call in witness of what I **assert** all Europeans who have lived in China.

5    Cooking, moreover, is in exact ratio to the state of civilization of each nation—the more developed the one, the more recherché[6] and the more perfect the other. France is the country in Europe which was civilized the first, and its cuisine is the most perfect in the West. So, instead of asking us whether we are in the habit of preparing such and such a fantastic dish, the European would do better to ask from what year our civilization dates. The answer to this question would at once show him that it is absurd to **attribute** to us the consumption of disgusting dishes, and that this is the work of mere imagination, vivid perhaps, but completely in the wrong.

## ✏ WRITE

NARRATIVE: Think of a time when a cultural norm, family tradition, or aspect of language you grew up perceiving as normal was met with curiosity, questions, or confusion by someone else. What happened? How did you react? What did you learn? Use descriptive details and reflection to engage your audience and communicate the significance of the event.

6. **recherché** obscure or arcane

# The New Food Fights:
## U.S. Public Divides Over Food Science

INFORMATIONAL TEXT
Cary Funk and Brian Kennedy
2016

## Introduction

This article digs deeper into a fascinating Pew Research Center survey about how Americans understand healthy eating—and how their understanding is impacted by the research of the scientific community. Broadly speaking, Americans' views of healthy eating are influenced by their peer groups, their levels of scientific knowledge, and even their political affiliations. This survey seeks to provide a better understanding of how Americans view what "healthy" means, how they make choices about what to eat, and how they are influenced, in this modern age of information, by the constant and daily stream of scientific food research in the news cycle.

# "Food studies and their conflicting findings abound, but most Americans see this as a sign of progress."

**Public views about Americans' eating habits**

1   The American food scene has undergone considerable change over the past two decades. During this period, the public has seen the introduction of genetically modified crops, the mainstreaming of organic foods into America's supermarkets, and the proliferation of chefs elevated to celebrity status within popular culture.

2   Over the same period, there has been a marked increase in public health concerns about the growing prevalence of obesity among both children and adults. Perhaps sparked by thinking from people such as Michael Pollan, Mark Bittman, and documentaries such as Morgan Spurlock's "Super Size Me," Americans' thinking about food has shifted dramatically.

3   Concerns about obesity, food allergies and other health effects of food are fueling a new level of scrutiny of chemicals and additives in foods and contribute to shifting notions about portion size, sugar and fat content. Consumption of sugary sodas has dropped to a 30-year low while sales of bottled and flavored water rose dramatically over the past few decades. Zero-calorie diet sodas long held allure for Americans concerned about their weight, but sales of diet sodas have also dropped, with at least some arguing that the decline has been fueled by growing public concern about ingesting artificial sweeteners and other food additives. America's love affair with fast-food chains is on the **wane**, with "fast casual" brands that offer convenient options which focus on natural, fresh ingredients gaining favor.

4   To some degree this is reflected in the emergence of distinct groups that can be identified by their focus on food issues and personal eating habits. New thinking about ways to eat healthy helped launch a number of eating "movements" with proponents arguing that Paleo, anti-inflammatory or vegan diets bring health benefits along with better weight control. Food and the way we eat has become a potential source of social friction as people follow their own ideologies about what to eat and how foods connect with people's **ailments**.

Skill: Technical Language

*Technical terms such as* calorie, artificial, *and* additives *demonstrate that the text is about food. The cumulative impact of the word choices stresses concerns about sweeteners and weight.*

5   During this same period, there have been sometimes strident public debates over science-related topics — most prominently on climate change, but also on a host of others including the environmental impacts of fracking and nuclear power, the safety of childhood vaccines and, of course, the safety of genetically modified foods. A previous Pew Research Center report showed that public attitudes on a wide range of science issues were widely **divergent** from those of members of the American Association of Advancement of Science (AAAS). In fact, the largest differences between the public and members of the AAAS were beliefs about the safety of eating genetically modified (GM) foods. Nearly nine-in-ten (88%) AAAS members said it is generally safe to eat GM foods compared with 37% of the general public, a difference of 51 percentage points. The wide differences of opinion over GM foods is connected with a broader public discourse over the role of science research and, perhaps, scientific expertise in understanding and crafting policy solutions.

6   This new Pew Research Center survey explores public thinking about scientists and their research on GM foods in some detail. As such, this survey can help address the ways in which public views of and trust in scientists may contribute to an opinion divide between the public and members of the scientific community on these issues.

7   In broad strokes, the survey shows that Americans believe the public is paying more attention to healthy eating today than they did 20 years ago. But, it is not clear to the public whether people are actually eating healthier today. About half of U.S. adults think the eating habits of Americans are *less* healthy today than they were 20 years ago and most point the blame at both the quantity and quality of what people eat.

8   Many Americans adopt their own food and eating philosophies because they have to — or want to. Some 15% of U.S. adults say they have at least mild allergies to one or more foods and another 17% have intolerances to foods. Food allergies are more common among women, blacks and people with chronic lung conditions such as asthma. A small minority of Americans describe themselves as either strictly or mostly eating vegan or vegetarian diets.

**Americans are paying attention to healthy eating, but many miss the mark**

9   Collectively, the American public is paying more attention to healthy eating, but not fully embracing what they learn. At least, that's how most Americans see things, according to this survey.

Skill: Technical Language

*Percentages and technical terms such as allergies, lung conditions, and asthma give the text a serious tone, showing that the authors know what they are talking about because of research. It doesn't sound biased.*

Skill: Informational Text Elements

*The authors begin to organize their ideas by presenting them with subheadings. The purpose of the subheading is to show that the article is moving into specific topics and to give an idea of what the section is about.*

10 

## Perceptions of the American appetite: More pay attention to healthy eating but fewer reach that goal

*% of U.S. adults who say that compared with twenty years ago ...*

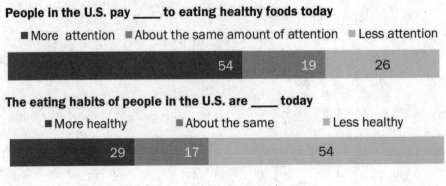

**People in the U.S. pay ____ to eating healthy foods today**

■ More attention ■ About the same amount of attention ■ Less attention

| 54 | 19 | 26 |

**The eating habits of people in the U.S. are ____ today**

■ More healthy ■ About the same ■ Less healthy

| 29 | 17 | 54 |

Note: Respondents who did not give an answer are not shown.
Source: Survey conducted May 10-June 6, 2016.
"The New Food Fights: U.S. Public Divides Over Food Science"

**PEW RESEARCH CENTER**

11  Some 54% of Americans say that compared with 20 years ago, people in the U.S. pay more attention to eating healthy foods today. Smaller shares say people pay less attention (26%) or about the same amount of attention (19%) to eating healthy today.

12  But 54% of Americans say eating habits in the U.S. are less healthy than they were 20 years ago. A minority (29%) say eating habits are healthier today, while 17% say they are about the same.

*The header, color key, and bar in this graphic feature illustrate the data and information explained in the following paragraph. Readers can see that the authors rely on data, and restating the data helps comprehension.*

13 

## A majority of the public says both quality and quantity of Americans' food consumption is a problem

*% of U.S. adults who say ____ is the bigger problem in the U.S. today*

■ The types of food people eat are not healthy enough
■ The total amount of food people eat is too much
■ Both are equally big problems

| 24 | 12 | 63 |

Note: Respondents who did not give an answer are not shown.
Source: Survey conducted May 10-June 6, 2016.
"The New Food Fights: U.S. Public Divides Over Food Science"

**PEW RESEARCH CENTER**

NOTES

14  The public points the finger at both quality and quantity in Americans' eating habits. When asked which is the bigger source of problems in Americans' eating habits, more say the issue is what people eat, not how much (24% vs. 12%). But a 63% majority says that both are equally big problems in the U.S. today.

15  These beliefs are somewhat tied to people's focus on food issues. People who care a great deal about the issue of GM foods are particularly likely to say Americans' eating habits have **deteriorated** over the past two decades: 67% hold this view, compared with 53% among those not at all or not too concerned about the GM foods issue. People focused on eating healthy and nutritious are relatively more inclined to say the types of food people eat is a bigger problem in the U.S. today than the overall amount (34%, compared with 21% among those not at all or not too focused on healthy and nutritious eating.)

16  ## Majority of Americans say healthy eating, physical exercise are key to a long and healthy life

*% of U.S. adults who say each of the following is _____ when it comes to improving a person's chances of a long and healthy life*

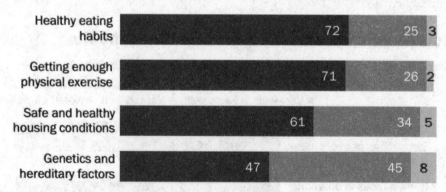

■ Very important  ■ Somewhat important  ■ Not too important/Not at all important

| | Very important | Somewhat important | Not too important/Not at all important |
|---|---|---|---|
| Healthy eating habits | 72 | 25 | 3 |
| Getting enough physical exercise | 71 | 26 | 2 |
| Safe and healthy housing conditions | 61 | 34 | 5 |
| Genetics and hereditary factors | 47 | 45 | 8 |

Note: Respondents who did not give an answer are not shown.
Source: Survey conducted May 10-June 6, 2016.
"The New Food Fights: U.S. Public Divides Over Food Science"

**PEW RESEARCH CENTER**

17  What's driving public attention to eating? One factor may be a belief in the oft-repeated adage "you are what you eat." Roughly seven-in-ten adults (72%) say that healthy eating habits are very important for improving a person's chances of living a long and healthy life.

18  A similar share (71%) says getting enough exercise is very important. Some 61% say safe and healthy housing conditions are very important. But fewer – 47% – believe genetics and hereditary factors are critical to improving a person's chances of a long and healthy life. Thus, most Americans consider

Please note that excerpts and passages in the StudySync® library and this workbook are intended as touchstones to generate interest in an author's work. The excerpts and passages do not substitute for the reading of entire texts, and StudySync® strongly recommends that students seek out and purchase the whole literary or informational work in order to experience it as the author intended. Links to online resellers are available in our digital library. In addition, complete works may be ordered through an authorized reseller by filling out and returning to StudySync® the order form enclosed in this workbook.

Reading & Writing Companion   **731**

their future health within their own grasps — if only they eat and exercise adequately.

19 People focused on food issues are particularly likely to believe that healthy eating habits are important. Fully 86% of those focused on eating healthy and nutritious say that healthy eating habits are very important, compared with 56% among those with little focus on eating healthy and nutritious. And, 87% of those with a deep personal concern about the issue of GM foods say that healthy eating habits are very important for a long and healthy life, compared with 68% among those with no or not too much concern about the GM foods issue.

**Americans have a variety of eating styles and philosophies about food**

20 Americans have many different approaches to eating. More say they focus on taste and nutrition than say they focus on convenience. Almost one-quarter (23%) of Americans say the statement "I focus on the taste sensations of every meal" describes them very well, while another 53% say this statement describes them fairly well. Similar shares say their "main focus is on eating healthy and nutritious," with 18% saying this statement describes them very well and 55% saying it describes them fairly well.

21 ## How Americans classify their own eating habits

*% of U.S. adults who say each of these statements describes them ...*

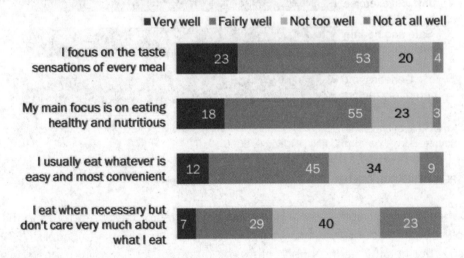

Note: Respondents who did not give an answer are not shown.
Source: Survey conducted May 10-June 6, 2016.
"The New Food Fights: U.S. Public Divides Over Food Science"

**PEW RESEARCH CENTER**

22 Smaller shares say the statements "I usually eat whatever is easy and most convenient" and "I eat when necessary but don't care very much about what I eat," describe them very well (12% and 7%, respectively). People with a particular concern about the GM foods issue and people focused on eating healthy and nutritious are less likely to describe themselves as unconcerned about what they eat.

23
## Most Americans feel they should eat healthier and they know who they are

*% of U.S. adults who say ...*

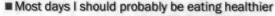

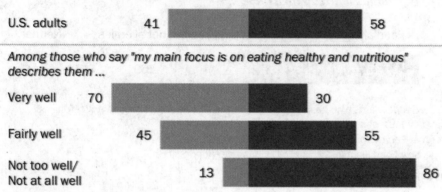

Note: Respondents who did not give an answer are not shown.
Source: Survey conducted May 10-June 6, 2016.
"The New Food Fights: U.S. Public Divides Over Food Science"

**PEW RESEARCH CENTER**

24 But, when Americans judge their own eating habits, a majority see themselves falling short. Some 58% of U.S. adults say that "most days I should probably be eating healthier." About four-in-ten (41%) hit their eating targets about right, saying they eat about what they should most days.

25 Those who are focused on eating healthy are, by and large, satisfied with their eating. Seven-in-ten (70%) of this group says they eat about what they should on most days. By contrast, 86% of people who describe themselves as not at all or not too focused on healthy eating say they should probably be eating healthier on most days.

26 There are more modest differences in eating assessments by degree of concern about the issue of GM foods; 51% of those who care a great deal about the issue of GM foods says they eat about they should most days, compared with 37% of those with no particular concern or not too much concern about this issue.

**Sizable minority of Americans have food allergies or intolerances to foods**

27  More children and adults are experiencing allergic reactions to foods today. Concern about food allergies and sensitivities can be seen in many places – from the regulations governing the public school lunch program to the way restaurants and food manufacturers package and offer alternatives to the most common allergens. For example, people with lactose intolerance can now choose from a wide range of milk and dairy alternatives made from soy and nuts. People allergic to the gluten in wheat can choose among special menu selections, even whole bakeries devoted to gluten-free options.

28  **15% of U.S. adults report at least one food allergy**

*% of U.S. adults who say they have ...*

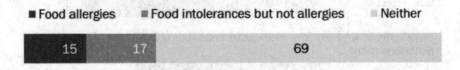

Note: Respondents who have severe, moderate or mild food allergies are combined. Respondents who did not give an answer are not shown.
Source: Survey conducted May 10-June 6, 2016.
"The New Food Fights: U.S. Public Divides Over Food Science"

**PEW RESEARCH CENTER**

29  About 15% of U.S. adults say they have severe, moderate or mild allergies to at least one kind of food. Another 17% of adults have food intolerances, but no food allergies. Roughly seven-in-ten of the adult public (69%) has no food intolerances or allergies.

30  More women than men report food allergies. About two-in-ten (19%) women say they have severe, moderate or mild food allergies, compared with 11% of men. And, blacks are more likely to say they have food allergies (27%) than either whites (13%) or Hispanics (11%). In other respects, those with food allergies reflect a mix of demographic and educational backgrounds.

31  The Center for Disease Control and Prevention reports a higher prevalence of asthma among children with food allergies. The Pew Research Center survey finds 29% of adults with asthma or another chronic lung condition have food allergies, compared with 12% among those who do not have chronic lung conditions.

**Vegans and vegetarians are a small minority of U.S., but they are a bit more common among younger generations and liberal Democrats**

32 Vegetarianism has been around for centuries and interest in following this diet – most commonly defined as omitting meat and fish – has **waxed** and waned over time. Today, vegetarian options are commonplace at many restaurants and food proprietors. Some of those who avoid meat and fish go a step further; vegans typically omit all foods that originate from animals including eggs and dairy products. But some people who consider themselves either vegetarian or vegan are "flexible" about what they eat and at least occasionally veer from these eating principles.

33

**More vegans and vegetarians in younger generations**

*% who say they are strictly or mostly vegan or vegetarian*

| | |
|---|---|
| U.S. adults | 9% |
| | |
| 18-29 | 12 |
| 30-49 | 12 |
| 50-64 | 5 |
| 65+ | 5 |
| | |
| Have food allergies | 21 |
| Have food intolerances, but no allergies | 8 |
| Have neither | 6 |
| | |
| Republican | 6 |
| Democrat | 12 |
| | |
| Conservative Rep | 4 |
| Mod/lib Republican | 8 |
| Mod/cons Democrat | 9 |
| Liberal Democrat | 15 |

Note: Republicans and Democrats include independents and other non-partisans who "lean" toward the parties. Respondents who do not lean to a political party not shown.
Source: Survey conducted May 10-June 6, 2016.
"The New Food Fights: U.S. Public Divides Over Food Science"

**PEW RESEARCH CENTER**

34 The Pew Research Center survey asked for people's own assessment of whether the terms vegan and vegetarian applied to them. A small minority – 9% – of U.S. adults identifies as either strict vegetarians or vegans (3%) or as mostly vegetarian or vegan (6%). The vast majority of Americans (91%) say they are neither vegetarian nor vegan.

35 Younger generations are more likely than others to identify as at least mostly vegan or vegetarian. Some 12% of adults ages 18 to 49 are at least mostly vegan or vegetarian, compared with 5% among those ages 50 and older. Men and women are equally likely to be vegan or vegetarian. There are no differences across region of the country, education or family income in the share who is vegan or vegetarian. There are more liberal Democrats in the vegan and vegetarian group, however. Some 15% of liberal Democrats are at least mostly vegan or vegetarian, compared 4% among conservative Republicans.

36 People who have food allergies are more likely to be vegan or vegetarian, suggesting that some food restrictions stem from **adverse** reactions to certain foods. Among adults with food allergies, 21% identify as strictly or mostly following vegan or vegetarian diets. Just 8% of adults with food intolerances (but no allergies) and 6% of adults with neither food allergies nor intolerances are vegan or vegetarian. Thus, about a third of people who identify as at least mostly vegan or vegetarian also report food allergies.

### Social networks: friends eat like friends

37 People tend to cluster together in social networks with others who are similar. The Pew Research Center survey finds this social pattern also occurs when it comes to people's eating philosophies and dietary habits.

38 ## Majority of the public says at least some of their family and friends focus on eating healthy and nutritious food

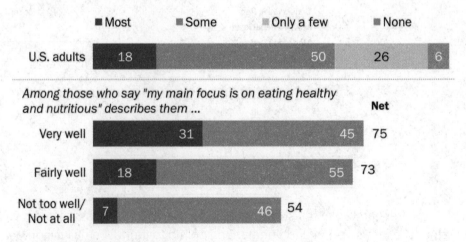

*% of U.S. adults who say _____ of their closest family and friends are focused on healthy and nutritious eating*

■ Most  ■ Some  ■ Only a few  ■ None

| | Most | Some | Only a few | None |
|---|---|---|---|---|
| U.S. adults | 18 | 50 | 26 | 6 |

*Among those who say "my main focus is on eating healthy and nutritious" describes them ...*

| | | | Net |
|---|---|---|---|
| Very well | 31 | 45 | 75 |
| Fairly well | 18 | 55 | 73 |
| Not too well/ Not at all | 7 | 46 | 54 |

Note: Respondents who did not give an answer are not shown.
Source: Survey conducted May 10-June 6, 2016.
"The New Food Fights: U.S. Public Divides Over Food Science"

**PEW RESEARCH CENTER**

39    Most Americans say that at least some of their closest friends and family focus on eating healthy and nutritious. Some 68% say this, while 32% say only a few or none of their friends and family does this.

40    Adults who say the statement "my main focus is on eating healthy and nutritious" describes them at least very or fairly well are more likely to say at least some of their closest family and friends do the same.

41    ## Minority of U.S. adults have close family and friends with food allergies or intolerances

*% of U.S. adults who say _____ of their closest family and friends have food intolerances or food allergies*

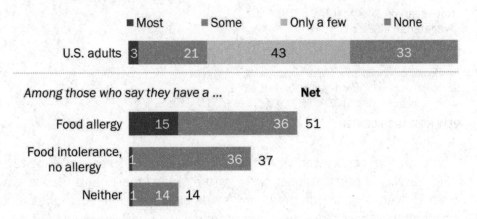

Note: Respondents who have severe, moderate or mild food allergies are combined. Respondents who did not give an answer are not shown.
Source: Survey conducted May 10-June 6, 2016.
"The New Food Fights: U.S. Public Divides Over Food Science"

**PEW RESEARCH CENTER**

42    A minority of the population (24%) says that most or some of their closest family and friends have food intolerances or food allergies. Among those who say that they, personally, have severe to mild allergies to some foods, a larger share (51%) says at least some of their closest family and friends also have intolerances or allergies.

NOTES

43

## More than half of Americans say none of their close family and friends are vegan or vegetarian

*% of U.S. adults who say _____ of their closest family and friends are vegan or vegetarian*

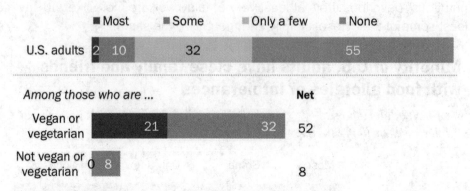

Note: Respondents who identify as strictly or mostly vegan/vegetarian are combined. Respondents who did not give an answer are not shown.
Source: Survey conducted May 10-June 6, 2016.
"The New Food Fights: U.S. Public Divides Over Food Science"

**PEW RESEARCH CENTER**

44 A similar pattern occurs when it comes to vegetarians and vegans. Some 12% of U.S. adults say that at least some of their close family and friends are vegan or vegetarian. But there are stark differences in social network composition among those who are, personally, vegan or vegetarian and those who are not. Fully 52% of people who are at least mostly vegan or vegetarian say that some or most of their closest family and friends also follow vegan or vegetarian diets. Just 8% of people who are not themselves vegan or vegetarian say the same.

**Many Americans say it's good party hosting behavior to inquire about food restrictions; few say it bothers them when guests ask for dietary accommodations**

45 Businesses have changed what foods they offer and how foods are packaged to accommodate Americans' **diverse** dietary needs and preferences over the past decade or more. What do people think about accommodating people's eating needs and preferences at private social gatherings? The Pew Research Center survey finds 37% of Americans say that, when hosting social gatherings, the host should always ask guests ahead of time if they have any food restrictions or allergies. One-quarter say they should do this sometimes, while 37% believe the host should never or not too often ask about food restrictions before hosting social gatherings.

NOTES

46 **Many Americans say hosts should ask about dietary needs, few bothered by guests asking for special foods**

*% of U.S. adults who say a host should _____ ask guests ahead of time if they have any food restrictions or food allergies*

■ Always   ■ Sometimes   ■ Not too often   ■ Never

| 37 | 25 | 21 | 16 |
|---|---|---|---|

*% of U.S. adults who say it bothers them _____ when guests ask for special food options at social gatherings they are hosting*

■ A lot   ■ Some   ■ Not too much   ■ Not at all

| 9 | 22 | 37 | 30 |
|---|---|---|---|

Note: Respondents who did not give an answer are not shown.
Source: Survey conducted May 10-June 6, 2016.
"The New Food Fights: U.S. Public Divides Over Food Science"

**PEW RESEARCH CENTER**

47 When they are the host, a minority (31%) of Americans say it bothers them at least some when guests ask for special kinds of food options at their social gatherings. Larger shares say it bothers them not too much (37%) or not at all (30%) when someone asks for special food accommodations at their social gatherings.

48

**Food-focused are more inclined to think hosts should ask guests for food needs**

*% of U.S. adults who say ...*

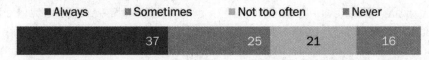

| | Host should _____ ask guests about food restrictions/allergies | | |
|---|---|---|---|
| | **Always** | **Sometimes** | **Not too often/ Never** |
| U.S. adults | 37 | 25 | 37 |
| *Among those who ___ about the issue of GM foods* | | | |
| Care a great deal | 49 | 26 | 24 |
| Care some | 38 | 28 | 33 |
| Care not too much/Not at all | 32 | 22 | 45 |
| *Among those who say "my main focus is on eating healthy and nutritious" describes them ...* | | | |
| Very well | 41 | 29 | 29 |
| Fairly well | 35 | 28 | 37 |
| Not too/Not at all well | 39 | 16 | 45 |
| *Among those with ...* | | | |
| Food allergies | 44 | 26 | 30 |
| Food intolerances | 40 | 21 | 37 |
| Neither | 35 | 26 | 39 |

Note: Respondents who did not give an answer are not shown.
Source: Survey conducted May 10-June 6, 2016.
"The New Food Fights: U.S. Public Divides Over Food Science"

**PEW RESEARCH CENTER**

49   Americans' beliefs about proper hosting behavior tend to be related to their own food ideologies. About half (49%) of those with a deep personal concern about the GM foods issue say that hosts should always ask guests about dietary needs; this compares with 32% of those with no or not too much concern about the GM foods issue. But people who themselves have food allergies are about equally likely as other adults to say that a host should ask about food allergies ahead of a gathering. And, like other Americans, a minority of those focused on food issues say they are bothered at least some when guests ask for special food options at a gathering they host.

**Food studies and their conflicting findings abound, but most Americans see this as a sign of progress**

50   A clear sign that many Americans are thinking about food is that they are paying attention to news and research studies on the subject. Fully two-thirds (66%) of the public says they hear or read news stories about the health effects of what people eat and drink every day (23%) or a few times a week (43%). About one-quarter (24%) say they see these news stories a few times a month while 9% report seeing these stories less often than that.

51   **Almost one-quarter of the public says they hear news stories about health effects of food every day**

*% of U.S. adults who say they hear or read news stories about the health effects of what people eat and drink ...*

■ Every day ■ A few times a week ■ A few times a month ■ Less often than that

| 23 | 43 | 24 | 9 |

Note: Respondents who did not give an answer are not shown.
Source: Survey conducted May 10-June 6, 2016.
"The New Food Fights: U.S. Public Divides Over Food Science"

**PEW RESEARCH CENTER**

52 **Food news 'whiplash' over conflicting studies is especially common among those who follow food and health news daily**

*% of U.S. adults who say they hear or read news stories about the health effects of food and drink which conflict with earlier news stories ...*

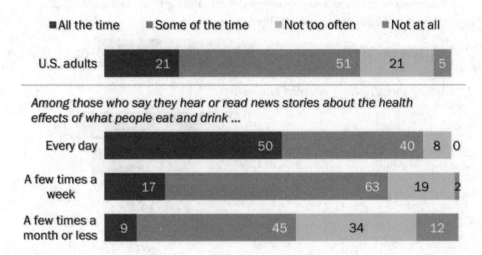

Note: Respondents who did not give an answer are not shown.
Source: Survey conducted May 10-June 6, 2016.
"The New Food Fights: U.S. Public Divides Over Food Science"

**PEW RESEARCH CENTER**

53 And many Americans perceive such studies as contradicting prior news reports at least some of the time. About half of U.S. adults (51%) say they hear or read news stories about the health effects of foods that conflict with earlier studies some of the time and roughly one-in-five (21%) say this occurs all the time. A minority of Americans (26%) say this does not occur at all or not too often.

54 People who regularly follow news about food and health issues are particularly likely to see news stories with **contradictory** findings. Some 50% of Americans who follow news about the health effects of foods on a daily basis say they see conflicting news reports about food all the time. Just 17% of those who hear or read food news a few times a week say that conflicting stories about the health effects of food and drink occur all the time and 9% of people who less regularly attend to food news say conflicting reports occur all the time.

55 There is considerable concern in the science community that this whiplash effect might confuse Americans and affect their views of the trustworthiness of science findings. The survey included two questions to shed light on how the public makes sense of contradictory findings about the health effects of foods.

56

## Most Americans say conflicting news stories about the health effects of food reflect improved understanding

*% of U.S. adults who say ...*

■ Research about the health effects of food cannot be trusted because many studies conflict

■ New research constantly improves understanding of foods' health effects so it makes sense findings conflict

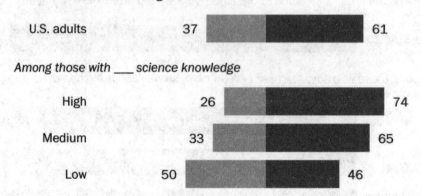

Note: Respondents who did not give an answer are not shown.
Source: Survey conducted May 10-June 6, 2016.
"The New Food Fights: U.S. Public Divides Over Food Science"

**PEW RESEARCH CENTER**

57    A majority of the American public (61%) says "new research is constantly improving our understanding about the health effects of what people eat and drink, so it makes sense that these findings conflict with prior studies," while a 37% minority says "research about the health effects of what people eat and drink cannot really be trusted because so many studies conflict with each other."

58    People's focus on food issues is not strongly related to beliefs about news stories with conflicting findings. Instead, people's general levels of knowledge about science, based on a nine-item index, tie to how people make sense of conflicting food studies in the news. Some 74% of those high in science knowledge say studies with findings that conflict with prior studies are signs that new research is constantly improving. But those in low science knowledge are closely divided over whether such studies are signs of improving research (46%) or show that food research cannot really be trusted (50%).

59 ## Despite conflicting reports, a majority of Americans say they understand the core ideas of healthy eating

*% of U.S. adults who say ...*

■ It is difficult to know how to eat healthy due to conflicting information

■ Even though studies conflict, the core ideas of healthy eating are pretty well understood

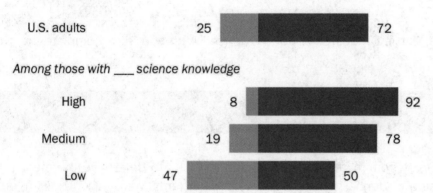

Note: Respondents who did not give an answer are not shown.
Source: Survey conducted May 10-June 6, 2016.
"The New Food Fights: U.S. Public Divides Over Food Science"

**PEW RESEARCH CENTER**

60 And, fully 72% of U.S. adults say even though new studies sometimes conflict with prior findings "the core ideas about how to eat healthy are pretty well understood." Only one-quarter of the public (25%) feels overwhelmed by the inconsistent findings, saying, "It is difficult to know how to eat healthy because there is so much conflicting information."

61 Here, too, beliefs are closely linked with people's level of knowledge about science. Fully 92% of those high in science knowledge say the core ideas about how to eat healthy are pretty well understood as do 78% of those with medium science knowledge. But those low in science knowledge are closely split with half (50%) saying the core ideas of how to eat healthy are pretty well understood and 47% saying it is difficult to know how to eat healthy because there is so much conflicting information. Thus, Americans with less grounding in science information appear to be more confused by and distrustful of research with contradictory findings about food and health effects.

"The New Food Fights: U.S. Public Divides Over Food Science." Pew Research Center, Washington, D.C. (December 1, 2016) http://www.pewinternet. org/2016/12/01/the-new-food-fights/

# First Read

Read "The New Food Fights: U.S. Public Divides Over Food Science." After you read, complete the Think Questions below.

 **THINK QUESTIONS**

1. What is the purpose of this survey from the Pew Research Center? Explain, using evidence from the text that supports your explanations.

2. What does the fourth diagram tell readers about what U.S. adults focus on most when choosing a meal? Explain, citing evidence from the text that supports your assertions.

3. Why do you think it is significant that "public attitudes on a wide range of science issues" are "widely divergent from those of members of the American Association of Advancement of Science?" Be sure to explain your answer and use evidence from the text.

4. Use context clues to determine the meaning of the word **divergent**. Write your definition, along with the words or phrases from the text that were most helpful in arriving at your conclusion. Finally, check a dictionary to confirm your understanding.

5. The word **adverse** stems from the Latin *adversus* meaning "turned toward or opposed." With this information in mind, write your best definition of *adverse* as it is used in this text. Be sure to also note any context clues that helped you determine the word's meaning.

# Skill:
# Technical Language

Use the Checklist to analyze Technical Language in "The New Food Fights: U.S. Public Divides Over Food Science." Refer to the sample student annotations about Technical Language in the text.

## ••• CHECKLIST FOR TECHNICAL LANGUAGE

In order to determine the meaning of words and phrases as they are used in a text, note the following:

- ✓ the subject of the book or article

- ✓ any unfamiliar words that you think might be technical terms

- ✓ graphic features such as charts or tables that accompany informational text

- ✓ words that have multiple meanings that change when used with a specific subject

- ✓ the possible contextual meaning of a word, or the definition from a dictionary

- ✓ the tone created by a word or phrase, such as serious or humorous

To analyze the effect of an author's word choices (including technical language) on the meaning and tone of an informational text, consider the following questions:

- ✓ What is the subject of the informational text?

- ✓ How does the use of technical language help establish the author as an authority on the subject?

- ✓ Are there any graphics, such as tables or charts, that supply context for the meaning of certain terms?

- ✓ How do technical terms reveal the meaning of the text?

- ✓ What is the tone of the text? Is it serious or humorous, for example? Is there bias?

- ✓ How does the cumulative, or increasing use, of technical language—as you might find in a government document—impact the meaning, tone, and readability of a text?

# Skill:
# Technical Language

Reread paragraphs 32 and 34 of "The New Food Fights: U.S. Public Divides Over Food Science." Then, using the Checklist on the previous page, answer the multiple-choice questions below.

## ↻ YOUR TURN

1. This question has two parts. First, answer Part A. Then, answer Part B.

   **Part A:** What is the cumulative effect of the technical language, including *vegetarian* and *vegan*, on the meaning of the paragraphs?

   ○ A. to show that animal as well as non-animal products are central to most American diets

   ○ B. to show the importance of eliminating certain foods from American diets

   ○ C. to define what it means to be vegetarian or vegan

   ○ D. to challenge American ideas about healthful eating, at home and in restaurants

   **Part B:** Which of the following details BEST supports your response to Part A?

   ○ A. "vegans typically omit all foods that originate from animals including eggs and dairy products"

   ○ B. "vegetarian options are commonplace at many restaurants and food proprietors"

   ○ C. "The vast majority of Americans (91%) say they are neither vegetarian nor vegan."

   ○ D. "some people who consider themselves either vegetarian or vegan are 'flexible' about what they eat"

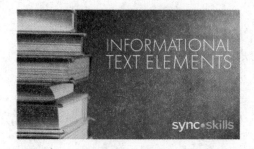

# Skill:
# Informational Text Elements

Use the Checklist to analyze Informational Text Elements in "The New Food Fights: U.S. Public Divides Over Food Science." Refer to the sample student annotations about Informational Text Elements in the text.

## ••• CHECKLIST FOR INFORMATIONAL TEXT ELEMENTS

In order to determine how the author unfolds an analysis or series of ideas or events, note the following:

- ✓ the subject of the informational text

- ✓ the order in which specific points are made

- ✓ how the author introduces and develops ideas or events

- ✓ key details in the text that describe or explain important ideas, events, or individuals

- ✓ other features, such as charts, maps, sidebars, and photo captions that might provide additional information outside of the main text

- ✓ similarities and differences between types of information in a text

- ✓ connections that are drawn between ideas and events

To analyze how the author unfolds an analysis or series of ideas or events, including the order in which the points are made, how they are introduced and developed, and the connections that are drawn between them, consider the following questions:

- ✓ What is the subject of the informational text?

- ✓ What are the author's key points and in what order are they made?

- ✓ In what order are the ideas or events the author presents introduced?

- ✓ How are ideas developed, and how does the author connect various ideas?

- ✓ What other features, if any, help readers to analyze the events, ideas, or individuals in the text?

Please note that excerpts and passages in the StudySync® library and this workbook are intended as touchstones to generate interest in an author's work. The excerpts and passages do not substitute for the reading of entire texts, and StudySync® strongly recommends that students seek out and purchase the whole literary or informational work in order to experience it as the author intended. Links to online resellers are available in our digital library. In addition, complete works may be ordered through an authorized reseller by filling out and returning to StudySync® the order form enclosed in this workbook.

Reading & Writing
Companion
**747**

# Skill:
# Informational Text Elements

Reread the subhead, paragraphs 20 and 22, and the accompanying graphic feature of "The New Food Fights: U.S. Public Divides Over Food Science." Then, using the Checklist on the previous page, answer the multiple-choice questions below.

## ↻ YOUR TURN

1. How does the subheading help the authors organize their ideas?

   ○ A. The subheading connects all the elements that follows in this section.
   ○ B. The subheading does not provide accurate information and needs further clarification.
   ○ C. The subheading summarizes the information from the last section.
   ○ D. The subheading does not relate to the information in the text that follows.

2. How does the graphic feature connect to the idea that Americans have different approaches to eating?

   ○ A. The graph depicts the percentage of people who want to improve their eating habits.
   ○ B. The graph illustrates different percentages from what is reported in the text.
   ○ C. The graph does not convey any additional information that is not reported in the text.
   ○ D. The graph clearly illustrates the response percentages of how people view their eating habits.

# Close Read

Reread "The New Food Fights: U.S. Public Divides Over Food Science." As you reread, complete the Skills Focus questions below. Then use your answers and annotations from the questions to help you complete the Write activity.

## ◎ SKILLS FOCUS

1. Identify examples of technical language used to discuss healthy eating and explain the effect of the language on the meaning of the article.

2. Analyze how the authors of the article use graphics to unfold and develop their points about healthy eating.

3. Explain how the authors' use of technical language in "Curry: A Tale of Cooks and Conquerors," "Chinese Cooking," and this article creates different tones.

4. Analyze how the authors use headings to connect the main points of the article.

5. Explain how Americans' relationship to food is connected to culture.

## ✎ WRITE

ARGUMENTATIVE: What do you think is the best way of encouraging healthy eating in kids? Use textual evidence as well as relevant anecdotal evidence to support your claim.

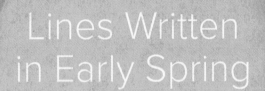

# Lines Written in Early Spring

POETRY
William Wordsworth
1798

## Introduction

Working with fellow English author Samuel Taylor Coleridge, William Wordsworth (1770–1850) co-wrote *Lyrical Ballads*, a collection of poems that helped to launch the Romantic movement in English literature. Romanticism celebrated nature and the natural world, in sharp contrast to the technological advancements of the Industrial Revolution. This poem, in particular, contrasts Wordsworth's appreciation for and connection to nature with his dark thoughts about the state of humanity.

# "And much it grieved my heart to think / What man has made of man."

1 I heard a thousand blended notes,
2 While in a grove I sate reclined,
3 In that sweet mood when pleasant thoughts
4 Bring sad thoughts to the mind.

5 To her fair works did Nature link
6 The human soul that through me ran;
7 And much it **grieved** my heart to think
8 What man has made of man.

9 Through primrose tufts, in that green **bower**,
10 The periwinkle trailed its wreaths;
11 And 'tis my faith that every flower
12 Enjoys the air it breathes.

13 The birds around me hopped and played,
14 Their thoughts I cannot measure:—
15 But the least motion which they made
16 It seemed a thrill of pleasure.

17 The **budding** twigs spread out their fan,
18 To catch the breezy air;
19 And I must think, do all I can,
20 That there was pleasure there.

21 If this belief from heaven be sent,
22 If such be Nature's holy plan,
23 Have I not reason to **lament**
24 What man has made of man?

William Wordsworth

✏ **WRITE**

LITERARY ANALYSIS: In Wordsworth's poem "Lines Written in Early Spring," the speaker sees a conflict between the natural world around him and the behaviors of humankind. How does Wordsworth use poetic devices and structure to contrast the natural world with the culture of humankind?

# B. Wordsworth

FICTION
V. S. Naipaul
1959

## Introduction

V. S. Naipaul (1932–2018) was a world-famous Caribbean novelist who wrote primarily in English. Born in Trinidad of Indian descent, Naipaul's grandfather came to Trinidad from India as an indentured servant. This story comes from one of Naipaul's earlier works, *Miguel Street*, which includes loosely connected stories based on his childhood in Port of Spain, Trinidad, in the 1940s. Naipaul lived for most of his adult life in London and was chosen as a recipient of both the Booker Prize and the Nobel Prize for Literature.

# "You're a poet, too, you know. And when you're a poet you can cry for everything."

1   Three beggars called punctually every day at the **hospitable** houses in Miguel Street. At about ten an Indian came in his dhoti and white jacket, and we poured a tin of rice into the sack he carried on his back. At twelve an old woman smoking a clay pipe came and she got a cent. At two a blind man led by a boy called for his penny.

2   Sometimes we had a **rogue**. One day a man called and said he was hungry. We gave him a meal. He asked for a cigarette and wouldn't go until we had lit it for him. That man never came again.

3   The strangest caller came one afternoon at about four o'clock. I had come back from school and was in my home-clothes. The man said to me, "Sonny, may I come inside your yard?"

4   He was a small man and he was tidily dressed. He wore a hat, a white shirt and black trousers.

5   I asked, "What you want?"

6   He said, "I want to watch your bees."

7   We had four small gru-gru palm trees and they were full of uninvited bees.

8   I ran up the steps and shouted, "Ma, it have a man outside here. He say he want to watch the bees."

9   My mother came out, looked at the man and asked in an unfriendly way, "What you want?"

10  The man said, "I want to watch your bees."

11  His English was so good, it didn't sound natural, and I could see my mother was worried.

12  She said to me, "Stay here and watch him while he watch the bees."

13  The man said, "Thank you, Madam. You have done a good deed today."

14  He spoke very slowly and very correctly as though every word was costing him money.

15  We watched the bees, this man and I, for about an hour, squatting near the palm trees.

16  The man said, "I like watching bees. Sonny, do you like watching bees?"

17  I said, "I ain't have the time."

18  He shook his head sadly. He said, "That's what I do, I just watch. I can watch ants for days. Have you ever watched ants? And scorpions, and centipedes, and congorees – have you watched those?"

19  I shook my head.

20  I said, "What you does do, mister?"

21  He got up and said, "I am a poet."

22  I said, "A good poet?"

23  He said, "The greatest in the world."

24  "What your name, mister?"

25  "B. Wordsworth[1]."

26  "B for Bill?"

27  "Black. Black Wordsworth. White Wordsworth was my brother. We share one heart. I can watch a small flower like the morning glory and cry."

28  I said, "Why you does cry?"

29  "Why, boy? Why? You will know when you grow up. You're a poet, too, you know. And when you're a poet you can cry for everything."

30  I couldn't laugh.

31  He said, "You like your mother?"

**Skill:**
**Theme**

The boy has never watched bees before. Maybe no one has encouraged him to take the time for it. This saddens the man. From this interaction, I infer a developing theme about the importance of taking time for observation.

**Skill:**
**Allusion**

"B. Wordsworth" alludes to William Wordsworth and also one of his subjects: flowers. B. Wordsworth explains the nature of poets, which helps to establish his character as a mentor to the boy.

---

1. **Wordsworth** William Wordsworth (1770–1850), a romantic English poet whose work was inspired by the Lake District where he spent most of his life

32    "When she not beating me."

33    He pulled out a printed sheet from his hip-pocket and said, "On this paper is the greatest poem about mothers and I'm going to sell it to you at a bargain price. For four cents."

34    I went inside and I said, "Ma, you want buy a poetry for four cents?"

35    My mother said, "Tell that blasted man I haul his tail away from my yard, you hear."

36    I said to B. Wordsworth, "My mother say she ain't have four cents."

37    B. Wordsworth said, "It is the poet's tragedy."

38    And he put the paper back in his pocket. He didn't seem to mind.

39    I said, "Is a funny way to go round selling poetry like that. Only calypsonians do that sort of thing. A lot of people does buy?"

40    He said, "No one has yet bought a single copy."

41    "But why you does keep on going round, then?"

42    He said, "In this way I watch many things, and I always hope to meet poets."

43    I said, "You really think I is a poet?"

44    "You're as good as me," he said.

45    And when B. Wordsworth left, I prayed I would see him again.

46    About a week later, coming back from school one afternoon, I met him at the corner of Miguel Street.

47    He said, "I have been waiting for you for a long time."

48    I said, "You sell any poetry yet?"

49    He shook his head.

50    He said, "In my yard I have the best mango tree in Port-of-Spain. And now the mangoes are ripe and red and very sweet and juicy. I have waited here for you to tell you this and to invite you to come and eat some of my mangoes."

Skill:
Theme

B. Wordsworth is always watching, noticing many things; this connects him to poets, inspiring the boy to think of himself as a poet. This develops the theme of taking time to observe, with more emotional connection.

51  He lived in Alberto Street in a one-roomed hut placed right in the center of the lot. The yard seemed all green. There was the big mango tree. There was a coconut tree and there was a plum tree. The place looked wild, as though it wasn't in the city at all. You couldn't see all the big concrete houses in the street.

52  He was right. The mangoes were sweet and juicy. I ate about six, and the yellow mango juice ran down my arms to my elbows and down my mouth to my chin and my shirt was stained.

53  My mother said when I got home, "Where you was? You think you is a man now and could go all over the place? Go cut a whip for me."

54  She beat me rather badly, and I ran out of the house swearing that I would never come back. I went to B. Wordsworth's house. I was so angry, my nose was bleeding.

55  B. Wordsworth said, "Stop crying, and we will go for a walk."

56  I stopped crying, but I was breathing short. We went for a walk. We walked down St. Clair Avenue to the Savannah and we walked to the race-course.

57  B. Wordsworth said, "Now, let us lie on the grass and look up at the sky, and I want you to think how far those stars are from us."

58  I did as he told me, and I saw what he meant. I felt like nothing, and at the same time I had never felt so big and great in all my life. I forgot all my anger and all my tears and all the blows.

59  When I said I was better, he began telling me the names of the stars, and I particularly remembered the **constellation** of Orion the Hunter, though I don't really know why. I can spot Orion even today, but I have forgotten the rest.

60  Then a light was flashed into our faces, and we saw a policeman. We got up from the grass.

61  The policeman said, "What you doing here?"

62  B. Wordsworth said, "I have been asking myself the same question for forty years."

63  We became friends, B. Wordsworth and I. He told me, "You must never tell anybody about me and about the mango tree and the coconut tree and the plum tree. You must keep that a secret. If you tell anybody, I will know, because I am a poet."

64   I gave him my word and I kept it.

65   I liked his little room. It had no more furniture than George's front room, but it looked cleaner and healthier. But it also looked lonely.

66   One day I asked him, "Mister Wordsworth, why you does keep all this bush in your yard? Ain't it does make the place damp?"

67   He said, "Listen, and I will tell you a story. Once upon a time a boy and girl met each other and they fell in love. They loved each other so much they got married. They were both poets. He loved words. She loved grass and flowers and trees. They lived happily in a single room, and then one day, the girl poet said to the boy poet, 'We are going to have another poet in the family.' But this poet was never born, because the girl died, and the young poet died with her, inside her. And the girl's husband was very sad, and he said he would never touch a thing in the girl's garden. And so the garden remained, and grew high and wild."

68   I looked at B. Wordsworth, and as he told me this lovely story, he seemed to grow older. I understood his story.

69   We went for long walks together. We went to the Botanical Gardens and the Rock Gardens. We climbed Chancellor Hill in the late afternoon and watched the darkness fall on Port-of-Spain, and watched the lights go on in the city and on the ships in the harbor.

70   He did everything as though he were doing it for the first time in his life. He did everything as though he were doing some church rite.

71   He would say to me, "Now, how about having some ice cream?"

72   And when I said, yes, he would grow very serious and say, "Now, which café shall we **patronize**?" As though it were a very important thing. He would think for some time about it, and finally say, "I think I will go and negotiate the purchase with that shop."

73   The world became a most exciting place.

74   One day, when I was in his yard, he said to me, "I have a great secret which I am now going to tell you."

75   I said, "It really secret?"

76   "At the moment, yes."

NOTES

77 I looked at him, and he looked at me. He said, "This is just between you and me, remember. I am writing a poem."

78 "Oh." I was disappointed.

79 He said, "But this is a different sort of poem. This is the greatest poem in the world."

80 I whistled.

81 He said, "I have been working on it for more than five years now. I will finish it in about twenty-two years from now, that is, if I keep on writing at the present rate."

82 "You does write a lot, then?"

83 He said, "Not any more. I just write one line a month. But I make sure it is a good line."

84 I asked, "What was last month's good line?"

85 He looked up at the sky, and said, *"The past is deep."*

86 I said, "It is a beautiful line."

87 B. Wordsworth said, "I hope to **distill** the experiences of a whole month into that single line of poetry. So, in twenty-two years, I shall have written a poem that will sing to all humanity."

88 I was filled with wonder.

89 Our walks continued. We walked along the sea-wall at Docksite one day, and I said, "Mr. Wordsworth, if I drop this pin in the water, you think it will float?"

90 He said, "This is a strange world. Drop your pin, and let us see what will happen."

91 The pin sank.

92 I said, "How is the poem this month?"

93 But he never told me any other line. He merely said, "Oh, it comes, you know. It comes."

94 Or we would sit on the sea-wall and watch the liners come into the harbor.

Skill:
Allusion

*B. Wordsworth, who lives in a place that is or was a British colony, is a poet, but unlike Wordsworth, B. Wordsworth struggles to do it. The narrator shows the joy and sadness the speaker of Wordsworth's poem feels.*

95  But of the greatest poem in the world I heard no more.

96  I felt he was growing older.

97  "How you does live, Mr. Wordsworth?" I asked him one day.

98  He said, "You mean how I get money?"

99  When I nodded, he laughed in a crooked way.

100  He said, "I sing calypsoes in the calypso season."

101  "And that last you the rest of the year?"

102  "It is enough."

103  "But you will be the richest man in the world when you write the greatest poem?"

104  He didn't reply.

105  One day when I went to see him in his little house, I found him lying on his little bed. He looked so old and so weak, that I found myself wanting to cry.

106  He said, "The poem is not going well."

107  He wasn't looking at me. He was looking through the window at the coconut tree, and he was speaking as though I wasn't there. He said, "When I was twenty I felt the power within myself." Then, almost in front of my eyes, I could see his face growing older and more tired. He said, "But that—that was a long time ago."

108  And then—I felt it so keenly, it was as though I had been slapped by my mother. I could see it clearly on his face. It was there for everyone to see. Death on the shrinking face.

109  He looked at me, and saw my tears and sat up.

110  He said, "Come." I went and sat on his knees.

111  He looked into my eyes, and he said, "Oh, you can see it, too. I always knew you had the poet's eye."

112  He didn't even look sad, and that made me burst out crying loudly.

113    He pulled me to his thin chest, and said, "Do you want me to tell you a funny story?" and he smiled encouragingly at me.

114    But I couldn't reply.

115    He said, "When I have finished this story, I want you to promise that you will go away and never come back to see me. Do you promise?"

116    I nodded.

117    He said, "Good. Well, listen. That story I told you about the boy poet and the girl poet, do you remember that? That wasn't true. It was something I just made up. All this talk about poetry and the greatest poem in the world, that wasn't true, either. Isn't that the funniest thing you have heard?"

118    But his voice broke.

119    I left the house, and ran home crying, like a poet, for everything I saw.

120    I walked along Alberto Street a year later, but I could find no sign of the poet's house. It hadn't vanished, just like that. It had been pulled down, and a big, two-storied building had taken its place. The mango tree and the plum tree and the coconut tree had all been cut down, and there was brick and concrete everywhere.

121    It was just as though B. Wordsworth had never existed.

"B. Wordsworth" from MIGUEL STREET by V. S. Naipaul. Copyright © 1959, copyright renewed 1987 by V. S. Naipaul, used by permission of The Wylie Agency LLC.

# First Read

Read "B. Wordsworth." After you read, complete the Think Questions below.

## ☁ THINK QUESTIONS

1. How does the boy's relationship with B. Wordsworth change over the course of the story? Cite evidence from the text to support your answer.

2. What things did the boy learn from B. Wordsworth? How did the poet change the boy's way of thinking? Include evidence from the text to support your answer.

3. In what ways do you think B. Wordsworth was truthful with the boy? In what ways was he not? Support your answer with evidence from the text.

4. Read the following dictionary entry:

**rogue**

rogue\rōg\*noun*

1. a dishonest or unprincipled man
2. a large animal with savage tendencies
3. a person with unpredictable behavior
4. a defective specimen

Decide which definition best matches **rogue** as it is used in this excerpt. Write that definition of *rogue* and indicate which clues found in the text helped you determine the meaning.

5. What is the meaning of the word **distill** as it is used in paragraph 87 of "B. Wordsworth"? Write your best definition of the word *distill*, along with a brief explanation of how you arrived at its meaning.

# Skill:
# Allusion

Use the Checklist to analyze Allusion in "B. Wordsworth." Refer to the sample student annotations about Allusion in the text.

## ••• CHECKLIST FOR ALLUSION

In order to identify an allusion, note the following:

- ✓ clues in a specific work that suggest an author has drawn on source material

- ✓ examples of how source material has been transformed, such as updating a location or time period

- ✓ a theme, event, character, topic, or situation in a text to which the allusion adds information

To better understand the source material an author used to create a new work, do the following:

- ✓ use a print or digital resource to look up the work and any other allusions

- ✓ list details about the work or allusion that are related to the newer work

To analyze how an author draws on and transforms source material in a specific work of fiction, consider the following questions:

- ✓ What theme/event/character from another work is referenced in the fiction I am reading? How do I know?

- ✓ How does that theme/event/character change or transform in this new text?

- ✓ How does the modern version of the work add to the earlier work?

Please note that excerpts and passages in the StudySync® library and this workbook are intended as touchstones to generate interest in an author's work. The excerpts and passages do not substitute for the reading of entire texts, and StudySync® strongly recommends that students seek out and purchase the whole literary or informational work in order to experience it as the author intended. Links to online resellers are available in our digital library. In addition, complete works may be ordered through an authorized reseller by filling out and returning to StudySync® the order form enclosed in this workbook.

Reading & Writing
Companion

763

# Skill:
# Allusion

Reread lines 1–8 of "Lines Written in Early Spring" and paragraphs 90–105 of "B. Wordsworth." Then, using the Checklist on the previous page, answer the multiple-choice questions below.

## ↻ YOUR TURN

1. This question has two parts. First, answer Part A. Then, answer Part B.

   **Part A:** In what way does the passage from "B. Wordsworth" allude to ideas in Wordsworth's poem, "Lines Written in Early Spring"?

   ○ A. The poem discusses ideas about nature, just as the story does.

   ○ B. This section of the poem is about the process of writing poetry, which is the same in the story.

   ○ C. The speaker of the poem is joyful about life, just as B. Wordsworth is in the story.

   ○ D. The speaker of the poem is sad even as he looks on something he loves, just as the boy does in the story.

   **Part B:** Which textual evidence from the poem and the story, respectively, BEST supports your answer in Part A?

   ○ A. "I heard a thousand blended notes,/ While in a grove I sate reclined" and "Or we would sit on the sea-wall and watch the liners come into the harbor."

   ○ B. "To her fair works did Nature link/ The human soul that through me ran" and "But of the greatest poem in the world I heard no more. I felt he was growing older."

   ○ C. "And much it grieved my heart to think /What man has made of man" and "He looked so old and so weak, that I found myself wanting to cry."

   ○ D. "In that sweet mood when pleasant thoughts/ Bring sad thoughts to the mind" and "When I nodded, he laughed in a crooked way. He said, 'I sing calypsoes in the calypso season.'"

# Skill:
# Theme

Use the Checklist to analyze Theme in "B. Wordsworth." Refer to the sample student annotations about Theme in the text.

## ••• CHECKLIST FOR THEME

In order to identify a theme or central idea of a text, note the following:

- ✓ the subject of the text and a theme that might be stated directly in the text

- ✓ details in the text that help to reveal theme

  - the title and chapter headings
  - description of the setting
  - the narrator's or speaker's tone
  - characters' thoughts, actions, and dialogue
  - the central conflict in a story's plot
  - the climax, or turning point in the story
  - the resolution of the conflict
  - shifts in characters, setting, or plot events

- ✓ specific details that shape and refine the theme

To determine a theme or central idea of a text and analyze in detail its development over the course of the text, including how it emerges and is shaped and refined by specific details, consider the following questions:

- ✓ What is a theme of the text? How and when does it emerge?

- ✓ What specific details shape and refine the theme?

- ✓ How does the theme develop over the course of the text?

# Skill: Theme

Reread paragraphs 105–112 of "B. Wordsworth." Then, using the Checklist on the previous page, answer the multiple-choice questions below.

## ↻ YOUR TURN

1. This question has two parts. First, answer Part A. Then, answer Part B.

   **Part A:** Which is the best statement of the theme that emerges in this passage?

   ○ A. Disappointment in the failure of friends is painful.

   ○ B. All friendships eventually have to end.

   ○ C. Creating poetry gives people a reason to live.

   ○ D. Acknowledging loss is a key part of human growth.

   **Part B:** Which detail from the text BEST supports to your answer from Part A?

   ○ A. "I could see his face growing older and more tired"

   ○ B. "Oh, you can see it, too. I always knew you had the poet's eye."

   ○ C. "he was speaking as though I wasn't there"

   ○ D. "He looked at me, and saw my tears and sat up."

# Close Read

Reread "B. Wordsworth." As you reread, complete the Skills Focus questions below. Then use your answers and annotations from the questions to help you complete the Write activity.

## ◎ SKILLS FOCUS

1. Identify a theme in the story and analyze its development over the course of the text using specific details.

2. In Wordsworth's poem "The Tables Turned," the speaker says, "Come forth into the light of things,/ let nature be your teacher." Using this quotation along with "Lines Written in Early Spring," analyze how Caribbean writer V.S. Naipaul draws on the work of British poet William Wordsworth to develop his story.

3. Analyze the character of B. Wordsworth over the course the story, including details that make him a complex character, such as dialogue and other interactions with the narrator.

4. Analyze the cultural experience reflected in the story from the point of view of the characters.

5. Discuss the "ingredients" of culture as shown in the short story.

## ✏ WRITE

LITERARY ANALYSIS: How does the author use a point of view and cultural setting to develop the theme? In your response, analyze details about at least two characters from the short story.

# Florida's Edible Wild Plants:
## A Guide to Collecting and Cooking

INFORMATIONAL TEXT
Peggy Sias Lantz
2014

## Introduction

Peggy Lantz is a native Floridian with more than 50 years of experience in gathering and preparing wild plants for consumption. Her 2014 compendium *Florida's Edible Wild Plants: A Guide to Collecting and Cooking* shares her formidable knowledge of this subject through a combination of practical advice, amusing anecdotes, and delicious recipes. This excerpt contains a portion of the opening chapter, followed by a specific example (Spanish needles) from the book's

# "1. Know what you're gathering. Don't guess."

1   For me, gathering wild foods is a hobby. I don't work too hard at it. When wild things are ready to eat, I'll add a few to the dinner or make jam just for fun.

2   I grew up in a family that always had a garden in the backyard. I picked and prepared a lot of beans and helped can tomatoes and make jelly. So I know the work that can go into preparing a dinner from scratch, even when I haven't had to go **foraging** for it.

3   I have been learning about and eating wild foods for over fifty years, and if I had to, I think I might be able to keep my husband and me alive on wild edibles. But it would be work. Just as prehistoric hunter-gatherers spent nearly all their waking hours finding, gathering, and preparing their foods, so would I, because nobody else would have picked or dug and washed and ground and peeled and chopped them for me. They don't come prebagged in plastic or frozen with cheese sauce on them.

4   Even when I'm giving only a short program on wild edibles, it takes me a couple of hours to gather the examples to take for my show-and-tell talk. Most of them grow in my, admittedly, large and wild yard, so I don't have to go far afield. But gathering the plants still takes time, and they still need to be prepared for putting on the table. Even so, you know this kind of food is fresh. You know where it comes from, and for me that's worth the effort.

5   So join me in this hobby, seriously if you wish, but mostly for pleasure—the pleasure of getting outdoors, of learning new things about plants, and of reaping where you have not sown.

6   The "wild" plants described in this book can be found in uncultivated places somewhere in Florida—maybe even in your yard, defying all your efforts to **eradicate** them. I refer to plants native to Florida, which means that they have been here since before the Spaniards arrived in the 1500s[1]. I also refer to some plants as naturalized. Many of these were brought over by later European settlers in Florida who used them to provide food or medicine or

---

1.   **Spaniards arrive in the 1500s** Ponce de León and his ships arrived in Florida in March of 1513 to search for gold, claiming the Eastern Coast of Florida for Spain and leading to the collapse of many native cultures by the end of the 1700s

as ornamentals especially cultivated for their beauty. Many of these transplants have since escaped from where they were intended to stay and now can survive without human care. Some naturalized plants (also called exotic pest plants) become invasive in the wild habitats they escape to, crowding out native plants and depriving wild animals of natural food and nesting places. Most of the wild plants here are not this type, and all those featured have benefits. As for the few pest plants? It makes all the more sense to eat them!

7   Before you start gathering samples of wild plants to eat, I have three very serious **caveats**. These are important, and I must state them right at the outset. I want you to be safe, and I want you to be a good naturalist when you pursue this hobby.

8   **1.** Know what you're gathering. Don't guess. Learn exactly what the plant and its edible parts look like.

9   Learn your edible plants one or two at a time. Don't try to absorb everything in this book at once and then go out to bring in supper.

10   Plant parts may be edible at different stages during a plant's life. Sometimes you'll need to learn how to identify a plant when it has grown beyond the tender edible stage. Study what the mature plant looks like until you know you can recognize it when it's young and fresh and without a flower. Go plant hunting with a friend now and then, someone who knows plants and can help you identify them. Picture books like this one help, but being sure of the real thing may elude you for a while.

11   Again, be sure. Don't guess. There are some poisonous plants out there, and you don't want to get sick on something you should have known not to eat (see chapter 4, What *Not* to Eat). And try things out in small doses in case you react badly to a particular plant.

12   **2.** Don't gather in areas where plants may have absorbed poisons. Don't gather along roadsides where cars and trucks spew exhaust full of heavy metals and other pollutants. Don't gather in your yard if you or a yard service sprays for weeds (the weeds are what you want to eat!) or if the next-door neighbor sprays his lawn with herbicides that blow or **leach** onto your property. Don't gather in polluted water. Be sure edible plants you gather are free of chemical pesticides.

13   **3.** Leave food for the wildlife. If you gather all the berries on a shrub or vine, there won't be any left for the birds to eat or for the plant to reproduce from. If you pick all the flowers, there will be no seeds. And many butterfly caterpillars need plant leaves to munch. Don't take it all.

14   And of course, as every gardener, outdoorsman, and camper knows, be careful where you put your hands. Fire ants might be crawling on a plant you're gathering, or poison ivy or a prickly blackberry might be growing next to it. A coral snake could be hiding under the leaves.

15  Finally, don't gather on private property without permission. Don't climb over fences or open gates. Don't gather in city, state, or national parks.

...

16  When Euell Gibbons[2] wrote his wonderful books on gathering wild foods in the 1960s, he was asked over and over again how their food value compared with common garden vegetables. He sent away several species to a lab for analysis. Turned out that all the wild plants tested had more nutrition in them than garden vegetables—more vitamin C, more vitamin A, more iron, more potassium, more everything. A lot more! Spinach and Swiss chard were the only vegetables that came close to matching the nutrients in wild plants.

17  Just so you know, I haven't personally gathered, prepared, and eaten every plant I describe here. I was born in Florida and have lived in central Florida for the better part of my quite long life, so I have never gathered walnuts in North Florida or made jelly from coco plums that grow in South Florida.

18  Some of the plants included here are ones I've only just identified and tried out this year while writing this book. One was shown to me by Green Deane, whom I met some years ago. He gathered the plant from the grass strip between a street and a sidewalk (which both of us agree is not the best place to gather edibles). Some plants I describe not on the basis of firsthand knowledge but from research or input provided by other knowledgeable people. Some plants I have chosen not to write about because they are uncommon and more important to wildlife than to us. And, of course, there are many more edible "weeds" out there that I haven't included or that I don't even know about yet.

19  Add wild foods to your dinner table one at a time. Learn an easy plant and **savor** it. Prepare it plain first or with a little salt to see what its real flavor is like. Maybe it's bland and needs other herbs or spices to spruce it up. Maybe it's sour and needs to be blended with other things. Then experiment and have fun. Cream it. Add it to scrambled eggs. Make it into a casserole with cheese.

20  I recommend that potherbs (leaves or stems to be eaten cooked rather than raw) be cooked in two waters. Use just enough water to cover the greens, bring them to a hard boil, discard the first water, then cover the greens again with some hot water and boil until tender. This process will help get rid of some of the bitterness and, we hope, any mild toxins.

21  Invite over some friends who might be curious about your new hobby for an unusual eating experience. I had a "wild dinner party" during the time our family lived for a few years in Minnesota. There, lots of wild edibles grew in my garden better than the beans and tomatoes I planted! I served dandelion

2. **Euell Gibbons** an author and advocate whose focus was on harvesting and cooking wild foods

NOTES

salad, lamb's quarters soup, cattails on the cob (from a nearby lake), milkweed blossoms (from the soybean fields across the road), homemade bread with homemade wild jellies and jams, and fried rabbit (the rabbit was caught in the barn). And for dessert, pie made with wild berries.

22  I took a lot of teasing from my teenage children, who thought their mother was a bit weird for feeding them "weeds," but they tried everything and would get out the canoe themselves to gather cattail blossom spikes in the spring. After we returned to Florida from Minnesota, I had a friend who wrote me letters addressed to "Weednut," which the postman **dutifully** delivered.

23  I encourage you to *enjoy* this new interest. You can be as casual about it—except for being sure of your identifications—or as industrious as you wish.

24  Get outdoors and have a wild time!

. . .

**Spanish Needles**

*Bidens alba*
**Part to eat:** Leaves, flowers
**When to gather:** Year-round
**Where to gather:** Disturbed sites throughout Florida

25  Spanish needles, or beggar ticks, *Bidens alba*, grows to three feet tall or more. Its leaves are opposite, lanceolate, smooth, and can be either single or trifoliate. The flowers have slightly toothed white petals that encircle a yellow floret[3]. Spanish needles ranges throughout Florida to Louisiana and the Carolinas.

26  Spanish needles have a ray of seeds with hooked ends that attach to anything passing by—your pants or socks or the dog's fur. It'll even prickle like a needle if your socks are thin. It's one of the weeds homeowners try the hardest to eradicate, but it is also a wonderful edible wild green.

27  Spanish needles is sometimes called beggar's tick, but I think that name should be reserved for a non-native pest plant called Caesarweed (*Urena lobata*), whose round, flat little seeds look more like ticks (and they happen to stick to socks or fur just as readily as Spanish needles).

28  The botanical name of Spanish needles is *Bidens alba*. *Bidens* comes from two Latin words—*bi*, which means "two," and *dens*, which means "teeth." It refers to the seeds, which are about half an inch long with two prongs on the end—the "teeth" that grab your socks. *Alba* refers to the white petals.

3. **floret** a smaller flower in a bouquet of larger ones

29 *Bidens alba* is another of the plants that is easier to learn to identify when it is tall and in bloom. Most gardeners are well acquainted with these yellow and white flowers, but they never knew they could be eaten. Spanish needles is prolific if left to its own devices.

30 When you've learned the characteristics of the leaves, you can find them when they are young, tender, and tastiest. Often you can find young sprouts alongside older plants in bloom.

31 You can use Spanish needles in many ways.

32 When you're learning to identify it, you can strip the smaller leaves from the stiff stem and cook them in a few changes of water to get rid of some of the bitterness. Try mixing them with some other greens that require cooking. Add some bacon bits or hard-cooked eggs. Top them with cheese. Chop them well and add them to scrambled eggs. Try using them in a quiche instead of spinach.

33 The young leaves can be added to a salad raw or cooked lightly like spinach. The small white and yellow blossoms can be thrown into a salad for a bit of edible color. As my friend Dick Deuerling likes to say, "If you don't like the weeds in your yard, eat them!"

34 Here's something else: I've been told that Spanish needles leaves will remove prickly pear cactus's painful glochids[4] from your skin if you crush the leaves in water and soak your hands in it. I've also heard that boat builders, after working with fiberglass, get relief from its irritation by taking a bath in Spanish needles water.

*Florida's Edible Wild Plants: A Guide to Collecting and Cooking* by Peggy Sias Lantz. Gainesville: University Press of Florida, 2014, pp. 1–6, 77–78. Reprinted with permission of the University Press of Florida.

✏️ **WRITE**

EXPLANATORY: Analyze how the author of *Florida's Edible Wild Plants: A Guide to Collecting and Cooking* adapts her style, including the use of informal language, formal language, and technical terms, to explain wild plants to a variety of audiences.

---

4. **glochid** a bristle on a cactus

# Maple Sugaring
## (in Aunt Alberta's Backyard)

POETRY
Diane Burns
1981

## Introduction

Diane Burns (1957—2006) is known for poetry that examines Native American life and identity, as well as for her associations with the renowned New York City poetry scene that included other famous poets like Allen Ginsberg. Burns grew up in both California and the Midwest, the daughter of two teachers who both taught at Native American boarding schools. In "Maple Sugaring," she describes the tenderness of a family tradition and how that tradition inspires deep bonds between family members.

# "tip birchbark basket into a bucket tree to tree to tree"

1 Me and Rex tramp through the slushy snow
2 almost warm enough to go without
3     bundled up and snowshoed
4 check the maple trail
5 collect a tiny amount of sap from each annoyed tree
6 tip birchbark basket into a bucket
7 tree to tree to tree
8 keep Rex from peeing on each tree
9 spirits soar like sap
10 sky so **tender** new and bright
11 hauling clear green maple sap
12 dumping it into the
13 pot
14 black iron kettle
15 like a cauldron
16 hangs above the fire
17 boil
18 boil
19 simmer
20 boil
21 stir with a long wooden spoon
22 stir
23 Stir
24     stir until your arms ache
25     and your eyes feel soaked with smoke.
26 Aunt Alberta watches **scowling** from the kitchen window
27 comes out to throw a little green wood under the kettle
28 Flaps her apron at the smoke
29 and says something like, "Well,
30 I guess if you stirred any slower we could just
31 chop it up and

Stage of the Outdoor Theatre at the Institute of American Indian Art, where Diane Burns spent her senior year of high school.

 NOTES

Skill: Language, Style, and Audience

*The style is free or open verse, broken across lines. Repeating the word* stir *creates a tone of tedium. The repetition of the* s *sound also makes the speaker sound deflated, emphasizing the work involved.*

NOTES

32  sprinkle it on our johnnie cakes[1]."

33  All that watery sap gets browner and browner

34  and smaller and smaller

35  stir   stir   stir

36  scrape the bottom

37  Every once in a while

38  **dribble** some sap onto the snow

39  and quick eat it

40  before

41  Alberta catches you not stirring.

42  Cousins always show up then:

43  "Gimme some why don't you!"

44  "Shhh!" and carelessly flop the spoon

45  over edge of the kettle

46  Whoops! spilled some (keep an eye on the kitchen window)

47  "Stir some then," I **command**

48  as little ones scramble for drops in the snow.

49  Beanie and Rusty take their turns

50  eyes watering, responsible and **solemn**.

51  "Try stirring faster," I say, "Scrape the bottom."

52  Dowie wants to try stirring so lift her over the edge,

53  the big wood spoon in her tiny hands

54  she stirs

55  tongue between teeth

56  scraping bottom as hard as she can

57  Her eyes turn red and watery

58  & I put her down finally.

59  "I can stir more," she says.

60  "You're too heavy," I say. "Look! Are those butterflies?"

61  "Catch me one, O.K.?"

62  They pelt off to the edge of the woods

63  while I stir quick and hard

64  hoping the syrup hasn't burned.

65  The wood spoon feels heavier

66  the sap is brown

67  and the spoon makes thick waves that

68      stand up

69      nearly solid.

70  Aunt Alberta comes out

71  Takes the spoon and gives it a few turns

72  And she dribbles some onto the snow and we both eat some.

73  "Do you know how to make johnnie cakes?" she asks, throwing

---

1. **johnnie cakes** cornmeal flatbread, a North American indigenous dish, also known as johnnycake or hoe cake

74  snow on the fire.
75  "If you come here tomorrow
76  early
77  I'll teach you."
78  And I feel as big as trees must feel
79  when they all sing together in the spring.

From *Riding the One-Eyed Ford* by Diane Burns. Published 1981, Contact II/
Strawberry Press.

Please note that excerpts and passages in the StudySync® library and this workbook are intended as touchstones to generate interest in an author's work. The excerpts and passages do not substitute for the reading of entire texts, and StudySync® strongly recommends that students seek out and purchase the whole literary or informational work in order to experience it as the author intended. Links to online resellers are available in our digital library. In addition, complete works may be ordered through an authorized reseller by filling out and returning to StudySync® the order form enclosed in this workbook.

Reading & Writing
Companion

777

# First Read

Read "Maple Sugaring (in Aunt Alberta's Backyard)." After you read, complete the Think Questions below.

## ☁ THINK QUESTIONS

1. Why does the speaker feel "as big as trees must feel / when they all sing together in the spring?" Use evidence from the text to back up your assertions.

2. What do you learn about the speaker from reading this poem? Explain, citing evidence from the text to support your response.

3. Based on what you read, how would you describe Aunt Alberta? Cite evidence from the text to support your explanation.

4. Use context clues to determine the meaning of the word **tender** as it is used in this poem. Write your best definition, along with the words or phrases that were most helpful in arriving at your conclusion. Finally, check a dictionary to confirm your understanding.

5. The word **solemn** stems from the Latin *sollemnis*, which means both "solemn observance" and "sacred or ceremonial." Explain how those definitions compare and connect to how the word is used in this poem. Write your definition of the word *solemn* as it is used in "Maple Sugaring," along with your explanations.

# Skill:
# Language, Style, and Audience

Use the Checklist to analyze Language, Style, and Audience in "Maple Sugaring (in Aunt Alberta's Backyard)." Refer to the sample student annotation about Language, Style, and Audience in the text.

## ••• CHECKLIST FOR LANGUAGE, STYLE, AND AUDIENCE

In order to determine an author's style, do the following:

- ✓ Identify and define any unfamiliar words or phrases.

- ✓ Analyze the surrounding words and phrases as well as the context in which the specific words are being used.

- ✓ Note the audience—both intended and unintended—and possible reactions to the author's word choice and style.

- ✓ Examine your reaction to the author's word choice and how the author's choice affected your reaction.

To analyze the cumulative impact of word choice on meaning and tone, ask the following questions:

- ✓ How did your understanding of the writer's language change during your analysis?

- ✓ How do the writer's cumulative word choice impact or create meaning in the text?

- ✓ How does the writer's cumulative word choice impact or create a specific tone in the text?

- ✓ What images, feelings, or ideas do the writer's cumulative word choices evoke?

- ✓ How could various audiences interpret this language? What different possible emotional responses can you list?

Please note that excerpts and passages in the StudySync® library and this workbook are intended as touchstones to generate interest in an author's work. The excerpts and passages do not substitute for the reading of entire texts, and StudySync® strongly recommends that students seek out and purchase the whole literary or informational work in order to experience it as the author intended. Links to online resellers are available in our digital library. In addition, complete works may be ordered through an authorized reseller by filling out and returning to StudySync® the order form enclosed in this workbook.

Reading & Writing Companion    779

# Skill:
# Language, Style, and Audience

Reread lines 37–48 of "Maple Sugaring (in Aunt Alberta's Backyard)." Then, using the Checklist on the previous page, answer the multiple-choice questions below.

## 🔄 YOUR TURN

1. This question has two parts. First, answer Part A. Then, answer Part B.

   **Part A:** How does the poet's word choice contribute to the tone of the poem?

   ○ A. The cousins' impatient language and the speaker's concern about upsetting Aunt Alberta help to establish an anxious tone.

   ○ B. The cousins' carelessness and the speaker's descriptions help to establish a carefree tone.

   ○ C. The speaker's fury over the spilled maple sap helps to establish an angry tone.

   ○ D. The younger cousins' focus and determination help to establish a serious tone.

   **Part B:** Which lines from the poem best illustrate your answer form Part A?

   ○ A. "'Stir some then,' I command" and "Cousins always show up then"

   ○ B. "as little ones scramble for drops in the snow" and "dribble some sap onto the snow"

   ○ C. "and quick eat it" and "over edge of the kettle"

   ○ D. "Gimme some why don't you!" and "(keep an eye on the kitchen window)"

2. What does the use of the word *command* in line 47 reveal about the speaker?

   ○ A. It shows that she is unsure about how to make the maple syrup.

   ○ B. It shows that she is bossy and disliked by her siblings and cousins.

   ○ C. It shows that she has a problem with doing the work of stirring herself.

   ○ D. It shows that she has a greater sense of responsibility than her cousins.

# Close Read

Reread "Maple Sugaring (in Aunt Alberta's Backyard)." As you reread, complete the Skills Focus questions below. Then use your answers and annotations from the questions to help you complete the Write activity.

## ◎ SKILLS FOCUS

1. Analyze how the author's language contributes to the tone of the poem.

2. Analyze how the language of the poem contributes to the meaning of the poem.

3. Analyze how the poet structures the poem to create an emotional effect.

4. Analyze how the poet develops a theme about how culture is passed on through tradition.

## ✎ WRITE

PERSONAL RESPONSE: What is one tradition in your family or personal experience that is as significant in your life as maple sugaring is to the poet Diana Burns? Write a personal response, which you might adapt to be in the form a poem, that paints a picture and evokes the feelings of that experience for a reader.

Please note that excerpts and passages in the StudySync® library and this workbook are intended as touchstones to generate interest in an author's work. The excerpts and passages do not substitute for the reading of entire texts, and StudySync® strongly recommends that students seek out and purchase the whole literary or informational work in order to experience it as the author intended. Links to online resellers are available in our digital library. In addition, complete works may be ordered through an authorized reseller by filling out and returning to StudySync® the order form enclosed in this workbook.

Reading & Writing Companion    **781**

# Ethiopia

POETRY
Audre Lorde
1986

## Introduction

Audre Lorde (1934–1992) was an African American writer and activist. She once remarked that the source of her poetry was "the intersection of me and my worlds." Her poetry collections include *The Black Unicorn*, *Coal*, and *Our Dead Behind Us*; in addition to poetry, Lorde wrote essays—some of which are collected in *Sister, Outsider*—and two highly regarded memoirs, *The Cancer Journals* and *Zami: A New Spelling of My Name*. First published in 1986, "Ethiopia" is an intimate portrait of a life impacted by the country's famine of the mid-1980s. The crisis made headlines around the globe and was the focus of highly publicized international relief efforts. By the time the famine ended, as many as eight million people had been affected by severe hunger and hundreds of thousands of people had died of starvation.

# "Seven years without milk means everyone dances for joy on your birthday"

*for Tifa*

1 Seven years without milk
2 means everyone dances for joy
3 on your birthday
4 but when you clap your hands
5 break at the wrist
6 and even grandmother's **ghee**
7 cannot **mend**
8 the delicate **embroideries**
9 of bone.

## ✏ WRITE

PERSONAL RESPONSE: In this unit, you have read two poems that shed light on traumatic global events: "Parsley" by Rita Dove and "Ethiopia" by Audre Lorde. A common way to learn about a historical event is through reading informational texts. However, it can be argued that poetry provides a more personal, emotional lens. How did reading this poem shape your understanding of the impact of the Ethiopian famine? What aspects of a historical event can poetry illuminate more effectively than an informational text? Use textual evidence from this poem and perhaps also from "Parsley," as well as original analysis, to support your response.

Extended
Writing
Project and
Grammar

EXTENDED
WRITING
PROJECT
ARGUMENTATIVE
WRITING

ARGUMENTATIVE
WRITING
PROCESS
PLAN

# Argumentative Writing Process: Plan

| PLAN | DRAFT | REVISE | EDIT AND PUBLISH |
|------|-------|--------|------------------|

Travel writer Deborah Cater once said, "You have to taste a culture to understand it." Similarly, according to novelist Jonathan Safran Foer, "Food is not just what we put in our mouths to fill up; it is culture and identity." Both writers are expressing the same idea—that one can get to know a particular culture or group of people through that group's food.

## WRITING PROMPT

**To what extent can you get to know a group of people through their food?**

Reflect on how the texts you have read throughout this unit, as well as your own personal experiences, inform your perspective on this topic. Choose a position that expresses your stance on this question. Write an argumentative essay in which you state a clear claim and support it with reasons and evidence from at least two of the unit texts as well as your own experience. Remember to include the following:

- an introduction with a thesis

- various types of reasons and relevant evidence

- transitions to clarify relationships between sections of text

- formal style

- a convincing conclusion

**Writing to Sources**

As you gather ideas and information from the texts in the unit, be sure to:

- include an arguable claim;

- address counterclaims, including alternate or opposing claims;

- use evidence from multiple sources; and

- avoid overly relying on one source.

Please note that excerpts and passages in the StudySync® library and this workbook are intended as touchstones to generate interest in an author's work. The excerpts and passages do not substitute for the reading of entire texts, and StudySync® strongly recommends that students seek out and purchase the whole literary or informational work in order to experience it as the author intended. Links to online resellers are available in our digital library. In addition, complete works may be ordered through an authorized reseller by filling out and returning to StudySync® the order form enclosed in this workbook.

Reading & Writing Companion    **785**

## Introduction to Argumentative Writing

An argumentative essay is a form of persuasive writing in which the writer makes a claim about a topic and then provides evidence—facts, details, examples, and quotations—to convince readers to accept and agree with the writer's claim. The writer may also address opposing viewpoints with counterarguments, or counterclaims. The characteristics of argumentative writing include:

- introduction
- claim or thesis
- valid reasoning
- relevant and sufficient evidence from several credible sources
- counterclaims
- conclusion

In addition to these characteristics, argumentative writers also carefully craft their work through their use of persuasive techniques, such as logical, emotional, and ethical appeals; transitions to link sections of text as well as clarify relationships between claims and reasons; and formal style. Effective arguments combine these genre characteristics and craft to convince the reader that a claim is valid.

As you continue with this Extended Writing Project, you'll receive more instruction and practice at crafting each of the characteristics of argumentative writing to create your own argument.

Before you get started on your own argumentative essay, read this essay that one student, Chloe, wrote in response to the writing prompt. As you read the Model, highlight and annotate the features of argumentative writing that Chloe included in her argumentative essay.

## ☰ STUDENT MODEL

NOTES

### Food: Simply Fuel or Fuel for Thought?

1 To many people, food is simply fuel for their bodies. However, the selections in this unit show that food is much more than a means of survival. Food can be a window into another culture—or a mirror that reflects a person's culture back to him or her. Examining ways that people prepare and eat food can reveal personal tastes, table manners, family roles, and cultural and geographical identities. As the authors of the texts "Chinese Cooking," *Curry: A Tale of Cooks and Conquerors,* and "The Latin Deli: An Ars Poetica" show, exploring and sharing food not only teaches people about new cuisine, but may also uncover misconceptions and provide deep understanding of an entire culture.

2 One cause of misconceptions about food and culture is ignorance. In "Chinese Cooking," Chen Jitong, the Chinese ambassador to France in the late 19th century, reveals the various food biases he encountered in Europe. In response to misconceptions, Chen Jitong examined how French and Chinese cuisines were similar: "It is true that we prepare our dishes in a different manner . . . but our dishes are nonetheless delicious." Lizzie Collingham describes a comparable conflict in *Curry: A Tale of Cooks and Conquerors.* Satya, a Punjabi woman, shows her cultural bias by commenting not only on what her Madrassi neighbor ate and how the food was prepared but also how she ate it—with her fingers. The neighbors never spoke again. In both cases, misconceptions about food and manners revealed biases based on assumptions and, essentially, ignorance of another's culture.

3 Another common assumption is that people from a particular geographic region must have a shared set of tastes or habits. However, in "The Latin Deli: An Ars Poetica," poet Judith Ortiz Cofer uses food to challenge this superficial idea about culture. In the

Please note that excerpts and passages in the StudySync® library and this workbook are intended as touchstones to generate interest in an author's work. The excerpts and passages do not substitute for the reading of entire texts, and StudySync® strongly recommends that students seek out and purchase the whole literary or informational work in order to experience it as the author intended. Links to online resellers are available in our digital library. In addition, complete works may be ordered through an authorized reseller by filling out and returning to StudySync® the order form enclosed in this workbook.

Reading & Writing
Companion

787

poem, a US grocery store owner attends to Spanish-speaking immigrants from different parts of Latin America searching for familiar foods in a grocery store. Each group has specific tastes. For example, Puerto Ricans seek out Bustelo coffee, while Cubans buy "*jamón y queso*" sandwiches "that would cost less at the A&P, but would not satisfy the hunger" for a taste of home. In other words, a simple ham and cheese sandwich is not really simple, depending on the way the ham is cured, and the type of cheese and bread used. The poem provides a glimpse into subtle cultural and geographical differences and preferences, but suggests that these differences only increase the variety of food experiences. In *Curry: A Tale of Cooks and Conquerors,* author Lizzie Collingham notices a similar pattern in India. She explains that "food on the Indian subcontinent does not divide into different culinary styles and dishes . . . so much as along . . . regional boundaries." As a result, what "curry" means varies greatly from area to area: Punjabi curry is heavy; Gujarati food is "sickly sweet"; Bengali curry is flavored with mustard oil; Telugu is "unbearably hot." These examples show how a common cultural food can become so specialized that any variation in a neighboring area is not considered "authentic." Studying a culture through the lens of food is a powerful way to learn about and come to appreciate any culture's unique variations.

4   Because practices and attitudes toward food can vary so much within a culture, some people might argue that it is impossible to understand a culture through its food. According to "The New Food Fights: U.S. Public Divides Over Food Science," Americans are deeply divided over issues such as vegetarianism, food allergies, and genetically modified foods. In one sense, this data shows that a group of people's beliefs and attitudes about food cannot be neatly categorized. However, the study also points out that nearly three-quarters of Americans agree that eating healthfully is "very important for improving a person's chances of living a long and healthy life." The study makes clear that despite the United States being a multicultural society rooted in many traditions and belief systems, most of us are united around the idea that eating healthful food is important. Perhaps if we started with what we have in common, such as the need to eat for health, we could begin to understand and appreciate our differences in other areas of our lives. Examining

food-based practices and attitudes, as the poets show, provides an entrypoint through which we can recognize shared values within and between cultures.

5    Despite our differences and whatever our culture, a memory of a favorite food seems to be a near-universal experience. On a personal level, reading how the patrons in Judith Ortiz Cofer's Latin deli linger over "the stale candy of everyone's childhood" made me remember my Nana's borscht, which is Russian beet soup. She made it from homegrown beets using an old family recipe. When I was nine, my favorite food was pizza, so when my family served borscht, I made a face and refused to eat the soup. I thought it tasted like dirt. My parents were embarrassed, but Nana was wise. She told me, "This soup is made from root vegetables that grow in the earth. To eat the soup is to taste the soil where you live. It ties you to your home, just as it did for your ancestors in Russia." Today, I love borscht because I understand that it is more than what it at first seemed; beneath its red surface, it tells the story of my ancestral origins. Food is one of the easiest ways to connect with and understand different cultures or even your own. A person does not have to speak the same language to express feelings of satisfaction and gratitude: "Mmm" is not too hard to translate.

Please note that excerpts and passages in the StudySync® library and this workbook are intended as touchstones to generate interest in an author's work. The excerpts and passages do not substitute for the reading of entire texts, and StudySync® strongly recommends that students seek out and purchase the whole literary or informational work in order to experience it as the author intended. Links to online resellers are available in our digital library. In addition, complete works may be ordered through an authorized reseller by filling out and returning to StudySync® the order form enclosed in this workbook.

Reading & Writing
Companion

789

# ✏️ WRITE

When writing, it is important to consider your audience and purpose so you can write appropriately for them. Your audience consists of your teacher and peers, and your purpose is implied within the writing prompt. Reread the prompt to determine your purpose for writing.

To begin, review the questions below and then select a strategy, such as brainstorming, journaling, reading, or discussing, to generate ideas.

After generating ideas, begin the prewriting process by writing a summary of your writing plan. In your summary, respond to the following questions:

- **Purpose**: What claim do you want to make, and why is it important?

- **Audience**: Who is your audience, and what idea do you want to express to them?

- **Introduction**: How will you introduce your topic? How will you engage an audience and preview what you plan to argue in your essay?

- **Claim**: What is your stance on the topic? How can you word your claim so it is clear and convincing to readers?

- **Rhetorical Appeals**: What kinds of techniques and language will you use to persuade your audience? How might you appeal to your audience's logic and emotions?

- **Textual Evidence**: Which texts from the unit support your ideas? What evidence will you use to support your claim? What facts, details, examples, and quotations will convince your audience to agree with your claim?

- **Counterclaim**: What counterclaim could you address? What might be your response to this counterclaim?

- **Conclusion**: How will you emphasize your point in the conclusion?

## Response Instructions

Use the questions in the bulleted list to write a one-paragraph summary. Your summary should include the claim you plan to make about the extent to which food can help you better understand a culture and note at least one text from which you plan to use evidence.

Don't worry about including all of the details now; focus only on the most essential and important elements. You will refer back to this short summary as you continue through the steps of the writing process.

Copyright © BookheadEd Learning, LLC

# Skill: Organizing Argumentative Writing

As you consider how to organize your writing for your argumentative essay, use the following questions as a guide:

- Have I identified my claim(s) and the evidence that supports it?

- Have I distinguished my claim from any alternate or opposing claims?

- Did I choose an organizational structure that establishes clear relationships between claims and counterclaims?

Follow these steps to organize your argumentative essay in a way that establishes a clear relationships among claim(s), counterclaims, reasons, and evidence:

- identify your precise, or specific, claim or claims and the evidence that supports it

- distinguish the claim or claims from alternate or opposing claims

- choose an organizational structure that establishes clear relationships among claims, and opposing or counterclaims, and the evidence presented to support your claim

- find evidence to distinguish counterclaims from your own claim

YOUR TURN

Read the examples of central claims below. Then, complete the chart by writing the organizational structure that would be most appropriate for the purpose, audience, topic, and context of the corresponding argumentative essay.

| Organizational Structure Options | | | |
| --- | --- | --- | --- |
| list advantages and disadvantages | cause and effect | compare and contrast | problem and solution |

| Central Claim | Structure |
| --- | --- |
| Cell phones can be extremely helpful in certain situations, but they can also have a negative effect on teens' lives. | |
| People who suffer from severe allergies may benefit from acupuncture. | |
| While llamas and alpacas may look similar, they are actually very different animals. | |
| Eliminating study hall periods will result in many students falling behind on their schoolwork. | |

Reading & Writing Companion

## ⟳ YOUR TURN

Complete the chart below by writing a short summary of what you will focus on in each paragraph of your essay. Make sure your ideas are appropriate for the purpose, audience, topic, and context of your essay.

| Outline | Summary |
|---|---|
| Introductory Statement: | |
| Claim: | |
| Main Idea 1: | |
| Main Idea 2: | |
| Main Idea 3 (Present and Refute Counterclaim): | |
| Concluding Statement: | |

# Skill:
# Thesis Statement

## ••• CHECKLIST FOR THESIS STATEMENT

Before you begin writing your thesis statement, ask yourself the following questions:

- What is the prompt asking me to write about?
- What claim do I want to make about the topic of this essay?
- Is my claim precise? How is it specific to my topic?
- Does my thesis statement introduce the body of my essay?
- Where should I place my thesis statement?

Here are some methods to introduce and develop a topic as well as a precise claim:

- think about your central claim of your essay
  - > identify a clear claim you want to introduce, thinking about:
    - o how closely your claim is related to your topic and specific to your supporting details
    - o any alternate or opposing claims (counterclaims)
  - > identify as many claims and counterclaims as you intend to prove

- your thesis statement should:
  - > let the reader anticipate the content of your essay
  - > begin your essay in an organized manner
  - > present your opinion clearly
  - > respond completely to the writing prompt

- consider the best placement for your thesis statement.
  - > if your response is short, you may want to get right to the point and present your thesis statement in the first sentence of the essay
  - > if your response is longer (as in a formal essay), you can build up to your thesis statement and place it at the end of your introductory paragraph

 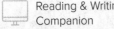

## ↻ YOUR TURN

Read the sentences below. Then, complete the chart by sorting them into those that are thesis statements and those that are statements of fact.

| | Sentences |
|---|---|
| A | In "Chinese Cooking," Chen Jitong reveals that two foods from different cultures can both be delicious even if they are very different. |
| B | People who Chen Jitong encountered revealed biases against foods from different cultures due to misconceptions and misunderstandings. |
| C | The idea that people from different cultural regions share the same tastes and habits suggests a superficial understanding of people's relationship to food. |
| D | In *Curry: A Tale of Cooks and Conquerors*, faulty assumptions lead to misconceptions and biases in different cultures. |
| E | The different women described in *Curry: A Tale of Cooks and Conquerors* reveal their prejudices against each others' foods and customs. |
| F | The speaker notes that Puerto Ricans seek out Bustelo coffee in a deli, while Cubans buy "*jamón y queso*" sandwiches. |

| Thesis Statements | Statements of Fact |
|---|---|
| | |
| | |
| | |

## ✎ WRITE

Use the questions in the checklist to draft a thesis statement for your argumentative essay.

# Argumentative Writing Process: Draft

| PLAN | DRAFT | REVISE | EDIT AND PUBLISH |
|------|-------|--------|------------------|

You have already made progress toward writing your argumentative essay. Now it is time to draft your argumentative essay.

## WRITE

Use your plan and other responses in your Binder to draft your argumentative essay. You may also have new ideas as you begin drafting. Feel free to explore those new ideas as you have them. You can also ask yourself these questions to ensure that your writing is focused, organized, and developed:

**Draft Checklist:**

☐ **Focused**: Have I made my claim clear to readers? Have I included only relevant supporting evidence and nothing extraneous that might confuse my readers?

☐ **Organized**: Does the organizational structure of my essay make sense? Will readers be engaged by the organization and persuaded by the ideas and evidence I present?

☐ **Developed**: Does my writing flow together naturally, or is it choppy? Will my readers be able to easily follow and understand how my reasons and evidence are connected? Is the progression of my ideas logical?

Before you submit your draft, read it over carefully. You want to be sure that you've responded to all aspects of the prompt.

Here is Chloe's argumentative essay draft. As you read, notice how Chloe develops her draft to be focused, organized, and developed. As she continues to revise and edit her essay, she will find and improve weak spots in her writing, as well as correct any language or punctuation mistakes.

## ☰ STUDENT MODEL: FIRST DRAFT

### Food: Fuel for Thought

1  ~~Some think food is simply fuel. However, the selections in this unit show that food is much more than a means of survival. Examining ways that people eat food can reveal personal tastes and cultural and geographical identities. The authors of the texts "Chinese Cooking", "Curry: A Tale of Cooks and Conquerors", and "The Latin Deli: An Ars Poetica" all show that exploring and sharing food teaches you about new cuisine, but also uncovers misconceptions and provides deep understanding of an entire culture.~~

To many people, food is simply fuel for their bodies. However, the selections in this unit show that food is much more than a means of survival. Food can be a window into another culture—or a mirror that reflects a person's culture back to him or her. Examining ways that people prepare and eat food can reveal personal tastes, table manners, family roles, and cultural and geographical identities. As the authors of the texts "Chinese Cooking," *Curry: A Tale of Cooks and Conquerors*, and "The Latin Deli: An Ars Poetica" show, exploring and sharing food not only teaches people about new cuisine, but may also uncover misconceptions and provide deep understanding of an entire culture.

2  ~~To begin with, peoples attitudes towards food can reflect cultural biases. In "Chinese Cooking," Chen Jitong, the Chinese ambassador to France, had to explain to a Frenchwoman that the Chinese don't eat dogs. The woman's concern reflected a cultural bias that Chinese food is different from French food and therefore inferior. That Chinese food is different from French food. And therefore inferior. In response, Jitong examined how French and Chinese cuisines are similar, through our misconceptions about food and manners our biases and assumptions are revealed.~~

> **Skill:**
> **Introductions**
>
> *Chloe revises her introduction by first strengthening her opening sentence and adding a "hook." Next, she realizes that she needs to clarify her topic and build up to her thesis. Then she crafts a stronger, clearer thesis by combining her ideas into one sentence to help clarify her claim for her reader.*

Please note that excerpts and passages in the StudySync® library and this workbook are intended as touchstones to generate interest in an author's work. The excerpts and passages do not substitute for the reading of entire texts, and StudySync® strongly recommends that students seek out and purchase the whole literary or informational work in order to experience it as the author intended. Links to online resellers are available in our digital library. In addition, complete works may be ordered through an authorized reseller by filling out and returning to StudySync® the order form enclosed in this workbook.

Reading & Writing Companion  **797**

NOTES

Skill: Reasons and
Relevant Evidence

*Chloe collects textual*
*evidence and writes*
*down her observations*
*and reactions. This*
*process helps her*
*identify reasons and*
*relevant evidence that*
*she can later*
*incorporate into her*
*essay. She also cites the*
*names of the sources*
*from which she gathers*
*her relevant evidence.*

One cause of misconceptions about food and culture is ignorance. In "Chinese Cooking," Chen Jitong, the Chinese ambassador to France in the late 19th century, reveals the various food biases he encountered in Europe. In response to misconceptions, Chen Jitong examined how French and Chinese cuisines were similar: "It is true that we prepare our dishes in a different manner . . . but our dishes are nonetheless delicious." Lizzie Collingham describes a comparable conflict in *Curry: A Tale of Cooks and Conquerors*. Satya, a Punjabi woman, shows her cultural bias by commenting not only on what her Madrassi neighbor ate and how the food was prepared but also how she ate it—with her fingers. The neighbors never spoke again. In both cases, misconceptions about food and manners revealed biases based on assumptions and, essentially, ignorance of another's culture.

3    A really common assumption is that people from a particular geographic region must have a shared set of tastes or habits. In "The Latin Deli," the author uses food to challenge this superficial idea about culture. In the poem, a grocery store owner attends to immigrants from different parts of Latin America searching for familiar foods. Each group has specific tastes. For readers unfamiliar with Latin American tastes, the poem reveals cultural differences and preferences. Lizzie Collingham explains that "food on the Indian subcontinent does not divide into different culinary styles and dishes . . . so much as along . . . regional boundaries." What "curry" means varies greatly from area to area. Punjabi curry is heavy. The phrase "sickly sweet" is used to describe Gujarati food. That a common cultural food can become so specalized that any variation in a neiboring area is not considered "authentic" is shown by these examples. Studying culture through the lens of food has been powerful. Way to learn about and come to apreciate their unique variations who shows the universal differences of food.

4    ~~Some people might argue that it is impossible to understand a culture through its food because a culture cannot be neatly categorized. "The New Food Fights: U.S. Public Divides Over Food Science" says that Americans are divided over issues such as vegetarianism, food allergies, and genetically modified foods. But it's clear that despite the United States being a multicultural society~~

~~rooted in many traditions and belief systems, most of us are united around the idea that eating healthy food is important. So, it seems that we have more in common than we have differences, at least when it comes to food. People's beliefs and attitudes toward food should provide a way to recognize shared values within and between cultures.~~

Because practices and attitudes toward food can vary so much within a culture, some people might argue that it is impossible to understand a culture through its food. According to "The New Food Fights: U.S. Public Divides Over Food Science," Americans are deeply divided over issues such as vegetarianism, food allergies, and genetically modified foods. In one sense, this data shows that a group of people's beliefs and attitudes about food cannot be neatly categorized. However, the study also points out that nearly three-quarters of Americans agree that eating healthfully is "very important for improving a person's chances of living a long and healthy life." The study makes clear that despite the United States being a multicultural society rooted in many traditions and belief systems, most of us are united around the idea that eating healthful food is important. Perhaps if we started with what we have in common, such as the need to eat for health, we could begin to understand and appreciate our differences in other areas of our lives. Examining food-based practices and attitudes, as the poets show, provides an entry point through which we can recognize shared values within and between cultures.

5

~~Most people would agree that food does reflect one's culture. Almost everyone has a memory of a favorite food. The speaker in Diane Burns's poem "Maple Sugaring (in Aunt Alberta's Backyard)" recalls the sweetness of homemade maple syrup, and I remember when I tried borscht I hated it. In the Latin deli the "candy of everyone's childhood" are lingered over. I understand that it is more than what it at first seemed it tells the story of my ancestral origins. Food is perhaps the easiest way to connect with and understand different cultures or even your own. You don't have to speak the same langauge to express your feelings. "MMMM" works in every culture.~~

Skill:
Transitions

*The opening of Chloe's fourth paragraph now includes a transition to link it to the previous paragraph. The transition phrase "According to" sets up Chloe's reference to a source that provides evidence in this paragraph. The phrase "In one sense" introduces a counterclaim, and the next sentence, which refutes this, begins with the transition word "However." The word "Perhaps" offers a gently persuasive transition to the idea of a shared view.*

NOTES

**Skill:**
**Conclusions**

*In order to strengthen her conclusion and show more of her own experience, Chloe decides to develop a personal anecdote about learning to love her grandmother's famous borscht soup that reflects her own culture and its relationship with food. She also links her experience with others in a way that shows food to be a language that allows us to understand each other. Chloe focuses the end of her argumentative essay on the connections between food, culture, and feelings.*

Despite our differences and whatever our culture, a memory of a favorite food seems to be a near-universal experience. On a personal level, reading how the patrons in Judith Ortiz Cofer's Latin deli linger over "the stale candy of everyone's childhood" made me remember my Nana's borscht, which is Russian beet soup. She made it from homegrown beets using an old family recipe. When I was nine, my favorite food was pizza, so when my family served borscht, I made a face and refused to eat the soup. I thought it tasted like dirt. My parents were embarrassed, but Nana was wise. She told me, "This soup is made from root vegetables that grow in the earth. To eat the soup is to taste the soil where you live. It ties you to your home, just as it did for your ancestors in Russia." Today, I love borscht because I understand that it is more than what it at first seemed; beneath its red surface, it tells the story of my ancestral origins. Food is one of the easiest ways to connect with and understand different cultures or even your own. A person does not have to speak the same language to express feelings of satisfaction and gratitude: "Mmm" is not too hard to translate.

# Skill: Introductions

Before you write your introduction, ask yourself the following questions:

- What is my claim? Have I recognized opposing claims that disagree with mine or use a different perspective? How can I use them to make my own claim more precise?

- How can I introduce my topic? How have I organized complex ideas, concepts, and information to make important connections and distinctions?

- How will I "hook" my reader's interest? I might:

  > start with an attention-grabbing statement

  > begin with an intriguing question

  > use descriptive words to set a scene

Below are two strategies to help you introduce your precise claim and topic clearly in an introduction:

- Peer Discussion

  > Talk about your topic with a partner, explaining what you already know and your ideas about your topic.

  > Review any notes and think about what will be your claim or controlling idea.

  > Briefly state your precise claim or thesis, establishing how it is different from other claims about your topic.

  > Write a possible "hook."

- Freewriting

  > Freewrite for 10 minutes about your topic. Don't worry about grammar, punctuation, or having fully formed ideas. The point of freewriting is to discover ideas.

  > Review your notes and think about what will be your claim or thesis.

  > Briefly state your precise claim or thesis, establishing how it is different from other claims about your topic.

  > Write a possible "hook."

**YOUR TURN**

Choose the best answer to each question.

1. Below is Chloe's introduction from a previous draft. The meaning of the underlined sentence is unclear. How can she rewrite the underlined sentence to make her idea clearer?

> Some think food is simply fuel. They don't consider how food can be a clue to the type of person you are as well as an insight. <u>Some people eat food in their own personal way that reflects the background and what they have been exposed to.</u>

- ○ A. People have all different ways of eating food that show who they are and what foods they like to eat.
- ○ B. Each person has their own personal way of eating food which helps them establish an identity that is unique.
- ○ C. People's personal tastes and where they come from are revealed by food that they eat and how they eat it.
- ○ D. Examining ways that people eat food can reveal personal tastes, and cultural and geographical identities.

2. The following introduction is from a previous draft of Chloe's essay. Chloe would like to add a hook to catch her audience's attention. Which sentence might she insert after sentence 2 to help best achieve this goal?

> (1) Some think food is simply fuel. (2) Many people feel that food can be a lot more than nourishment. (3) Examining ways that people eat food can reveal personal tastes, and cultural and geographical identities.

- ○ A. Food is love, memory, and magic in every bite.
- ○ B. Fuel can take many forms, but it is not gasoline or kerosene.
- ○ C. Very few humans like food at all except to wolf it down.
- ○ D. But what is food really and does it bring us more than a full stomach?

 **WRITE**

Use the questions in the checklist to revise the introduction of your argumentative essay to meet the needs of the purpose, audience, topic, and context.

# Skill: Reasons and Relevant Evidence

## ••• CHECKLIST FOR REASONS AND RELEVANT EVIDENCE

As you begin to determine what reasons and relevant evidence will support your claim(s), use the following questions as a guide:

- Is my claim precise, specific, and clearly stated?

- How is my claim different from any alternate or opposing claims? How can I make my claim more specific to my topic and ideas?

- What are the relationships between the claims, counterclaims, reasons, and evidence I have presented? What kinds of transitional devices or organizational patterns might improve these relationships?

- What is my counterclaim? How can I use it to strengthen my claim?

Use the following steps as a guide to help you introduce a precise claim(s), distinguish the claim(s) from alternate or opposing claims, and create an organization that establishes clear relationships among argument elements:

- identify the precise claim or claims you will make in your argument, refine it by:

  > eliminating any gaps of information or vague ideas

  > using vocabulary that clarifies your ideas

  > evaluating how it is distinguished, or different, from other claims and counterclaims on your topic

- assess any connections between your claim and the counterclaim, which is another claim made to refute or disprove a previous claim

- choose or create an organizational pattern, such as compare and contrast, that will establish clear relationships among claim(s), counterclaims, reasons, and evidence

## ⟳ YOUR TURN

Read each piece of textual evidence from *Curry: A Tale of Cooks and Conquerors* below. Then, complete the chart by sorting them into those that are relevant and those that are not relevant to the writing topic of "the link between food and culture."

| | Textual Evidence |
|---|---|
| A | This catalogue of dishes conjures up the aroma of fried onions; windows adorned with bright red fairy lights, white tablecloths, patchy service, Indian music humming in the background, and a two-course meal for under $20. |
| B | The food of Bangladesh belongs to the culinary world of Bengal. Punjabis share a food culture although their region was split in two with the creation of Pakistan. These are just two of the many culinary regions on the Indian subcontinent. |
| C | The range of culinary styles within India means that authenticity is more accurately tied to a region. But the regional subdivisions of Indian food are complicated by local patterns of consumption. |
| D | When the chef whipped together a can of Campbell's tomato soup, some cream, and a few spices to provide a gravy for the offending chicken, he produced a **mongrel** dish of which, to their shame, Britons now eat at least 18 tons a week. |

| Relevant Evidence | Not Relevant Evidence |
|---|---|
| | |
| | |

## ↻ YOUR TURN

Complete the chart below by identifying three texts you may want to write about. Then, provide reasons for choosing each text, as well as relevant evidence from each text to help develop your own writing ideas.

| Text | Reasons | Relevant Evidence |
|---|---|---|
|  |  |  |
|  |  |  |
|  |  |  |

Please note that excerpts and passages in the StudySync® library and this workbook are intended as touchstones to generate interest in an author's work. The excerpts and passages do not substitute for the reading of entire texts, and StudySync® strongly recommends that students seek out and purchase the whole literary or informational work in order to experience it as the author intended. Links to online resellers are available in our digital library. In addition, complete works may be ordered through an authorized reseller by filling out and returning to StudySync® the order form enclosed in this workbook.

Reading & Writing
Companion

805

# Skill:
# Transitions

Copyright © BookheadEd Learning, LLC

## ••• CHECKLIST FOR TRANSITIONS

Before you revise your current draft to include transitions, think about:

- the key ideas you discuss in your body paragraphs
- the relationships among your claim(s), reasons, and evidence
- the relationship between your claim(s) and counterclaims
- the logical progression of your argument

Next, reread your current draft and note areas in your essay where:

- the relationships between your claim(s), counterclaims, and the reasons and evidence are unclear, identifying places where you could add linking words or other transitional devices to make your argument more cohesive. Look for:

  > sudden jumps in your ideas

  > breaks between paragraphs where the ideas in the next paragraph are not logically following from the previous

Revise your draft to use words, phrases, and clauses to link the major sections of the text, create cohesion, and clarify the relationships between claim(s) and reasons, between reasons and evidence, and between claim(s) and counterclaims, using the following questions as a guide:

- Are there unifying relationships between the claims, reasons, and evidence I present in my argument?
- How do my claim(s) and counterclaim relate?
- Have I clarified, or made clear, these relationships?
- What linking words (such as conjunctions), phrases, or clauses could I add to my argument to clarify the relationships between the claims, reasons, and evidence I present?

## ⟳ YOUR TURN

Choose the best answer to each question.

1.  The following section is from an earlier draft of Chloe's argumentative essay. In the underlined sentence, Chloe did not use an appropriate transition to show the relationship between ideas. Which of the following transitions should Chloe use to replace *whereas* to make her writing more coherent and appropriate for the purpose, audience, topic, and context of her essay?

> Is it true that if you come from the same geographic region, you share food tastes or habits with everyone else? Most people would disagree, whereas Judith Ortiz Cofer, whose poem "The Latin Deli" uses food to challenge this biased idea.

- ○ A. since
- ○ B. on the other hand
- ○ C. because
- ○ D. including

2.  Below is a section from a previous draft of Chloe's argumentative essay. The connection between the ideas in the underlined sentence and the previous sentence is unclear. Which revision of the sentence uses a transition that best improves the clarity of the relationship? Choose the transition that makes her writing more coherent and is most appropriate for the purpose, audience, topic, and context of her essay.

> Most Americans think that all curry is the same, but Lizzie Collingham explains that Punjabi curry is heavy, Guranjati food is "sickly sweet," and Telugu is "unbearably hot." Curry dishes vary greatly depending on the region they are from.

- ○ A. On the other hand, curry dishes vary greatly depending on the region they are from.
- ○ B. Similarly, curry dishes vary greatly depending on the region they are from.
- ○ C. In other words, curry dishes vary greatly depending on the region they are from.
- ○ D. As a result, curry dishes vary greatly depending on the region they are from.

## ✎ WRITE

Use the checklist to revise the transitions in a section of your argumentative essay. Make sure that you use transitions that make your writing more coherent and appropriate for your purpose, audience, topic, and context.

# Skill:
# Conclusions

## ••• CHECKLIST FOR CONCLUSIONS

Before you write your conclusion, ask yourself the following questions:

- How can I restate the thesis or claim in my concluding section or statement? What impression can I make on my reader?

- How can I write my conclusion so that it supports and follows logically from my argument?

- Should I include a call to action?

- How can I conclude with a memorable comment?

Below are two strategies to help you provide a concluding statement or section that follows from and supports the argument presented:

- Peer Discussion

  > After writing your introduction and body paragraphs, talk with a partner and decide what you want readers to remember, writing notes about your discussion.

  > Review your notes and think about what you wish to express in your conclusion.

  > Do not simply restate your claim or thesis statement. Rephrase your main idea to show the depth of your knowledge, the importance of your idea, and encourage readers to adopt your view.

  > Write your conclusion.

- Freewriting

  > Freewrite for 10 minutes about what you might include in your conclusion. Don't worry about grammar, punctuation, or having fully formed ideas.

  > Review your notes and think about what you wish to express in your conclusion.

  > Rephrase your main idea to show the depth of your knowledge, support for the importance of your idea, and encourage readers to adopt your view.

  > Write your conclusion.

  Reading & Writing Companion

**YOUR TURN**

Choose the best answer to each question.

1. Below is part of the conclusion from a revised version of Chloe's argumentative essay. Which sentence below supports and follows logically from Chloe's thesis, that "exploring and sharing food not only teaches people about new cuisine, but may also uncover misconceptions and provide deep understanding of an entire culture"?

> Today, I love borscht because I understand that it is more than what it at first seemed; beneath its red surface, it tells the story of my ancestral origins. Food is perhaps the easiest way to connect with and understand different cultures or even your own. A person doesn't have to speak the same language to express feelings of satisfaction and gratitude: "Mmm" is not too hard to translate.

- ○ A. "Today, I love borscht because I understand that it is more than what it at first seemed; beneath its red surface, it tells the story of my ancestral origins."
- ○ B. "Food is perhaps the easiest way to connect with and understand different cultures or even your own."
- ○ C. "A person doesn't have to speak the same language to express feelings of satisfaction and gratitude"
- ○ D. "'Mmm' is not too hard to translate."

2. Read another part of the conclusion from Chloe's revised version below. Which sentence most nearly restates the claim that "exploring and sharing food not only teaches people about new cuisine, but may also uncover misconceptions and provide deep understanding of an entire culture"?

> Most people would agree that food does reflect one's culture. Almost everyone has a memory of a favorite food. For example, the speaker in Diane Burns's poem "Maple Sugaring (in Aunt Alberta's Backyard)" recalls the sweetness of homemade maple syrup. Likewise, the patrons in the Latin deli linger over the "candy of everyone's childhood."

- ○ A. "Most people would agree that food does reflect one's culture."
- ○ B. "Almost everyone has a memory of a favorite food."
- ○ C. "For example, the speaker in Diane Burns's poem 'Maple Sugaring (in Aunt Alberta's Backyard)' recalls the sweetness of homemade maple syrup."
- ○ D. "Likewise, the patrons in the Latin deli linger over the 'candy of everyone's childhood.'"

✎ **WRITE**

Use the questions in the checklist section to revise the conclusion of your argumentative essay so that it restates your claim or argument while summarizing the evidence provided and leaves readers with a memorable final impression.

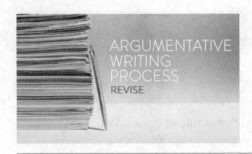

# Argumentative Writing Process: Revise

| PLAN | DRAFT | REVISE | EDIT AND PUBLISH |
|------|-------|--------|------------------|

You have written a draft of your argumentative essay. You have also received input from your peers about how to improve it. Now you are going to revise your draft.

##  REVISION GUIDE

Examine your draft to find areas both within and between sentences for revision. Use the guide below to help you review:

| Review | Revise | Example |
|--------|--------|---------|
| **Clarity** | | |
| Revisit the original title and see if it reflects the current version of the essay. | Add to, delete, or revise the title to reflect the genre and style of the essay. For example, identify two different views in the title to signal that the essay is an argument. | **Food: Simply Fuel or Fuel for Thought?** |
| Identify information that may seem important but is actually not needed. Upon reflection you realize that it is cluttering up the conclusion and is not all that crucial to the overall writing. | Avoid generalizations that cannot be substantiated. Remove unneeded information from the concluding paragraph, since the impact of the conclusion is weakened by a last-minute reference to a source that has not been previously discussed. Finally, add a transition to link the conclusion to the previous paragraph(s). | Despite our differences and whatever our culture, ~~Most people would agree that food does reflect one's culture.~~ ~~Almost everyone has~~ a memory of a favorite food ~~seems to be~~ a near-universal experience. ~~The speaker in Diane Burns's poem "Maple Sugaring (in Aunt Alberta's Backyard)" recalls the sweetness of homemade maple syrup.~~ |

| Review | Revise | Example |
|---|---|---|
| **Development** | | |
| Identify the reasons that support your claims. Annotate places where you determine there is not enough evidence or commentary to support your claims. | Focus on a single idea or claim and add support, supporting it with textual evidence or analysis. | Each group has specific tastes. For example, Puerto Ricans seek out Bustelo coffee, while Cubans buy "*jamón y queso*" sandwiches "that would cost less at the A&P, but would not satisfy the hunger" for a taste of home. For readers unfamiliar with Latin American tastes, the poem reveals cultural differences and preferences. |
| **Organization** | | |
| Review your body paragraphs. Identify and annotate any sentences that don't flow in a logical way. | Rewrite ideas and details so they appear in a clear and logical order, starting with a strong transition or topic sentence. Delete details that are repetitive or not essential to support your claim. | ~~To begin with, peoples attitudes toward food can reflect cultural biases.~~ One cause of misconceptions about food and culture is ignorance. |
| **Style: Word Choice** | | |
| Identify words or phrases that could be strengthened to help persuade readers of the validity of your claim. | Replace weak or unclear words or phrases with more persuasive and precise ones to increase rhetorical appeal. Remove extraneous language. | ~~For readers unfamiliar with Latin American tastes, t~~The poem ~~reveals~~ provides a glimpse into subtle cultural and geographical differences and preferences. . . . |

| Review | Revise | Example |
|---|---|---|
| **Style: Sentence Effectiveness** | | |
| Read aloud your argumentative essay and notice places where your sentences are repetitive, short and choppy, or unclear. Annotate places where adding a conjunction, transition, dependent clause, or punctuation could make a sentence longer and more interesting. | Remove repetitive sentences. Join together shorter sentences to form compound or complex sentences by moving a phrase or clause and using conjunctions, transitions, and/or punctuation. Use a dependent clause to modify an independent clause when additional information or clarification is needed. | ~~Through exploring and sharing something as basic as food, a person not only learns about new cuisine, but can also uncover misconceptions and gain deep understanding of an entire culture.~~ As ~~T~~the authors of the texts "Chinese Cooking," *Curry: A Tale of Cooks and Conquerors,* and "The Latin Deli: An Ars Poetica" ~~all~~ show, ~~that~~ exploring and sharing food not only teaches ~~you~~ people about new cuisine, ~~and can~~ but may also uncover misconceptions and provide deep understanding of an entire culture. |

## ✏ WRITE

Use the guide above, as well as your peer reviews, to help you evaluate your argumentative essay to determine areas that should be revised.

# Skill: Style

## ••• CHECKLIST FOR STYLE

First, reread the draft of your argumentative essay and identify the following:

- slang, colloquialisms, contractions, abbreviations, or a conversational tone

- areas where you could use domain-specific (subject-specific) or academic language in order to help persuade or inform your readers

- the use of first person (*I*) or second person (*you*)

- areas where you could vary sentence structure and length, emphasizing compound, complex, and compound-complex sentences

- statements that express judgment or emotion, rather than an objective tone that relies on facts and evidence

- incorrect uses of the conventions of standard English for grammar, spelling, capitalization, and punctuation

Establish and maintain a formal style in your essay, using the following questions as a guide:

- Have I avoided slang in favor of academic language?

- Did I consistently used a third-person perspective, using third-person pronouns (*he*, *she*, *they*)?

- Have I maintained an objective tone without expressing my own judgments and emotions?

- Have I used varied sentence lengths and different sentence structures?

  > Where should I make some sentences longer by using conjunctions to connect independent clauses, dependent clauses, and phrases?

  > Where should I make some sentences shorter by separating independent clauses?

- Did I follow the conventions of standard English?

- Have I referenced a style guide as needed?

Reading & Writing Companion

## ↻ YOUR TURN

Choose the best answer to each question.

1.  Below is a section from a previous draft of Chloe's essay. The underlined sentence lacks a formal style. What changes should Chloe make to improve the formal style of the sentence?

> Because practices and attitudes toward food can vary so much within a culture, some people might argue that it's impossible to understand a culture through its food. According to "The New Food Fights: U.S. Public Divides Over Food Science," Americans are deeply divided over issues such as vegetarianism, food allergies, and genetically modified foods.

- ○ A. Change *might* to *can*.
- ○ B. Change *people* to *humans*.
- ○ C. Change *it's* and to *it is*.
- ○ D. Change *its* to *it's*.

2.  Chloe wants to make sure her essay has an objective tone. How can she best revise the underlined sentence to make it more objective?

> A really common assumption is that people from a particular geographic region have got a shared set of tastes or habits. In "The Latin Deli," the author uses food to challenge this superficial idea about culture. In the poem, a grocery store owner attends to immigrants from different parts of Latin America searching for familiar foods.

- ○ A. A really messed-up assumption is that people from a particular geographic region have got a shared set of tastes or habits.
- ○ B. A totally common assumption is that people from a particular geographic region must have a shared set of tastes or habits.
- ○ C. A really common assumption is that people from any old geographic region have got a shared set of tastes or habits.
- ○ D. Another assumption is that people from a particular geographic region must have a shared set of tastes or habits.

## ⟳ YOUR TURN

Complete the chart by revising the sentences below to achieve a more formal style and objective tone.

| Sentence | Revision |
| --- | --- |
| Although I really liked the story, the characters made decisions that hurt others. | |
| The coolest lesson from the article was that money alone can't make a difference without leaders who know what to do with it and where it can go. | |
| Nobody's perfect, sure, but this story shows that if you don't at least try to learn from your mistakes, what's the point? | |

Please note that excerpts and passages in the StudySync® library and this workbook are intended as touchstones to generate interest in an author's work. The excerpts and passages do not substitute for the reading of entire texts, and StudySync® strongly recommends that students seek out and purchase the whole literary or informational work in order to experience it as the author intended. Links to online resellers are available in our digital library. In addition, complete works may be ordered through an authorized reseller by filling out and returning to StudySync® the order form enclosed in this workbook.

Reading & Writing
Companion

815

# Grammar:
# Adverb Clauses

Adverb clauses are subordinate clauses that often modify the verb in the main clause of a complex sentence. They can also modify adjectives or adverbs.

Adverb clauses tell when, *where*, *how*, *why*, or *under what conditions* the action in the sentence occurs.

| Text | Explanation |
|------|-------------|
| **Since the United States government is for the people and by the people**, public opinion should matter in deciding this issue.<br><br>Burning the American Flag: First Amendment Right or a Crime? | The adverb clause *since the United States government is for the people and by the people* modifies the verb *should matter*. It tells *why* public opinion should matter. |
| Chris had purchased the secondhand yellow Datsun **when he was a senior in high school.**<br><br>Into the Wild | The adverb clause *when he was a senior in high school* modifies the verb *had purchased*. It tells *when* Chris purchased the Datsun. |
| **If you will comply with my conditions,** I will leave them and you at peace.<br><br>Frankenstein | The adverb clause *if you will comply with my conditions* modifies the verb *will leave*. It tells *under what conditions* the speaker will leave. |

Adverb clauses begin with subordinating conjunctions.

| Common Subordinating Conjunctions | | | | |
|------|------|------|------|------|
| although<br>because | before<br>since | than<br>unless | when<br>whenever | wherever<br>while |

An adverb clause that seems to have missing words is called "elliptical." The words that are left out are understood in the clause.

| Text | Explanation |
|------|-------------|
| Amy was three years younger **than I.**<br><br>An American Childhood | The adverbial clause *than I* should be read as *than I* was. The word *was* is left out of the clause. |

## ⟳ YOUR TURN

1. How should this sentence be changed to include an adverb clause?

> People frequently confuse our names.

- ○ A. People frequently confuse our names, but it does not bother us.
- ○ B. Because we are identical twins, people frequently confuse our names.
- ○ C. People frequently confuse our names in class.
- ○ D. No change needs to be made to this sentence.

2. How should this sentence be changed to include an adverb clause?

> Hakim did more work for the recycling project.

- ○ A. Hakim did more work for the recycling project today.
- ○ B. Hakim did more work for the recycling project outside.
- ○ C. Hakim did more work for the recycling project than she.
- ○ D. No change needs to be made to this sentence.

3. How should this sentence be changed to include an adverb clause?

> The house will be hard to sell if it is old.

- ○ A. The house will be hard to sell if it is old, but we can do it.
- ○ B. Until the spring, the house will be hard to sell if it is old.
- ○ C. The house will be hard to sell in this market if it is old.
- ○ D. No change needs to be made to this sentence.

4. How should this sentence be changed to include an adverb clause?

> Jerry will wash his car.

- ○ A. Jerry will wash his car before the end of the day.
- ○ B. Jerry will wash his car in his own time.
- ○ C. Jerry will wash his car unless it rains.
- ○ D. No change needs to be made to this sentence.

# Grammar: Relative Clauses

## Relative Pronouns, Relative Adverbs, and Relative Clauses

Relative pronouns and relative adverbs are pronouns and adverbs that are used to begin a subject-verb word group called a relative clause. A relative clause is a clause that acts like an adjective. Because of this, they are also known as adjective clauses. Relative clauses contain a subject and a verb, but cannot stand alone as a sentence.

Relative pronouns include *who, whoever, whom, whomever, what, whatever, which, whichever, that, whose.* Sometimes, the relative pronoun is left out. For example, *The shirt that I'm wearing* becomes *The shirt I'm wearing.*

Relative adverbs include *when, where,* and *why.* Sometimes, the modified noun is left out. For example, *I don't know the reason why Jerome left early* becomes *I don't know why Jerome left early.*

Sometimes, the relative pronoun acts as the subject in that clause. In the sentence, "Brutus was the senator who stabbed Julius Caesar last," the relative pronoun *who* is the subject of the relative clause *who stabbed Julius Caesar last.* It connects the relative clause to the rest of the sentence.

When the subject of an adjective clause is a relative pronoun, the verb in the clause must agree with the antecedent of the relative pronoun. The antecedent is the word or group of words to which the pronoun refers.

| Example | Explanation |
|---|---|
| I have a calculator **that** prints out results. | *That* is the subject of the adjective clause *that prints out results. Calculator* is the antecedent of *that.* The verb *prints* is singular, which agrees with the singular noun *calculator.* |

## ⟳ YOUR TURN

1. How should this sentence be changed?

   > The lady what car is parked in the driveway is visiting Mom.

   - ○ A. Change **what** to **which**.
   - ○ B. Change **what** to **whose**.
   - ○ C. Change **what** to **whatever**.
   - ○ D. No change needs to be made to this sentence.

2. How should this sentence be changed?

   > The dormitory is one of the buildings that was damaged in the earthquake.

   - ○ A. Change **is** to **are**.
   - ○ B. Change **was** to **were**.
   - ○ C. Change **that** to **those**.
   - ○ D. No change needs to be made to this sentence.

3. How should this sentence be changed?

   > The bike race will begin where you hear the sound of the horn.

   - ○ A. Change **where** to **when**.
   - ○ B. Change **where** to **who**.
   - ○ C. Change **where** to **why**.
   - ○ D. No change needs to be made to this sentence.

4. Which sentence best incorporates a relative clause?

   > When called upon to answer, Marvin stood reluctantly before his classmates.

   - ○ A. When called upon to answer, Marvin stood reluctantly, shy and timid before his classmates.
   - ○ B. When called upon to answer, shy and timid Marvin stood reluctantly before his classmates.
   - ○ C. When called upon to answer, Marvin, who is shy and timid, stood reluctantly before his classmates.
   - ○ D. None of the above.

# Argumentative Writing Process: Edit and Publish

| PLAN | DRAFT | REVISE | EDIT AND PUBLISH |
|------|-------|--------|------------------|

You have revised your argumentative essay based on your peer feedback and your own examination.

Now, it is time to edit your argumentative essay. When you revised, you focused on the content of your essay. You probably looked at your thesis statement, reasons and relevant evidence, and transitions. When you edit, you focus on the mechanics of your essay, paying close attention to things like grammar and punctuation.

## Use the checklist below to guide you as you edit:

☐ Have I used various types of phrases and clauses to convey specific meanings and add variety to my writing?

☐ Have I used adverb clauses to tell *when*, *where*, *how*, *why*, or *under what conditions* the action in the sentence occurs?

☐ Have I used relative pronouns and clauses appropriately and in a way that is consistent with my purpose throughout my essay?

☐ Do I have any sentence fragments or run-on sentences?

☐ Have I used parallel structure where needed?

☐ Have I spelled everything correctly?

☐ Have I punctuated correctly?

## Notice some edits Chloe has made:

- Added a phrase to connect ideas within a paragraph.

- Used a colon to set off a list.

- Combined sentences using semicolons.

- Made a sentence parallel with the others in a list.

- Added a subordinating conjunction to make an adverbial clause and fix a sentence fragment.

- Corrected a verb tense to make it consistent.

- Replaced a pronoun with an unclear antecedent.

- Removed an unnecessary and confusing relative clause.

- Corrected several spelling errors.

As a result, ~~w~~What "curry" means varies greatly from area to area~~:~~. Punjabi curry is heavy~~;~~. ~~The phrase~~ Gujarati food is "sickly sweet" ~~is used to describe Gujarati food.~~; Bengali curry is flavored with mustard oil~~.~~; Telugu is "unbearably hot." These examples show how ~~That~~ a common cultural food can become so ~~specalized~~ specialized that any variation in a ~~neiboring~~ neighboring area is not considered "authentic." ~~is shown by these examples.~~ Studying a culture through the lens of food is ~~has been~~ a powerful ~~Way~~ way to learn about and come to ~~apreciate~~ appreciate ~~their~~ any culture's unique variations. ~~who shows the universal differences of food.~~

## ✏ WRITE

Use the questions above, as well as your peer reviews, to help you evaluate your argumentative essay to determine areas that need editing. Then edit your essay to correct those errors.

Once you have made all your corrections, you are ready to publish your work. You can distribute your writing to family and friends, hang it on a bulletin board, or post it on your blog. If you publish online, share the link with your family, friends, and classmates.

Please note that excerpts and passages in the StudySync® library and this workbook are intended as touchstones to generate interest in an author's work. The excerpts and passages do not substitute for the reading of entire texts, and StudySync® strongly recommends that students seek out and purchase the whole literary or informational work in order to experience it as the author intended. Links to online resellers are available in our digital library. In addition, complete works may be ordered through an authorized reseller by filling out and returning to StudySync® the order form enclosed in this workbook.

Reading & Writing Companion     821

# The Science of Genetically Altering Foods:

## Should We Do It?

INFORMATIONAL

## Introduction

New technology promises healthier crops, with higher yield and greater nutritional value. But do these advances carry with them potential problems?

**VOCABULARY**

**enhanced**

improved upon or made better

**modified**

somewhat changed

**lethal**

deadly or fatal

**species**

a group of animals or plants that are similar and can produce young animals or plants

**manipulation**

the process of influencing, controlling, or changing something

 **READ**

 NOTES

**The Science of Genetically Altering Foods: Should We Do It?**

**Point:** Genetic modification of plants is justified. It dramatically improves the quality and quantity of crops.

1   Genetic modification involves the **manipulation** of DNA to introduce a totally different gene. The action changes the structure of the plant. Genetically **modified** crops are more resistant to diseases and pests. That resistance is appealing to farmers because insects cause huge crop losses every year. Farmers make less money when they lose crops. Fewer crops also mean less food for people.

2   Farmers tend to use a lot of pesticides. Modified plants would most likely need only one pesticide application. Farmers would save time and money. In addition, not reapplying pesticides helps the environment.

3   The demand for improved crops is increasing. One reason for the increase is that modified corn and soybean seeds make more crops. One seed developer claims up to eight percent more crops. The plants also can be changed to provide better nutrition. Hunger could end in countries where malnutrition is a problem. For example, scientists are developing "golden rice." That rice will stimulate the body to develop vitamin A. The rice will improve the health of millions of children in developing countries. They will go blind without the vitamin A.

4   Science has helped change plants and animals throughout history. One example is that humans crossbred a mustard **species** to create broccoli, Brussels sprouts, and cabbage. Generations of plant breeding have improved taste, size, and yields of different foods. Those changes took time. On the other hand, genetic modification can change seeds in one generation.

5   The research and development of modified crops are very expensive. It is true. However, the long-term benefits are worth the cost. Farmers can save on pesticides. They can grow larger and disease-resistant crops. Finally, more crops will eliminate world hunger.

**Counterpoint:** Genetic modification of plant material is both potentially **lethal** and dangerous.

6   Genetic modification introduces other elements to the DNA of plants. Bacteria and fungus can be introduced. Those elements could have a horrible effect on the human body. No long-term studies have been made on the effects. That is concerning.

7   Just as concerning is the idea that scientists can introduce genes from unrelated species. They might add a nut gene into a corn plant. They could add a fish gene into a soybean. The scientists think the new gene will improve the original plant. However, it could also introduce new allergens. Many people are already seriously allergic to some foods. Scientists assume there will be no problems. They have made this assumption before. They were proven wrong. For example, a common pesticide used after World War II caused deadly problems for people and the environment.

8   Genetically modified seed development is profit driven. Modified seed prices are high. Farmers in developing countries could not pay for those seeds. The "eliminate world hunger" argument is a public relations device. It will not help people who cannot get the **enhanced** seeds. Another problem is caused when huge amounts of modified crops are produced. A lot of crops would end the need for those food imports. Stopping food imports hurts the economies of other countries that rely on the sales.

Copyright © BookheadEd Learning, LLC

9  The problems with genetically altered crops cannot be ignored. Genetic modification is unnatural. Scientists should not hurry a plant's natural growth. They should not change how much food it makes. They also should not mix unrelated genes.

10  Consumers are usually unaware of the way food has been strangely modified. Biotechnology firms have developed and sold modified seeds too quickly. Testing, research, and public discussion have been limited if they occurred at all.

Please note that excerpts and passages in the StudySync® library and this workbook are intended as touchstones to generate interest in an author's work. The excerpts and passages do not substitute for the reading of entire texts, and StudySync® strongly recommends that students seek out and purchase the whole literary or informational work in order to experience it as the author intended. Links to online resellers are available in our digital library. In addition, complete works may be ordered through an authorized reseller by filling out and returning to StudySync® the order form enclosed in this workbook.

Reading & Writing
Companion

825

THE SCIENCE OF
GENETICALLY ALTERING FOODS:
SHOULD WE DO IT?

# First Read

Read "The Science of Genetically Altering Foods: Should We Do It?." After you read, complete the Think Questions below.

## ☁ THINK QUESTIONS

1. According to the Point author, what are the benefits of genetic modification?

   Genetic modification improves _____.

2. How did humans create broccoli and cabbage?

   To create broccoli and cabbage, humans _____.

3. According to the Counterpoint author, what is one possible negative result of introducing new genes into plants? Include a line from the text to support your response.

   Introducing new genes into plants may _____.

   The author says, "_____."

4. Use context to confirm the meaning of the word *enhanced* as it is used in "The Science of Genetically Altering Foods: Should We Do It?" Write your definition of *enhanced* here.

   *Enhanced* means _____.

   A context clue is _____.

5. What is another way to say that a chemical is *lethal*?

   The chemical is _____.

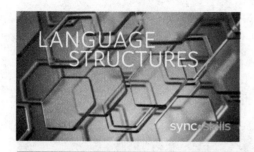

# Skill:
# Language Structures

## ★ DEFINE

In every language, there are rules that tell how to **structure** sentences. These rules define the correct order of words. In the English language, for example, a **basic** structure for sentences is subject, verb, and object. Some sentences have more **complicated** structures.

You will encounter both basic and complicated **language structures** in the classroom materials you read. Being familiar with language structures will help you better understand the text.

## ••• CHECKLIST FOR LANGUAGE STRUCTURES

To improve your comprehension of language structures, do the following:

✓ Monitor your understanding.

- Ask yourself: Why do I not understand this sentence? Is it because I do not understand some of the words? Or is it because I do not understand the way the words are ordered in the sentence?

✓ Break down the sentence into its parts.

- In English, adjectives almost always come before the noun. Example: He had a **big dog.**

> A **noun** names a person, place, thing, or idea.

> An **adjective** modifies, or describes, a noun or a pronoun.

> If there is more than one adjective, they usually appear in the following order separated by a comma: quantity or number, quality or opinion, size, age, shape, color.
Example: He had a **big, brown dog.**

> If there is more than one adjective from the same category, include the word *and*.
Example: He had a **brown and white dog.**

- Ask yourself: What are the nouns in this sentence? What adjectives describe them? In what order are the nouns and adjectives?

✓  Confirm your understanding with a peer or teacher.

## ↻ YOUR TURN

Read paragraph 7 of the text. Then, using the Checklist on the previous page, answer the multiple-choice questions below.

---

from **"The Science of Genetically Altering Foods: Should We Do It?"**

Just as concerning is the idea that scientists can introduce genes from unrelated species. They might add a nut gene into a corn plant. They could add a fish gene into a soybean. The scientists think the new gene will improve the original plant. However, it could also introduce new allergens. Many people are already seriously allergic to some foods. Scientists assume there will be no problems. They have made this assumption before. They were proven wrong. For example, a common pesticide used after World War II caused deadly problems for people and the environment.

---

1.  Which adjective modifies the noun *species*?

    ○  A.  genes
    ○  B.  introduce
    ○  C.  unrelated
    ○  D.  concerning

2.  Which adjective describes the noun *foods*?

    ○  A.  some
    ○  B.  seriously
    ○  C.  many
    ○  D.  already

3.  In the phrase "nut gene," to which category of adjectives does *nut* belong?

    ○  A.  quality or opinion
    ○  B.  size
    ○  C.  shape
    ○  D.  type

 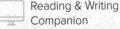

Choose the best answer to each question.

4. Which sentence orders the adjectives and noun correctly?

   ○ A. I own several vigorous old green plants.

   ○ B. I own vigorous old several green plants.

   ○ C. I own several green plants vigorous old.

   ○ D. I own old several green vigorous plants.

5. Which sentence orders the adjectives and noun correctly?

   ○ A. Luis bought a new blue beautiful short coffee table.

   ○ B. Luis bought a beautiful short new blue coffee table.

   ○ C. Luis bought a coffee table beautiful short new blue.

   ○ D. Luis bought a blue beautiful new coffee short table.

# Skill:
# Comparing and Contrasting

## ★ DEFINE

To **compare** is to show how two or more pieces of information or literary elements in a text are similar. To **contrast** is to show how two or more pieces of information or literary elements in a text are different. By comparing and contrasting, you can better understand the **meaning** and the **purpose** of the text you are reading.

## ••• CHECKLIST FOR COMPARING AND CONTRASTING

In order to compare and contrast, do the following:

✓ Look for information or elements that you can compare and contrast.

• Ask yourself: How are these two things similar? How are they different?

✓ Look for signal words that indicate a compare-and-contrast relationship.

• Ask yourself: Are there any words that indicate the writer is trying to compare and contrast two or more things?

✓ Use a graphic organizer, such as a Venn diagram or chart, to compare and contrast information.

**YOUR TURN**

Read paragraphs 3 and 8 from the text. Then, using the Checklist on the previous page, complete the chart below to compare and contrast the passages.

---

from **"The Science of Genetically Altering Foods: Should We Do It?"**

*Point Author*
The plants also can be changed to provide better nutrition. Hunger could end in countries where malnutrition is a problem. For example, scientists are developing "golden rice." That rice will stimulate the body to develop vitamin A. The rice will improve the health of millions of children in developing countries. They will go blind without the vitamin A.

*Counterpoint Author*
Genetically modified seed development is profit driven. Modified seed prices are high. Farmers in developing countries could not pay for those seeds. The "eliminate world hunger" argument is a public relations device. It will not help people who cannot get the enhanced seeds. Another problem is caused when huge amounts of modified crops are produced. A lot of crops would end the need for those food imports. Stopping food imports hurts the economies of other countries that rely on the sales.

---

| | Examples |
|---|---|
| **A** | Growing nutritious plants from genetically modified seeds would help with hunger. People who do not have enough food also do not get the nutrition they need to be healthy. |
| **B** | Genetically modified seeds cannot solve global nutrition or hunger problems. Farmers in the poorest countries cannot afford to buy enhanced seeds. |
| **C** | Genetically modified seeds can produce nutritious plants. |

| Point Author | Both | Counterpoint Author |
|---|---|---|
| | | |

THE SCIENCE OF
GENETICALLY ALTERING FOODS:
SHOULD WE DO IT?

# Close Read

---

## ✏ WRITE

ARGUMENTATIVE: Do you think that genetically altering food is beneficial or dangerous? Write a paragraph explaining your opinion. Compare and contrast both sides of the argument to support your claim. Pay attention to and edit for main and helping verbs.

---

**Use the checklist below to guide you as you write.**

☐ Do you agree more with the Point or the Counterpoint?

☐ Which side has the strongest reasons and evidence?

☐ How would you explain your opinion to someone else?

**Use the sentence frames to organize and write your argument.**

I think that genetically altering food is _____.

Although the (Point / Counterpoint) _____

author argues that genetically altering food is _____,

I agree with the (Point / Counterpoint) _____

author because this author explains how genetically altering food _____,

and it also _____.

This leads me to think that genetically altering food is _____.

## The Tomato in History, Art, and Imagination

INFORMATIONAL

## Introduction

The tomato has a rich global history and an important place in art and culture. How did the tomato get its start? And how has its image changed over time?

## V VOCABULARY

**achieve**

to accomplish through effort or skill

**resilient**

tending to bounce back or restore oneself quickly after experiencing misfortune

**develop**

start to exist or grow

**ubiquity**

the state of appearing everywhere

**millennium**

plural is **millennia**; a period of one thousand years

NOTES

## ≡ READ

1 Many of the foods we eat today have traveled the globe before reaching our plates. Take the bacon, lettuce, and tomato sandwich, for example. Thousands of years ago, Chinese farmers made the first bacon. Egyptians grew lettuce over four **millennia** ago. Tomatoes first grew in 700 AD as weed-like bushes in the Andes Mountains. Tomatoes then traveled north to the Aztec Empire. Spanish explorer Hernán Cortés and other conquistadors came across the tomato in 1519 and took seeds back to Europe. At that time, no one could have predicted the fame and **ubiquity** that the tomato has today.

2 Initially, the tomato had a mixed reception in Europe. The French people called it *pomme d'amour*, or love apple. The French used it as a decorative plant, not as a food. In northern Europe, many people thought tomatoes were poisonous. The acid in tomatoes drew lead out of the pewter dishes that the upper classes used. This caused lead poisoning. As a result, the tomato **developed** a dangerous reputation on that part of the continent. Meanwhile, Italians in southern Europe loved the tomato and used it as a topping for pizza.

3  Later, tomatoes came to symbolize bad performances. The movie review website *Rotten Tomatoes* gets its name from the old practice of throwing rotten tomatoes at performers. In 1883, the *New York Times* reported that John Ritchie was on a stage in Long Island when the audience got out of hand. Audience members became rowdy and threw rotten tomatoes at him. Even though the audience continued to bust his chops, Ritchie hung in there and continued his performance. Richie finally ran off stage after a tomato hit him in the face. It is not clear why the audience found Ritchie's act disappointing, but they did not beat around the bush when it came to giving their opinion.

4  By the end of the 19th century, modern tomatoes were much more famous than the first tomatoes that grew wild in the Andes. Some of the world's most famous artists have even found inspiration in the tomato. In the summer of 1944, just before the end of World War II, the tomato inspired Pablo Picasso to create a series of paintings. In these paintings, the tomato is a symbol of strength. The contrast of a green plant against a grey window symbolizes **resilient** life that continues during war. Two decades later, Andy Warhol famously used cans of tomato soup as symbols of consumer culture.

5  Today, the tomato stars in two large festivals. The Tomato Art Festival in Nashville, Tennessee, includes tomato crafts and a parade. La Tomatina, another festival, sells 20,000 tickets every year. For La Tomatina, people travel from all over the world to a small village in Spain. During the festival, they throw tomatoes at each other in the streets.

Pablo Picasso, *Plant de Tomates*, 1944

NOTES

Andy Warhol, *Campbell's Soup Can (Tomato)*, 1962

6    As the tomato's meaning has shifted over time, it remains a basic ingredient in a variety of foods, including pico de gallo, marinara sauce, and ketchup. The tomato has come a long way from its beginnings as a weed growing on the mountainside. Perhaps no other plant can claim the level of symbolism that the tomato has **achieved**.

# First Read

Read "The Tomato in History, Art, and Imagination." After you read, complete the Think Questions below.

## ☁ THINK QUESTIONS

1. What caused the tomato's dangerous reputation in northern Europe?

   The tomato had a dangerous reputation because _____.

2. Name two famous artists who used tomatoes in art.

   Two famous artists who used tomatoes in art were _____ and_____.

3. What is special about La Tomatina? Include a line from the text to support your response.

   La Tomatina is special because _____,

   The text says " _____."

4. Use context to confirm the meaning of the word *millennia* as it is used in "The Tomato in History, Art, and Imagination." Write your definition of *millennia* here.

   *Millennia* means _____

   A context clue is _____.

5. What is another way to say that a person who was sick last week is *resilient*?

   The person is _____.

Please note that excerpts and passages in the StudySync® library and this workbook are intended as touchstones to generate interest in an author's work. The excerpts and passages do not substitute for the reading of entire texts, and StudySync® strongly recommends that students seek out and purchase the whole literary or informational work in order to experience it as the author intended. Links to online resellers are available in our digital library. In addition, complete works may be ordered through an authorized reseller by filling out and returning to StudySync® the order form enclosed in this workbook.

Reading & Writing
Companion    **837**

# Skill:
# Analyzing Expressions

## ★ DEFINE

When you read, you may find English expressions that you do not know. An **expression** is a group of words that communicates an idea. Three types of expressions are idioms, sayings, and figurative language. They can be difficult to understand because the meanings of the words are different from their **literal**, or usual, meanings.

An **idiom** is an expression that is commonly known among a group of people. For example, "It's raining cats and dogs" means it is raining heavily. **Sayings** are short expressions that contain advice or wisdom. For instance, "Don't count your chickens before they hatch" means do not plan on something good happening before it happens. **Figurative** language is when you describe something by comparing it with something else, either directly (using the words *like* or *as*) or indirectly. For example, "I'm as hungry as a horse" means I'm very hungry. None of the expressions are about actual animals.

## ••• CHECKLIST FOR ANALYZING EXPRESSIONS

To determine the meaning of an expression, remember the following:

✓ If you find a confusing group of words, it may be an expression. The meaning of words in expressions may not be their literal meaning.

- Ask yourself: Is this confusing because the words are new? Or because the words do not make sense together?

✓ Determining the overall meaning may require that you use one or more of the following:

- context clues

- a dictionary or other resource

- teacher or peer support

✓ Highlight important information before and after the expression to look for clues.

YOUR TURN

Read each sentence in the chart below. Then, complete the chart by identifying the expression in each sentence and writing what you think the expression means.

| Expression Options | |
|---|---|
| A | "beat around the bush" |
| B | "out of hand" |
| C | "came across" |
| D | "hung in there" |

| Sentence | Expression | Meaning |
|---|---|---|
| Conquistadors came across the tomato in 1519. | | |
| In 1883, the *New York Times* reported that John Ritchie was on a stage in Long Island when the audience got out of hand. | | |
| Ritchie hung in there and continued his performance. | | |
| They did not beat around the bush when it came to giving their opinion. | | |

Please note that excerpts and passages in the StudySync® library and this workbook are intended as touchstones to generate interest in an author's work. The excerpts and passages do not substitute for the reading of entire texts, and StudySync® strongly recommends that students seek out and purchase the whole literary or informational work in order to experience it as the author intended. Links to online resellers are available in our digital library. In addition, complete works may be ordered through an authorized reseller by filling out and returning to StudySync® the order form enclosed in this workbook.

Reading & Writing
Companion

839

## Skill:
## Visual and Contextual Support

---

### ★ DEFINE

**Visual support** is an image or an object that helps you understand a text. **Contextual support** is a **feature** that helps you understand a text. By using visual and contextual supports, you can develop your vocabulary so you can better understand a variety of texts.

First, preview the text to identify any visual supports. These might include illustrations, graphics, charts, or other objects in a text. Then, identify any contextual supports. Examples of contextual supports are titles, headers, captions, and boldface terms. Write down your **observations**.

Then, write down what those visual and contextual supports tell you about the meaning of the text. Note any new vocabulary that you see in those supports. Ask your peers and your teacher to **confirm** your understanding of the text.

---

### ••• CHECKLIST FOR VISUAL AND CONTEXTUAL SUPPORT

To use visual and contextual support to understand texts, do the following:

✓ Preview the text. Read the title, headers, and other features. Look at any images and graphics.

✓ Write down the visual and contextual supports in the text.

✓ Write down what those supports tell you about the text.

✓ Note any new vocabulary that you see in those supports.

✓ Create an illustration for the reading and write a descriptive caption.

✓ Confirm your observations with your peers and teacher.

## ↻ YOUR TURN

Complete the chart below by matching each vocabulary word with the support that could best help a reader understand the meaning of the word.

| | Answer Bank |
|---|---|
| A | an illustration of John Ritchie's performance as reported by the *New York Times* |
| B | an image of ornamental apples in France |
| C | millenia |
| D | rowdy |
| E | a timeline showing when different foods developed |
| F | a footnote that defines "consumer culture" |
| G | decoration |
| H | consumer culture |

| Vocabulary | Supports |
|---|---|
| | |

**THE TOMATO**
IN HISTORY, ART,
AND IMAGINATION

# Close Read

---

## ✏ WRITE

PERSONAL RESPONSE: Foods can have both symbolic and nutritional value. Whether it's birthday cake or something that your family makes on holidays, think about a food that has symbolic value. Explain why that food is important to you. Include details that will help your audience understand the food's symbolic meaning. Pay attention to and edit for homophones.

---

**Use the checklist below to guide you as you write.**

☐ What is one food that is a symbol for you?

☐ What makes this food important to you?

☐ What words and phrases can help you explain why this food matters to you?

**Use the sentence frames to organize and write your personal response.**

One food with symbolic value for me is _____.

This food has _____ special meaning for me because _____.

(It's / Its) _____

a symbol of _____, and I remember eating it when _____.

(It's / Its) _____ special because _____.

For me, this food means _____.

# studysync®

ASSIGNMENTS   BINDER   LIBRARY

## Origin Stories

**UNIT 6**

# Origin Stories

How does who we were guide who we will become?

Genre Focus: **TEXTS THAT BLEND GENRES**

## Texts

 Paired Readings

# Extended Writing Project and Grammar

# Unit 6: Origin Stories

## How does who we were guide who we will become?

**NIKOLAI GOGOL**

Nikolai Gogol (1809–1852) was born in Ukraine to a gentleman farmer who also wrote Ukrainian folk comedies. Gogol would become a central figure of 19th-century Russian literature, known for his use of absurd humor and surrealism in the bizarre social and political satires that shaped his novels, plays, and short stories. One of his best-known short stories, "The Nose" (1836), presents an unflattering portrayal of Russian aristocratic society.

**GABRIEL GARCÍA MÁRQUEZ**

Although he's known for his contributions to the literary genre known as magical realism, Gabriel García Márquez (1927–2014) has said that there's not a single line in all of his work that does not have a basis in reality. One of the main life events that would shape his writing style was revisiting the place where he was born, a small town near the Caribbean coast in Colombia, when he was twenty-two. He said of his visit, "It was as if everything I saw had already been written."

**SAROJINI NAIDU**

Poet and political activist Sarojini Naidu (1879–1949) was the first Indian woman to become president of the Indian National Congress, the political party founded in 1885 that led the movement for independence from Great Britain. With Mahatma Gandhi, Naidu opposed British colonial rule in India, serving multiple prison sentences for her anti-British activity. Also a writer and intellectual, Naidu published her first volume of poetry, *The Golden Threshold*, in 1905.

**LOUIS PASTEUR**

The contributions of French chemist and microbiologist Louis Pasteur (1822–1895) to the fields of science, technology, and medicine in the 19th century were fundamental to the emergence of modern science. Out of the research he conducted on microorganisms and infectious diseases, he developed various vaccines and a process for eliminating pathogens from food, known as pasteurization. In his 1888 address to his colleagues, Pasteur emphasized the importance of constantly questioning one's scientific findings.

**ANNA QUINDLEN**

As a native New Yorker and a journalist, who at one point had been a staff writer for *The New York Times*, Anna Quindlen (b. 1952) was greatly affected by the 9/11 terrorist attacks when they happened. Published just weeks after the attacks, her piece "A Quilt of a Country" (2001) reflects on the state of the nation at that time, and calls for the preservation of American values such as unity, equality, and tolerance.

## NAJLA SAID

Although writer and actress Najla Said (b. 1974) was born in Boston to a Palestinian father and a Lebanese mother, she was baptized Episcopalian. As the daughter of famed intellectual Edward Said, she grew up around world-renowned scholars and frequent political debates. Yet attending a private girls' school in New York's wealthy Upper East Side, she often just wanted to fit in with her peers. Said's memoir follows her journey of self-discovery, framing it within the context of America's fraught relationship with the Middle East.

## AMY TAN

Born in Oakland, California, to Chinese immigrant parents, Amy Tan (b. 1952) was inspired to write her first novel, *The Joy Luck Club* (1989), when she visited China for the first time with her mother. An often humorous portrayal of family dynamics across generations and cultures, the novel incorporates semi-autobiographical material, family stories, and traditions. Tan's many books often draw from her own family history in their depictions of Chinese American women and the immigrant experience.

## URSULA VILLARREAL-MOURA

Born and raised in San Antonio, Texas, Ursula Villarreal-Moura (b. 1978) writes fiction and essays dealing with personal and family history, relationships, and identity, and has said that her writing often addresses themes of loss and abandonment. In her essay, "Coming-of-Age Traditions from Around the World," Villarreal-Moura surveys a wide range of coming-of-age rituals from China to Mexico and the United States to the Amazon.

## THI BUI

Thi Bui (b. 1975) was born three months before the end of the Vietnam War and fled with her family to the United States in 1978 after the fall of South Vietnam. Bui has said that her illustrated memoir, *The Best We Could Do* (2017), was a way for her to make sense of the stories she heard growing up. The book contextualizes her parents' anecdotes within a broader political and historical narrative, and recalls the difficulties she and her family faced as immigrants in the United States.

## LAGNAJITA MUKHOPADHYAY

At seventeen, Lagnajita Mukhopadhyay (b. 1998) became Nashville, Tennessee's first Youth Poet Laureate. An immigrant from India, she is committed to increasing the visibility of the diverse backgrounds and experiences that make up American culture. While Mukhopadhyay has played various instruments and has written songs from a young age, she thinks of her poetry as having a different function in that it can be a means of broadening the worldview of her readers.

## ANGIE SHUMOV

Angie Shumov's article "Creation Myths from Around the World" delves into the narratives told across cultures and throughout history about the origins of the world. It discusses the myths of ancient civilizations, in addition to the commonalities among the origin stories of Christianity, Judaism, and Islam.

## Introduction

This informational text provides readers with cultural and historical background information about the origins of magical realist literature. Magical realism, at first only a term used to describe art, became its own literary genre in the 1940s. Used to describe literature that blends the real with the supernatural, magical realism often shares characteristics with other genres such as surrealism. Literary giants Isabel Allende and Gabriel García Márquez are some of the most well-known authors of magical realism, with their masterpieces *The House of the Spirits* and *One Hundred Years of Solitude*. Discover how writers of magical realism play with time and metaphor to lend attention to political and social structures in the real world.

# "Time is elastic and ever changing in works of magical realism."

1   Have you ever had a dream that felt completely real? Perhaps you dreamed you were in a familiar place, like home or school. Then suddenly you realized that you were flying or breathing underwater and your sense of time seemed to stretch and bend. If these things happened in real life, they'd be mind-blowing, but in a dream, they seem perfectly natural. Magical realism is a form of literature that resembles a dreamlike state. Magical realism is a genre of narrative fiction and film that blends the real and the magical in a totally believable way.

## The Origins of Magical Realism

2   Before magical realism became an official literary movement, authors experimented with bending reality. In his 1915 novella *The Metamorphosis*, the Czech novelist Franz Kafka describes how the main character, Gregor Samsa, deals with the fact that he has turned into an insect overnight. Readers accustomed to realistic fiction might wonder, "Did the man really turn into a bug?" It doesn't matter, because the narrator and the main character believe that he has. In treating the story's conflict in this matter-of-fact way, Kafka blurred the lines between the real and the unreal in a way that hadn't been done before outside of mythology or tales of fantasy.

3   The term *magical realism* was introduced ten years later by the German art critic Franz Roh, who used it to describe art that injected bizarre images into **realistic** depictions of the world. Literary magical realism originated in Latin America beginning in the 1940s. It is a genre primarily associated with the works of a group of writers from that region. They include Cuban Alejo Carpentier, Colombian Gabriel García Márquez, Argentines Julio Cortázar and Jorge Luis Borges, and Chilean Isabel Allende. Cortázar's *Rayuela* (Hopscotch) (1963) and García Márquez's *One Hundred Years of Solitude* (1970) are considered two of the first major novels of magical realism. Translations of these and other works spread the influence of magical realism around the world. Toni Morrison, Alice Hoffman, and Salman Rushdie have incorporated magical realism into their novels, as have filmmakers like Guillermo del Toro. His films *The Devil's Backbone* and *Pan's Labyrinth* tell dark stories that blend myth and fantasy with the reality of their wartime

NOTES

settings. Magical realism also inspired artists, such as Italian painter Giorgio de Chirico and American painter Philip Evergood, both of whom blended realist and surrealist aspects to evoke a dreamlike reality.

Giorgio de Chirico, Italian painter, among some of his works, 1925.

**Timely and Timeless Stories**

4 Magical realists were influenced by folk and fairy tales, mythology, and the literary movements of early twentieth century European writers, especially the writings of Kafka. Their works—mostly stories and novels—are characterized by complicated plots that weave together the **mundane**, the magical, and the political. Time is elastic and ever-changing in works of magical realism. It might jump forward or backward or even stand still for long stretches. The settings are often ordinary places where **supernatural** events happen to characters who have magical qualities. For example, in García Márquez's story "The Handsomest Drowned Man in the World," the women in a fishing village fall in love with and adopt a sailor whose dead body has washed ashore. A character in Isabel Allende's multigenerational novel *The House of the Spirits* has green hair and yellow eyes. The **fantastical** events in magical realist literature are often metaphorical. They disguise an implicit critique of social or political institutions. For example, neither the villagers nor the priests in García Márquez's story "A Very Old Man With Enormous Wings" treat the angel with much respect. The angel himself is the antithesis of angelic; he's smelly, grumpy, and uncommunicative. García Márquez seems to be commenting on the traditional ideas about religion.

5 Another feature of magical realism is its **indifferent** tone. Narrators describe real and fantastical events with a lack of surprise. They are not impressed or amazed by the fantastical elements in the story. As a result, the readers follow their lead, taking the surreal events in stride and treating them as perfectly ordinary and normal.

*Dowager in a Wheelchair* (1952) by Philip Evergood.

## Overlaps with Other Genres

6   Magical realism, which is also sometimes known as magic realism, shares many qualities with other literary genres from the modern and postmodern periods, including surrealism and, fantasy. Like surrealism, magical realism borrows archetypes and inexplicable and fantastical elements from the world of dreams; however, in magical realism, their purpose is to comment on the external world, not to explore the author's inner psyche. Like fantasy, magical realism borrows supernatural events and fantastical characters from myth, folklore, and fairy tales, but magical realism lacks fantasy's sense of wonder and impossibility, replacing it with a tone of indifference.

7   **Major Concepts**

- Magical realism incorporates elements of mythology, folktales, fairy tales, and fantasy.

- The stories, novels, and films in the magical realist tradition have plots that blend the surreal and fantastical and the real and mundane. Neither the characters, the narrator, nor the readers question the supernatural elements that arise in the stories.

- The mundane settings and supernatural elements in the stories often provide cover for a critique of social, cultural, or political institutions.

8   **Style**

- Literary works of magical realism primarily take the form of novels and stories.

- These works feature realistic and mundane settings that serve as the backdrop for magical or even surreal events and characters with fantastical traits.

- The works have a realistic tone. The narrators tell the story in a straight-forward, almost indifferent manner. Magical events are described as if they are ordinary and normal.

- Time is often not linear in works of magical realism. It may bend, skip forward or backward, or stand still.

9   Magical realism is a thoughtful blend of the everyday and the surreal, the serious and the supernatural. Since the 1960s, readers have been enthralled by magical realists' stories of love and death set in mundane yet magical villages. The original authors of magical realistic literature have mostly passed away, yet they have left a powerful legacy behind. Where do you see elements of magical realism in the books, stories, films, and videos you read and watch?

# Literary Focus

Read "Literary Focus: Magical Realism." After you read, complete the Think Questions below.

☁ **THINK QUESTIONS**

1. What are several early influences on the literary movement of magical realism? Be sure to cite evidence directly from the text.

2. How do the elements of magical realism help disguise its critique of social or political institutions?

3. Based on your reading of the text, what effect does the blending of the mundane and the magical have on the readers of magical realism?

4. Use context clues to determine the meaning of the word **indifferent**. Write your best definition, along with the words and phrases that were most helpful in determining the word's meaning. Then, check a dictionary to confirm your understanding.

5. The word *supernatural* comes from the Latin *super*, meaning "above" or "beyond" and *naturalis*, meaning "birth." With this information in mind, write your best definition of the word **supernatural** as it used in this text. Cite any words or phrases that were particularly helpful in coming to your conclusion.

# The City that Never Stops Giving

POETRY
Lagnajita Mukhopadhyay
2015

## Introduction

Poet and avid guitar-player Lagnajita Mukhopadhyay was born in India, and as a child moved with her family to Nashville, Tennessee. In 2015, at the age of 17, she published a book of poetry, *This is Our War*, and was named Nashville's first Youth Poet Laureate. Her poem "The City that Never Stops Giving" was inspired by the location of her high school in downtown Nashville, and captures the buzz and energy of a major urban area, at once particular and universal.

# "From this crosswalk, electricity ripples through the crooked streets of the city."

1    The city never stops giving
2    on the corner of 6th and Broadway
3    where downtown traffic is a **harrowing**
4    consistency, when the light turns green,
5    it doesn't always mean go.
6    Where Roy Orbison wrote "Oh Pretty Woman[1],"
7    emboldened by the femme[2] of mercy
8    below his apartment balcony
9    where tourists and the music
10   leave a warm taste of **affinity**,
11   by the Starbucks in the Renaissance[3]
12   that snags money from teenagers
13   who **rendezvous** before school.
14   They never spell my name right
15   on the little cups filled with magic.
16   From this crosswalk, electricity ripples
17   through the crooked streets of the city.
18   The paths of headlights **mature** into veins
19   of a breathing atmosphere.
20   The wait is forgiving, and when
21   we don't like what we see and
22   all significance is lost, we turn
23   around softly and walk the other way.
24   A newfangled[4] story in a blink and a sigh,
25   blinkers signaling a right turn,
26   people staring straight ahead,
27   headlong into the bright eyes
28   of a **symmetrical** world. So begins
29   the journey across the black and white,
30   when everyone becomes familiar

---

1. **"Oh Pretty Woman"** a hit 1964 song performed by Roy Orbison
2. **femme** woman
3. **Renaissance** the name of a building
4. **newfangled** fancy or modern, objectionably so

NOTES

31 and nothing feels strange. Every step
32 falls into the heartbeats of a million
33 lonely people, and when the crosswalk ends,
34 so does another chance encounter
35 with a supreme stranger that you
36 never would have otherwise met—
37 a James, a Taylor, a small life changer,
38 the old love of a never ending family
39 meets the new love of a never ending home,
40 and the city never stops giving.

"The City that Never Stops Giving" by Ladnajita Mukhopadhyay, 2015 Nashville Youth Poet Laureate. Used by permission of the National Youth Poet Laureate Program, www.youthlaureate.org.

## ✏ WRITE

**PERSONAL RESPONSE:** In her poem "The City that Never Stops Giving," poet Lagnajita Mukhopadhyay's speaker offers a personal guide to Nashville, Tennessee. In response to this poem, write a poem or short prose piece of your own, entitled, "The [Place] that _____," in which you guide readers in how to see the bond you have with the place where you live or have grown up. Include descriptive details, figurative language, and other elements to create a rich and meaningful response.

# Past and Future

POETRY
Sarojini Naidu
1905

## Introduction

K nown as "the Nightingale of India," Sarojini Naidu (1879–1949) was an activist, poet, and politician. She was a strong proponent of the Indian Congress Movement, led by Mahatma Gandhi, which opposed British rule and called for Indian independence in the years surrounding the Second World War. She became the first Indian female president of the National Congress in 1925. The subjects of her poems, many of which she composed and published prior to her activism, range from patriotism to ancient wisdom. In "Past and Future," published in Naidu's first collection of poems, *The Golden Threshold*, she personifies the "Soul," depicting its transition from old memories to new beginnings.

# "The new hath come and now the old retires. . ."

1  The new hath come and now the old retires:
2  And so the past becomes a mountain-cell,
3  Where lone, apart, old hermit-memories dwell
4  In **consecrated** calm, forgotten yet
5  Of the keen heart that hastens to forget
6  Old longings in fulfilling new desires.

7  And now the Soul stands in a **vague**, intense
8  Expectancy and **anguish** of suspense,
9  On the dim chamber-threshold . . . lo! he sees
10 Like a strange, fated bride as yet unknown,
11 His **timid** future shrinking there alone,
12 Beneath her marriage-veil of mysteries.

Sarojini Naidu and Mahatma Gandhi on their way to break the Salt Laws in India, 1930.

## ✏ WRITE

LITERARY ANALYSIS: For some, the past is something to be escaped, while for others, it is something to long for. Which is it for the speaker of this poem? Locate poetic elements and identify structural techniques in the text to support your interpretation.

# The Joy Luck Club

FICTION
Amy Tan
1989

## Introduction

Chinese American author Amy Tan (b. 1952) grew up in Oakland, California, as the daughter of immigrant parents. *The Joy Luck Club*, her first published book, was a critical and commercial success that catapulted her into the literary mainstream. Constructed of episodic stories drawing on her own heritage, the book explores the relationships between a group of Chinese American women and their immigrant mothers, offering a compelling portrait of their interwoven lives across generations. In the story presented here, "Two Kinds," a mother has high expectations for her daughter, hoping she will become "a Chinese Shirley Temple" or a classically trained pianist on *The Ed Sullivan Show.*

# "For unlike my mother, I did not believe I could be anything I wanted to be. I could only be me."

"Jing-Mei Woo: Two Kinds"

1  My mother believed you could be anything you wanted to be in America. You could open a restaurant. You could work for the government and get good retirement. You could buy a house with almost no money down. You could become rich. You could become instantly famous.

 **Skill: Textual Evidence**

*The mother wants her daughter to succeed when she says, "you can be prodigy" and "best anything." She is competing with Auntie Lindo to have the best daughter when she says, "Her daughter, she is only best tricky."*

2  "Of course you can be prodigy[1], too," my mother told me when I was nine. "You can be best anything. What does Auntie Lindo know? Her daughter, she is only best tricky."

3  America was where all my mother's hopes lay. She had come here in 1949 after losing everything in China: her mother and father, her family home, her first husband, and two daughters, twin baby girls. But she never looked back with regret. There were so many ways for things to get better.

. . .

4  We didn't immediately pick the right kind of prodigy. At first my mother thought I could be a Chinese Shirley Temple[2]. We'd watch Shirley's old movies on TV as though they were training films. My mother would poke my arm and say, "*Ni kan*"—You watch. And I would see Shirley tapping her feet, or singing a sailor song, or pursing her lips into a very round O while saying, "Oh my goodness."

5  "*Ni kan*," said my mother as Shirley's eyes flooded with tears. "You already know how. Don't need talent for crying!"

6  Soon after my mother got this idea about Shirley Temple, she took me to the beauty training school in the Mission district and put me in the hands of a student who could barely hold the scissors without shaking. Instead of getting

---

1. **prodigy**  an exceptionally talented child or young person
2. **Shirley Temple**  a child star in the 1930s, Shirley Temple (1928–2014) became a diplomat and was ambassador to Czechoslovakia during the fall of the Berlin Wall

big fat curls, I **emerged** with an uneven mass of crinkly black fuzz. My mother dragged me off to the bathroom and tried to wet down my hair.

7   "You look like Negro Chinese," she lamented, as if I had done this on purpose.

8   The instructor of the beauty training school had to lop off these soggy clumps to make my hair even again. "Peter Pan is very popular these days" the instructor assured my mother. I now had hair the length of a boy's, with straight-across bangs that hung at a slant two inches above my eyebrows. I liked the haircut and it made me actually look forward to my future fame.

9   In fact, in the beginning, I was just as excited as my mother, maybe even more so. I pictured this prodigy part of me as many different images, trying each one on for size. I was a dainty ballerina girl standing by the curtains, waiting to hear the right music that would send me floating on my tiptoes. I was like the Christ child lifted out of the straw manger, crying with holy indignity. I was Cinderella stepping from her pumpkin carriage with sparkly cartoon music filling the air.

10  In all of my imaginings, I was filled with a sense that I would soon become *perfect*. My mother and father would adore me. I would be beyond reproach. I would never feel the need to sulk for anything.

11  But sometimes the prodigy in me became impatient. "If you don't hurry up and get me out of here, I'm disappearing for good," it warned. "And then you'll always be nothing."

12  Every night after dinner my mother and I would sit at the Formica kitchen table. She would present new tests, taking her examples from stories of amazing children she had read in *Ripley's Believe It or Not*, or *Good Housekeeping*, *Reader's Digest*, and a dozen other magazines she kept in a pile in our bathroom. My mother got these magazines from people whose houses she cleaned. And since she cleaned many houses each week, we had a great assortment. She would look through them all, searching for stories about remarkable children.

13  The first night she brought out a story about a three-year-old boy who knew the capitals of all the states and even most of the European countries. A teacher was quoted as saying that the little boy could also pronounce the names of the foreign cities correctly.

14  "What's the capital of Finland?" my mother asked me, looking at the magazine story.

15  All I knew was the capital of California, because Sacramento was the name of the street we lived on in Chinatown. "Nairobi!" I guessed, saying the most foreign word I could think of. She checked to see if that was possibly one way to pronounce "Helsinki" before showing me the answer.

16  The tests got harder—multiplying numbers in my head, finding the queen of hearts in a deck of cards, trying to stand on my head without using my hands, predicting the daily temperatures in Los Angeles, New York, and London.

17  One night I had to look at a page from the Bible for three minutes and then report everything I could remember. "Now Jehoshaphat had riches and honor in abundance and... that's all I remember, Ma," I said.

18  And after seeing my mother's disappointed face once again, something inside me began to die. I hated the tests, the raised hopes and failed expectations. Before going to bed that night, I looked in the mirror above the bathroom sink and when I saw only my face staring back—and that it would always be this ordinary face—I began to cry. Such a sad, ugly girl! I made high-pitched noises like a crazed animal, trying to scratch out the face in the mirror.

19  And then I saw what seemed to be the prodigy side of me—a face I had never seen before. I looked at my reflection, blinking so I could see more clearly. The girl staring back at me was angry, powerful. This girl and I were the same. I had new thoughts, willful thoughts, or rather thoughts filled with lots of won'ts. I won't let her change me, I promised myself. I won't be what I'm not.

20  So now on nights when my mother presented her tests, I performed listlessly, my head propped on one arm. I pretended to be bored. And I was. I got so bored I started counting the bellows of the foghorns out on the bay while my mother drilled me in other areas. The sound was comforting and reminded me of the cow jumping over the moon. And the next day, I played a game with myself, seeing if my mother would give up on me before eight bellows. After a while I usually counted only one, maybe two bellows at most. At last she was beginning to give up hope.

21  Two or three months went by without any mention of my being a prodigy. And then one day my mother was watching *The Ed Sullivan Show* on TV. The TV was old and the sound kept shorting out. Every time my mother got halfway up from the sofa to adjust the set, the sound would go back on and Ed would be talking. As soon as she sat down, Ed would go silent again. She got up, the TV broke into loud piano music. She sat down. Silence. Up and down, back and forth, quiet and loud. It was like a stiff embraceless dance between her and the TV set. Finally she stood by the set with her hand on the sound dial.

22    She seemed entranced by the music, a little frenzied piano piece with this mesmerizing quality, sort of quick passages and then teasing lilting ones before it returned to the quick playful parts.

23    "*Ni kan*," my mother said, calling me over with hurried hand gestures. "Look here."

24    I could see why my mother was fascinated by the music. It was being pounded out by a little Chinese girl, about nine years old, with a Peter Pan haircut. The girl had the sauciness of a Shirley Temple. She was proudly modest like a proper Chinese child. And she also did this fancy sweep of a curtsy, so that the fluffy skirt of her white dress cascaded slowly to the floor like the petals of a large carnation.

25    In spite of these warning signs, I wasn't worried. Our family had no piano and we couldn't afford to buy one, let alone reams of sheet music and piano lessons. So I could be generous in my comments when my mother bad-mouthed the little girl on TV.

26    "Play note right, but doesn't sound good! No singing sound," complained my mother.

27    "What are you picking on her for?" I said carelessly. "She's pretty good. Maybe she's not the best, but she's trying hard." I knew almost immediately that I would be sorry I had said that.

28    "Just like you," she said. "Not the best. Because you not trying." She gave a little huff as she let go of the sound dial and sat down on the sofa.

29    The little Chinese girl sat down also, to play an encore of "Anitra's Tanz," by Grieg. I remember the song, because later on I had to learn how to play it.

30    Three days after watching *The Ed Sullivan Show* my mother told me what my schedule would be for piano lessons and piano practice. She had talked to Mr. Chong, who lived on the first floor of our apartment building. Mr. Chong was a retired piano teacher and my mother had traded housecleaning services for weekly lessons and a piano for me to practice on every day, two hours a day, from four until six.

31    When my mother told me this, I felt as though I had been sent to hell. I whined and then kicked my foot a little when I couldn't stand it anymore.

32    "Why don't you like me the way I am? I'm *not* a genius! I can't play the piano. And even if I could, I wouldn't go on TV if you paid me a million dollars!" I cried.

33   My mother slapped me. "Who ask you to be genius?" she shouted. "Only ask you be your best. For you sake. You think I want you to be genius? Hnnh! What for! Who ask you!"

34   "So ungrateful," I heard her mutter in Chinese, "If she had as much talent as she has temper, she'd be famous now."

35   Mr. Chong, whom I secretly nicknamed Old Chong, was very strange, always tapping his fingers to the silent music of an invisible orchestra. He looked ancient in my eyes. He had lost most of the hair on the top of his head and he wore thick glasses and had eyes that always looked tired and sleepy. But he must have been younger that I thought, since he lived with his mother and was not yet married.

36   I met Old Lady Chong once and that was enough. She had this peculiar smell like a baby that had done something in its pants. And her fingers felt like a dead person's, like an old peach I once found in the back of the refrigerator; the skin just slid off the meat when I picked it up.

37   I soon found out why Old Chong had retired from teaching piano. He was deaf. "Like Beethoven!" he shouted to me. "We're both listening only in our head!" And he would start to **conduct** his frantic silent sonatas.

38   Our lessons went like this. He would open the book and point to different things, explaining their purpose: "Key! Treble! Bass! No sharps or flats! So this is C major! Listen now and play after me!"

39   And then he would play the C scale a few times, a simple chord, and then, as if inspired by an old, unreachable itch, he gradually added more notes and running trills and a pounding bass until the music was really something quite grand.

40   I would play after him, the simple scale, the simple chord, and then I just played some nonsense that sounded like a cat running up and down on top of garbage cans. Old Chong smiled and applauded and then said, "Very good! But now you must learn to keep time!"

41   So that's how I discovered that Old Chong's eyes were too slow to keep up with the wrong notes I was playing. He went through the motions in half-time. To help me keep rhythm, he stood behind me, pushing down on my right shoulder for every beat. He balanced pennies on top of my wrists so that I would keep them still as I slowly played scales and arpeggios. He had me curve my hand around an apple and keep that shape when playing chords. He marched stiffly to show me how to make each finger dance up and down, staccato like an obedient little soldier.

42  He taught me all these things, and that was how I also learned I could be lazy and get away with mistakes, lots of mistakes. If I hit the wrong notes because I hadn't practiced enough, I never corrected myself. I just kept playing in rhythm. And Old Chong kept conducting his own private reverie.

43  So maybe I never really gave myself a fair chance. I did pick up the basics pretty quickly, and I might have become a good pianist at the young age. But I was so determined not to try, not to be anybody different that I learned to play only the most ear-splitting preludes, the most discordant hymns.

44  Over the next year, I practiced like this, dutifully in my own way. And then one day I heard my mother and her friend Lindo Jong both talking in a loud bragging tone of voice so others could hear. It was after church, and I was leaning against the brick wall wearing a dress with stiff white petticoats. Auntie Lindo's daughter, Waverly, who was about my age, was standing farther down the wall about five feet away. We had grown up together and shared all the closeness of two sisters **squabbling** over crayons and dolls. In other words, for the most part, we hated each other. I thought she was snotty. Waverly Jong had gained a certain amount of fame as "Chinatown's Littlest Chinese Chess Champion."

45  "She bring home too many trophy," lamented Auntie Lindo that Sunday. "All day she play chess. All day I have no time do nothing but dust off her winnings." She threw a scolding look at Waverly, who pretended not to see her.

46  "You lucky you don't have this problem," Auntie Lindo said with a sigh to my mother.

47  And my mother squared her shoulders and bragged: "Our problem worser than yours. If we ask Jing-mei wash dish, she hear nothing but music. It's like you can't stop this natural talent."

48  And right then, I was determined to put a stop to her foolish pride.

49  A few weeks later, Old Chong and my mother conspired to have me play in a talent show which would be held in the church hall. By then, my parents had saved up enough to buy me a secondhand piano, a black Wurlitzer spinet with a scarred bench. It was the showpiece of our living room.

50  For the talent show, I was to play a piece called "Pleading Child," from Schumann's *Scenes from Childhood*. It was a simple, moody piece that sounded more difficult than it was. I was supposed to memorize the whole thing, playing the repeat parts twice to make the piece sound longer. But I dawdled over it, playing a few bars and then cheating, looking up to see what

notes followed. I never really listened to what I was playing. I daydreamed about being somewhere else, about being someone else.

51    The part I liked to practice best was the fancy curtsy: right foot out, touch the rose on the carpet with a pointed foot, sweep to the side, left leg bends, look up and smile.

52    My parents invited all the couples from the Joy Luck Club[3] to witness my debut. Auntie Lindo and Uncle Tin were there. Waverly and her two older brothers had also come. The first two rows were filled with children both younger and older than I was. The littlest ones got to go first. They recited simple nursery rhymes, squawked out tunes on miniature violins, twirled Hula Hoops, practiced in pink ballet tutus, and when they bowed or curtsied, the audience would sigh in unison, "Awww," and then clap enthusiastically.

53    When my turn came, I was very confident. I remember my childish excitement. It was as if I knew, without a doubt, that the prodigy side of me really did exist. I had no fear whatsoever, no nervousness. I remember thinking to myself, This is it! This is it! I looked out over the audience, at my mother's blank face, my father's yawn, Auntie Lindo's stiff-lipped smile, Waverly's sulky expression. I had on a white dress layered with sheets of lace, and a pink bow in my Peter Pan haircut. As I sat down I envisioned people jumping to their feet and Ed Sullivan rushing up to introduce me to everyone on TV.

54    And I started to play. It was so beautiful. I was so caught up in how lovely I looked that at first I didn't worry about how I would sound. So it was a surprise to me when I hit the first wrong note and I realized something didn't sound quite right. And then I hit another and another followed that. A chill started at the top of my head and began to trickle down. Yet I couldn't stop playing, as though my hands were bewitched. I kept thinking my fingers would adjust themselves back, like a train switching to the right track. I played this strange jumble through two repeats, the sour notes staying with me all the way to the end.

55    When I stood up, I discovered my legs were shaking. Maybe I had just been nervous and the audience, like Old Chong, had seen me go through the right motions and had not heard anything wrong at all. I swept my right foot out, went down on my knee, looked up and smiled. The room was quiet, except for Old Chong, who was beaming and shouting "Bravo! Bravo! Well done!" But then I saw my mother's face, her stricken face. The audience clapped weakly, and as I walked back to my chair, with my whole face quivering as I

---

3. **the Joy Luck Club**  the name of the mahjong club organized by the four immigrant Chinese women whose stories comprise *The Joy Luck Club*, Amy Tan's debut novel

tried not to cry, I heard a little boy whisper loudly to his mother, "That was awful," and mother whispered back, "Well, she certainly tried."

56 And now I realized how many people were in the audience, the whole world it seemed. I was aware of eyes burning into my back. I felt the shame of my mother and father as they sat stiffly through the rest of the show.

57 We could have escaped during intermission. Pride and some strange sense of honor must have anchored my parents to their chairs. And so we watched it all: the eighteen-year-old boy with a fake mustache who did a magic show and juggled flaming hoops while riding a unicycle. The breasted girl with white makeup who sang from *Madama Butterfly* and got honorable mention. And the eleven-year-old boy who won first prize playing a tricky violin song that sounded like a busy bee.

58 After the show, the Hsus, the Jongs, and the St. Clairs from the Joy Luck Club came up to my mother and father.

59 "Lots of talented kids," Auntie Lindo said vaguely, smiling broadly.

60 "That was somethin' else," my father said, and I wondered if he was referring to me in a humorous way, or whether he even remembered what I had done.

61 Waverly looked at me and shrugged her shoulders. "You aren't a genius like me," she said matter-of-factly. And if I hadn't felt so bad, I would have pulled her braids and punched her stomach.

62 But my mother's expression was what devastated me: a quiet, blank look that said she had lost everything. I felt the same way, and it seemed as if everybody were now coming up, like gawkers at the scene of an accident, to see what parts were actually missing. When we got on the bus to go home, my father was humming the busy-bee tune and my mother was silent. I kept thinking she wanted to wait until we got home before shouting at me. But when my father unlocked the door to our apartment, my mother walked in and then went to the back, into the bedroom. No accusations. No blame. And in a way, I felt disappointed. I had been waiting for her to start shouting, so that I could shout back and cry and blame her for all my misery.

63 I assumed my talent-show fiasco meant I never had to play the piano again. But two days later, after school, my mother came out of the kitchen and saw me watching TV.

64 "Four clock," she reminded me as if it were any other day. I was stunned, as though she were asking me to go through the talent-show torture again. I wedged myself more tightly in front of the TV.

65   "Turn off TV," she called from the kitchen five minutes later.

66   I didn't budge. And then I decided. I didn't have to do what mother said anymore. I wasn't her slave. This wasn't China. I had listened to her before and look what happened. She was the stupid one.

67   She came out of the kitchen and stood in the arched entryway of the living room. "Four clock," she said once again, louder.

68   "I'm not going to play anymore," I said nonchalantly. "Why should I? I'm not a genius."

69   She walked over and stood in front of the TV. I saw that her chest was heaving up and down in an angry way.

70   "No!" I said, and I now felt stronger, as if my true self had finally emerged. So this was what had been inside me all along.

71   "No! I won't!" I screamed.

72   She yanked me by the arm, pulled me off the floor, snapped off the TV. She was frighteningly strong, half pulling, half carrying me towards the piano as I kicked the throw rugs under my feet. She lifted me up onto the hard bench. I was sobbing by now, looking at her bitterly. Her chest was heaving even more and her mouth was open, smiling crazily as if she were pleased that I was crying.

73   "You want me to be someone that I'm not!" I sobbed. "I'll never be the kind of daughter you want me to be!"

74   "Only two kinds of daughters," she shouted in Chinese. "Those who are obedient and those who follow their own mind! Only one kind of daughter can live in this house. Obedient daughter!"

75   "Then I wish I wasn't your daughter. I wish you weren't my mother," I shouted. As I said these things I got scared. It felt like worms and toads and slimy things crawling out of my chest, but it also felt good, as if this awful side of me had surfaced, at last.

76   "Too late to change this," said my mother shrilly.

77   And I could sense her anger rising to its breaking point. I wanted to see it spill over. And that's when I remembered the babies she had lost in China, the ones we never talked about. "Then I wish I'd never been born!" I shouted. "I wish I were dead! Like them."

78   It was as if I had said magic words. Alakazam!—and her face went blank, her mouth closed, her arms went **slack**, and she backed out of the room, stunned, as if she were blowing away like a small brown leaf, thin, brittle, lifeless.

• • •

79   It was not the only disappointment my mother felt in me. In the years that followed, I failed her so many times, each time asserting my own will, my right to fall short of expectations. I didn't get straight As. I didn't become class president. I didn't get into Stanford. I dropped out of college.

80   For unlike my mother, I did not believe I could be anything I wanted to be. I could only be me.

81   And for all those years, we never talked about the disaster at the recital or my terrible accusations afterward at the piano bench. All that remained unchecked, like a betrayal that was now unspeakable. So I never found a way to ask her why she had hoped for something so large that failure was **inevitable**.

82   And even worse, I never asked her what frightened me the most: Why had she given up hope?

83   For after our struggle at the piano, she never mentioned my playing again. The lessons stopped. The lid to the piano was closed, shutting out the dust, my misery, and her dreams.

84   So she surprised me. A few years ago, she offered to give me the piano, for my thirtieth birthday. I had not played in all those years. I saw the offer as a sign of forgiveness, a tremendous burden removed.

85   "Are you sure?" I asked shyly. "I mean, won't you and Dad miss it?"

86   "No, this your piano," she said firmly. "Always your piano. You only one can play."

87   "Well, I probably can't play anymore," I said. "It's been years."

88   "You pick up fast," said my mother, as if she knew this was certain. "You have natural talent. You could been genius if you want to."

89   "No, I couldn't."

90   "You just not trying," said my mother. And she was neither angry nor sad. She said it as if to announce a fact that could never be disproved. "Take it," she said.

Please note that excerpts and passages in the StudySync® library and this workbook are intended as touchstones to generate interest in an author's work. The excerpts and passages do not substitute for the reading of entire texts, and StudySync® strongly recommends that students seek out and purchase the whole literary or informational work in order to experience it as the author intended. Links to online resellers are available in our digital library. In addition, complete works may be ordered through an authorized reseller by filling out and returning to StudySync® the order form enclosed in this workbook.

Reading & Writing
Companion

869

91 But I didn't at first. It was enough that she had offered it to me. And after that, every time I saw it in my parents' living room, standing in front of the bay windows, it made me feel proud, as if it were a shiny trophy that I had won back.

92 Last week I sent a tuner over to my parents' apartment and had the piano reconditioned, for purely sentimental reasons. My mother had died a few months before and I had been been getting things in order for my father, a little bit at a time. I put the jewelry in special silk pouches. The sweaters she had knitted in yellow, pink, bright orange—all the colors I hated—I put those in moth-proof boxes. I found some old Chinese silk dresses, the kind with little slits up the sides. I rubbed the old silk against my skin, then wrapped them in tissue and decided to take them home with me.

93 After I had the piano tuned, I opened the lid and touched the keys. It sounded even richer than I remembered. Really, it was a very good piano. Inside the bench were the same exercise notes with handwritten scales, the same secondhand music books with their covers held together with yellow tape.

94 I opened up the Schumann book to the dark little piece I had played at the recital. It was on the left-hand side of the page, "Pleading Child." It looked more difficult than I remembered. I played a few bars, surprised at how easily the notes came back to me.

95 And for the first time, or so it seemed, I noticed the piece on the right-hand side. It was called "Perfectly Contented." I tried to play this one as well. It had a lighter melody but the same flowing rhythm and turned out to be quite easy. "Pleading Child" was shorter but slower; "Perfectly Contented" was longer but faster. And after I played them both a few times, I realized they were two halves of the same song.

---

# First Read

Read *The Joy Luck Club*. After you read, complete the Think Questions below.

 **THINK QUESTIONS**

1. What does the mother in the excerpt want from her daughter? Use details from the text to support your answer.

2. How does the narrator's attitude toward the idea of being a prodigy change over the course of the text? Support your answer with evidence from the text.

3. After her performance at the piano recital, explain why the narrator is disappointed when her mother does not yell at her. Support your answer using ideas from the text that are directly stated or implied.

4. Use context clues to determine the meaning of the word **squabble** as it is used in the text. Write your definition of *squabble*, and explain which clues helped you understand it.

5. Keeping in mind that the Latin word *evitar* means "to avoid," and the Latin prefix *in-* means "not," write your definition of the word **inevitable** as it is used in the text. Then, use a print or an online dictionary to verify your understanding.

# Skill:
# Textual Evidence

Use the Checklist to analyze Textual Evidence in *The Joy Luck Club*. Refer to the sample student annotation about Textual Evidence in the text.

## ••• CHECKLIST FOR TEXTUAL EVIDENCE

In order to support an analysis by citing evidence that is explicitly stated in the text, do the following:

✓ Read the text closely and critically.

✓ Identify what the text says explicitly.

✓ Find the most relevant textual evidence that supports your analysis.

✓ Consider why an author explicitly states specific details and information.

✓ Cite the specific words, phrases, sentences, or paragraphs from the text that support your analysis.

In order to interpret implicit meanings in a text by making inferences, do the following:

✓ Combine information directly stated in the text with your own knowledge, experiences, and observations.

✓ Cite the specific words, phrases, sentences, or paragraphs from the text that led to and support this inference.

In order to cite textual evidence to support an analysis of what the text says explicitly as well as inferences drawn from the text, consider the following questions:

✓ Have I read the text closely and critically?

✓ What inferences am I making about the text?

✓ What textual evidence am I using to support these inferences?

✓ Am I quoting the evidence from the text correctly?

✓ Does my textual evidence logically relate to my analysis or the inference I am making?

# Skill:
# Textual Evidence

Reread paragraphs 12–20 of *The Joy Luck Club*. Then, using the Checklist on the previous page, answer the multiple-choice questions below.

## ⟳ YOUR TURN

1. The textual evidence that best supports the inference that Jing-mei is not a prodigy is —

   ○ A. "My mother got these magazines from people whose houses she cleaned. And since she cleaned many houses each week, we had a great assortment. She would look through them all, searching for stories about remarkable children."

   ○ B. "All I knew was the capital of California, because Sacramento was the name of the street we lived on in Chinatown. "Nairobi!" I guessed, saying the most foreign word I could think of."

   ○ C. "The tests got harder—multiplying numbers in my head, finding the queen of hearts in a deck of cards, trying to stand on my head without using my hands, predicting the daily temperatures in Los Angeles, New York, and London."

   ○ D. "And after seeing my mother's disappointed face once again, something inside me began to die."

2. Which of the interpretations below is best supported by textual evidence in paragraphs 19 and 20?

   ○ A. Jing-mei realizes that she has no idea who she truly is.
   ○ B. Jing-mei is frightened by how angry her mother has made her with the endless tests.
   ○ C. Jing-mei realizes that the power to resist her mother makes her a kind of prodigy.
   ○ D. Jing-mei promises herself that she will continue to try her best with her mother's tests.

Please note that excerpts and passages in the StudySync® library and this workbook are intended as touchstones to generate interest in an author's work. The excerpts and passages do not substitute for the reading of entire texts, and StudySync® strongly recommends that students seek out and purchase the whole literary or informational work in order to experience it as the author intended. Links to online resellers are available in our digital library. In addition, complete works may be ordered through an authorized reseller by filling out and returning to StudySync® the order form enclosed in this workbook.

Reading & Writing Companion    873

# Close Read

Reread *The Joy Luck Club*. As you reread, complete the Skills Focus questions below. Then use your answers and annotations from the questions to help you complete the Write activity.

◎ SKILLS FOCUS

1. Irony occurs when the author reveals an outcome that is not what readers or characters are expecting (situational irony), or uses language to mean the opposite of what is literally stated in order to create humor (verbal irony). Identify an example of irony in the text and cite evidence to explain what makes the example ironic.

2. Identify a scene in which the daughter's upbringing conflicts with her mother's. Explain why she chooses to reject her mother's influence and the effect this has on the theme.

3. Explain the central plot as well as how the author weaves in other reflections or events to help develop and enrich the narrative. Discuss the effect(s) the structure creates.

4. Reread the last two paragraphs of the story. Analyze the conclusion to discuss the theme that a person's past informs his or her identity in the present.

✎ WRITE

LITERARY ANALYSIS: This excerpt from the novel is titled "Two Kinds: Jing-Mei Woo." How does the idea of being "two kinds" posed in the title of this excerpt provide insight into the narrator's character? In your response, cite textual evidence to trace the development of this complex character over the course of the text.

# The Best We Could Do:
## An Illustrated Memoir

INFORMATIONAL TEXT
Thi Bui
2017

## Introduction

A fter Thi Bui moved across the continental United States to be closer to her aging parents, she came to understand the cold distance between them. In her bestselling illustrated memoir, *The Best We Could Do*, Bui recounts her family's nautical escape from Vietnam in 1978 and her roots in that war-scarred country, "thinking that," she writes, "if I bridged the gap between the past and the present I could fill the void between my parents and me." In this excerpt from her National Book Critics Circle finalist book, Bui articulates the ways "proximity and

# "I keep looking toward the past, tracing our journey in reverse . . ."

**Skill:
Media**

I notice big waves and a swaying boat that suggest a dangerous journey from Vietnam to the United States. The first voiceover explains the context, while the second shares the adult Bui's self-deprecating point of view.

**Page 1**

**Page 2**

 Skill:
Media

The harsh sound of the moving truck and the worried look on Bui's face show her anxiety about moving to be closer to her parents. The fourth panel emphasizes the emotional distance between them.

**Page 3**

Page 4

**Page 5**

**Page 6**

**Page 7**

**Page 8**

Please note that excerpts and passages in the StudySync® library and this workbook are intended as touchstones to generate interest in an author's work. The excerpts and passages do not substitute for the reading of entire texts, and StudySync® strongly recommends that students seek out and purchase the whole literary or informational work in order to experience it as the author intended. Links to online resellers are available in our digital library. In addition, complete works may be ordered through an authorized reseller by filling out and returning to StudySync® the order form enclosed in this workbook.

Reading & Writing
Companion

883

**Page 9**

**Page 10**

Please note that excerpts and passages in the StudySync® library and this workbook are intended as touchstones to generate interest in an author's work. The excerpts and passages do not substitute for the reading of entire texts, and StudySync® strongly recommends that students seek out and purchase the whole literary or informational work in order to experience it as the author intended. Links to online resellers are available in our digital library. In addition, complete works may be ordered through an authorized reseller by filling out and returning to StudySync® the order form enclosed in this workbook.

Reading & Writing Companion

885

**Page 11**

**Page 12**

# First Read

Read *The Best We Could Do*. After you read, complete the Think Questions below.

 **THINK QUESTIONS**

1. Why does Bui feel guilty? What does this guilt reveal about her and the situation she is in? Cite evidence from the text to support your response.

2. How is Bui's relationship with her mother different from Bui's relationship with her father? What do both relationships have in common? Explain, citing examples from the text in support of your response.

3. Explain what you learned about the relationship between Bui's father and his father, citing evidence from the text.

4. Use context clues to determine the meaning of the word **chasm** as it is used in the excerpt. Write your definition and identify clues that helped you figure out its meaning.

5. Use context clues to determine the meaning of the word **origin** as it is used in the excerpt. Write your definition of *origin*, along with those words and phrases from the text that helped you determine its meaning.

# Skill: Media

Use the Checklist to analyze Media in *The Best We Could Do.* Refer to the sample student annotations about Media in the text.

## ••• CHECKLIST FOR MEDIA

In order to determine the representation of a subject or a key scene in two different artistic mediums, do the following:

✓ Note the artistic medium and its features.

✓ Identify what is emphasized or absent in each treatment of a subject or a key scene.

✓ Examine why the same subject receives completely different treatments in different media.

✓ Consider sources, as a story about a historical event might refer, directly or indirectly, to letters, paintings, plays, or photographs from the same place and time as the events that took place.

To analyze the representation of a subject or a key scene in two different artistic mediums, including what is emphasized or absent in each treatment, consider the following questions:

✓ Is the content informational or fictional? How does this affect the treatment of the key scene or subject?

✓ What are the strengths and weaknesses of each artistic medium? How does this affect the treatment of the key scene or subject?

✓ What is emphasized and what is absent, or left out of each medium's version of events?

# Skill:
# Media

Reread pages 7–8 of *The Best We Could Do*. Then, using the Checklist on the previous page, answer the multiple-choice questions below.

## ↻ YOUR TURN

1. This question has two parts. First, answer Part A. Then, answer Part B.

   **Part A:** The voiceover on the bottom panel on page 7 indicates that—

   ○ A. the narrator feels incomplete because of her lack of knowledge about her heritage.

   ○ B. the narrator made a decision to get a large tattoo of Vietnam on her back.

   ○ C. Vietnam is now more important to the author than her parents are.

   ○ D. the narrator finally cares about Vietnam the way her parents do.

   **Part B:** Which of the following images best connects to the voiceovers to support your answer from Part A?

   ○ A. the waves behind her

   ○ B. the Vietnam-shaped hole in her back

   ○ C. the image of her writing

   ○ D. her hair blowing in the wind

2. The illustration of the narrator and her mother in the first panel on page 8 and the voiceovers in all of the panels on page 8 work together to illustrate the idea that—

   ○ A. the narrator's mother remembers the boat trip from Vietnam to America.

   ○ B. she finds an ocean-front view helps her remember Vietnam.

   ○ C. the ocean is behind everything the narrator thinks about.

   ○ D. there is distance between Bui and her mother.

# Close Read

Reread *The Best We Could Do*. As you reread, complete the Skills Focus questions below. Then use your answers and annotations from the questions to help you complete the Write activity.

## ◎ SKILLS FOCUS

1. Analyze how the illustrations and the text work together to develop the memoir, including what is emphasized in each depiction of events.

2. Identify the central or main idea of the memoir and analyze its development over the course of the text.

3. On the second page of the graphic memoir, the narrator notes that "proximity and closeness are not the same." Discuss the denotations of each word, the connotations of the words, and analyze how the nuances of the word meanings affect your understanding of the text.

4. Analyze the memoir to explain how the text and illustrations show the impact of the past on the present life of the author.

## ✏ WRITE

INFORMATIVE: In this graphic novel excerpt, author Thi Bui illustrates the sacrifices her family made in their search for a better future. Create your own illustrated memoir, in your writer's notebook or in a digital format, about a time in your life where you or your family made a sacrifice. Be sure that elements of your illustrated memoir work together to convey a distinct tone and central idea. Then, write a response explaining how you used elements of media to communicate meaning. Support your response with evidence from the text you created.

Please note that excerpts and passages in the StudySync® library and this workbook are intended as touchstones to generate interest in an author's work. The excerpts and passages do not substitute for the reading of entire texts, and StudySync® strongly recommends that students seek out and purchase the whole literary or informational work in order to experience it as the author intended. Links to online resellers are available in our digital library. In addition, complete works may be ordered through an authorized reseller by filling out and returning to StudySync® the order form enclosed in this workbook.

Reading & Writing Companion    891

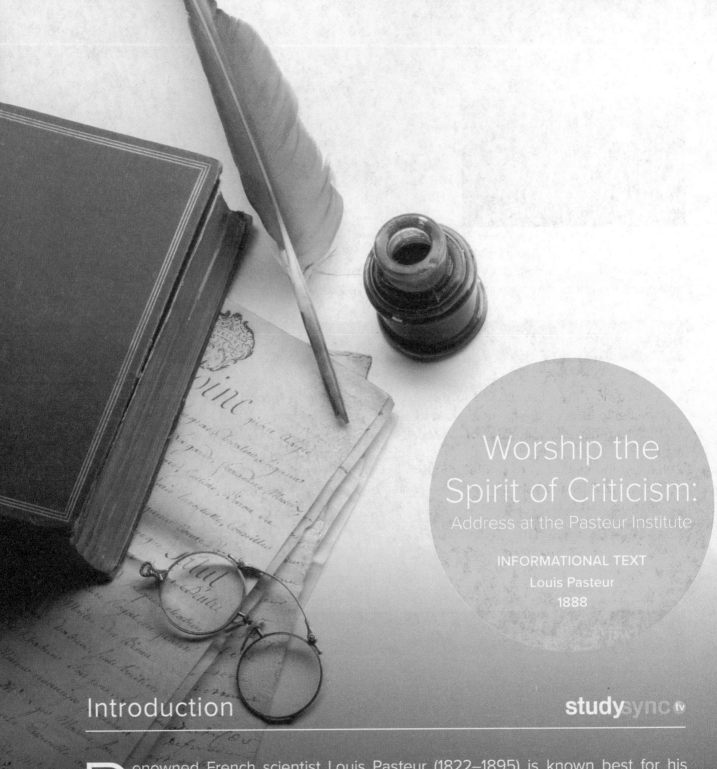

# Worship the Spirit of Criticism:
## Address at the Pasteur Institute

**INFORMATIONAL TEXT**
Louis Pasteur
1888

## Introduction

**study**sync tv

Renowned French scientist Louis Pasteur (1822–1895) is known best for his trailblazing research into infectious diseases, which has led to longer and healthier lives for millions of people. On November 14, 1888, he addressed his colleagues at the opening of the Pasteur Institute in Paris. In an effort to encourage the advancement of science, Pasteur exhorted his peers to "worship the spirit of criticism" by questioning their own findings. Pasteur's speech also helped define the relationship between science and society as he pressed future generations of scientists to seek "new means of delivering man from the scourges which beset him."

# "Never advance anything that cannot be proved in a simple and decisive fashion."

*Excerpt from a speech by Louis Pasteur given in 1888 on the occasion of the opening of the Pasteur Institute[1] in Paris:*

Portrait of Louis Pasteur

1   It is now finished, this great building, of which it might be said that there is not a stone but what is the material sign of a generous thought. All the virtues have subscribed to build this dwelling place for work.

2   Alas! mine is the bitter grief that I enter it, a man "vanquished by time," deprived of my masters, even of my companions in the struggle, Dumas, Bouley, Paul Bert, and lastly Vulpian, who, after having been with you, my dear Grancher[2], my counselor at the very first, became the most energetic, the most convinced champion of this method[3].

3   However, if I have the sorrow of thinking that they are no more, after having valiantly taken their part in discussions which I have never provoked but I have had to endure; if they cannot hear me proclaim all that I owe to their counsels and support; if I feel their absence as deeply as on the morrow of their death, I have at least the consolation of believing that all we struggled for together will not perish. The collaborators and students who are now here share our scientific faith.... Keep your early enthusiasm, dear **collaborators**, but let it ever be regulated by rigorous examinations and tests. Never advance anything that cannot be proved in a simple and decisive fashion.

---

1. **Pasteur Institute** a French research foundation established in 1888 to study biology and microorganisms
2. **Grancher** Jacques-Joseph Grancher (1843–1907) was a French microbiologist who made significant advances in the treatment of tuberculosis and rabies
3. **this method** referring to the scientific method, a process for experimentation and testing hypotheses with evidence

NOTES

4    Worship the spirit of criticism. If reduced to itself, it is not an awakener of ideas or a **stimulant** to great things, but, without it, everything is **fallible**; it always has the last word. What I am now asking you, and you will ask of your pupils later on, is what is most difficult to an inventor.

5    It is indeed a hard task, when you believe you have found an important scientific fact and are feverishly anxious to publish it, to constrain yourself for days, weeks, years sometimes, to fight with yourself, to try and ruin your own experiments and only to proclaim your discovery after having exhausted all contrary hypotheses.

6    But when, after so many efforts, you have at last arrived at a certainty, your joy is one of the greatest which can be felt by a human soul, and the thought that you have contributed to the honor of your country renders that joy still deeper.

7    If science has no country, the scientist should have one, and ascribe to it the influence which his works may have in this world.... Two contrary laws seem to be wrestling with each other nowadays; the one, a law of blood and death, ever imagining new means of destruction and forcing nations to be constantly ready for the battlefield—the other, a law of peace, work and health, ever evolving new means of delivering man from the **scourges** which beset him.

8    The one seeks violent conquests; the other, the relief of humanity. The latter places one human life above any victory; while the former would sacrifice hundreds and thousands of lives to the **ambition** of one. The law of which we are the instruments seeks, even in the midst of carnage, to cure the sanguinary ills of the law of war; the treatment inspired by our sanguinary methods may preserve thousands of soldiers. Which of those two laws will **ultimately** prevail, God alone knows. But we may assert that French science will have tried, by obeying the law of humanity, to extend the frontiers of life.

### ✏ WRITE

RHETORICAL ANALYSIS: How does Louis Pasteur use rhetorical devices to persuade his audience of his purpose and point of view? In your response, be sure to identify Pasteur's audience and purpose, and analyze several examples of rhetorical devices he uses to achieve his purpose.

# A Very
# Old Man with
# Enormous Wings

FICTION
Gabriel García Márquez
(Translated by Gregory Rabassa)
1955

# Introduction

Colombian author Gabriel García Márquez (1927–2014) is renowned as a literary giant of the 20th century. He is praised as one of the fathers of magical realism, a style in which the natural and supernatural are woven together with vivid detail. His novels and short stories often reveal deep truths hidden in universal human experiences, such as solitude—a recurring theme in many of his works. In one of his most anthologized short stories, "A Very Old Man with Enormous Wings," García Márquez provides subtle social commentary as he narrates the story of a peculiar man who captivates a small village.

# "The world had been sad since Tuesday."

NOTES

Skill: Point of View

*García Márquez, the author, is Colombian. Details such as the crabs, the name "Pelayo," and the courtyard suggest a culture from outside the US. The comment about the world shows an omniscient narrator.*

1   On the third day of rain they had killed so many crabs inside the house that Pelayo had to cross his drenched courtyard and throw them into the sea, because the newborn child had a temperature all night and they thought it was due to the stench. The world had been sad since Tuesday. Sea and sky were a single ash-gray thing and the sands of the beach, which on March nights glimmered like powdered light, had become a stew of mud and rotten shellfish. The light was so weak at noon that when Pelayo was coming back to the house after throwing away the crabs, it was hard for him to see what it was that was moving and groaning in the rear of the courtyard. He had to go very close to see that it was an old man, a very old man, lying face down in the mud, who, in spite of his tremendous efforts, couldn't get up, impeded by his enormous wings.

2   Frightened by that nightmare, Pelayo ran to get Elisenda, his wife, who was putting compresses on the sick child, and he took her to the rear of the courtyard. They both looked at the fallen body with a mute stupor. He was dressed like a ragpicker. There were only a few faded hairs left on his bald skull and very few teeth in his mouth, and his pitiful condition of a drenched great-grandfather took away any sense of grandeur he might have had. His huge buzzard wings, dirty and half-plucked, were forever entangled in the mud. They looked at him so long and so closely that Pelayo and Elisenda very soon overcame their surprise and in the end found him familiar. Then they dared speak to him, and he answered in an incomprehensible dialect with a strong sailor's voice. That was how they skipped over the inconvenience of the wings and quite intelligently concluded that he was a lonely castaway from some foreign ship wrecked by the storm. And yet, they called in a neighbor woman who knew everything about life and death to see him, and all she needed was one look to show them their mistake.

3   "He's an angel," she told them. "He must have been coming for the child, but the poor fellow is so old that the rain knocked him down."

4   On the following day everyone knew that a flesh-and-blood angel was held captive in Pelayo's house. Against the judgment of the wise neighbor woman, for whom angels in those times were the fugitive survivors of a celestial

conspiracy, they did not have the heart to club him to death. Pelayo watched over him all afternoon from the kitchen, armed with his bailiff's club, and before going to bed he dragged him out of the mud and locked him up with the hens in the wire chicken coop. In the middle of the night, when the rain stopped, Pelayo and Elisenda were still killing crabs. A short time afterward the child woke up without a fever and with a desire to eat. Then they felt **magnanimous** and decided to put the angel on a raft with fresh water and provisions for three days and leave him to his fate on the high seas. But when they went out into the courtyard with the first light of dawn, they found the whole neighborhood in front of the chicken coop having fun with the angel, without the slightest reverence, tossing him things to eat through the openings in the wire as if he weren't a supernatural creature but a circus animal.

5   Father Gonzaga arrived before seven o'clock, alarmed at the strange news. By that time onlookers less frivolous than those at dawn had already arrived and they were making all kinds of conjectures concerning the captive's future. The simplest among them thought that he should be named mayor of the world. Others of sterner mind felt that he should be promoted to the rank of five-star general in order to win all wars. Some visionaries hoped that he could be put to stud in order to implant the earth a race of winged wise men who could take charge of the universe. But Father Gonzaga, before becoming a priest, had been a robust woodcutter. Standing by the wire, he reviewed his catechism in an instant and asked them to open the door so that he could take a close look at that pitiful man who looked more like a huge decrepit hen among the fascinated chickens. He was lying in the corner drying his open wings in the sunlight among the fruit peels and breakfast leftovers that the early risers had thrown him. Alien to the **impertinences** of the world, he only lifted his antiquarian[1] eyes and murmured something in his dialect when Father Gonzaga went into the chicken coop and said good morning to him in Latin. The parish priest had his first suspicion of an imposter when he saw that he did not understand the language of God or know how to greet His ministers. Then he noticed that seen close up he was much too human: he had an unbearable smell of the outdoors, the back side of his wings was strewn with parasites and his main feathers had been mistreated by terrestrial winds, and nothing about him measured up to the proud dignity of angels. Then he came out of the chicken coop and in a brief sermon warned the curious against the risks of being ingenuous. He reminded them that the devil had the bad habit of making use of carnival tricks in order to confuse the unwary. He argued that if wings were not the essential element in determining the difference between a hawk and an airplane, they were even less so in the recognition of angels. Nevertheless, he promised to write a letter to his bishop so that the latter would write his primate so that the latter would write to the Supreme Pontiff in order to get the final verdict from the highest courts.

 Skill: Point of View

*The appearance of a priest and an angel, along with the desire to put the angel into positions of power, show the culture is religious. The narrator judges, perhaps humorously, "less frivolous," "simplest," and "sterner."*

1. **antiquarian** relating to antiques or a person who collects or specializes in them

6    His **prudence** fell on sterile hearts. The news of the captive angel spread with such rapidity that after a few hours the courtyard had the bustle of a marketplace and they had to call in troops with fixed bayonets to disperse the mob that was about to knock the house down. Elisenda, her spine all twisted from sweeping up so much marketplace trash, then got the idea of fencing in the yard and charging five cents admission to see the angel.

7    The curious came from far away. A traveling carnival arrived with a flying acrobat who buzzed over the crowd several times, but no one paid any attention to him because his wings were not those of an angel but, rather, those of a sidereal bat. The most unfortunate invalids on earth came in search of health: a poor woman who since childhood has been counting her heartbeats and had run out of numbers; a Portuguese man who couldn't sleep because the noise of the stars disturbed him; a sleepwalker who got up at night to undo the things he had done while awake; and many others with less serious ailments. In the midst of that shipwreck disorder that made the earth tremble, Pelayo and Elisenda were happy with fatigue, for in less than a week they had crammed their rooms with money and the line of pilgrims waiting their turn to enter still reached beyond the horizon.

8    The angel was the only one who took no part in his own act. He spent his time trying to get comfortable in his borrowed nest, befuddled by the hellish heat of the oil lamps and sacramental candles that had been placed along the wire. At first they tried to make him eat some mothballs, which, according to the wisdom of the wise neighbor woman, were the food prescribed for angels. But he turned them down, just as he turned down the papal lunches that the penitents brought him, and they never found out whether it was because he was an angel or because he was an old man that in the end ate nothing but eggplant mush. His only supernatural virtue seemed to be patience. Especially during the first days, when the hens pecked at him, searching for the stellar parasites that proliferated in his wings, and the cripples pulled out feathers to touch their defective parts with, and even the most merciful threw stones at him, trying to get him to rise so they could see him standing. The only time they succeeded in arousing him was when they burned his side with an iron for branding steers, for he had been motionless for so many hours that they thought he was dead. He awoke with a start, ranting in his hermetic[2] language and with tears in his eyes, and he flapped his wings a couple of times, which brought on a whirlwind of chicken dung and lunar dust and a gale of panic that did not seem to be of this world. Although many thought that his reaction had not been one of rage but of pain, from then on they were careful not to annoy him, because the majority understood that his passivity was not that of a hero taking his ease but that of a cataclysm in **repose**.

_____

2. **hermetic** ascribing to an old, non-scientific belief system composed of elements of astrology, alchemy, and speculation of the afterlife

9 Father Gonzaga held back the crowd's frivolity with formulas of maidservant inspiration while awaiting the arrival of a final judgment on the nature of the captive. But the mail from Rome showed no sense of urgency. They spent their time finding out if the prisoner had a navel, if his dialect had any connection with Aramaic, how many times he could fit on the head of a pin, or whether he wasn't just a Norwegian with wings. Those meager letters might have come and gone until the end of time if a providential event had not put and end to the priest's tribulations.

10 It so happened that during those days, among so many other carnival attractions, there arrived in the town the traveling show of the woman who had been changed into a spider for having disobeyed her parents. The admission to see her was not only less than the admission to see the angel, but people were permitted to ask her all manner of questions about her absurd state and to examine her up and down so that no one would ever doubt the truth of her horror. She was a frightful tarantula the size of a ram and with the head of a sad maiden. What was most heartrending, however, was not her outlandish shape but the sincere affliction with which she recounted the details of her misfortune. While still practically a child she had sneaked out of her parents' house to go to a dance, and while she was coming back through the woods after having danced all night without permission, a fearful thunderclap rent the sky in two and through the crack came the lightning bolt of brimstone that changed her into a spider. Her only nourishment came from the meatballs that charitable souls chose to toss into her mouth. A spectacle like that, full of so much human truth and with such a fearful lesson, was bound to defeat without even trying that of a haughty angel who scarcely deigned to look at mortals. Besides, the few miracles attributed to the angel showed a certain mental disorder, like the blind man who didn't recover his sight but grew three new teeth, or the paralytic who didn't get to walk but almost won the lottery, and the leper whose sores sprouted sunflowers. Those consolation miracles, which were more like mocking fun, had already ruined the angel's reputation when the woman who had been changed into a spider finally crushed him completely. That was how Father Gonzaga was cured forever of his insomnia and Pelayo's courtyard went back to being as empty as during the time it had rained for three days and crabs walked through the bedrooms.

11 The owners of the house had no reason to lament. With the money they saved they built a two-story mansion with balconies and gardens and high netting so that crabs wouldn't get in during the winter, and with iron bars on the windows so that angels wouldn't get in. Pelayo also set up a rabbit warren close to town and gave up his job as a bailiff for good, and Elisenda bought

Skill:
Summarizing

*Summary: A spider-woman arrives with a traveling show. She recounts how this happened to her. The townspeople are moved because the woman explains herself; they feel the angel is behaving as if he is above them.*

some satin pumps with high heels and many dresses of iridescent silk, the kind worn on Sunday by the most desirable women in those times. The chicken coop was the only thing that didn't receive any attention. If they washed it down with creolin and burned tears of myrrh inside it every so often, it was not in homage to the angel but to drive away the dungheap stench that still hung everywhere like a ghost and was turning the new house into an old one. At first, when the child learned to walk, they were careful that he not get too close to the chicken coop. But then they began to lose their fears and got used to the smell, and before the child got his second teeth he'd gone inside the chicken coop to play, where the wires were falling apart. The angel was no less standoffish with him than with the other mortals, but he tolerated the most ingenious infamies with the patience of a dog who had no illusions. They both came down with the chicken pox at the same time. The doctor who took care of the child couldn't resist the temptation to listen to the angel's heart, and he found so much whistling in the heart and so many sounds in his kidneys that it seemed impossible for him to be alive. What surprised him most, however, was the logic of his wings. They seemed so natural on that completely human organism that he couldn't understand why other men didn't have them too.

12   When the child began school it had been some time since the sun and rain had caused the collapse of the chicken coop. The angel went dragging himself about here and there like a stray dying man. They would drive him out of the bedroom with a broom and a moment later find him in the kitchen. He seemed to be in so many places at the same time that they grew to think that he'd be duplicated, that he was reproducing himself all through the house, and the exasperated and unhinged Elisenda shouted that it was awful living in that hell full of angels. He could scarcely eat and his antiquarian eyes had also become so foggy that he went about bumping into posts. All he had left were the bare cannulae of his last feathers. Pelayo threw a blanket over him and extended him the charity of letting him sleep in the shed, and only then did they notice that he had a temperature at night, and was **delirious** with the tongue twisters of an old Norwegian. That was one of the few times they became alarmed, for they thought he was going to die and not even the wise neighbor woman had been able to tell them what to do with dead angels.

13   And yet he not only survived his worst winter, but seemed improved with the first sunny days. He remained motionless for several days in the farthest corner of the courtyard, where no one would see him, and at the beginning of December some large, stiff feathers began to grow on his wings, the feathers of a scarecrow, which looked more like another misfortune of

NOTES

decrepitude. But he must have known the reason for those changes, for he was quite careful that no one should notice them, that no one should hear the sea chanteys that he sometimes sang under the stars. One morning Elisenda was cutting some bunches of onions for lunch when a wind that seemed to come from the high seas blew into the kitchen. Then she went to the window and caught the angel in his first attempts at flight. They were so clumsy that his fingernails opened a furrow in the vegetable patch and he was on the point of knocking the shed down with the ungainly flapping that slipped on the light and couldn't get a grip on the air. But he did manage to gain altitude. Elisenda let out a sigh of relief, for herself and for him, when she watched him pass over the last houses, holding himself up in some way with the risky flapping of a senile vulture. She kept watching him even when she was through cutting the onions and she kept on watching until it was no longer possible for her to see him, because then he was no longer an annoyance in her life but an imaginary dot on the horizon of the sea.

Gabriel Garcia Marquez. "Un señor muy viejo con unas alas enormes", La increíble y triste historia de la cándida Erendira y de se abuela desalmada. © Gabriela García Márquez, 1972 and Heirs of Gabriel García Márquez. All pages from "A VERY OLD MAN WITH ENORMOUS WINGS" from LEAF STORM AND OTHER STORIES by GABRIEL GARCIA MARQUEZ. Translated by Gregory Rabassa. Copyright © 1971 by Gabriel García Márquez. Reprinted by permission of HarperCollins Publishers.

A VERY OLD MAN
WITH ENORMOUS WINGS

# First Read

Read "A Very Old Man with Enormous Wings." After you read, complete the Think Questions below.

## ☁ THINK QUESTIONS

1. What are the townspeople's first impressions of the old man? How do they interpret his appearance? Cite specific evidence from the text to support your answer.

2. What happens when the people learn of the "spider-woman"? How does their reaction compare to when they first discovered the old man? Make sure to include examples from the story.

3. How does the old man transform physically throughout the story? Use specific examples from the text to support your answer.

4. Use the surrounding context to infer the definition of **impertinences** as it is used in paragraph 5 of the story. Write your definition, explaining how you came to this meaning. Then, verify your understanding of the word with a print or an online dictionary.

5. The Latin word *prudentia* is translated "foresight, or practical judgment." Keeping this in mind, come up with your best definition of the word **prudence** as it is used in paragraph 6. Write your definition, and explain which clues led you to arrive at it.

# Skill:
# Point of View

Use the Checklist to analyze Point of View in "A Very Old Man with Enormous Wings." Refer to the sample student annotations about Point of View in the text.

## ••• CHECKLIST FOR POINT OF VIEW

In order to identify the point of view or cultural experience reflected in a work of literature from outside the United States, note the following:

✓ the country of origin of the characters or speaker and author

✓ scenes and details that reflect a culture outside the United States

✓ ideas and observations from the narrator or speaker

✓ inferences made by drawing on a wide reading from world literature, such as

- dramas, plays, poetry, and short stories written by international authors

- stories that reflect an indigenous person's experience in another country

To analyze the point of view or cultural experience reflected in a work of literature from outside the United States, drawing on a wide reading of world literature, consider the following questions:

✓ What is the country of origin of the author and of the characters in the text? What details show that?

✓ What texts have you read previously from these nations or cultures? How does this help you analyze the cultural experience in this text?

✓ What is the author's, narrator's, or speaker's point of view? How do you know?

✓ How does this text use point of view to present a cultural experience different from that of the United States? How do you know?

✓ Is the narrator or speaker objective or unreliable? How does that affect the understanding of culture?

Please note that excerpts and passages in the StudySync® library and this workbook are intended as touchstones to generate interest in an author's work. The excerpts and passages do not substitute for the reading of entire texts, and StudySync® strongly recommends that students seek out and purchase the whole literary or informational work in order to experience it as the author intended. Links to online resellers are available in our digital library. In addition, complete works may be ordered through an authorized reseller by filling out and returning to StudySync® the order form enclosed in this workbook.

Reading & Writing
Companion

903

# Skill:
# Point of View

Reread paragraph 12 from "A Very Old Man with Enormous Wings." Then, using the Checklist on the previous page, answer the multiple-choice questions below.

## ♻ YOUR TURN

1. This question has two parts. First, answer Part A. Then, answer Part B.

   **Part A:** How has the family's point of view concerning the existence of the angel shifted by this stage of the story?

   ○ A. He is considered a holy creature to be treated with reverence.

   ○ B. He has become an annoyance.

   ○ C. He has made the people fearful.

   ○ D. He has brought joy and humor.

   **Part B:** Which of the following details BEST supports your answer from Part A?

   ○ A. "Pelayo threw a blanket over him and extended him the charity of letting him sleep in the shed."

   ○ B. "He could scarcely eat and his antiquarian eyes had also become so foggy that he went about bumping into posts."

   ○ C. "They would drive him out of the bedroom with a broom and a moment later find him in the kitchen."

   ○ D. "All he had left were the bare cannulae of his last feathers."

# Skill:
# Summarizing

Use the Checklist to analyze Summarizing in "A Very Old Man with Enormous Wings." Refer to the sample student annotation about Summarizing in the text.

## ••• CHECKLIST FOR SUMMARIZING

In order to determine how to write an objective summary of a text, note the following:

- ✓ how the theme or central idea develops over the course of the text

- ✓ how a theme emerges and is then shaped and refined by specific details

- ✓ answers to the basic questions *who, what, where, when, why,* and *how*

- ✓ avoidance of personal thoughts, judgments, or opinions

To provide an objective summary of a text, consider the following questions:

- ✓ What are the answers to basic *who, what, where, when, why,* and *how* questions in literature and works of nonfiction?

- ✓ What is the theme or central idea of the text?

- ✓ Does my summary include how the theme or central idea is developed over the course of the text?

- ✓ Does my summary demonstrate how that theme is shaped and refined by choosing only important details?

- ✓ Is my summary objective, or have I added my own thoughts, judgments, and personal opinions?

Please note that excerpts and passages in the StudySync® library and this workbook are intended as touchstones to generate interest in an author's work. The excerpts and passages do not substitute for the reading of entire texts, and StudySync® strongly recommends that students seek out and purchase the whole literary or informational work in order to experience it as the author intended. Links to online resellers are available in our digital library. In addition, complete works may be ordered through an authorized reseller by filling out and returning to StudySync® the order form enclosed in this workbook.

Reading & Writing
Companion

905

# Skill:
# Summarizing

Reread paragraph 13 of "A Very Old Man with Enormous Wings." Then, using the Checklist on the previous page, answer the multiple-choice questions below.

## ⟳ YOUR TURN

1. This question has two parts. First, answer Part A. Then, answer Part B.

   **Part A:** Which of the following is the BEST summary of the events in paragraph 13?

   ○ A. The angel survives the winter. He starts to grow new feathers and is very protective of them, hiding them so that people can't see them. He spends a lot of time hiding in the corner of the courtyard.

   ○ B. The angel survives the winter and flies away.

   ○ C. The angel survives the winter, grows new feathers, and flies away. The family is relieved but they shouldn't be because now they have no way to make more money.

   ○ D. The angel survives the winter and begins gaining strength. He grows new feathers and one day he flies away, to the relief of the family.

   **Part B:** Which of the following details are the MOST important for your summary from part A?

   ○ A. "large, stiff feathers began to grow on his wings"

   ○ B. "One morning Elisenda was cutting some bunches of onions for lunch"

   ○ C. "They were so clumsy that his fingernails opened a furrow in the vegetable patch"

   ○ D. "the feathers of a scarecrow, which looked more like another misfortune of decrepitude"

A VERY OLD MAN
WITH ENORMOUS WINGS

# Close Read

Reread "A Very Old Man with Enormous Wings." As you reread, complete the Skills Focus questions below. Then use your answers and annotations from the questions to help you complete the Write activity.

## ◎ SKILLS FOCUS

1. Summarize the short story, briefly and objectively.

2. Discuss how a particular cultural experience is reflected in this Colombian short story.

3. Determine the theme or central idea of the short story and analyze how it is shaped using two or three specific details.

4. García Márquez's short story reflects such source material as the myth of Icarus, the work of medieval theologians such as Thomas Aquinas (concerning angels), as well as the Catholicism of the people of South America. Research one of these allusions and analyze how the new representation uses the allusion for effect or to reveal a theme.

5. Discuss how the angel's arrival affects or guides the lives of the people in this village. Cite evidence from the text to support your ideas.

## ✎ WRITE

LITERARY ANALYSIS: García Márquez uses this work of magical realism to convey a social and moral point of view to the reader. What elements of the story are magical? What elements are realistic? How does the combination of magic and realism help convey a social and moral point of view in a way that other methods cannot? Use textual evidence and original analysis in your response.

Please note that excerpts and passages in the StudySync® library and this workbook are intended as touchstones to generate interest in an author's work. The excerpts and passages do not substitute for the reading of entire texts, and StudySync® strongly recommends that students seek out and purchase the whole literary or informational work in order to experience it as the author intended. Links to online resellers are available in our digital library. In addition, complete works may be ordered through an authorized reseller by filling out and returning to StudySync® the order form enclosed in this workbook.

Reading & Writing Companion

907

# The Nose

FiCTION
Nikolai Gogol
1836

## Introduction

Nikolai Gogol (1809–1852) was one of the preeminent Russian writers of the 19th century. While he is a central figure of the natural school of Russian realism (a group whose members also included towering Russian authors like Turgenev and Dostoevsky), Gogol's work was also darkly humorous, surreal, and grotesque. In the city of St. Petersburg, Russia, in the early 1800s, a barber awakens. He slices into his morning roll and makes an unexpected discovery: inside the roll, a nose! What's more, he recognizes it as the nose of one of his customers—a bureaucrat named Kovalev. What ensues is an uproarious satire of Russian society, bureaucracy, and vanity, as the reader follows Kovalev on his journey to find his

# "Ivan Yakovlevitch was dumbfounded. He thought and thought, but did not know what to think."

I

1   ON 25 March an unusually strange event occurred in St. Petersburg. For that morning Barber Ivan Yakovlevitch, a dweller on the Vozkresensky Prospekt (his name is lost now—it no longer figures on a signboard bearing a portrait of a gentleman with a soaped cheek, and the words: "Also, Blood Let Here")—for that morning Barber Ivan Yakovlevitch awoke early, and caught the smell of newly baked bread. Raising himself a little, he perceived his wife (a most respectable dame, and one especially fond of coffee) to be just in the act of drawing newly baked rolls from the oven.

Portrait of Nikolai Gogol

2   "Prascovia Osipovna," he said, "I would rather not have any coffee for breakfast, but, instead, a hot roll and an onion,"—the truth being that he wanted both but knew it to be useless to ask for two things at once, as Prascovia Osipovna did not fancy such tricks.

3   "Oh, the fool shall have his bread," the dame reflected. "So much the better for me then, as I shall be able to drink a second lot of coffee."

4   And duly she threw on to the table a roll.

5   Ivan Yakovlevitch donned a jacket over his shirt for politeness' sake, and, seating himself at the table, poured out salt, got a couple of onions ready, took a knife into his hand, assumed an air of importance, and cut the roll asunder. Then he glanced into the roll's middle. To his intense surprise he saw something glimmering there. He probed it cautiously with the knife—then poked at it with a finger.

6   "Quite solid it is!" he muttered. "What in the world is it likely to be?"

7   He thrust in, this time, all his fingers, and pulled forth—a nose! His hands dropped to his sides for a moment. Then he rubbed his eyes hard. Then again he probed the thing. A nose! Sheerly a nose! Yes, and one familiar to him, somehow! Oh, horror spread upon his feature! Yet that horror was a trifle compared with his spouse's overmastering wrath.

8   "You brute!" she shouted frantically. "Where have you cut off that nose? You villain, you! You drunkard! Why, I'll go and report you to the police myself. The brigand, you! Three customers have told me already about your pulling at their noses as you shaved them till they could hardly stand it."

9   But Ivan Yakovlevitch was neither alive nor dead. This was the more the case because, sure enough, he had recognised the nose. It was the nose of Collegiate Assessor[1] Kovalev—no less: it was the nose of a gentleman whom he was accustomed to shave twice weekly, on each Wednesday and each Sunday!

10  "Stop, Prascovia Osipovna!" at length he said. "I'll wrap the thing in a clout, and lay it aside awhile, and take it away altogether later."

11  "But I won't hear of such a thing being done! As if I'm going to have a cut-off nose kicking about my room! Oh, you old stick! Maybe you can just strop a razor still; but soon you'll be no good at all for the rest of your work. You loafer, you wastrel, you bungler, you blockhead! Aye, I'll tell the police of you. Take it away, then. Take it away. Take it anywhere you like. Oh, that I'd never caught the smell of it!"

12  Ivan Yakovlevitch was dumbfounded. He thought and thought, but did not know what to think.

13  "The devil knows how it's happened," he said, scratching one ear. "You see, I don't know for certain whether I came home drunk last night or not. But certainly things look as though something out of the way happened then, for bread comes of baking, and a nose of something else altogether. Oh, I just can't make it out."

14  So he sat silent. At the thought that the police might find the nose at his place, and arrest him, he felt frantic. Yes, already he could see the red collar with the smart silver braiding—the sword! He shuddered from head to foot.

15  But at last he got out, and donned waistcoat and shoes, wrapped the nose in a clout, and departed amid Prascovia Osipovna's forcible objurgations.

---

1. **Collegiate Assessor** a position in the relative middle of the Table of Ranks, a hierarchy of social standing established in the early 18th century by Tsar Peter I (Peter the Great)

16    His one idea was to rid himself of the nose, and return quietly home—to do so either by throwing the nose into the gutter in front of the gates or by just letting it drop anywhere. Yet, unfortunately, he kept meeting friends, and they kept saying to him: "Where are you off to?" or "Whom have you arranged to shave at this early hour?" until seizure of a fitting moment became impossible. Once, true, he did succeed in dropping the thing, but no sooner had he done so than a constable pointed at him with his truncheon, and shouted: "Pick it up again! You've lost something," and he perforce had to take the nose into his possession once more, and stuff it into a pocket. Meanwhile his desperation grew in proportion as more and more booths and shops opened for business, and more and more people appeared in the street.

17    At last he decided that he would go to the Isaakievsky Bridge, and throw the thing, if he could, into the Neva. But here let me confess my fault in not having said more about Ivan Yakovlevitch himself, a man estimable in more respects than one.

18    Like every decent Russian tradesman, Ivan Yakovlevitch was a terrible tippler. Daily he shaved the chins of others[2], but always his own was unshorn, and his jacket (he never wore a top-coat) piebald—black, thickly studded with greyish, brownish-yellowish stains—and shiny of collar, and adorned with three pendent tufts of thread instead of buttons. But, with that, Ivan Yakovlevitch was a great cynic. Whenever Collegiate Assessor Kovalev was being shaved, and said to him, according to custom: "Ivan Yakovlevitch, your hands do smell!" he would retort: "But why should they smell?" and, when the Collegiate Assessor had replied: "Really I do not know, brother, but at all events they do," take a pinch of snuff[3], and soap the Collegiate Assessor upon cheek, and under nose, and behind ears, and around chin at his good will and pleasure.

19    So the worthy citizen stood on the Isaakievsky Bridge, and looked about him. Then, leaning over the parapet, he feigned to be trying to see if any fish were passing underneath. Then gently he cast forth the nose.

20    At once ten puds-weight seemed to have been lifted from his shoulders. Actually he smiled! But, instead of departing, next, to shave the chins of chinovniki, he bethought him of making for a certain establishment inscribed "Meals and Tea," that he might get there a glassful of punch.

21    Suddenly he sighted a constable standing at the end of the bridge, a constable of smart appearance, with long whiskers, a three-cornered hat, and a sword

---

2. **Daily he shaved the chins of others** around 1698, Peter the Great also imposed a "beard tax" because he didn't want Russian men to wear beards; he wanted them to look more "modern"

3. **snuff** chewing tobacco

complete. Oh, Ivan Yakovlevitch could have fainted! Then the constable, beckoning with a finger, cried:

22 "Nay, my good man. Come here."

23 Ivan Yaklovlevitch, knowing the proprieties, pulled off his cap at quite a distance away, advanced quickly, and said:

24 "I wish your Excellency the best of health."

25 "No, no! None of that 'your Excellency,' brother. Come and tell me what you have been doing on the bridge."

26 "Before God, sir, I was crossing it on my way to some customers when I peeped to see if there were any fish jumping."

27 "You lie, brother! You lie! You won't get out of it like that. Be so good as to answer me truthfully."

28 "Oh, twice a week in future I'll shave you for nothing. Aye, or even three times a week."

29 "No, no, friend. That is rubbish. Already I've got three barbers for the purpose, and all of them account it an honour. Now, tell me, I ask again, what you have just been doing?"

30 This made Ivan Yakovlevitch blanch, and——

31 Further events here become enshrouded in mist. What happened after that is unknown to all men.

II

32 COLLEGIATE ASSESSOR KOVALEV also awoke early that morning. And when he had done so he made the "B-r-rh!" with his lips which he always did when he had been asleep—he himself could not have said why. Then he stretched himself, had handed to him a small mirror from the table near by, and set himself to inspect a pimple which had broken out on his nose the night before. But, to his unbounded astonishment, there was only a flat patch on his face where the nose should have been! Greatly alarmed, he called for water, washed, and rubbed his eyes hard with the towel. Yes, the nose indeed was gone! He prodded the spot with a hand—pinched himself to make sure that he was not still asleep. But no; he was not still sleeping. Then he leapt from the bed, and shook himself. No nose had he on him still! Finally, he bade his clothes be handed him, and set forth for the office of the Police Commissioner at his utmost speed.

33   Here let me add something which may enable the reader to perceive just what the Collegiate Assessor was like. Of course, it goes without saying that Collegiate Assessors who acquire the title with the help of academic diplomas cannot be compared with Collegiate Assessors who become Collegiate Assessors through service in the Caucasus, for the two species are wholly **distinct,** they are——Stay, though. Russia is so strange a country that, let one but say anything about any one Collegiate Assessor, and the rest, from Riga to Kamchatka, at once apply the remark to themselves—for all titles and all ranks it means the same thing. Now, Kovalev was a "Caucasian" Collegiate Assessor, and had, as yet, borne the title for two years only. Hence, unable ever to forget it, he sought the more to give himself dignity and weight by calling himself, in addition to "Collegiate Assessor," "Major."

34   "Look here, good woman," once he said to a shirts' vendor whom he met in the street, "come and see me at my home. I have my flat in Sadovaia Street. Ask merely, 'Is this where Major Kovalev lives?' Anyone will show you." Or, on meeting fashionable ladies, he would say: "My dear madam, ask for Major Kovalev's flat." So we too will call the Collegiate Assessor "Major."

35   Major Kovalev had a habit of daily promenading the Nevsky Prospekt in an extremely clean and well-starched shirt and collar, and in whiskers of the sort still observable on provincial surveyors, architects, regimental doctors, other officials, and all men who have round, red cheeks, and play a good hand at "Boston." Such whiskers run across the exact centre of the cheek—then head straight for the nose. Again, Major Kovalev always had on him a quantity of seals, both of seals engraved with coats of arms, and of seals inscribed "Wednesday," "Thursday," "Monday," and the rest. And, finally, Major Kovalev had come to live in St. Petersburg because of necessity. That is to say, he had come to live in St. Petersburg because he wished to obtain a post befitting his new title—whether a Vice-Governorship or, failing that, an Administratorship in a leading department. Nor was Major Kovalev altogether set against marriage. Merely he required that his bride should possess not less than two hundred thousand rubles in capital. The reader, therefore, can now judge how the Major was situated when he perceived that instead of a not unpresentable nose there was figuring on his face an extremely uncouth, and perfectly smooth and uniform patch.

36   Ill luck prescribed, that morning, that not a cab was visible throughout the street's whole length; so, huddling himself up in his cloak, and covering his face with a handkerchief (to make things look as though his nose were bleeding), he had to start upon his way on foot only.

37   "Perhaps this is only imagination?" he reflected. Presently he turned aside towards a restaurant (for he wished yet again to get a sight of himself in a mirror). "The nose can't have removed itself of sheer idiocy."

38   Luckily no customers were present in the restaurant—merely some waiters were sweeping out the rooms, and rearranging the chairs, and others, sleepy-eyed fellows, were setting forth trayfuls of hot pastries. On chairs and tables last night's newspapers, coffee-stained, were strewn.

39   "Thank God that no one is here!" the Major reflected. "Now I can look at myself again."

40   He approached a mirror in some trepidation, and peeped therein. Then he spat.

41   "The devil only knows what this vileness means!" he muttered. "If even there had been something to take the nose's place! But, as it is, there's nothing there at all."

42   He bit his lips with vexation, and hurried out of the restaurant. No; as he went along he must look at no one, and smile at no one. Then he halted as though riveted to earth. For in front of the doors of a mansion he saw occur a phenomenon of which, simply, no explanation was possible. Before that mansion there stopped a carriage. And then a door of the carriage opened, and there leapt thence, huddling himself up, a uniformed gentleman, and that uniformed gentleman ran headlong up the mansion's entrance-steps, and disappeared within. And oh, Kovalev's horror and astonishment to perceive that the gentleman was none other than—his own nose! The unlooked-for spectacle made everything swim before his eyes. Scarcely, for a moment, could he even stand. Then, deciding that at all costs he must await the gentleman's return to the carriage, he remained where he was, shaking as though with fever. Sure enough, the Nose did return, two minutes later. It was clad in a gold-braided, high-collared uniform, buckskin breeches, and cockaded hat. And slung beside it there was a sword, and from the cockade on the hat it could be inferred that the Nose was purporting to pass for a State Councillor. It seemed now to be going to pay another visit somewhere. At all events it glanced about it, and then, shouting to the coachman, "Drive up here," re-entered the vehicle, and set forth.

43   Poor Kovalev felt almost demented. The astounding event left him utterly at a loss. For how could the nose which had been on his face but yesterday, and able then neither to drive nor to walk independently, now be going about in uniform?—He started in pursuit of the carriage, which, luckily, did not go far, and soon halted before the Gostiny Dvor.

44   Kovalev too hastened to the building, pushed through the line of old beggar-women with bandaged faces and apertures for eyes whom he had so often scorned, and entered. Only a few customers were present, but Kovalev felt so upset that for a while he could decide upon no course of action save to

scan every corner in the gentleman's pursuit. At last he sighted him again, standing before a counter, and, with face hidden altogether behind the uniform's stand-up collar, inspecting with absorbed attention some wares.

45     "How, even so, am I to approach it?" Kovalev reflected. "Everything about it, uniform, hat, and all, seems to show that it is a State Councillor now. Only the devil knows what is to be done!"

46     He started to cough in the Nose's vicinity, but the Nose did not change its position for a single moment.

47     "My good sir," at length Kovalev said, compelling himself to boldness, "my good sir, I——"

48     "What do you want?" And the Nose did then turn round.

49     "My good sir, I am in a difficulty. Yet somehow, I think, I think, that—well, I think that you ought to know your proper place better. All at once, you see, I find you—*where*? Do you not feel as I do about it?"

50     "Pardon me, but I cannot apprehend your meaning. Pray explain further."

51     "Yes, but how, I should like to know?" Kovalev thought to himself. Then, again taking courage, he went on:

52     "I am, you see—well, in point of fact, you see, I am a Major. Hence you will realise how unbecoming it is for me to have to walk about without a nose. Of course, a peddler of oranges on the Vozkresensky Bridge could sit there noseless well enough, but I myself am hoping soon to receive a——Hm, yes. Also, I have amongst my acquaintances several ladies of good houses (Madame Chektareva, wife of the State Councillor, for example), and you may judge for yourself what that alone signifies. Good sir"—Major Kovalev gave his shoulders a shrug—"I do not know whether you yourself (pardon me) consider conduct of this sort to be altogether in accordance with the rules of duty and honour, but at least you can understand that——"

53     "I understand nothing at all," the Nose broke in. "Explain yourself more satisfactorily."

54     "Good sir," Kovalev went on with a heightened sense of dignity, "the one who is at a loss to understand the other is I. But at least the immediate point should be plain, unless you are determined to have it otherwise. Merely—you are my own nose."

55     The Nose regarded the Major, and contracted its brows a little.

56 "My dear sir, you speak in error," was its reply. "I am just myself—myself separately. And in any case there cannot ever have existed a close relation between us, for, judging from the buttons of your undress uniform, your service is being performed in another department than my own."

57 And the Nose definitely turned away.

58 Kovalev stood dumbfounded. What to do, even what to think, he had not a notion.

59 Presently the agreeable swish of ladies' dresses began to be heard. Yes, an elderly, lace-bedecked dame was approaching, and, with her, a slender maiden in a white frock which outlined delightfully a trim figure, and, above it, a straw hat of a lightness as of pastry. Behind them there came, stopping every now and then to open a snuffbox, a tall, whiskered beau in quite a twelve-fold collar.

60 Kovalev moved a little nearer, pulled up the collar of his shirt, straightened the seals on his gold watch-chain, smiled, and directed special attention towards the slender lady as, swaying like a floweret in spring, she kept raising to her brows a little white hand with fingers almost of transparency. And Kovalev's smiles became broader still when peeping from under the hat he saw there to be an alabaster, rounded little chin, and part of a cheek flushed like an early rose. But all at once he recoiled as though scorched, for all at once he had remembered that he had not a nose on him, but nothing at all. So, with tears forcing themselves upwards, he wheeled about to tell the uniformed gentleman that he, the uniformed gentleman, was no State Councillor, but an impostor and a knave and a villain and the Major's own nose. But the Nose, behold, was gone! That very moment had it driven away to, **presumably**, pay another visit.

61 This drove Kovalev to the last pitch of desperation. He went back to the mansion, and stationed himself under its portico, in the hope that, by peering hither and thither, hither and thither, he might once more see the Nose appear. But, well though he remembered the Nose's cockaded hat and gold-braided uniform, he had failed at the time to note also its cloak, the colour of its horses, the make of its carriage, the look of the lackey seated behind, and the pattern of the lackey's livery. Besides, so many carriages were moving swiftly up and down the street that it would have been impossible to note them all, and equally so to have stopped any one of them. Meanwhile, as the day was fine and sunny, the Prospekt was thronged with pedestrians also—a whole kaleidoscopic stream of ladies was flowing along the pavements, from Police Headquarters to the Anitchkin Bridge. There one could descry an Aulic Councillor whom Kovalev knew well. A gentleman he was whom Kovalev always addressed as "Lieutenant-Colonel," and especially in the presence of

others. And there there went Yaryzhkin, Chief Clerk to the Senate, a crony who always rendered forfeit at "Boston" on playing an eight. And, lastly, a like "Major" with Kovalev, a like "Major" with an Assessorship acquired through Caucasian service, started to beckon to Kovalev with a finger!

62  "The devil take him!" was Kovalev's muttered comment. "Hi, cabman! Drive to the Police Commissioner's direct."

63  But just when he was entering the drozhki he added:

64  "No. Go by Ivanovskaia Street."

65  "Is the Commissioner in?" he asked on crossing the threshold.

66  "He is not," was the doorkeeper's reply. "He's gone this very moment."

67  "There's luck for you!"

68  "Aye," the doorkeeper went on. "Only just a moment ago he was off. If you'd been a bare half-minute sooner you'd have found him at home, maybe."

69  Still holding the handkerchief to his face, Kovalev returned to the cab, and cried wildly:

70  "Drive on!"

71  "Where to, though?" the cabman inquired.

72  "Oh, straight ahead!"

73  "'Straight ahead'? But the street divides here. To right, or to left?"

74  The question caused Kovalev to pause and recollect himself. In his situation he ought to make his next step an application to the Board of Discipline—not because the Board was directly connected with the police, but because its dispositions would be executed more speedily than in other departments. To seek satisfaction of the the actual department in which the Nose had declared itself to be serving would be sheerly unwise, since from the Nose's very replies it was clear that it was the sort of individual who held nothing sacred, and, in that event, might lie as unconscionably as it had lied in asserting itself never to have figured in its proprietor's company. Kovalev, therefore, decided to seek the Board of Discipline. But just as he was on the point of being driven thither there occurred to him the thought that the impostor and knave who had behaved so shamelessly during the late encounter might even now be using the time to get out of the city, and that in that case all further pursuit of the rogue would become vain, or at all events last for, God preserve us! a

full month. So at last, left only to the guidance of Providence, the Major resolved to make for a newspaper office, and publish a circumstantial description of the Nose in such good time that anyone meeting with the truant might at once be able either to restore it to him or to give information as to its whereabouts. So he not only directed the cabman to the newspaper office, but, all the way thither, prodded him in the back, and shouted: "Hurry up, you rascal! Hurry up, you rogue!" whilst the cabman intermittently responded: "Aye, barin," and nodded, and plucked at the reins of a steed as shaggy as a spaniel.

75  The moment that the drozhki halted Kovalev dashed, breathless, into a small reception-office. There, seated at a table, a grey-headed clerk in ancient jacket and pair of spectacles was, with pen tucked between lips, counting sums received in copper.

76  "Who here takes the advertisements?" Kovalev exclaimed as he entered. "A-ah! Good day to you."

77  "And my respects," the grey-headed clerk replied, raising his eyes for an instant, and then lowering them again to the spread out copper heaps.

78  "I want you to publish——"

79  "Pardon—one moment." And the clerk with one hand committed to paper a figure, and with a finger of the other hand shifted two accounts markers. Standing beside him with an advertisement in his hands, a footman in a laced coat, and sufficiently smart to seem to be in service in an aristocratic mansion, now thought well to display some knowingness.

80  "Sir," he said to the clerk, "I do assure you that the puppy is not worth eight grivni even. At all events I wouldn't give that much for it. Yet the countess loves it—yes, just loves it, by God! Anyone wanting it of her will have to pay a hundred rubles. Well, to tell the truth between you and me, people's tastes differ. Of course, if one's a sportsman one keeps a setter or a spaniel. And in that case don't you spare five hundred rubles, or even give a thousand, if the dog is a good one."

81  The worthy clerk listened with gravity, yet none the less accomplished a calculation of the number of letters in the advertisement brought. On either side there was a group of charwomen, shop assistants, doorkeepers, and the like. All had similar advertisements in their hands, with one of the documents to notify that a coachman of good character was about to be disengaged, and another one to advertise a koliaska imported from Paris in 1814, and only slightly used since, and another one a maid-servant of nineteen experienced in laundry work, but prepared also for other jobs, and another one a sound

drozhki save that a spring was lacking, and another one a grey-dappled, spirited horse of the age of seventeen, and another one some turnip and radish seed just received from London, and another one a country house with every amenity, stabling for two horses, and **sufficient** space for the laying out of a fine birch or spruce plantation, and another one some second-hand footwear, with, added, an invitation to attend the daily auction sale from eight o'clock to three. The room where the company thus stood gathered together was small, and its atmosphere confined; but this closeness, of course, Collegiate Assessor Kovalev never perceived, for, in addition to his face being muffled in a handkerchief, his nose was gone, and God only knew its present habitat!

82  "My dear sir," at last he said impatiently, "allow me to ask you something: it is a pressing matter."

83  "One moment, one moment! Two rubles, forty-three kopeks. Yes, presently. Sixty rubles, four kopeks."

84  With which the clerk threw the two advertisements concerned towards the group of charwomen and the rest, and turned to Kovalev.

85  "Well?" he said. "What do you want?"

86  "Your pardon," replied Kovalev, "but fraud and knavery has been done. I still cannot understand the affair, but wish to announce that anyone returning me the rascal shall receive an adequate reward."

87  "Your name, if you would be so good?"

88  "No, no. What can my name matter? I cannot tell it you. I know many acquaintances such as Madame Chektareva (wife of the State Councillor) and Pelagea Grigorievna Podtochina (wife of the Staff-Officer), and, the Lord preserve us, they would learn of the affair at once. So say just 'a Collegiate Assessor,' or, better, 'a gentleman ranking as Major.'"

89  "Has a household serf of yours absconded, then?"

90  "A household serf of mine? As though even a household serf would perpetrate such a crime as the present one! No, indeed! It is my nose that has absconded from me."

91  "Gospodin Nossov, Gospoding Nossov? Indeed a strange name, that![4] Then has this Gospodin Nossov robbed you of some money?"

4. **Indeed a strange name, that!:** *Noss* means "nose" in Russian, and *Gospodin* is equivalent to the English "Mr."

92    "I said nose, not Nossov. You are making a mistake. There has disappeared, goodness knows whither, my nose, my own actual nose. Presumably it is trying to make a fool of me."

93    "But how could it so disappear? The matter has something about it which I do not fully understand."

94    "I cannot tell you the exact how. The point is that now the nose is driving about the city, and giving itself out for a State Councillor —wherefore I beg you to announce that anyone apprehending any such nose ought at once, in the shortest possible space of time, to return it to myself. Surely you can judge what it is for me meanwhile to be lacking such a conspicuous portion of my frame? For a nose is not like a toe which one can keep inside a boot, and hide the absence of if it is not there. Besides, every Thurdsay I am due to call upon Madame Chektareva (wife of the State Councillor): whilst Pelagea Grigorievna Podtochina (wife of the Staff-Officer, mother of a pretty daughter) also is one of my closest acquaintances. So, again, judge for yourself how I am situated at present. In such a condition as this I could not possibly present myself before the ladies named."

95    Upon that the clerk became thoughtful: the fact was clear from his tightly compressed lips alone.

96    "No," he said at length. "Insert such an announcement I cannot."

97    "But why not?"

98    "Because, you see, it might injure the paper's reputation. Imagine if everyone were to start proclaiming a disappearance of his nose! People would begin to say that, that—well, that we printed absurdities and false tales."

99    "But how is this matter a false tale? Nothing of the sort has it got about *it*."

100   "You think not; but only last week a similar case occurred. One day a chinovnik brought us an advertisement as you have done. The cost would have been only two rubles, seventy-three kopeks, for all that it seemed to signify was the running away of a poodle. Yet what was it, do you think, in reality? Why, the thing turned out to be a libel, and the 'poodle' in question a cashier—of what department precisely I do not know."

101   "Yes, but here am I advertising not about a poodle, but about my own nose, which, surely, is, for all intents and purposes, myself?"

102   "All the same, I cannot insert the advertisement."

Copyright © BookheadEd Learning, LLC

103 "Even when actually I have lost my own nose!"

104 "The fact that your nose is gone is a matter for a doctor. There are doctors, I have heard, who can fit one out with any sort of nose one likes. I take it that by nature you are a wag, and like playing jokes in public."

105 "That is not so. I swear it as God is holy. In fact, as things have gone so far, I will let you see for yourself."

106 "Why trouble?" Here the clerk took some snuff before adding with, nevertheless, a certain movement of curiosity: "However, if it really won't trouble you at all, a sight of the spot would gratify me."

107 The Collegiate Assessor removed the handkerchief.

108 "Strange indeed! Very strange indeed!" the clerk exclaimed. "And the patch is as uniform as a newly fried pancake, almost unbelievably uniform."

109 "So you will dispute what I say no longer? Then surely you cannot but put the announcement into print. I shall be extremely grateful to you, and glad that the present occasion has given me such a pleasure as the making of your acquaintance"—whence it will be seen that for once the Major had decided to climb down.

110 "To print what you want is nothing much," the clerk replied. "Yet frankly I cannot see how you are going to benefit from the step. I would suggest, rather, that you commission a skilled writer to compose an article describing this as a rare product of nature, and have the article published in *The Northern Bee*" (here the clerk took more snuff), "either for the instruction of our young" (the clerk wiped his nose for a finish) "or as a matter of general interest."

111 This again depressed the Collegiate Assessor: and even though, on his eyes happening to fall upon a copy of the newspaper, and reach the column assigned to theatrical news, and encounter the name of a beautiful actress, so that he almost broke into a smile, and a hand began to finger a pocket for a Treasury note (since he held that only stalls were seats befitting Majors and so forth)—although all this was so, there again recurred to him the thought of the nose, and everything again became spoilt.

112 Even the clerk seemed touched with the awkwardness of Kovalev's plight, and wishful to lighten with a few sympathetic words the Collegiate Assessor's depression.

113 "I am sorry indeed that this has befallen," he said. "Should you care for a pinch of this? Snuff can dissipate both headache and low spirits. Nay, it is good for haemorrhoids as well."

114   And he proffered his box-deftly, as he did so, folding back underneath it the lid depicting a lady in a hat.

115   Kovalev lost his last shred of patience at the thoughtless act, and said heatedly:

116   "How you can think fit thus to jest I cannot imagine. For surely you perceive me no longer to be in possession of a means of sniffing? Oh, you and your snuff can go to hell! Even the sight of it is more than I can bear. I should say the same even if you were offering me, not wretched birch bark, but real rappee."

117   Greatly incensed, he rushed out of the office, and made for the ward police inspector's residence. Unfortunately he arrived at the very moment when the inspector, after a yawn and a stretch, was reflecting: "Now for two hours' sleep!" In short, the Collegiate Assessor's visit chanced to be exceedingly ill-timed. Incidentally, the inspector, though a great patron of manufacturers and the arts, preferred still more a Treasury note.

118   "That's the thing!" he frequently would say. "It's a thing which can't be beaten anywhere, for it wants nothing at all to eat, and it takes up very little room, and it fits easily to the pocket, and it doesn't break in pieces if it happens to be dropped."

119   So the inspector received Kovalev very drily, and intimated that just after dinner was not the best moment for beginning an inquiry—nature had ordained that one should rest after food (which showed the Collegiate Assessor that at least the inspector had some knowledge of sages' old saws), and that in any case no one would purloin the nose of a *really* respectable man.

120   Yes, the inspector gave it Kovalev between the eyes. And as it should be added that Kovalev was extremely sensitive where his title or his dignity was concerned (though he readily pardoned anything said against himself personally, and even held, with regard to stage plays, that, whilst Staff-Officers should not be assailed, officers of lesser rank might be referred to), the police inspector's reception so took him aback that, in a dignified way, and with hands set apart a little, he nodded, remarked: "After your insulting observations there is nothing which I wish to add," and betook himself away again.

121   He reached home scarcely hearing his own footsteps. Dusk had fallen, and, after the unsuccessful questings, his flat looked truly dreary. As he entered the hall he perceived Ivan, his valet, to be lying on his back on the stained old leathern divan, and spitting at the ceiling with not a little skill as regards

successively hitting the same spot. The man's coolness rearoused Kovalev's ire, and, smacking him over the head with his hat, he shouted:

122 "You utter pig! You do nothing but play the fool." Leaping up, Ivan hastened to take his master's cloak.

123 The tired and despondent Major then sought his sitting-room, threw himself into an easy-chair, sighed, and said to himself:

124 "My God, my God! why has this misfortune come upon me? Even loss of hands or feet would have been better, for a man without a nose is the devil knows what—a bird, but not a bird, a citizen, but not a citizen, a thing just to be thrown out of window. It would have been better, too, to have had my nose cut off in action, or in a duel, or through my own act: whereas here is the nose gone with nothing to show for it—uselessly—for not a groat's profit!— No, though," he added after thought, "it's not likely that the nose is gone for good: it's not likely at all. And quite probably I am dreaming all this, or am fuddled. It may be that when I came home yesterday I drank the vodka with which I rub my chin after shaving instead of water—snatched up the stuff because that fool Ivan was not there to receive me."

125 So he sought to ascertain whether he might not be drunk by pinching himself till he fairly yelled. Then, certain, because of the pain, that he was acting and living in waking life, he approached the mirror with diffidence, and once more scanned himself with a sort of inward hope that the nose might by this time be showing as restored. But the result was merely that he recoiled and muttered:

126 "What an absurd spectacle still!"

127 Ah, it all passed his understanding! If only a button, or a silver spoon, or a watch, or some such article were gone, rather than that anything had disappeared like this—for no reason, and in his very flat! Eventually, having once more reviewed the circumstances, he reached the final conclusion that he should most nearly hit the truth in supposing Madame Podtochina (wife of the Staff-Officer, of course—the lady who wanted him to become her daughter's husband) to have been the prime agent in the affair. True, he had always liked dangling in the daughter's wake, but also he had always fought shy of really coming down to business. Even when the Staff-Officer's lady had said point blank that she desired him to become her son-in-law he had put her off with his compliments, and replied that the daughter was still too young, and himself due yet to perform five years service, and aged only forty-two. Yes, the truth must be that out of revenge the Staff-Officer's wife had resolved to ruin him, and hired a band of witches for the purpose, seeing that the nose could not **conceivably** have been cut off—no one had entered his private

room lately, and, after being shaved by Ivan Yakovlevitch on the Wednesday, he had the nose intact, he knew and remembered well, throughout both the rest of the Wednesday and the day following. Also, if the nose had been cut off, pain would have resulted, and also a wound, and the place could not have healed so quickly, and become of the uniformity of a pancake.

128  Next, the Major made his plans. Either he would sue the Staff-Officer's lady in legal form or he would pay her a surprise visit, and catch her in a trap. Then the foregoing reflections were cut short by a glimmer showing through the chink of the door—a sign that Ivan had just lit a candle in the hall: and presently Ivan himself appeared, carrying the candle in front of him, and throwing the room into such clear radiance that Kovalev had hastily to snatch up the handkerchief again, and once more cover the place where the nose had been but yesterday, lest the stupid fellow should be led to stand gaping at the monstrosity on his master's features.

129  Ivan had just returned to his cupboard when an unfamiliar voice in the hall inquired:

130  "Is this where Collegiate Assessor Kovalev lives?"

131  "It is," Kovalev shouted, leaping to his feet, and flinging wide the door. "Come in, will you?"

132  Upon which there entered a police-officer of smart exterior, with whiskers neither light nor dark, and cheeks nicely plump. As a matter of fact, he was the police-officer whom Ivan Yakovlevitch had met at the end of the Isaakievsky Bridge.

133  "I beg your pardon, sir," he said, "but have you lost your nose?"

134  "I have—just so."

135  "Then the nose is found."

136  "What?" For a moment or two joy deprived Major Kovalev of further speech. All that he could do was to stand staring, open-eyed, at the officer's plump lips and cheeks, and at the tremulant beams which the candlelight kept throwing over them. "Then how did it come about?"

137  "Well, by the merest chance the nose was found beside a roadway. Already it had entered a stage-coach, and was about to leave for Riga with a passport made out in the name of a certain chinovnik. And, curiously enough, I myself, at first, took it to be a gentleman. Luckily, though, I had my eyeglasses on me. Soon, therefore, I perceived the 'gentleman' to be no more than a nose. Such

is my shortness of sight, you know, that even now, though I see you standing there before me, and see that you have a face, I cannot distinguish on that face the nose, the chin, or anything else. My mother-in-law (my wife's mother) too cannot easily distinguish details."

138    Kovalev felt almost beside himself.

139    "Where is the nose now?" cried he. "Where, I ask? Let me go to it at once."

140    "Do not trouble, sir. Knowing how greatly you stand in need of it, I have it with me. It is a curious fact, too, that the chief agent in the affair has been a rascal of a barber who lives on the Vozkresensky Prospekt, and now is sitting at the police station. For long past I had suspected him of drunkenness and theft, and only three days ago he took away from a shop a button-card. Well, you will find your nose to be as before."

141    And the officer delved into a pocket, and drew thence the nose, wrapped in paper.

142    "Yes, that's the nose all right!" Kovalev shouted. "It's the nose precisely! Will you join me in a cup of tea?"

143    "I should have accounted it indeed a pleasure if I had been able, but, unfortunately, I have to go straight on to the penitentiary. Provisions, sir, have risen greatly in price. And living with me I have not only my family, but my mother-in-law (my wife's mother). Yet the eldest of my children gives me much hope. He is a clever lad. The only thing is that I have not the means for his proper education."

144    When the officer was gone the Collegiate Assessor sat plunged in vagueness, plunged in inability to see or to feel, so greatly was he upset with joy. Only after a while did he with care take the thus recovered nose in cupped hands, and again examine it attentively.

145    "It, undoubtedly. It, precisely," he said at length. "Yes, and it even has on it the pimple to the left which broke out on me yesterday."

146    Sheerly he laughed in his delight.

147    But nothing lasts long in this world. Even joy grows less lively the next moment. And a moment later, again, it weakens further. And at last it remerges insensibly with the normal mood, even as the ripple from a pebble's impact becomes remerged with the smooth surface of the water at large. So Kovalev relapsed into thought again. For by now he had realised that even yet the affair was

Please note that excerpts and passages in the StudySync® library and this workbook are intended as touchstones to generate interest in an author's work. The excerpts and passages do not substitute for the reading of entire texts, and StudySync® strongly recommends that students seek out and purchase the whole literary or informational work in order to experience it as the author intended. Links to online resellers are available in our digital library. In addition, complete works may be ordered through an authorized reseller by filling out and returning to StudySync® the order form enclosed in this workbook.

Reading & Writing Companion    925

not wholly ended, seeing that, though retrieved, the nose needed to be re-stuck.

148 "What if it should fail so to stick!"

149 The bare question thus posed turned the Major pale.

150 Feeling, somehow, very nervous, he drew the mirror closer to him, lest he should fit the nose awry. His hands were trembling as gently, very carefully he lifted the nose in place. But, oh, horrors, it would not *remain* in place! He held it to his lips, warmed it with his breath, and again lifted it to the patch between his cheeks—only to find, as before, that it would not retain its position.

151 "Come, come, fool!" said he. "Stop where you are, I tell you."

152 But the nose, obstinately wooden, fell upon the table with a strange sound as of a cork, whilst the Major's face became convulsed.

153 "Surely it is not too large now?" he reflected in terror. Yet as often as he raised it towards its proper position the new attempt proved as vain as the last.

154 Loudly he shouted for Ivan, and sent for a doctor who occupied a flat (a better one than the Major's) on the first floor. The doctor was a fine-looking man with splendid, coal-black whiskers. Possessed of a healthy, comely wife, he ate some raw apples every morning, and kept his mouth extraordinarily clean—rinsed it out, each morning, for three-quarters of an hour, and polished its teeth with five different sorts of brushes. At once he answered Kovalev's summons, and, after asking how long ago the calamity had happened, tilted the Major's chin, and rapped the vacant site with a thumb until at last the Major wrenched his head away, and, in doing so, struck it sharply against the wall behind. This, the doctor said, was nothing; and after advising him to stand a little farther from the wall, and bidding him incline his head to the right, he once more rapped the vacant patch before, after bidding him incline his head to the left, dealing him, with a "Hm!" such a thumb-dig as left the Major standing like a horse which is having its teeth examined.

155 The doctor, that done, shook his head.

156 "The thing is not feasible," he pronounced. "You had better remain as you are rather than go farther and fare worse. Of course, I *could* stick it on again—I could do that for you in a moment; but at the same time I would assure you that your plight will only become worse as the result."

157 "Never mind," Kovalev replied. "Stick it on again, pray. How can I continue without a nose? Besides, things could not possibly be worse than they are

now. At present they are the devil himself. Where can I show this caricature of a face? My circle of acquaintances is a large one: this very night I am due in two houses, for I know a great many people like Madame Chektareva (wife of the State Councillor), Madame Podtochina (wife of the Staff-Officer), and others. Of course, though, I shall have nothing further to do with Madame Podtochina (except through the police) after her present proceedings. Yes," persuasively he went on, "I beg of you to do me the favour requested. Surely there are means of doing it permanently? Stick it on in any sort of a fashion—at all events so that it will hold fast, even if not becomingly. And then, when risky moments occur, I might even support it gently with my hand, and likewise dance no more—anything to avoid fresh injury through an unguarded movement. For the rest, you may feel assured that I shall show you my gratitude for this visit so far as ever my means will permit."

158  "Believe me," the doctor replied, neither too loudly nor too softly, but just with incisiveness and magnetic "when I say that I never attend patients for money. To do that would be contrary alike to my rules and to my art. When I accept a fee for a visit I accept it only lest I offend through a refusal. Again I say—this time on my honour, as you will not believe my plain word—that, though I could easily re-affix your nose, the proceeding would make things worse, far worse, for you. It would be better for you to trust merely to the action of nature. Wash often in cold water, and I assure you that you will be as healthy without a nose as with one. This nose here I should advise you to put into a jar of spirit: or, better still, to steep in two tablespoonfuls of stale vodka and strong vinegar. Then you will be able to get a good sum for it. Indeed, I myself will take the thing if you consider it of no value."

159  "No, no!" shouted the distracted Major. "Not on any account will I sell it. I would rather it were lost again."

160  "Oh, I beg your pardon." And the doctor bowed. "My only idea had been to serve you. What is it you want? Well, you have seen me do what I could."

161  And majestically he withdrew. Kovalev, meanwhile, had never once looked at his face. In his distraction he had noticed nothing beyond a pair of snowy cuffs projecting from black sleeves.

162  He decided, next, that, before lodging a plea next day, he would write and request the Staff-Officer's lady to restore him his nose without publicity. His letter ran as follows:

163  DEAR MADAME ALEXANDRA GRIGORIEVNA, I am at a loss to understand your strange conduct. At least, however, you may rest assured that you will benefit nothing by it, and that it will in no way further force me to marry your daughter. Believe me, I am now aware of all the circumstances connected

with my nose, and know that you alone have been the prime agent in them. The nose's sudden disappearance, its subsequent gaddings about, its masqueradings as, firstly, a chinovnik and, secondly, itself—all these have come of witchcraft practised either by you or by adepts in pursuits of a refinement equal to your own. This being so, I consider it my duty herewith to warn you that if the nose should not this very day reassume its correct position, I shall be forced to have resort to the law's protection and defence. With all respect, I have the honour to remain your very humble servant, PLATON KOVALEV.

164 "MY DEAR SIR," wrote the lady in return, "your letter has greatly surprised me, and I will say frankly that I had not expected it, and least of all its unjust reproaches. I assure you that I have never at any time allowed the chinovnik whom you mention to enter my house—either masquerading or as himself. True, I have received calls from Philip Ivanovitch Potanchikov, who, as you know, is seeking my daughter's hand, and, besides, is a man steady and upright, as well as learned; but never, even so, have I given him reason to hope. You speak, too, of a nose. If that means that I seem to you to have desired to leave you with a nose and nothing else, that is to say, to return you a direct refusal of my daughter's hand, I am astonished at your words, for, as you cannot but be aware, my inclination is quite otherwise. So now, if still you wish for a formal betrothal to my daughter, I will readily, I do assure you, satisfy your desire, which all along has been, in the most lively manner, my own also. In hopes of that, I remain yours sincerely, ALEXANDRA PODTOCHINA.

165 "No, no!" Kovalev exclaimed, after reading the missive. "She, at least, is not guilty. Oh, certainly not! No one who had committed such a crime could write such a letter." The Collegiate Assessor was the more expert in such matters because more than once he had been sent to the Caucasus to institute prosecutions. "Then by what sequence of chances has the affair happened? Only the devil could say!"

166 His hands fell in bewilderment.

167 It had not been long before news of the strange occurrence had spread through the capital. And, of course, it received additions with the progress of time. Everyone's mind was, at that period, bent upon the marvellous. Recently experiments with the action of magnetism had occupied public attention, and the history of the dancing chairs of Koniushennaia Street also was fresh. So no one could wonder when it began to be said that the nose of Collegiate Assessor Kovalev could be seen promenading the Nevski Prospekt at three o'clock, or when a crowd of curious sightseers gathered there. Next, someone declared that the nose, rather, could be beheld at Junker's store, and the throng which surged thither became so massed as to necessitate a summons

to the police. Meanwhile a speculator of highly respectable aspect and whiskers who sold stale cakes at the entrance to a theatre knocked together some stout wooden benches, and invited the curious to stand upon them for eighty kopeks each; whilst a retired colonel who came out early to see the show, and penetrated the crowd only with great difficulty, was disgusted when in the window of the store he beheld, not a nose, but merely an ordinary woollen waistcoat flanked by the selfsame lithograph of a girl pulling up a stocking, whilst a dandy with cutaway waistcoat and receding chin peeped at her from behind a tree, which had hung there for ten years past.

168 "Dear me!" irritably he exclaimed. "How come people so to excite themselves about stupid, improbable reports?"

169 Next, word had it that the nose was walking, not on the Nevski Prospekt, but in the Taurida Park, and, in fact, had been in the habit of doing so for a long while past, so that even in the days when Khozrev Mirza had lived near there he had been greatly astonished at the freak of nature. This led students to repair thither from the College of Medicine, and a certain eminent, respected lady to write and ask the Warden of the Park to show her children the phenomenon, and, if possible, add to the demonstration a lesson of edifying and instructive tenor.

170 Naturally, these events greatly pleased also gentlemen who frequented routs, since those gentlemen wished to entertain the ladies, and their resources had become exhausted. Only a few solid, worthy persons deprecated it all. One such person even said, in his disgust, that comprehend how foolish inventions of the sort could circulate in such an enlightened age he could not—that, in fact, he was surprised that the Government had not turned its attention to the matter. From which utterance it will be seen that the person in question was one of those who would have dragged the Government into anything on earth, including even their daily quarrels with their wives.

171 Next——

172 But again events here become enshrouded in mist. What happened after that is unknown to all men.

III

173 FARCE really does occur in this world, and, sometimes, farce altogether without an element of probability. Thus, the nose which lately had gone about as a State Councillor, and stirred all the city, suddenly reoccupied its proper place (between the two cheeks of Major Kovalev) as though nothing at all had happened. The date was 7 April, and when, that morning, the major awoke as usual, and, as usual, threw a despairing glance at the mirror, he this time,

Please note that excerpts and passages in the StudySync® library and this workbook are intended as touchstones to generate interest in an author's work. The excerpts and passages do not substitute for the reading of entire texts, and StudySync® strongly recommends that students seek out and purchase the whole literary or informational work in order to experience it as the author intended. Links to online resellers are available in our digital library. In addition, complete works may be ordered through an authorized reseller by filling out and returning to StudySync® the order form enclosed in this workbook.

Reading & Writing
· Companion    929

beheld before him, what?—why, the nose again! Instantly he took hold of it. Yes, the nose, the nose precisely! "Aha!" he shouted, and, in his joy, might have executed a trepak about the room in bare feet had not Ivan's entry suddenly checked him. Then he had himself furnished with materials for washing, washed, and glanced at the mirror again. Oh, the nose was there still! So next he rubbed it vigorously with the towel. Ah, still it was there, the same as ever!

174 "Look, Ivan," he said. "Surely there is a pimple on my nose?" But meanwhile he was thinking: "What if he should reply: 'You are wrong, sir. Not only is there not a pimple to be seen, but not even a nose'?"

175 However, all that Ivan said was:

176 "Not a pimple, sir, that isn't. The nose is clear all over."

177 "Good!" the Major reflected, and snapped his fingers. At the same moment Barber Ivan Yakovlevitch peeped round the door. He did so as timidly as a cat which has just been whipped for stealing cream.

178 "Tell me first whether your hands are clean?" the Major cried.

179 "They are, sir."

180 "You lie, I'll be bound."

181 "By God, sir, I do not!"

182 "Then go carefully."

183 As soon as Kovalev had seated himself in position Ivan Yakovlevitch vested him in a sheet, and plied brush upon chin and a portion of a cheek until they looked like the blanc mange served on tradesmen's namedays.

184 "Ah, you!" Here Ivan Yakovlevitch glanced at the nose. Then he bent his head askew, and contemplated the nose from a position on the flank. "It looks right enough," finally he commented, but eyed the member for quite a little while longer before carefully, so gently as almost to pass the imagination, he lifted two fingers towards it, in order to grasp its tip—such always being his procedure.

185 "Come, come! Do mind!" came in a shout from Kovalev. Ivan Yakovlevitch let fall his hands, and stood disconcerted, dismayed as he had never been before. But at last he started scratching the razor lightly under the chin, and, despite the unhandiness and difficulty of shaving in that quarter without also grasping the organ of smell, contrived, with the aid of a thumb planted firmly

Reading & Writing Companion·

upon the cheek and the lower gum, to overcome all obstacles, and bring the shave to a finish.

186 Everything thus ready, Kovalev dressed, called a cab, and set out for the restaurant. He had not crossed the threshold before he shouted: "Waiter! A cup of chocolate!" Then he sought a mirror, and looked at himself. The nose was still in place! He turned round in cheerful mood, and, with eyes contracted slightly, bestowed a bold, satirical scrutiny upon two military men, one of the noses on whom was no larger than a waistcoat button. Next, he sought the chancery of the department where he was **agitating** to obtain a Vice-Governorship (or, failing that, an Administratorship), and, whilst passing through the reception vestibule, again surveyed himself in a mirror. As much in place as ever the nose was!

187 Next, he went to call upon a brother Collegiate Assessor, a brother "Major." This colleague of his was a great satirist, but Kovalev always met his quarrelsome remarks merely with: "Ah, you! I know you, and know what a wag you are."

188 Whilst proceeding thither he reflected:

189 "At least, if the Major doesn't burst into laughter on seeing me, I shall know for certain that all is in order again."

190 And this turned out to be so, for the colleague said nothing at all on the subject.

191 "Splendid, damn it all!" was Kovalev's inward comment.

192 In the street, on leaving the colleague's, he met Madame Podtochina, and also Madame Podtochina's daughter. Bowing to them, he was received with nothing but joyous exclamations. Clearly all had been fancy, no harm had been done. So not only did he talk quite a while to the ladies, but he took special care, as he did so, to produce his snuffbox, and deliberately plug his nose at both entrances. Meanwhile inwardly he said:

193 "There now, good ladies! There now, you couple of hens! I'm not going to marry the daughter, though. All this is just—*par amour*, allow me."

194 And from that time onwards Major Kovalev gadded about the same as before. He walked on the Nevski Prospekt, and he visited theatres, and he showed himself everywhere. And always the nose accompanied him the same as before, and evinced no signs of again purposing a departure. Great was his good humour, replete was he with smiles, intent was he upon pursuit of fair ladies. Once, it was noted, he even halted before a counter of the Gostini

Dvor, and there purchased the riband of an order. Why precisely he did so is not known, for of no order was he a knight.

195 To think of such an affair happening in this our vast empire's northern capital! Yet general opinion decided that the affair had about it much of the improbable. Leaving out of the question the nose's strange, unnatural removal, and its subsequent appearance as a State Councillor, how came Kovalev not to know that one ought not to advertise for a nose through a newspaper? Not that I say this because I consider newspaper charges for announcements excessive. No, that is nothing, and I do not belong to the number of the mean. I say it because such a proceeding would have been *gauche*, derogatory, not the thing. And how came the nose into the baked roll? And what of Ivan Yakovlevitch? Oh, I cannot understand these points—absolutely I cannot. And the strangest, most unintelligible fact of all is that authors actually can select such occurrences for their subject! I confess this too to pass my comprehension, to——But no; I will say just that I do not understand it. In the first place, a course of the sort never benefits the country. And in the second place—in the second place, a course of the sort never benefits anything at all. I cannot divine the use of it.

196 Yet, even considering these things; even conceding this, that, and the other (for where are not incongruities found at times?) there may have, after all, been something in the affair. For no matter what folk say to the contrary, such affairs do happen in this world—rarely of course, yet none the less really.

## ✏ WRITE

LITERARY ANALYSIS: Nikolai Gogol's absurdist satire, "The Nose," is a forerunner of the genre known as magical realism. In what ways does Gogol's story of Major Kovalev reflect the traits of magical realism while putting forth a particular point of view of Russian society? Incorporate textual evidence that supports your claim.

# A Quilt of a Country

INFORMATIONAL TEXT
Anna Quindlen
2001

## Introduction

A nna Quindlen (b. 1952) is a decorated American journalist and author. She is a bestselling author of nine novels, three of which were made into movies. Anna also won the Pulitzer Prize for Commentary in 1992 for her op-ed column in the *New York Times*. "A Quilt of a Country" was written mere weeks after the September 11 terrorist attacks that devastated Americans. Quindlen's thoughts about America, especially in the wake of terrorism and fear, are poignant and personal since New York is her home. She dissects her homeland to its core, evaluating equality and tolerance—or lack thereof—in the contemporary American landscape.

# "America is an improbable idea. A mongrel nation built of ever-changing disparate parts . . ."

Copyright © BookheadEd Learning, LLC

Skill: Figurative Language

*Two metaphors: 1) a quilt is many different pieces of fabric put together to make a whole blanket; 2) a mongrel is a mix of different breeds. Different people from many backgrounds together form the nation.*

1   America is an improbable idea. A mongrel[1] nation built of ever-changing **disparate** parts, it is held together by a notion, the notion that all men are created equal, though everyone knows that most men consider themselves better than someone. "Of all the nations in the world, the United States was built in nobody's image," the historian Daniel Boorstin wrote. That's because it was built of bits and pieces that seem discordant, like the crazy quilts that have been one of its great folk-art forms, velvet and calico and checks and brocades. Out of many, one. That is the ideal.

2   The reality is often quite different, a great national striving consisting frequently of failure. Many of the oft-told stories of the most pluralistic nation on earth are stories not of tolerance, but of **bigotry**. Slavery and sweatshops, the burning of crosses and the ostracism of the other. Children learn in social-studies class and in the news of the lynching of blacks, the denial of rights to women, the murders of gay men. It is difficult to know how to convince them that this amounts to "crown thy good with brotherhood," that amid all the failures is something spectacularly successful. Perhaps they understand it at this moment, when enormous tragedy, as it so often does, demands a time of reflection on enormous blessings.

3   This is a nation founded on a conundrum[2], what Mario Cuomo has characterized as "community added to individualism." These two are our defining ideals; they are also in constant conflict. Historians today bemoan the ascendancy of a kind of prideful apartheid[3] in America, saying that the clinging to ethnicity, in background and custom, has undermined the concept of unity. These historians must have forgotten the past, or have gilded it. The New York of my children is no more Balkanized[4], probably less so, than the Philadelphia of my father, in which Jewish boys would walk several blocks out

1. **mongrel** of mixed descent; crossbred (often pejorative)
2. **conundrum** a confusing or difficult puzzle or problem
3. **apartheid** an institutionally enforced policy of racial separation, most commonly in reference to South Africa from after World War II until the 1990s
4. **Balkanized** separated into small and mutually hostile parts; the reference is derived from the countries of the Balkan region of southeastern Europe leading up to and after Yugoslavian unification

of their way to avoid the Irish divide of Chester Avenue. (I was the product of a mixed marriage, across barely bridgeable lines: an Italian girl, an Irish boy. How quaint it seems now, how incendiary then.) The Brooklyn of Francie Nolan's famous tree, the Newark of which Portnoy complained, even the uninflected WASP suburbs of Cheever's characters: they are ghettos, pure and simple. Do the Cambodians and the Mexicans in California coexist less easily today than did the Irish and Italians of Massachusetts a century ago? You know the answer.

4    What is the point of this splintered whole? What is the point of a nation in which Arab cabbies chauffeur Jewish passengers through the streets of New York—and in which Jewish cabbies chauffeur Arab passengers, too, and yet speak in theory of hatred, one for the other? What is the point of a nation in which one part seems to be always on the verge of fisticuffs with another, blacks and whites, gays and straights, left and right, Pole and Chinese and Puerto Rican and Slovenian? Other countries with such divisions have in fact divided into new nations with new names, but not this one, impossibly interwoven even in its hostilities.

5    Once these disparate parts were held together by a common enemy, by the fault lines of world wars and the electrified fence of communism. With the end of the cold war there was the creeping concern that without a focus for hatred and distrust, a sense of national identity would evaporate, that the left side of the hyphen—African-American, Mexican-American, Irish-American—would overwhelm the right. And slow-growing domestic traumas like economic unrest and increasing crime seemed more likely to emphasize division than community. Today the citizens of the United States have come together once more because of armed conflict and enemy attack. Terrorism has led to devastation—and unity.

6    Yet even in 1994, the overwhelming majority of those surveyed by the National Opinion Research Center agreed with this statement: "The U.S. is a unique country that stands for something special in the world." One of the things that it stands for is this vexing notion that a great nation can consist entirely of refugees from other nations, that people of different, even warring religions and cultures can live, if not side by side, than on either side of the country's Chester Avenues. Faced with this diversity there is little point in trying to isolate anything remotely resembling a national character, but there are two strains of behavior that, however tenuously, **abet** the concept of unity.

7    There is that Calvinist[5] undercurrent in the American psyche that loves the difficult, the demanding, that sees mastering the impossible, whether it be

**Skill: Word Patterns and Relationships**

*I know the noun* splinter, *like a splinter of wood in my finger. I see that* splintered *here is an adjective describing* whole. *A splintered nation is broken up in some way, in this case ethnically.*

**Skill: Word Patterns and Relationships**

*The verb* vex *means "to cause distress." The addition of* -ing *makes it an adjective modifying* notion, *or idea. The author uses* vexing *sarcastically, since refugees living peacefully should not cause distress.*

---

5. **Calvinist** referring to the Reform tradition of Protestant Christianity established by French religious reformer John Calvin (1509–1564)

prairie or subway, as a test of character, and so glories in the struggle of this fractured **coalescing**. And there is a grudging fairness among the citizens of the United States that eventually leads most to admit that, no matter what the English-only advocates try to suggest, the new immigrants are not so different from our own parents or grandparents. Leonel Castillo, former director of the Immigration and Naturalization Service and himself the grandson of Mexican immigrants, once told the writer Studs Terkel proudly, "The old neighborhood Ma-Pa stores are still around. They are not Italian or Jewish or Eastern European any more. Ma and Pa are now Korean, Vietnamese, Iraqi, Jordanian, Latin American. They live in the store. They work seven days a week. Their kids are doing well in school. They're making it. Sound familiar?"

8   Tolerance is the word used most often when this kind of coexistence succeeds, but tolerance is a vanilla-pudding word, standing for little more than the allowance of letting others live unremarked and unmolested. Pride seems excessive, given the American willingness to endlessly complain about them, them being whoever is new, different, unknown or currently under suspicion. But patriotism is partly taking pride in this unlikely ability to throw all of us together in a country that across its length and breadth is as different as a dozen countries, and still be able to call it by one name. When photographs of the faces of all those who died in the World Trade Center destruction are assembled in one place, it will be possible to trace in the skin color, the shape of the eyes and the noses, the texture of the hair, a map of the world. These are the representatives of a mongrel nation that somehow, at times like this, has one spirit. Like many improbable ideas, when it actually works, it's a wonder.

Skill: Arguments and Claims

Repeating *improbable* reinforces the idea introduced in paragraph 1, that America is an "improbable idea." Quindlen reinforces her claim that an improbable idea can work: America can have unity.

A QUILT OF A COUNTRY

# First Read

Read "A Quilt of a Country." After you read, complete the Think Questions below.

## ☁ THINK QUESTIONS

1. Why does Quindlen refer to America as a quilt? Does this symbolism have a positive or negative connotation? Use evidence from the text to support your answer.

2. What defines "unity" in America, according to the author? Use textual evidence from paragraphs 5–7 to explain your response.

3. Quindlen mentions "pride" throughout the essay; in what ways does pride affect the cultural climate of America? Explain your answer using textual evidence.

4. The Latin word *alescere* means "to grow up." Using this knowledge and clues from the text, write your best definition of the word **coalescing**, and indicate which clues helped you with your definition.

5. Quindlen writes, "Many of the oft-told stories of the most pluralistic nation on earth are stories not of tolerance, but of **bigotry**." Using context clues from the text, write your best definition of **bigotry**.

# Skill:
# Figurative Language

Use the Checklist to analyze Figurative Language in "A Quilt of a Country." Refer to the sample student annotation about Figurative Language in the text.

## ••• CHECKLIST FOR FIGURATIVE LANGUAGE

In order to determine the meaning of a figure of speech in context, note the following:

✓ words that mean one thing literally and suggest something else

✓ similes, metaphors, or personification

✓ figures of speech, including

- oxymorons, or a figure of speech in which apparently contradictory terms appear in conjunction, such as

  > a description such as "deafening silence"

  > sayings such as "seriously funny"

- euphemisms, or a mild or indirect word or expression substituted for one considered to be too harsh when referring to something unpleasant or embarrassing, such as

  > saying someone has "passed away" instead of "died"

  > using the term "correctional facility" instead of "prison"

In order to interpret a figure of speech in context and analyze its role in the text, consider the following questions:

✓ Where is there figurative language in the text and what seems to be the purpose of the author's use of it?

✓ Why does the author use a figure of speech rather than literal language?

✓ How do euphemisms or oxymorons affect the meaning of the text?

✓ How does the figurative language develop the message or theme of the literary work?

Copyright © BookheadEd Learning, LLC

# Skill:
# Figurative Language

Reread paragraph 5 of "A Quilt of a Country." Then, using the Checklist on the previous page, answer the multiple-choice questions below.

## ↻ YOUR TURN

1. What is the BEST interpretation of Quindlen's use of the twin metaphors of "fault lines" and "electrified fences" as they are used in the first sentence?

   ○ A. The metaphors are used to describe how in the past Americans were forced to get along because of rules set down by the government.

   ○ B. The metaphors are used to describe national boundaries and protections, as a fault line in the land divides an area, or an electrified fence keeps out a common enemy.

   ○ C. The metaphor is used to describe how Americans used to be so afraid of communism that they feared their neighbors and didn't get to know each other.

   ○ D. The metaphor is used to describe the trench warfare and barbed wire that was used during World War I.

2. What is the BEST interpretation of the figure of speech, "the left side of the hyphen," as used in the second sentence?

   ○ A. The figure of speech is meant to question a person's citizenship in the country.

   ○ B. The figure of speech is describing the political "left" as opposed to the political "right."

   ○ C. The figure of speech suggests that some believe a person's ethnic identity will feel more important than his or her American identity.

   ○ D. The figure of speech is used to describe economic unrest and increasing crime.

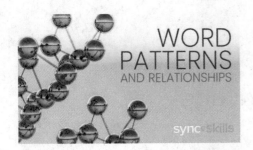

# Skill:
# Word Patterns and Relationships

Use the Checklist to analyze Word Patterns and Relationships in "A Quilt of a Country." Refer to the sample student annotations about Word Patterns and Relationships in the text.

## ••• CHECKLIST FOR WORD PATTERNS AND RELATIONSHIPS

In order to identify patterns of word changes to indicate different meanings or parts of speech, do the following:

- ✓ determine the word's part of speech

- ✓ when reading, use context clues to make a preliminary determination of the meaning of the word

- ✓ when writing a response to a text, check that you understand the meaning and part of speech and that it makes sense in your sentence

- ✓ consult a dictionary to verify your preliminary determination of the meanings and parts of speech, including morphological elements such as base or root words, prefixes, and suffixes

- ✓ be sure to read all of the definitions, and then decide which definition, form, and part of speech makes sense within the context of the text

To identify and correctly use patterns of word changes that indicate different meanings or parts of speech, consider the following questions:

- ✓ What is the intended meaning of the word?

- ✓ Do I know that this word form is the correct part of speech? Do I understand the word patterns for this particular word?

- ✓ When I consult a dictionary, can I confirm that the meaning I have determined for this word is correct? Do I know how to use it correctly?

# Skill:
# Word Patterns and Relationships

Reread paragraph 4 of "A Quilt of a Country." Then, using the Checklist on the previous page, answer the multiple-choice questions below.

## ⟳ YOUR TURN

1. What part of speech is the word *divisions*?

   ○ A. adjective
   ○ B. plural noun
   ○ C. verb
   ○ D. noun

2. What part of speech is the word *divided*?

   ○ A. noun
   ○ B. adjective
   ○ C. verb
   ○ D. adverb

3. What meaning is gained from analyzing the author's use of the patterns of the word changes, *divisions* and *divided*, in the context of the essay?

   ○ A. The use of the word patterns *divisions* and *divided* highlights the similarities between the United States and other countries facing similar challenging ideas.
   ○ B. The use of the word patterns *divisions* and *divided* highlights the differences between the United States and other countries facing similar challenging ideas.
   ○ C. The use of the word patterns *divisions* and then *divided* highlights the similarities and differences between the United States and other countries facing similar challenging ideas.
   ○ D. The use of the word patterns *divisions* and then *divided* highlights the ethnic differences in the United States.

# Skill:
# Arguments and Claims

Use the Checklist to analyze Arguments and Claims in "A Quilt of a Country." Refer to the sample student annotation about Arguments and Claims in the text.

## ••• CHECKLIST FOR ARGUMENTS AND CLAIMS

In order to identify the speaker's argument and claims, note the following:

- ✓ clues that reveal the author's opinion in the title, opening remarks, or concluding statement

- ✓ declarative statements that come before or follow a speaker's anecdote or story

To delineate a speaker's argument and specific claims, do the following:

- ✓ note the information that the speaker introduces in sequential order

- ✓ describe the speaker's argument in your own words

To evaluate the argument and specific claims, consider the following questions:

- ✓ Does the writer support each claim with reasoning and evidence?

- ✓ Is the reasoning sound and the evidence sufficient?

- ✓ Do the writer's claims work together to support the writer's overall argument?

- ✓ Which claims are not supported, if any?

# Skill:
# Arguments and Claims

Reread paragraph 7 of "A Quilt of a Country." Then, using the Checklist on the previous page, answer the multiple-choice questions below.

## ↻ YOUR TURN

1.  This question has two parts. First, answer Part A. Then, answer Part B.

    **Part A:** What is the author's claim in this paragraph?

    ○ A. Ma-Pa stores no longer exist in today's modern American society.

    ○ B. Modern immigrants struggle to find opportunities similar to those of earlier immigrants.

    ○ C. Calvinists are making it more difficult for immigrants to do things like ride the subway.

    ○ D. A Calvinist work ethic unifies both new immigrants and long-time Americans.

    **Part B:** What is the BEST reason or piece of evidence the author uses to support her claim?

    ○ A. "There is that Calvinist undercurrent in the American psyche"

    ○ B. "Leonel Castillo, former director of the Immigration and Naturalization Service"

    ○ C. "the new immigrants are not so different from our own parents or grandparents"

    ○ D. "Ma and Pa are now Korean, Vietnamese, Iraqi, Jordanian, Latin American."

A QUILT OF A COUNTRY

# Close Read

Reread "A Quilt of a Country." As you reread, complete the Skills Focus questions below. Then use your answers and annotations from the questions to help you complete the Write activity.

## ◎ SKILLS FOCUS

1. Analyze Quindlen's title in relation to the essay, and explain how her use of figurative language helps her to build her argument.

2. Discuss the many times Quindlen uses some form of the word *nation*—including as singular noun, plural noun, and adjective—and explain the effect of the usage of this word on her essay. Be sure to identify and correctly use the word patterns you mention.

3. Delineate and evaluate Quindlen's central argument in this essay.

4. Analyze how the author's use of words related to the idea of difference—including *different* and *disparate*—as well as the identification of specific ethnic and religious groups help to develop and refine her ideas and claims.

5. Explain how, according to Quindlen, America's past informs its identity today.

## ✏ WRITE

EXPLANATORY: Rather than separating her essay into a series of clear claims with evidence, the author uses a string of seemingly unrelated examples to build the foundation of her argument. How does this structure help develop her central idea of America as a quilt? It might be helpful to think about how her argument or message would be changed if the essay were structured more traditionally.

# Creation Myths from Around the World

INFORMATIONAL TEXT
Angie Shumov
2016

## Introduction

Ancient cultures, without the benefit of modern science and without being in contact with one another, passed down stories to explain the natural phenomena they saw around them. Some of these stories were told to explain the oldest of mysteries, the beginning of the world itself, and they are as different as the cultures to which they were born.

# "All around the world, creation myths help us make sense of man's origin."

1   Where did we come from and how did we get here? The answer to life's most **fundamental** question may remain unknown, but that doesn't stop narratives from telling of the world's beginning and how man came to be.

2   Neither proved right or wrong, creation myths have been passed down person to person, across generations and cultures since the beginning of time. Some speak of birth and a Supreme Being while others say the elements formed life. Even stories from the same cultural origins have different versions and **interpretations**.

### He the Creator

3   Christian, Jewish, and Islamic faiths share a common creation story. In the Book of Genesis, God says "let there be light" and in six days he creates the sun, moon, land and sky and all living creatures. He tells all to "be fruitful and multiply." Another **adaptation** goes on to speak of God creating Adam, the first man, out of the earth's dust. He then created a female companion out of Adam's rib who was given the name Eve, meaning mother of all living. Adam and Eve lived happily in God's Garden of Eden until one day, a serpent who lived in the tree of forbidden fruit, persuaded the humans to eat an apple. As God had forbidden them to touch this fruit, their disobedience brought the awareness of good and evil in the world.

### A Balanced Beginning

4   In one Chinese creation story, first there was a cosmic[1] egg made up of two balanced opposites: yin and yang. The egg held P'an Ku, the divine embryo. P'an Ku grew until the egg could not hold him, causing the shell to burst. So P'an Ku went to work right away making the world, with a hammer in hand. He dug out valleys, made way for rivers, and piled up mountains. But the earth was not complete until P'an Ku passed away. It wasn't until death that his flesh became soil and his bones the rocks. His eyes became the sun and moon

---

1. **cosmic** related to the universe as a whole, rather than just earth

and his head the sky. From what was once his sweat and tears was now rain and the fleas that covered his body became mankind.

## The Sacrifice

5 The earliest Vedic[2] text in the Hindu religion, the Rig Veda, tells the tale of Purusha. He who had a thousand heads, eyes, and feet could envelop the earth with his fingers. The gods sacrificed Purusha and his body turned to butter, **transforming** into animals, elements, the three gods Agni, Vayu, and Indra, and even the four castes of Hindu society. Later on, a different interpretation developed that spoke of the trinity of creation. Brahma the creator, Vishnu the preserver, and Shiva the destroyer makes a universal cycle of the world's beginning and end.

## Water of Life

6 The ancient Egyptians had numerous creation myths that all begin with the chaotic waters of Nun. Atum, while considered genderless, appeared as the first god or goddess. It is said he created himself from his thoughts and will. From the dark waters of Nun, emerged a hill for Atum to stand upon. This is where he made Shu, the god of air and Tefnut, the goddess of moisture. Shu and Tefnut created Geb, the earth, and Nut, the sky. And from Geb and Nut came even more gods and goddesses. While the world's order formed over time, Shu and Tefnut got lost in darkness. Atum sent his all-seeing eye to search for them and upon their return, he wept tears of joy. The tears struck the earth and turned into the first men.

## Three Tries

7 A Mayan creation story tells the tale of Tepeu, the maker and Gucumatz, the feathered spirit. After the two built the world with their thoughts, they decided they needed beings to look after their earth and to praise them for their creation. First, they made animals from birds and snakes to deer and panthers, but realized these creatures could not communicate their admiration. They had to produce another kind of being that was capable of worshiping them.

8 They first created man from wet clay but when he tried to speak, he crumbled apart. In a second attempt, they made men out of wood and while they could talk, they were empty headed and empty hearted, producing words with no meaning behind them. The third time around, they made four men out of the white and yellow corn. To their satisfaction, these men could think

---

2. **Vedic** the language, religion, or world view of the Vedas, the Aryan precursors of the Hindu peoples and religion

and feel and speak words out of love and respect. To ensure the human race continued, the gods created women as their mates and so mankind lived on.

9   All around the world, creation myths help us make sense of man's origin. While many variations exist, these stories have built the **foundation** of the world's largest religions and cultures. There may not be a universal understanding but these legends, true or false, are the real roots of society today.

By Angie Shumov. Used by permission of National Geographic Creative.

 **WRITE**

PERSONAL RESPONSE: How did this text shape your understanding of the purpose of storytelling? According to this text, what meaning is attached to creation stories? Do you think humans nowadays tell stories for the same reasons or different reasons than in ancient times? Use as evidence at least one account or story of a subject told in different mediums, such as a photo on social media and a text message, in your response.

# Looking for Palestine:
## Growing Up Confused in an Arab-American Family

INFORMATIONAL TEXT
Najla Said
2013

## Introduction

Author, actress, and playwright Najla Said (b. 1974) is the daughter of leading Palestinian American intellectual Edward Said. In her memoir *Looking for Palestine: Growing Up Confused in an Arab-American Family*, she describes her life as a "hyphenated" American. In this excerpt from the beginning of the memoir, Said introduces readers to her struggle to make sense of her identity as the daughter of immigrants—and as a member of a culture about which many Americans are deeply suspicious.

# "It's mainly because of my father that people now say 'Asian American' instead of 'Oriental.'"

1   I am a Palestinian-Lebanese-American Christian woman, but I grew up as a Jew in New York City.

2   I began my life, however, as a WASP[1].

3   I was born in Boston to an Ivy League[2] literature professor and his wife, baptized into the Episcopal Church at the age of one, and, at five, sent to an all-girls private school on the Upper East Side of Manhattan, one that boasts among its alumnae such perfectly formed and well-groomed American blue bloods as the legendary Jacqueline Onassis. It was at that point that I realized that something was seriously wrong — with me.

4   With my green seersucker tunic, its matching bloomers (worn underneath for gym and dance classes), the white Peter Pan collar of my blouse, and my wool knee socks, I was every bit the Chapin[3] schoolgirl. I was proud of my new green blazer with its fancy school emblem and my elegant shoes from France. But even the most elaborate uniform could not protect against my instant awareness of my differences. I was a dark-haired rat in a sea of blond perfection. I didn't live on the Upper East Side, where everyone else in my class seemed to live, but on the Upper West Side, or, rather, so far beyond the boundaries of what was then considered the Upper West Side as to be unacceptable to many. I did not have a canopy bed, an uncluttered bedroom, and a perfectly decorated living room the way my classmates did or like the homes I saw on TV. I had books piled high on shelves and tables, pipes, pens, Oriental rugs, painted walls, and strange house guests. I was surrounded at home not only by some of the Western world's greatest scholars and writers — Noam Chomsky, Lillian Hellman, Norman Mailer, Jacques Derrida, Susan Sontag, Joan Didion — but by the creme de la creme[4] of the Palestinian Resistance[5].

---

1. **WASP** White Anglo-Saxon Protestant
2. **Ivy League** a group of eight elite, private colleges in the U.S. Northeast, including Brown, Columbia Cornell, Dartmouth, Harvard, Penn, Princeton, and Yale
3. **Chapin** a girls' school in Manhattan, New York, founded in 1901
4. **creme de la creme** (French) "the cream of the cream," i.e., the very best
5. **Palestinian Resistance** insurgency of the inhabitants of Palestine against the state of Israel after its establishment in 1948

5    I know today there are probably lots of children of immigrants growing up similarly confused by the mixed messages of their lives, pertaining to everything from class to culture to standards of beauty. For me, though, growing up the daughter of a Lebanese mother and a **prominent** Palestinian thinker in New York City in the 1980s and '90s was confusing and unsettling. I constantly questioned everything about who I was and where I fit in the world, constantly judged my own worthiness and compared myself to others, and I struggled desperately to find a way to reconcile the beautiful, comforting, loving world of my home, culture, and family with the supposed "barbaric" and "backward" place and society others perceived it to be. I wondered why I was "an exception" to the rule of what both Arabs and Americans were "supposed" to be like, and why I was stuck in such an uneasy position.

6    After years of trying desperately to convince people that they didn't really understand me or the place my family came from, I stopped trying, especially since there was never anyone around to make me feel less alone in my **assertions**. I resigned myself to believing that everything people said about my culture was true, because it was exhausting and futile to try to convince anyone otherwise. Strangely, though, I also held on tightly to what I knew to be accurate and real about my family and culture. My parents and extended family are entirely responsible for that. I spent years simultaneously pushing them away and drawing them close, until I found a place where I could exist together with them and completely apart from them. Letting go of the idea that I had to have one identity, one way to describe myself, one "real me" hasn't left me any less confused about who I am, but it has certainly left me inspired, engaged, interested, complicated, and aware. And I'd rather be all of those things than just plain old "American," or plain old "Arab."

7    With the exception of my birth in Boston and a year-and-a-half-ish stint in Palo Alto, and then Southern California, I spent the first thirteen years of my life in an apartment building on Morningside Drive between West 119th and 120th streets. My father was a "teacher of English and Comparative Lit-er-a-ture at Columbia University." I learned to pronounce that impressive-sounding title at the age of four, though I had no idea what it meant. When people asked me what my daddy's job was, I'd wrap my brain and articulators around the phrase with great effort and draw it out.

8    I did recognize the word "Columbia," and I knew what that was (the park where we played after school and on weekends). I also knew that he did something in an office in that campus-park.

9    To very smart people who study a lot, Edward Said is the "father of **postcolonial** studies" or, as he told me once when he insisted I was wasting my college education by taking a course on postmodernism and I told him he didn't even know what it was:

10    "Know what it is, Najla? I invented it!!!" I still don't know if he was joking or serious.

11    To others, he is the author of Orientalism[6], the book that everyone reads at some point in college, whether in history, politics, Buddhism, or literature class. He wrote it when I was four.

12    As he explained once, when I pressed him to put it into simple English: "The basic concept, is that . . . historically, through literature and art, the 'East,' as seen through a Western lens, becomes **distorted** and degraded so that anything 'other' than what we Westerners recognize as familiar is not just exotic, mysterious, and sensual but also inherently inferior."

13    You know, like Aladdin.

14    It's mainly because of my father that people now say "Asian American" instead of "Oriental."

15    To other people, he is the symbol of Palestinian self determination, a champion of human rights, equality, and social justice. A "humanist" who "spoke truth to power."

16    And then still other people insist he was a terrorist, though anyone who knew him knows that's kind of like calling Gandhi a terrorist.

17    To me, he was my daddy, a **dapper** man in three-piece suits tailor-made in London. A cute old guy who yelled at me passionately in his weird sometimes British, sometimes American accent and then (five minutes later) forgot he had been upset; the one who brought me presents from all over the world, talked to me about Jane Eyre — my favorite book when I was twelve — and held me when I cried. He played tennis and squash, drove a Volvo, smoked a pipe, and collected pens. He was a professor. He was my father.

Excerpted from *Looking for Palestine: Growing Up Confused in an Arab-American Family* by Najla Said, published by Riverhead Books.

6. ***Orientalism*** a term coined by Edward W. Said in his 1978 book of the same name; it refers to the exotic aura and images projected onto Middle and Far East cultures by Western colonial nations who maintain indirect power over them

WRITE

ARGUMENTATIVE: The unit texts you have read so far deal with the role of traditions in shaping both individuals and communities. With these texts in mind, defend, challenge, or qualify the following statement: A person's identity is shaped by his or her surroundings. In your response, synthesize evidence from this text and at least one other text from the unit to support your position on the statement. Consider focusing on characters or speakers who react against or uphold traditions.

Please note that excerpts and passages in the StudySync® library and this workbook are intended as touchstones to generate interest in an author's work. The excerpts and passages do not substitute for the reading of entire texts, and StudySync® strongly recommends that students seek out and purchase the whole literary or informational work in order to experience it as the author intended. Links to online resellers are available in our digital library. In addition, complete works may be ordered through an authorized reseller by filling out and returning to StudySync® the order form enclosed in this workbook.

Reading & Writing          953
Companion

# Coming-of-Age Traditions from Around the World

INFORMATIONAL TEXT
Ursula Villarreal-Moura
2018

## Introduction

**studysync** tv

Ursula Villarreal-Moura (b. 1978) is a writer whose essays and fiction have been widely published in literary journals from *Tin House* to the *Nashville Review*. This essay surveys coming-of-age rituals from China to Mexico, from the United States to the Amazon. Read about a mitten filled with stinging ants, a dance routine that scintillated the internet, and a host of other traditions that serve as the bridge between adolescence and adulthood.

# "For those who choose to celebrate, a fun time is almost guaranteed."

NOTES

1   Entrance into adulthood is an important and oftentimes celebrated tradition around the world. Many coming-of-age traditions are considered joyous occasions marked by dancing and the lavishing of gifts while other adolescents are expected to provide evidence of their fortitude and bravery. Regardless of the rituals or requirements, becoming an adult frequently means welcoming new social expectations and duties.

2   Centuries ago, many cultures prepared younger generations for marriage, war, and other significant endeavors. Depending on the society in which young people come of age now, rites of passage can still signify a young person's maturity and their readiness to date or consider romantic relationships.

3   The timeline for when young people leave behind childhood and join the ranks of teenagers or young adults varies from culture to culture. For some, the transition is celebrated at age eleven while in other parts of the globe, a person must turn thirteen, fifteen, or, in the case of Guan Li candidates in China, men must wait until their eighteenth or twentieth birthdays.

4   In the United States, for many teenagers obtaining a driver's license or a part-time job is a **quintessential** rite of passage. Whereas previously the teen was dependent on a parent, guardian, or friend for transportation needs, with the ability to drive comes newfound freedom—even if it requires sharing a vehicle. Similarly, an after-school or summer job is often a teen's first taste of financial independence, one hallmark of adulthood.

5   While many young people enjoy partaking in long-standing cultural traditions, not everyone finds these rites of passage representative of their emerging identity. For some individuals, status quo traditions serve as a reminder of times when social or cultural obligations were rarely questioned, and people behaved as was expected of them. Such rituals may be rooted in religious beliefs or strict standards regarding gender roles. Some customs have evolved with time to suit current generations, who might wish for less public pomp and circumstance.

Skill: Textual Evidence

*Gaining freedom and financial independence is "one hallmark of adulthood," supported by explicit evidence: getting a driver's license and a part-time job are rites of passage, like an American declaration of independence.*

6   For those who choose to celebrate, a fun time is almost guaranteed. After all, nothing confirms some *joie de vivre* like a boisterous party.

**Quinceañera**

7   The Latin American counterpart to the Sweet Sixteen celebration is the *quinceañera*. Quinceañeras, believed to have originated in Mexico, mark the end of a young girl's childhood and her introduction into society as a mature young woman. Celebrated when girls are fifteen, quinceañeras are lavish **soirees** in which the honoree dons an extravagant ball gown. Accessories often include expensive jewelry and a tiara.

8   Celebration festivities traditionally begin with a Catholic mass in which the young girl renews her baptismal commitment and is blessed by a priest, godparents, and her parents. Part of her shift from childhood into womanhood is marked by vows to honor herself, her family, and her religion.

9   Festivities typically include several rounds of dancing and meals, a candle ceremony, and a toast made to the quinceañera herself. Often the price of such a celebration can range up to several thousands of dollars, with high-ticket items including the honoree's dress and jewelry, hired photographers, live music, catered food, and an enormous cake, as well as gifts the young woman can use as she transitions into womanhood.

A photograph of a young woman on her quinceanera day.

10  In 2016, a Houston native named Jasmine Cortinas decided she wanted her quinceañera to be memorable for guests as well as representative of her musical tastes. While a father-daughter dance is traditionally part of the party's events, Jasmine opted for a dance routine that incorporated contemporary music and dance styles that would challenge both her and her father's dance skills. The result was a choreographed dance routine that went viral on YouTube and likely inspired many other young women to tailor their own celebrations to their unique tastes and personalities.

11  While most quinceañeras are well attended, in 2016 Rubi Ibarra's party invitation went viral on Facebook after her father publicly posted details about his daughter's celebration, allowing the time and location of the bash to be shared by thousands of users. While the party in the northern Mexico town of Villa de Guadalupe was intended solely for Rubi's friends and family, over a million people from all over the world RSVPed. In total, between 20,000 and 30,000 people were reported to have attended her birthday. In addition to the party's lineup of many rounds of catered food, and plenty of dancing and live music, it included an outdoor horse race.

**Tchoodi**

12  In the West Africa country of Mali, Fulani women undergo a facial tattooing process known interchangeably as *tchoodi* or *socou-gol*. In order to avoid mockery by peers and signal their readiness to marry, beginning at puberty young girls signal their bravery by allowing other women to darken their lips, mouth, and oftentimes gums with black ink. The ritual occurs while the fully conscious young girl lays on her back as older Fulani women transform her face from girlhood to womanhood.

13  During the custom, black pigment is applied by repeatedly poking an ink-soaked scorching needle or sharp piece of wood into the young girl's lips and the surrounding facial area. A time-consuming process, tchoodi causes profuse bleeding and swelling, which Fulani girls are expected to endure with stoicism and bravery. Such coloring is believed to highlight a girl's smile and her white teeth, a sign of exquisite beauty and fertility in the culture.

14  Since dark lips and a ringed mouth are considered aesthetically attractive, Fulani men are expected to marry young women who have undergone this beautification ritual. Women aren't the only ones believed to become more attractive with pigmentation, though. In neighboring Senegal, Fulani men often undergo a similar process in which their gums are blackened. This related custom is considered both a marker of attraction as well as a sign of dental health in their community.

NOTES

Skill: Textual Evidence

*I can infer that personalizing a coming-of-age tradition is rewarding. The author states that because Jasmine personalized her dance routine to her tastes, she likely inspired other girls to do the same.*

Please note that excerpts and passages in the StudySync® library and this workbook are intended as touchstones to generate interest in an author's work. The excerpts and passages do not substitute for the reading of entire texts, and StudySync® strongly recommends that students seek out and purchase the whole literary or informational work in order to experience it as the author intended. Links to online resellers are available in our digital library. In addition, complete works may be ordered through an authorized reseller by filling out and returning to StudySync® the order form enclosed in this workbook.

Reading & Writing
Companion     957

NOTES

This teenage girl's facial tattoo is evidence of her entrance into womanhood.

15   **Recovery** time for tchoodi can last up to three weeks, when young girls subsist on liquids ingested through a straw. Since bravery is an integral part of this African culture, girls are not known to shy away from the ritual. In fact, continuing the Fulani way of life and custom—known as *pulaaku*— is of utmost importance to the tribe and enduring tchoodi is one way in which traditions live on generation after generation.

**Sateré-Mawé**

16   In the Amazon, young Sateré-Mawé boys prove their readiness to become warriors by enduring an agonizing **initiation** known as *dança da tucandeira*, involving many tucandeiras or poisonous bullet ants.

17   At age 13, Sateré-Mawé boys enter the jungle to hunt for bullet ants to use for their initiation ritual. Hundreds of bullet ants are first sedated then woven onto palm frond gloves resembling oven mitts. Ants stingers are intentionally woven pointing inward as the goal is to endure as much pain as nature intends. In preparation for the endurance test, youths have their hands and forearms covered in a black paint that is said to protect them from the inevitable stings.

18   Sateré-Mawé boys are fitted with the mitts and subjected to the ants stinging for up to ten minutes at a time. Considered thirty times more painful than a bee sting, the pain of a bullet ant bite is sometimes likened to being shot, hence the name "bullet" ant. Ant venom causes the boys' hands and arms to

swell and it is common for the initiant to experience temporary paralysis or convulsions following the ritual. Few boys are said to cry out, as manhood among the Sateré-Mawé is defined by tolerance to agony. However, the relief of removing the mitt is short-lived as the process will be repeated up to twenty times over several months in order for the boy to prove his manhood.

## Ji Li and Guan Li

19    An ancient tradition, the Confucian coming-of-age ceremonies of *Ji Li* (笄禮 or hair pinning) and *Guan Li* (冠禮 or capping) are now experiencing a resurgence. Known as coronation ceremonies, the rituals involve both young women and young men having their hair pinned or capped as proof of their sexual maturity and readiness to marry.

20    In China, the coming-of-age tradition Ji Li occurs for young women at age fifteen, and for young men between the ages of eighteen and twenty. The ceremony involves wearing traditional Han clothing and includes honoring Huangdi, a former emperor.

21    Since having long, strong hair is considered a symbol of beauty, some young girls in China wear their hair in braids until their Ji Li ceremony. The initiation involves honorees having their hair washed, parted, and pulled into a knot or bun. The gathered hair is then held tight with pins made of wood, jade, or gold. Modern-day Ji Li celebrations are community affairs with groups of girls publicly taking vows of adulthood.

A Ji Li honoree is attended to by an elder who prepares her hair.

22  Prior to Guan Li, a young man is required to select a guest of honor to perform the ceremony, typically a teacher, and another guest to cap him. During the ritual, the honoree is presented with a cap and scarf. In the presence of his family, his hair is pulled into a bun and he is capped by his chosen assistant after which the young man delivers a speech. Given the importance of respect, the honoree bows and kneels throughout the ceremony to his teacher and parents, and listens as they offer advice and usher him into the next stage of his **development**.

23  Part of the coronation ceremony for Ji Li and Guan Li includes honorees receiving a courtesy or style name that replaces their birth name and welcomes them as adults with new responsibilities. Style names may be self-selected by the honoree or chosen by a mentor, teacher, or parent.

**Celebrating the Transition From Child to Adult**

24  Youths across the globe embrace passage into adulthood in a variety of styles and manners. All the traditions discussed—quinceañera, tchoodi, dança da tucandeira, and Ji Li and Guan Li—involve participation from parents, mentors, or community members.

25  Often, traditions can be modernized to reflect contemporary styles or attitudes as evidenced by Jasmine Cortinas' choreographed father-daughter dance. Other times preserving traditions for decades is a sign of respect and unwavering dedication to one's ancestors, as in the case of tchoodi.

26  Sometimes the journey from childhood to adulthood happens without much fanfare. Gaining the right to vote and to enlist in the military are two long-standing American rites of passage that occur when a teen turns eighteen. Exercising the right to vote imbues an individual with a political voice and the potential to shape far-reaching legislative policies. Likewise, joining the the military is an opportunity to demonstrate patriotism through service to our country. Both these coming of age traditions acknowledge increased expectations that accompany mature citizenship.

27  All rites of passage, whether private or public, near or far, serve as important milestones for generation after generation.

# First Read

Read "Coming-of-Age Traditions from Around the World." After you read, complete the Think Questions below.

 **THINK QUESTIONS**

1. How are driver's licenses and after-school jobs steps toward adulthood in America? Explain, citing evidence from the text.

2. How do quinceañeras and the Chinese coming-of-age traditions involve elders of the community? Cite evidence from the text to support your answer.

3. Explain what rituals from the text have evolved to include more "modern tastes" and which rituals have adhered to tradition. Refer to the text as you develop your answer.

4. Use context clues to determine the meaning of **soiree** as it is used in the text. Write your best definition, along with a brief explanation of the which clues helped you determine its meaning.

5. Keeping in mind that the Latin word *initiō* means "to begin," what do you think the word **initiation** means as it is used in the text? Write your definition, and explain how you determined its meaning.

Please note that excerpts and passages in the StudySync® library and this workbook are intended as touchstones to generate interest in an author's work. The excerpts and passages do not substitute for the reading of entire texts, and StudySync® strongly recommends that students seek out and purchase the whole literary or informational work in order to experience it as the author intended. Links to online resellers are available in our digital library. In addition, complete works may be ordered through an authorized reseller by filling out and returning to StudySync® the order form enclosed in this workbook.

Reading & Writing Companion   961

# Skill:
# Textual Evidence

Use the Checklist to analyze Textual Evidence in "Coming-of-Age Traditions from Around the World." Refer to the sample student annotations about Textual Evidence in the text.

In order to support an analysis by citing evidence that is explicitly stated in the text, do the following:

✓ Read the text closely and critically.

✓ Identify what the text says explicitly.

✓ Find the most relevant textual evidence that supports your analysis.

✓ Consider why an author explicitly states specific details.

✓ Cite the specific words, phrases, lines, or stanzas from the text that support your analysis.

In order to interpret implicit meanings in a text by making inferences, do the following:

✓ Combine information directly stated in the text with your own knowledge, experiences, and observations.

✓ Cite the specific words, phrases, sentences, or paragraphs from the text that led to and support this inference.

In order to cite textual evidence to support an analysis of what the text says explicitly as well as inferences drawn from the text, consider the following questions:

✓ Have I read the text closely and critically?

✓ What inferences am I making about the text?

✓ What textual evidence am I using to support these inferences?

✓ Am I quoting the evidence from the text correctly?

✓ Does my textual evidence logically relate to my analysis or the inference I am making?

# Skill:
# Textual Evidence

Reread paragraph 15 of "Coming-of-Age Traditions from Around the World." Then, using the Checklist on the previous page, answer the multiple-choice questions below.

## ⟳ YOUR TURN

1. This question has two parts. First, answer Part A. Then, answer Part B.

   **Part A:** What can be inferred about important coming-of-age traditions in this paragraph?

   ○ A. Preserving a cultural tradition is more important than temporary discomfort.

   ○ B. Women have more pain tolerance than men during rituals in the Fulani culture.

   ○ C. Coming-of-age traditions like this one should be modernized.

   ○ D. Traditions that have an element of pain endurance should be more respected than others.

   **Part B:** Which piece of textual evidence BEST supports your answer from Part A?

   ○ A. "Since bravery is an integral part of this African culture, girls are not known to shy away from the ritual."

   ○ B. "In fact, continuing the Fulani way of life and custom—known as *pulaaku*— is of utmost importance to the tribe"

   ○ C. "enduring tchoodi is one way in which traditions live on generation after generation"

   ○ D. "Recovery time for tchoodi can last up to three weeks."

Please note that excerpts and passages in the StudySync® library and this workbook are intended as touchstones to generate interest in an author's work. The excerpts and passages do not substitute for the reading of entire texts, and StudySync® strongly recommends that students seek out and purchase the whole literary or informational work in order to experience it as the author intended. Links to online resellers are available in our digital library. In addition, complete works may be ordered through an authorized reseller by filling out and returning to StudySync® the order form enclosed in this workbook.

Reading & Writing Companion

963

# Close Read

Reread "Coming-of-Age Traditions from Around the World." As you reread, complete the Skills Focus questions below. Then use your answers and annotations from the questions to help you complete the Write activity.

## ◎ SKILLS FOCUS

1. Highlight details in the text that suggest complex emotions are involved in coming-of-age traditions. Cite strong textual evidence to explain several emotions that are evoked.

2. Identify the author's purpose in writing this essay and explain how the author's choice of language helps to support that purpose.

3. Discuss how the use of headings, photographs, and captions helps to connect sections of text.

4. Analyze how rites of passage, according to this essay, affect the lives of the people who celebrate them.

## ✏ WRITE

DISCUSSION: Traditions are customs, stories, beliefs, rituals, and/or routines that are passed down in a family from one generation to another. Research has proven that traditions are part of healthy families, provide a foundation for shared identity, and help build strong bonds between generations. In your opinion, what positive effects can traditions have on individuals, families, and/or communities? Synthesize textual evidence from this text and at least one other text from the unit, as well as relevant personal anecdotes, to support your answer to this question. To prepare for the discussion, write down your thoughts about this question and explain your reasoning.

Extended Writing Project and Grammar

EXTENDED
WRITING
PROJECT
RESEARCH WRITING

# Research Writing Process: Plan

| PLAN | DRAFT | REVISE | EDIT AND PUBLISH |

Mythologist Joseph Campbell once said, "If you're going to have a story, have a big story, or none at all." People across time and place have invented ways to explain how we came to be the way we are now. Origin stories can play a role in nations, families, cultures, and religions. Examples of origin stories include the biblical story of Genesis, the Iroquois story of the Great Turtle, and the Greek story of Zeus.

## WRITING PROMPT

**What do origin stories reveal about our perceptions of the world?**

Choose one origin story relating to a religion, culture, or nation that you would like to learn more about. Write a research paper explaining this origin story and how it has shaped a particular community. As part of your research process, select a research question, develop a research plan, gather and evaluate source materials, and synthesize and present your research findings. Regardless of which origin story you choose, be sure your research project includes the following:

- an introduction
- relevant information synthesized from at least three authoritative print and digital sources
- a clear text structure
- appropriate formatting, graphics, and multimedia, as needed
- a conclusion
- citations for sources

**Writing to Sources**

As you gather ideas and information from a variety of authoritative print and digital sources, be sure to:

- use and cite evidence from multiple sources;
- avoid plagiarism, or including source information without credit; and
- avoid overly relying on one source.

## Introduction to Informative Research Writing

Informative research writing examines a topic and conveys ideas and information through comparisons, description, and explanation. Good informative research writing includes genre characteristics and craft, such as a clear **thesis statement** and **supporting facts and details** from **reliable sources** that clarify and support the central idea or thesis statement. The characteristics of informative research writing include:

- an **introduction** with a clear controlling idea or thesis statement
- **body paragraphs** with supporting details, such as definitions, quotations, examples, and facts that are cited accurately and back up the central idea or thesis
- a clear and logical **text structure**
- a **formal style**
- integration of **print features**, such as headers; **graphics**, such as maps or charts; and **multimedia**, including audio or video, as needed for comprehension
- a **conclusion** that wraps up your ideas
- proper citation of sources, including a **works cited list**

In addition to these characteristics, writers also carefully narrow the focus of their research by generating research questions and developing a research plan. The research process requires patience as you evaluate the validity and usefulness of sources related to your topic. Researchers develop over time their skills of locating and assessing the appropriateness of a source.

As you continue with this Extended Writing Project, you'll receive more instruction and practice at crafting each of the characteristics of informative research writing to create your own Informative research paper.

Please note that excerpts and passages in the StudySync® library and this workbook are intended as touchstones to generate interest in an author's work. The excerpts and passages do not substitute for the reading of entire texts, and StudySync® strongly recommends that students seek out and purchase the whole literary or informational work in order to experience it as the author intended. Links to online resellers are available in our digital library. In addition, complete works may be ordered through an authorized reseller by filling out and returning to StudySync® the order form enclosed in this workbook.

Reading & Writing Companion **967**

Before you get started on your own informative research paper, read this paper that one student, Josh, wrote in response to the writing prompt. As you read the Model, highlight and annotate the features of informative research writing that Josh included in his paper.

NOTES

## STUDENT MODEL

### The *Popol* Vuh and the Maya: Keeping Meaning Across Time

**The Maya Beginning**

1  "Who am I?" and "How do I fit into this world?" are not just questions we ask ourselves as we grow up. These questions have been around for ages. To answer these important life questions, ancient humans used observations and imagination to explain how things came to be. The world's oldest cultures developed origin stories that explain the existence of good and evil, for example, as well as the creation of earth, sky, water, crops, animals, and humans. The Maya of what is now Guatemala are one such ancient culture. Part of their origin story, the *Popol Vuh*, describes how the gods created humankind after multiple failed attempts. Carefully studying the *Popol Vuh* and the research around it provides insight into how the Maya have understood time, the divine, and human nature. Studying ancient texts like the *Popol Vuh* serves to remind all human beings of the distances human progress has traveled through centuries, and also how much wisdom the ancients had that is still worth understanding today.

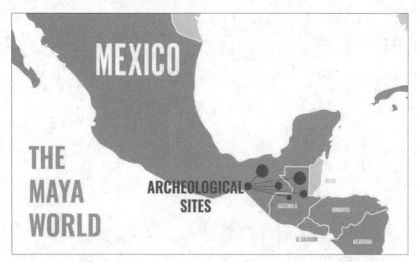

Spreading from what is now Guatemala and beyond, the Maya civilization was one of the most advanced in what is now Latin America. ("The Maya World")

### A Book for the Ages

2  According to Lewis Spence, translator of a 1908 English edition of the *Popol Vuh*, "The name 'Popol Vuh' signifies 'Record of the Community,' and its literal translation is 'Book of the Mat,' from the Kiché word 'pop' or 'popol,' a mat or rug of woven rushes or bark on which the entire family sat, and 'vuh' or 'uuh,' paper or book, from 'uoch' to write" (Spence). For centuries, the *Popol Vuh* has shaped Maya understanding of life as a cycle. The story begins with the gods gathering to create the earth. After building the world, the gods wanted to fill it with creatures who would worship them (Shumov).

3  • First, they created humans from wet clay, but these humans could not speak, so the gods destroyed them in a flood.

4  • On their second attempt, the gods created humans out of wood; however, as Shumov explains, while these humans could talk, "they were empty headed and empty hearted." So, the gods destroyed the human race a second time.

5  • Finally, on the third attempt, the gods "made four men out of the white and yellow corn" and were satisfied that "these men could think and feel and speak words out of love and respect" (Shumov). In Maria Gomez's retelling, these humans were actually "too wise." Rather than destroy the human race for a third time, however, one of the gods "clouded their minds and eyes so they would become less wise" (Gomez).

6  This ancient story told in the *Popol Vuh* shows the power of the gods and reveals a cycle of creation and destruction that has shaped the way the Maya understand time, the divine, and their rulers.

### Humanity in Time

7  The three creations of humanity, as described in the *Popol Vuh,* have had a great influence on Maya culture, which can be seen in the Maya's relationship with time. Because gods destroyed humanity twice before, the Maya believe the gods could do so again. However, because humans were then re-created, the Maya believe this, too, will happen again. These interpretations of the *Popol Vuh* relate to the Maya belief in time as an endless cycle of beginnings and endings. To record these never-ending cycles of creation and

destruction, the Maya invented "one of the most accurate calendar systems in human history" ("The Calendar System"). The Calendar Round records dates 52 days into the future (Mark). The Long Count Calendar, started in 3114 BCE, calculates dates far into the future. The current cycle started in December 2012. This way of timekeeping is still seen in Maya society today. To track the different cycles of time, Maya communities have "daykeepers." Daykeepers are responsible for keeping the cycles going with the proper rituals and ceremonies. Drawing on centuries of knowledge, they keep track of the calendar, and serve as healers for the Maya people ("The Modern Calendar Priests"). In Maya culture, a calendar is more than a grid or list of dates used for keeping appointments; this calendar encompasses entire life cycles.

This shows the features of a Calendar Round. One view of the daykeepers is that the world is constantly dying, and the daykeepers reset it. ("The Modern Calendar Priests," Getty Images)

8    Beyond the Calendar Round, the Maya origin story has also influenced the Maya's understanding of divine forces and human nature. According to the *Popol Vuh*, humanity was created in order to worship the gods. The gods are to be respected because they have the power to both create and destroy humanity. This aspect of their religion can be seen in the Maya pyramids. The structure of the pyramids is symbolic. For example, the pyramids were built with flat tops, which created space on which rituals of bloodletting and human sacrifice could be performed to honor the gods by returning "life force" to them (Jarus). In addition to emphasizing Maya respect for

the gods, ancient Maya structures also reveal Maya understanding of human nature. In the city of Palenque, an ancient burial tomb for a Maya king, Pakal, was discovered in 1952. This tomb is decorated with carvings that show the king's ancestors as well as his rebirth (Jarus). These depictions of the king's life, death, and rebirth reveal a belief in life as a series of beginnings and endings and connect back to the cycle of creation and destruction described in the *Popol Vuh*.

**The Web of Life**

9    Thousands of years ago, the Maya first told creation stories in an attempt to understand the world and to answer life's big questions, such as "Who am I?," "Why am I here?," and "Why is the world the way it is?" In attempting to answer these questions, the Maya origin stories described the world and beyond as places "where time is cyclical and all things are interconnected" ("Connecting Earth and Sky"). In other words, time is an intricately woven web that connects all beings and events. These creation stories also describe a special bond between humanity and the gods, as well as a careful balance of creation and destruction. Indeed, for the Maya who are alive today, these stories serve as an important cultural foundation and link to the past. For the world, links to ancient cultures can serve as guideposts: no matter what the future holds, human beings must find a way, as the Daykeepers did, to adjust their settings and keep on going.

Please note that excerpts and passages in the StudySync® library and this workbook are intended as touchstones to generate interest in an author's work. The excerpts and passages do not substitute for the reading of entire texts, and StudySync® strongly recommends that students seek out and purchase the whole literary or informational work in order to experience it as the author intended. Links to online resellers are available in our digital library. In addition, complete works may be ordered through an authorized reseller by filling out and returning to StudySync® the order form enclosed in this workbook.

Reading & Writing
Companion

971

NOTES

## Works Cited

"The Calendar System." *Living Maya Time: Sun, Corn, and the Calendar*, Smithsonian National Museum of the American Indian, maya.nmai.si.edu/calendar/calendar-system. Accessed 8 Apr. 2018.

"Connecting Earth and Sky." *Living Maya Time: Sun, Corn, and the Calendar*, Smithsonian National Museum of the American Indian, maya.nmai.si.edu/the-maya/connecting-earth-and-sky. Accessed 7 Apr. 2018.

Gomez, Maria C. "Maya Religion." *Ancient History Encyclopedia*, www.ancient.eu/Maya_Religion/#references. Accessed 8 Apr. 2018.

Jarus, Owen. "The Maya: History, Culture & Religion." *LiveScience*, 22 Aug. 2017, www.livescience.com/41781-the-maya.html. Accessed 9 Apr. 2018.

Mark, Joshua J. "Maya Civilization." *Ancient History Encyclopedia*, www.ancient.eu/Maya_Civilization/. Accessed 8 Apr. 2018.

"The Maya World." *Living Maya Time: Sun, Corn, and the Calendar*, Smithsonian National Museum of the American Indian, maya.nmai.si.edu/the-maya/maya-world. Accessed 7 Apr. 2018.

"The Modern Calendar Priests." *Archaeology Magazine*, www.archaeology.org/issues/44-1211/features/306-calendar-priests. Accessed 8 Apr. 2018.

Shumov, Angie. "Creation Myths from Around the World." StudySync. 2016.

Spence, Lewis. "The Popol Vuh." *Project Gutenberg.* 1908. http://www.gutenberg.org/files/56550/56550-h/56550-h.htm. Accessed 4 Apr. 2018.

# ✏ WRITE

When writing, first consider your purpose, keeping in mind who your audience is so you can write appropriately for them. Your audience for this project consists of your teacher and peers, and your purpose is implied within the writing prompt. Reread the prompt to determine your purpose for writing.

To begin, review the questions below and then select a strategy, such as brainstorming, journaling, reading, or discussing, to generate ideas.

After generating ideas, begin the prewriting process by writing a summary of your writing plan. In your summary, respond to the following questions:

- **Purpose:** Which origin story would you like to write about? What does it tell us about the culture it came from?

- **Audience:** Who is your audience? What background information will you need to include about your topic? What new information do you want them to learn?

- **Question:** How can you use a research question to focus your research?

- **Sources:** What kinds of sources will help you answer that question?

- **Structure:** How can you effectively share the information you find with readers?

## Response Instructions

Use the questions in the bulleted list to write a one-paragraph summary. Your summary should describe what you plan to research and inform your audience about in this research paper. Include possible research questions of your own based on the prompt.

Don't worry about including all of the details now; focus only on the most essential and important elements. You will refer back to this short summary as you continue through the steps of the writing process.

Please note that excerpts and passages in the StudySync® library and this workbook are intended as touchstones to generate interest in an author's work. The excerpts and passages do not substitute for the reading of entire texts, and StudySync® strongly recommends that students seek out and purchase the whole literary or informational work in order to experience it as the author intended. Links to online resellers are available in our digital library. In addition, complete works may be ordered through an authorized reseller by filling out and returning to StudySync® the order form enclosed in this workbook.

Reading & Writing Companion    **973**

# Skill:
# Planning Research

## ••• CHECKLIST FOR PLANNING RESEARCH

In order to conduct a short or more sustained research project to answer a question or solve a problem, do the following:

- Select a topic or problem to research.

- Think about what you want to find out and where you might search.

- Start to formulate your major research question by asking open-ended questions that begin "How...?" and "Why...?" and choose one that you are interested in exploring.

- Narrow or broaden your inquiry when appropriate, sorting information or items so they are easily distinguishable from one another.

- Locate multiple sources on the subject to:

  > synthesize information from different points of view.

  > demonstrate understanding of the subject under investigation.

In order to conduct a short or more sustained research project to answer a question or solve a problem, consider the following questions:

- Does the question allow me to explore a new issue, an important problem worth solving, or a fresh perspective on a topic?

- Can I research my question within my given time frame and with the resources available to me?

- Can I synthesize information from multiple sources on the question or problem, looking for different points of view?

- Will I be able to demonstrate understanding of the subject under investigation in my research project?

## ♻ YOUR TURN

Read the research questions below. Then, complete the chart by matching each question into the correct category.

| | Research Questions |
|---|---|
| A | What does the Chinese creation story tell us about the prominence of nature in ancient Chinese culture? |
| B | How many different origin stories exist in China and how have they changed over time? |
| C | What are some Egyptian creation stories? |
| D | What was the relationship of ancient Egyptians to bodies of water? |
| E | What artistic representation best reveals how the Chinese creation story portrays nature? |
| F | What do Egyptian stories tell us about the ancient Egyptians' relationship with nature? |

| Too Narrow | Appropriate | Too Broad |
|---|---|---|
| | | |
| | | |
| | | |

## ♻ YOUR TURN

With your teacher's guidance, generate questions for formal research. Using the questions in the checklist, evaluate each question to determine whether it is too narrow, too broad, or just right. Select a just-right question. Then, complete the chart by writing a short plan for how you will go about doing research for your paper.

| Questions | My Response |
|---|---|
| Possible Research Questions: | |
| Selected Research Question: | |
| Step 1: | |
| Step 2: | |
| Step 3: | |

# Skill:
# Evaluating Sources

## ••• CHECKLIST FOR EVALUATING SOURCES

First, reread the sources you gathered and identify the following:

- what kind of source it is, including video, audio, or text, and where the source comes from
- where information seems inaccurate, biased, or outdated
- where information seems irrelevant or tangential to your research question

In order to use advanced searches to gather relevant, credible, and accurate print and digital sources, use the following questions as a guide:

- Is the material published by a well-established source or expert author?
- Is the material up-to-date or based on the most current information?
- Is the material factual, and can it be verified by another source?
- Are there specific terms or phrases in my research question that I can use to adjust my search?
- Can I use "and," "or," or "not" to expand or limit my search?
- Can I use quotation marks to search for exact phrases?

In order to integrate multiple sources of information presented in diverse media formats, ask the following:

- Have I included information from a variety of media?

- Am I relying too heavily on one source or source type?

- Have I varied the points at which I reference a particular source over the course of the speech or paper?

- As I listen to a presentation, am I aware of the speaker's use of sources? Where applicable, do the diverse media formats work well together?

**YOUR TURN**

Read the factors below. Then, complete the chart by sorting them into those that show a source is credible and reliable and those that do not.

| | Factors |
|---|---|
| A | The website is a personal blog written by a person who enjoys learning about the subject matter. |
| B | The author is a journalist working for an internationally recognized newspaper. |
| C | The text avoids personal judgments and includes several different viewpoints that are properly cited. |
| D | The article states only the author's personal opinions and leaves out other positions as well as sources. |
| E | The text relies on questionable premises and broad generalizations to persuade readers. |
| F | The article includes citations and a list of sources the author referenced. |

| Credible and Reliable | Not Credible or Reliable |
|---|---|
| | |
| | |
| | |

**YOUR TURN**

Complete the chart below by filling in the title and author of a source and answering questions about it.

| Source Title and Author: | |
|---|---|
| **Reliability:** Has the source material been published in a well-established book, periodical, or website? | |
| **Reliability:** Is the source material up-to-date or based on the most current information? | |
| **Credibility:** Is the source material written by a recognized expert on the topic? | |
| **Credibility:** Is the source material published by a well-respected author or organization? | |
| **Bias:** Is the source material connected to persons or organizations that are objective and unbiased? | |
| **Evaluation:** Is this a source I should use in my project? | |

Please note that excerpts and passages in the StudySync® library and this workbook are intended as touchstones to generate interest in an author's work. The excerpts and passages do not substitute for the reading of entire texts, and StudySync® strongly recommends that students seek out and purchase the whole literary or informational work in order to experience it as the author intended. Links to online resellers are available in our digital library. In addition, complete works may be ordered through an authorized reseller by filling out and returning to StudySync® the order form enclosed in this workbook.

Reading & Writing Companion  **979**

# Skill:
# Research and Notetaking

## ••• CHECKLIST FOR RESEARCH AND NOTETAKING

In order to conduct short as well as more sustained research projects to answer a question (including a self-generated question) or solve a problem, do the following:

- answer a question for a research project, or think of your own, self-generated question that you would like to have answered

- look up your topic in an encyclopedia to find general information

- find specific, up-to-date information in books and periodicals, on the Internet, and if appropriate, from interviews with experts

- narrow or broaden your inquiry when appropriate

  > if you find dozens of books on a topic, your research topic may be too broad

  > if it is difficult to write a research question, narrow your topic so it is more specific

- synthesize your information by organizing your notes from various sources to see what they have in common and how they differ

To conduct short as well as more sustained research projects to answer a question (including a self-generated question) or solve a problem, consider the following questions:

- Where could I look to find additional information?

- How does new information I have found affect my research question?

- How can I demonstrate understanding of the subject I am investigating?

## ↻ YOUR TURN

Read the notes from a student's research below. Then, complete the chart by sorting them into those that are relevant and those that are not relevant to the topic of what the Chinese origin story of Pan Gu reveals about the Chinese people's attitude toward divine forces.

| | Notes |
|---|---|
| A | According to one Chinese origin story, the first man was named Pan Gu. He separated heaven and earth and divided the seas. |
| B | The Mien people of southern China primarily believe in Daoism, which is focused on the origin story of Pan Gu. |
| C | One important principle that surfaces throughout the story of Pan Gu is the idea of "inescapable duality." |
| D | Representations of Pan Gu are embroidered on many traditional Chinese items of clothing. |

| Relevant to Topic | Not Relevant to Topic |
|---|---|
| | |
| | |

Please note that excerpts and passages in the StudySync® library and this workbook are intended as touchstones to generate interest in an author's work. The excerpts and passages do not substitute for the reading of entire texts, and StudySync® strongly recommends that students seek out and purchase the whole literary or informational work in order to experience it as the author intended. Links to online resellers are available in our digital library. In addition, complete works may be ordered through an authorized reseller by filling out and returning to StudySync® the order form enclosed in this workbook.

Reading & Writing Companion    981

## ⟳ YOUR TURN

Complete the chart by synthesizing and recording information from each of four sources relevant to your subject. Remember to number and cite each source.

| Information from Sources | Synthesis |
| --- | --- |
| | |
| | |
| | |
| | |

# Research Writing Process: Draft

| PLAN | DRAFT | REVISE | EDIT AND PUBLISH |

You have already made progress toward writing your research paper. Now it is time to draft your research paper.

## ✏ WRITE

Use your plan and other responses in your Binder to draft your research paper. You may also have new ideas as you begin drafting. Feel free to explore those new ideas as you have them. You can also ask yourself these questions to ensure that your writing is focused, organized, and developed:

**Draft Checklist:**

☐ **Focused:** Have I made my thesis statement clear to readers? Have I included only relevant information and details and nothing extraneous that might confuse my readers?

☐ **Organized:** Does the organizational structure in my paper make sense? Will readers be engaged by the organization and interested in the way I present information and evidence?

☐ **Developed:** Does my writing flow together naturally, or is it choppy? Will my readers be able to follow my ideas? Will they understand the purpose of my research?

Before you submit your draft, read it over carefully. You want to be sure that you've responded to all aspects of the prompt.

Here is Josh's informative research paper draft. As you read, notice how Josh develops his draft to be focused, organized, and developed. As he continues to revise and edit his paper, he will find and improve weak spots in his writing, as well as correct any language or punctuation mistakes.

NOTES

### Skill: Print and Graphic Features

Josh adds headings throughout his paper to group the information and help readers better understand his thesis. By including print and graphic features, as well as synthesizing multiple sources, including multimedia sources, Josh communicates information more effectively and supports his thesis in a more thorough manner.

---

## ☰ STUDENT MODEL: FIRST DRAFT

### The *Popol Vuh* and the Maya

#### The Maya Beginning

To answer important life questions, ancient humans came up with creation stories. The world's oldest cultures all have origin stories that explain good and evil and telling the creation of earth, sky, water, crops, animals, and humans. The Maya were one such ancient culture. Part of their origin story, the *Popol Vuh*, describes how the gods created humankind after multiple, failed attempts. Carefully studying the *Popol Vuh* provides insight into how the Maya have understood time, the divine and human nature.

#### A Book for the Ages

The Popol Vuh has shaped Mayan understanding of life as a cycel. The story begins with the gods gathering to create the earth. After building the world, the gods wanted to fill it with creatures who would worship them. First they created humans from wet clay, but these humans could not speak so the gods destroyed them in a flood. On their second attempt the gods created men out of wood, however, while these men could talk, they were empty headed and empty hearted. So the gods destroyed the human race a second time. Finaly on the third attempt the gods made four men out of white and yellow corn and satisfied that these men could think and feel and speak words out of love and respect. In one retelling, these humans were actualy "too wise." Rather than destroy the human race for a third time, however, one of the gods "clouded their minds and eyes so they would become less wise." This ancient story told in the Popol Vuh shows the power of the gods and reveals a cycel of creation and destruction that has shaped the way the Maya understand time, the divine, and their rulers.

- Finally, on the third attempt, the gods "made four men out of the white and yellow corn" and were satisfied that "these men could think and feel and speak words out of love and respect" (Shumov). In Maria Gomez's retelling, these humans were actually "too wise." Rather than destroy the human race for a third time, however, one of the gods "clouded their minds and eyes so they would become less wise" (Gomez).

This ancient story told in the *Popol Vuh* shows the power of the gods and reveals a cycle of creation and destruction that has shaped the way the Maya understand time, the divine, and their rulers.

**Humanity in Time**

~~The three creations of humanity influenced the Mayas' relationship with time. Because gods destroyed humanity twice before, the Maya beleive the gods could do so again, and because humans were then re-created, the Maya beleive this, too will happen again. These interpretations of the Popol Vuh relate to the Maya belief in time as an endless cycle of beginnings and also is a cycle of endings. To record these never-ending cycles the Mayans invented, "one of the most accurate calendar systems in human history" ("The Calendar System"). The Calendar Round records dates 52 days into the future ("Maya Civilization.").~~

The three creations of humanity, as described in the *Popol Vuh*, have had a great influence on Maya culture, which can be seen in the Maya's relationship with time. Because gods destroyed humanity twice before, the Maya believe the gods could do so again. However, because humans were then re-created, the Maya believe this, too, will happen again. These interpretations of the *Popol Vuh* relate to the Maya belief in time as an endless cycle of beginnings and endings. To record these never-ending cycles of creation and destruction, the Maya invented "one of the most accurate calendar systems in human history" ("The Calendar System"). The Calendar Round records dates 52 days into the future (Mark). The Long Count Calendar, started in 3114 BCE, calculates dates far into the future. The current cycle started in December 2012. This way of timekeeping is still seen in Maya society today. To track the different cycles of

**Skill:
Paraphrasing**

Josh feels confident that he is paraphrasing information and integrates it selectively in order to maintain the logical flow of ideas and the original meaning of the text. He avoids plagiarism by acknowledging his sources for both paraphrased and quoted material and continues to be sure to include information from more than one source.

**Skill: Critiquing Research**

Josh suspects that by relying primarily on a single source for information, he is missing some deeper understanding of the Maya's relationship with time. He decides to find additional sources. As Josh reads more about the Maya calendar system, he revises and expands his paragraph. He adds information from the new source and revises his discussion. He also realizes he had incorrectly cited one of his sources.

time, Maya communities have "daykeepers." Daykeepers are responsible for keeping the cycles going with the proper rituals and ceremonies. Drawing on centuries of knowledge, they keep track of the calendar, and serve as healers for the Maya people ("The Modern Calendar Priests"). In Maya culture, a calendar is more than a grid or list of dates used for keeping appointments; this calendar encompasses entire life cycles.

According to the Popol Vuh, humanity was created in order to worship the gods. The gods are to be shown respect because they have a lot of power. They have the power to both create and end humanity. The structure of the pyramids is symbolic. The pyramids were built with flat tops. These flat tops created space for rituals. These depictions reveal a belief in life as a series of beginnings and endings.

**The Web of Life**

Thosands of years ago, the Maya first told creation stories in an attempt to understand the world and answering life's big questions, such as, "Who am I?," "Why am I here?," and "Why is the world the way it is?" In answering these questions, the Maya origin stories described the world and beyond as places, "where time is cyclical and all things are interconnected" "Connecting Earth and Sky". These creation stories also describe a special bond between humanity and the gods, as well as a careful balance of creation and destruction, for the Maya who are alive today, these stories serve as an important cultural foundation and are linking it to the past.

### Sources

Spence, Lewis. "The Popol Vuh." *Project Gutenberg*. 1908. http://www.gutenberg.org/files/56550/56550-h/56550-h.htm. Apr. 4, 2018.

"The Calendar System." maya.nmai.si.edu/calendar/calendar-system.

Shumov, Angie. "Creation Myths from Around the World." 2016.

Gomez, Maria C. Ancient History Encyclopedia, "Maya Religion." www.ancient.eu/Maya_Religion/#references.

Gomez, Maria C. "Maya Religion." *Ancient History Encyclopedia*, www.ancient.eu/Maya_Religion/#references. Accessed 8 Apr. 2018.

Jarus, Owen. "The Maya: History, Culture & Religion." *LiveScience*, 22 Aug. 2017, www.livescience.com/41781-the-maya.html. Accessed 9 Apr. 2018.

NOTES

Skill: Sources and Citations

Josh adjusts the style of the website title and adds the date he accessed it to the Gomez citation. He inserts the Jarus citation in his works cited list, including all of the required information. Josh gives proper credit to the sources he uses in his research paper.

Please note that excerpts and passages in the StudySync® library and this workbook are intended as touchstones to generate interest in an author's work. The excerpts and passages do not substitute for the reading of entire texts, and StudySync® strongly recommends that students seek out and purchase the whole literary or informational work in order to experience it as the author intended. Links to online resellers are available in our digital library. In addition, complete works may be ordered through an authorized reseller by filling out and returning to StudySync® the order form enclosed in this workbook.

Reading & Writing Companion

987

# Skill:
# Critiquing Research

## ••• CHECKLIST FOR CRITIQUING RESEARCH

In order to conduct short or sustained research projects to answer a question or solve a problem, drawing on several sources, do the following:

- narrow or broaden the question or inquiry as necessary when researching your topic

- synthesize and integrate multiple sources on a subject

- use advanced search terms effectively when looking for information online, such as using unique terms that are specific to your topic (i.e., "daily life in Jamestown, Virginia" rather than just "Jamestown, Virginia")

- assess the usefulness of each source

- integrate information from multiple sources to maintain a flow of ideas

- quote or paraphrase the information without plagiarizing, or copying your source

- provide information about your sources in a works cited list

To evaluate and use relevant information while conducting short or sustained research projects, consider the following questions:

- Have I successfully synthesized and integrated multiple sources on my topic?

- Did I broaden or narrow my research inquiry as needed?

- Are there specific terms or phrases in my research question that I can use to adjust my search?

- Can I use *and, or,* or *not* to expand or limit my search?

- Can I use quotation marks to search for exact phrases?

- Did I quote or paraphrase information without plagiarizing?

- Have I integrated information to maintain a flow of ideas?

- Have I included a works cited list of the sources I have used?

**YOUR TURN**

Choose the best answer to each question.

1.  Below is a section from a previous draft of Josh's research paper. Josh has two sources that discuss the religious significance of Maya pyramids. One source mentions the purpose of the ancient practice of human sacrifice, and one does not. What should Josh do to confirm the reliability of the source in the underlined sentence?

> According to the *Popol Vuh*, the gods created humans because they wanted someone to worship them. Human's submissiveness to the gods is reflected in the design and purpose of Maya pyramids. The structure of the pyramids is deeply symbolic. Each level of a pyramid represents a level of the underworld (Cartwright). <u>At the top of Maya pyramids, rituals of bloodletting and human sacrifice used to be performed for the purpose of returning precious "life force" to the gods (Jarus).</u>

- ○ A.  Cite "Cartwright" as well as "Jarus."
- ○ B.  Josh should trust the source and not worry about it.
- ○ C.  Delete the reference to the purpose of the rituals.
- ○ D.  Check additional sources to confirm the information.

2.  Josh critiqued his research process at each step. He began his first draft using the following major research question: How did the origin stories in the *Popol Vuh* shape the ancient Maya's perception of time? As he learned more about the topic, he realized that the Maya still exist today and still practice their religious and cultural beliefs. What should Josh do?

- ○ A.  Modify his research question and revise his research plan.
- ○ B.  Stick with his original research question.
- ○ C.  Reevaluate the validity of his sources.
- ○ D.  Look for additional sources.

 **WRITE**

Use the questions in the checklist to critique your research process and identify any necessary changes. When you have finished implementing changes to your draft, write out a new version.

# Skill: Paraphrasing

## ••• CHECKLIST FOR PARAPHRASING

In order to integrate information into a text, note the following:

- make sure you understand what the author is saying after reading the text carefully

- words and phrases that are important to include in a paraphrase to maintain the meaning of the text

- any words or expressions that are unfamiliar

- avoid plagiarism by acknowledging all sources for both paraphrased and quoted material, as well as over reliance on any one source

- integrate information selectively to maintain a logical flow of ideas

To integrate information into a text, consider the following questions:

- Do I understand the meaning of the text?

- Does my paraphrase of the text maintain its original meaning? Have I missed any key points or details?

- Have I determined the meanings of any words from the text that are unfamiliar to me?

- Did I integrate information selectively to maintain a logical flow of ideas?

- Have I avoided plagiarism by acknowledging all my sources for both paraphrased and quoted material, and avoided over reliance on any one source?

**YOUR TURN**

Josh wants to paraphrase a quotation from the article "The Modern Calendar Priests" in *Archaeology Magazine*. Read the quotation that he wants to paraphrase, and use the checklist on the previous page to answer the multiple-choice questions that follow it.

"According to Christenson, the Daykeepers' role in the community is to keep track of different cycles of time, to perform the proper rituals to keep the cycles running, and to heal people when they are sick" ("The Modern Calendar Priests").

1. This is an excerpt from a draft of Josh's paper. It shows his first attempt to paraphrase a quotation. What is incorrect about this paraphrasing?

The current cycle started in December 2012. This way of timekeeping is still seen in Maya society today. "According to Christenson, the Daykeepers' role in the community is to keep track of different cycles of time, to perform the proper rituals to keep the cycles running, and to heal people when they are sick" ("The Modern Calendar Priests").

- A. It is incorrect because it summarizes the information, rather than paraphrasing it.
- B. It is incorrect because it quotes the text directly, rather than paraphrasing it.
- C. It is incorrect because the original meaning of the text is not maintained.
- D. It is incorrect because key points are missing, and this alters the original meaning..

2. What would be the best, most accurate and complete paraphrase of the source?

- A. To track the different cycles of time, Maya communities have "daykeepers." Daykeepers are responsible for keeping the cycles going with the proper rituals and ceremonies ("The Modern Calendar Priests").
- B. The Daykeepers track the different cycles of time and are responsible for keeping up with rituals and ceremonies the community need ("The Modern Calendar Priests").
- C. The Daykeepers are like doctors in that they cure illness and keep time for the community by maintaining the cycles ("The Modern Calendar Priests").
- D. People won't get sick if the rituals perform the cycles and the Daykeepers keep the time correctly ("The Modern Calendar Priests").

**WRITE**

Use the questions in the checklist to paraphrase and integrate a source into a paragraph of your informative research paper. When you have finished, write out the whole paragraph.

# Skill:
# Sources and Citations

## ••• CHECKLIST FOR SOURCES AND CITATIONS

In order to cite and gather relevant information from multiple, authoritative print and digital sources, do the following:

- gather information from a variety of print and digital sources using search terms effectively to narrow your search

- check that sources are useful:

  > find information on authors to see if they are experts on a topic

  > look at the publication date to see if the information is current

  > quote or paraphrase the data you find and cite it to avoid plagiarism, using parenthetical citations, footnotes, or endnotes to credit sources

- integrate information from various sources selectively to maintain a logical flow of ideas in the text, using transitional words and phrases

- include all sources in a bibliography or works cited list, following a standard format:

  > Halall, Ahmed. *The Pyramids of Ancient Egypt.* Central Publishing, 2016.

  > for a citation, footnote, or endnote, include the author, title, and page number

To check that sources are gathered and cited correctly, consider the following questions:

- Did I cite the information I found using a standard format to avoid plagiarism?

- Have I relied on one source, instead of looking for different points of view on my topic in other sources?

- Did I include all my sources in my bibliography or works cited list?

YOUR TURN

Choose the best answer to each question.

1. Below is a section from a previous draft of Josh's research paper. In it, he cites a printed book he read about origin stories. What change should Josh make to improve the clarity of his citations?

> In the introduction to her book *Primal Myths,* religion professor Barbara C. Sproul says that creation myths helped humans explain "first causes" and provided a way for humans to "organize the way we perceive facts and understand ourselves in the world" (Sproul). The Maya were one such ancient culture.

- ○ A. Delete Sproul's name from the parentheses following the quotation.
- ○ B. Add the page number in the parentheses following the quotation.
- ○ C. Add the title of the book to the parentheses following the quotation.
- ○ D. No change needs to be made.

2. Below is a section from a previous draft of Josh's works cited list. Which revision best corrects his style errors?

> Boyd, Mildred. "The Modern Maya." *Mexico's Culture and History*, www.chapala.com/chapala/magnifecentmexico/modernmaya/modernmaya.html.

- ○ A. www.chapala.com/chapala/magnifecentmexico/modernmaya/modernmaya.html. Accessed Dec. 13, 2018. Boyd, Mildred. The Modern Maya." *Mexico's Culture and History*.
- ○ B. Boyd, Mildred. *Mexico's Culture and History*, "The Modern Maya." www.chapala.com/chapala/magnifecentmexico/modernmaya/modernmaya.html.
- ○ C. Mildred Boyd. "The Modern Maya." *Mexico's Culture and History*, www.chapala.com/chapala/magnifecentmexico/modernmaya/modernmaya.html.
- ○ D. Boyd, Mildred. "The Modern Maya." *Mexico's Culture and History*, www.chapala.com/chapala/magnifecentmexico/modernmaya/modernmaya.html. Accessed 13 Dec. 2018.

 WRITE

Use the questions in the checklist to revise your academic citations and works cited list of source materials for your research paper. When you have finished revising your sources and citations, write out a new copy.

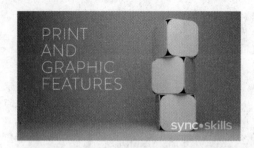

# Skill:
# Print and Graphic Features

## ••• CHECKLIST FOR PRINT AND GRAPHIC FEATURES

First, reread your draft and ask yourself the following questions:

- To what extent would including formatting, graphics, or multimedia be effective in achieving my purpose?
- Which formatting, graphics, or multimedia seem most important for conveying information to the reader?
- How is the addition of the formatting, graphics, or multimedia useful to aiding comprehension?

To include formatting, graphics, and multimedia, use the following questions as a guide:

- How can I use formatting to better organize information? Consider adding:

  > titles

  > headings

  > subheadings

  > bullets

  > boldface and italicized terms

How can I use graphics to better convey information? Consider adding:

  > charts, graphs, and/or tables

  > timelines, diagrams, and/or maps

How can I use multimedia to add interest and variety? Consider adding a combination of the following, including captions:

  > photographs

  > art

  > audio

  > video

Copyright © BookheadEd Learning, LLC

## ⟳ YOUR TURN

Choose the best answer to each question.

1. Reread the paragraph from a previous draft of Josh's research paper. Which of the following headings best represents the content of the passage and would help his audience focus on the main idea?

> Thousands of years ago, the Maya first told creation stories in an attempt to understand the world and to answer life's big questions, such as "Who am I?," "Why am I here?," and "Why is the world the way it is?" In attempting to answer these questions, the Maya origin stories described the world and beyond as places "where time is cyclical and all things are interconnected" ("Connecting Earth and Sky"). In other words, time is an intricately woven web that connects all beings and events. These creation stories also describe a special bond between humanity and the gods, as well as a careful balance of creation and destruction. For the Maya who are alive today, these stories serve as an important cultural foundation and link to the past. For the world, links to ancient cultures can serve as guideposts: no matter what the future holds, human beings must find a way, as the Daykeepers did, to adjust their settings and keep on going.

- ○ A. Questions of Life
- ○ B. The Web of Life
- ○ C. Balancing Creations and Destruction
- ○ D. The Daykeepers

2. Josh also considers adding an image, graph, or table to help his audience understand the Maya creation story. Which of the following graphic elements would be most helpful for readers?

- ○ A. An image of a web as a series of cycles.
- ○ B. A timeline showing the calendar of the Maya.
- ○ C. A graphic displaying the various types of humans created by the Mayan gods.
- ○ D. An image showing Mayan ruins with carvings that show the cycle of life.

## ✎ WRITE

Use the questions in the checklist to add at least three headings, two graphics, and one piece of multimedia to your research paper. When you have finished revising your draft, write out a new copy.

# Research Writing Process: Revise

| PLAN | DRAFT | REVISE | EDIT AND PUBLISH |

You have written a draft of your research paper. You have also received input from your peers about how to improve it. Now you are going to revise your draft.

## ⟵ REVISION GUIDE

Examine your draft to find areas for revision. Use the guide below to help you review:

| Review | Revise | Example |
|---|---|---|
| **Clarity** | | |
| Identify difficult concepts or complex quoted language in your research paper. Annotate places in which additional explanation or clarification might be helpful to readers. | Follow challenging material with a restatement in simpler terms to assist your audience's understanding. | In attempting to answering these questions, the Maya origin stories described the world and beyond as places "where time is cyclical and all things are interconnected" ("Connecting Earth and Sky"). In other words, time is like an intricately woven web that connects all beings and events. |

| Review | Revise | Example |
|---|---|---|
| **Development** | | |
| Synthesize key ideas from multiple sources. Annotate places where additional description or information could help develop your ideas. | Integrate quoted material with paraphrased material, avoiding over-reliance on one source of information. Use commas and other punctuation for clarification. Cite all sources. | Finally, on the third attempt, the gods "made four men out of white and yellow corn" and were satisfied that "these men could think and feel and speak words out of love and respect" (Shumov). In Maria Gomez's retelling, these humans were actually "too wise." Rather than destroy the human race for a third time, however, one of the gods "clouded their minds and eyes so they would become less wise" (Gomez). |
| **Organization** | | |
| Review your writing for opportunities to use print features to clarify information. | Add transitions to connect information across paragraphs. Use bulleted lists to break down information or sequence complex information to enhance reader comprehension. Include citations. | For centuries, the *Popol Vuh* has shaped Mayan understanding of life as a cycel. The story begins with the gods gathering to create the earth. After building the world, the gods wanted to fill it with creatures who would worship them (Shumov). <br>• First, they created humans from wet clay, but these humans could not speak, so the gods destroyed them in a flood. <br>• On their second attempt, the gods created humans out of wood; however, as Shumov explains, while these humans could talk, "they were empty headed and empty hearted." So, the gods destroyed the human race a second time. |

| Review | Revise | Example |
|---|---|---|
| **Style: Word Choice** | | |
| Identify weak or repetitive words or phrases that do not clearly or precisely express your ideas to the reader. | Replace weak and repetitive words and phrases with more descriptive or precise ones that better convey your ideas. | The gods are to be ~~shown~~ respected because they ~~have a lot of power. They~~ have the power to both create and ~~end~~ destroy humanity. |
| **Style: Sentence Effectiveness** | | |
| Read your research paper aloud. Annotate places where you have too many short sentences in a row. Using relative pronouns to link closely related sentences or independent clauses can add clarity by associating ideas. Vary your sentence beginnings. | Combine short sentences that are closely related by linking them together using relative pronouns. Add details that provide more complete information. | The structure of the pyramids is symbolic. ~~For example, the~~ The pyramids were built with flat tops. ~~These flat tops,~~ which created space ~~for~~ on which rituals. ~~The rituals~~ of bloodletting and human sacrifice were performed to honor the gods by returning "life force" to the gods (Jarus). |

## ✎ WRITE

Use the guide above, as well as your peer reviews, to help you evaluate your research paper to determine areas that should be revised.

# Skill:
# Using a Style Guide

## ••• CHECKLIST FOR USING A STYLE GUIDE

In order to write your work so that it conforms to the guidelines in a style manual, do the following:

- When doing research, keep careful bibliographic notes (type of work, publishing information, location of information) on each source you use and the information you will cite from that source.

- Determine which style guide (e.g., *MLA Handbook*, *Turabian's Manual for Writers*) you should use *before* you write your draft.

  > Follow the choice as directed by a teacher or assignment requirements.

  > Familiarize yourself with that guide and check your writing against the guide when you edit.

- As you draft, write in-text citations following the style guide.

- Once your draft has been revised, compile your works cited list or bibliography following the style of the chosen guide. The guide is organized by type of source—book, magazine, newspaper, website—number of authors (if known), and other relevant bibliographic data.

To edit your work so that it conforms to the guidelines in a style manual, consider the following questions:

- Have I followed the conventions for spelling, punctuation, capitalization, sentence structure, and formatting according to the style guide?

- Does each in-text citation conform to the style guide?

- Do I have an entry in my works cited list or bibliography for each reference used?

- Have I followed the correct style, including capitalization and punctuation, for each entry?

**YOUR TURN**

Read the types of information below. Then, complete the chart by sorting them into those that are found in a style guide and those that are not.

| Types of Information | | | |
|---|---|---|---|
| **A** | how to cite Internet sources | **F** | how to write an outline |
| **B** | synonyms for a word | **G** | how to format a bibliography |
| **C** | a list of possible research topics | **H** | the definition of a word |
| **D** | when to use italics | **I** | how to select a thesis |
| **E** | proper punctuation for quotations | **J** | when to use a hyphen |

| In a Style Guide | Not in a Style Guide |
|---|---|
| | |
| | |
| | |
| | |
| | |

**WRITE**

Use the checklist to help you choose a convention that has been problematic for you. Use a credible style guide to check and correct any errors related to that convention in your research paper.

# Grammar: Conjunctive Adverbs

## Conjunctive Adverb

A conjunctive adverb is a special kind of adverb that is used to connect related ideas in two different sentences. Conjunctive adverbs are usually more formal than coordinating conjunctions.

| Use | Examples |
| --- | --- |
| to replace *and* | also, besides, furthermore, moreover |
| to replace *but* | however, nevertheless, still, instead |
| to show cause and effect | consequently, therefore, thus |
| to compare or contrast | equally, likewise, similarly, conversely |
| to state an opinion | fortunately, unfortunately, ironically |
| to reinforce an argument | certainly, indeed |
| to show order of time | subsequently, afterwards, then |

Conjunctive adverbs are used to join two independent clauses. Usually, a semicolon separates the two clauses and a comma follows the conjunctive adverb. The conjunctive adverb clarifies the relationship between the two ideas in the clauses.

| Correct | Incorrect |
| --- | --- |
| Many theories now accepted by science were once scorned; **therefore**, we should be careful not to dismiss any new theory too quickly. | Many theories now accepted by science were once scorned; likewise, we should be careful not to dismiss any new theory too quickly. |

## ⟳ YOUR TURN

1. How should this sentence be changed?

> The plays of Sophocles and Euripides entertained and enlightened the audiences of ancient Greece; instead, they are still being performed today.

- ○ A. Replace the semicolon with a comma.
- ○ B. Replace **instead** with **moreover**.
- ○ C. Replace **instead** with **therefore**.
- ○ D. No change needs to be made to this sentence.

2. How should this sentence be changed?

> A common theme in stories about war is how fighting changes the soldier; consequently, the same stories often stress how the fighting does not change the military situation.

- ○ A. Replace **consequently** with **ironically**.
- ○ B. Replace **consequently** with **subsequently**.
- ○ C. Replace **consequently** with **fortunately**.
- ○ D. No change needs to be made to this sentence.

3. How should this sentence be changed?

> In *Animal Farm*, George Orwell analyzes how power develops within a society; unfortunately, Orwell's tale demonstrates that society's members are partly responsible for their own powerlessness.

- ○ A. Replace **unfortunately** with **so**.
- ○ B. Replace **unfortunately** with **instead**.
- ○ C. Replace **unfortunately** with **conversely**.
- ○ D. No change needs to be made to this sentence.

4. How should this sentence be changed?

> Personal electronic communication, which can be tracked, will completely transform commerce and politics; nevertheless, there are already ways to monitor the hashtags that appear in social media.

- ○ A. Replace **nevertheless** with **however**.
- ○ B. Replace **nevertheless** with **therefore**.
- ○ C. Replace **nevertheless** with **indeed**.
- ○ D. No change needs to be made to this sentence.

# Grammar: Commonly Misspelled Words

By following a few simple steps, you can learn to spell new words—even words that are unfamiliar or difficult. As you write, keep a list of words you have trouble spelling. Refer to online or print resources for pronunciation, Latin or Greek roots, and other information that may help you. Then use the steps below to learn to spell those words.

**Say it.** Look at the word again and say it aloud. Say it again, pronouncing each syllable clearly.

**See it.** Close your eyes. Picture the word. Visualize it letter by letter.

**Write it.** Look at the word again and write it two or three times. Then write the word without looking at the printed version.

**Check it.** Check your spelling. Did you spell it correctly? If not, repeat each step until you can spell it easily.

Here are some words that can sometimes confuse even strong spellers.

| Commonly Misspelled Words | | |
|---|---|---|
| abdomen | acquaintance | admission |
| advertisement | aerial | bibliography |
| bureaucrat | coming | cataclysm |
| colonel | concede | conscientious |
| discrimination | dissatisfaction | forfeit |
| gauge | grammatically | hindrance |
| ingenious | livelihood | luxurious |
| marriageable | mathematics | negotiable |
| parliament | personnel | significant |
| succession | twelfth | variety |

## ⟳ YOUR TURN

1. How should this sentence be changed?

> When buraucrat Mike Smithson revealed his sources, the rest of the members were stunned by the admision.

- ○ A. Change **buraucrat** to **bureaucrat** and **admision** to **admission**.
- ○ B. Change **buraucrat** to **buracrat** and **admision** to **admition**.
- ○ C. Change **buraucrat** to **buraecrat** and **admision** to **admition**.
- ○ D. No change needs to be made to this sentence.

2. How should this sentence be changed?

> At that point, most of the members were forced to consede that Smithson's revelation was a significant one.

- ○ A. Change **consede** to **conscede** and **significant** to **significent**.
- ○ B. Change **consede** to **concede** and **significant** to **significant**.
- ○ C. Change **consede** to **conceed** and **significant** to **singnifigant**.
- ○ D. No change needs to be made to this sentence.

3. How should this sentence be changed?

> Melanie was amazed by the huge variety of the sources she found in the bibliografy of her chemistry textbook.

- ○ A. Change **variety** to **vareity**.
- ○ B. Change **bibliografy** to **bibliography**.
- ○ C. Change **variety** to **varietie** and **bibliografy** to **bibbliografy**.
- ○ D. No change needs to be made to this sentence.

4. How should this sentence be changed?

> It was impossible to gauge the full extent of the damage, but many people called last week's hurricane a cataclysm.

- ○ A. Change **gauge** to **guage**.
- ○ B. Change **cataclysm** to **cataclism**.
- ○ C. Change **gauge** to **gage** and **cataclysm** to **cateclysm**.
- ○ D. No change needs to be made to this sentence.

# Research Writing Process: Edit and Publish

| PLAN | DRAFT | REVISE | EDIT AND PUBLISH |
|------|-------|--------|------------------|

You have revised your research paper based on your peer feedback and your own examination.

Now, it is time to edit your research paper. When you revised, you focused on the content of your research paper. You probably critiqued your research process and carefully evaluated your sources and citations. When you edit, you focus on the mechanics of your research paper, paying close attention to things like grammar and punctuation.

**Use the checklist below to guide you as you edit:**

☐ Have I used commas correctly to set off source material?

☐ Have I used parallel construction?

☐ Have I avoided misusing commas that result in comma splices?

☐ Do I have any sentence fragments or run-on sentences?

☐ Have I used conjunctive adverbs correctly, with or without a semicolon?

☐ Have I spelled everything correctly?

**Notice some edits Josh has made:**

- Added a comma after an introductory phrase.

- Edited text to make two sections parallel.

- Replaced a comma with a period to avoid a comma splice.

- Deleted an unnecessary comma before a quotation.

- Added parentheses around an in-text citation.

- Added a conjunctive adverb to create transition.

- Corrected two spelling errors.

Please note that excerpts and passages in the StudySync® library and this workbook are intended as touchstones to generate interest in an author's work. The excerpts and passages do not substitute for the reading of entire texts, and StudySync® strongly recommends that students seek out and purchase the whole literary or informational work in order to experience it as the author intended. Links to online resellers are available in our digital library. In addition, complete works may be ordered through an authorized reseller by filling out and returning to StudySync® the order form enclosed in this workbook.

Reading & Writing Companion 1005

~~Thosands~~ **Thousands** of years ago, the Maya first told creation stories in an attempt to understand the world and ~~answering~~ **to answer** life's big questions, such as~~,~~ "Who am I?," "Why am I here?," and "Why is the world the way it is?" In attempting to answer these questions, the Maya origin stories described the world and beyond as places "where time is cyclical and all things are interconnected" ("Connecting Earth and Sky"). . . . These creation stories also describe a special bond between ~~humanty~~ **humanity** and the gods, as well as a careful balance of creation and destruction~~;. for~~ **Indeed, for** the Maya who are alive today, these stories serve as an important cultural foundation and ~~are linking it~~ **a link** to the past.

## ✏ WRITE

Use the questions above, as well as your peer reviews, to help you evaluate your research paper to determine areas that need editing. Then edit your research paper to correct those errors.

Once you have made all your corrections, you are ready to publish your work. You can distribute your writing to family and friends, hang it on a bulletin board, or post it on your blog. If you publish online, share the link with your family, friends, and classmates.

# Tiger Moms and Trophies for Everyone

INFORMATIONAL TEXT

## Introduction

Tiger Mom Amy Chua faced a lot of criticism for her parenting style. But is parenting one-size-fits-all? Or do different cultural groups have their own traditions and values to uphold as parents?

# VOCABULARY

## approach
a method or technique

## culture
the beliefs, customs, and practices that distinguish one group or society from another

## conflict
a serious disagreement or argument

## obedience
compliance or submission to another's authority

## controversial
causing disagreement or debate

# READ

1   Parenting is a **controversial** topic. People have many different ideas about the best way to raise kids. Parenting strategies include free-range parenting, helicopter parenting, tiger parenting, and elephant parenting. Amy Chua, known as the tiger mom, faced criticism when she wrote about her **approach** to parenting. Chua acknowledges that while her parenting style is common among Chinese parents, it may seem harsh to people who are familiar with a more Western parenting style. After excerpts from her book were published online, many people challenged her for demanding perfection from her daughters. Looking carefully at both sides of the issue can be helpful before deciding who is right.

2   In Chinese **culture**, each year on the lunar calendar has its own animal sign. Chua was born during the year of the tiger, and she explains that the tiger is a symbol of authority. For Chua, being Chinese means that her parenting style is not just a personal choice. She says that Chinese culture values **obedience**. As a Chinese tiger mom, she expects her daughters to obey her rules. These rules include not being allowed to watch TV or play video games and not being allowed to perform in a school play. She forces her daughters

to practice violin and piano for hours every day. She expects them to get straight As on every report card. Chua argues that many Chinese parents think that being strict and having the highest standards for their children prepares them for the future. They believe that this style of parenting gives kids confidence and strong work habits.

3    Chua's parenting style has its roots in the Chinese cultural tradition of filial piety, or respect for elders. The rule of filial piety says that you must respect and obey people who are older than you, especially your parents. A collection of folktales from around the 13th century, *The Twenty-Four Stories of Filial Piety*, gives examples of filial sons putting their parents' needs before their own. In one story, Jiang Ge carries his mother on his back to his cousin's village. Once they arrive in his cousin's village, Jiang Ge has lost his clothes and shoes. Without clothes or shoes, he starts working to support his mother. Other stories show children obeying their parents' wishes even when their parents are unkind. In one example, Wang Xiang's father and stepmother are cruel to him. His stepmother likes to eat fish, but the river is frozen solid in winter. Wang Xiang lies down on the ice to melt it with his body. Once the ice melts, he catches fresh fish to serve his stepmother. Filial piety is an important Chinese cultural value, and parents like Chua honor their cultural roots by keeping these traditions alive.

4    As an alternative to tiger parenting and its focus on respect for elders, Western parenting styles often prioritize the well-being of the child. Researchers at the University of Arizona report that Western parents tend to give kids positive support and set moderate expectations. According to their research, this kind of parenting is healthy for kids. Parents who follow a Western model are more likely to worry about kids' self-esteem, and their family culture is warmer and more affectionate.

5    But is it possible to worry too much about kids' self-esteem? Can anti-tiger parenting have negative effects too? A growing trend among Western parents is to give awards to all the kids who participate in an event, not just the winners. Supporters of this practice say that children should be rewarded for their efforts no matter the outcome. They say that they are protecting kids' feelings. But others argue that handing out trophies to all participants in a sports tournament, for example, sends kids the wrong message. Instead of preparing them for the real world where not everyone is a winner, this practice teaches kids that they can be rewarded for just showing up.

6    The Western parenting model does focus more on the child's self-image, but these children may not be prepared to deal with **conflict** and challenges. They might not have skills to cope with disappointment or rejection. Evaluating both sides helps consider the details before deciding who is right.

An obedient son in *The Twenty-Four Stories of Filial Piety* strangles a tiger to protect his father from being attacked.

Jiang Ge carries his mother on his back.

Wang Xiang melts ice with his body and catches a fish for his stepmother.

# First Read

Read "Tiger Moms and Trophies for Everyone: How Culture Influences Parenting." After you read, complete the Think Questions below.

## ☁ THINK QUESTIONS

1. What are some of the rules that Amy Chua, the tiger mom, expects her daughters to follow?

   Tiger mom Amy Chua's rules include _____

   _____.

2. What is the Chinese cultural tradition of filial piety?

   In the tradition of filial piety, children must _____.

3. What are some examples of filial piety? Include textual evidence to support your response.

   One example of filial piety is _____.

   The text says "_____."

4. Use context to confirm the meaning of the word *obedience* as it is used in "Tiger Moms and Trophies for Everyone." Write your definition of *obedience* here.

   *Obedience* means _____.

   A context clue is _____.

5. What is another way to say that a topic is *controversial*?

   The topic is _____.

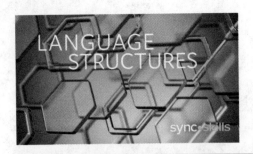

# Skill:
# Language Structures

## ★ DEFINE

In every language, there are rules that tell how to **structure** sentences. These rules define the correct order of words. In the English language, for example, a **basic** structure for sentences is subject, verb, and object. Some sentences have more **complicated** structures.

You will encounter both basic and complicated **language structures** in the classroom materials you read. Being familiar with language structures will help you better understand the text.

## ••• CHECKLIST FOR LANGUAGE STRUCTURES

To improve your comprehension of language structures, do the following:

✓ Monitor your understanding.

- Ask yourself: Why do I not understand this sentence? Is it because the sentence is long? Or is it because I do not understand the logical relationship between the ideas in this sentence?

- Pay attention to coordinating conjunctions.

  > **Coordinating conjunctions** show an equal emphasis on the ideas in a sentence.

  > The coordinating conjunction *and* shows that two or more things are true of a person, object, or event.
  Example: Josefina is a good athlete **and** student.

  > The coordinating conjunction *or* shows a choice between different possibilities.
  Example: Josefina can either do her homework **or** go for a run.

  > The coordinating conjunction *but* shows a contrast between people, objects, or events.
  Example: Josefina wants to run **but** should finish her homework first.

- Break down the sentence into its parts.

  > Ask yourself: what ideas are expressed in this sentence? Are there conjunctions that join ideas or show contrast?

✓ Confirm your understanding with a peer or teacher.

## ↻ YOUR TURN

Read the following excerpt from paragraph 3 of "Tiger Moms and Trophies for Everyone." Then, using the Checklist on the previous page, answer the multiple-choice questions below.

---

from **"Tiger Moms and Trophies for Everyone"**

(1) In one example, Wang Xiang's father and stepmother are cruel to him. (2) His stepmother likes to eat fish, but the river is frozen solid in winter. (3) Wang Xiang lays down on the ice to melt it with his body. (4) Once the ice melts, he catches fresh fish to serve his stepmother. (5) Filial piety is an important Chinese cultural value, and parents like Chua honor their cultural roots by keeping these traditions alive.

---

1. Which sentences use coordinating conjunctions?

   ○ A. sentences 2 and 3
   ○ B. sentences 3 and 4
   ○ C. sentences 2 and 5
   ○ D. sentences 4 and 5

2. What is the subordinating conjunction in sentence 4?

   ○ A. once
   ○ B. melts
   ○ C. to
   ○ D. he

3. What is true about the clauses in sentence 5?

   ○ A. The first clause is more important than the second.
   ○ B. The second clause is more important than the first.
   ○ C. The clauses are both subordinate.
   ○ D. The clauses are equally important.

# Skill: Visual and Contextual Support

## ★ DEFINE

**Visual support** is an image or an object that helps you understand a text. **Contextual support** is a **feature** that helps you understand a text. By using visual and contextual supports, you can develop your vocabulary so you can better understand a variety of texts.

First, preview the text to identify any visual supports. These might include illustrations, graphics, charts, or other objects in a text. Then, identify any contextual supports. Examples of contextual supports are titles, headers, captions, and boldface terms. Write down your **observations**.

Then, write down what those visual and contextual supports tell you about the meaning of the text. Note any new vocabulary that you see in those supports. Ask your peers and your teacher to **confirm** your understanding of the text.

## ••• CHECKLIST FOR VISUAL AND CONTEXTUAL SUPPORT

To use visual and contextual support to understand texts, do the following:

- ✓ Preview the text. Read the title, headers, and other features. Look at any images and graphics.

- ✓ Write down the visual and contextual supports in the text.

- ✓ Write down what those supports tell you about the text.

- ✓ Note any new vocabulary that you see in those supports.

- ✓ Create an illustration for the reading and write a descriptive caption.

- ✓ Confirm your observations with your peers and teacher.

## ⟳ YOUR TURN

Read each example of visual and contextual supports below. Then, complete the chart by sorting them into those that are visual supports and those that are contextual supports.

| Visual and Contextual Supports | |
|---|---|
| **A.** the title of a scientific study | **E.** an infographic about immigration to America |
| **B.** a boldface vocabulary word | **F.** headers dividing an article into sections |
| **C.** a sketch of a main character | **G.** a photograph of an author |
| **D.** a pie chart showing a state's budget | **H.** a caption that describes an image |

| Visual Supports | Contextual Supports |
|---|---|
| | |
| | |
| | |
| | |

# Close Read

---

✏️ **WRITE**

INFORMATIVE: Think about the different parenting styles presented in "Tiger Moms and Trophies for Everyone" and about other parenting styles that you have experienced or learned about. Write a paragraph that explains how families' cultural backgrounds influence their parenting styles. Support your conclusions with details and evidence from the text and from your own knowledge and personal experiences. Pay attention to and edit for the formation of plural nouns.

**Use the checklist below to guide you as you write.**

☐ What does "Tiger Moms and Trophies for Everyone" explain about culture and parenting?

☐ What have you seen in your own family or community that connects cultural values with parenting styles?

☐ How do you think culture influences parenting styles?

**Use the sentence frames to organize and write your informational response.**

Families' cultural backgrounds influence their parenting styles because parents pass on their families'

_____ ,

customs, and practices. For example, Amy Chua's parenting style is influenced by _____ .

In my experience, parents get ideas about the best way to raise kids from their _____ .

For example, my _____ believes in _____ .

I know that _____ influenced (his / her) parenting style.

# Karima

FICTION

## Introduction

Karima's life as an immigrant is complicated—she constantly faces the expectations of everyone around her, including her parents, her Arabic school friends, and her American high school peers. Can she maintain an independent sense of herself as she navigates through awkward social situations, encounters prejudice toward Arabs, and deals with the feelings of being misunderstood?

## VOCABULARY

**assimilate**

to fully become part of the culture of a population or group

**subtle**

not obvious

**culture**

a group's beliefs, customs, and social behavior that separate them from another group

NO
IMAGE
PROVIDED

**xenophobia**

the fear or dislike of people from other countries

VOTE

**exercise**

to use or implement

NOTES

## READ

CHARACTERS:
Karima, 15
Karima's Mom, 40
Karima's Dad, 45
Sarah, 15
Malcolm, 16
Rabia, 15
Ahmed, 15

**Scene 1** - Karima's home.

1 *Karima and her parents are in spirited but friendly discussion. They are having tea and bread in the family's living room. Because this play happens in Karima's own head—from her point of view—she occasionally addresses the audience with comments/asides. Karima's parents speak English with strong Levantine Arabic accents. Karima speaks English with a slight accent.*

**2   KARIMA**

It's absolutely ridiculous! "Go back to where you come from"?! I mean, HELLO, she's from Dallas! She was born here. Just because she covers her head, just because she's Muslim!

**3   KARIMA'S MOM**

(shaking her head)
It's terrible, I know. I'm so proud of you for sticking beside your friend. *That's who we are.*

**4   KARIMA**

Of course I did. And you know what? I'm thinking of starting to wear my hijab to school, too, like Rabia—

**5   KARIMA'S MOM**

No, Karima, don't be silly, why do that?

**6   KARIMA**

Why not? Why do I wear it everywhere else then? It seems like I'm trying to make them feel comfortable instead of **exercising** my right in this country!

**7   KARIMA'S DAD**

People are afraid of what they don't understand. Every time they talk about us on the news it's with the word *terrorist* attached—*Arab terrorist*—and this naturally leads to violence. But I agree with your mother. You shouldn't call attention to yourself at school. It's important to **assimilate**, to get along—

**8   KARIMA'S MOM**

Yes! it's okay to want to fit in, Karima. It's okay to have an American high school experience while keeping close to your Palestinian identity and family.

**9   KARIMA**

(to audience, rolls eyes)
Thanks, Mom, why didn't *I* think of that?
(back to scene)
But I'm proud of our **culture**, why should I have to hide it?

**10   KARIMA'S DAD**

It's not about hiding, Karima! It's about being comfortable with anyone, anywhere. The most important thing is your—

**11   KARIMA**

My education, I know.
(to the audience)

The thing about parents is that they're the same everywhere: they repeat the same things over and over like you're deaf or something. . .

12  KARIMA'S MOM
We're so proud of you. The world needs more brilliant women going into STEM fields. You're an exceptional student. In the end, that's what matters most.

13  KARIMA'S DAD
Yes, it's undoubtedly difficult to be a target of **xenophobia** in your own country, as a contributing citizen! But at the same time, you, Karima, with hard work, are going to be able to be and do anything you want. *Anything. (holding back tears)* That is why we're here.

14  KARIMA
(to audience)
Oh no, this is where he starts tearing up. I'm grateful, I really am, but it makes me uncomfortable when he starts talking about everything they sacrificed for me. It's a lot of pressure.

15  KARIMA'S DAD
(suddenly stern, a warning)
As long as you remember that the most important thing is your—

16  KARIMA
(to audience)
Say it with me now. . .Wait for it. . ."Education!"

17  KARIMA'S MOM
You're not getting bullied are you?

18  KARIMA
No, at school they just think I'm weird and nerdy. It's like I'm not American enough for high school, but I'm also not Arab enough for my Arab friends. It's like I don't quite fit anywhere. . .

19  KARIMA'S DAD
Pffff. Don't let anyone tell you who you are. You're my Karima. You're perfect, exactly as you are.

20  KARIMA
(to audience)
First of all, my dad is not *always* so cool. Sometimes he doesn't think I'm so perfect when I bring home less than a perfect grade, for example. Second, I wouldn't tell my parents because they'd worry, but it still *feels* like I'm being

bullied even though I can't point to one big thing. It's way more **subtle** than having GO BACK TO WHERE YOU CAME FROM spray painted on your locker, like what happened to Rabia today. She couldn't help but cry in the hallway, in front of everyone. That's what she said hurt her the most when we finally got to be alone at her house. She just didn't want them to see her cry. But she just couldn't help it. So I guess I shouldn't complain because everyone's kind of nice to me. But they ask so many questions like I'm a zoo animal. And all the questions make me want to hide in my books and shut the world out. But, I guess, maybe that's partly why I'm so smart? (Laughs at herself) And also modest, of course. Oh no, I'm late for school. . .

21 *Karima runs to the other side of the stage into. . .*

**Scene 2** - *A public high school in Texas. Karima is getting books out of her locker, when two classmates, SARAH and COURTNEY, approach her. They're overly friendly.*

22 SARAH
Hey Ka. . .um. . .

23 KARIMA
Karima.

24 SARAH
I knew that!

25 COURTNEY
Karina, right. See? I *told* you.

26 KARIMA
No, it's actually Karima, with an m.

27 SARAH
SO cute! Where is that name from? My name is SO BORING. Sarah. Barf.

28 COURTNEY
Mine toooo! Courtney is just like. . .blah. Bored. So where are you from again?

29 KARIMA
I'm from, my family's from Palestine. My name means generous in Arabic.

30 SARAH
Wow. That's *crazy*. And your accent is *adorbs*.

31 KARIMA
Um. . .ok?

32 **COURTNEY**

So we were just wondering if you wanted to hang out with us this weekend? Like, wanna go to the game with us? We pre-game at Dan's house, it's really fun and chill.

33 **SARAH**

Ok fine we'll tell you!! But top secret, ok? Full disclosure: our friend who also happens to be my second cousin and *really* good friend Ben has a *massive* crush on you. So we're asking for him.

34 **COURTNEY**

Not that we don't wanna hang, too.

35 **SARAH**

Oh duh definitely want to hang! But Ben's been asking us. . .

36 **KARIMA**

(turning bright red)
Really? Wow. That sounds fun. . .

37 **SARAH & COURTNEY**

SO FUN!!

38 **KARIMA**

(realizing, backtracking)
But, actually, I'm not really allowed to go to the games, or out on weekends. I mean, I would, I just. . .can't. Sorry. But thanks for inviting me.

39 **SARAH**

Tragic. What do you do on weekends then!?

40 **KARIMA**

(unsure, doesn't want to say)
Um. . .family stuff, mostly.

41 **SARAH**

Wow is that like an Arab thing?

42 **COURTNEY**

Where *is* Palestine, exactly? Like what language do you speak?

43 **SARAH & COURTNEY IN UNISON, GROWING IN SPEED AND VOLUME**

What do you eat there? Do you eat the same stuff here? Why did you leave? Why does your friend wear a scarf on her head? What does it mean? Do your parents wear weird stuff too? Do Arabs like Americans? Do you know any terrorists? Are you religious?

44  *Karima turns to the audience, shuts her eyes tight and covers her ears and SCREAMS. The voices and characters disappear. BLACK OUT.*

**Scene 3** - *Outside of Karima's Arabic School, Saturday afternoon*

45  *Karima with her two closest Arabic school friends, Rabia and Ahmed. They walk and talk as they hit the sidewalk. All three speak to each other in Arabic, with a few English words thrown in. Rabia and Karima both have their heads covered.*

46  KARIMA
(in Arabic)
Ok, should we go to Ahmed's?

47  RABIA
(in Arabic)
I'm hungry!

48  AHMED
(in Arabic)
You're always hungry.

49  *Rabia shoves Ahmed playfully. This makes Ahmed back up into Sarah, who is walking down the street in the opposite direction. Sarah is wearing workout gear and headphones.*

50  SARAH
Hey, watch it!

51  AHMED
Sorry, sorry, it was her fault.

52  *Sarah brushes it off. She is about to move on when she recognizes Karima.*

53  SARAH
Karina? Hey!

54  *Karima looks at her friends and back at Sarah.*

55  RABIA
It's *Karima.*

56  SARAH
We missed you last night! Ben was totally asking about you.

57 **AHMED**
Last night?

58 *Karima flushes. Ahmed and Rabia give Karima a look like: Seriously?*

59 **KARIMA**
Thank you for inviting me. These are my friends Rabia and Ahmed. Rabia, Ahmed this is Sarah.

60 *They all look at each other, nodding awkwardly.*

61 **SARAH**
So what is this?

62 **KARIMA**
This is our other school, on the weekends. It's Arabic school.

63 **SARAH**
Double school, whoa.

64 **KARIMA**
It's actually fun.

65 **SARAH**
Cool, well hopefully we can hang out sometime. Rabia, Ahmed, it was really nice to meet you. See ya!

66 *Sarah runs off and waves. Rabia and Ahmed give Karima a look: huh, she was nice. Karima smiles.*

67 **KARIMA**
Wow. She only asked one question.

68 *They continue walking along, talking again in Arabic.*

**Scene 4** - *Karima stands alone on stage*

69 **KARIMA**
(to audience)
You know, sometimes it feels like I'm split right down the middle. There's the Karima who goes to this big loud American high school in the middle of Texas, and really wants to fit in and be normal. And then there's the one that wants to hold on to my family and my culture so tightly. And feel like I have this *place* in the world that's way bigger than me, where everyone understands me, down to my bones. These two Karimas, most of the time, feel worlds apart. Like, they don't even text each other. But then, sometimes, there's just. . .me.

Like when I'm alone, in my room, listening to music or reading a book I really love. It's just me. And I don't feel torn at all. I just feel okay. Just like you. I guess just like everybody.

70  BLACKOUT.

# First Read

Read "Karima." After you read, complete the Think Questions below.

1. What happened to Rabia that made Karima upset?

   Karima is upset because _____.

2. Where does Scene 2 take place?

   Scene 2 takes place _____.

3. At the end of the play, how does Karima explain having two identities? Include evidence from the text to support your response.

   Karima says that one part of her is _____ and another part _____.

   She explains this by saying "_____."

4. Use context to confirm the meaning of the word **assimilate** as it is used in "Karima." Write your definition of *assimilate* here.

   *Assimilate* means _____.

   A context clue is _____.

5. What is another way to say that a message is *subtle*?

   The message is _____.

# Skill:
# Analyzing Expressions

## ★ DEFINE

When you read, you may find English expressions that you do not know. An **expression** is a group of words that communicates an idea. Three types of expressions are idioms, sayings, and figurative language. They can be difficult to understand because the meanings of the words are different from their **literal**, or usual, meanings.

An **idiom** is an expression that is commonly known among a group of people. For example, "It's raining cats and dogs" means it is raining heavily. **Sayings** are short expressions that contain advice or wisdom. For instance, "Don't count your chickens before they hatch" means do not plan on something good happening before it happens. **Figurative** language is when you describe something by comparing it with something else, either directly (using the words *like* or *as*) or indirectly. For example, "I'm as hungry as a horse" means I'm very hungry. None of the expressions are about actual animals.

## ••• CHECKLIST FOR ANALYZING EXPRESSIONS

To determine the meaning of an expression, remember the following:

✓ If you find a confusing group of words, it may be an expression. The meaning of words in expressions may not be their literal meaning.

- Ask yourself: Is this confusing because the words are new? Or because the words do not make sense together?

✓ Determining the overall meaning may require that you use one or more of the following:

- context clues

- a dictionary or other resource

- teacher or peer support

✓ Highlight important information before and after the expression to look for clues.

## ⟳ YOUR TURN

Read paragraph 69 from the text. Then, using the Checklist on the previous page, answer the multiple-choice questions below.

---

from **"Karima"**

**Scene 4** - *Karima stands alone on stage*

KARIMA
(to audience)
(1) You know, sometimes it feels like I'm split right down the middle. (2) There's the Karima who goes to this big loud American high school in the middle of Texas, and really wants to fit in and be normal. (3) And then there's the one that wants to hold on to my family and my culture so tightly. (4) And I feel like I have this place in the world that's way bigger than me, where everyone understands me, down to my bones. (5) These two Karimas, most of the time, feel worlds apart. (6) Like, they don't even text each other. (7) But then, sometimes, there's just...me. (8) Like when I'm alone, in my room, listening to music or reading a book I really love. (9) It's just me. (10) And I don't feel torn at all. (11) I just feel okay. (12) Just like you. (13) I guess just like everybody.

---

1.  In sentence 2, the expression "fit in" most closely means —

    ○ A. to act out in an angry way

    ○ B. to be in harmony with others

    ○ C. to wear the right sized clothes

    ○ D. to be physically active

2.  When Karima says that she "wants to hold on to my family and my culture so tightly" in sentence 3, what does she mean?

    ○ A. She wants to literally hold her family and culture tightly.

    ○ B. Karima wants to stay connected to her family and culture.

    ○ C. Karima thinks that she should copy Anglo-American culture.

    ○ D. She thinks that hugging family members is a good thing.

3. If people are "worlds apart" (sentence 5), it means that they—

○ A. live on different hemispheres

○ B. live far away from each other

○ C. cannot understand each other

○ D. seem different from each other

4. When Karima says "I don't feel torn" (sentence 10), what does she mean?

○ A. She feels focused and whole.

○ B. She feels well-dressed.

○ C. She feels uninjured.

○ D. She feels like a book character.

Please note that excerpts and passages in the StudySync® library and this workbook are intended as touchstones to generate interest in an author's work. The excerpts and passages do not substitute for the reading of entire texts, and StudySync® strongly recommends that students seek out and purchase the whole literary or informational work in order to experience it as the author intended. Links to online resellers are available in our digital library. In addition, complete works may be ordered through an authorized reseller by filling out and returning to StudySync® the order form enclosed in this workbook.

Reading & Writing Companion

1029

# Skill: Analyzing and Evaluating Text

## ★ DEFINE

**Analyzing** and **evaluating** a text means reading carefully to understand the author's **purpose** and **message**. In informational texts, authors may provide information or opinions on a topic. They may be writing to inform or persuade a reader. In fictional texts, the author may be **communicating** a message or lesson through their story. They may write to entertain, or to teach the reader something about life.

Sometimes authors are clear about their message and purpose. When the message or purpose is not stated directly, readers will need to look closer at the text. Readers can use textual evidence to make inferences about what the author is trying to communicate. By analyzing and evaluating the text, you can form your own thoughts and opinions about what you read.

## ••• CHECKLIST FOR ANALYZING AND EVALUATING TEXT

In order to analyze and evaluate a text, do the following:

✓ Look for details that show why the author is writing.

- Ask yourself: Is the author trying to inform, persuade, or entertain? What are the main ideas of this text?

✓ Look for details that show what the author is trying say.

- Ask yourself: What is the author's opinion about this topic? Is there a lesson I can learn from this story?

✓ Form your own thoughts and opinions about the text.

- Ask yourself: Do I agree with the author? Does this message apply to my life?

## ⟳ YOUR TURN

Read paragraph 69 from the text. Then, using the Checklist on the previous page, answer the multiple-choice questions below.

---

from **"Karima"**

**Scene 4** - *Karima stands alone on stage*

KARIMA
(to audience)
You know, sometimes it feels like I'm split right down the middle. There's the Karima who goes to this big loud American high school in the middle of Texas, and really wants to fit in and be normal. And then there's the one that wants to hold on to my family and my culture so tightly. And feel like I have this place in the world that's way bigger than me, where everyone understands me, down to my bones. These two Karimas, most of the time, feel worlds apart. Like, they don't even text each other. But then, sometimes, there's just...me. Like when I'm alone, in my room, listening to music or reading a book I really love. It's just me. And I don't feel torn at all. I just feel okay. Just like you. I guess just like everybody.

---

1.  Repetition of the phrase "just me" serves to—

    ○ A. remind the audience that this is a play about a student named Karima

    ○ B. show how Karima likes to spend her time alone with books or music

    ○ C. show that Karima has an identity independent of how others see her

    ○ D. demonstrate how minor Karima's problems are compared to her parents

2.  How can you tell that this excerpt is narrative text?

    ○ A. It features debatable opinions in addition to facts.

    ○ B. It tells a story and gives a character's point of view.

    ○ C. It requires the reader to choose one side of a debate.

    ○ D. It gives information about a topic related to history.

3. How does this aside from Karima support the author's purpose?

  ○ A. It illustrates how Karima feels pressure to fit into two cultures.

  ○ B. It shows that Texans are friendly and welcoming of immigrants.

  ○ C. It indicates that the world is bigger than just one high school.

  ○ D. It reveals that the narrator is not alone in being bullied.

4. How might asides like this one make the audience feel?

  ○ A. surprised by the break in the dialogue

  ○ B. annoyed at having to hear a lecture

  ○ C. amused by Karima's foolishness

  ○ D. involved in Karima's world

# Close Read

---

✏️ **WRITE**

LITERARY ANALYSIS: In this drama, the main character finds herself being one way around her Arab friends and another way around her American high school peers. How does Karima express the idea of having different identities? Look at what she says and how she acts around these two peer groups. Use details and evidence from the text to support your response. Pay attention to and edit for negatives and contractions.

**Use the checklist below to guide you as you write.**

☐ What are Karima's two identities?

☐ What does Karima say to the audience that shows her two identities?

☐ What does Karima say and do around her peers to show that she has two identities?

**Use the sentence frames to organize and write your literary analysis.**

In the play "Karima," the main character has two _____.

Karima says she wants to fit in with her American _____

when she tells Sarah and Courtney that she would like to attend their party, but she _____.

Karima shows that she respects her Palestinian _____

when she acts _____ to introduce her Arab friends to Sarah.

At the end of the play, Karima says that when she's by herself she _____

have to think about trying to fit in with (anyone / no one).

---

## PHOTO/IMAGE CREDITS:

p. iii, ©iStock.com/xijian
p. iii, ©iStock.com/ferrantraite
p. iii, iStock.com/BrianAJackson
p. iii, iStock.com/PeopleImages
p. iii, iStock.com/Chalabala
p. iii, ©iStock.com/ooyoo
p. v, iStock.com/DNY59
p. vi, ©iStock.com/DWalker44
p. vii, ©iStock.com/DWalker44
p. vii, iStock.com/deimagine
p. viii, ©iStock.com/DWalker44
p. viii, ©iStock.com/halbergman
p. viii, iStock.com/DragonImages
p. viii, iStock.com/Petar Chernaev
p. viii, iStock.com/Kirby Hamilton
p. viii, iStock.com/EricFerguson
p. ix, iStock.com/hanibaram, iStock.com/seb_ra, iStock.com/
Martin Barraud
p. xi, ©iStock.com/xijian
p. xi, iStock.com/borchee
p. xiii, ©iStock.com/xijian
p. xiv, Chinua Achebe - Eliot Elisofon/Contributor/The LIFE Picture
Collection/Getty Images
p. xiv, Hayan Charara - Rachel de Cordova
p. xiv, Joseph Conrad - George C. Beresford/Stringer/Hulton
Archive/Getty Images
p. xiv, Patrick Henry - benoitb/DigitalVision Vectors/Getty Images
p. xiv, Franz Kafka - Stringer/Contributor/Hulton Archive/Getty
Archive Photos/
p. xv, Mohja Kahf - courtesy of Wendi La Fey
p. xv, Martin Luther King Jr. - Bettmann/Contributor/Bettmann/
Getty Images
p. xv, Francis La Flesche - Public Domain
p. xv, Ursula K. LeGuin - Michael Buckner/Stringer/Getty Images
North America
p. 0, ©iStock.com/DWalker44
p. 5, ©iStock.com/Delpixart/
p. 6, ©iStock.com/Delpixart/
p. 7, ©iStock.com/DWalker44
p. 8, ©istock.com/urbancow
p. 9, ©istock.com/urbancow
p. 10, ©iStock.com/deimagine
p. 11, ©iStock.com/deimagine
p. 12, ©iStock.com/DWalker44
p. 13, istock.com/diegograndi
p. 15, Getty: NurPhoto/Contributor/NurPhoto
p. 16, Getty: AFP/Stringer/AFP
p. 18, ©istock.com/diegograndi
p. 19, ©iStock.com/PetarPaunchev
p. 22, ©istock.com/RapidEye
p. 26, ©istock.com/RapidEye
p. 27, ©iStock.com/ooyoo
p. 28, ©iStock.com/ooyoo
p. 29, ©iStock.com/Dominique_Lavoie
p. 30, ©iStock.com/Dominique_Lavoie
p. 31, ©iStock.com/Martin Barraud
p. 32, ©iStock.com/Martin Barraud
p. 34, ©istock.com/RapidEye
p. 35, ©istock.com/MidwestWilderness
p. 36, Public Domain
p. 41, ©istock.com/funky-data
p. 45, ©istock.com/
p. 48, ©iStock.com/Rauluminate
p. 49, ©iStock.com/Dominique_Lavoie
p. 50, ©iStock.com/Dominique_Lavoie

p. 51, ©iStock.com/yipengge
p. 52, ©iStock.com/yipengge
p. 53, ©istock.com/
p. 54, ©iStock.com/jdemast
p. 58, ©iStock.com/dblight
p. 63, Bettmann/Contributor/Getty Images
p. 78, Bettmann/Contributor/Getty Images
p. 79, ©iStock.com/ThomasVogel
p. 80, ©iStock.com/ThomasVogel
p. 81, ©iStock.com/DNY59
p. 82, ©iStock.com/DNY59
p. 83, ©iStock/pixhook
p. 84, ©iStock/pixhook
p. 85, Bettmann/Contributor/Getty Images
p. 86, ©iStock.com/GoodLifeStudio
p. 89, iStock.com/
p. 90, Public Domain
p. 93, iStock.com/
p. 94, ©iStock.com/Brostock
p. 95, ©iStock.com/Brostock
p. 96, iStock.com/unoL
p. 97, iStock.com/unoL
p. 98, ©iStock.com/Martin Barraud
p. 99, ©iStock.com/Martin Barraud
p. 100, ©iStock.com/
p. 102, iStock.com/hanibaram, iStock.com/seb_ra, iStock.com/
Martin Barraud
p. 103, ©iStock.com/Martin Barraud
p. 108, ©iStock.com/fstop123
p. 111, ©iStock.com/gopixa
p. 113, ©iStock.com/Dominik Pabis
p. 115, ©iStock.com/Martin Barraud
p. 119, ©iStock/bo1982
p. 121, ©iStock/Jeff_Hu
p. 124, ©iStock.com/stevedangers
p. 126, ©iStock.com/Martin Barraud
p. 128, iStock.com/Fodor90
p. 131, iStock.com/efks
p. 133, iStock/Vimvertigo
p. 135, iStock.com/Piotr_roae
p. 137, ©iStock.com/Martin Barraud
p. 139, ©iStock.com/halbergman
p. 140, DragonImages/iStock.com
p. 140, Petar Chernaev/iStock.com
p. 140, SolStock/iStock.com
p. 140, EricFerguson/iStock.com
p. 140, Kirby Hamilton/iStock.com
p. 142, ©iStock.com/halbergman
p. 143, ©iStock.com/BlackJack3D
p. 145, ©iStock.com/BlackJack3D
p. 147, ©iStock.com/halbergman
p. 148, ©iStock.com/EcoPic
p. 149, SergeyNivens/iStock.com
p. 149, burwellphotography/iStock.com
p. 149, pkline/iStock.com
p. 149, enciktep/iStock.com
p. 149, Olga_Danylenko/iStock.com
p. 152, ©iStock.com/EcoPic
p. 153, ©iStock.com/Ales_Utovko
p. 156, ©iStock.com/eugenesergeev
p. 159, ©iStock.com/EcoPic

p. 161, iStock.com/borchee
p. 161, ©iStock.com/ferrantraite
p. 163, ©iStock.com/ferrantraite
p. 164, Chinua Achebe - Eliot Elisofon/Contributor/The
LIFE Picture Collection/Getty Images
p. 164, Amanda Gorman - Charley Gallay/Stringer/Getty
Images Entertainment
p. 164, Rashema Melson - The Washington Post/
Contributor/The Washington Post/Getty Images
p. 164, Louise Munson - courtesy of Louise Munson
p. 165, Plato - Print Collector/Contributor/Hulton Archive/
Getty Images
p. 165, Ellen Johnson Sirleaf - Liesa Johannssen/
Contributor/Photothek Collection/Getty Images
p. 165, Rigoberta Tum - Tony Barson/Contributor/
FilmMagic/Getty Images
p. 165, Elie Wiesel - Kasia/Contributor/Contour/Getty Images
p. 166, ©iStock.com/tunart
p. 168, Public Domain
p. 169, JMN/Contributo/Getty Images
p. 171, ©iStock.com/MinistryOfJoy
p. 171, ©iStock.com/esolla
p. 174, ©iStock.com/da-kuk
p. 175, Bettmann/Bettmann/GettyImages
p. 175, StudySync Graphic
p. 180, ©iStock.com/da-kuk
p. 181, ©iStock.com/donatas1205
p. 182, ©iStock.com/donatas1205
p. 183, ©iStock.com/Caval
p. 184, ©iStock.com/Caval
p. 185, iStock.com/Smithore
p. 186, iStock.com/Smithore
p. 187, ©iStock.com/da-kuk
p. 188, ©iStock.com/PeopleImages
p. 192, ©iStock.com/ajiravan/
p. 193, Public Domain
p. 195, Public Domain
p. 197, ©iStock.com/ajiravan/
p. 198, ©iStock.com/Andrey_A
p. 199, ©iStock.com/Andrey_A
p. 200, ©iStock.com/altanaka
p. 201, ©iStock.com/altanaka
p. 202, ©iStock.com/ajiravan/
p. 203, ©iStock.com/Mlenny
p. 208, ©iStock.com/Caslav Lazic
p. 210, ©iStock.com/Mlenny
p. 211, ©iStock.com/donatas1205
p. 212, ©iStock.com/donatas1205
p. 213, ©istock.com/urbancow
p. 214, ©istock.com/urbancow
p. 215, ©iStock.com/ThomasVogel
p. 216, ©iStock.com/ThomasVogel
p. 217, ©iStock.com/Mlenny
p. 218, ©iStock.com/nirat
p. 221, ©iStock.com/cokada
p. 226, Bettmann/Bettmann/GettyImages
p. 227, StudySync Graphic
p. 228, StudySync Graphic
p. 229, ©iStock.com/cokada
p. 230, ©iStock.com/peepo
p. 231, ©iStock.com/peepo
p. 233, iStock.com/elementals
p. 234, iStock.com/elementals
p. 235, ©iStock.com/cokada
p. 236, ©iStock.com/arocas
p. 240, iStock.com/Sadeugra
p. 246, iStock.com/yangphoto
p. 251, ©iStock.com/yangphoto
p. 252, ©iStock.com/Caval
p. 253, ©iStock.com/Caval
p. 254, ©iStock.com/janrysavy
p. 255, ©iStock.com/janrysavy
p. 256, ©iStock.com/yangphoto
p. 257, ©iStock.com/ToprakBeyBetmen
p. 262, ©iStock.com/trevkitt
p. 268, iStock.com/hanibaram, iStock.com/seb_ra,
iStock.com/Martin Barraud
p. 269, ©iStock.com/Martin Barraud
p. 275, ©iStock.com/ThomasVogel
p. 278, ©iStock.com/gopixa
p. 280, ©iStock.com/Tevarak
p. 282, ©iStock.com/Martin Barraud
p. 286, ©iStock.com/bo1982
p. 288, ©iStock/Jeff_Hu
p. 291, ©iStock.com/peepo
p. 294, ©iStock.com/stevedangers
p. 296, ©iStock.com/Martin Barraud
p. 298, ©iStock.com/Fodor90
p. 301, iStock/Vimvertigo
p. 303, iStock/borchee
p. 305, iStock.com/Piotr_roae
p. 307, ©iStock.com/Martin Barraud
p. 309, ©iStock.com/wundervisuals
p. 310, fotofrog/iStock.com
p. 310, iStock.com/pixalot
p. 310, Cameron Strathdee/iStock.com
p. 310, Terry J Alcorn/iStock.com
p. 310, Gajus/iStock.com
p. 312, ©iStock.com/wundervisuals
p. 313, ©iStock.com/Ales_Utovko
p. 316, ©iStock.com/Zoran Kolundzija
p. 318, ©iStock.com/wundervisuals
p. 319, ©iStock.com/mediaphotos
p. 320, Istock.com/
p. 320, Istock.com/
p. 320, Istock.com/
p. 320, Istock.com/
p. 320, Istock.com/
p. 322, ©iStock.com/mediaphotos
p. 323, ©iStock.com/BlackJack3D
p. 325, ©iStock.com/Zoran Kolundzija
p. 328, ©iStock.com/mediaphotos

p. 329, ©iStock.com/BrianAJackson
p. 329, ©iStock.com/eyewave, ©iStock.com/subjug, ©iStock.com/Ivantsov, iStock.com/borchee, iStock.com/seb_ra
p. 331, ©iStock.com/BrianAJackson
p. 332, Kimberly Blaeser - Used by permission of Kimberly M. Blaeser
p. 332, Allison Adelle Hedge Coke - Chris Felver/Contributor/Premium Archive/Getty Images
p. 332, Salvador Dali - Hulton Archive/Stringer/Archive Photos/Getty
p. 332, Sigmund Freud - Hans Casparius/Stringer/Hulton Archive/Getty
p. 332, Rachel Kolb - courtesy of Rachel Kolb
p. 332, Ngo Tu Lap - Nguyen Le Tam via Milkweed Editions.
p. 333, Edna St. Vincent Millay - PhotoQuest/Contributor/Archive Photos/Getty
p. 333, Mike Price - courtesey of Mike Price
p. 333, Santha Rama-Rau - Bettmann/Contributor/Bettmann/Getty
p. 333, Marjane Satrapi - Alessandra Benedetti - Corbis/Contributor/Corbis Entertainment/Getty
p. 333, Rebecca Skloot - Daniel Boczarski/Stringer/Getty Images Entertainment
p. 334, ©iStock.com/zorazhuang
p. 336, Public Domain
p. 337, Universal History Archive/Contributor/Universal Images Group
p. 338, DEA PICTURE LIBRARY/Contributor/De Agostini/Getty
p. 340, ©iStock.com/zorazhuang
p. 341, ©iStock.com/Xantana
p. 348, ©iStock.com/cirano83
p. 351, Sean Gallup/Staff/Getty Images News
p. 352, ©iStock.com/cirano83
p. 353, ©iStock.com/Caval
p. 354, ©iStock.com/Caval
p. 355, ©iStock.com/fotogaby
p. 356, ©iStock.com/fotogaby
p. 358, iStock.com/unoL
p. 359, iStock.com/unoL
p. 360, ©iStock.com/cirano83
p. 361, ©istock.com/elenaleonova
p. 371, ©istock.com/elenaleonova
p. 372, ©iStock.com/Orla
p. 373, ©iStock.com/Orla
p. 374, ©iStock.com/Hohenhaus
p. 375, ©iStock.com/Hohenhaus
p. 376, ©iStock.com/elenaleonova
p. 377, ©iStock.com/FooTToo
p. 379, ©iStock.com/UliU
p. 381, ©iStock.com/UliU
p. 382, ©iStock.com/Orla
p. 383, ©iStock.com/Orla
p. 384, ©iStock.com/Andrey_A
p. 385, ©iStock.com/Andrey_A
p. 387, ©iStock.com/UliU
p. 388, iStock.com/SensorSpot
p. 390, CARLOS CRIVELLI AND SERGIO JARILLO
p. 393, iStock.com/SensorSpot
p. 394, ©iStock.com/ThomasVogel
p. 395, ©iStock.com/ThomasVogel
p. 396, iStock.com/Smithore
p. 397, iStock.com/Smithore
p. 398, ©iStock.com/Orla
p. 399, ©iStock.com/Orla
p. 401, ©iStock.com/SensorSpot
p. 402, iStock.com/cassp
p. 403, ©iStock.com/RomoloTavani
p. 409, ©iStock.com/elleon
p. 412, ©iStock.com/skodonnell
p. 417, ©iStock.com/Vikram Raghuvanshi
p. 421, ©iStock.com/Tarzan9280
p. 422–429, The Shabbat from PERSEPOLIS: THE STORY OF A CHILDHOOD by Marjane Satrapi, translation copyright © 2003 by L'Association, Paris, France. Used by permission of Pantheon Books, an imprint of the Knopf Doubleday Publishing Group, a division of Penguin Random House LLC. All rights reserved.
p. 430, ©iStock.com/Tarzan9280
p. 431, ©iStock.com/deimagine
p. 432, ©iStock.com/deimagine
p. 433, ©iStock.com/ValentinaPhotos
p. 434, ©iStock.com/ValentinaPhotos
p. 435, ©iStock.com/Hohenhaus
p. 436, ©iStock.com/Hohenhaus
p. 437, ©iStock.com/Tarzan9280
p. 438, ©iStock.com/JurgaR
p. 445, iStock.com/hanibaram, iStock.com/seb_ra, iStock.com/Martin Barraud
p. 446, ©iStock.com/Martin Barraud
p. 451, ©iStock.com/oonal
p. 454, ©iStock.com/truelight
p. 456, ©iStock.com/Martin Barraud
p. 460, ©iStock.com/Jinnawat
p. 462, ©iStock/Jeff_Hu
p. 465, ©iStock/Jasmina007
p. 467, ©iStock.com/stevedangers
p. 469, ©iStock.com/Martin Barraud
p. 472, ©iStock.com/JStaley401
p. 474, iStock.com/peeterv
p. 476, iStock/Vimvertigo
p. 478, iStock.com/efks
p. 480, ©iStock.com/Martin Barraud
p. 482, Alfred Eisenstaedt/Getty Images
p. 483, aydinmutlu/iStock.com
p. 483, skynesher/iStock.com
p. 483, Image_Source_/iStock.com
p. 483, Mordolff/iStock.com
p. 483, aprott/iStock.com
p. 485, Alfred Eisenstaedt/Getty Images
p. 486, ©iStock.com/Ales_Utovko
p. 488, ©iStock.com/Mlenny
p. 490, Alfred Eisenstaedt/Getty Images
p. 491, ©iStock.com/DEVASHISH_RAWAT
p. 492, ©iStock.com/hidesy
p. 492, ©iStock.com/Lefteris_
p. 492, ©iStock.com/simarik
p. 492, ©iStock.com/RuslanDashinsky
p. 494, ©iStock.com/DEVASHISH_RAWAT
p. 495, ©iStock.com/BlackJack3D
p. 498, ©iStock.com/14951893
p. 500, ©iStock.com/DEVASHISH_RAWAT

p. 501, ©iStock.com/PeopleImages
p. 501, ©iStock.com/eyewave, ©iStock.com/subjug, ©iStock.com/Ivantsov, iStock.com/borchee, ©iStock.com/seb_ra
p. 503, ©iStock.com/PeopleImages
p. 504, Gloria Anzaldúa - Photograph by Margaret Randall
p. 504, Daniel Chacón - photo courtesey of Daniel Chacón
p. 504, Alice Dunbar-Nelson - Interim Archives/Contributor/Archive Photos/Getty Images
p. 504, Terry George - Photo 12/Alamy Stock Photo
p. 504, Roni Jacobson - NBC/Contributor/NBCUniversal/Getty Images
p. 504, Naomi Shabib Nye - Roberto Ricciuti/Contributor/Getty Images Entertainment
p. 505, Keir Pearson - Allstar Picture Library/Alamy Stock Photo
p. 505, William Shakespeare - istock.com/MarsBars
p. 505, Michelangelo di Lodovico Buonarroti Simoni - IanDagnall Computing/Alamy Stock Photo
p. 506, iStock.com/AZemdega
p. 508, Print Collector/Hulton Fine Art Collection/Getty Images
p. 509, Heritage Images/Hulton Archive/Getty Images
p. 511, iStock.com/AZemdega
p. 512, ©iStock.com/aniszewski
p. 515, iStock.com/anthonyjhall
p. 517, Print Collector/Hulton Archive/Getty Images
p. 522, iStock.com/anthonyjhall
p. 523, ©iStock.com/deimagine
p. 524, ©iStock.com/deimagine
p. 525, iStock.com/Smithore
p. 526, iStock.com/Smithore
p. 527, ©iStock.com/Hohenhaus
p. 528, ©iStock.com/Hohenhaus
p. 529, iStock.com/anthonyjhall
p. 530, iStock.com/tunart
p. 532, Bettmann/Bettmann/Getty Images
p. 537, iStock.com/tunart
p. 538, iStock.com/Spanishalex
p. 539, iStock.com/Spanishalex
p. 540, ©iStock.com/fotogaby
p. 541, ©iStock.com/fotogaby
p. 542, iStock.com/yipengge
p. 543, iStock.com/yipengge
p. 544, iStock.com/tunart
p. 545, iStock.com/PeopleImages
p. 546, Public Domain Image
p. 551, iStock.com/PeopleImages
p. 552, iStock.com/Brostock
p. 553, iStock.com/Brostock
p. 554, iStock.com/eskaylim
p. 555, iStock.com/eskaylim
p. 556, ©iStock.com/Hohenhaus
p. 557, ©iStock.com/Hohenhaus
p. 558, iStock.com/PeopleImages
p. 560, peeterv/Getty Images
p. 567, peeterv/Getty Images
p. 568, iStock.com/Spanishalex
p. 569, iStock.com/Spanishalex
p. 570, peeterv/Getty Images
p. 571, iStock.com/EJ-J
p. 576, iStock.com/Tabitazn
p. 580, iStock.com/Tabitazn
p. 581, iStock.com/eskaylim
p. 582, iStock.com/eskaylim
p. 583, iStock.com/Orla

p. 584 - iStock.com/Orla
p. 585, iStock.com/
p. 586, iStock.com/
p. 587, iStock.com/Tabitazn
p. 588, iStock.com/tverkhovinets
p. 589, GraphicaArtis/Archive Photos/Getty Images
p. 590, Mondadori Portfolio/Hulton Fine Art Collection/Getty Images
p. 591, iStock.com/Nicholas Vettorel
p. 598, iStock.com/Vimvertigo
p. 604, iStock.com/Victoria Avvacumova
p. 605, Interim Archives/Archive Photos/Getty Images
p. 610, iStock.com/Victoria Avvacumova
p. 611, iStock.com/janrysavy
p. 612, iStock.com/janrysavy
p. 613, iStock.com/ValentinaPhotos
p. 614, iStock.com/ValentinaPhotos
p. 615, iStock.com/Victoria Avvacumova
p. 616, iStock.com/Vasyl Dolmatov
p. 619, Stock.com/hanibaram, iStock.com/seb_ra, iStock.com/Martin Barraud
p. 620, iStock.com/Martin Barraud
p. 623, "Victory Over Polio." U-I News. Universal Newsreels, 1955.
p. 626, StudySync
p. 629, iStock.com/Mutlu Kurtbas
p. 632, iStock.com/BilevichOlga
p. 635, iStock.com/Martin Barraud
p. 638, iStock.com/Martin Barraud
p. 643, iStock.com/polesnoy
p. 646, iStock/Peepo
p. 649, iStock.com/tofumax
p. 652, iStock.com/SasinParaksa
p. 655, iStock.com/Martin Barraud
p. 659, iStock.com/
p. 661, iStock.com/Mr_Twister
p. 663, iStock.com/Mr_Twister
p. 665, iStock.com/Martin Barraud
p. 667, JTKPHOTOz/iStock.com
p. 668, iStock.com/alexh
p. 668, iStock.com/zeljkosantrac
p. 668, iStock.com/qingwa
p. 668, iStock.com/
p. 668, iStock.com/stocksnapper
p. 670, JTKPHOTOz/iStock.com
p. 671, iStock.com/BlackJack3D
p. 674, ©iStock.com/serggn
p. 676, JTKPHOTOz/iStock.com
p. 677, iStock.com/Martin Dimitrov
p. 678, iStock.com/
p. 678, iStock.com/
p. 678, iStock.com/michaelbwatkins
p. 678, iStock.com/Tim-e
p. 678, iStock.com/PeopleImages
p. 679, iStock/skynesher
p. 680, iStock/SolStock
p. 682, iStock.com/Martin Dimitrov
p. 683, iStock.com/Ales_Utovko
p. 685, ©iStock.com/AlexandrBognat
p. 687, iStock.com/Martin Dimitrov

p. 689, iStock.com/Chalabala

p. 689, ©iStock.com/eyewave, ©iStock.com/subjug, ©iStock.com/Ivantsov, iStock.com/borchee, ©iStock.com/seb_ra

p. 691, iStock.com/Chalabala

p. 692, Matsuo Bansho - Photo 12/Alamy Stock Photo

p. 692, Judith Ortiz Cofer - CREDIT: "University of Georgia Marketing & Communications. All rights reserved."

p. 692, Lizzie Collingham - C45JD0, Jeff Morgan 13/Alamy Stock Photo

p. 692, Rita Dove - Getty Images Europe: Barbara Zanon/Contributor

p. 692, Chen Jitong - Public Domain

p. 692, Audre Lorde - Jack Mitchell/Contributor/Archive Photos/Getty Images

p. 693, V.S Naipaul - Awakening/Contributor/Corbis Entertainment/Getty Images

p. 693, William Wordsworth - Hulton Archive/Stringer/Hulton Archive/Getty Images

p. 694, iStock.com/sharrocks

p. 697, James Leynse/Corbis Historical/Getty Images

p. 697, Anadolu Agency/Anadolu Agency/Getty Images

p. 699, iStock.com/sharrocks

p. 700, iStock.com

p. 702, iStock.com/

p. 703, iStock/Rainer Lesniewski

p. 706, iStock.com/

p. 707, istock.com/urbancow

p. 708, istock.com/urbancow

p. 709, iStock.com/Orla

p. 710, iStock.com/Orla

p. 711, iStock.com/

p. 712, iStock.com/DamianPEvans

p. 715, iStock.com/DamianPEvans

p. 716, iStock.com/fotogaby

p. 717, iStock.com/fotogaby

p. 718, iStock.com/DamianPEvans

p. 719, iStock.com/bonniecaton

p. 724, iStock.com/VvoeVale

p. 725, adoc-photos/Corbis Historical/Getty Images

p. 727, iStock.com/ollinka

p. 730–743, "The New Food Fights: U.S. Public Divides Over Food Science." Pew Research Center, Washington, D.C. (December 1, 2016) http://www.pewinternet.org/2016/12/01/the-new-food-fights/

p. 744, iStock.com/ollinka

p. 745, iStock/Orla

p. 746, iStock/Orla

p. 747, iStock.com/eskaylim

p. 748, iStock.com/eskaylim

p. 749, iStock.com/ollinka

p. 750, iStock.com/elenaleonova

p. 751, Bob Thomas/Popperfoto/Popperfoto/Getty Images

p. 753, iStock.com/olindana

p. 762, iStock.com/olindana

p. 763, iStock.com/ooyoo

p. 764, iStock.com/ooyoo

p. 765, iStock.com/Dominique_Lavoie

p. 766, iStock.com/Dominique_Lavoie

p. 767, iStock.com/olindana

p. 768, iStock.com/wonry

p. 774, iStock.com/bgfoto

p. 775, GE Kidder Smith/Corbis Historical/Getty Images

p. 778, iStock.com/bgfoto

p. 779, iStock.com/unoL

p. 780, iStock.com/unoL

p. 781, iStock.com/bgfoto

p. 782, iStock.com/marthof

p. 784, Stock.com/hanibaram, iStock.com/seb_ra, iStock.com/Martin Barraud

p. 785, iStock.com/Martin Barraud

p. 791, iStock.com/fstop123

p. 794, iStock.com/gopixa

p. 796, iStock.com/Martin Barraud

p. 801, iStock.com/bo1982

p. 803, iStock.com/Domin_domin

p. 806, iStock.com/Jeff_Hu

p. 808, iStock.com/stevedangers

p. 810, iStock.com/Martin Barraud

p. 813, iStock/Fodor90

p. 816, iStock/Vimvertigo

p. 817, iStock/Vimvertigo

p. 820, iStock.com/Martin Barraud

p. 822, iStock.com/D-Keine

p. 823, iStock.com/

p. 823, iStock.com/grinvalds

p. 823, iStock.com/Robert Kirk/

p. 823, iStock.com/

p. 823, iStock.com/tunart

p. 826, iStock.com/D-Keine

p. 827, iStock.com/BlackJack3D

p. 830, iStock.com/RazvanDP

p. 832, iStock.com/D-Keine

p. 833, iStock.com/Labylullaby

p. 834, ©iStock.com/Wavebreakmedia

p. 834, istock.com/

p. 834, istock.com/

p. 834, istock.com/

p. 834, istock.com/

p. 835, DANIEL LEAL-OLIVAS/AFP/Getty Images

p. 836, EMMANUEL DUNAND/AFP/Getty Images

p. 837, iStock.com/Labylullaby

p. 838, iStock.com/Ales_Utovko

p. 840, iStock.com/AlexandrBognat

p. 842, iStock.com/Labylullaby

# studysync

## Text Fulfillment Through StudySync

If you are interested in specific titles, please fill out the form below and we will check availability through our partners.

### ORDER DETAILS

Date:

| TITLE | AUTHOR | Paperback/ Hardcover | Specific Edition *If Applicable* | Quantity |
|-------|--------|----------------------|----------------------------------|----------|
|  |  |  |  |  |
|  |  |  |  |  |
|  |  |  |  |  |
|  |  |  |  |  |
|  |  |  |  |  |
|  |  |  |  |  |
|  |  |  |  |  |

### SHIPPING INFORMATION

Contact:

Title:

School/District:

Address Line 1:

Address Line 2:

Zip or Postal Code:

Phone:

Mobile:

Email:

### BILLING INFORMATION ☐ *SAME AS SHIPPING*

Contact:

Title:

School/District:

Address Line 1:

Address Line 2:

Zip or Postal Code:

Phone:

Mobile:

Email:

### PAYMENT INFORMATION

☐ CREDIT CARD

Name on Card:

Card Number:　　　　　Expiration Date:　　　　　Security Code:

☐ PO

Purchase Order Number:

StudySync Text Fulfillment, BookheadEd Learning, LLC
610 Daniel Young Drive | Sonoma, CA 95476